AA

KEYGUIDE

CROATIA

218

CONTENTS

84

60
149

3

UNDERSTANDING CROATIA

Understanding Croatia is an introduction to Croatia, its economy, history and
its people, giving a real insight into the country. Living Croatia gets under the
skin of the country today, while The Story of Croatia takes you through its past.

UNDERSTANDING CROATIA

The young Republic of Croatia (Republika Hrvatska) is a fascinating blend of Balkan, Central European and Mediterranean cultures. Born in 1991 out of the collapse of the former Yugoslavia, it is fast emerging as one of Europe's most beguiling holiday destinations. Historic towns and cities have become lively cultural centres, none more so than Dubrovnik, spectacularly risen from the ashes of war. Ruled at various times in its history by Rome, Venice, Vienna, Budapest and Belgrade, Croatia has adopted influences from them all. This is a land of vivid colours—green pines, purple lavender, golden stone, azure sea and bright Mediterranean skies.

THE CROATS

The Croats were a Slavic race who migrated to the Balkans in the seventh century AD at the same time as the Serbs. Before that Croatia was occupied by Illyrian hill tribes, including the Histri in present-day Istria and the Liburnians in Kvarner Bay. It had also been part of the Roman empire, one of whose greatest emperors, Diocletian (CAD245–313), was born in Dalmatia. During its medieval golden age, Croatia was a nation ruled by its own dukes and kings. Legend states that the last king cursed Croatia to a millennium of foreign rule. In fact, it took just over 900 years for the 'thousand-year dream' of Croatian independence to be realized.

NEVER MIND THE BALKANS

Until 1991, Croatia was part of Yugoslavia, with Serbia, Montenegro, Macedonia, Bosnia-Herzegovina and Slovenia. Together with others such as Albania, Bulgaria and Greece, these countries are often referred to as the Balkans. While this is geographically correct—the Balkan peninsula extends from the Adriatic to the Black Sea—it is politically controversial. Croatia has always looked north and west, and its leaders refer to it as a Central European rather than a Balkan country. This is partly to distance it from Serbia, but also because the word balkanization implies fragmentation into small, ungovernable states.

The divisions in the Balkans can be traced to the partition of the Roman empire, its boundary roughly along today's borders of Croatia and Bosnia-Herzegovina.

Famously described by Pope Leo X as 'the ramparts of Christendom', Croatia has always tended to see itself as a nation on the front line of different civilizations, and the last bastion of Catholic Europe before the Orthodox and Muslim worlds of the Balkans. For this reason, the term Balkan is loaded with historical symbolism and visitors should be wary of using it.

THE HOMELAND WAR

It is impossible to understand Croatia without reference to the Domovinski Rat (Homeland War), a war of independence from Yugoslavia fought between 1991 and 1995 (▷ 24–25). At that time Croatia was also involved in a bloody three-way conflict in Bosnia-Herzegovina. The war has left an indelible mark on Croatia and continues to dominate political debate, especially the issue of alleged war criminals and the war crimes tribunal at The Hague. Nationalism is still a potent force in Croatia and visitors should exercise caution when voicing opinions on the war.

There are few visible signs of war damage on the coast, but bombed-out houses and abandoned villages are a common sight near the Bosnian and Serbian borders, especially in Vukovar and the Krajina region of northern Dalmatia. Landmines are still a problem in remote areas—over 400 people have been killed by mines since the end of the war—so keep to main roads and footpaths and heed warning signs.

Above *The 15th-century Knežev Dvor, Dubrovnik*

PEOPLE

A 2009 estimate put the population of Croatia at just over 4.5 million, of whom almost 1 million live in Zagreb. The next biggest cities are Split, Rijeka and Osijek. Around 90 per cent of the population are Croats and 4 per cent are Serbs. Before 1991, some 15 per cent were Serbs, but many left during the Homeland War; at the same time many Croat refugees arrived from Bosnia-Herzegovina. Several million Croats live abroad, with large communities in the USA and Canada, as well as Australia, Great Britain and Germany.

Religion is divided along ethnic lines, with 88 per cent of Croatia's population Roman Catholic, 4 per cent Serbian Orthodox and 1 per cent Muslim. Although church attendance is low, there has been a revival of popular religion since independence and there are strong links between Catholicism and nationalism.

The official language is Croatian (Hrvatski), a branch of the Serbo-Croat languages of the Balkans. However, largely for political reasons, it is now treated as distinct from Bosnian and Serbian. Croatian uses the Latin script while Serbia uses Cyrillic, but many words are otherwise identical. Most young people speak a foreign language, usually English, German or Italian, and there is a significant Italian-speaking minority in Istria.

CROATIA'S REGIONS

Zagreb is the political and cultural capital of Croatia, home to around 20 per cent of the country's population.

Inland Croatia stretches from the Kvarner highlands in the west to the River Danube in the east via the fertile Slavonia plains. Apart from the Plitvice Lakes, tourism has yet to make an impact here. The areas bordering Bosnia and Serbia suffered badly in the war.

Istria (Istra) is a peninsula in the northern Adriatic. Once occupied by Italy, it reflects a strong Italian influence. Pula has well-preserved Roman monuments, while the west coast has some of the biggest resorts in Croatia.

Kvarner is a large bay separating Istria from Dalmatia, including Croatia's two largest islands, Cres and Krk. Rijeka, Croatia's third city, is a busy port.

Dalmatia (Dalmacija) is a long, narrow coastal region, with hundreds of islands and a beautiful shoreline. The main cities are Zadar, Šibenik and Split

Dubrovnik and Beyond includes the gem of the Croatian coast, Dubrovnik, and other sights within day-trip distance.

THE BEST OF CROATIA

ZAGREB

Gornji Grad (▷ 54) Take the funicular to the top of the city for churches and museums on cobbled streets.

Hrvatsko Narodno Kazalište (▷ 58) Spend an evening amid the Habsburg splendour of the National Theatre.

Kula Lotrščak (▷ 54) Clamber up this tower in the Gornji Grad at noon to witness the firing of the midday cannon.

Maksimirski perivoj (▷ 60) Pack a picnic and relax on the grassy expanses of one of Europe's oldest parks.

Medvednica (▷ 60) Take the cable car to the summit of Zagreb's mountain for fresh air, walks and views.

Tkalčićeva (▷ 65) Join the beautiful people for an evening *korzo* (stroll) on Zagreb's prettiest street.

Trg Bana Jelačića (▷ 63) Soak up city life and enjoy people-watching from a café table on the main square.

INLAND CROATIA

Lonjsko Polje (▷ 86–87) See black storks and relax for a night in a wooden cottage by the River Sava.

Osijek (▷ 88–89) Gaze up at the grand baroque, neoclassical and art nouveau facades in Osijek, the bustling capital of the Slavonia region.

Plitvička Jezera (▷ 91–93) Follow boardwalk trails around the beautiful lakes and waterfalls of this famous national park.

Samobor (▷ 94) Tuck into *samoborska kremšnita*, a delicious local custard tart, in this pretty town a short hop from Zagreb.

Varaždin (▷ 97–99) Stroll through the streets admiring the baroque architecture of Croatia's former capital.

Vukovar (▷ 95) Ponder the horror and futility of war in this once beautiful town on the River Danube.

Zagorje (▷ 100–103) Journey through northern Croatia's rolling hills, stopping off at medieval hilltop castles and atmospheric churches along the way.

ISTRIA

Brijuni (▷ 118–119) Explore the luxuriant islands in the Brijuni archipelago off the Istrian coast, once Tito's presidential playground and now a national park.

Eufrazijeva Basilika (▷ 125) Gaze in awe at the gleaming Byzantine icons on display at the Basilica of Euphrasius in Poreč.

Hum (▷ 121) Send a postcard home from Hum to prove you've been to the smallest town in the world.

Motovun (▷ 122) Discover exquisite fortified hilltop towns such as Motovun and Grožnjan (▷ 120).

Pula (▷ 127–129) Imagine gladiators and Christians being thrown to the lions at the magnificent Roman arena.

Rovinj (▷ 130–132) Dip your feet in the sea while sipping cocktails at Istria's most attractive seaside resort.

Zigante (▷ 143) Feast on Istrian truffles and local wine in this truffle-themed restaurant in Livade.

KVARNER

Caput Insulae, Cres (▷ 160–161) Explore the stone labyrinth on an eco-trail from Beli.

Krk (▷ 150) Relax at Baška beach on the south coast of Krk Island, one of the finest stretches of sand you'll find in the Adriatic.

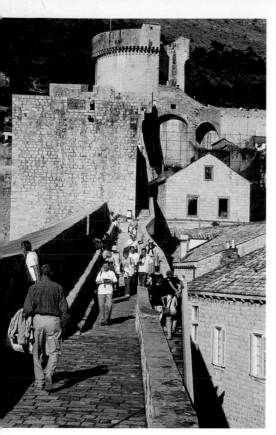

Split (▷ 189–193) Wander around the remains of the palatial retirement home of Roman emperor Diocletian.
Vis (▷ 195) Take a boat from Split to this remote and seldom visited island, formerly a Yugoslav military base and only open to visitors since 1989.

DUBROVNIK AND BEYOND

Elafitski Otoci (▷ 226) Take the ferry to these peaceful islands, with their sandy beaches and gentle walks.
Gradske Zidine (▷ 219–220) Everyone does it, but you simply have to make the circuit atop Dubrovnik's splendid city walls.
Lokanda Peskarija (▷ 236) Dine on fresh fish, salad and chilled white wine at a table beside the harbour.
Lokrum (▷ 227) Escape Dubrovnik's crowds by hopping over to peaceful Lokrum Island for some cooling woodland shade and nudist beaches.
Mljet (▷ 228–229) Take a few days to cycle or walk this beautiful island, the western end of which has been designated a national park.
Stradun (▷ 220–221) Sit at a pavement (sidewalk) café and watch the crowds on this beautiful street in Dubrovnik's old town.
Summer Festival (▷ 235) See Shakespeare's *Hamlet* performed at Fort Lovrijenac.

Opposite Spectacular Skradinski Buk waterfall in Krka National Park
Left The approach to Tvrđava Minčeta, on Dubrovnik's city walls
Below The first-century AD Roman amphitheatre at Pula, Istria

Gorski Kotar (▷ 164) Ski in winter with a view of the sea, or walk in the highlands in summer.
Opatija (▷ 152) Relive the *fin-de-siècle* days of the Austro Hungarian empire on the Lungomare seafront.
Rab (▷ 154–155) Uncover the layers of history on a stroll through one of Croatia's most appealing island towns.
Rijeka (▷ 156–157) Delve into the story of the Glagolitic alphabet (▷ 21) at an exhibition in the university library.
Sjeverni Velebit (▷ 153) Pull on hiking boots for a spot of trekking in these limestone peaks that trace the line of the coast.

DALMATIA

Hvar (▷ 172–173) Dubbed the Croatian St. Tropez, Hvar Town is where the rich and famous come to see and be seen.
Korčula (▷ 177–179) See a performance of the *moreška* sword dance and stroll around the Venetian town.
Kornati (▷ 182) Cruise through the remote and eerily beautiful islands of this archipelago near Zadar.
Krka (▷ 180–181) Swim beneath the cascades, then take a boat trip through the dramatic Krka canyon.
Morske Orgulje, Zadar (▷ 197) Sit on the steps of Zadar's seafront promenade at sunset and enjoy a symphony of nature from the sea organ below.

TOP EXPERIENCES

Charter your own yacht and sail among the Dalmatian islands, tying up at a different port each night.

Drive the Magistrala highway between Dubrovnik and Split, one of Europe's most spectacular coast roads—best in low season.

Get away from it all with a night in a farmhouse in Istria, Slavonia or the Zagorje, dining on local food.

Go island-hopping on the excellent network of local ferries (▷ 38–39).

Enjoy a summer concert in a magical outdoor setting. The Dubrovnik Summer Festival (▷ 235), when the city turns itself into an open-air stage, and Split's Summer Festival (▷ 207), with open-air opera performances in the Peristil courtyard of Diocletian's Palace, are the most prestigious, but every town has a summer festival.

Sip *prošek* (sweet red wine) on a summer evening by the sea, on the café-lined Riva (waterfront promenade) to be found in all coastal towns.

Take a walk in the mountains in summer, enjoying cool breezes, stunning scenery and magnificent sea views.

Taste *pršut* (cured ham) with *paški sir* (Pag cheese), olives and crusty bread—heaven on a plate.

Throw off your clothes and go as nature intended on one of Croatia's many nudist beaches—if you are ever going to shed your inhibitions, this is the place to do it.

Unwind and give in to the spirit of *fijaka*—a feeling of indolent pleasure, best captured in lazy days by the sea.

Dance the night away at the traditional Shrovetide carnival in Rijeka, capital of the Kvarner region, where carnival celebrations are the liveliest in Croatia (▷ 165).

Motor through the Zagorje, inland Croatia's most attractive region (▷ 100–103).

Take a night-time tour of Diocletian's Palace in Split to experience the Roman remains minus the crowds of other visitors (▷ 190).

Watch a Zadar sunset while listening to the soothing music of the *Morske orgulje* (Sea Organ, ▷ 197)—it is *the* way to end the day.

Sample some Istrian truffles, one of Croatia's finest delicacies, at Zigante (▷ 143), the famed truffle restaurant in the village of Livade.

Below *The unspoiled island of Vis, a remote Adriatic outpost, has become a popular destination for sailors*

LIVING CROATIA

A NEW NATION

No visitor to Croatia can fail to notice the Croats' immense pride in their country since independence in 1991. Symbols of nationhood are everywhere, from the ubiquitous red, white and blue tricolour flying from government buildings to the checkered *hrvatski grb* seen on everything from policemen's uniforms to soccer shirts. Streets and squares once named after Tito (▷ 23) now carry names of Croatian nationalist heroes. Soccer fans wave banners proclaiming 'Proud to be Croat'. Traditional festivals are being revived, and the language is now always *hrvatski* (Croatian), rather than Serbo-Croat. Religion in the shape of the Roman Catholic Church is also seen as an integral part of being Croatian. As Croatia embraces the 21st century and looks towards EU membership, nationalism has proved an obstacle and fuelled the swell of Euro scepticism in the country. The EU has done little to make itself popular in Croatia, insisting on progress in bringing individuals seen by many as war heroes to trial and opening the door to poorer neighbours Romania and Bulgaria first.

LEAPS OF FAITH
Another sign of resurgent nationalism is the growth in support for the Roman Catholic Church, after decades of marginalization under communism. Figures in the 2001 census show some 88 per cent of Croatia's population are Roman Catholics, a rise of 12 per cent in 10 years. In part, this reflects post-war demographic changes, the majority of Orthodox Serbs having fled to Bosnia, but it also shows that many Croats see Catholicism as deeply entwined with national identity and politics. As a result, religious festivals are celebrated with fervour and churches struggle to accommodate huge congregations. Despite ties with Rome, abortion and homosexuality are legal.

Clockwise from above *Soccer fans celebrate Croatia's winning goal during a match against Austria in Euro 2008; pilgrims at the Church of Our Lady of the Snows at Marija Bistrica in the Zagorje; the emblem of Hajduk Split soccer team includes the distinctive red-and-white* hrvatski grb

MODEL MODERN CROAT

The businessman Goran Štrok is typical of the new breed of Croatian expatriate entrepreneurs who are investing their cash in the rebuilding of their country. Born in Zagreb in 1947, this son of one of Tito's generals was a professional motor-racing driver, winning seven national championships before moving to London in 1977. In 1995, he bought his first hotel in Rijeka and now owns a chain of smart Croatian hotels, the flagship being the restored Dubrovnik Palace. It was opened in 2004 by President Stjepan Mesić, after a €45 million investment. Štrok's wife Renata is an interior designer and his daughter Vanja is one of the fashion duo Gharani Štrok, with such clients as Madonna and Nicole Kidman. The Štroks support charitable projects in Croatia—Goran set up the Izidor Štrok Memorial Fund in memory of his father, and Renata sponsors children who were orphaned in the Homeland War.

KNIGHTS IN ARMOUR

The ugly side of Croatian nationalism occasionally rears its head, especially in former war zones that still have an undercurrent of anti-Serb hostility. The medieval Sinjska Alka festival (▷ 207) in the Dalmatian town of Sinj is a heady brew of patriotism and religious fervour, in an area with a large military presence where memories of the war are still fresh. In 2001 the event was taken over by supporters of General Mirko Norac, a local soldier who was elected Duke of Sinjska Alka, despite being dismissed from the Army and accused of war crimes for which he was later sentenced to 12 years in prison. In his support, the local *alkari* (knights) returned the traditional gift sent by Croatian president Stjepan Mesić, who responded by cutting off state funding for the festival until 2005. The event went ahead with supporters chanting General Norac's name and waving flags and insignia of the Ustaše period.

MONEY TALKS

Even the currency is a political statement in Croatia. Officially introduced in October 1993, the kuna takes its name from the pine marten, whose furs were traded in medieval times. Critics, however, saw it as a throwback to an earlier era of nationalism, recalling that the kuna had last been used by the Fascist Ustaše regime which occupied Croatia during World War II. The 1-, 2- and 5-kuna coins feature an image of the pine marten on one side, with a nightingale, tuna and brown bear respectively on the reverse. Banknotes are adorned with Croatian poets, dukes, politicians and iconic landmarks, such as the Eltz Palace at Vukovar and the King Tomislav statue in Zagreb. Ironically, for all its controversy and symbolism, the kuna is already on its way out. Croatia will introduce the euro by 2012.

CHECK MATE

The red and white checkerboard known as the *hrvatski grb* (Croatian shield) is one of the oldest national symbols in Europe, dating back at least 500 years. According to mythology, its origins lie in a game of chess, in which a 10th-century Croatian king defeated a Venetian prince to preserve Croatia's freedom. The shield is at the centre of the national flag, topped by a crown made up of five smaller shields representing the historic coats of arms of Croatia, Dubrovnik, Dalmatia, Istria and Slavonia. This potent symbol of nationalism is often derided by opponents because of its associations with the repressive Ustaše régime, but it has been used by Croatian rulers of every political complexion, from Austrian emperors and Serbian kings to Communist Yugoslavia.

THE GREAT OUTDOORS

It may seem hard to believe amid the bustle of Zagreb or on the crowded Adriatic beaches in summer, but Croatia is still largely a wilderness country. Around 40 per cent of the landmass is taken up with karst limestone mountains, while another 30 per cent comprises forests of oak, pine, beech, spruce and fir. Add pristine lakes, unpolluted rivers and hundreds of desert islands, and what you have is a giant outdoor adventure playground. At weekends Croatians flee the cities to go hiking in the mountains, or hunting and fishing in the forests and rivers. Adrenaline addicts get their fix from rafting, canoeing, kayaking, caving and climbing. In summer, people go camping in alpine huts or sail their yachts to remote islands; in winter, at the first sign of snow, they pack up their skis and head for the hills. It is not only humans who enjoy Croatia's spectacular natural landscapes. Among the wildlife to be found in the forest and mountain regions of Croatia are lynx, wolves, wild boar, red and roe deer, pine-marten, golden eagles, peregrine falcons and brown bears.

YACHTING

Dropping anchor in one of Croatia's pretty harbours or off one of its 1,000 or so islands is *de rigueur* among the yachting set. And, it is gaining in popularity. Ask any local who lives by the Adriatic and he or she will tell you about the multi-million-dollar yachts that have docked in their town and about the antics of their well-heeled owners.

Chartering a boat is a great way to see uninhabited islands, secluded coves and deserted beaches that are otherwise inaccesible. Countless companies charter luxury yachts. If you're a novice, your boat will come with a skipper. Motor launches and even full-blown sailing ships are also available for rental.

Clockwise from above *A population of some 400 brown bears live in Croatia, mostly in the Gorski Kotar and Velebit massifs; Croatia's first naturist beach opened in 1934 and today there are more than 30 official resorts; Croatia's own dog, the distinctive black-and-white spotted Dalmatian*

BEAR NECESSITIES

Once brown bears roamed over much of the planet, but today they are reduced to a few pockets of Europe and North America. The brown bear is one of the largest living land carnivores on earth, weighing up to 300kg (660lb). There are an estimated 400 bears in Croatia, living mostly in the Gorski Kotar and Velebit massifs. They are typically shy animals, coming down to the lower slopes at night to hunt. Although protected within national parks, bears can be legally hunted in Croatia and are prized for meat, medicinal uses and fur. Travellers may be shocked to see smoked bear salami and pâté on sale in shops. It is forbidden to hunt mothers and young bear cubs, but inevitably some do get killed. The Refugium Ursorum bear sanctuary at Kuterevo, near Otočac in the Kvarner region, supports bear cubs orphaned as a result of illegal hunting (▷ 165).

SPOTTED DOGS

The black-and-white spotted dogs known as Dalmatians were immortalized in the 1961 Disney film *101 Dalmatians*, based on the children's story by Dodie Smith (1896–1990), in which the wicked Cruella de Vil kidnaps Dalmatian puppies to make a fur coat. However, the Dalmatian is much more than a cuddly cartoon character. In 1994 the World Canine Federation officially recognized Croatia's claim to be the origin of the breed. First seen in ancient Egyptian and Greek art, the Dalmatian was popular as a carriage dog in 19th-century England, running alongside horses to protect carriages and their occupants from attack. They were also used in the Balkans by bands of *Roma* (gypsy) musicians and circus performers, and have been adopted as mascots by fire stations across the USA. A little-known fact is that the puppies are born white all over, the distinctive black spots develop later.

THE NAKED TRUTH

One sign of Croatia's back-to-nature approach is its laid-back attitude to nudity. The first naturist beach opened in 1934 on the island of Rab in Kvarner Bay, and today there are more than 30 official naturist resorts, plus many where nudity is tolerated. In the 1960s Yugoslavia was the first country to commercialize naturism, and the Istrian coast was heavily promoted in Germany and Austria as a naturist destination. Koversada, which opened in 1961 on an islet off Vrsar, has become Europe's biggest nudist colony, accommodating 5,000. Beaches where naturism is encouraged are indicated by the letters FKK (*freikörperkultur* or 'free body culture') but in practice clothing is optional at most remote beaches and islands. Visitors can go to the harbour at any popular resort in summer and find boatmen offering trips to nudist beaches. More information on naturism in Croatia is available at www.cronatur.com

BOTTLENOSE DOLPHINS

If dolphins are a sign of a healthy marine environment, then the waters around Cres and Lošinj are some of the cleanest in the Mediterranean. The Adriatic Dolphin Project in Veli Lošinj has identified and photographed around 160 individual bottlenose dolphins, whose behaviour is closely monitored by researchers. Among the biggest threats to the survival of dolphins here are overfishing, which forces them to hunt farther afield for food, and the engine noise from motorboats, which has a disrupting effect on their navigational senses. In 2006 the Croatian government announced the establishment of the Lošinj Dolphin Reserve off the coasts of Cres and Lošinj, the first such protected area in the Mediterranean. If you want to help, Blue World (▷ 164) offers 'adopt a dolphin' sponsorship or you could join one of the volunteer research programmes in summer. Swimming with dolphins is illegal in Croatia.

SPORTING HEROES

For a country of 4.5 million people which has been in existence for less than 20 years, Croatia has achieved a remarkable level of sporting success. Sport is seen by many Croats as a source of national pride and a way of gaining international recognition. Ask a people in Germany or Britain what they know about Croatia, and they will probably reel off the names of soccer stars such as Dado Pršo, Igor Tudor and brothers Robert and Niko Kovač, or tennis players Ivan Ljubičić and Mario Ančić, heroes of the Davis Cup-winning team of 2005. Since first entering the Olympic Games as an independent nation in 1992, Croatia has won medals in tennis, basketball, water polo, swimming, weightlifting, rowing and skiing, with Janica Kostelić (▷ opposite) becoming the most successful female skier ever. The greatest results have come in handball, at which Croatia traditionally excels. Croatian athletes made up the bulk of the Yugoslav handball team that won the first Olympic gold medal at Munich in 1972, and Croatia went on to win handball gold at Atlanta in 1996 and Athens in 2004.

SLAVEN BILIĆ

Slaven Bilić, born in Split in 1968, played for the Croatian national soccer team, as well as English teams West Ham and Everton, before injury brought an early end to his playing career. Bilić was appointed coach of Croatia's national squad in 2006, the youngest man ever to hold the job. Success wasn't long in coming, and in 2008 Bilić guided the team to the European championships in Austria and Switzerland, famously knocking England out along the way. He is recognized as one of the best managers in the world, and the top European clubs such as Inter Milan, Real Madrid and Barcelona are likely to come knocking for his services when his contract runs out with the Croatian national team.

Clockwise from above *Croatian footballing legend Dado Pršo in action during a 2006 World Cup qualifier against Hungary; Dražen Petrović faces Michael Jordan of the USA during the 1992 Olympics in Barcelona; Goran Ivanišević wins the inaugural 2009 Chengdu Open in China*

GOLDEN BOOTS

In 1998, playing in their first World Cup, the Croatian national soccer team finished third, going out in the semi-finals to the hosts, and eventual champions, France. The star was Davor Šuker of Real Madrid and Croatia, winner of the Golden Boot for the World Cup's leading scorer (six goals in seven games). He now runs a soccer academy in Zagreb. The Croatian captain was Zvonimir Boban, who played for AC Milan for nine years. Since his retirement he has gained a history degree at Zagreb University and been a commentator for Croatian and Italian TV. He also owns a restaurant in Zagreb. Defender Slaven Bilić (▷ opposite), now manager of the national team, was another key member of the 1998 squad. Although the Vatreni (Fiery Ones) have not reached such heights since 1998, with success in the qualifiers for the 2010 World Cup eluding them, Croatia continues to be a force in world soccer.

FROM REFUGEE TO CHAMPION

Born in 1979 in Banja Luka, Bosnia, Ivan Ljubičić faced a disrupted childhood when his family was forced to flee to Croatia in 1992 as a result of ethnic cleansing by Bosnian Serbs. Thirteen years later he virtually single-handedly won the Davis Cup, the world's premier international men's team tennis tournament. With first round victories over Americans Andre Agassi and Andy Roddick, he won seven of his eight singles matches and all of his doubles during the year, culminating in defeating Slovakia in the final. One of his teammates was Goran Ivanišević, formerly the most famous sportsman in Croatia after winning Wimbledon as a wild card entry in 2001. Known for his striking good looks and an erratic temperament, he had reached, but lost, the final three times in the 1990s. Typically, perhaps, he came back to win when everybody least expected it.

BORN TO SKI

Despite the lack of high-class winter sports facilities, Croatia has produced probably the greatest female skier of all time. Born in Zagreb in 1982, Janica Kostelić took her first tentative steps on the slopes of Medvednica when she was just three years old. At 16 she competed in the Nagano Winter Olympics, finishing eighth in the combined downhill and slalom. In 2002 at Salt Lake City, she created Olympic history, becoming the first Alpine skier to win four medals in a single Olympic Games, including gold in the slalom, giant slalom and combined. Following knee operations, serious illness and the removal of her thyroid gland, she took part in the 2006 Winter Olympics in Turin, winning another gold in the combined event and silver in the Super-G to become the most successful female skier in Olympic history. Her brother Ivica also got in on the act, winning a silver medal in the men's combined event.

BASKETBALL GIANT

The great propensity of the Croats to grow tall gives them a considerable advantage when it comes to basketball, and no one made better use of his height than the 195cm (6ft 5in) Dražen Petrović (1964–93), a legendary player who has achieved iconic status since his death in a car crash at the age of 28. Born in Šibenik, Petrović first made his name playing for Cibona of Zagreb, where he once scored an astounding 112 points in a single game. Later he represented the Portland Blazers and the New Jersey Nets in the American NBA (National Basketball Association) and led Croatia to a silver medal in the 1992 Olympics, behind the USA 'Dream Team'. Petrović is still idolized by fans in Zagreb, and the Cibona stadium is named after him. He was posthumously admitted to the Basketball Hall of Fame and is honoured with a memorial in the Olympic park at Lausanne, in Switzerland.

ADRIATIC JET SET

With over a thousand uninhabited islands, Croatia's Adriatic coastline is perfect for escaping the attentions of the paparazzi, especially if you are rich enough to have your own private yacht. In recent years it has become the destination of choice for royalty, film stars and A-list celebrities seeking Mediterranean seclusion. Hollywood actor John Malkovich has been spotted cruising the Adriatic from his villa near Dubrovnik; Princess Caroline of Monaco owns an island off the Istrian coast, and stars such as Andre Agassi, Gwyneth Paltrow, Robert De Niro and Sharon Stone have all been visitors. Billionaire soccer club owner Roman Abramovich, Microsoft magnate Bill Gates and Formula One motor-racing supremo Bernie Ecclestone all enjoy Croatian island cruising.

ANYONE FOR POLO?
The Brijuni islands (▷ 118–119) off the west coast of Istria were the favoured resort of the Habsburg aristocracy in the dying days of the Austro-Hungarian empire. During the Communist era Brijuni was Tito's private retreat, where he entertained movie stars appearing at the Pula Film Festival. In an attempt to revive Brijuni's exclusive image, Italian fashion house Brioni reintroduced the sport of polo in 2004, after a 70-year absence. The Brioni Polo Classic is now an annual event, with specially imported polo ponies and guests arriving by yacht and private jet. Brijuni has recovered its cachet and is once again the place to be seen in Croatia in summer.

THE RIGHT FORMULA
Bernie Ecclestone (b1930), Formula One motor-racing supremo, is a big fan of Croatian island cruising and his 190ft yacht *Petara*, named after his two daughters Petra and Tamara, is a frequent visitor to places like Brač, Hvar and Korčula. He was married to a Croat, former Armani model Slavica Radić, 28 years his junior, and before their divorce in 2008, they were often to be found living the high life at the Dalmatian coast's celebrity hotspots. In 2001 they famously flew Wimbledon champion Goran Ivanišević (▷ 17) in their private plane on his triumphant return to his home town of Split.

Above *A view from the scenic Bol to Murvica road, on Brač, the largest island off the Dalmatian coast*

THE STORY OF CROATIA

AT THE CROSSROADS OF EMPIRES

The partition of the Roman empire into east and west in AD395 redrew the map of the Balkans, creating a fault line which still exists today as the boundary of the Catholic and Orthodox worlds. When Slavic tribes migrated to the Balkans in the seventh century the Croats settled on the coast, while the Serbs occupied the interior. Croatia's golden age began in 925, when Tomislav was crowned its first king, and ended with the death of King Zvonimir in 1089. According to legend, Zvonimir was murdered by Croat nobles, and swore on his deathbed that Croatia would be ruled by foreigners for a thousand years. After entering a union with Hungary in 1102, Croatia spent the next eight centuries torn between powerful neighbours, with Austria-Hungary to the north, Ottoman Turkey to the south and Venice, which controlled much of Istria, Kvarner and Dalmatia, to the west. The Habsburg emperors formed the Vojna Krajina (Military Frontier) and recruited Serb soldiers from Bosnia to defend it against the Turks—a decision that was to have far-reaching consequences as it established the presence of a large Serbian minority in Croatia.

BAN POWER

Born into the Croatian aristocracy in 1801, Josip Jelačić rose through the military ranks to become Ban (governor) of Croatia in 1848. During the Hungarian revolution, which was seen as a threat to the Habsburg Empire and to Croatian autonomy, Jelačić fought many battles against the Hungarians, remaining loyal to the emperor throughout. In the years after hostilities concluded, he is credited with ending serfdom in Croatia, expanding the right to vote and introducing economic reforms, though he also oversaw a period of Germanization. He died while still in office in 1859. The main square in Zagreb was named after him in 1866 and his face appears on Croatian banknotes.

Above *The walled city of Dubrovnik, in medieval times a wealthy mercantile city-state to rival Venice*

RAGUSA

Medieval Dubrovnik was the republic of Ragusa (1358–1808), a city state with a fleet to rival Venice and possessions stretching from Lastovo to the Bay of Kator. Wealth bought freedom, paying Turkish, Hungarian and Austrian rulers to leave it alone, and artists, mathematicians, poets, philosophers, architects and playwrights all flourished here. The nominal ruler, the rector, elected each month by all male nobles, was confined to the Rector's Palace during his term of office. Ragusa was abolished and taken into the French Illyrian provinces by Napoleon, then ceded to Austria in 1815. Much of the ruling class took a vow of celibacy rather than serve under a foreign power.

Above *Traditional costume*
Right *Statue of Josip Jelačić, in Zagreb's Trg Bana Jelačića*

SLAVIC SCRIPT

One notable feature of the early Croatian state was the use of the Glagolitic script, devised in the ninth century by Macedonian brothers Cyril and Methodius to present the scriptures in the Slavic languages of the Croats and Serbs. Based on the ancient Greek alphabet, it featured around 40 characters in intricate geometric forms. The 10th-century bishop of Nin, Grgur Ninski, clashed repeatedly with the Pope after Ninski championed the use of the Glagolitic alphabet and Croatian language to replace Latin in church. Glagolitic was widely used in Istria and Kvarner, where it survived as recently as the 19th century. It was also the forerunner of the Cyrillic alphabet, still used in Serbia and Macedonia today. There is a permanent exhibition of Glagolitic writings in the university library at Rijeka (▷ 156).

A FEUDAL CONSPIRACY

During the Middle Ages, power, wealth and influence in Croatia rested in the hands of two aristocratic families, granted large estates by the Hungarian and Austrian kings as a reward for military service against the Turks. The Frankopan and Zrinski families supplied several Croatian *bans* (governors) and owned more than 40 castles, from Krk to the Hungarian border. Related by marriage, the two dynasties died out at the same time after a conspiracy by Petar Zrinski (1621–71) and his brother-in-law Fran Krsto Frankopan (1643–71) against the Austrian emperor. When the plot was discovered the two men were summoned to Vienna and publicly beheaded, and their properties in Croatia confiscated. In 1919, their bodies were transferred to Zagreb cathedral. The two conspirators are now proudly displayed on the 5kn banknote. In 2002, a family claiming to be descendants of the Frankopans signed a contract allowing them to return to one of their castles near Karlovac.

RENAISSANCE MAN

The 19th century saw a flowering of Croatian language, arts and literature in the movement known as the Croatian National Revival, accompanied by growing political support for Croatian independence. A key figure was Josip Juraj Strossmayer (1815–1905), bishop of his home diocese of Đakovo for 55 years until his death. As leader of the National Party from 1860 to 1873, he advocated *Jugoslavenstvo* — the unity of all southern Slavs, including Croats and Serbs, within the Austro-Hungarian empire. In the light of what has happened since, this may seem an idea doomed to failure, but at the time many Croats saw an alliance with Serbia as the best way of standing up to Vienna. Strossmayer saw no conflict between Croatian nationalism and support for the concept of Yugoslavia. As well as being a priest and politician, he was an art collector and lover of Lipizzaner horses and fine wine. He also spoke several languages fluently and helped to found the University of Zagreb.

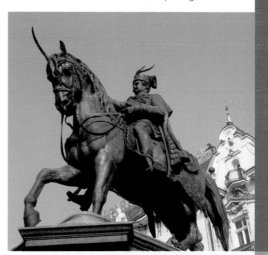

BROTHERHOOD AND DISUNITY

World War I began in the Balkans with the assassination of Austrian Archduke Franz Ferdinand by a Serb gunman in the Bosnian capital Sarajevo. Thus Croatia entered the war on the Austro-Hungarian side, but there was a growing southern Slav consciousness and many Croats saw their future with Serbia. When the Habsburg empire collapsed in 1918 Croatia entered the Kingdom of Serbs, Croats and Slovenes under the Serbian monarch in Belgrade. Despite becoming Yugoslavia (Land of the Southern Slavs) in 1929, the kingdom was effectively run by Serbs. In 1934, on a visit to France, King Aleksandar was assassinated by Croatian nationalists of the Fascist Ustaše movement. In 1941 Yugoslavia was invaded by Germany and Italy, who established a puppet regime in Croatia under Ustaše leader Ante Pavelić. The Ustaše were opposed both by royalist Serbian Chetniks and Tito's Partisan liberation army, which gained control of Yugoslavia in 1945, ushering in Communism. After Tito's death in 1980 Yugoslavia fell apart as Slobodan Milošević (1941–2006) fought disastrous wars in Croatia, Bosnia and Kosovo in his quest for a Greater Serbia.

SPRINGTIME IN CROATIA

The Croatian Spring was a largely intellectual and student movement demanding greater rights for Croatia within the Yugoslav federal setup. In addition to demonstrations and strikes, some of the protests took on a linguistic approach; the politically charged 1967 Declaration on the Status and Name of the Croatian Standard Language and the 1971 publication of a Croatian Orthography both challenged the status of Serbo-Croat as the official language of the federation. Some of the disquiet was down to an unjust economic situation which saw 50 per cent of foreign earnings coming through Croatia but only 7 per cent remaining in the country. Tito suppressed the movement and around 2,000 people were detained and some imprisoned. In 1974, a new constitution gave each republic more autonomy, largely fulfilling the movement's demands.

Clockwise from above *Dr. Ante Pavelić, leader of the post-war puppet state NDH, with members of the Ustaše youth in 1941; statesman Marshal Tito, who held Yugoslavia together for 35 years; Alojzije Stepinac, a much-loved but deeply controversial figure*

TITO'S YUGOSLAVIA

Born in Kumrovec, Josip Broz Tito (1892–1980) had a Croatian father and a Slovenian mother. Joining the Austro-Hungarian military as a conscript, he was imprisoned by the Russians, and, inspired by Bolshevik ideals, fought with the Red Army on his release. Returning to Yugoslavia, he rose rapidly through the ranks of the Communist Party and, after leading the Partisans to victory in 1945, became president for life. He formed six socialist republics, linked by the slogan 'brotherhood and unity', and his unique form of communism rejected both western capitalism and the Soviet model. Tito held Yugoslavia together for 35 years; a measure of his achievement is that after his death, brotherhood and unity quickly gave way.

IVAN MEŠTROVIĆ

Ivan Meštrović (1883–1962) was undeniably one of the greatest sculptors of the 20th century. At the age of 15 he was apprenticed to a stonemason in Split and spent much of the next two decades abroad. Returning to Croatia, he was later imprisoned by the Ustaše and spent his final years living in exile in the USA. Meštrović worked in wood, bronze and stone, with influences ranging from Balkan history and religion to classical Greek sculpture and the work of his mentor, Auguste Rodin (1840–1917). In 1952, he presented his house and studio in Zagreb (▷ 55) and his summer villa in Split (▷ 192–193) to the nation. His public works include monuments to Grgur Ninski in Split (▷ 191) and Bishop Strossmayer (▷ 62) in Zagreb.

THE USTAŠE

The occupying powers in World War II set up the NDH (Independent State of Croatia), ostensibly a Croatian nationalist regime but really a puppet state of Nazi Germany, with Ustaše leader Ante Pavelić as Poglavnik (Führer). It encompassed most of present-day Croatia and Bosnia-Herzegovina, but the Dalmatian coast was largely ceded to Italy. The Ustaše unleashed a reign of terror across Croatia, with thousands of Serbs and Jews murdered at concentration camps such as Jasenovac (▷ 83). It was official policy to eliminate Serbs from Croatia by deporting a third, killing a third and converting the rest to Catholicism. The spectre of the Ustaše continues to haunt politics here, and accounts for the deep fear felt by many Croatian Serbs at the revival of Croatian nationalism. President Franjo Tuđman (▷ 25) was accused of rehabilitating the Ustaše and pandering to extremists when he questioned the number of deaths at Jasenovac concentration camp and allowed the return of Ustaše insignia.

A TURBULENT PRIEST

The Blessed Alojzije Stepinac (1898–1960) is a much-loved but deeply controversial figure. As Archbishop of Zagreb in 1941, he initially gave his blessing to the Ustaše régime, but although he continued to view the Ustaše leaders as patriots, he is said to have cried when he learnt of the horrors of Jasenovac (▷ 83) and personally intervened to save the lives of many Jews. He even wrote to the Ustaše leader Pavlević condemning violence against all men and imploring him not to kill Serbs. The only religious leader in Zagreb to survive the war, he was arrested on Tito's orders in 1946, charged with collaboration and sentenced to 16 years in prison. After five years in Lepoglava prison he spent the rest of his life under house arrest in Krašić (▷ 83) and is buried in Zagreb Cathedral. In 1952 Pope Pius XII appointed Stepinac a cardinal, causing Tito to break diplomatic relations with the Vatican. Beatified in 1990, he is revered by many Croats, though questions remain about the role of the Church during the war and its links with the Ustaše.

WAR AND PEACE

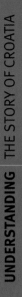

In 1990 the first multi-party elections for over 50 years resulted in victory for Franjo Tuđman's HDZ (Croatian Democratic Union). Alarmed by Tuđman's nationalist rhetoric, Croatia's minority Serb population began organizing resistance, supported by the Yugoslav army. When Croatia declared independence from Yugoslavia in 1991, rebel Serbs established the Republic of Serbian Krajina at Knin. Soon, almost a third of Croatia was in Serbian hands, including a swathe of Northern Dalmatia, cutting road and rail links between Zagreb and Split and leaving Croatia's unity dependent on a ferry crossing from Pag. Croats were murdered or driven from their homes in an operation known as *etničko čišćenje* (ethnic cleansing). Serbs living in Croatian areas were subject to revenge attacks and the fighting escalated into all-out war, with at least 10,000 killed between 1991 and 1995. The Homeland War ended in August 1995, when Croatian forces led by Ante Gotovina captured the Krajina in Operation Oluja (Storm), thought to be the largest land offensive in Europe since World War II. Over 200,000 Serbs fled across the border, but parts of Slavonia remained under UN control and were only returned to Croatia in 1998.

Clockwise from above *In 1991 the small town of Vukovar suffered severe damage from Yugoslav shelling; Milan Babić, president of the Republic of Serbian Krajina, on trial in The Hague for war crimes; Slobodan Milošević at the 1995 peace negotiations in Paris, at which the Dayton Peace Agreement was signed and an end brought to the war*

THE BATTLE FOR VUKOVAR

One of the first acts of the Homeland War was the massacre of 12 Croatian policemen by Serbian paramilitaries in Vukovar in May 1991. From August to November, the town was besieged by the Yugoslav army, with a volunteer force of under 2,000 trying to hold out against at least 40,000 well-equipped troops, supported by 600 tanks and 100 planes. During the three-month battle at least 2,000 Croat civilians were killed, along with many Serbian soldiers. The most shocking incident occurred a day after the fall of the town, when 200 wounded were taken from Vukovar hospital and executed in a field before being buried in a mass grave at Ovčara.

FATHER OF THE NATION

Croatia's war leader was Dr. Franjo Tuđman (1922–99), who, as the first president of independent Croatia, is widely seen as the father of the nation. A former Communist who fought with the Partisans and became a general in Tito's army, he was later expelled from the party and imprisoned for anti-Yugoslav activity. By 1990 he had emerged as a hardline nationalist, famously declaring during the election campaign:'I am glad that my wife is neither a Serb nor a Jew.' He was criticized for his authoritarian tendencies and his role in the Bosnian war, but he is still a hero to many Croats—though had he lived, it is likely that he would have ended up on trial in The Hague for war crimes alongside his old adversary Slobodan Milošević.

STORM TROOPERS

Operation Oluja (Storm) in early August 1995 took back parts of Croatia that had been occupied by Serb separatists for up to four years. Controversially, the four-day operation saw the Serb exodus from Knin, capital of the Republic of Serbian Krajina, as civilians fled the fighting. Few have returned. General Ante Gotovina (▷ 26) has been indicted for war crimes allegedly committed during Operation Storm, but 5 August, the day Croatian forces took Knin, is still celebrated in Croatia as Victory Day. This military initiative is regarded as a contributing factor in bringing the Serbs to the negotiating table and the eventual signing of the Dayton Peace Agreement, which ended the war in Yugoslavia.

THE SIEGE OF DUBROVNIK

The war in Croatia came to the world's attention through television footage of shells raining down on the medieval walls in Dubrovnik. From October 1991 to May 1992 the city came under constant attack from the Yugoslav army, aided by Montenegrin reservists and Bosnian Serbs from the nearby hills. Around 80 per cent of houses in the old town took direct hits, 45 bombs landed on Stradun and over 80 civilians were killed. Many people retreated to their cellars, without adequate food, water or electricity. Unlike other key battlegrounds in Croatia, Dubrovnik had no significant Serbian minority and was of no obvious strategic interest. There has long been suspicion that both sides manipulated the siege of Dubrovnik for their own ends. The Serbs saw it as a chance to destroy Croatia's tourist industry and strike at a powerful historic and cultural symbol; the Croats used it as an opportunity to rally international opinion to the defence of a World Heritage city.

A DENTIST FROM KNIN

Milan Babić (1956–2006) was a provincial dentist whose Serbian parents were nearly murdered by a Croatian Ustaše neighbour before he was born. In 1990 he was elected President of the Municipal Assembly of Knin and leader of the Serbian Democratic Party. He became president of the Republic of Serbian Krajina and one of the architects of the ethnic cleansing of Croatian villages. In 1995 he fled to become a chicken farmer in Belgrade. Seven years later he surrendered to the international war crimes tribunal at The Hague, testifying in court against his former mentor Slobodan Milošević. Babić is one of the few convicted war criminals to show remorse for his actions, telling the tribunal he felt a 'deep sense of shame' and begging his 'brother Croats' to forgive him. 'These crimes and my participation in them can never be justified,' he said. Jailed for 13 years for crimes against humanity, he was found dead in his cell in The Hague in 2006, having committed suicide.

CONFÉRENCE DE PAIX SUR L'EX-YOUGOSLAVIE
PARIS

INTO THE FUTURE

Croatian politics has settled down since the death of President Tuđman, with the parties campaigning on the economy and taxation rather than nationalism. Nevertheless, the government's cooperation with the UN war crimes tribunal remains a source of controversy, with many Croats accusing leaders of betraying national heroes for the sake of international acceptance. In 2003, the former Communist Ivica Račan of the Social Democratic Party was replaced as prime minister by Ivo Sanader of the HDZ, who has led his party away from nationalism toward mainstream European Christian democracy. Talks with the European Union met delays in 2005 over the failure to arrest Ante Gotovina (▷ right), but Croatia is on course to join the EU and NATO at the end of 2010. Sanader resigned in 2009, opening the way for Jadranka Kosor, Croatia's first female prime minister, to take office.

Above left *Stjepan Mesić, president of Croatia for 10 years until his resignation in 2010*
Above right *Jadranka Kosor, Croatia's first woman prime minister*

A MESIĆ OF PEACE

If Franjo Tuđman was a natural war leader, Stjepan (Stipe) Mesić, president of Croatia from 2000 until his retirement in 2010, was the man for peace. A former Communist mayor, he was actually the last president of Yugoslavia before it collapsed in 1991. In 1994 he split with Tuđman over the war in Bosnia-Herzegovina, and formed the Croatian People's Party. Elected as president following Tuđman's death, he was branded a traitor by nationalists for being a witness at The Hague. He has also encouraged the return of Serbian refugees. Re-elected in 2005, Mesić saw out his second term without achieving one of his main goals, to see Croatia join the EU. He was succeeded by Ivo Josipović, a former composer and university professor.

HERO OR VILLAIN?

The arrest of General Ante Gotovina (b1955) on the Spanish island of Tenerife in December 2005 brought crowds onto the streets in Croatia. To many Croats, especially veterans of the Homeland War, he is regarded as a patriotic hero who liberated Croatia from Serbian aggression. To prosecutors at The Hague, he is a war criminal who allowed his troops to murder and deport Croatian Serbs during Operation Storm in 1995. The arrest highlighted the dilemmas for the Croatian government in its dealings with the war crimes tribunal, as it attempts to tread a delicate balance between international obligations and public opinion. Director Jack Baric's 2009 film *Searching for a Storm* questions whether Gotovina was made a scapegoat by the UN at the war crimes tribunal to justify its own failures in the war.

ON THE MOVE

On the Move gives you detailed advice and information about the various options for travelling to Croatia before explaining the best ways to get around the country once you are there. Handy tips help you with everything from buying tickets to renting a car.

ARRIVING BY AIR

Croatia is well served by flights from other European countries, with major international airports at Zagreb, Split and Dubrovnik having flights all year. Pula, Rijeka and Zadar airports are busiest in summer, with many charter flights and a number of budget airlines. All airports have facilities including currency exchange, ATMs and car hire, while bigger terminals at Zagreb, Split and Dubrovnik have banks, post offices, cafés and shops. There is also an airport at Osijek, mostly for domestic flights, and international airfields on Brač and Lošinj, used by smaller planes.

SCHEDULED FLIGHTS

The national carrier, Croatia Airlines, flies to Zagreb from major European cities including Amsterdam, Berlin, Brussels, Frankfurt, London, Munich, Paris, Rome, Sarajevo, Stockholm, Vienna and Zurich. It also operates connecting flights from Zagreb to regional airports, and direct international services to Pula, Rijeka, Split, Zadar and Dubrovnik year round (tel 020 8563 0022, UK). Alternatively, visit www.croatiaairlines.hr.

From the UK, British Airways flies from Gatwick to Dubrovnik.

GETTING INTO CITIES FROM THE AIRPORT

AIRPORT	ZAGREB (ZAG)	PULA (PUY)	RIJEKA (RJK)
INFORMATION	Tel 01 456 2222 www.zagreb-airport.hr	Tel 052 530105 www.airport-pula.hr	Tel 051 842132 www.rijeka-airport.hr
LOCATION	15km (9.5 miles) south of Zagreb at Pleso	8km (5 miles) northeast of Pula	30km (19 miles) south of Rijeka on the island of Krk
BY BUS	Croatia Airlines shuttle buses depart every 30–60 minutes from 7am–8pm, with later buses linked to flight arrival times. The bus terminates at Zagreb's main bus station, from where tram 6 goes to the city centre. Journey time: 30 minutes Price: 30kn	Brioni buses run twice weekly, departing Tuesday 10.50am and Thursday 9am. Journey time: 15 minutes Price: 29kn	Autotrans buses meet incoming flights for the transfer to Jelačićev Trg in the city centre. Journey time: 30 minutes Price: 30kn
BY TAXI	Approximately 200kn to downtown Zagreb	Approximately 80kn to city centre	Approximately 250kn to city centre

Other airlines with direct flights from Europe include Aer Lingus, Air France, Alitalia, Austrian Airlines, CSA, KLM, Lufthansa, Malev and SAS.

There are currently no direct flights to Croatia from North America. Travellers from outside Europe should fly to a European city such as London and pick up a connecting flight.

BUDGET AIRLINES

The low-cost airline revolution has reached Croatia, with a growing number of budget carriers operating flights, particularly to the coastal airports during the summer. Routes change with the seasons and prices vary from day to day, so you should shop around online for the most competitive prices or look on an internet search engine such as www. skyscanner.net.

Budget airlines flying to Croatia from the UK include easyJet from Gatwick and Bristol to Split, and Gatwick and Liverpool to Dubrovnik; Wizz Air from Luton to Zagreb, and Ryanair from Edinburgh and Stansted to Pula. European budget airlines operating to Croatia include German Wings and TUI from Germany, and Norwegian Air Shuttle from Norway. New flights may appear over the next few years, so keep an eye out for new routes to destinations such as Osijek and Zadar.

Ryanair usually offers the cheapest fares on flights from Stansted to Italy's Adriatic coast. You can fly to Ancona, Bari, Pescara, Trieste or Venice and continue to Croatia by ferry or bus.

CHARTER FLIGHTS

During the busy summer season tour operators have charter flights to Croatia from a number of regional airports across Europe. Although many of the seats are booked by the tour operators for passengers on their package holidays, it is often possible to buy seat-only tickets on these flights. Among the major operators of charter flights to Croatia are Holiday Options and Thomson in the UK.

BUDGET AIRLINES WEBSITES

easyJet	www.easyjet.com
German Wings	www.germanwings.com
Norwegian Air Shuttle	www.norwegian.no
Ryanair	www.ryanair.com
SN Brussels	www.flysn.com
TUI	www.tuifly.com
Wizz Air	www.wizzair.com

ZADAR (ZAD)

Tel 023 205800
www.zadar-airport.hr
8km (5 miles) southeast of Zadar

Croatia Airlines shuttle buses coincide with flight arrival times for the transfer to the city bus station and ferry port.
Journey time: 15 minutes
Price: 25kn

Approximately 100kn to city centre

SPLIT (SPU)

Tel 021 733100
www.split-airport.hr
25km (16 miles) west of Split near Trogir

Croatia Airlines shuttle buses coincide with flight arrival times. The bus terminates at the east end of the Riva, close to the ferry port.
Journey time: 30 minutes
Price: 30kn
Local bus 37 from Trogir runs every 20 minutes throughout the day, passing the airport on its way to Split.
Journey time: 45 minutes
Price: 15kn

Approximately 250kn to city centre

DUBROVNIK (DBV)

Tel 020 773377
www.airport-dubrovnik.hr
20km (12 miles) south of Dubrovnik at Čilipi

Croatia Airlines and Atlas shuttle buses coincide with flight arrival times. The buses terminate at the main bus station at Gruž, and also stop by the entrance to the old town at Pile Gate.
Journey time: 30 minutes
Price: 35kn

Approximately 200kn to Dubrovnik and 100kn to Cavtat

ARRIVING BY SEA

The many ferry services linking Croatia to Italy across the Adriatic Sea are a convenient option for travellers driving across Europe or those taking budget flights to Italy. Most ferry ports are right in the city centre, and standing on deck watching the ship sail into the harbour is undoubtedly the most romantic way to arrive in Croatia. Main year-round routes are Ancona to Zadar, Ancona to Split and Bari to Dubrovnik. Additional seasonal services include fast ferries from Venice to Istria in summer.

CAR FERRIES

Jadrolinija has overnight car and passenger ferries from Ancona to Zadar (8 hours), Ancona to Split (10 hours) and Bari to Dubrovnik (8 hours). In summer there are also services from Pescara to Split (6–12 hours), Pescara to Stari Grad (9 hours), Ancona to Stari Grad (12 hours) and Ancona to Korčula (15 hours). These ferries link with the main Jadrolinija coastal route between Rijeka and Dubrovnik.

SEM Blueline operates year-round car ferries from Ancona to Split, with seasonal services to Stari Grad and Vis. Car ferries are also run by Azzurra Line to Dubrovnik from Bari. From June to September both Sanmar and SNAV offer high-speed jetfoil services from Pescara to Stari Grad (3.5 hours) and Split (5 hours). SNAV also run catamarans from Ancona to Split (4.5 hours). These are much faster than traditional car ferries, but you can't go on deck.

PASSENGER FERRIES

In summer, Venezia Lines operates high-speed catamarans from Venice to Pula, Poreč, Rovinj, Rabac and Mali Lošinj, with sailing times of between 2 and 4 hours. These ferries mostly cater for foot passengers, but it is also possible to take cars and motorcycles on the routes from Venice to Pula and Rovinj.

Emilia Romagna offers high-speed catamarans in summer from the Italian ports of Pesaro, Ravenna and Rimini to Pula, Rovinj, Mali Lošinj, Hvar and Dugi Otok. Mia Tours operates fast boats in summer from Ancona to Zadar and Hvar.

PRACTICALITIES

» Foot passengers can usually buy tickets on arrival at the ferry terminal, but for vehicles, particularly if you plan to travel at peak times, it is best to make a reservation, either direct with the company or online at www.traghettionline.net.
» Large car ferries have a full range of facilities, including restaurants, bars, shops cabins, reclining seats and couchettes.
» The port at Dubrovnik is at Gruž, 4km (2.5 miles) west of the old town; take bus 1A or 1B to Pile.

USEFUL TELEPHONE NUMBERS AND WEBSITES		
FERRY COMPANY	TELEPHONE	WEBSITE
Azzurra Line	+39 080 592 8400	www.azzurraline.com
Emilia Romagna	+39 054 767 5157	www.emiliaromagnalines.it
Jadrolinija	+385 051 666111	www.jadrolinija.hr
Mia Tours	+385 023 254300	www.miatours.hr
Sanmar	+39 085 451 0873	www.sanmar.it
SEM Blueline	+385 021 352553	www.bli-ferry.com
SNAV	+39 071 207 6116	www.snav.it
Venezia Lines	+39 041 242 4000	www.venezialines.com

Croatia shares land borders with Slovenia, Hungary, Bosnia-Herzegovina, Serbia and Montenegro. The majority of border crossings are open 24 hours a day. Travellers arriving from Slovenia and Hungary can expect minimal delays at the border, but be prepared for delays and extensive checks of paperwork if entering from Bosnia, Serbia or Montenegro.

BY CAR

Drivers entering Croatia must show their driver's licence, car registration documents and insurance certificate (green card). International driving licences are not valid in Croatia, but EU and other national driver's licences are valid for six months. If you are bringing your own car or motorcycle, arrange insurance and obtain the relevant documents from your insurance company before you leave home.

If you hire a car outside Croatia you will need to show rental documents at the border. It is important to check that the insurance covers Croatia. Because of the number of visitors arriving in Croatia via low-cost flights to Italy, car rental agencies in Trieste and Venice are used to this situation and will usually stamp your documents at no extra cost to confirm that your insurance is valid in Croatia. If you book online be sure to read the small print regarding insurance in other countries.

It is compulsory for all drivers to carry a first-aid kit, warning triangle, reflective jacket and set of replacement bulbs. In winter, you are also strongly advised to carry snow chains, particularly if travelling in mountain and highland regions. Car hire companies usually supply these at no extra charge.

Before arriving, familiarize yourself with driving regulations in Croatia (▷ 33–35). All drivers should be aware that dipped (low beam) headlights are compulsory at all times and that driving with any alcohol in the system is forbidden for drivers under 24 years of age. For drivers over the age of 24 the legal limit is 0.05 per cent of alcohol in the blood.

Roadside assistance and repairs are available from the Hrvatski Autoklub 24 hours a day by calling 987; a charge is made for this service. Alternatively, take out European breakdown cover before you leave home with an organization like the Automobile Association (AA). Car hire firms provide their own breakdown/rescue service.

BY BUS

Croatia is served by international bus services from across Europe.

EMERGENCY TELEPHONE NUMBERS	
Police	92
Fire	93
Ambulance	94
All emergencies	112
Roadside assistance	987
	(+385 1 987 from a mobile phone)

Most buses arrive at the central bus station in Zagreb. There are also daily services from the Italian city of Trieste to Poreč, Pula, Rovinj, Opatija, Rijeka, Zadar, Split and Dubrovnik. Travellers to Croatia can fly to Trieste, take a local bus from the airport to the city bus station and pick up a connection from there.

BY TRAIN

There are direct rail links to Zagreb from Budapest, Ljubljana, Munich, Venice and Vienna, and indirect links from other European cities. The Inter Rail and Eurail passes are valid for journeys both to and within Croatia. Border formalities are completed on the train.

GETTING AROUND

Croatia has a comprehensive and well-integrated public transportation network. Bus and train stations in the main towns and cities are generally close together, and buses also link with ferry timetables, making it easy to switch from one mode of transport to another. Most of the sights in this book are accessible by public transport, but to get the most out of your visit, consider hiring a car to explore the countryside, national parks and out-of-the-way areas.

BY CAR

Driving in Croatia is mostly straightforward once you have got used to the somewhat cavalier attitude to overtaking (passing) of many Croatian drivers. Speed limits (▷ 34) and the ban on drink-driving for under 24s are strictly enforced by the police, so stick to the law irrespective of what the locals do. Much of the time Croatia's roads are pleasantly free of traffic, though major routes to the Adriatic coast get very clogged up on summer weekends and the single-lane Magistrala coast road is a nightmare in July and August.

New motorways from Zagreb to Rijeka and Split have reduced journey times to the coast and linked Croatia into the European route network. Although motorways are less scenic than many of the alternatives, they are also much faster and the volume of traffic regulated by the high cost of tolls (▷ 35).

BY BUS

Buses are the most common form of public transport in Croatia, and range from luxury air-conditioned vehicles on inter-city and long-distance routes to rickety old buses linking remote villages. A plethora of private companies provide a network that covers virtually the entire country. It is possible to get just about anywhere by bus, though you may need to change buses along the way and some remote destinations are served very infrequently. Bus journeys between the mainland and the islands include travel by ferry. Larger cities such as Zagreb, Split, Dubrovnik, Rijeka and Osijek have their own municipal bus and tram services.

BY TRAIN

Croatia's rail network is concentrated in the north and east of the country. There are no trains to Dubrovnik and few trains to other coastal cities. Train travel in inland Croatia is safe and

comfortable, but tends to be slower than the equivalent journey by bus.

BY FERRY

The only way to reach the outlying islands is by ferry. Most ferries are operated by Jadrolinija, together with various local companies. Car and passenger ferries run throughout the year, with extra services in summer. During the peak holiday months of July and August long lines build up at the ferry ports so it is essential to arrive in good time if you plan to take a car on the ferry.

ORGANIZED TOURS

Local tour operators in the main towns and resorts offer a wide variety of organized excursions. Although these invariably work out more expensive than doing your own thing, they make a good alternative to public transport if you want to visit remote areas, such as the Plitvice Lakes, without hiring a car.

Driving is the quickest and easiest method of travelling around Croatia, and the only way to reach some of the more remote villages and mountain areas. Roads vary from well-maintained motorways (highways) to dirt roads.

BRINGING YOUR OWN VEHICLE

Before bringing your car or motorcycle to Croatia, ensure that it is properly serviced and that you have adequate insurance and breakdown cover. For more details, see Arriving By Land (▷ 31).

CAR RENTAL

» International car rental chains have offices at airports, ports and in city centres. You will also find local companies in main towns and resorts. Rental can be arranged through travel agents and hotels.
» It is usually cheaper to book in advance. The best deals are available online, through individual rental company websites or at www. holidayautos.co.uk. Definitely book in advance if you need a car for the duration of your visit or want to collect it on arrival at the airport. If you only want a car for a few days, it may be better to wait until you arrive, when you have a better idea of where you want to go.
» If you require extras such as child seats, luggage racks and snow chains remember that these should be booked in advance.
» You will need to show a passport, national driver's licence and credit card. The credit card deposit will be used as security in case you return the vehicle damaged or without fuel.
» The minimum age is usually 21, or 25 if you wish to rent a larger vehicle, and you must have held a valid licence for at least two years.
» Check that you have adequate insurance. Your rental agreement should include the minimum legal requirements for third-party insurance, but you are strongly advised to take out CDW (collision damage waiver) and theft protection. Without these, you will be liable for the full repair or replacement cost in the event of accident or theft
» Insurance policies usually include an excess of around €400, meaning that you will pay the first part of any claim. You may be offered a waiver for an additional payment.
» If you plan to drive into neighbouring countries, make sure the insurance covers you for this. Some policies exclude driving in Serbia and Montenegro. If you rent a car outside Croatia, check that the insurance is valid in Croatia and get confirmation of this on the rental documents.
» Check the condition of the vehicle before driving it and get the rental company to note damage.
» Check the procedure for returning the car. Most companies have designated parking at airports. Always return the keys and documents to the office inside the airport—never to anyone in the car park (parking lot) claiming to be an employee of the car rental company.
» Most cars are supplied with a full tank of fuel and should be returned at the end of the rental period with a full tank.
» Always keep your passport, driver's licence and rental documents with you; never leave them unattended in the car.

CAR RENTAL AGENCIES		
NAME	TELEPHONE	WEBSITE
Avis	062 222226	www.avis.com.hr
Budget	01 480 5688	www.budget.hr
Europcar	0800 443322	www.europcar.hr
Hertz	01 484 6777	www.hertz.hr
National	01 6215924	www.nationalcar.com
Sixt	01 665 1599	www.sixt.hr

RULES OF THE ROAD

» Drive on the right and overtake (pass) on the left.

» At roundabouts give way to cars from the left.

» The minimum driving age is 18.

» Children under 12 must sit in a rear seat.

» It is illegal to use a mobile phone while driving.

» Dipped (low beam) headlights must be on at all times.

» The driver and all passengers must wear safety belts.

» Safety helmets must be worn when riding mopeds and motorcycles.

» Speed limits (▷ panel pposite) are strictly enforced. There is a minimum speed limit of 40kph (25mph) on motorways.

» Croatia's drink-driving laws are strict. Drivers over the age of 24 are permitted to have 0.05 per cent of alcohol in the blood. However, the regulation zero per cent still applies to under 24s and is strictly enforced. Never drive if you think you may be over the limit and allow 24 hours for any alcohol to leave the system.

» The police can impose fixed on-the-spot fines, ranging from 300kn for driving without headlights to 3,000kn for speeding or drink-driving. Fines must be paid into a bank within eight days and the police may hold your passport until you do so.

MAJOR ROUTES
Motorways (Highways)

» Croatia has a rapidly developing system of motorways *(autoceste)* linked into the European route network. All have at least two traffic lanes plus an emergency lane in each direction. Overhead electronic signs display traffic information, such as temperature, wind velocity and temporary speed limits. There are regular service areas *(odmorište)*.

» The A1 motorway, also known as the Dalmatina, connects Zagreb with Split (380km/236 miles). Completed in 2005, it is a remarkable feat of engineering, with two tunnels of around 5.6km (3.5 miles) beneath the Velebit and Mala Kapela mountains. The section south to Ploče opened

in 2008 and by 2012 the ribbon of tarmac should extend to Dubrovnik.

» The A3 motorway runs west from Zagreb to the Slovenian border and east to the Serbian border. This is the Croatian section of the Autocesta, the major route across the former Yugoslavia, linking Zagreb with Ljubljana and Belgrade. It forms part of European route E70.

» Other motorways include the A2 from Zagreb to the Slovenian border via Krapina; A4 from Zagreb to the Hungarian border via Varaždin; and A6 from Zagreb to Rijeka. The A7 links Rijeka with the Slovenian border at Rupa.

» The A8 and A9 form the 'Istrian ypsilon', a Y-shaped motorway network linking Rijeka, Pula and Slovenia.

» Projects under way include a motorway from Zagreb to Sisak, and a north–south motorway across Slavonia linking Hungary and Bosnia via Osijek and Đakovo.

Main Roads

» The D1 is the old main road from Zagreb to Split via Karlovac, the Plitvice Lakes, Knin and Sinj. This follows a scenic route through the Lika and Krajina regions, but is single-lane each way.

» The D2 runs across northern Croatia from Varaždin to Osijek, with one lane in each direction.

» The D8, also known as the Magistrala or Adriatic Highway, follows the coast for 600km (372 miles) from Rijeka to Dubrovnik. A stunning drive, it gets very busy in summer and there are few opportunities for overtaking. It forms part of European route E65.

The Neum Corridor

Between Ploče and Dubrovnik, the Magistrala travels through a short section of Bosnia-Herzegovina for 9km (5.5 miles) around the Bosnian town of Neum. There are minimal formalities at the border, but have your passport and vehicle documents ready and check that your insurance covers you. The only way of avoiding this is to take a ferry from Ploče to

Trpanj, but plans to build a bridge from Ploče to Pelješac by 2010 will make it possible to drive from Zagreb to Dubrovnik within Croatia.

Tolls

» A toll is payable on all motorways, with the exception of the southern ring road around Zagreb, which links the various parts of the motorway network together.

» Collect a ticket on entering the motorway and pay at the toll booth on exit. Tolls can be paid in either Croatian kunas or euros. Payment can also be made by using one of the major credit cards.

» The A8 and A9 in Istria are largely toll-free, except for the Učka tunnel linking Rijeka with Istria and the bridge over the River Mirna between Poreč and Novigrad.

» There is also a toll for using the road bridge between Rijeka and Krk.

ACCIDENTS AND BREAKDOWNS

» If you are involved in an accident, you must call the police. If driving a rental car, failure to get a police report will invalidate your insurance and you will be liable for the full cost of repairs.

» Hrvatski Autoklub provides a breakdown service with a fixed scale of charges. Mechanics can carry out minor repairs at the roadside or transfer you and your vehicle up to 200km (125 miles) after an accident or breakdown.

SPEED LIMITS
» 50kph (31mph) in built-up areas
» 90kph (56mph) outside built-up areas
» 110kph (68mph) on expressways
» 130kph (80mph) on motorways

TOLL FEES	
Zagreb–Varaždin	23kn
Zagreb–Rijeka	56kn
Zagreb–Zadar	105kn
Zagreb–Split	157kn
Krk bridge	30kn
Mirna bridge	14kn
Učka tunnel	28kn
(All prices correct as of October 2009)	

TRAFFIC INFORMATION

Hrvatski Autoklub provides a 24-hour information service (tel 01 464 0800) covering traffic and weather, ferry times and road closures.

FUEL

» Petrol (gas) stations open daily from 7am to 8pm; many stay open until 10pm in summer. At motorway service areas, on main roads and in major cities, petrol stations remain open 24 hours.
» Most petrol stations are staffed by attendants, but some are self-service.
» Fuel includes Eurosuper 95, Superplus 98 and Eurodiesel.
» The majority of petrol stations accept payment by credit card.

PARKING

» Car parking can be a problem in towns and cities, especially between June and September. Most towns have car parking (lots) just outside the historic centre.
» On-street parking is indicated by blue lines. Pay cash at the meter and display the ticket clearly.
» You can pay parking by SMS (text message) in some cities. Send a text with your registration number (without spaces) to the telephone number on the meter and you will receive confirmation that your mobile phone account has been debited.
» Check the details of any parking restrictions, as these vary from town to town. In some, parking is free between October and May, while in others there is a charge all year.
» Do not be tempted to park illegally, especially in large cities. Your car will probably be towed away and the fee for getting it back will be high.

TIPS

» Try to avoid driving in big cities.
» There are few fuel stations on the islands, so fill up before you go.
» Carry snow chains in winter, particularly if travelling in mountain or highland regions.
» Be suspicious of anyone indicating that you have a problem with your car, or flagging you down by the roadside, as thieves have been known to operate in this way.

The chart below shows the distances in kilometres of a car journey between key destinations in Croatia.

	Đakovo	Dubrovnik	Karlovac	Knin	Makarska	Nova Gradiška	Ogulin	Osijek	Pula	Rijeka	Rovinj	Šibenik	Sinj	Sisak	Split	Trogir	Varaždin	Virovitica	Vukovar	Zadar
Dubrovnik	850																			
Karlovac	297	553																		
Knin	540	310	243																	
Makarska	684	166	387	144																
Nova Gradiška	104	705	195	395	539															
Ogulin	342	540	45	230	374	240														
Osijek	37	887	334	577	721	125	379													
Pula	527	703	230	388	537	475	206	564												
Rijeka	421	597	124	282	431	319	100	458	106											
Rovinj	512	688	215	373	522	410	191	549	43	91										
Šibenik	596	288	299	56	122	451	286	633	431	325	416									
Sinj	605	245	308	65	79	460	295	642	453	347	438	80								
Sisak	202	605	95	295	439	100	140	239	325	219	310	351	360							
Split	634	228	337	94	62	489	324	671	475	369	460	60	29	389						
Trogir	634	250	317	74	84	489	324	671	460	354	445	38	51	369	22					
Varaždin	218	683	130	373	517	200	175	235	360	254	345	429	438	145	467	447				
Virovitica	110	724	214	414	558	113	259	127	444	338	429	657	666	119	695	695	108			
Vukovar	52	902	349	592	736	156	394	35	579	473	564	648	657	254	686	686	270	162		
Zadar	530	369	233	102	203	385	188	567	327	221	312	71	154	285	145	113	363	447	582	
Zagreb	248	603	50	293	437	150	95	285	280	174	265	349	358	65	387	367	80	165	306	283

BUSES

Long-distance bus travel in Croatia is fast, reliable and efficient, and a good way to meet local people. Modern, air-conditioned buses travel between the major cities, while local routes serve outlying towns and villages. Services are run by a variety of private companies, with competition keeping prices low and standards high.

BUYING TICKETS

» Major cities have large, central bus stations, always open, with such facilities as left luggage (baggage check), toilets and ATMs.
» Departures are usually displayed on a board. Major routes have hourly services, but others may only be daily or a few times a week.
» Buy a ticket from one of the ticket windows. The ticket should show the destination, departure time, platform and seat numbers and name of the bus company. At some bus stations different companies have their own ticket windows, so compare times and prices before you buy.
» Tickets are valid for a particular bus, not for the route. Round-trip tickets usually work out cheaper, but mean you must travel with the same company in both directions.

» Children under 12 usually travel for half-price and under-4s travel free, though this may vary.
» On popular routes it is worth booking your seat a day or two in advance, but this is usually only possible if you get on in the city where the bus originates.
» To join an inter-city bus at a point on its route, buy a ticket when the bus arrives or pay the driver.

PRACTICALITIES

» Smoking is banned.
» Large items of luggage go in the hold (for a fee of 7kn).
» Not all buses have toilets. Comfort

breaks are taken every two hours.
» Timetables for all services across Croatia can be checked online at www.autobusni-kolodvor.com.

LOCAL BUSES

» Major cities have municipal bus networks, extending to the suburbs and including popular tourist routes.
» In Rijeka and Split local buses depart from a suburban bus station, not the main inter-city station.
» Tickets can be bought from the driver but may be cheaper if bought in advance from a kiosk. Validate tickets at the start of your journey in the machine behind the driver.

MAIN BUS STATIONS

CITY	TELEPHONE
Dubrovnik	060 305070
Pula	060 304090
Rijeka	060 302010
Split	060 327777
Zadar	023 211555
Zagreb	060 313333

INTER-CITY ROUTES

FROM	TO	TIME	SINGLE FARE
Dubrovnik	Korčula	3 hours	100kn
Dubrovnik	Split	4 hours	112kn
Dubrovnik	Zagreb	11 hours	200kn
Pula	Rijeka	2 hours	93kn
Pula	Zagreb	4 hours	209kn
Zadar	Zagreb	4 hours	130kn
Zagreb	Osijek	4 hours	150kn
Zagreb	Samobor	30 minutes	25kn
Zagreb	Split	6 hours	120kn
Zagreb	Varaždin	2 hours	60kn
(All prices correct as of October 2009)			

TRAINS

Croatia's rail network was developed in the days of the Austro-Hungarian empire to link Zagreb with other parts of the empire to the north. As a result, train travel in Croatia is largely restricted to the north and east of the country, making it most useful for journeys to and from Zagreb. There are no trains to Dubrovnik, and only slow branch lines to Dalmatian coastal cities such as Šibenik and Zadar. Travelling by train is generally slower but marginally cheaper than making the equivalent journey by bus. The exception is the high-speed rail link from Zagreb to Split, with modern, well-equipped trains complete with personal headphones and laptop connections making the journey in under six hours.

WHERE TO START
The central railway station in Zagreb is a magnificent Austro-Hungarian edifice, built in 1892 as a stop on the Orient Express. Now restored, it has a currency exchange, newsagents, ATMs and a left luggage (baggage check) facility.

TRAIN AND TICKET TYPES
» *Putnički* (passenger trains) are slow trains that stop at every station. All seating is second-class, unreserved and non-smoking. The only facilities are toilets.
» *Brzi* (express) and Inter-City trains are much faster, stopping only at major stations, and usually have first- and second-class carriages, with a choice of smoking or non-smoking. Booking is recommended, and is compulsory on certain rush-hour services. Trains are modern, comfortable and have air-conditioning and toilets, with buffet cars on some services.
» First-class rail tickets cost 50 per cent more than the standard second-class ticket.

» A return fare is usually twice the cost of one-way, but a few inter-city routes offer cheaper returns.
» Children under 12 travel half price and under-4s travel free.
» On overnight trains from Zagreb to Split you can pay extra for a berth in a sleeping car or couchette.

RAIL PASSES
» Inter Rail, available to citizens of European countries, offers unlimited travel in 30 countries for up to a month. The pass is only useful if your visit to Croatia is part of a larger trip, including other European countries.
» Eurail is for people living outside Europe and offers unlimited travel in 21 European countries. Passes from 10 days to three months are available.
» European residents can buy a Euro

Domino pass in their home country, giving unlimited rail travel in Croatia for between three and eight days in a given calendar month. This is only worth doing if you plan to travel extensively by rail.

INFORMATION
Timetables are available at main railway stations, or contact Hrvatske Željeznice (Croatian Railways); tel 060 333444; www.hznet.hr

GLOSSARY	
CROATIAN	**ENGLISH**
blagajna	ticket office
dolazak	arrival
odlazak	departure
putnički	slow train
vozni red	timetable

INTER-CITY ROUTES			
FROM	**TO**	**TIME**	**SINGLE (SECOND-CLASS)**
Zagreb	Osijek	3–4 hours	114kn
Zagreb	Split	5–6 hours	105kn
Zagreb	Varaždin	2–3 hours	56kn
(All prices correct as of October 2009)			

FERRIES

Ferries are an essential part of Croatia's transport network and the only way to reach the Adriatic islands. Car and passenger ferries run throughout the year, providing a lifeline for islanders and an enjoyable experience for visitors.

CAR FERRIES

» Most routes are operated by Jadrolinija (tel 051 666111; www.jadrolinija.hr), which has offices in Rijeka, Zadar, Split, Dubrovnik and on the major islands.

» SEM Blueline (tel 021 352553; www.splittours.hr) competes with Jadrolinija on the busy Split–Supetar route, with three ferries a day in winter and more in summer, at prices around 20 per cent lower than Jadrolinija.

» In a few places, the service is provided by a local company, such as Rapska Plovidba, which runs to the island of Rab.

» The majority of routes link the islands directly with the mainland, making them less useful for island-hopping. Exceptions are the summer service from Baška (Krk) to Lopar (Rab) and the year-round service from Korčula to Lastovo.

» Split is the major point of departure for the Dalmatian islands, with ferries to Brač, Hvar, Korčula, Lastovo, Šolta and Vis. The large, modern passenger terminal has ticket offices, toilets, parking and ATMs.

» The nearest islands to the mainland can be reached by short hops of 20–40 minutes from ports directly opposite the island. Routes include Brestova to Porozina (Cres), Jablanac to Mišnjak (Rab) and Orebić to Dominće (Korčula). In summer these provide an almost continuous roll-on, roll-off service, with departures at least hourly during the day. Buses from Rijeka and Dubrovnik use these ferries on their way to Cres, Lošinj, Rab and Korčula.

» Jadrolinija also operates a coastal ferry from Rijeka to Dubrovnik via Split, Stari Grad and Korčula. The frequency varies from twice a week in winter to daily in summer. Boats leave Rijeka in the evening, travelling overnight to Split (10 hours) and continuing by day to Dubrovnik (20 hours).

TIMETABLES AND TICKETS

» Jadrolinija publishes timetables twice a year, covering June to

JADROLINIJA OFFICES	
PORT	**TELEPHONE**
Dubrovnik	020 418000
Korčula	020 715410
Rijeka	051 211444
Split	021 338333
Stari Grad	021 765048
Supetar	021 631357
Vis	021 711032
Zadar	023 254800

September and October to May. They are available at Jadrolinija offices and ferry ports. A basic service operates year-round, with more frequent departures in summer.

» Tickets for departures from Split can be bought at the Jadrolinija ticket office inside the terminal. You can also purchase them from kiosks outside the terminal building.

» Tickets for most island ferries can be bought at kiosks on the quayside around 30 minutes before departure.

» It is possible to buy tickets in advance, but this does not guarantee a reservation. Foot passengers can always get onto the boat, but cars must join a line. At busy times, especially in July and August, you should aim to arrive at the harbour at least two hours before departure. If the ticket office is not open, park your car in the line and wait.

» There are separate charges for passengers and vehicles, including cars, motorcycles and bicycles. You must buy a ticket for all passengers, including the driver. Children aged 3 to 12 pay half price. The cost of tickets rises by around 20 per cent between June and September.

» Tickets for the coastal route can be booked in advance. Accommodation ranges from deck passage to couchettes and private cabins. Prices are quoted in euros but can be paid in Croatian kuna. A journey from Rijeka to Dubrovnik in high season costs 250kn for deck passage and 670kn for a berth in a two-bed inside cabin with shower and toilet, plus 700kn for a car. Cabin prices include breakfast, and other meals can be booked in advance. There is a 20 per cent discount for return journeys. Foot passengers can break their journey for up to a week

FARES

FROM	TO	PASSENGER	CAR
Baška	Lopar	37kn	225kn
Brestova	Porozina	16kn	108kn
Drvenik	Sućuraj	12kn	86kn
Dubrovnik	Lopud	15kn	n/a
Dubrovnik	Sobra	38kn	259k
Orebić	Dominče	12kn	58kn
Split	Stari Grad	38kn	259kn
Split	Supetar	28kn	127kn
Split	Vela Luka	42kn	374kn
Split	Vis	41kn	270kn

All prices correct for high season 2009

at no extra charge, provided their ticket is validated by the purser at each stop.

PRACTICALITIES

» Ferries on the major routes from Rijeka, Split and Dubrovnik begin embarkation 1–2 hours before sailing. Most island ferries embark around 10–15 minutes prior to departure, but it is best to arrive well before this.

» There are limited facilities at most ports. As well as a Jadrolinija ticket booth, there may be a café and newspaper kiosk.

» Most ferries have a café on board for hot and cold drinks and snacks. The main coastal ferry from Rijeka to Dubrovnik has a full restaurant.

» Smoking is only permitted on deck.

FAST FERRIES

» Jadrolinija operates high-speed catamarans all year to the islands of Rab, Cres, Lošinj, Brač, Hvar, Korčula and Lastovo. High-speed services are also run by SEM Blueline (Split to Vis), Krilo Express (Split to Hvar and Korčula), and Atlantagent (Dubrovnik to Mljet).

» Catamarans take foot passengers only. They tend to be quicker than conventional ferries, but are more expensive and you cannot go on deck to enjoy the view, which is one of the pleasures of travelling by ferry. Smoking is not permitted.

» Most of these services are subsidised by the state and the timetable is geared to the needs of islanders, usually with one departure from the island in early morning and a return service in late afternoon. This makes them useful for day-trips from the islands to the mainland, but means an overnight stay if you are travelling to the islands. An exception is the daily Dubrovnik to Mljet catamaran (▷ above).

» In summer, taxi and excursion boats from the main harbours and resorts offer day-trips to islands and island-hopping trips.

GETTING AROUND IN ZAGREB

Zagreb has an efficient and integrated public transportation system, operated by ZET. The city centre is served by trams, while buses link Zagreb with the outlying suburbs.

TRAMS
» Trams run every 5–10 minutes from 4am to midnight. Line 3 operates weekdays only.
» A network map is displayed at all stops. The busiest interchange is Trg Bana (Josipa) Jelačića, with seven different lines.
» The route number and destination are displayed at the front of the tram.
» Night trams run every 30–40 minutes from midnight to 5am. Most useful is No. 31, from Črnomerec to Savski Most.
» Beware of pickpockets on crowded trams.

BUSES
» Buses serve districts beyond the city centre. Most suburban bus routes begin at the end of tram lines. Bus stations and the destinations they serve are shown on the tram map.
» Buses for Mirogoj depart in front of the cathedral; for Samobor from the main bus station and Črnomerec, at the end of tram lines 2, 6 and 11; for Velika Gorica from behind the railway station.
» Smoking is not allowed on buses or trams.

TICKETS AND PASSES
» Bus and tram tickets can be bought from the driver, but are cheaper in advance from ZET or newspaper kiosks, found in Trg Bana Jelačića and all major transport termini.
» A ticket for Zone 1 costs 8kn in advance and 10kn from the driver. This covers the tram network and most local buses, and is valid for 90 minutes. A one-day pass, valid until 4am, costs 25kn and also includes the funicular.
» A ticket for Zone 2 costs 16kn in advance and 20kn from the driver. It covers journeys to Velika Gorica.
» Children under 6 and people over 65 travel free.
» Tickets must be validated in the machine behind the driver. Passes must be validated the first time of use and shown on request.
» Fines of 210kn are levied for travelling without a ticket or with a non-validated ticket.
» The Zagreb Card, which is available from tourist offices, gives unlimited travel on buses, trams, the funicular and Medvednica cable car. Cards cost 60kn for 24 hours or 90kn for 72 hours.

FUNICULAR AND CABLE CAR
» A funicular railway (uspinjača), built in 1890, connects the upper and lower towns, departing from Tomićeva every 10 minutes from 6.30am to 9pm for Gornji Grad. A single ticket costs 4kn.
» The Sljeme cable car (žičara) makes the 20-minute trip to the summit of Medvednica from near the Dolje tram terminus, leaving on the hour from 8am to 8pm. A single fare costs 11kn, a return 17kn.

TAXIS
» There are taxi ranks outside the Croatian National Theatre on Trg Maršala Tita, south of Trg Bana Jelačića at junction of Gajeva and Teslina, and north of Trg Bana Jelačića near the cathedral.
» You can get a taxi 24 hours a day by dialling 970 or 01 660 0671.
» Fares are metered, with a basic fare of 19kn, plus 7kn per kilometre and 3kn per item of luggage (more on Sundays, public holidays and from 10pm–5am).

USEFUL TRAM LINES
2 Črnomerec–rail station–bus station–Savišče
6 Črnomerec–Trg Bana Jelačića–rail station–bus station–Sopot
11 Črnomerec–Trg Bana Jelačića–Maksimir–Dubec
12 Ljubljanica–Trg Maršala Tita–Trg Bana Jelačića–Maksimir–Dubrava

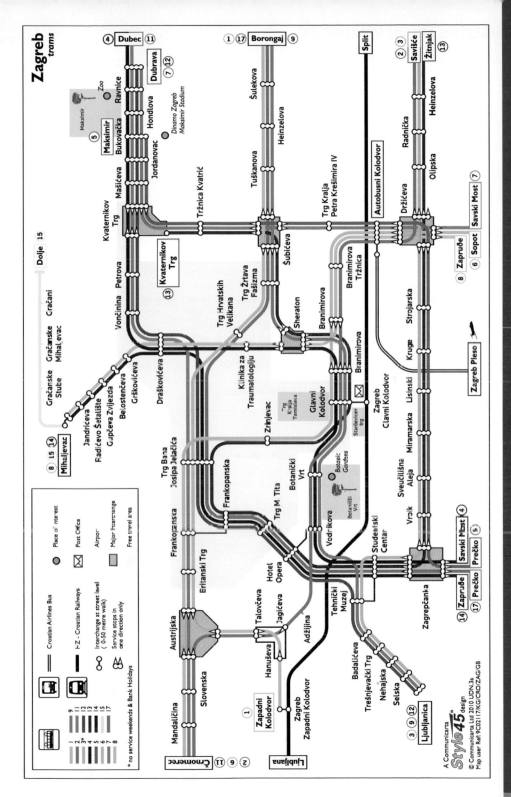

GETTING AROUND IN DUBROVNIK

The old town of Dubrovnik is easily explored on foot, and traffic is banned within the city walls. Buses connect the old town with the hotels on the Lapad peninsula, and boat trips link Dubrovnik with nearby islands.

BUSES
» Buses are operated by Libertas (www.libertasdubrovnik.com). The city bus network is concentrated to the west of the old town, with buses leaving from a terminus outside Pile Gate for Gruž harbour and the Lapad and Babin Kuk peninsulas.
» Timetables are shown at bus stops and available from tourist offices. On busy routes, buses run every 15–20 minutes from 6am to midnight.
» A single ticket costs 8kn from news kiosks or Libertas counters at the bus station and Pile Gate, or 10kn on the bus. You need the exact money as drivers don't give change.
» Tickets must be validated in the machine beside the driver as you board.
» Buses for Cavtat leave from the long-distance bus station at Gruž harbour.
» Smoking is not allowed on buses.
» Beware of pickpockets on crowded buses.

TAXIS
» There are taxi ranks outside Pile and Ploče gates, at Gruž harbour, the bus station and on the main street of Lapad.
» You can get a taxi 24 hours a day by dialling 970 or 0800 1441.
» Fares are metered, and the basic fare is 25kn, plus 8kn per km, and 2kn per piece of luggage.

FERRIES
» Ferries and catamarans to the Elafiti Islands and Mljet depart from the harbour at Gruž.
» Taxi and excursion boats depart from the Old Port for Cavtat and Lokrum in summer.
» Between June and September Nova (tel 020 313599; www.nova-dubrovnik.com) operates a fast shuttle service between Dubrovnik and the Elafiti Islands, as well as boats to Lokrum and a daily shuttle between Gruž harbour and the old

town, which stops at various hotels on the Lapad peninsula. Sample fares are 15kn from the Old Port to Lokrum, 60kn from the Old Port to Gruž, 60kn from Gruž to Lopud, and 30kn from Lopud to Šipan. Children under 7 travel free. You can also buy a one-day pass for 150kn and there are various family and weekly passes available.
» Between April and October an old-fashioned rowing boat ferry *(barkariol)* makes the morning journey across the bay from Lapad to Gruž, as it has done for more than 100 years. Although it only saves a short walk, this is a delightfully nostalgic trip. The journey lasts 10 minutes and costs 5kn.

CAR PARKING
» There are car parks (parking lots) open 24 hours a day outside Pile Gate (10kn/hour) and the northern entrance to the city walls (5kn/hour).
» There is also a long-term car park at Gruž harbour, where you can leave your car for 40kn per day and travel into the city by bus.
» The nearest free parking to the old town is at Gradac, outside Pile Gate, though you will be very lucky to find a space here.
» Do not be tempted to park illegally, especially in the vicinity of the old town, as your car will be clamped or towed away and you will pay a hefty fee for its return.

USEFUL BUS ROUTES

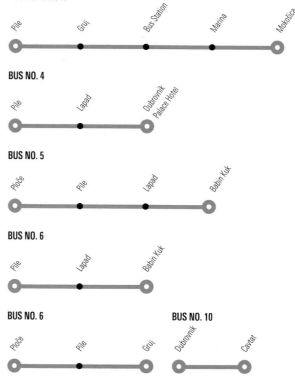

CYCLING IN CROATIA

Croatia has a wealth of unspoiled countryside, coastal scenery and sleepy villages that are perfect for exploring on two wheels.

Options range from challenging mountain-bike trails in the national parks to gentle bike rides on the islands.

TAKING YOUR OWN BICYCLE

» Service your bicycle before you go and take spare lights, reflectors and tyres, which may not be available in Croatia.

» Check that your airline will carry a bicycle.

» Check your insurance policy covers bicycling in Croatia, including personal accidents.

BICYCLE RENTAL

» Tourist offices and hotels can give details of local bicycle rental outlets.

» Most coast and island resorts have at least one bicycle rental shop. You can also rent from hotels and travel agents.

» Typical charges are 20kn per hour or 100kn per day, with discounts for longer rentals.

SAFETY

» Bicycles are forbidden on motorways, and drivers on main roads do not always pay attention to cyclists. Take particular care on the busy Magistrala coast road.

» Check lights, brakes, reflectors and tyres each time you set off.

» Wear bright reflective clothing and a bicycle helmet. Children under 16 must always wear a helmet or face a fine.

RESOURCES

» For information on a range of trails around Zagreb and Samobor, visit www.pedala.hr

» Get *Istra Bike*, with maps and routes around Istria. It is available from tourist offices.

» *Kvarner by Bike* has 19 cycle routes in the Kvarner region.

FAMILY TRAILS

These flat, easy bicycle trails are located in places of scenic beauty, with bicycle rental facilities available in summer.

» Lake Jarun, Zagreb

» On the island of Veli Brijun

» Zlatni Rt forest park, Rovinj

» Around the shores of Vransko Jezero, Pakoštane

» Around the shores of Veliko Jezero, Mljet

» Park Prevlaka, Dubrovnik

CYCLING HOLIDAYS IN CROATIA

COMPANY	TELEPHONE	WEBSITE
Explore	0845 013 1537	www.explore.co.uk
Pure Adventures	+1 480 905 1235	www.pure-adventures.com
Saddle Skedaddle	+44 0191 2651110	www.skedaddle.co.uk
2 Wheel Treks	+44 01483 271212	www.2wheeltreks.co.uk

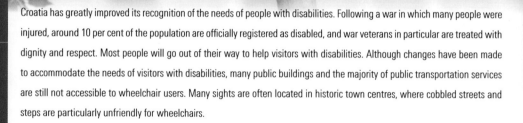

Croatia has greatly improved its recognition of the needs of people with disabilities. Following a war in which many people were injured, around 10 per cent of the population are officially registered as disabled, and war veterans in particular are treated with dignity and respect. Most people will go out of their way to help visitors with disabilities. Although changes have been made to accommodate the needs of visitors with disabilities, many public buildings and the majority of public transportation services are still not accessible to wheelchair users. Many sights are often located in historic town centres, where cobbled streets and steps are particularly unfriendly for wheelchairs.

BEFORE YOU GO

» Ask your tour operator or airline about the facilities they can provide. Although most airlines will transport wheelchairs free of charge and most airports have wheelchair transfer on arrival, this may have to be booked in advance.

» Be clear about your needs and discuss them in detail with your hotel or tour operator before you book. The majority of recently built or renovated hotels are adapted for disabled visitors, but older hotels may not even have ramps.

GETTING AROUND ZAGREB

» The city of Zagreb offers a free dial-a-ride service for wheelchair users in a fleet of adapted vehicles. Companions must pay a fare. The service must be booked at least one day in advance, or on Friday for travel the following Saturday, Sunday or Monday (tel 01 299 5956).

» Old-style buses and trams are being phased out in favour of the new low-floor type which provide wheelchair access. Most buses are now accessible, and the first low-floor trams came into service in 2005.

» The funicular railway between the upper and lower towns is fully wheelchair-accessible.

GETTING AROUND CROATIA

» Airports, bus and train stations in the major cities have wheelchair access, including to toilets.

» Buses, trains and ferries in Croatia are not generally adapted for travellers with disabilities. Getting on and off ferries can be a problem as most boats do not have ramps, but the steward and crew will usually help out.

» Taxis are ordinary cars and are rarely adapted for travellers with disabilities. However, if you specify your needs when booking, a larger vehicle may be provided.

» There are designated disabled parking spaces in most towns and cities.

» In Zagreb and other large cities low-level public phone kiosks are provided.

CROATIA
SOIH (Association of Organizations of Disabled People in Croatia)
Savska 3, Zagreb
Tel 01 482 9394; www.soih.hr

UK
Tourism for All
Tel 0845 124 9974
www.tourismforall.org.uk

USA
SATH (Society for Accessible Travel and Hospitality)
Tel 212 447 7284
www.sath.org

REGIONS

This chapter is divided into six regions of Croatia (▷ 6–7). Region names are for the purposes of this book only and places of interest are listed alphabetically in each region.

Croatia's Regions 46–240

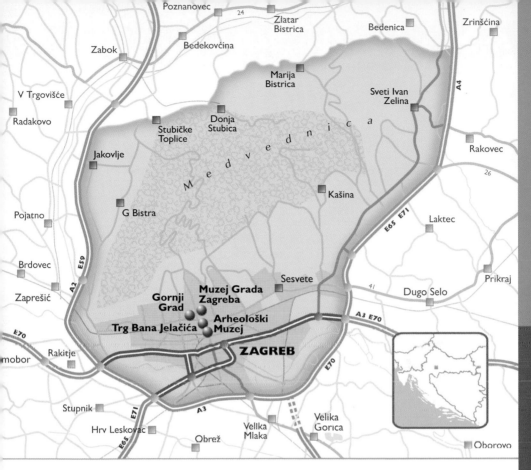

ZAGREB

Home to a quarter of the country's population, the Croatian capital is an energetic, self-confident city, with theatres and concert halls, lively nightlife and the country's best shopping. Somewhat overlooked by sun-seekers hurrying to the coast, Zagreb tempts visitors with striking Austro-Hungarian architecture, intriguing museums and galleries, and atmospheric restaurants, which are open year-round, no matter what the weather. The city also serves as transport hub, linking inland Croatia with the coast.

Zagreb brims with green spaces, wide boulevards and medieval thoroughfares, all centred on Trg Bana Jelačića, the city's ever-busy main square. The city centre is in two parts: Gornji Grad (Upper Town) and Donji Grad (Lower Town). Gornji Grad, reached by perhaps the world's shortest funicular railway, the *Uspinjača* from Ilica, can easily be explored on foot. The sights of Donji Grad are more spread out, with the city's biggest museums set in gardens and parks.

Away from its cultural delights, Zagreb has much else to offer visitors. Mount Medvednica, looming over the city at 1,032m (3,385ft), is easily accessible by a short cable-car or bus ride, and is perfect for a spot of light summer hiking, lazy picnicking or winter skiing at its modern ski resort. Shopping has become a major draw in recent years, with retailers big and small opening outlets in the city.

Getting around this compact city is easy with Zagreb's blue trams grinding shallow rails that criss-cross the city. When the gradients get too steep, cable cars and funiculars take over. But part of the joy of exploring the Croatian capital is aimless wandering on foot, stopping by at a museum along the way, refuelling at a traditional eatery and enjoying the bustle of this central European metropolis.

ZAGREB

ZELENGAJ

0   250 m
0   250 yds

Medvednica,
Mirogoj

GORNJI
GRAD

Muzej
Grada
Zagreba

KAPTOL

Miklou-
šićeva

Hrvatski
Prirodoslovni
Muzej

Atelier
Meštrović

Markov
Trg

Sabor
Sv
Marka

Kamenita
Vrata

Kamenita

Hrvatski Povijesni Muzej

Hrvatski Muzej
Naivne Umjetnosti

Galerija
Klovićevi
Dvori

Katarinin
Trg

Trg A
Stepinca

Sv
Katarina

Trg B/J
Langa

Kula Lotrščak

Uspinjača

Dolac

Katedrala

CENTAR

Trg Bana
Jelačića

ILICA

ILICA

JURIŠIĆEVA

Britanski
Trg

ILICA

AMRUŠEVA

Trg
Petra
Preradovića

Bogovićeva

Kordunska

Arheološki
Muzej

N TESLE

Đorđićeva

Berislavićeva

PRILAZ GJURE DEŽELIĆA

Trg Nikole
Šubića
Zrinjskog

R BOŠKOVIĆEVA

KLAIĆEVA

Trg Maršala
Tita

Muzej za
Umjetnost i Obrt

Hrvatsko
Narodno
Kazalište

Strossmayerova
Galerija Starih Majstora

JAGIĆEVA

Rooseveltov
Trg

Strossmayerova
Trg

MAGAZINSKA

Muzej
Mimara

Etnografski Muzej

DONJI GRAD

Mažuranićev
Trg

KRŠNJAVOGA

BARUNA TRENKA

P HATZA

J ŽERJAVIĆA

Marulićev
Trg

Zagrebačko
Kazalište
Lutaka

Trg Kralja
Tomislava

A Šenoe

VODNIKOVA

MIHANOVIĆEVA

MIHANOVIĆEVA

Grgurova

GLAVNI
KOLODVOR

Botanički Vrt

Tehnički
Muzej

KRANJČEVIĆEVA

TRATINSKA

Koncertna
Dvorana
Vatroslava
Lisinskog

Trg Stjepan
Radica

A   B   C

Šuflaja

Suhinova

Galdekova

Mesićeva

Šalata

Novakova

Helež

Rubetićeva

Horvatovac

VOČARSKA CESTA

VONĆNINA

HORVATOVAC

American
International
School of Zagreb

Zeleni dol

Zelenjak

Wickenhauserova

Babonićeva

Mikulićeva

Čačkovićeva

Horvatova

Vočarsko
naselje

Jurkovica

PETROVA

VLAŠKA

SREBRNJAK

Srebrnjak

PETROVA

Cctovica

Laginlina

Trg Otokara
Keršovanija

Strapceval

Kvaternikov
Trg

LAŠČINA

LAŠČINSKA

Zalčeva

Krjesnice

Dobri dol

Pražnica

Filipoviceva

Klanicic

PETROVA

Klančić

Podvrsje

Jordanovac

Gornji pr

Gorjanoviceva

Donji prećac

Osredak

KIŠPATIĆEVA

Jordanovac

Pokornoja

Mandroviceva

Kluska

Flanova

Dzeguliceva

Semljegova

Trnskog

Nemciceva

Racićeva

Rendićeva

Bukovce
trg

MAKSIMIRSKA CESTA

Šuljekova

Kušlanova

Škriceva

Smolkova

ŠTOUŠOVA

Buzanova

Kušlanova

Maksimirski
Perivoj

J DRASKOVIĆA

Iblerov
Trg

Smičiklasova

F RAČKOG

Patačiceva

Tomaš

Bulićeva

Lopašiceva

MARTIĆEVA

ANTUNA BAUERA

Vojnoviceva

Barčićeva

Brešćenskog

PAVLA SUPICA

Tra F Grabovca

Tuškanova

Matanceva

HEINZELOVA

RAKOVČEVA

Livadiceva

Rusanova

KRALJA ZVONIMIRA

Buzanova

Strgina

Stara
Pešćenica I.

Černina

K DRŽISLAVA

K J DRASKOV-ĆEVA

Trg
žrtava
Fašizma

KRALJA ZVONIMIRA

K MISLAVA

Križanićeva

Švear

Stanetićeva

Cmenog kr

Noallova

Bogisćeva

Vrbaniceva

Prisavskog

I Banjavčica

KNEZA BRANIMIRA

HEINZELOVA

K J DRAŠKOV-ĆEVA

Kneza

Borne

Hrvoj

KNEZA VISEŠLAVA

Kruźceva

Kneza

Ljudevita

ZAVRTNICA

Trpimirova

Domagojeva

Ercodvjeva

K Jelene

Zaharova

Vrtic 1

Vrtic

Eugena Počujupskog

HEINZELOVA

KNEZA BRANIMIRA

Autobusni
Kolodvor

Strolarska
cesta

Trg L
Botića

Supilova

RADNICKA CESTA

Zaharova

Strolarska cesta

Dubravkin
trg

Menceticeva

Tanllu

Bunićeva

Zoraniceva

UL GRADA VUKOVARA

D

E

F

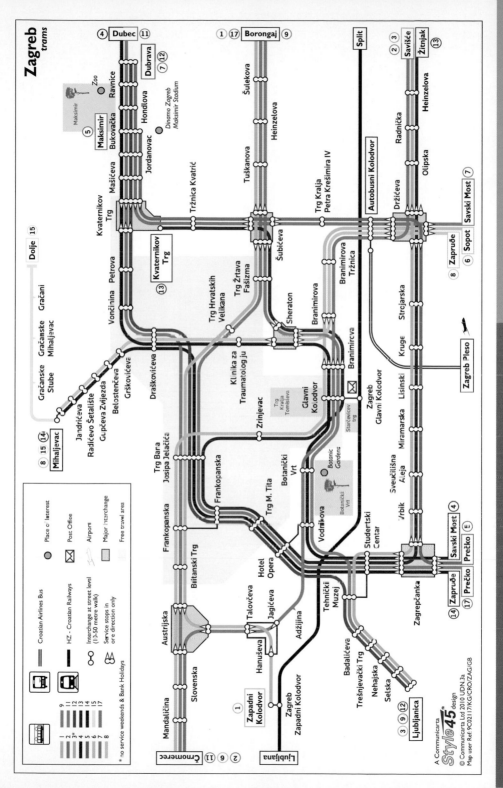

Zagreb
trams

ARHEOLOŠKI MUZEJ (ARCHAEOLOGICAL MUSEUM)

Housed in a late 19th-century palace overlooking Zrinjevac, Zagreb's favourite park, the museum contains artefacts spanning over 5,000 years of Croatian history. The chronologically arranged exhibits start on the top floor with the prehistory collection, the wealth of objects an indication of the rich cultures in Croatia before the arrival of the Greeks, Romans and Slavs. Pride of place goes to the Vučedol culture, which thrived in Vukovar around 2,500BC, including the Vučedolska Golubica (Vučedol Dove), a three-legged, geometrically patterned vessel in the shape of a bird. Look out, too, for the 14th-century BC Idol of Dalj.

THE ZAGREB MUMMY

Also on the top floor is the Egyptian collection, with sarcophagi and burial goods from ancient Egyptian tombs. The star attraction is the Zagreb Mummy, brought back from Egypt by Croatian noble Mihael Barić in 1848. When examined, it was found that its linen shroud contained the world's longest surviving Etruscan script, from the fourth century BC, thought to be a liturgical calendar.

ROMAN TO MEDIEVAL

The second-floor galleries contain several fine Roman sculptures, including the head of a girl from Salona, beautifully carved in marble in the third century BC. The medieval collection includes the earliest known Croatian stone carving, an altarpiece dated AD888 and inscribed with the name of Prince Branimir.

INFORMATION

www.amz.hr

48 C3 | Trg Nikole Šubića Zrinjskog 19 | 01 487 3101 | Tue, Wed, Fri 10–5, Thu 10–8, Sat–Sun 10–1 | Adult 20kn, child 10kn | Tram 6,13 | Lapidarium courtyard café

TIP

» Don't miss the Lapidarium in the museum courtyard, displaying a collection of Roman stone monuments from the first to fourth centuries AD. In summer, the courtyard doubles up as a pleasant outdoor café.

Above *The ancient bronze statue of Apoxyomenos, recovered from the sea off Veli Lošinj, at the Arheološki Muzej*
Opposite *Trg Bana Jelačića, Zagreb's central square*

INFORMATION

🕂 48 B2 🚇 Funicular from Tomićeva

INTRODUCTION

Gornji Grad, the oldest part of Zagreb, is an attractive, compact district of old houses, leafy lanes and cobbled streets. Set on a wooded hill above the city, it is accessible by funicular railway (▷ Tips, 55) or a steep climb up the steps, and is best explored on foot.

The district has its origins in the 13th century, when in 1242, following a Tatar assault on Zagreb, King Bela IV established a free royal city on Gradec hill. In a document known as the Golden Bull, the king granted privileges to the citizens of Gradec, including the right to trade and hold markets, but in return he required them to build defensive walls around the city. Since the 16th century, Gradec has been the seat of government in Croatia. The walls were pulled down in the 17th century. The term Gornji Grad (Upper Town) usually refers to Gradec, but also includes the neighbouring district of Kaptol, which lies across the Medveščak stream, on the site of today's Tkalčićeva.

WHAT TO SEE

KULA LOTRŠČAK

Kula Lotrščak (Burglars' Tower) is the only surviving part of the 13th-century fortifications that once enclosed the free royal city of Gradec. Its name reflects the *campana latrunculorum* (bell of thieves), which used to chime from the watchtower each night to announce the closing of the city's four gates. The modern equivalent is the Grič cannon, fired from the tower at noon each day by a cannoneer in military uniform. The tradition dates back to New Year's Eve 1877 and has been observed every day since. Climb the spiral staircase to see

Above *The* Uspinjača *(funicular railway) connects Gornji Grad (Upper Town) with Donji Grad (Lower Town)*

the ceremony take place, then go up to the observation platform for views over the city.

🕆 48 B2 ✉ Strossmayerovo Šetalište 9 ☎ 01 485 1926 🕘 Apr–end Oct Tue–Sun 11–7 💷 Adult 10kn, child 5kn

TRG SVETOG MARKA/MARKOV TRG (ST. MARK'S SQUARE)

St. Mark's Square is the symbolic heart of power in Croatia, surrounded by key state institutions including the Sabor (Parliament), Banski Dvor (seat of the Croatian government) and Ustavni Sud (the highest constitutional court). At the centre of the square is St. Mark's Church, dating from the 13th century. The church was rebuilt in the late 19th century by Hermann Bollé, with the addition of colourful mosaic roof tiles featuring the historic coats of arms of Croatia, Slavonia, Dalmatia and Zagreb. Also of note are the Gothic south portal and the sculptures by Ivan Meštrović inside the church.

🕆 48 B2

HRVATSKI POVIJESNI MUZEJ (CROATIAN HISTORY MUSEUM)

www.hismus.hr

Set in a fine baroque townhouse, built in 1764 as a palace for the Vojković family, this museum stages changing exhibitions on themes from Croatian history, ranging from Josip Jelačić, the last Ban of Croatia, to works of Croatian sculpture, historical uniforms and religious treasures. A pair of solid oak doors leads into the entrance hall, which was designed to provide enough space for carriages to turn around. From here, climb the steps to the first-floor ballroom, a focal point for aristocratic social life in Habsburg Zagreb. Next come the private apartments, where you can glimpse the lifestyle of the 18th-century elite.

🕆 48 B2 ✉ Ulica Matoševa 9 ☎ 01 485 1900 🕘 Mon–Fri 10–6, Sat–Sun 10–1 💷 Adult 10kn, child 5kn 📷

ATELIER MEŠTROVIĆ

www.mdc.hr/mestrovic

The sculptor Ivan Meštrović (▷ 23) lived in this house from 1924 until he left Croatia in 1942. The building was renovated in the 1950s and 1960s and eventually opened as a museum of his work. The collection includes more than 300 sculptural works in wood, bronze, marble and stone, as well as an

TIPS

» The easiest way of getting to Gornji Grad is on the *Uspinjača* (funicular railway) which leaves from Tomićeva every 10 minutes from 6.30am to 9pm. In continuous operation since 1893, this was the city's first form of public transport and it continues to be held in great affection by the people of Zagreb. It takes less than a minute to make the ascent, but it saves a steep climb up the steps. If you do want to walk, you can take the staircase alongside the funicular tracks or head up Radićeva from the northwest corner of Trg Bana Jelačića and enter through Kamenita Vrata.

» Time your visit to coincide with the noon firing of the Grič cannon. However, if you are nervous about loud noises or have small children with you, it is best to avoid midday.

» Pod Gričkim Topom (▷ 75), near the upper funicular station, makes a good spot for lunch, with views over Donji Grad from the terrace.

Left *The tiled patterns depicting historic coats of arms on St. Mark's Church date from the 19th century*
Below *Architectural detail, Gornji Grad*

assortment of drawings. Pieces on display range from large-scale works in the garden to intimate portraits of his family and a beautiful walnut carving of a *Mother and Child* (1942). On the second floor are plaster reliefs of Meštrović, his mother and father, wife, son and daughter, designed for the bronze doors of the family mausoleum at his childhood home in Otavice, Dalmatia. The originals were destroyed during the Homeland War (1991–95), making these surviving copies all the more valuable.

✚ 48 B2 ✉ Ulica Mletačka 8 ☎ 01 485 1123 🕐 Tue–Fri 10–6, Sat–Sun 10–2 ✋ Adult 20kn, child 10kn 🎫

CRKVA SVETA KATARINE/SV KATARINA (ST. CATHERINE'S CHURCH)

Depending on your taste, you will either find this church beautiful or completely over the top. Built by Jesuit priests between 1620 and 1632, it is considered the city's baroque masterpiece. The ceiling and walls are covered in pink stucco adorned with angels and plant motifs, while behind the main altar is a fresco of St. Catherine by Slovenian artist Kristofor Andrija Jelovšek. The gleaming white facade was remodelled after the 1880 earthquake and features statues of Mary and the four evangelists in niches.

✚ 48 B3 ✉ Katarinski Trg

KAMENITA VRATA (STONE GATE)

The Stone Gate is all that remains of the four original entrance gates to the medieval city. According to legend, when fire swept through this district in 1731, destroying most of the wooden houses, a painting of the Virgin was found unharmed in the ashes, and a shrine was built to house it. The image is kept behind a wrought silver grid inside the gate, attracting large numbers of pilgrims who pause here to pray and light candles.

✚ 48 C2

Below *Lined with old houses, the attractive streets of Gornji Grad are a pleasant place to stroll*

Above *Self-portrait by celebrated naive painter Ivan Generalić, Hrvatski Muzej Naivne Umjetnosti*
Left *Bronze sculpture, Atelier Meštrović*
Below *The Katedrala (cathedral), in the Kaptol district*

MORE TO SEE

HRVATSKI PRIRODOSLOVNI MUZEJ
(CROATIAN NATURAL HISTORY MUSEUM)

www.hpm.hr

Fossils, rocks, stuffed animals, birds and unidentified creatures preserved in formaldehyde are displayed in old-fashioned cabinets at this huge museum. The museum's extensive collection (almost 2 million specimens) also includes the original remains of Krapina Man (▷ 101), but these are not on display and can be seen only by appointment.

🏛 40 D2 ✉ Ulica Demetrova 1 ☎ 01 485 1700 🕐 Tue–Fri 10–5, Sat–Sun 10–1 ✋ Adult 15kn, child 7kn

HRVATSKI MUZEJ NAIVNE UMJETNOSTI
(CROATIAN NAIVE ART MUSEUM)

www.hmnu.org

The Croatian naive art movement began in the village of Hlebine (▷ 82), and this museum features paintings and sculptures by artists including Ivan Generalić (1914–92) and his son Josip (1936–2004), as well as other well-known exponents of the genre, including Mijo Kovačić (1935–), Emerik Feješ (1904–69) and Ivan Rabuzin (1921–2008).

🏛 48 B3 ✉ Ulica Ćirila i Metoda 3 ☎ 01 485 1911 🕐 Tue–Fri 10–6, Sat–Sun 10–1 ✋ Adult 20kn, child 10kn

MUZEJ GRADA ZAGREBA

▷ 61.

GALERIJA KLOVIĆEVI DVORI (KLOVIĆ GALLERY)

www.galerijaklovic.hr

Occupying a former Jesuit College, this is Zagreb's top exhibition space for temporary shows of modern art by Croatian and big-name international artists such as Picasso and Chagall. The gallery's gift shop is a superb place to pick up unusual souvenirs.

🏛 48 B3 ✉ Jezuitski Trg 4 ☎ 01 485 1926 🕐 Tue–Sun 11–7 ✋ Prices vary 🚋 Tram 1, 6, 11, 12, 13, 14, 17 to Trg Bana Jelačića

ETNOGRAFSKI MUZEJ (ETHNOGRAPHIC MUSEUM)

www.emz.hr

In a Viennese Secession trades hall dating from 1904, this museum features folk costumes and crafts from Croatia and abroad. The first floor is devoted to Croatian folk culture, particularly traditional costume from the late 19th and early 20th centuries. Look out for golden embroidery from Slavonia, silk embroidery from the Konavle region, and beautiful lace costumes from Pag. The collection also includes jewellery, musical instruments, agriculture and rural crafts. The ground floor has non-European items, with many objects brought back by explorers Mirko and Stjepan Seljan, brothers from Karlovac, such as Native American headdresses, African masks, Aboriginal bark paintings and samurai swords.

Before leaving, pause to admire the building itself, one of Zagreb's finest examples of art nouveau.
🏛 48 B4 ✉ Trg Mažuranića 14 ☎ 01 482 6220 🕐 Tue–Thu 10–6, Fri–Sun 10–1 💰 Adult 15kn; child 10kn; free on Thu 🚋 Tram 12,13,14,17 🏛

HRVATSKO NARODNO KAZALIŠTE (CROATIAN NATIONAL THEATRE)

www.hnk.hr

With trumpet-blowing angels on the balcony and classical columns adorning a mustard-coloured facade, the ostentatiously baroque Croatian National Theatre is in the tradition of grand Central European opera houses. Designed by the Viennese architects Ferdinand Fellner and Hermann Helmer, it was opened by Franz Josef I on a state visit in 1895. The main auditorium is a riot of baroque details, with plush furnishing and sculpted cherubs, while the first-floor hall, with a balcony overlooking the square, has ceiling frescoes and busts of distinguished actors.

This is the most prestigious venue in Croatia for ballet, opera and drama. The season usually runs from October to June and it is worth attending a performance if you get the chance (▷ 70). Outside the theatre is a sculpture by Ivan Meštrović, a group of interesting bronze figures known as *Zdenac Života* (Well of Life).
🏛 48 B4 ✉ Trg Maršala Tita 15 ☎ 01 488 8418 🚋 Tram 12,13,14,17

KATEDRALA (CATHEDRAL)

The cathedral's twin spires are the tallest structures in Zagreb, at 105m (344ft). The first church was begun on this site in 1094, but today's neo-Gothic structure was largely built by Hermann Bollé (1845–1926) after the 1880 earthquake. The baroque marble pulpit is a survivor from the 17th century, while the 1846 stained-glass windows in the sanctuary are the oldest in Croatia. Behind the main altar, a sarcophagus contains an effigy of Cardinal Stepinac (▷ 23), which attracts a stream of pilgrims. His actual tomb is in the north wall, with a relief by Ivan Meštrović depicting Stepinac kneeling before Christ. Near here is the sacristy, with some rare 13th-century frescoes, and the treasury of precious objects, including an embroidered cloak of King Ladislav, founder of the Zagreb diocese in 1094. The statue outside the cathedral, with the Virgin at the head of a column surrounded by gilded angels, is by Anton Fernkorn (1813–78).
🏛 48 C3 ✉ Kaptol 31 ☎ 01 481 4727 🕐 Mon–Sat 10–5, Sun 1–5; for Mass at other times 💰 Free

Left *Hrvatsko Narodno Kazalište, home of Croatian theatre, ballet and opera*
Opposite *The stunning Katedrala (cathedral)*
Below *Displays at the Etnografski Muzej*

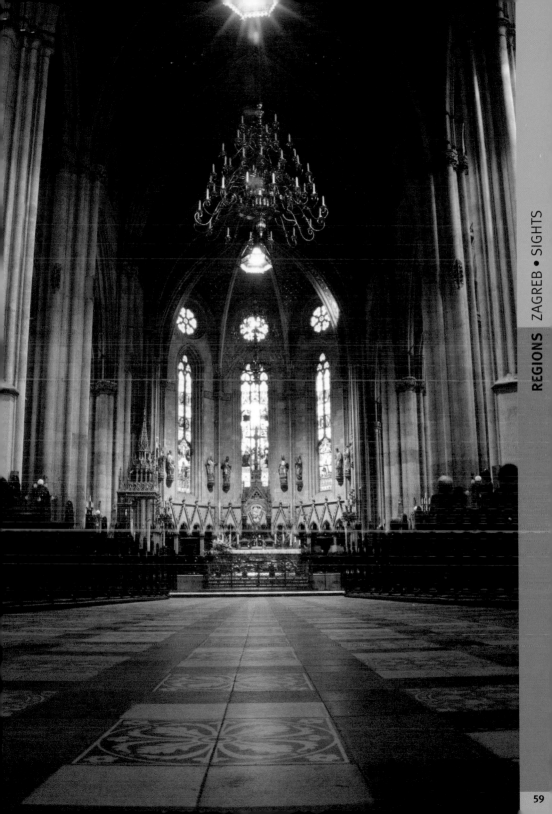

Above *The café in leafy Maksimirski Perivoj, one of Europe's oldest parks*

Left *The beautiful arcades at the entrance to Mirogoj cemetery, designed by architect Hermann Bollé*

MAKSIMIRSKI PERIVOJ (MAKSIMIR PARK)

Opened in 1794, this is one of Europe's oldest public parks and is named after its founder, Bishop Maksimilian Vrhovec (1752–1827). With lakes, meadows, oak woods, pavilions, sculptures and bridges, it is a lovely place to stroll. A wide avenue leads to the *vidikovac*, a three-storey belvedere built in 1843 which now houses a summer café. Near here is the zoo (tel 01 230 2198; May–end Sep daily 9–8, Oct–end Apr 9–4; www.zoo.hr). A path from the belvedere leads to Mogila, an artificial hill of soil from more than 100 places in Croatia, beneath which are buried items of cultural heritage. The hill is topped by a statue of a falcon, and the Croatian flag and coat of arms. Opposite the main entrance, Maksimir Stadium is the home of Dinamo Zagreb and the national football team.

🚇 Off map 49 F2 ✉ Maksimirska Cesta 🚊 Tram 11,12 ☕

MEDVEDNICA

www.pp-medvednica.hr

The wooded mountain overlooking the city makes a popular retreat for the people of Zagreb, who come here to hike in summer and ski in winter. Getting there is part of the fun, on the *žičara* (cable car) which makes the dramatic 20-minute journey to the summit (daily 8–8). From the Dolje tram terminus, walk through the tunnel and climb through the woods to reach the lower cable car station. It is also possible to walk up in about two hours, or take the cable car up and walk back down. The cable car drops you beneath the summit of Sljeme (1,033m/3,388ft), from where there is an extensive network of trails. An easy path leads to the Church of Our Lady of Sljeme, built in 1932 at a height of 1,000m (3,280ft) to commemorate the millennium of the medieval Croatian kingdom. A longer hike goes to the 13th-century fortress at Medvedgrad, with its Altar of the Homeland and an eternal flame honouring the Croatian victims of war. Other sights include the reconstructed Zrinski silver mine (Sat–Sun 10–4) and the underground Veternica cave (guided tours only, Apr–end Oct Sat–Sun).

🚇 Off map 48 C1 ℹ️ Park Prirode Medvednica, Bliznec ☎ 01 458 6317 🚊 Tram 8,14 to Mihaljevac then 15 to Dolje

MIROGOJ

This cemetery was designed by Hermann Bollé, who built the arcades at the entrance. With tombs and memorials by famous sculptors such as Ivan Rendić, Ivan Meštrović and Antun Augustinčić, this is virtually an open-air museum of 19th- and 20th-century Croatian sculpture. Look in the arcade to the right for the tomb of Stjepan Radić (1871–1928), the assassinated leader of the Croatian Peasants Party and campaigner for independence. Behind the chapel, the granite tomb of former president Dr. Franjo Tuđman (▷ 25) attracts many visitors, who lay candles and flowers in his honour. Thousands of citizens are buried here too, with each tombstone bearing the symbols of their religion, and others engraved with the red star of Tito's Partisans.

Outside the cemetery gates lies the memorial park for the victims of the Homeland War. Beneath the park, the Zid Boli (Wall of Pain), is a pile of bricks, each representing a missing person. Built by the victims' families on a street corner in central Zagreb, it was moved here in 2005.

🚇 Off map 48 C1 🕐 Summer daily 6–8; winter daily 7.30–6 🚌 Bus 106 from Kaptol

MUZEJ GRADA ZAGREBA (ZAGREB CITY MUSEUM)

The Zagreb City Museum tells the city's story using models, maps, photographs and original artefacts. One of the main exhibits is the building itself, the 17th-century convent of the nuns of St. Clare. Iron Age remains excavated in the basement form the opening galleries, including a reconstructed blacksmith's workshop from the first century BC. The museum also incorporates parts of Popov Toranj (Priests' Tower), a 13th-century fortress at the northern gate of Gradec, which has housed the city observatory since 1903.

THE EARLY YEARS

The ground-floor concentrates on early history. Room 4 contains a copy of Felician's Charter (1134), the first recorded document to mention Zagreb, while Room 5 has a copy of the Golden Bull (1242) in which Bela IV established the royal city of Gradec. The oldest coat of arms of Zagreb, carved in stone in 1499, is in Room 9.

CITY LIFE

The first-floor galleries follow Zagreb's development through such themes as parks and promenades, clubs and societies, theatres, shops and domestic life. Highlights include the silver hammer used by Franz Josef I at the opening of the Croatian National Theatre (Room 35) and a reconstructed bathing shed (Room 40). The finale is a sobering display of furniture and crockery from the presidential palace, broken by Yugoslav rockets in October 1991.

INFORMATION

www.mgz.hr

✚ 48 C2 ✉ Ulica Opatička 20 ☎ 01 485 1361 🕐 Tue, Wed, Fri 10–6, Thu 10–10, Sat 11–7, Sun 10–2 💰 Adult 20kn, child 10kn 🚊 Tram 1, 6, 11, 12, 13, 14, 17 to Trg Bana Jelačića, then a five-minute walk. Funicular from Tomićeva 🎧 Free tours, Sat–Sun 11am 🍴 Stara Vura 🛗 ♿

TIPS

» Allow at least a couple of hours, with a break for lunch in the Stara Vura restaurant.

» Look out for the pillar in the reception area, displaying old museum posters. This is an original from 19th-century Zagreb and similar examples can still be seen in the city today.

Below *Detail from one of the historic parchments in the museum's collection*

slobodno biraju gradskog suca iz koj
ada umre bez nasljednika. neka mu s
ši se sa sugrađanima. neka ostavi su
adležnosti grada. K tomu, ako tko u
odredi, razdijeliti siromasima i crkvi
onedjeljkom i četvrtkom: neka se po
naime, ugarski kralj krene u ratni p
odinu kralju, kada on glavom kren
da, dužni su dati polovicu spomenut
anovanja, stotinu kruhova i jednu l
godina, a kad prođe tih pet godina,
Grič. U svrhu pak uzdržavanja gra
noga Dionizija, bana sveukupne Sla
ci koja se naziva Kraljev Brod, uz gl
ver, prelazeći vodu koja se naziva M
Alaku stiže do glavnog puta, što se
rič ide ravno na sjever, pružajući se
točića koji se naziva Sopotnica, a za
rebačkim Kaptolom: druga je međa
do međe Mikulinih sinova koja se
koje se nalazi križ, a pokraj njega
se tako njime, malo skreće na zap

MUZEJ MIMARA

This extensive museum reflects the eclectic tastes of Croatian businessman Ante Topić Mimara (1898–1987), whose collection of art, amassed from around the world, was donated to the state shortly before his death.

Born in Korusča, Mimara first left his homeland during World War I. His passion for collecting began when he was just 19 years old; he bought an ancient Christian chalice, made in Alexandria in the third century AD, in Rome in 1918. Over the years, his collection grew to encompass Egyptian antiquities and glassware, Chinese porcelain and jade, Turkish carpets, Spanish tapestries, Italian Renaissance sculpture and paintings by European masters including Rembrandt, Rubens and Raphael. Among the collection's treasures is *The Bather* by Pierre Auguste Renoir (1841–1919), which is on display in Room 40.

Room 17 has a 14th-century carved ivory English hunting horn; Room 26 has the 17th-century carved ivory sceptre used by Polish kings.

✚ 48 B4 ✉ Rooseveltov Trg 5 ☎ 01 482 8100 ⏱ Tue–Wed, Fri–Sat 10–5, Thu 10–7, Sun 10–2 💵 Adult 20kn, child 10kn 🚃 Tram 12,13,14,17 ☕ 🏛

MUZEJ ZA UMJETNOST I OBRT (ARTS AND CRAFTS MUSEUM)

www.muo.hr

Like the Muzej Mimara (▷ left), this museum offers a broad sweep through the arts, but Croatia and Central Europe are the theme. Founded in 1880 to preserve traditional arts and crafts and housed in a Hermann Bollé neo-Renaissance palace, the collections include furniture, ceramics, textiles, clocks and watches, paintings and sculpture, musical instruments, and graphic and industrial design. Of particular interest is the religious art collection, with polychrome wooden sculptures from the 15th to 18th centuries and an altarpiece of the Madonna from the church of Remetinec, near Varaždin.

✚ 48 B4 ✉ Trg Maršala Tita 10 ☎ 01 488 2111 ⏱ Tue–Wed, Fri–Sat 10–7, Thu 10–10, Sun 10–2 💵 Adult 30kn, child 20kn 🚃 Tram 12,13,14,17 V11 and 5 🍴 ☕ 🏛

STROSSMAYEROVA GALERIJA STARIH MAJSTORA (STROSSMAYER GALLERY OF OLD MASTERS)

www.mdc.hr/strossmayer

This collection of paintings is in the Academy of Sciences and Arts, an Italian Renaissance-style building commissioned by Josip Juraj Strossmayer (1815–1905) and opened in 1884. As well as being Bishop of Đakovo, Strossmayer was a key figure in 19th-century Croatian politics and a patron of the arts, and his personal collection of European art from the 15th to 19th centuries forms the core of this gallery. Heavily biased towards religious painting, with a handful of portraits, landscapes and rural scenes, the collection includes works by artists from the Italian, Dutch and Flemish schools, among them Carpaccio, Fra Angelico and El Greco. Look in particular for a St. Mary Magdalene by El Greco (Room 5) and a self-portrait by Jean Fragonard (Room 9). Behind the building is a statue of Strossmayer by renowned sculptor Ivan Meštrović (▷ 23).

Among the museum's treasures is the original Bašćanska Ploča (Baška Stone), which is on display in the entrance lobby. Inscribed on the 11th-century tablet is one of the oldest examples of the Glagolitic script (▷ 21) that was once widely used in Istria and Kvarner.

✚ 48 C4 ✉ Trg Nikole Šubića Zrinjskog 11 ☎ 01 489 5117 ⏱ Tue 10–1, 5–7, Wed–Sun 10–1 💵 Adult 10kn, child 5kn 🚃 Tram 6,13

Left *The statue of St. George and the Dragon outside the Muzej za Umjetnost i Obrt*
Below *The stately entrance to Muzej Mimara*

TRG BANA JELAČIĆA

Trg Bana Jelačića lies at the meeting point of the upper and lower towns, and is the heart and soul of Zagreb. Originally a fairground and market place, it has been the main square since 1850. At first, it was called Manduševac after the spring on its eastern side, which is now a pretty fountain but until 1878 supplied the city with water. The current name dates from 1866, when the statue of Josip Jelačić was erected.

THE STATUE

An equestrian statue of Josip Jelačić (1801–59), by Anton Fernkorn, is at the square's centre. Appointed by Vienna as *ban* (governor) of Croatia, Jelačić was a popular figure who abolished slavery and united Croatia, Slavonia and Dalmatia into a single state. He became an icon of Croatian nationalism, particularly during the Communist era when the statue was removed and the square renamed Trg Republike (Republic Square). In 1990 it was restored to its pedestal following a petition and now acts as a rallying point for political demonstrations and a meeting place for young people at the start of the evening *korzo* (stroll) along nearby Tkalčićeva.

THE MARKET

An archway behind the statue leads to Dolac (Mon–Sat 6–2, Sun 6–noon), the city's main market since 1930. The raised outdoor terrace is where farmers sell fresh fruit, vegetables and home-made cottage cheese. Meat and fish are sold at indoor market halls, and there are flower stalls on nearby Ulica Splavnica.

INFORMATION

✚ 48 C3 🚏 Trg Bana Jelačića 11
☎ 01 481 4051 ⏰ Jul to mid-Sep
Mon–Fri 8.30am–9pm, Sat 9–5, Sun
10–2; mid-Sep to end May Mon–Fri
8.30–8, Sat 9–5, Sun 10–2 🚋 Tram
1,6,11,12,13,14,17

TIPS

» The best way to enjoy Trg Bana Jelačića is from one of the café terraces. Mala Kavana is a good choice.
» The streets around Trg Bana Jelačića are the main venues for the evening *korzo* (promenade)—especially Tkalčićeva to the north and Bogovićeva to the south.

Above *Zagreb's central square is a vibrant hive of activity from morning to night*

OLD ZAGREB

This short walk explores the upper town of Gornji Grad, historically divided between Gradec (the citizens' district) and Kaptol (the ecclesiastical capital). With several interesting museums and churches en route, it can easily be extended to last all day.

THE WALK

Distance: 3km (2 miles)
Allow: 1–2 hours plus visits
Start/end: Trg Bana Jelačića
✚ 48 C3

HOW TO GET THERE

Trams 1, 6, 11, 12, 13, 14 and 17 all stop at Trg Bana Jelačića.

★ Start the walk at Trg Bana Jelačića (▷ 63), Zagreb's central square. With the statue of Josip Jelačić behind you, begin by heading down Ulica Ljudevita Gaja (Gajeva) on the southern side of the square. Turn right into Bogovićeva, a busy shopping street with café tables out on the pavement (sidewalk). The street ends in Trg Petra Preradovića.

❶ Trg Petra Preradovića is named after the poet Petar Preradović (1818–72), whose statue stands on the square. Most locals refer to it as Cvjetni Trg (Flower Square) because of the florists who sell here. On the right-hand corner with Bogovićeva, Oktogon is the finest of Zagreb's Viennese-style shopping arcades, erected in 1899 and topped by a stained-glass dome.

Cross Trg Petra Preradovića diagonally to your right, passing the Orthodox Church of the Transfiguration to arrive on Ilica. Turn left and then immediately right into Ulica Tomića (Tomićeva). From here, you can take the funicular railway or walk up the steps to Gornji Grad.

❷ The *Uspinjača* (funicular) is popularly known as the old lady of Zagreb. First opened in 1890, it is sometimes said to be the shortest public transport journey in the world, travelling 66m (72 yards) at a gradient of 1:2 in around 55 seconds.

Emerging from the funicular station opposite Kula Lotrščak (▷ 54), you arrive on Strossmayerovo Šetalište.

❸ This shady promenade occupies the site of the former defensive wall of Gradec, and offers fine views. A short diversion to the right brings you to a sculpture depicting the Croatian writer Antun Gustav Matoš (1873–1914) sitting on a bench.

Turn back to walk along Strossmayerovo Šetalište. Continue past the funicular station and take the Grič alley to your right to arrive on Markovićev Trg. From here, turn left along Ulica Matoševa.

❹ This pretty street is lined with 18th- and 19th-century houses, including the baroque mansion housing the Hrvatski Povijesni Muzej (Croatian History Museum; ▷ 50).

At the end of Ulica Matoševa, turn left then right onto Ulica Demetrova, passing the Hrvatski Prirodoslovni Muzej (Croatian Natural History Museum; ▷ 57). Stay on this road as it bends to the right towards the Muzej Grada Zagreba (Zagreb City Museum; ▷ 61). At the end of the road, turn right onto Ulica Opatička.

❺ This short stretch of Ulica Opatička has two very handsome buildings. Narodni Dom (National Hall) is a neoclassical mansion, built in the 1830s and used variously as a museum, reading room, casino and ballroom. The nearby Zlatni Dvorana (Golden Palace) is notable for its wrought-iron gates, designed by the architect Hermann Bollé and topped by the coats of arms of Croatia, Dalmatia and Slavonia. Now home to the Croatian History Institute, the walls are decorated with scenes from Croatian history.

Take the next right along Ulica 29 Listopad 1918 to arrive on Markov Trg (St. Mark's Square).

❻ St. Mark's Square (▷ 55) is the focal point of Gradec and the heart of Croatian political life. The Sabor (Parliament) is on one side and the Banski Dvor (the former Governor's palace, now the seat of the Croatian government) on the other. Walk around St. Mark's Church to admire the mosaic roof tiles from the far side of the square.

Keep straight ahead towards Kula Lotrščak and turn left on Katarinin Trg, with the church of Sveta Katarina (St. Catherine) ahead of you. Bear left in front of the church to arrive on Jezuitski Trg.

❼ Jezuitski Trg takes its name from the Jesuit monastery which used to stand on this site. The monastery buildings now house Klovićevi Dvori, a gallery hosting changing exhibitions of modern art.

Turn right on Ulica Kamenita to pass through the Kamenita Vrata (▷ 56). Beyond the gate, turn right by a statue of St. George and the Dragon onto Ulica Radićeva. Walk down this steep, cobbled shopping street and turn left onto Krvavi Most.

❽ Krvavi Most (Bloody Bridge) stands on the site of the historic boundary between Gradec and Kaptol, which were separated by the Medveščak stream. Its name reflects centuries of confrontation between the two districts.

At the end of Krvavi Most, turn left onto Ulica Tkalčić (Tkalčićeva).

❾ Tkalčićeva is Zagreb's most popular promenade, where the young and beautiful strut on summer nights. It was built on the site of a dried-up riverbed where the Medveščak

stream once flowed. In the 19th century, this was the city's artisan quarter, and many of the townhouses and workshops from then, with their pastel facades, are now art galleries and terrace bars. A short way up on the left, look out for a bronze statue of a woman holding an umbrella. This is Marija Jurić Zagorka (1873–1957), Croatia's first female journalist and the author of novels including *Grička Vještica (The Witch from Grič)*.

Continue along Tkalčićeva until you see the Oliver Twist pub on your right. Beside the pub is a surviving section of the city wall that once enclosed Kaptol. Walk through a gap in the wall and up the steps to a small park.

❿ Opatovina park is named after a Cistercian abbey which once stood nearby. Across the park is the church of Sveti Frane (St. Francis of Assisi), with stained-glass windows by Ivo Dulčić (1916–75).

Walk past the church and turn right along Kaptol, passing the Komedija theatre and the cathedral on your return to the start.

Above *A wall sign on Ulica Kaptol*
Opposite *The stained-glass dome of the late 19th-century Oktogon shopping arcade*

WHERE TO EAT
IVICA I MARICA
▷ 74.

KAPTOLSKA KLET
▷ 74.

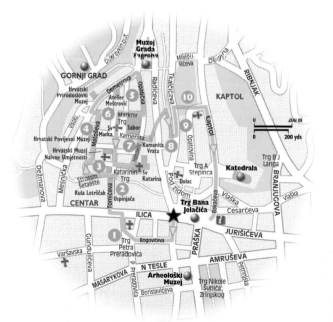

ZAGREB'S GREEN HORSESHOE

Donji Grad (Lower Town) is the setting for this relaxing walk, which follows a series of elegant parks, avenues and squares laid out in a horseshoe shape by Milan Lenuci (1849–1924) in the late 19th century. Along the way, you pass the grand cultural institutions of Habsburg-era Zagreb and several important works by the sculptor Ivan Meštrović.

THE WALK
Distance: 2km (1.2 miles)
Allow: 1 hour
Start: Trg Maršala Tita ✚ 48 B4
End: Trg Bana Jelačića ✚ 48 C3

HOW TO GET THERE
Trams 12, 13, 14 and 17 all stop at Trg Maršala Tita. Alternatively, it is a short walk from Trg Bana Jelačića.

★ Trg Maršala Tita, named after the Yugoslav leader Tito, is surrounded by impressive Austro-Hungarian buildings. On the north side is the rectorate of Zagreb University. At the foot of the steps leading up to the building is one of Meštrović's most famous works, a bronze statue of a seated woman known as *History of the Croats* (1932). Facing the

university is the imposing Hrvatsko Narodno Kazalište (▷ 58). Another sculpture by Meštrović, the mildly erotic *Zdenac Života* (Well of Life), is in front of the theatre.

Begin by the sculpture and walk around the theatre with the Muzej za Umjetnost i Obrt (▷ 62) to your right. Keep going south across a succession of green squares. Walk across Mažuranićev Trg with the Etnografski Muzej (▷ 58) on your right and cross the road to reach Marulićev Trg.

❶ Marulićev Trg is named after Marko Marulić (1450–1524), known as the father of Croatian literature. His portrait is featured on the 500 kuna banknote. A statue of him sits

at the heart of the square. Ahead is the former University Library, now housing the State Archive. Designed by Rudolf Lubinsky in 1912, this is considered Zagreb's finest Viennese Secession-style building. Walk to the front for a closer look at the facade. A statue of archaeologist Frane Bulić stands outside.

Facing you across the street is the Botanički Vrt (Botanical Garden). Cross the road to enter the gardens, then stroll through the park before leaving via the gate at the far end.

❷ This English-style landscape garden, with ponds, paths, bridges and arboretums, was founded in 1889 and contains over 10,000 species of plants from around the world. From November to March, when the gardens are usually closed, walk along Vodnikova.

Follow Mihanovićeva past the headquarters of Hrvatske Željeznice (Croatian Railways) on the left and the Regent Esplanade hotel (▷ 77) on the right, then take the steps down into Trg Ante Starčevića, an attractive park laid out with flowerbeds, lawns and a fountain.

❸ On your right is the main train station, built in 1892 and at one time a major stop on the Orient Express. Across from the station is a statue of Tomislav, the first Croatian king (925–28), on horseback and wielding a sword. The statue, by Robert Mihanović, was placed here in 1947. Behind the statue, the lawns of Trg Kralja Tomislava stretch to the yellow Umjetnički Paviljon (Art Pavilion), which was built for the Millennium Exhibition in Budapest in 1896 before being dismantled and moved to Zagreb. Art exhibitions are still held here and it also houses a famous restaurant, Paviljon (▷ 75).

Walk around the Art Pavilion and cross the main road to reach Strossmayerova Trg.

❹ Strossmayerova Trg is named after Josip Strossmayer (1815–1905), the Bishop of Đakovo and an early campaigner for Croat-Serb unity. A statue of Strossmayer stands in the square, behind the Croatian Academy of Arts and Sciences. The building contains the Strossmayerova Galerija Starih Majstora (▷ 62) and the original Bašćanska Ploča (Baška Stone) from Krk, one of the earliest examples of the Glagolitic script in Croatia (▷ 21).

Cross Ulica A Hebranga to arrive on Trg Nikole Šubića Zrinskog, known as Zrinjevac.

❺ Founded as a cattle fair in 1826, Zrinjevac is Zagreb's favourite park,

with fountains, tree-lined avenues and a bandstand. The benches around the park are popular trysting spots for young couples. On the west side of the square is the Arheološki Muzej (▷ 53).

From the northwest corner of the square, a short walk along Ulica Praška leads to Trg Bana Jelačića.

WHERE TO EAT
PAVILJON
▷ 75.

PLACE TO VISIT
BOTANIČKI VRT
☎ 01 484 4002 ⏰ Apr–end Oct Wed–Sun 9–7, Mon–Tue 9–2.30 💲 Free

Below *Detail of Ivan Meštrović's* Well of Life, *in front of the Hrvatsko Narodno Kazalište*

WHAT TO DO

SHOPPING

ALGORITAM

www.algoritam.hr

This bookstore beneath Hotel Dubrovnik is the best place for foreign-language books and magazines. It has books about Croatia, including history, fiction, travel guides and maps.

✉ Gajeva 1, Zagreb ☎ 01 488 1555 🕔 Mon–Fri 8.30am–9pm, Sat 8.30–3 🚋 Tram 1, 6, 11, 12, 13, 14, 17 to Trg Bana Jelačića

AQUARIUS

www.aquarius-records.com

A branch of Croatia's leading music store selling CDs, from international pop releases to Croatian folk, jazz and classical music.

✉ Varšavska 13, Zagreb ☎ 01 639 1673 🕔 Mon–Fri 8–8, Sat 8–3 🚋 Tram 1, 6, 11, 12, 13, 14, 17 to Trg Bana Jelačića

AROMATICA

www.aromatica.hr

Aromatica sells natural cosmetics and toiletries made from Adriatic plants and herbs, including a range of aromatic massage oils and shampoos. You can make your own selection and have it individually wrapped in an attractive gift box.

✉ Vlaška 7, Zagreb ☎ 01 481 1584 🕔 Mon–Fri 8–8, Sat 8–3 🚋 Tram 1, 6, 11, 12, 13, 14, 17 to Trg Bana Jelačića

BAKINA KUĆA

www.bakina-kuca.hr

This little cellar sells products from across Croatia, including truffles, olive oil, honey, wine, liqueurs and natural cosmetics.

✉ Strossmayerova Trg 7, Zagreb ☎ 01 485 2525 🕔 Mon–Fri 8am–8.30pm, Sat 9–5 🚋 Tram 6, 13 to Zrinjevac

CENTAR KAPTOL

www.centarkaptol.hr

This US-style shopping mall has trendy bars and boutiques, a cinema and a branch of British chain Marks and Spencer. There are entrances on the road above the cathedral and on Medvedgradska, a continuation of Tkalčićeva.

✉ Nova Ves 17, Zagreb ☎ 01 486 0241 🕔 Most shops open Mon–Sat 9–9 🚋 Tram 1, 6, 11, 12, 13, 14, 17 to Trg Bana Jelačića

CROATA

www.croata.hr

The main branch of Croata is in the Oktogon passage, a lovely Viennese shopping arcade built in 1899. It sells silk ties, scarves and other accessories. There is another branch near the cathedral at Kaptol 13.

✉ Prolaz Oktogon, Ilica 5, Zagreb ☎ 01 481 2726 🕔 Mon–Fri 8–8, Sat 8–3 🚋 Tram 1, 6, 11, 12, 13, 14, 17 to Trg Bana Jelačića

DOLAC

Zagreb's vivid central market is held daily on a raised terrace above the main square, where farmers sell an array of fruit, vegetables and cheese. There are indoor halls for meat, fish and dairy products.

✉ Dolac, Zagreb ☎ 01 481 4400 🕔 Mon–Sat 6–2, Sun 6am–noon 🚋 Tram 1, 6, 11, 12, 13, 14, 17 to Trg Bana Jelačića

ETNO-BUTIK MARA

This tiny boutique is on the first floor of the Croatian Chamber of Trade, a historic trades hall on Ilica. The owner makes and sells her own clothing, bags and gifts, made from natural materials embroidered with Croatian designs and motifs.

✉ Ilica 49, Zagreb ☎ 01 480 6511
🕐 Mon–Fri 9–8, Sat 9–2 🚊 Tram 6, 11, 2 to Frankopanska

GHARANI ŠTROK

www.gharanistrok.co.uk
Founded by Croatian designer Vanya Štrok and Iranian Nargess Gharani, this store has dressed some of the world's most famous women, including Nicole Kidman, Madonna and Kylie Minogue. In 2005, the company launched its first shop in Zagreb, offering quality ready-to-wear, sexy clothes for women.

✉ Dežmanov Prolaz 5, Zagreb ☎ 01 484 6152 🕐 Mon–Fri 9–8, Sat 9–2 🚊 Tram 1, 6, 11 to Frankopanska

HERUC GALERIA

www.herucgaleria.hr
This chain, with branches across Croatia, offers Italian and Croatian fashions at sensible prices for both men and women.

✉ Ilica 26, Zagreb ☎ 01 483 3569
🕐 Mon–Fri 8–8, Sat 8–3 🚊 Tram 1, 6, 11, 12, 13, 14, 17 to Trg Bana Jelačića

HRELIĆ

This vast, sprawling flea market takes place every Sunday morning on the south bank of the River Sava in Novi Zagreb. Hawkers sell everything from car parts to second-hand furniture and posters of nationalist heroes. This is a great place to soak up some Croatian atmosphere, but it is not a standard tourist experience, so take care of all your possessions. An antiques market is also held on Sunday mornings at Britanski Trg.

✉ Sajam Jakuševec, Novi Zagreb
☎ 01 660 9900 🕐 Sun 7–3 🚌 Bus 295 from behind the railway station

ILOČKI PODRUMI

www.ilocki-podrumi.hr
This small shop, hidden away in a car park near the cathedral, sells white wines from the Slavonian town of Ilok, which was devastated during the Homeland War but is now producing quality wines once again.

✉ Kaptol 12, Zagreb ☎ 01 481 4593
🕐 Mon–Sat 8–8 🚊 Tram 1, 6, 11, 12, 13, 14, 17 to Trg Bana Jelačića

IMAGE HADDAD

www.image-haddad.com
This is the flagship store of Croatian designer Zrinka Haddad, whose boutiques throughout the country offer affordable, stylish clothes for women, characterized by their elegant lines and feminine design.

✉ Ilica 6, Zagreb (also at Ilica 21)
☎ 01 483 1035 🕐 Mon–Fri 8–8, Sat 8–3 🚊 Tram 1, 6, 11, 12, 13, 14, 17 to Trg Bana Jelačića

KRAŠ

www.kras.hr
Kraš chocolates and confectionery are popular all over Croatia, with 11 branches in Zagreb alone. This shop sells all the favourites, from hand-made chocolates to gift packs for adults and children.

✉ Trg Bana Jelačića 12, Zagreb ☎ 01 481 0443 🕐 Mon–Sat 7am–8pm 🚊 Tram 1, 6, 11, 12, 13, 14, 17 to Trg Bana Jelačića

LAZER ROK

Jeweller Lazer Lumezi's unusual designs have attracted a cult following in Zagreb. You can see how jewellery meets cutting-edge art at the open-plan studio.

✉ Tkalčićeva 53, Zagreb ☎ 01 481 4030
🕐 Mon–Fri 10–8, Sat 10–3 🚊 Tram 1, 6, 11, 12, 13, 14, 17 to Trg Bana Jelačića

NAMA

www.nama.hr
The large domed building on the corner of Ilica and Trg Bana Jelačića was built in 1880 and was the leading state-owned department store in Yugoslavia. It now looks dated but is worth a visit for its history alone.

✉ Ilica 4, Zagreb ☎ 01 480 3111
🕐 Mon–Fri 8am–8.30pm, Sat 8–3 🚊 Tram 1, 6, 11, 12, 13, 14, 17 to Trg Bana Jelačića

NATURA CROATICA

www.naturacroatica.com
It is hard to resist this tempting delicatessen, which sells only Croatian products made from natural ingredients. Among the items on sale are candied fruits, Istrian truffles, olive oil, wild boar salami, pepper biscuits, herbal brandy, liqueurs and aromatic wines. There is another shop in the Westin Zagreb hotel at Kršnjavoga 1 (▷ 77).

✉ Preradovićeva 8, Zagreb ☎ 01 485 5076
🕐 Mon–Fri 9–9, Sat 10–4 🚊 Tram 6, 13 to Zrinjevac

PROFIL MEGASTORE

www.profil.hr
Three floors full of books, films, music and computer games are on sale at this multimedia megastore. It also has a gift shop and internet café.

✉ Bogovićeva 7, Zagreb ☎ 01 487 7325
🕐 Mon–Sat 9am–10pm 🚊 Tram 1, 6, 11, 12, 13, 14, 17 to Trg Bana Jelačića

PRŠUT GALERIJA

This small deli near the cathedral specializes in Dalmatian and Istrian ham—anything from a sandwich to an entire leg of *pršut* (cured ham). It also sells Pag sheep's cheese, olive oil, wines and brandies.

✉ Stara Vlaška 7, Zagreb ☎ 01 481 6129
🕐 Mon–Fri 9–8, Sat 9–2 🚊 Tram 1, 6, 11, 12, 13, 14, 17 to Trg Bana Jelačića

SUVENIR PURGER

This fun souvenir shop at the main market sells a large range of traditional souvenirs such as carved wooden boxes, felt slippers, and almost anything emblazoned with the Croatian flag. Or you could choose a clock featuring Glagolitic numerals (▷ 21), which bear no relation to ordinary digits.

✉ Dolac 1, Zagreb ☎ 01 789 8111
🕐 Mon–Sat 8–8, Sun 8–3 🚊 Tram 1, 6, 11, 12, 13, 14, 17 to Trg Bana Jelačića

VALENTINO MODA

If you need to buy a gift for a soccer fan, this shop, on the corner of the main square, sells the official Croatian national football shirts as well as club scarves and caps.

✉ Jurišićeva 1, Zagreb ☎ 01 481 3401
🕐 Mon–Fri 10–8, Sat 9–2 🚊 Tram 1, 6, 11, 12, 13, 14, 17 to Trg Bana Jelačića

VINARIJA

This wonderfully atmospheric cellar sells Zagreb County wine straight from the barrel. Old men gather here to drink Graševina by the glass, or you can get your own plastic bottle filled for 20kn per litre.

✉ Kaptol 14, Zagreb ☎ 01 481 4675 🕓 Mon–Fri 8–2, 4–7, Sat 8–2, Sun 9–1 🚊 Tram 1, 6, 11, 12, 13, 14, 17 to Trg Bana Jelačića

VINOTEKA BORNSTEIN

www.bornstein.hr
Bornstein has an extensive cellar of Croatian and foreign wines, together with olive oil and cheese. It also sells wooden gift boxes that can be filled with Croatian wines, spirits and liqueurs.

✉ Kaptol 19, Zagreb ☎ 01 481 2361 🕓 Mon–Fri 9–8, Sat 9–2 🚊 Tram 1, 6, 11, 12, 13, 14, 17 to Trg Bana Jelačića

ŽITNJAK

www.zitnjak.hr
This ordinary-looking grocery store, on a corner near the main square, has a surprisingly well-stocked cellar, including wines from Zagreb, Slavonia, Istria and Dalmatia.

✉ Ulica Nikole Tesle 7, Zagreb ☎ 01 487 2576 🕓 Mon–Fri 7am–9pm, Sat 8–1 🚊 Tram 1, 6, 11, 12, 13, 14, 17 to Trg Bana Jelačića

ZLATARNA KRIŽEK

www.zlatarna-krizek.hr
In the Oktogon passage near Croata, Križek is the official seller of *morčić* jewellery, which originated in Rijeka and features an enamel figure of a Moor's head. The design comes in the shape of earrings, brooches, necklaces and chains.

✉ Prolaz Oktogon, Ilica 5, Zagreb ☎ 01 492 1931 🕓 Mon–Fri 9–1, 4–8, Sat 9–2 🚊 Tram 1, 6, 11, 12, 13, 14, 17 to Trg Bana Jelačića

ENTERTAINMENT AND NIGHTLIFE

AQUARIUS

www.aquarius.hr
At Aquarius, founding father of the Zagreb club scene, electronic and hip-hop music plays to more than 2,000 people spread over two dance floors, five bars and a large summer terrace. In summer, the club hosts big-name Croatian acts. It also runs a beach club on the island of Pag.

✉ Aleja Matije Ljubeka, Zagreb ☎ 01 364 0231 🕓 Tue–Sun 10pm–5am 🖐 Varies 🚊 Tram 5, 17 to Jarun

BP CLUB

www.bpclub.hr
This intimate jazz club near Trg Bana Jelačića is owned by Croatian jazz legend Boško Petrović, who still plays here some nights. There is live jazz and blues most evenings.

✉ Ulica Nikole Tesle 7, Zagreb ☎ 01 481 4444 🕓 Daily 5pm–1am, music from 10pm 🖐 30–40kn 🚊 Tram 1, 6, 11, 12, 13, 14, 17 to Trg Bana Jelačića

BROADWAY 5 TKALČA

www.broadway-kina.com
This multiplex inside the Centar Kaptol shopping mall has five screens and comfortable seats. It shows the latest international films in their original language with subtitles in Croatian. The Candy Bar sells snacks.

✉ Nova Ves 17, Zagreb ☎ 01 466 7686 🕓 Daily 12–11 🖐 20–30kn 🖵 🚊 Tram 1, 6, 11, 12, 13, 14, 17 to Trg Bana Jelačića

CINESTAR

www.blitz-cinestar.hr
This 13-screen cinema is situated inside the Branimir shopping centre near the railway station.

✉ Branimirova 29, Zagreb ☎ 060 323233 🕓 Box office open Mon–Fri 1–9.30, Sat–Sun 10am–11.30pm 🖐 20–30kn 🍴 🚊 Tram 2, 6, 8 to Branimirova

HRVATSKI GLAZBENI ZAVOD

www.hageze.org
The Croatian Music Institute was founded in 1827 and is one of the oldest cultural institutions in Zagreb. Its concert hall near Trg Bana Jelačića hosts recitals of chamber music and occasional performances by a big band jazz orchestra.

✉ Gundulićeva 6, Zagreb ☎ 01 483 0822 🕓 Box office open Mon–Fri 11–1 and one hour before performance 🖐 Varies 🍴 🚊 Tram 1, 6, 11 to Frankopanska

HRVATSKO NARODNO KAZALIŠTE (CROATIAN NATIONAL THEATRE)

www.hnk.hr
The Croatian National Theatre is housed in a Habsburg-era opera house on Trg Maršala Tita, which is also home to the National Ballet and National Opera. The season usually runs from October to June.

✉ Trg Maršala Tita 15, Zagreb ☎ 01 488 8418 🕓 Box office open Mon–Fri 10–2 and 90 minutes before performance 🖐 Drama 45–80kn, ballet and opera 80–150kn 🍴 🚊 Tram 12, 13, 14, 17 to Trg Maršala Tita

KAZALIŠTE KOMEDIJA

www.komedija.hr
Opened in 1950, this small theatre near the cathedral hosts operettas, musicals and dramatic performances in Croatian. The box office is in Oktogon passage, Ilica 5.

✉ Kaptol 9, Zagreb ☎ 01 481 3200. Box office: 01 481 2657 🕓 Box office open Mon–Fri 8–5.30, Sat 8–1; at theatre one hour before performance 🖐 Drama 40–60kn, musicals 60–120kn 🍴 🚊 Tram 1, 6, 11, 12, 13, 14, 17 to Trg Bana Jelačića

KONCERTNA DVORANA VATROSLAV LISINSKI

www.lisinski.hr
Zagreb's main concert hall, built in 1973, was named after composer Vatroslav Lisinski (1819–54). It is home to the Zagreb Philharmonic Orchestra and also hosts visiting orchestras from abroad.

✉ Trg Stjepana Radića 4, Zagreb ☎ 01 612 1166 🕓 Box office open Mon–Fri 10–8, Sat 9–2, and one hour before performance 🖐 Varies 🍴 🚊 Tram 3, 5, 13 to Lisinski

THE MOVIE PUB

www.the-movie-pub.com
This popular bar on the outskirts of Zagreb has been decked with Hollywood film memorabilia. There is live music most nights, and karaoke on Wednesday and Thursday.

✉ Savska Cesta 141, Zagreb ☎ 01 605 5045 🕓 Mon–Wed 7am–2am, Thu–Sat 7am–4am, Sun 9am–2am 🚊 Tram 4, 5, 14, 17 to Prisavlje

SAX

www.sax-zg.hr

This busy central basement club has live music every night, ranging from jazz and blues to rock and pop. It closes for a summer break in July and August.

✉ Palmotićeva 22, Zagreb ☎ 01 487 2836 ⊙ Daily 9am–3am, music from 10pm ✋ Varies 🚋 Tram 1, 6, 11, 12, 13, 14, 17 to Trg Bana Jelačića

ŠKOLA

Everything is white except the plants at this popular, ultra-trendy lounge bar, situated above a bookshop and the terrace bars of Bogovićeva. The restaurant serves Japanese-inspired cuisine and the bar offers a range of unusual and expensive cocktails. If you are feeling flush, try the Champagne with gold flakes.

✉ Bogovićeva 7, Zagreb ☎ 01 482 8196 ⊙ Mon–Sat 10am–1am, Sun 11am–1am 🚋 Tram 1, 6, 11, 12, 13, 14, 17 to Trg Bana Jelačića

TVORNICA

www.tvornica-kulture.hr

This multitasking cultural centre stages live concerts, dance nights, theatre performances and myriad other events. The centre's offbeat café-bar is open throughout the day but the action really starts here around 8pm.

✉ Šubićeva 2, Zagreb ☎ 01 777 8673 ⊙ 8am–4am ✋ 40kn–130kn 🚋 Tram 5, 7 to Trg Kralja Petra Krešimira IV

SPORTS AND ACTIVITIES

CIBONA

www.cibona.com

Croatia's top basketball team plays at the Dražen Petrović stadium, named after a famous former player (▷ 17). Euroleague matches take place between September and April. The best mid-price tickets are in the red and blue sections on either side of the court.

✉ Savska 30, Zagreb ☎ 01 484 3333 ⊙ Call or check press for match times ✋ 20–300kn 🚋 Tram 3, 4, 9, 12, 13, 14, 17 to Tehnički Muzej or Studentski Centar

GOLF & COUNTRY CLUB ZAGREB

www.gcczagreb.hr

This short nine-hole (par 30) course opened in 2004 on the Sava river embankment in Novi Zagreb. There is also a golf academy and driving range. There are plans to build a full 18-hole championship course here.

✉ Jadranska Avenija 6, Zagreb ☎ 01 653 1177 ⊙ All year ✋ Adult 300kn 🍴 🚌 🚗 Cross the River Sava, take the highway to Karlovac and turn right after first gas station

DINAMO ZAGREB

www.nk-dinamo.hr

Dinamo are the biggest club in Croatia and were league champions in 2009. They play at the Maksimir stadium, which seats 40,000 spectators and is also used by the Croatian national team. The

domestic season runs from August to May, with a winter break between December and February. Tickets are inexpensive and can usually be bought on the gate, the exception being for matches against the team's arch-rivals Hajduk Split.

✉ Maksimirska Cesta 128, Zagreb ☎ 01 232 3234 ⊙ Call or check press for match times ✋ From 30kn 🚋 Tram 11, 12 to Bukovačka

JARUN

On this artificial lake you can swim from beaches, canoe, kayak, sail or windsurf, or take a scuba-diving course. There are jogging and cycle paths, lakeside walks, bicycle rental, mini-golf, table-tennis, volleyball, basketball and handball courts, plus bars and cafés.

✉ Jarun, Zagreb ☎ 01 303 1888 ⊙ All year ✋ Varies according to activity 🚌 Tram 5, 17 to Jarun

KLIZALIŠTE VELESAJAM

Just south of the river, this is possibly the city's best ice rink. During the week the building is used by professional figure skaters and ice hockey teams, but it is open to the public at weekends.

✉ Jozefa Antala bb ☎ 01 655 4357 ⊙ Fri–Sun, hours vary

Below *The bustling daily market at Dolac, where farmers from the surrounding countryside sell their fresh produce*

SLJEME

www.sljeme-skijanje.com

Olympic medallists Janica and Ivica Kostelić learned to ski on the ski slopes of Medvednica. In winter, you can ski without leaving the city, with pistes ranging from white (easy) to red (challenging). There is also a snowboard park, and sledging (sledding) for children. Skis and boots can be hired. In January, Sljeme plays host to the FIS World Cup Snow Queen trophy.

✉ Sljeme, Zagreb ☎ 01 467 3006
🕐 Dec–end Mar daily 9–4 ✋ Ski pass 70kn per day, 50kn per half-day 🚋 Tram 8, 14 to Mihaljevac then 15 to Dolje followed by cable car

FOR CHILDREN
MAKSIMIRSKI PERIVOJ

www.park-maksimir.hr

Maksimir Park (▷ 60) is a paradise for children, with playgrounds, swings and open spaces to explore as well as the city's zoo (▷ right). Or children can let off steam in central parks. The best are Ribnjak and Zrinjevac.

✉ Maksimirska Cesta, Zagreb
☎ 01 232 0460 🕐 Open during daylight hours 🚻 🚋 Tram 11, 12 to Bukovačka

MEĐUNARODNI CENTAR ZA USLUGE U KULTURI

www.mcuk.hr

The multitasking International Centre for Cultural Services often stages performances for children, especially around Christmas. These usually come in the form of puppet shows and fairy tales. Performances are held at the centre and at various venues around town. Check the website or call for details about what's on.

✉ Magovca 17 ☎ 01 660 1626

TEHNIČKI MUZEJ (TECHNICAL MUSEUM)

www.mdc.hr/tehnicki

This enjoyable science museum has planetarium shows and an underground tour of a reconstructed mine. Kids will enjoy the transport gallery, with cars, planes and trains.

There are free tram rides at 9.30am on Sundays.

✉ Savska 18, Zagreb ☎ 01 435446
🕐 Tue–Fri 9–5, Sat–Sun 9–1; mine tours Tue–Fri 3, Sat–Sun 11; planetarium Tue–Fri 4, Sat–Sun 12 ✋ Adult 15kn, child 10kn; planetarium 15kn 🚋 Tram 3, 4, 9, 12, 13, 14, 17 to Tehnički Muzej or Studenstski Centar

ZOO ZAGREB

www.zgzoo.com

The city zoo, on an island in Maksimir Park, has native animals, including brown bears and wolves, as well as other species ranging from elephants to lions, tigers, chimpanzees, crocodiles and penguins.

✉ Maksimirski Perivoj, Zagreb ☎ 01 230 2198 🕐 May–end Aug daily 9–8; Sep–end Apr shorter hours (see website for details)
✋ Adult 30kn, child 20kn 🚋 Tram 11, 12 to Bukovačka

Below left to right *Commemorative statue at the Dražen Petrović Basketball Hall; Zagreb Zoo*

FESTIVALS AND EVENTS

APRIL

BIENNALE OF NEW MUSIC
www.mbz.hr
Held on odd-numbered years (2011 and 2013 for example), this biennial festival showcases contemporary classical music from Croatia and abroad.
✉ Croatian Composers Society, Berislavićeva 9, Zagreb ☎ 01 487 2370

QUEER ZAGREB
www.queerzagreb.org
This annual festival is five days of cinema, theatre, music and dance on gay and lesbian themes at venues across the city.

APRIL/MAY

ST. MARK'S FESTIVAL
www.festivalsvmarka.hr
Chamber, orchestral and sacred music at St. Mark's Church and venues such as the Croatian Music Institute.
✉ Trg Svetog Marka 5, Zagreb ☎ 01 482 1175

MAY–SEPTEMBER

PROMENADE CONCERTS
Big bands, children's choirs and chamber orchestras play at the bandstand in Zrinjevac park on Saturday mornings from Easter to the end of September.
✉ Trg Nikole Šubića Zrinjskog, Zagreb
🕐 Sat 11–1 🚋 Tram 6, 13 to Zrinjevac

JULY

EUROKAZ
www.eurokaz.hr
International and multilingual, this popular contemporary theatre festival attracts companies from across the globe. Reservations in advance.
✉ Various city centre venues ☎ 01 484 7856

INTERNATIONAL FOLKLORE FESTIVAL
www.msf.hr
Founded in 1966, this well-respected festival has Croatian and international folk groups performing on an outdoor stage in Trg Bana Jelačića, along with dance workshops, world music and a concert at Vatroslav Lisinski concert hall.
✉ Zagreb Concert Management, Kneza Mislava 18, Zagreb ☎ 01 450 1200

JULY AND AUGUST

ZAGREB SUMMER EVENINGS
www.kdz.hr
Classical and chamber music concerts take place in the cathedral and Gornji Grad.
✉ Zagreb Concert Management, Kneza Mislava 18, Zagreb ☎ 01 450 1200

AUGUST AND SEPTEMBER

INTERNATIONAL PUPPET THEATRE FESTIVAL
www.mcuk.hr
Puppet theatre has a long tradition in southeast Europe and this festival features a week of performances in the Komedija theatre and venues across the city.
✉ Božidara Magovca 17, Travno, Zagreb ☎ 01 660 1626

OCTOBER

ZAGREB FILM FESTIVAL
www.zagrebfilmfestival.com
The annual film festival at the Student Centre showcases feature films, short films and documentaries, with an emphasis on a different country each year.
✉ Savska 25, Zagreb ☎ 01 482 9477
🚋 Tram 3, 4, 13, 14, 17 to Studenstski Centar

DECEMBER

ADVENT IN THE HEART OF ZAGREB
Throughout the month of December Trg Bana Jelačića is turned into a winter playground, with Christmas markets, stalls selling hot dogs and mulled wine, and evening concerts held on an open-air stage. There are also a variety of special events for children, including miniature train rides with Santa.
✉ Trg Bana Jelačića 🕐 5–22 Dec

Below *Dancers performing at the annual International Folklore Festival*

EATING

PRICES AND SYMBOLS

The restaurants are listed alphabetically. The prices given are the average for a two-course lunch (L) and a three-course dinner (D) for one person, without drinks. The wine price is for a litre of table wine followed by the least expensive bottle of quality wine. All the restaurants listed accept credit cards unless otherwise stated.

For a key to the symbols, ▷ 2.

AGAVA

www.restaurant-agava.hr
A casually stylish place on trendy Tkalčićeva Street, with historic views, this central eatery specializes in Mediterranean cuisine with a Croatian twist. The menu offers an interesting selection of pastas, risotto, meat and fish, although the choice of desserts is rather limited.
✉ Tkalčićeva 39, Zagreb ☎ 01 482 9826
🕓 Daily noon–11pm 🍴 L 150kn, D 180kn, Wine from 150kn 🚊 Tram 1, 6, 11, 12, 13, 14, 17 to Trg Bana Jelačića

BOBAN

www.boban.hr
This brick-vaulted cellar off the main square attracts a buzzy crowd for its Italian cuisine and faux antique décor. Choose from classics such as tagliatelle with truffles, cream and brandy, or order a 'hunter's platter' of venison salami, ham and smoked cheese to share.
✉ Gajeva 9, Zagreb ☎ 01 481 1549
🕓 Daily 10am–midnight 🍴 L 90kn, D 130kn, Wine 70/110kn 🚊 Tram 1, 6, 11, 12, 13, 14, 17 to Trg Bana Jelačića

GOSTIONICA TIP-TOP

Be transported back in time at this old-fashioned eatery, a popular choice among locals. Here you can enjoy Adriatic seafood dishes on checked tablecloths, followed by a dessert of pancakes with walnuts or wine mousse. The restaurant is sometimes known by its old name 'Blato', a word synonymous with Zagreb's literary and arts scene.
✉ Gundulićeva 18, Zagreb ☎ 01 483 0349 🕓 Mon–Sat 7am–10pm 🍴 L 70kn, D 110kn, Wine 90/140kn 🚊 Tram 6, 13 to Zrinjevac

IVICA I MARICA

www.ivicaimarica.com
Vegetarian cooking is raised to an art form at this modern restaurant, which combines Hansel-and-Gretel cottage décor and waiters in folk costume with a *nouvelle cuisine* approach to food. There are some meat and fish dishes but most are meat-free, such as *štrukli* (cottage cheese and spinach parcels), vegetarian goulash and grilled mushrooms. The owners have a cake shop next door.
✉ Tkalčićeva 70, Zagreb ☎ 01 482 8999
🕓 Mon–Sat 12–11, Sun 1–9.30
🍴 L 100kn, D 140kn, Wine from 110kn
🚊 Tram 1, 6, 11, 12, 13, 14, 17 to Trg Bana Jelačića

K PIVOVARI

www.kpivovari.com
This busy pub is attached to the Ožujsko brewery. In summer, you can enjoy draught beers in the garden; in winter, tuck into plates of sausages, baked potatoes and mixed grills.
✉ Ilica 222, Zagreb ☎ 01 375 1808
🕓 Mon–Thu 10am–11pm, Fri–Sat 10am–midnight 🍴 L 70kn, D 100kn, Beer from 15kn 🚊 Tram 2, 6,11 to Slovenska

KAPTOLSKA KLET

www.kaptolska-klet.hr
Choose from a crowded beer hall with communal wooden tables and

Opposite In restaurants, the more expensive wines are sold by the bottle

a terrace facing the cathedral, or a pretty courtyard restaurant serving a wider variety of Zagreb and Zagorje-style dishes. At lunchtime, the pub offers inexpensive, filling fare such as goulash, stuffed peppers, bean stew, sausages and scones with bacon.

✉ Kaptol 5, Zagreb ☎ 01 481 4838 🕓 Daily 9am–midnight 🖐 L 60kn, D 110kn, Wine 100/150kn 🚋 Tram 1, 6, 11, 12, 13, 14, 17 to Trg Bana Jelačića

KEREMPUH

www.kerempuh.hr

This famous restaurant above Dolac market is popular with Zagreb's professionals, who come here to enjoy good, freshly prepared Croatian cooking. The menu changes daily according to what is in the market, with an emphasis on meat dishes. Arrive early to grab a seat on the terrace. Lunch only.

✉ Kaptol 3, Zagreb ☎ 01 481 9000 🕓 Mon–Sat 6am–midnight, Sun 7–4 🖐 L 80kn, Wine 100/110kn 🚋 Tram 1, 6, 11, 12, 13, 14, 17 to Trg Bana Jelačića

KONOBA DIDOV SAN

www.konoba-didovsan.com

This superb little tavern in the Gornji Grad serves up mouth-watering traditional meat and fish dishes under hefty timber beams. Desserts are freshly made, the wine crisp and the welcome friendly. There's another branch at Bencekovićeva 28 just south of the river, near the hippodrome.

✉ Mletačka 11, Zagreb ☎ 01 485 1154 🕓 Mon–Sat 10am–11pm, Sun 11am–10pm 🖐 L 150kn, D 180kn, Wine 65/120kn 🚋 Tram 1, 6, 11, 12, 13, 14, 17 to Trg Bana Jelačića

KONOBA MAŠKLIN I LATA

www.konoba-masklinilata.com

This surprisingly light and airy cellar restaurant serves authentic Dalmatian and Istrian fish specialities as well as meat and pasta dishes. With its abstract nautical theme and a friendly welcome, it's a particularly cosy place to eat in wintertime.

✉ Hebranga 11, Zagreb ☎ 01 481 8273 🕓 Daily 9am–11pm 🖐 L 190kn, D 220kn, Wine from 140kn 🚋 Tram 6, 13 to Zrinjevac

NOVA

www.novarestoran.com.hr

Vegetarians often feel neglected in Croatia, where meat figures prominently in the diet, but this long-established macrobiotic vegan eatery in central Zagreb can quickly put that right. Organic juices, dairy-free desserts and simple pastas are just the ticket for vegetarians, as well as offering meat-eaters the chance to detox if they've overdone it on Croatia's red meat delights.

✉ Ilica 72, Zagreb ☎ 01 481 0059 🕓 Mon–Sat 12–10 🖐 L 100kn, D 120kn 🚋 Tram 1, 6, 11 to Britanski Trg

OKRUGLJAK

www.okrugljak.hr

This top-notch restaurant at the base of Mount Medvednica has been pleasing taste buds for more than a century. The gourmet food, attentive service and old-world ambience come at a price, but it's well worth it. The extensive wine list features Croatian table varieties as well as vintage reds and whites, and the menu is imaginative while remaining largely traditional.

✉ Mlinovi 28, Zagreb ☎ 01 467 4112 🕓 Daily 11am–midnight 🖐 L 200kn, D 250kn, Wine 110/150kn 🚌 102 to Pirovac

PAVILJON

www.restaurant-paviljon.com

Housed in the splendid setting of the 19th-century Art Pavilion, this is one of Zagreb's top restaurants. Chef Stanko Erceg creates modern Croatian classics such as swordfish carpaccio, broccoli and shrimp soup and his signature dish, crispy roast duck with red cabbage and figs. On some nights a grand piano plays. Dress up to come here or you will feel out of place.

✉ Trg Kralja Tomislava 22, Zagreb ☎ 01 481 3066 🕓 Mon–Sat 12–12 🖐 L 150kn, D 250kn, Wine from 140kn 🚋 Tram to Glavni Kolodvor (train station)

PIVNICA TOMISLAV

The no-frills Tomislav beer hall serves up just about the cheapest sit-down meals in the capital, with the set lunch menu coming in at between 30kn and 35kn. It is understandably popular with ravenous local office workers by day and fans of the half-litre glass by night and its tiled floors and pine-clad walls reverberate with lively Slavic banter at all times of the day.

✉ Trg Kralja Tomislava 18, Zagreb ☎ 01 492 2255 🕓 Mon–Sat 7am–11pm, Sun 9–9 🖐 L 35kn, D 50kn, Beer 13kn 🚋 Tram 6, 13 to Zrinjevac

POD GRIČKIM TOPOM

With a flower-filled terrace overlooking the city, the restaurant is perfect on a summer evening. The menu focuses on steaks and fish, and also includes veal schnitzel stuffed with ham and cheese. Get there by climbing the steps or taking the funicular to Gradec.

✉ Zakmardijeve Stube 5, Zagreb ☎ 01 483 3607 🕓 Mon–Sat 11am–midnight, Sun 11–5 🖐 L 120kn, D 150kn, Wine 110/240kn 🚡 Funicular to Gradec

RUBELJ

www.rubelj-grill.hr

This flagship of a chain of fast-food restaurants offering *ćevapčići* (meatballs), sausages and kebabs is on the terrace of Dolac market. It isn't fancy, but the perfectly grilled meat is served with crusty bread and *ajvar* (aubergine/eggplant and pepper relish). Just the place for a filling lunchtime snack.

✉ Dolac 2, Zagreb ☎ 01 481 8777 🕓 Daily 8am–11pm 🖐 L 50kn, D 70kn, Beer from 15kn 🚋 Tram 1, 6, 11, 12, 13, 14, 17 to Trg Bana Jelačića

STARI FIJAKER

The pub, one of Zagreb's oldest, has model carriages hanging from the ceiling. The cuisine includes Zagorje-style soup, cottage cheese *štrukli* and pasta with roast duck and turkey.

✉ Mesnička 6, Zagreb ☎ 01 483 3829 🕓 Mon–Sat 7am–11pm, Sun 9am–10pm 🖐 L 80kn, D 120kn, Wine 70/170kn 🚋 Tram 1, 6, 11 to Frankopanska

PRICES AND SYMBOLS

Prices are the lowest for a double room for one night. Breakfast is included unless noted otherwise. All the hotels listed accept credit cards unless otherwise stated. Note that rates vary widely throughout the year.

For a key to the symbols, ▷ 2.

ARCOTEL ALLEGRA

www.arcotel.cc/allegra

Designed by Viennese artist Harald Schreiber, the Allegra is full of bright colours and funky touches, and all rooms include DVD players and mobile tables which double up as desks or for breakfast in bed. The buffet breakfast here is one of the best in town, and the restaurant does an excellent all-you-can-eat Sunday brunch. The sixth-floor fitness centre provides sauna and massage. The hotel is part of a modern shopping mall, which also includes a cinema, near the railway station.

✉ Branimirova 29, Zagreb ☎ 01 469 6000 ✋ €85 ⓘ 151 🔄 📺 🚌 Tram 2, 6, 8 to Branimirova or a short walk from railway station

CENTRAL

www.hotel-central.hr

Directly opposite the railway station, this functional but comfortable hotel provides a convenient mid-price base within walking distance of the central Zagreb. If you can, opt for one of the rooms on the top floor, from where there are fine views of the cathedral across the city.

✉ Branimirova 3, Zagreb ☎ 01 484 1122 ✋ 780kn ⓘ 79 🔄 🚌 Tram 2, 4, 6, 9, 13 to railway station

DUBROVNIK

www.hotel-dubrovnik.hr

Built in 1929, the Dubrovnik occupies a prime position in a corner of Trg Bana Jelačića, the heart and soul of the city. Some rooms overlook the square. You enter through a striking glass wing on Gajeva, central to Zagreb's open-air café life. The hotel is a good choice if you are looking for four-star comforts in the heart of the city.

✉ Gajeva 1, Zagreb ☎ 01 486 3555 ✋ €132 ⓘ 266 🔄 🚌 Tram 1, 6, 11, 12, 13, 14, 17 to Trg Bana Jelačića

GARNY

www.hotel-garny.hr

This family-run hotel in the vicinity of Zagreb airport makes a good choice for anyone with an early flight to catch the next morning. The rooms are tastefully decorated with bright colours, warm furnishings and paintings by contemporary Croatian artist Vladimir Zopf. This is an unexpectedly special place and a world away from the standard image of airport hotels.

✉ Mikulčićeva 7a, Velika Gorica ☎ 01 625 3600 ✋ 750kn ⓘ 19 🔄 🏊 Indoor 📺 🚌 Follow the signs off the airport approach road just before you reach the terminal

HOTEL AS

www.hotel-as.hr

North of central Zagreb in the city's green hinterland, the hotel allows guests to combine a peaceful stay in tranquil surroundings with the bustle of the Croatian capital. Rooms are elegantly modern, there's an on-site restaurant and café, and Trg Bana Jelačića is a mere 15-minute walk

away. Accessible by taxi, private car or on foot.
✉ Zelengaj 2, Zagreb ☎ 01 4609 111 ✋ 980kn ⓘ 20

HOTEL I
www.hotel-i.hr
This mid-range hotel just south of the Sava River has comfortable rooms with everything you're likely to need during your stay and a list of services as long as your arm. It's popular among businesspeople visiting the Croatian capital thanks to its easy transport links to the airport, trade fair grounds and city centre.
✉ Remetinečka cesta 106 ☎ 01 654 2238 ✋ 790kn ⓘ 214 🚌 Tram 7, 14

ILICA
www.hotel-ilica.hr
Although the rooms are on the small side, this friendly hotel, just two tram stops from Trg Bana Jelačića, offers the best budget option in central Zagreb. The 12 rooms are divided into singles, doubles and triples, all with private bathrooms. Reserve in advance. No credit cards.
✉ Ilica 102, Zagreb ☎ 01 377 7522 ✋ 599kn ⓘ 12 🚌 Tram 1, 6, 11 to Britanski Trg

JAEGERHORN
www.hotel-pansion-jaegerhorn.hr
The main appeal of this small hotel is its setting, in the attractive 19th-century Lovački Rog shopping arcade, which is reached through an arch just off the main square. Rooms are simple and functional, and there is a lovely garden restaurant, where you dine by a waterfall at the foot of the steps leading up to Gradec.
✉ Ilica 14, Zagreb ☎ 01 483 3877 ✋ 690kn ⓘ 13 🚌 Tram 1, 6, 11, 12, 13, 14, 17 to Trg Bana Jelačića

MOVIE HOTEL
www.themoviehotel.com
Zagreb's first theme hotel opened in 2006 above The Movie Pub, a popular English-style pub on the outskirts of town filled with Hollywood memorabilia. Rooms are named after famous film stars, and the Hollywood theme runs throughout.
✉ Savska Cesta 141, Zagreb ☎ 01 600 3600 ✋ 590kn ⓘ 41 🚌 Tram 4, 5, 14, 17 to Prisavlje

PALACE
www.palace.hr
Built as the Austro-Hungarian Schlessinger Palace in 1891 and converted to a hotel in 1907, the Palace is the oldest hotel in Zagreb and one of the oldest in Central Europe. Recent renovations have introduced modern facilities such as internet access in the rooms, but the hotel still exudes old-world style and art nouveau design. Most of the rooms overlook a series of pretty parks and squares between the railway station and the main square. There is a delightful Viennese-style café on the ground floor, a good place to meet friends over coffee.
✉ Strossmayerova Trg 10, Zagreb ☎ 01 489 9600 ✋ 1,050kn ⓘ 123 🚌 Tram 6, 13 to Zrinjevac or a short walk from railway station or Trg Bana Jelačića

REGENT ESPLANADE
www.theregentzagreb.com
The *grande dame* of Zagreb hotels opened in 1925 for train passengers arriving on the Orient Express, and the guest list has included Tito, Orson Welles and Pele. After a complete renovation by Regent Hotels in 2004, the Esplanade is once again the classiest address in town. From the moment you step into the art deco marble and walnut lobby, you feel the hotel's history and elegance. Rooms are luxuriously decorated with rich fabrics and fresh flowers, together with marble bathrooms and walk-in showers. Modern touches include free WiFi throughout the hotel.
✉ Mihanovićeva 1, Zagreb ☎ 01 456 6666 ✋ €150 ⓘ 209 🚌 Tram 2, 4, 6, 9, 13 to railway station

SLIŠKO
www.slisko.hr
This small family-run hotel in a quiet street near the bus station makes a convenient choice for travellers arriving on the airport bus. Rooms are simply furnished but comfortable, and guests have free access to a computer to check their email.
✉ Bunečeva 7, Zagreb ☎ 01 618 4777 ✋ 517kn ⓘ 15 🚌 Tram 2, 5, 6, 7, 8 to Autobusni Kolodvor (bus station)

TOMISLAVOV DOM
www.hotel-tomislavovdom.com
This mountain lodge, surrounded by pine woods at a height of 1,000m (3,300ft), allows you to combine a visit to Zagreb, accessible by cable car and then tram, with some walking in summer or skiing in winter. Just beneath the summit of Medvednica, a short distance from the ski slopes, the hotel has an indoor pool and excellent spa facilities, including sauna and massage treatments. ✉ Sljeme bb, Zagreb ☎ 01 456 0400 ✋ 570kn ⓘ 42 🏊 Indoor 🚌 Tram 15 to Dolje followed by cable car

VILLA TINA
www.vilatina.com.hr
Set in a large house high above Maksimir Park, just a short tram ride from the city, Villa Tina offers a peaceful retreat, with a tasteful modern interior decorated with art and antiques. The hotel also has an indoor pool and fitness centre.
✉ Bukovačka Cesta 213, Zagreb ☎ 01 244 5138 ✋ €90 ⓘ 26 🏊 Indoor 🚌 Bus 203 from Maksimir Park 🚌 Take Maksimirska Cesta out of the city and turn left up Bukovačka Cesta just before Maksimir Park

WESTIN ZAGREB
www.westin.com/zagreb
The Westin Zagreb (formerly the Hotel Opera) is a high-rise Zagreb landmark, towering over the city close to the Mimara Museum and Croatian National Theatre. It offers modern luxury and comforts, including the signature Heavenly Bed with its layers of plush white sheets. The top floors have some of the best views in Zagreb.
✉ Kršnjavoga 1, Zagreb ☎ 01 489 2000 ✋ €135 ⓘ 378 🏊 Indoor 🚌 Tram 12, 13, 14, 17 to Hotel Opera

REGIONS ZAGREB • STAYING

INLAND CROATIA

Croatia's least visited region is divided between the undulating hills of the Zagorje in the west and the wide plains along the Danube and Sava rivers to the south and east. The traditionally minded region of Slavonia, centred on Osijek, the tumbling waterfalls of the Plitvice Lakes National Park and the region's Hungarian influences are just some of the highlights of Croatia's brooding hinterland.

Off the beaten track and seen by few sun-seekers, this is not the Croatia of the beach-and-swimming-pool tourist brochures. With its grand Habsburg-era baroque and neoclassical architecture, busy café culture and the formal frills and stiffer etiquette of Central Europe, Croatia's other face is turned away from the sun, seafood and hybrid culture of Dalmatia and Istria, and more towards central Europe.

Away from the cities, Inland Croatia abounds in natural beauty; Croatia's first national park was established at the Plitvice Lakes, now one of the country's top attractions. The Danube and Sava flood plains provide wetland nesting sites for migrating birds, most notably at Kopački Rit and Lonjsko Polje, while other wildlife seeks sanctuary in the gentle wooded hills of the Zagorje. The region is given a splash of folksy colour by festivals held across the region, such as those in Slavanski Brod and Đakovo, and lashings of paprika and garlic lend a dash of spice to the local cuisine.

Recent history shattered the peaceful scene for a few terrible years at the beginning of the 1990s, when the region formed the backdrop to fighting during the Homeland War. Today, in numerous villages along the border, newly repaired houses stand alongside bombed-out ruins, and many areas are still dangerous due to landmines (minefields are very well marked). However, the regions' towns have been restored to their former glory, and in most cases look even better than they did before hostilities began.

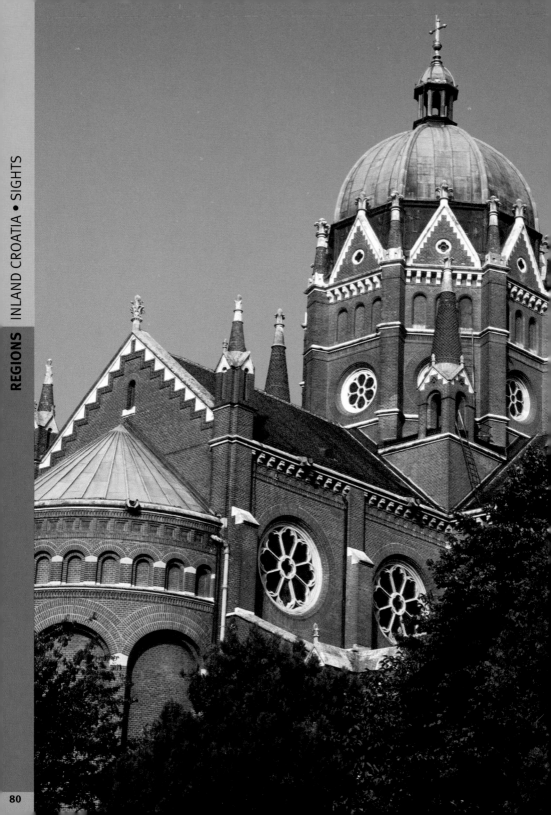

ČAKOVEC

www.tourism-cakovec.hr

Čakovec, 16km (10 miles) north of Varaždin and near the Hungarian border, was the northern stronghold of the Zrinski dynasty, aristocrats and soldiers who were granted the town in 1547 for their services to the Habsburg emperor. It was Nikola Šubić Zrinski (1508–66), a former governor of Croatia, who began the castle that dominates the town. His great-grandson, Nikola (1620–64), was killed in a wild boar hunt and is recalled in a memorial in the nearby park. The restored castle is now the Muzej Međimurja (Tue–Fri 10–3, Sat–Sun 10–1; adult 15kn, child 10kn), a museum with exhibits ranging from archaeology and local history to Carnival masks, modern art and a reconstruction of an old pharmacy. The town centre is based around Trg Kralja Tomislava, an elongated main square leading to wide pedestrianized shopping streets. On the main square, opposite the tourist office, is the former trades hall (1908), a striking red-brick building that now contains the city library. Look for the Zrinski coat of arms above the portal of the parish church.

Čakovec is the main town of Međimurje, a fertile region of farmland between the Mura and Drava rivers. The village of Štrigova is known for its excellent white wines.

➕ 280 E1 🛈 Trg Kralja Tomislava 1, ☎ 040 313319 🕙 Mon–Fri 8–7, Sat 8–1 🚌 From Varaždin and Zagreb 🚂 From Varaždin and Zagreb

ĐAKOVO

www.tz-djakovo.hr

The approach to Đakovo is dominated by the twin spires of its neo-Gothic cathedral, 84m (275ft) tall and towering over the city. The interior has painted ceilings, frescoes and a central cupola. The cathedral was built between 1866 and 1882 for Bishop Josip Strossmayer (▷ 21) and as you explore the city, it can start feeling like a Strossmayer memorial park. His tomb lies in the crypt, his statue stands outside, the city park is named after him,

and there is also a small museum (Mon–Fri 8–6, Sat 8–1.30) devoted to his life.

Ulica Hrvatskih Velikana — known as the *korzo* — runs north from the cathedral to the small whitewashed church of Svi Svetih (All Saints), housed in a converted 16th-century Turkish mosque. A short walk from the centre leads to the Lipizzaner stud farm (tel 031 813286; www.ergela-djakovo.hr; visits by appointment), founded in 1506 to breed white horses for the imperial court in Vienna.

➕ 283 J3 🛈 Ulica Kralja Tomislava 3 ☎ 031 812319 🕙 Mon–Fri 8–3 🚌 From Osijek and Slavonski Brod

HLEBINE

▷ 82.

ILOK

www.turizamilok.hr

The easternmost town in Croatia, Ilok sits above a bend in the River Danube, with views across the river to the neighbouring Serbian city of Novi Sad. It is built around a 14th-century fortress, within whose walls is the parish church of Sveti Ivan Kapistran, dedicated to the Franciscan priest who died defending the town from the Turks in 1456. For more than 100 years, Ilok was part of the Ottoman empire and you can see the remains of a Turkish bath in the castle.

The nearby hills of Fruška Gora have been known for their vineyards since Roman times. After a lull, the vineyards are productive again; the wine harvest fair in September is a joyous occasion.

➕ 283 K3 🛈 Trg Nikole Iločkog 2 ☎ 032 590020 🕙 Mon–Fri 9–5 🚌 From Osijek and Vukovar

Above *The historic town of Čakovec, close to the Hungarian border*

Opposite *Đakovo's imposing red-brick, neo-Gothic cathedral*

INFORMATION
www.generalic.com
✚ 281 F1 ℹ Trg Ivana Generalića 1,
Koprivnica ☎ 048 836139 🕓 Mon–Fri
8–4, Sat 8–12

TIPS

» A map outside Galerija Hlebine shows the location of around 20 studios in the village, all of which can be visited to see and buy.

» Galerija Koprivnica (tel 048 622564; Tue–Fri 10–1, 5–8, Sat–Sun 10–1), on the main square in Koprivnica, also has exhibitions of naive art.

» There are no restaurants in Hlebine, but Pivnica Kraluš in Koprivnica serves filling fare at reasonable prices (▷ 110).

Below A Dance in the Mountains *by Ivan Generalić, father of naive art in Croatia*

HLEBINE

This small rural village is known throughout Croatia as the birthplace of the Croatian naive art movement. This began in the 1930s when the artist Krsto Hegedušić (1901–75) returned from Paris to find villagers in Hlebine producing colourful scenes of rural life reminiscent of the work of French primitive painter Henri Rousseau (1844–1910). The first generation of naive artists, such as Ivan Generalić (1914–92), Mirko Virius (1889–1943) and Franjo Mraz (1910–81), were self-taught, but Hegedušić helped develop their technique and exhibited their work in Zagreb.

FROM FATHER...

Galerija Hlebine (tel 048 836075; Mon–Fri 10–4, Sat 10–2; adult 10kn, child 5kn) in the village has exhibitions of work by local artists. One room is devoted to Ivan Generalić, considered the father of naive art. It reveals the development of his style, from youthful portraits and landscapes to experiments with fantasy and magical realism. The highlight is a striking triptych of Christ crucified among the snows of Hlebine.

...TO SON

Ivan's son Josip (1936–2004) also worked in Hlebine and his home is now the Galerija Josip Generalić (tel 048 836071; visits by appointment). Among his works are portraits of his father, plus fanciful images of Sophia Loren and The Beatles in Hlebine. Also here is Ivan's house and studio, now a small museum with photographs and posters from exhibitions. The family tradition is continued by grandson Goran (b.1971), who has an online gallery in nearby Koprivnica.

JASENOVAC

www.jusp-jasenovac.hr

Jasenovac was the site of a notorious concentration camp run by the Ustaše regime during the Independent State of Croatia (1941–45). No one knows how many people were murdered here, but estimates range from 50,000 to over 100,000. The majority of victims were ethnic Serbs, but others included Jews, Roma (gypsies), Bosnian Muslims and Croats opposed to the regime. The camp was razed to the ground, and in its place now stands a large concrete lotus flower. The monument was designed by Bogdan Bogdanović (b.1922), a Serbian artist and former mayor of Belgrade who now lives in exile in Vienna. The walkway to the monument is constructed out of railway sleepers; nearby stands an old cattle train, similar to those that transported inmates to the camp. During the 1991–95 war Jasenovac was occupied by Serbian troops and the Memorial Museum was looted, with many exhibits ending up in Belgrade. Many of these items have been returned and a new museum opened at the site in 2006.

✚ 281 F3 ℹ Jasenovac Memorial Museum ☎ 044 672319 ◷ Tue–Fri 9–5, Sat–Sun 10–4 🚆 From Zagreb

KARLOVAC

www.karlovac-touristinfo.hr

Karlovac was established at the junction of four rivers in 1579 as a military base on the southern border of the Austro-Hungarian empire. The walls that once surrounded the citadel were torn down in the 19th century, but their outline can still be seen in the tree-lined promenades encircling the town. The 2.5km (1.5-mile) circuit makes a pleasant walk, through green parks overlooking a moat. The prettiest section is along Šetalište Tuđmana, where there is a restored 19th-century theatre, Zorin Dom. Inside the walls, the old town keeps its baroque feel, particularly around the central square, Trg Bana Jelačića, with its 1691 plague pillar. The nearby Gradski Muzej (Tue–Fri 8–3, Sat–Sun 10–12) has displays of local history, archaeology and folk costumes. Just 5km (3 miles) south of the town, at the confluence of the Korana and Mrežnica rivers, Turanj was the frontline of the Homeland War. An open-air memorial museum displays tanks and anti-aircraft guns from the war. There are plans for a permanent museum on this site.

✚ 280 D3 ℹ Ulica Petra Zrinskog 3 ☎ 047 600606 ◷ Jun–end Sep Mon–Fri 8–3, Sat 9–1, 5–8; Oct–end May Mon–Fri 8–3, Sat 9–12 🚌 From Zagreb 🚆 From Zagreb

KOPAČKI RIT

▷ 84.

KRAŠIĆ

This small village has become an important place of pilgrimage to Cardinal Alojzije Stepinac (▷ 23). Stepinac grew up in Krašić and held his first Mass here. He also spent the last years of his life in Krašić, under house arrest. His apartment behind the church is a now a memorial museum. The statue of Stepinac in front of the parish church was erected in 1998 on the centenary of his birth; crowds flock here every year on his birthday (8 May).

✚ 280 D3 ℹ Krašić 101 ☎ 01 627 0910 ◷ Tue and Fri 8–12

Below left *The memorial at Jasenovac, site of an infamous Ustaše concentration camp*
Below *An archery lesson at Dubovac castle, which overlooks the town of Karlovac*

INFORMATION

www.kopacki-rit.com

✚ 283 J2 ✉ Park Prirode Kopački Rit, Kopačevo ☎ 031 752320 ⏰ Daily 9–5 ✋ Adult/child 10kn 🍴 ▣ 🏛

TIPS

» Mosquitoes can be a problem in summer, so wear long sleeves and trousers and use insect repellent.

» If you want to stay overnight, several families in the village of Bilje offer cheap rooms in private houses.

Above *Kopački Rit Nature Park lies at the confluence of the Danube and Drava rivers*

KOPAČKI RIT

The flood plain of the River Danube, on the borders of Croatia, Hungary and Serbia, is a significant wetland habitat, and around 180sq km (70sq miles) is protected as Kopački Rit Nature Park. Among the wildlife here are 44 species of fish, 11 species of amphibians including frogs, 10 species of reptiles, 55 species of mammals and more than 140 species of nesting birds. Less appealing are the 7 species of mosquito that terrorize unwitting visitors in summer.

SEEING THE PARK

The visitor centre is close to Kopačevo, 3km (2 miles) from Bilje and 12km (7.5 miles) from Osijek. Get there by heading north from Osijek towards Hungary, turning right at the crossroads in Bilje and following signs to the park. The staff can issue maps of footpaths and bicycle trails. From April to October, the best introduction is to take a boat trip on Lake Sakadaš, on an old steamer that departs from a dock near the entrance. Take some binoculars to see herons, cormorants and geese as you travel through the marshes. Among other birds to nest here are white-tailed eagles, black storks, little egrets and the endangered ferruginous duck, with its red-brown plumage.

IN THE WOODS

Deeper in the park, you encounter swathes of willow and oak forest, home to populations of red deer, wild boar and wild cats. The best place to walk is in the oak woods around the old hunting lodge, once used by Tito as a hunting retreat. The building has since been transformed into an eco-friendly hotel and restaurant complex. When walking in the park, be aware that it was heavily mined during the Homeland War and wandering off marked trails is unwise.

KUMROVEC

Kumrovec, now transformed into an enjoyable open-air museum of rural life, is a typical Zagorje village, with characteristic whitewashed, thatched wooden cottages and a stream running through the middle. What makes the village different is that this is where the Yugoslav leader Tito was born in 1892. His parents, Franjo and Marija Broz, owned a blacksmith's workshop here and lived in the first brick house in the village. A statue of Tito by local artist Antun Augustinčić (1900–79) stands outside.

THE MUSEUM

The origins of the Staro Selo (Old Village) museum go back to 1953, when the Broz family house was opened as a branch of the Ethnographic Museum in Zagreb. Much later, after Tito's death, the museum expanded to take over the entire village. Some 40 buildings, including farmhouses, barns, pigsties and wells have been reconstructed to recreate the conditions familiar to the young Tito at the end of the 19th century. There are stables, potteries and a toymaker's workshop. From April to October, craftspeople demonstrate rural activities such as cider-making and weaving, and sell *štrukli* (cottage cheese parcels) in the old wine-cellar Zagorski Klet.

THE VILLAGE

All of the buildings have been restored in situ, with the result that Kumrovec has the feel of a real village rather than a museum piece. When restoration was taking place in the 1980s, a few families refused to leave their houses; they continue to go about their everyday lives among the renovated cottages and actors in folk costume.

INFORMATION

www.mdc.hr/kumrovec

✚ 280 D2 ✉ Staro Selo, Kumrovec
☎ 049 225830 (guided tours)
🕐 Apr–end Sep daily 9–7; Oct–end Mar daily 9–4 ✋ Adult 20kn, child 10kn
🚌 From Zagreb 🍴 🚻 📷

TIP

» Take a walk along the main street of the village to see the school that Tito attended from 1900 to 1905.

Above *The village of Kumrovec has been restored to its 19th-century appearance and is now an open-air museum*

LONJSKO POLJE

INFORMATION
www.pp-lonjsko-polje.hr
✚ 281 F3 ℹ️ Park Prirode Lonjsko Polje,
Krapje 30 ☎ 044 672080 📖 Adult 25kn,
child 20kn

INTRODUCTION

Established in 1990, the Lonjsko Polje Nature Park is the largest protected wetland area in Croatia and is included on the Ramsar list of internationally important wetland habitats. Much of the park consists of the flood plain of the River Sava. These flood plains provide a refuge for numerous migrant birds, including the much-loved white storks that nest here in spring and summer. When the waters rise each winter, the low-lying meadows flood, filling with waterlilies as well as carp and frogs, which provide nourishing food for migrant birds. The Lonjsko Polje also acts as a valuable flood defence system for Zagreb, which would otherwise be threatened by the rising waters of the Sava. The farmers of the Lonjsko Polje still use traditional farming methods. Sturdy Posavina horses roam freely on the marshes, and spotted Turopolje pigs (an indigenous breed unique to this region) can be found in the oak forests, feeding off wild acorns.

Although it covers an area of some 500sq km (190sq miles), Lonjsko Polje's main sights are strung out along the 70km (44-mile) road that follows the east bank of the River Sava from Sisak to Jasenovac. The park headquarters is in Krapje, but there is also an information office in Čigoć (open throughout the year), where you can pick up leaflets and maps. The best time to visit the park is between April and August, when storks nest on the roofs and the meadows are carpeted with wild flowers; from November to March, much of the Lonjsko Polje is under water.

Above *Horses grazing in the fertile meadows of the park*

WHAT TO SEE
ČIGOĆ

Čigoć has been designated the first European Stork Village because of its large population of white storks, which arrive each spring to build their nests and stay here until departing for Africa in late summer. You can see storks in other villages—notably Mužilovčica—but the greatest concentration is in Čigoć. During the season, almost every house in the village has a stork's nest on the roof. The information office, housed in a typical wooden cottage at the centre of the village, has details of local walks, including a 30-minute stroll through the forest and a two-hour hike along the flood dyke. Also in Čigoć is the Sučić ethnographic museum, with collections of textiles, embroidery, and farming and fishing tools displayed in a family house (tel 044 715184; included in price of park entry ticket).

🛈 Čigoć 26 ☎ 044 715115 🕓 Daily 8–4 🏛

KRAPJE

The village of Krapje is known for its traditional Posavina oak houses, with steep-sided roofs and wooden staircases to the first floor. Some of these houses are more than 200 years old. There has been a move to restore traditional cottages in the Lonjsko Polje and some families in the village offer rooms to visitors. Just outside Krapje, Krapje Đol was Croatia's first ornithological reserve; it provides a nesting ground for waterfowl such as herons and spoonbill.

🛈 Krapje 1 ☎ 098 222086 🕓 Apr–end Oct daily 8–4 🏛

TIPS
» Mosquitoes can be a problem in summer, so wear long sleeves and trousers and protect yourself with insect repellent.
» If you plan to go walking in this area, remember that it can be flooded at any time of year and good boots are essential.

Left *A traditional oak farmhouse*
Below *Winter fuel reserves*

OSIJEK

gREGIONS INLAND CROATIA • SIGHTS

INFORMATION
www.tzosijek.hr

283 J2 Županijska 2 031 203755 Mon–Fri 7–4, Sat 8–12; also at Trg Križanićeva 6, Tvrđa From Đakovo, Vukovar and Zagreb From Zagreb

INTRODUCTION

Osijek is the biggest city in eastern Croatia. Standing on the south bank of the River Drava near its confluence with the Danube, it has always been strategically important. Destroyed by the Ottomans in 1526, it was recaptured by Austrian troops in 1687. In 1712, they began building Tvrđa, a baroque garrison town with barracks, government buildings, churches, schools and houses, with defensive walls and gates. The walls were demolished in 1926. After bombardment in the 1991–95 Homeland War, Osijek was restored and has since recovered its easy-going atmosphere. It is now a relaxing place of avenues and parks.

The city is divided between the fortress at Tvrđa and the 19th-century district of Gornji Grad. With its baroque churches and grand public buildings, Tvrđa has the character of an open-air museum, while Gornji Grad houses most of the hotels, restaurants and shops. The two are linked by Europska Avenija, a fine avenue of art nouveau townhouses served by tram 1 during the day. The two districts are also linked by a riverside path.

WHAT TO SEE
TRG SVETOG TROJSTVA (HOLY TRINITY SQUARE)
The central square of Tvrđa is lined with fine public buildings dating from the early 18th century. At the centre of the square is a beautiful baroque plague column, erected in 1729 by the widow of General Maksimilijan Petraš, who had died in a plague epidemic. This monument was offered to God in the hope that Osijek would be delivered from the plague.

MUZEJ SLAVONIJE (MUSEUM OF SLAVONIA)
The former magistrates court is now the Museum of Slavonia, with collections of archaeology, geology, coins and metallurgy. The archaeological exhibits include finds from the Roman colony of Mursa as well as bronze jewellery from the 15th century BC. The metallurgy section has a fascinating variety of household items from the 19th and 20th centuries.

Trg Svetog Trojstva 6 031 250730 Tue–Wed, Fri 8–2, Thu 8–8, Sat–Sun 10–1 Adult 15kn, child 10kn

Above *The plague monument in the middle of Trg Svetog Trojstva, Tvrđa's central square*

Fri88

GALERIJA LIKOVNIH UMJETNOSTI (GALLERY OF FINE ARTS)

www.gluo.hr

The Gallery of Fine Arts occupies a Renaissance mansion, and holds changing exhibitions, some of which feature the works of the homegrown 19th-century Osijek School. Its permanent collections range from the baroque period to contemporary artists, with many works the erstwhile property of the Slavonian nobility.

✉ Europska Avenija 9 ☎ 031 251280 🕐 Tue, Wed, Fri 10–6, Thu 10–8, Sat–Sun 10–1 🖐 Adult 10kn, child 5kn 📧

CRKVA SV PETRA I PAVLA (CHURCH OF SS PETER AND PAUL)

This neo-Gothic red-brick church, built in 1894 as a rival to the cathedral at Đakovo (▷ 81), is known in the city as the cathedral, although it is only a parish church. At 90m (295ft) tall, its tower is higher than those at Đakovo and it dominates the heart of Gornji Grad.

MORE TO SEE

TVRĐA CHURCHES

Erected on the site of an Ottoman-era mosque, the 18th-century Crkva uzvišenja sv. (Church of the Holy Cross), belonging to the Franciscan monastery, lies at the western end of Tvrđa. It has an ornate but dimly lit baroque interior with an impressive baroque altar. The restored Jesuit church of Sveti Mihovil (church of St. Michael) stands on the other side of Tvrđa. Its two typically baroque onion-domed spires and yellow facade are a highlight amid the surrounding war-damaged buildings, but inside, the church is plain. Built on the site on an earlier mosque, the present church dates from 1725.

✉ Church of the Holy Cross: Franjevačka. Church of St. Michael. Trg J. Križanića

ERNESTINOVO

The village of Ernestinovo, 14km (8.5 miles) south from Osijek, is home to a colony of naive art sculptors, first established in the early 1970s. August, when a large open-air exhibition of wood sculptures takes place, is the best time to visit. At other times of the year you can view and buy works from local galleries that specialize in naive art.

TIPS

» Car parking in the city centre is a nightmare; it is easier to leave your car in one of the side streets around Tvrđa.

» To explore both Tvrđa and Gornji Grad, walk one way along the riverbank and return by tram, or follow the walk on pages 106–107.

» You can make a tour of Osijek on a 1926 vintage tram, complete with costumed driver and conductor.

Left *The baroque bell tower of the Church of Sveti Mihovil, Tvrđa*

Below *Sculptural detail from the plague monument on Trg Svetog Trojstva*

PLITVIČKA JEZERA (PLITVICE LAKES)

INTRODUCTION

Established in 1949, Plitvice Lakes is the oldest national park in Croatia; its ecological importance was underlined when it was awarded UNESCO World Heritage status in 1979. The park covers an area of almost 300sq km (116sq miles), with the biggest lake, Jezero Kozjak, lying at 535m (1,755ft) above sea level. Although the lakes and waterfalls are the main attractions, most of the park consists of karst limestone covered in forests of beech, fir, pine and maple. This unique ecosystem attracts a wide range of fauna and flora. The rivers and lakes teem with trout, newts, frogs, toads, salamanders, lizards and water snakes. Around 140 species of birds have been identified, including black stork and several varieties of woodpecker. Brown bears, wolves and lynx inhabit the mountains. The now peaceful environment of Plitvice is a far cry from 31 March 1991, when, in the so-called Bloody Easter incident, forces of the Republic of the Serbian Krajina took over the park and Croatian policeman Josip Jović became the first casualty of the Homeland War.

The park is 75km (47 miles) south of Karlovac, on the old main road from Zagreb to Split. It is signposted from the A1 motorway; you can also get there from the coast by taking the mountain roads that climb inland from the Kvarner Bay towns of Senj and Karlobag. Among the public transport options, regular Zagreb–Split buses stop at the entrance to the park, and there are also two daily departures from Zagreb, leaving in the early morning and returning late afternoon to allow you a full day at the lakes. In addition, tour operators offer organized excursions to Plitvice from resorts in Istria, Kvarner and Northern Dalmatia.

Visiting independently gives you the chance to explore the park at your own pace, or even to stay overnight and enjoy the colours of dawn and dusk and the peace after the day-trippers have left. On the other hand, it is a long drive from the coast and for many people an organized tour will be the best option. Although you could spend several days here, it is so well geared up for day-trippers that you can see the main sights in a few hours.

HIGHLIGHTS

VELIKI SLAP

Veliki Slap (Big Waterfall) is an apt description for the most famous sight in the park, where the Plitvica stream empties into the River Korana by plunging 70m (230ft) over a cliff. This is also the easiest sight to see, with an observation terrace overlooking the waterfall just inside Ulaz 1 (Entrance 1). From here, paths continue down to the foot of the cascade; you can climb to the top for views over the falls, or follow the lakeside trail past Kaluđerovac, Gavanovac and Milanovac lakes to arrive at the dock for the boat trip across Jezero Kozjak.

THE LAKES

The lakes at Plitvice are formed from travertine (a mixture of moss and eroded limestone) and fed by numerous rivers, brooks and streams. There are 16 major lakes altogether, joined by waterfalls which force them to descend more than 150m (490ft) from Prošćansko Jezero, the highest lake, to the River Korana. The colour of the lakes varies from light turquoise to deep emerald green, reflecting the forests and the wild flowers that grow on the cliffs. A network of footpaths criss-crosses the lakes, allowing you to get up close. To escape the crowds, head for the more remote upper lakes. Take the shuttle bus from Ulaz 2 (Entrance 2) to the Labudovac falls at the head of Prošćansko Jezero. From here, you can make a complete circuit of the lake on foot, or follow a path up into the mountains to the source of the spring. Alternatively, stay on the red trail along the shores of Okrugljak, Galovac and Gravinsko until you reach Jezero Kozjak, the largest lake,

INFORMATION

www.np-plitvicka-jezera.hr

✚ 285 D5 ✉ Plitvička Jezera

☎ 053 751132; 751015 (hotel reservations) ◷ Summer 7am–8pm; spring and autumn 8–6; winter 8–4

✋ Apr–end Oct: adult 110kn, child 55kn; Nov–end Mar: adult 80kn, child 40kn

🚌 From Zagreb 🍴 🛍 🏛

Opposite *Wooden boardwalks and paths link the lakes, allowing visitors to appreciate their beauty at close quarters*

INLAND CROATIA • SIGHTS

REGIONS

91

TIPS

» Of the two park entrances, Ulaz 1 is close to Veliki Slap and the lower lakes, while Ulaz 2 gives access to the upper lakes. In practice you can use either entrance, as the admission price includes shuttle bus and boat rides in summer, allowing you to explore the lower and upper lakes in a single day. Wooden boardwalks travel around and between the lakes, passing above and beneath the waterfalls for spectacular views. With a map, you can work out your own route, but there are also a number of colour-coded itineraries, clearly signposted and designed to take between two and six hours using buses, boats and on foot. Note that the shuttle buses and boats do not operate between November and April.

» Go early or late in the day to see the park at its best: There are fewer visitors, the light is better for photography and you have more chance of seeing animals.

» Always take an extra layer of clothing; it can be surprisingly cool in summer and bitterly cold in winter.

Below Trout thrive in the clear waters

where you can catch a boat downstream towards Veliki Slap. The circuit takes approximately six hours.

FLORA AND FAUNA

Among the larger mammals to inhabit the park are wolves, foxes, lynx, badgers, pine marten, roe deer and brown bear. You are unlikely to see any of these, though you stand the best chance in the early morning, twilight or just after dusk. Some of these species are seriously endangered: There are thought to be fewer than 50 wolves living in Croatia, and around 60 pairs of lynx, who returned to Plitvice in 1980 after an absence of 80 years. You are far more likely to see some of the 70 species of nesting birds who have made Plitvice their home, including the black woodpecker, mountain titmouse and mountain owl.

Almost 1,150 species of flora can be found in the national park. This diversity is due to differences in temperature and elevation within the park, which range from 417m (1,367ft) on the River Korana and 1,289m (4,228ft) at the top of Seliski vrh. These produce a wide range of microclimates and habitats. Species typical for the Mediterranean, Southern Europe, the Carpathian Mountains, Boreal regions and the Eurasian steppes can sometimes be found within a few hundred metres of each other, and many are endemic to the Plitvička Jezera. Remember never to pick any plants in the park as they may be protected by law.

MEDVJEĐAK TRAIL

If you are exploring the park on your own and have your hiking boots with you, a great morning or afternoon walk leads to the top of Mount Medvjeđak. From the ridge rise three peaks: Oštri Medvjeđak (884m/2,899ft), Tupi Medvjeđak (868m/2,847ft) and Turčić (801m/2,627ft). A path to the top of these was specially created for visitors in the late 19th century. The views from the top are incredible, with the entire park spread out below. The brown bears that gave

the mountain its name (*medvjeđ* means 'bear' in Croatian) still roam its forested slopes, although it is unlikely that you will encounter any. There are two walking tours described on the national park's website, one a relatively easy one-and-a-half hour route, the other a longer, slightly more demanding two-hour trek. Useful route maps can also be downloaded from the site.

WHEN TO GO

The lakes are lovely at any time of year, but take on a different character with the seasons. Spring (May to June) is a good time to visit for birdsong, wild flowers and rushing water as the winter snows melt, increasing the flow over the falls. Summer (July to August) is by far the busiest time, though it is easy enough to escape the crowds if you head away from the major points of interest. Autumn (September to October) is when the colours begin to turn on the trees. In winter (November to April), the park is frequently covered in a blanket of snow; the national park buses and boats do not run, and the footpaths are sometimes closed to visitors. With the snow-covered landscape and frozen waterfalls, some people regard this as the most attractive time of all.

HUCK FINN ADVENTURE TRAVEL

This company (Vukovarska 271, Zagreb; tel 01 618 3333; www.huck-finn.hr) specializes in canoeing, kayaking, rafting, walking, bicycling and swimming in the Plitvice Lakes National Park, with itineraries ranging from half a day to a week and accommodation in village houses by the River Korana.

Above *A network of paths link the lakes*
Below left *Tour boats operate in summer*
Below *Paths lead right up to the waterfalls, allowing spectacular views*

INFORMATION

www.tz-samobor.hr
✚ 280 D2 🛈 Trg Kralja Tomislava 5
☎ 01 336 0044 🕐 Mon–Fri 8–7, Sat
9–5, Sun 10–5 🚌 From Zagreb

TIPS

» Restaurants in Samobor sell garlic
sausages accompanied by local mustard.
You can buy mustard at the Filipec family
shop (Mon–Sat 8–7), just off the main
square (▷ 108).
» Walk off the calories by taking Ulica
Svete Ane behind the church and climbing
through the woods to the ruined castle,
Stari Grad.

Above *Pretty Samobor, a weekend retreat*
for citizens of Zagreb
Opposite *The beautiful cloister at the*
Franciscan monastery at Slavonski Brod

SAMOBOR

Just 20km (12.5 miles) from the capital and served by regular buses, Samobor
is where the people of Zagreb head when they want a weekend break in the
country. This pretty provincial town is a real delight, with a stream running
through the middle and a square lined with 19th-century townhouses,
overlooked by a Habsburg yellow onion-domed church. Most visitors seem to
spend their time in cafés, enjoying Samobor's delicious custard tart, *samoborska
kremšnita*. The best place to try this local speciality is at Kavana Livadić (Trg Kralja
Tomislava 1), which opened in 1800 and is still the social hub, with its elegant
salons and summer patio.

MUSIC AND ART

During the 19th century, Samobor was at the heart of the Croatian National
Revival in politics, music and the arts. A key figure was Ferdo Livadić (1799–
1879), composer of the patriotic song 'Još Hravatska nij Propala' (Croatia Has
Not Fallen Yet). His home is now the town museum, Gradski Muzej (tel 01 336
1014; Tue–Fri 9–3, Sat–Sun 9–6; adult 8kn, child 5kn), with archaeology and
geology displays, 19th-century portraits and furniture, and occasional piano
recitals. A scale model shows how Samobor looked in 1764; the only buildings
surviving from this period are the Livadić manor house and the parish church.
Above the church, Muzej Marton (Jurjevska 7, tel 01 332 6426; Sat–Sun 10–1
in summer; adult 20kn, child 15kn) was Croatia's first private museum when it
opened in 2003, with collections of Austro-Hungarian furniture, porcelain, glass,
paintings and clocks displayed in a 19th-century mansion.

SLAVONSKI BROD

www.tzgsb.hr

This busy town on the north bank of the River Sava grew up around its star-shaped Tvrđava (fortress), built in 1715 to guard the historic Vojna Krajina (Military Frontier) between the Habsburg and Ottoman empires. Today, the river forms a natural border between Bosnia and Croatia. Slavonski Brod suffered extensive shelling during the Homeland War and the damage to the Tvrđava is clearly visible. A section of the restored fortress houses the Galerija Ružić (tel 035 411510; Tue–Fri 9–1, 5–8, Sat–Sun 10–2), with sculptures by locally born artist Branko Ružić (1919–97) displayed in the former casemates. A short walk along the riverbank leads to the 18th-century Franciscan monastery, with a beautiful baroque cloister. The nearby Muzej Brodskog Posavlja (Regional Museum) was damaged during the war and is currently under restoration.

✚ 282 H3 🛈 Trg Pobjede 30 ☎ 035 445765 ⓦ Jul–end Aug daily 7am–7.30pm; Sep–end Jun Mon–Sat 7am–7.30pm; also an information kiosk at Tvrđava mid-Jun to mid-Sep 🚌 From Đakovo, Osijek and Zagreb 🚆 From Zagreb

VARAŽDIN

▷ 97–99.

VELIKA GORICA

www.tzvg.hr

When you arrive at Zagreb airport, you are actually landing in Velika Gorica, which would be Croatia's seventh-largest city were it not effectively a suburb of Zagreb. To get there, walk through the tunnel beneath the railway station in Zagreb and catch the bus, which leaves every 10 minutes. The farmers' market in a hall beside the bus station is a reminder that this is the main town of the rural Turopolje region. The bright orange building on the edge of the central park is the former town hall, built in 1765. It is now the Muzej Turopolja (tel 01 622 1325; Tue–Fri 9–4, Sat–Sun 10–1), with collections of archaeology, folk costumes and local history.

Velika Gorica is known for its wooden chapels, built out of local oak. The simple 18th-century Kapela Ranjenog Isusa (Chapel of the Wounded Christ) is dramatically floodlit at night.

✚ 280 E3 🛈 Ulica Matije Slatinskog 11 ☎ 01 622 1666 ⓦ Mon–Fri 8–4 🚌 268 from Zagreb

VUKOVAR

www.turizamvukovar.hr

Vukovar is a name that evokes strong feelings across Croatia. Until 1991, this was a peaceful provincial town; now it has become synonymous with the suffering of war. For three months, the people of Vukovar held out under siege from Serbian forces. At least 2,000 people were killed and thousands more are missing, believed to be buried in mass graves. When the town finally fell, the surviving Croats fled; most have never returned. Vukovar today is a shadow of its former self. The baroque Eltz Palace, now the Town Museum (tel 032 441270; Mon–Fri 7–3), has been stripped of its treasures and the building has been undergoing renovation for years following war damage. The only reason to go to Vukovar is to contemplate the horrors of war and pay tribute to the victims at the large white cross by the Danube. The memorial cemetery, just outside town on the road to Ilok, contains the graves of the defenders of Vukovar and rows of unmarked white crosses recalling the bodies that were never found.

✚ 283 K3 🛈 Strossmayerova 15 ☎ 032 442889 ⓦ Mon–Fri 7–3 🚌 From Osijek

VARAŽDIN

INTRODUCTION
This delightful city to the north of Zagreb contains the most perfect baroque architectural ensemble in Croatia, while street artists, musicians and festivals give it a relaxed, easy-going feel.

Varaždin was founded in 1181 and was declared a free and royal city by King Andrija II in 1209, more than 30 years before Zagreb. In 1756, it became the seat of the Croatian governor and parliament, and in 1767 a decree by Empress Maria Teresa of Austria made Varaždin the capital of the tripartite kingdom of Croatia, Slavonia and Dalmatia. Its status as capital lasted less than 10 years, until a fire—said to have been started by a peasant boy who tripped over a pig and dropped the cigarette he was carrying into a haystack—destroyed 80 per cent of the town in 1776. Rebuilt from scratch, the resulting town is a harmonious blend of late 18th-century baroque architecture unrivalled in Croatia.

The easiest way to see Varaždin is on a day trip from Zagreb. Buses make the journey in less than two hours, though the three-hour train ride offers constantly changing views over the rolling countryside of the Zagorje. Cars cannot be taken into the city centre and the best place to leave them is at the free car park outside the cemetery, west of the castle. The centre is compact and easily explored on foot. The finest baroque palaces and churches are concentrated in the traffic-free streets around Trg Kralja Tomislava. As you walk, look out for architectural details.

The best time of year to be in Varaždin is during the famous Varaždin Baroque Evenings (▷ 109) in September, when Croatian and international orchestras specializing in music of the period perform at venues around the town.

WHAT TO SEE
TRG KRALJA TOMISLAVA
Renovated in early 2009, the main square is dominated by the town hall, whose present appearance dates from 1791 when the clock tower was added. Above the entrance, look for the coat of arms of Varaždin, with a red-and-white striped shield watched over by an angel. This is one of the oldest surviving coats of arms in Europe, first used in 1464 and revived in 1990. On the east side of the square, Kavana Grofica Marica is the city's most popular meeting place, while the nearby Palača Drašković briefly acted as the Croatian parliament building. On the western side, take a close look at Kraš, a confectionery shop in the former Casa Jaccomini: A mermaid hangs above the door; inside, the stucco decorations on the ceiling include the initials of owner Daniela Jaccomini and the date 1777.

If you are here on a Saturday in summer, be sure to see the Changing of the Guard, which takes place at 11am in front of the town hall. The best place to see the ceremony, performed by the members of the Purgari (City Guard), in their blue uniforms and bearskin hats, is from a seat outside Kavana Grofica Marica.

BAROQUE PALACES
The city's two finest baroque buildings are found side by side on Franjevački Trg, just off the main square. Palača Patačić, with its cream-coloured rococo facade, was built in 1764 and was the social heart of 18th-century Varaždin; next door is the peach-coloured palace of the county governor, dating from 1768. Across the street, outside the Franciscan monastery church, is a bronze statue of Grgur Ninski by Ivan Meštrović—a smaller version of the one in Split (▷ 191).

URŠULINSKA CRKVA (URSULINE CHURCH)
The Ursuline sisters arrived in Varaždin at the beginning of the 18th century at the invitation of Countess Magdalena Drašković, the owner of the castle, whose

INFORMATION
www.tourism-varazdin.hr
✚ 280 E1 🛈 Ulica Padovca 3 ☎ 042 210987 🕘 Apr–end Oct Mon–Fri 8–7, Sat 8–4, Sun 10–1; Nov–end Mar Mon–Fri 8–4, Sat 10–1 🚌 From Zagreb 🚆 From Zagreb

REGIONS INLAND CROATIA • SIGHTS

Opposite The town hall's 18th-century clock tower dominates Trg Kralja Tomislava, Varaždin's main square

TIPS

» If you are in Varaždin in late August, you'll catch the town's Špancirfest, a festival featuring street theatre, acrobats, crafts and performances of world music. September, when the city stages the famous Varaždin Baroque Evenings, is also a good time to visit.

» The old-style Vienna coffee house Kavana Grofica Marcia is the best place in town for a drink (Trg Kralja Tomislava 2; tel 042 320914). The opulent interior features dark wood, mirrors, chandeliers and red velvet benches, while the terrace makes the perfect spot to observe the evening *korzo* (promenade).

own daughter was a member of the order. The single-nave baroque church was built between 1707 and 1712, but the most striking feature is the tower, which was added in 1726. Slender and tall, pink and white, with a fresco set into the niche and topped by an onion-dome, it acts as a city landmark just outside the castle gates.

✉ Uršulinska Ulica 3

STARI GRAD (OLD CASTLE)

www.gmv.hr

Set in a red-roofed, whitewashed Renaissance palace surrounded by a dried-up medieval moat, the old castle dominates Varaždin. Get there by crossing the drawbridge and passing through the 16th-century watchtower. From here, you can follow the promenade around the protective earth ramparts, now an attractive park. The castle itself, with a beautiful galleried courtyard at the centre, is home to the city museum. Exhibits in the museum's first-floor galleries include the town magistrate's mace and seal from 1464 and a charter signed by Ferdinand II of Austria in 1621 granting legal rights to the city's tailors. The upper floor galleries display furniture from different periods, revealing the changing tastes of Croatia's nobility from the 16th to 20th centuries. A balcony leads to the chapel of Sveti Lovre (St. Lawrence) and the adjoining sacristy, set in a circular defence tower.

✉ Strossmayerovo Šetalište ☎ 042 658754 🕐 Apr–end Oct Tue–Sat 10–6, Sun 10–1; Nov–end Mar Tue–Fri 10–5, Sat–Sun 10–1 ✋ Adult 20kn, child 10kn 📖 70kn 📅

GROBLJE (CEMETERY)

Situated on the outskirts of Varaždin, 500m (550 yards) west of the castle, the peaceful town cemetery is a lovely place, with wide, shady avenues planted with beech, birch and magnolia amid the tombstones and statuary. Herman Haller, who designed the cemetery in 1905, was determined that rather than being sad and gloomy, it should be uplifting for all who visited it; the result is a beautiful memorial garden for the people of Varaždin.

✉ Hallerova Aleja ☎ 042 330316 🕐 May–end Sep daily 7am–9pm; Oct–end Apr daily 7–5 ✋ Free

Below *The streets in central Varaždin are traffic free and easily explored on foot*

MORE TO SEE

GALERIJA STARIH I NOVIH MAJSTORA (GALLERY OF OLD AND NEW MASTERS)

The baroque Sermage palace opposite the castle houses an interesting array of works dating from the 15th to the 20th century, but mostly from the 17th and 18th centuries. The 3,000 pieces in the gallery's possession include works by minor members of the Rubens and Canaletto schools as well as large collections of 19th-century portraits and Croatian modern art. It also holds a large collection of works by Croatian painter Miljenko Stančić (1926–77), who was born in Varaždin.

✉ Trg Miljenka Stančića 3 ☎ 042 214172 🕒 Tue–Fri 10–2, Sat–Sun 10–1 ✋ Adult 15kn, child 10kn

ENTOMOLOŠKI MUZEJ (ENTOMOLOGICAL MUSEUM)

A branch of Varaždin's city museum, the Entomological Museum is housed in an 18th-century baroque palace that once belonged to the Herczer family. It is worth a half-hour visit, even if you have no real interest in the incredible collection of insects on display. The collection was donated to the museum by local entomologist Franjo Košćec in 1954, and he became its first curator. The 4,500 exhibits cover around 1,000 species of insect and include nests and burrows as well as the insects themselves. There is also a reconstruction of Košćec's study.

✉ Franjevački Trg 6 ☎ 042 213491 🕒 Tue–Fri 10–2, Sat–Sun 10–1 ✋ Adult 15kn, child 10kn

KATEDRALA

This Jesuit monastery church, now the cathedral of the Varaždin Diocese, was built between 1642 and 1646. The later baroque portal shows the coat of arms belonging to the Drašković family, one of the country's oldest noble families; the baroque facade dates from the 18th century. The most impressive feature inside the church is the 18th-century main altar with an altarpiece depicting the Assumption of the Virgin Mary. Several local artists contributed to the decoration of this fine building.

✉ Pavlinska 5 🕒 During morning and evening services only

Above *Trg Kralja Tomislava, Varaždin's main square*
Below *The tower of St. John the Baptist Church*

ZAGORJE

INFORMATION
www.tz-zagorje.hr
✚ 280 D2 🛈 Zagrebačka 6, Krapinske
Toplice ☎ 049 233653 🕐 Mon–Fri 8–4

INTRODUCTION

The Zagorje (highlands) occupies the area north of Zagreb between the Medvednica mountain range and the Slovenian border. This bucolic region of gently rolling hills dotted with picture-book castles and churches is known throughout Croatia for its beauty. Ruled as an independent principality from the 13th to 15th centuries, the Zagorje region contains more than 40 castles and mansions, reflecting its strategic location between Zagreb, Slovenia and Hungary. This was the birthplace of both the Yugoslav leader Tito and Croatian president Franjo Tuđman, who was born in the village of Veliko Trgovišće in 1922. The people of the Zagorje, especially around Krapina, speak a dialect of Croatian known as *kajkavski*.

The sights are spread out across the region, and there are only a few main roads, so you will need to allow plenty of time. Buses connect Zagreb with Krapina and Marija Bistrica, but to get the most out of the Zagorje you will need your own car. It is possible to make a circuit of the Zagorje in a single day (▷ 104–105), but to explore the region in depth and visit the castles at Veliki Tabor and Trakošćan, consider staying overnight at one of the growing number of farmhouses offering rural accommodation.

WHAT TO SEE
TRAKOŠĆAN

www.mdc.hr/trakoscan

A castle in Croatia usually means a stately country house, but Trakošćan is everyone's idea of what a proper castle should look like, standing proud on a wooded hillside, with white walls and crenellated towers reflected in an artifical lake. Begun in the 13th century as part of the defence network of what was then the Zagorje principality, the castle takes its present romantic appearance from a 19th-century restoration by the Drašković family, who were granted the estate by the Habsburg emperor in 1584 as a reward for military service. It remained in their possession until it was confiscated by the state and turned into a museum in Tito's Yugoslavia. Cross the drawbridge and climb the steep path to the castle, where exhibits reflect the lifestyles of the Austro-Hungarian nobility, with family portraits, tapestries, hunting trophies, firearms, ceramic braziers and furniture, including a splendid 19th-century card table. Don't miss the study of Julijana

Above *Gently rolling green hills dotted with vineyards—a characteristic Zagorje landscape*

Erdödy-Drašković (1847–1901), the first recognized female painter in Croatia, whose piano is preserved alongside her paintings of rural life. Afterwards, you can walk around the lakeshore or take a boat out on the lake.

✚ 280 E1 ☎ 042 796422 🕐 Apr–end Oct daily 9–6; Nov–end Mar daily 9–3 ✋ Adult 30kn, child 15kn 📖 Guidebook 50kn, miniguide 10kn 🖥 🏛

VELIKI TABOR
www.veliki-tabor.hr

Standing on a hill 334m (1,095ft) high with views across the Zagorje, the castle at Veliki Tabor is the finest surviving example of a late medieval fortress in Croatia. It was built during the 16th century by the Ratkay family, who lived here for almost 300 years. The castle is pentagonal, with four semicircular towers around an arcaded courtyard. Inside is a museum containing halberds and pikes, but the real attractions are the views. Following the demise of the Ratkay family, the castle changed hands several times; during World War II it was run as an orphanage by Franciscan nuns. It became a museum in 1993 but it is still in a poor state of repair and restoration is likely to be ongoing for some time.

During restoration work in 1982, the skull of a young woman was found, giving credence to a local legend. According to the tale, the handsome son of Count Herman of Celje, owner of the castle, fell in love with a beautiful girl, called Veronika. The count disapproved of the relationship, so the young lovers escaped to Slovenia, where they married in secret. When the count found out, he sent his soldiers to arrest the couple and had his son imprisoned in a tower. An even worse fate awaited Veronika, she was drowned and her body walled into the castle.

✚ 280 D2 ✉ Desinić ☎ 049 343963 🕐 Apr–end Sep daily 10–5; Oct–end Mar daily 9–3 ✋ Adult 10kn, child 5kn

MUZEJ KRAPINSKOG PRAČOVJEKA (MUSEUM OF EVOLUTION)
www.krapina.com

The region's main town of Krapina is best known for the discovery of *Homo krapinensis*, a Neanderthal human who lived here some 30,000 years ago, whose bones were found in a cave on the Hušnjakovo hill in 1899. The originals are kept

TIP
» A speciality of the Zagorje region is the *licitarsko srce*, a gingerbread heart decorated with red icing and displayed in the home rather than eaten. You can buy them at shops in the church square at Marija Bistrica.

Left *Romantically situated Trakošćan castle, on a hilltop overlooking a lake*
Below *The Church of Our Lady of the Snows at Marija Bistrica, an important place of pilgrimage*

in the Croatian Natural History Museum in Zagreb (▷ 57), but a new high-tech museum on the site, opened in 2009, has plenty of interest, with interactive exhibits as well as reproductions of human skulls, prehistoric tools and a full skeleton of a cave bear. Walk up the hill behind the museum to see the cave itself, marked by life-size sculptures of humans and animals. The museum offers guided tours.

✉ Šetalište Sluge, Krapina ☎ 049 371491 🕐 Apr–end Sep daily 9–5; Oct–end Mar Tue–Sun 9–3 💰 Adult 20kn, child 10kn

MARIJA BISTRICA

www.info-marija-bistrica.hr

The Church of Our Lady of the Snows at Marija Bistrica is the most important pilgrimage site in Croatia. The object of veneration is the Black Madonna, a dark wooden statue of the Virgin and Child, probably dating from the 15th century. According to tradition, the statue was walled into the church by the parish priest to protect it from Turkish invaders and was discovered in 1684 when a miraculous beam of light revealed its hiding place. In 1935 the Black Madonna was proclaimed Queen of the Croats by the Archbishop of Zagreb. The present church was built in 1883 by Hermann Bollé, architect of Zagreb's cathedral. Pope John Paul II made the pilgrimage here in 1998 to announce the beatification of Cardinal Alojzije Stepinac (▷ 23); the square in front of the church is now named after the pontiff. Climb the Via Crucis (Way of the Cross) on the hill behind the church for good views.

✚ 280 E2 ℹ Zagrebačka ☎ 049 468380 🕐 Apr–end Oct daily 7–5; Nov–end Mar Mon–Fri 7–3 🚌 From Zagreb

KUMROVEC

▷ 85.

MORE TO SEE

GALERIJA AUGUSTINČIĆ

www.mdc.hr/augustincic

Sculptures by Antun Augustinčić (▷ 105) on display in the village of Klanjec.

✚ 280 D2 ✉ Trg Antun Mihanovića 10, Klanjec ☎ 049 550343 🕐 Apr–end Sep daily 9–5; Oct–end Mar, Tue–Sun 9–3 💰 Adult 20kn, child 10kn

BELEC

A minor road from Zlatar leads to the village of Belec and the church of Sveta Marije Snježne (St. Mary of the Snows). This 18th-century church is one of the finest baroque creations in Croatia, a riot of extravagant detail with sculpted angels and saints, and beautifully restored frescoes by Ivan Ranger (1700–53).

✚ 280 E2

Opposite *The castle at Veliki Tabor, a late-medieval gem*
Below *Statues by Croatian sculptors depicting the 14 Stations of the Cross line the Via Crucis at Marija Bistrica*

DRIVE

THROUGH THE ZAGORJE

The Zagorje region north of Zagreb is Croatia's little Switzerland, an enchanting land of alpine meadows, vineyards, castles and forested hills. This circuit of the region takes in all of the main sights and passes through some delightful rural scenery along the way.

THE DRIVE
Distance: 160km (100 miles)
Allow: 3–4 hours
Start/end: Donja Stubica ✚ 280 E2

★ Donja Stubica is on the main road from Marija Bistrica to Stubičke Toplice. Beside the parish church is an attractive park, with a bridge-spanned brook. The nearby spa town of Stubičke Toplice is in the foothills of Medvednica (▷ 60). A road from here leads to the summit of Sljeme and over the mountain to Zagreb.

Leave Donja Stubica in the direction

of Stubičke Toplice. Reaching the town, follow the road round to the right and climb towards Oroslavje. Take the second exit at the roundabout (signposted Zabok and Kumrovec) and stay on this road as it passes beneath the Zagreb–Krapina highway, passing through a green valley before climbing to the village of Klanjec with views to your left.

❶ Klanjec sits on the east bank of the River Sutla, which forms a natural border between Croatia and Slovenia. The village was the birthplace of Antun Augustinčić (1900–79), who

was a pupil of Ivan Meštrović. Augustinčić became the official Yugoslav state artist and his sculpture *Peace* stands outside the United Nations headquarters in New York. His works are displayed in a gallery and sculpture park off Klanjec's main square. Also here is a memorial to Antun Mihanović (1796–1861), author of the Croatian national anthem, 'Lijepa Naša Domovino' (Our Beautiful Homeland).

Stay on this road as it drops down to the Sutla valley, running beside the river on its way to Kumrovec (▷ 85).

Beyond Kumrovec, take the right fork just before the Slovenian border and keep on this minor road as it climbs to the hilltop village of Zagorska Sela, dominated by the mustard-coloured church of Sveta Katarina (St. Catherine). After passing through Plavić, turn right in Miljana and continue until you see the castle of Veliki Tabor high on a hill to your left.

❷ Veliki Tabor (▷ 101) is worth a visit for the views across the Zagorje to all sides.

Continue to Desinić and turn left to Pregrada. Arriving in Pregrada, turn right towards Zagreb and stay on this road for 4km (2.5 miles) before taking a left turn towards Krapina beside Dvorac Bezanec hotel. The road rises and falls through the vineyards before snaking down the hillside to Krapina (▷ 101).

❸ A short detour to your left leads to the Museum of Evolution.

Cross the railway line and turn right, skirting the centre and following signs to Maribor (Slovenia). When you see the church ahead of you, turn right to climb to the highway and bridge above the town. Turn right here and stay on the main road, passing through tunnels. When you reach the Slovenian border, fork right onto a forest road which leads to Trakošćan.

❹ Trakošćan (▷ 100–101) has a superb castle and lakeside walks.

Turn right at Trakošćan and follow the Bednja valley to Lepoglava.

❺ Lepoglava is notable for its fortress-like Pauline monastery, founded in 1400. The monks established Croatia's first grammar school here in the early 16th century. From 1854 to 2001 the monastery was a notorious prison, whose inmates included Tito and the future Croatian president Franjo Tuđman. In 2001 the monastery was returned to the Church.

Above *Trakošćan castle's towers and crenellations stand proud of the surrounding countryside*
Opposite *The entrance to the Church of Our Lady of the Snows, Marija Bistrica*

Turn right at the junction on the outskirts of Lepoglava and stay on this road for the next 5km (3 miles), then turn left, following signs for Zlatar and Marija Bistrica. Pass through Zlatar and Zlatar Bistrica, continuing to Marija Bistrica (▷ 102). Arriving in Marija Bistrica, keep straight ahead to visit the town or fork right and turn right again to return to Donja Stubica.

WHERE TO EAT
GREŠNA GORICA
▷ 111.

PLACE TO VISIT
GALERIJA AUGUSTINČIĆ, KLANJEC
www.mdc.hr/augustincic
☎ 049 550343 🕐 Apr–end Sep daily 9–5; Oct–end Mar Tue–Sun 9–3 ✋ Adult 20kn, child 10kn

WALK

ALONG THE RIVER AT OSIJEK

This walk links the 18th-century fortress at Tvrđa with Gornji Grad, the heart of modern Osijek. You walk one way along Europska Avenija, a grand boulevard lined with parks and art nouveau townhouses, then return along a pleasant riverside promenade.

THE WALK

Distance: 5km (3 miles)
Allow: 2 hours
Start/end: Trg Svetog Trojstva

HOW TO GET THERE

The Tvrđa district is situated 2km (1.2 miles) east of the centre. Tram No. 1 runs from Trg Ante Starčevića in front of the cathedral, with a stop on Europska Avenija near Tvrđa.

★ Trg Svetog Trojstva (Holy Trinity Square) is the main square of Tvrđa. Originally known as Weinplatz because of the wine market that was held here, it has had many changes of name, reflecting the political upheavals of the last 200 years. It

has variously been named after the Austrian emperor Franz Josef I, the Serbian Karađorđe dynasty and Tito's Partisan liberation movement. The column in the middle of the square was erected in 1730 by the widow of a plague victim as a plea to God to deliver the people of Osijek from an epidemic that was sweeping through the town. Among the fine Austro-Hungarian buildings surrounding the square is the former City Guard in the northwest corner, with its distinctive clock tower and ground-floor arcades.

Begin by taking the street alongside the City Guard, which leads to the church of Sveti Mihovil (St. Michael).

❶ The parish church of St. Michael, with its twin onion-domed spires and restored yellow facade, stands out among the war-damaged buildings of Tvrđa. It was begun in 1704 on the site of the old Turkish mosque, though the present church dates from 1725.

Follow the road to the left in front of the church, and turn right on Kuhačeva to emerge by a park.

❷ Perivoj Kralja Tomislava (King Tomislav Park) was laid out in the 18th century. On your left, notice a small section of Turkish wall, the only remains of the Ottoman fortifications that once encircled Tvrđa.

Opposite Osijek is built around an 18th-century fortress on the banks of the Drava

Walk across the park to arrive on Europska Avenija and continue along the pavement. At the junction with Ulica Kardinala Alozija Stepinac, cross to the other side of the road to admire the triangular 1912 Post Office building.

❸ The next stretch of Europska Avenija is lined with fine houses built in the Viennese Secession style, an Austrian equivalent of art nouveau, in the first years of the 20th century for wealthy German, Austrian and Hungarian industrialists. Look out for details such as sculpted angels on the pastel-coloured, stuccoed facades.

Continue along the southern side of Europska Avenija, passing the Galerija Likovnih Umjetnosti (▷ 89). Cross back to the northern side at the next junction with Ulica Stjepana Radića (Radićeva).

❹ Kino Urania, on the right, is a Viennese Secession-style cinema, opened in 1912 and still in use. In front of the cinema, a pair of stone sphinxes marks the entrance to Šetalište Petar Preradovića, a small park promenade lined with busts of local notables. The park ends at another cinema, Kino Europa, in a 1939 modernist building.

Keep straight ahead on the pedestrian shopping street Kapucinska to arrive at Trg Ante Starčevića, the large open square in front of the parish church.

❺ The enormous Gothic red-brick church of Sv Petra i Pavla (Ss Peter and Paul) is universally referred to as the cathedral, though in fact it does not have cathedral status.

Turn right here and walk down to the Zimska Luka (Winter Harbour). When you reach the river, turn right and follow the riverside promenade past Hotel Osijek until you come to a footbridge across the Drava.

❻ This elegant suspension bridge, built in 1980, managed to survive the 1991–95 war. Its total span is 210m (690ft) and the pylons have a height of 30m (100ft). The bridge was built to connect the city centre with the Copacabana summer recreation area on the north bank. On both sides of the river are promenades.

From here you have a choice. For a short walk, keep straight ahead along the south bank and take the footpath to your right at the end of the park to return to Tvrđa. For a longer walk, cross the footbridge and follow the Drava's north bank, passing Copacabana beach club with views of Tvrđa across the river. Climb the steps to the road bridge, walk across, and descend the steps to the south bank and take the riverside path to enter Tvrđa via Vodena Vrata (Water Gate), the only surviving gateway to the fortress.

WHERE TO EAT
MIRNA LUKA
▷ 110.

PLACES TO VISIT
GALERIJA LIKOVNIH UMJETNOSTI
▷ 89.

MUZEJ SLAVONIJE
▷ 88.

Below *The bell tower of the Jesuit church of Sveti Mihovil, in the Tvrđa district*

WHAT TO DO

ILOK

ILOČKI PODRUMI
www.ilocki-podrumi.hr
The wine cellars of Ilok produce first-class Slavonian white wines, including Graševina, Traminac and Chardonnay. Ask about a visit to the Stari Podrumi, the atmospheric old wine cellars inside the castle, which were looted by Serbian troops during the war but are now open for tours.
✉ Franje Tuđmana 72, Ilok ☎ 032 590003
🕐 Mon–Fri 8–8, Sat 8–2

OSIJEK

COPACABANA
Cool down in summer by crossing the footbridge to this sports and recreation centre on the north bank of the River Drava, optimistically named after the famous Rio beach. There are open-air pools, a sandy riverside beach, waterslides, beach volleyball and a restaurant.
✉ Tvrđavica, Osijek ☎ 031 285000
🕐 Jun–end Sep

HRVATSKO NARODNO KAŽALISTE (CROATIAN NATIONAL THEATRE)
Housed in a magnificent Austro-Hungarian casino dating from the mid-19th century and restored after the Homeland War, the Croatian National Theatre is the city's venue for serious drama and opera.
✉ Županijska 9, Osijek ☎ 031 220700
🕐 Box office open Mon–Fri 9–1, Sat 9–noon, and one hour before performance
✋ 30–120kn 🏆

KINO URANIA
This, the oldest movie house in Osijek, was built in 1912 in Viennese Secession style on the corner of a pretty park. It is worth going in here just to admire the art deco lobby.
✉ Šetalište Vjekoslava Hengla 1, Osijek
☎ 031 211560 🕐 Varies ✋ 20kn

OSIJEK ZOO
Osijek's zoo was closed during the war but has reopened on the north bank of the River Drava. The elephants have not returned but you can see lions, tigers, wolves, monkeys, crocodiles, snakes and birds. There are pony rides for children in summer. Get there by walking west along the north bank of the river, or by ferry from the heart of the city.
✉ Sjevernodravska Obala 1, Osijek
☎ 031 285234 🕐 May–end Sep daily 9–7; Oct–end Apr daily 9–5 ✋ Adult 10kn, child 5kn 🚌 7 🚗 Cross the bridge towards Bilje and turn left along the north bank, following signs to the zoo

RUKOTVORINE
For handmade items from the Slavonia region, head to this wonderful little shop near the Croatian National Theatre.
✉ Županijska 15, Osijek ☎ 031 212217
🕐 Mon–Fri 8.30–12.30, 4–7, Sat 8.30–2

TUFNA
www.tufna.hr
This new club is one of the leading lights on Osijek's nightlife scene, attracting the city's young and beautiful. On weekends, the two floors resound to the latest sounds until the early hours. The nightclub even has its own (somewhat noisy) backpacker hostel.
✉ Kuhačeva 10, Osijek ☎ 031 215020
🕐 From 10pm

SAMOBOR

OBITELJ FILIPEC
The Filipec family produces *bermet*, an aromatic vermouth flavoured with carob and herbs, and sweet, spicy Samobor mustard. Both local specialities date back to the occupation by French troops in 1808. You can buy them at the small shop in an alley off the main square; if the shop is closed, just ring the bell.
✉ Stražnička 1A, Samobor ☎ 01 336 4835
🕐 Mon–Sat 8–7

FESTIVALS AND EVENTS

ŽUMBERAČKO EKO SELO

Deep in the forests of the Žumberak Nature Park, this eco-lodge and ranch offers a range of activities including horse and pony rides, and quad-biking, plus rustic food and accommodation in alpine huts.
✉ Kravlak 13, Koretići ☎ 01 338 7472 🕒 All year

SLAVONSKI BROD
ZDJELAREVIĆ

www.zdjelarevic.hr

This family-run winery and hotel was established in 1991, at a time when everyone else was fleeing war-torn Slavonia. The cellars beneath the hotel stock white wines from the vineyards, including Chardonnay, Manzoni and Rizling.
✉ Vinogradska 102, Brodski Stupnik ☎ 035 427775 🕒 Ask at hotel 🚗 Take the road from Slavonski Brod to Nova Gradiska and turn right after 7km (4 miles) in Brodski Stupnik

VARAŽDIN
AQUACITY

www.aquacity.hr

An artificial lake in a former gravel pit has become Varaždin's city beach, crowded with locals on hot summer days. As well as bathing, other attractions include tennis and beach volleyball courts.
✉ Medimurska 26, Varaždin ☎ 042 350555 🕒 Jun–end Sep 🚗 3km (2 miles) from Varaždin on the road to Koprivnica

HRVATSKO NARODNO KAZALIŠTE

www.hnkvz.hr

The Croatian National Theatre was designed by Viennese architect Hermann Helmer in 1873. This grand old theatre hosts classic drama and operatic performances, as well as recitals during the two-week Varaždin Baroque Evenings festival in September (▷ opposite).
✉ Ulica A. Cesarca 1, Varaždin ☎ 042 214688 🕒 Box office open Mon–Sat 10–12, 6–7.30, and one hour before performance ✋ 30–100kn 🚻

FEBRUARY
CARNIVAL

www.samoborski-fasnik.com

For two weeks in February Samobor hosts some wild Carnival celebrations, with traditions dating back to 1827. They include masked dances, fancy dress balls and parades of Carnival floats on the final weekend. It all culminates with a bonfire and firework display.
✉ Samobor ☎ 01 336 0044 🕒 Dates vary according to Easter

MAY
FESTIVAL TAMBURAŠKE GLAZBE (FESTIVAL OF TAMBURICA MUSIC)

The *tamburica* (mandolin) was introduced to Croatia by the Ottoman Turks and has become an authentic expression of Slavonian folk music. This week-long festival has tamburica concerts in Osijek and Vukovar.
✉ Osijek ☎ 031 283253 🕒 Late May

JUNE
BRODSKO KOLO

www.fa-broda.hr

The oldest folk festival in Croatia attracts musicians and dancers from across Croatia. It lasts two weeks, but the central Sunday has parades of wedding carriages and horse-riding and a beauty contest with girls wearing traditional costume.
✉ Slavonski Brod ☎ 035 445801 🕒 Mid-Jun

INTERNATIONAL FIREWORK FESTIVAL

www.vatromet.com

Music and fireworks take place on an open-air stage at the football stadium in Samobor over four days in June.
✉ Samobor ☎ 01 333 1000 🕒 Mid-Jun

JUNE/JULY
ĐAKOVAČKI VEZOVI (ĐAKOVO EMBROIDERY)

www.tz-djakovo.hr

A large festival of Slavonian folk culture. Much of the action takes place in Strossmayer Park, but there are also organ concerts in the cathedral.
✉ Đakovo ☎ 031 812319 🕒 Late Jun and early Jul

OSJEČKO LJETO KULTURE (OSIJEK SUMMER OF CULTURE)

www.tzosijek.hr

Like most towns in Croatia, Osijek puts on a summer festival, with open-air drama and concerts of classical and jazz music.
✉ Osijek ☎ 031 229229 🕒 Late Jun to late Aug

AUGUST
ŠPANCIRFEST

www.spancirfest.com

For 10 days each year, the streets of Varaždin come alive with musicians, acrobats, mime artists, jugglers, traditional craftsmen, and elegant lords and ladies in baroque costume, as part of the annual 'street promenaders' festival. It also includes pop and world music concerts on outdoor stages across the city.
✉ Varaždin ☎ 042 210987 🕒 Late Aug

SEPTEMBER
ILOČKA BERBA GROŽĐA (ILOK GRAPE FAIR)

The annual grape fair in Ilok is a major harvest festival. Dancers in folk costume perform the *kolo* (circle dance) while everyone else drinks wine and throws bunches of grapes into the air.
✉ Ilok ☎ 032 590020 🕒 Second or third Sat in Sep

VARAŽDINSKE BAROKNE VEČERI (VARAŽDIN BAROQUE EVENINGS)

www.vbv.hr

One of Croatia's major cultural festivals, featuring two weeks of baroque music recitals.
✉ Varaždin ☎ 042 212907 🕒 Mid- to late Sep

EATING

PRICES AND SYMBOLS

The restaurants are listed alphabetically. The prices given are the average for a two-course lunch (L) and a three-course dinner (D) for one person, without drinks. The wine price is for a litre of table wine followed by the least expensive bottle of quality wine. All the restaurants listed accept credit cards unless otherwise stated.

For a key to the symbols, ▷ 2.

JASENOVAC
KOD RIBIĆA

If you are heading into the Lonjsko Polje, stop for lunch at this simple fish restaurant. The fish soup is almost a meal in itself, or you can choose from spicy *fiš paprikaš* (spicy fish stew) or fried catfish.
✉ Ulica Vladimira Nazora 24, Jasenovac ☎ 044 672066 ⏰ Mon–Sat 8am–10pm ✋ L 50kn, D 100kn, Wine 70/120kn

KARLOVAC
POD STARIMI KROVOVI

This traditional restaurant in a baroque house on the main street of the old town is staffed by students from the local catering school. Dishes such as steak with oyster mushroom sauce, cranberry jam and semolina croquettes lean towards the heavy side, but there are lighter choices such as grilled trout with Swiss chard and potatoes.
✉ Radićeva 8, Karlovac ☎ 047 615420 ⏰ Mon–Sat 9am–10pm ✋ L 60kn, D 80kn, Wine 70/90kn

KOPRIVNICA
PIVNICA KRALUŠ

A wooden carving of beer drinkers in the naive art style of Hlebine adorns the door of this atmospheric beer cellar on the main square of Koprivnica, with brick arches, flagstoned floors and low benches around a traditional chimney at the centre. It serves hearty pub food such as beer sausages, venison casserole and hard Podravina cheese.
✉ Zrinski Trg 10, Koprivnica ☎ 048 622302 ⏰ Daily 8am–11pm ✋ L 40kn, D 60kn, Beer from 15kn

OSIJEK
KAVANA OSIJEK

The tang of freshly crushed coffee beans permeates the air at this trendy, very popular coffee-and-cakes shop on the ground floor of the Hotel Osijek complex (▷ 113). Make your way to one of the trendy leather armchairs gathered around minimalist glass tables or mix your caffeine with some fresh air on the terrace with river views.
✉ Šamačka 4, Osijek ☎ 031 230356 ⏰ Mon–Thu 7am–11pm, Fri–Sun 7am–midnight

MIRNA LUKA

It's hard to beat the setting of this fish restaurant, on a barge moored in the Winter Harbour beneath the glass skyscraper of the Hotel Osijek. In summer, tables are laid out on the deck with views over the River Drava. House specials include fresh grilled fish, fish casserole, seafood risotto, stuffed squid and fried river carp.
✉ Zimski, Osijek ☎ 031 781 8963 ⏰ Daily 11–11 ✋ L 80kn, D 100kn, Wine 70/100kn

SLAVONSKA KUĆA

Tuck into a plate of spicy food at this rustic cottage, where you'll find chunky timber furniture, pretty lace curtains and a real Slavonian welcome. Trout features significantly on the menu, and this is a great

Opposite Summertime dining overlooking the River Drava, Osijek

place to have your first taste of *riblji paprikaš* (spicy fish soup).

✉ Kamila Firingera 26a, Osijek ☎ 031 369955 🕐 Mon–Sat 9pm–11pm, Sun 12–4 ✋ L 100kn, D 120kn, Wine from 70kn

STROSSMAYER

Forget the usual checked tablecloths and Italian-style kitsch, this great pizzeria just a short walk west from Trg Ante Starčevića has a wonderfully styled art nouveau interior with lots of curving wrought iron and oriental rugs. The pizza's not bad either or you could plump for a pasta dish, risotto or just a sandwich.

✉ Strossmayerova 133, Osijek ☎ 031 375888 🕐 Mon–Sat 8am–11pm, Sun 10–11 ✋ L 90kn, D 110kn, Wine from 130kn

SAMOBOR
PRI STAROJ VURI

The name of this restaurant means 'at the old clock' and it is found in an 18th-century yellow-painted house behind the church, decorated with old clocks and Carnival masks. It serves dishes based on 19th-century recipes, as well as the more modern *štrukli*, soup and Samobor sausages with sauerkraut and mustard. Try a glass of *bermet*, local vermouth, with a complimentary canapé.

✉ Giznik 2, Samobor ☎ 01 336 0548 🕐 Mon–Sat 12–11, Sun 11–6 ✋ L 90kn, D 125kn, Wine 80/120kn

SAMOBORSKA KLET

www.samoborska-klet.hr
As is customary away from the coast, meat dominates the menu at this popular local restaurant. A truly belt-busting meal here might start with some superb beef soup, followed by a first course of venison stew, a main of grilled boar or *Samoborski kotlet* (steak) and traditional pancakes to finish off. In the old dining room, images of old Samobor line the walls and a huge ceramic stove keeps things toasty in winter.

✉ Trg Kralja Tomislava 7, Samobor ☎ 01 332 6536 🕐 Daily 8am–11pm ✋ L 110kn, D 180kn, Wine 60/150kn

SAMOBORSKA PIVNICA

Traditional red-and-white checked tablecloths match the waiters' waistcoats at this folksy underground beer hall just off the main square. Start with a plate of salami or beef tongue, followed by local sausages with mashed potato or a mixed sausage platter for two, best washed down with an Ožujsko or Tomislav beer from Zagreb.

✟ Šmidhenova 3, Samobor ✉ 01 336 1623 🕐 Sun–Thu 9am–11pm, Fri–Sat 9am–midnight ✋ L 70kn, D 90kn, Wine 70kn/90kn

SLAVONSKI BROD
ZDJELAREVIĆ

www.zdjelarevic.hr
The restaurant attached to Croatia's first wine hotel (▷ 113) serves excellent dishes to accompany Graševina, Rizling, Chardonnay or Manzoni white wines from the hotel vineyards. Specialities include chicken with wild thyme sauce, beef in Samobor mustard sauce, venison ragout and a 'vineyard plate' with a selection of cured meats.

✉ Brodski Stupnik ☎ 035 427040 🕐 Tue–Sat 11–11, Sun–Mon 12–8 ✋ L 80kn, D 130kn, Wine 80kn 🚗 Take the road from Slavonski Brod to Nova Gradiska and turn right after 7km (4 miles) in the village of Brodski Stupnik.

VARAŽDIN
PIVNICA RAJ

Join local office workers for a filling meal in a basic but friendly old-school pub atmosphere. *Mlinci* (baked noodles) feature frequently on the daily set menu. The beer is the best, and cheapest, in town.

✉ Gundulića 11, Varaždin ☎ 042 213146 🕐 8am–10pm ✋ L and D under 50kn, Beer 13kn

ZLATNA GUŠKA

Set in a brick-vaulted cellar beneath a 17th-century palace, the 'Golden Goose' recreates the feel of the Austro-Hungarian empire, with pikestaffs and coats of arms on the walls. Dishes include the Daggers of the Count of Brandenburg (skewers of pork, chicken and beef with strawberries) and Countess Julijana's Flower (pancakes with fruit).

✉ Habdelićeva 4, Varaždin ☎ 042 213393 🕐 Mon–Fri 7am–11pm, Sat 7am–midnight, Sun 7am–10pm ✋ L 80kn, D 130kn, Wine 60/110kn

ZLATNE RUKE

www.zlatneruke.com
At this 90-seat restaurant just off Trg Kralja Tomislava, Varaždin's main square, all dishes are prepared with a golden touch (the name means 'golden hands'). House specialities including wild boar, venison steak tartare, goose liver with peaches, goulash and home-made cakes, can be enjoyed in a relaxing beige-and-cream dining room resplendent with retro 1970s pod chairs and exposed stone walls.

✉ Ivana Kukuljevića 13, Varaždin ☎ 042 320650 🕐 Daily 10–11 ✋ L 190kn, D 220kn, Wine from 140kn

ZAGORJE
GREŠNA GORICA

www.gresna-gorica.com
This farmhouse restaurant with a terrace overlooking Veliki Tabor castle has children's play areas and farm animals to keep little ones amused. It serves good, down-to-earth Zagorje home cooking such as cheese, sausages, veal with mushrooms and venison goulash with dumplings, accompanied by home-made wine.

✉ Tahorgradska 3, Desinić ☎ 049 343001 🕐 Daily 10–10 ✋ L 100kn, D 120kn, Wine 70kn/110kn 🚗 Off the road from Miljana to Desinić

Below An appetizing dish of mussels

PRICES AND SYMBOLS

Prices are the lowest for a double room for one night. Breakfast is included unless noted otherwise. All the hotels listed accept credit cards unless otherwise stated. Note that rates vary widely throughout the year.

For a key to the symbols, ▷ 2.

KARLOVAC

KORANA

www.hotelkorana.hr

Set on the edge of a park on the banks of the River Korana, this former sanatorium has re-emerged as one of Croatia's most stylish small hotels. Breakfast is served on a summer terrace overlooking the river and city beach. The old town is a 10-minute walk away.

✉ Perivoj Josipa Vrbanića 8, Karlovac
☎ 047 609090 🛏 From 875kn 🛈 16
🔄 🏊 Indoor

KOPAČKI RIT

GALIĆ

Snježana Galić is one of several hosts offering private rooms in the village of Bilje, near the entrance to Kopački Rit Nature Park. There are two rooms in the main house, with a shared bathroom, and four rooms with private bathrooms in a bungalow in the garden. The hearty Slavonian breakfast will set you up for the day. If this place is full, the tourist office on the main street has details of families offering accommodation.

✉ Ritska 1, Bilje ☎ 031 750393 🛏 328kn
🛈 6 🅿 Off the main street, near Kod Varge restaurant

LONJSKO POLJE

RAVLIĆ

The guest room of this 200-year-old oak cottage has wooden beds, antique furniture and shutters opening to a view of the River Sava.

The Ravlić family welcome visitors seeking a back-to-nature experience. Horse-riding, boating and fishing can be arranged, and meals are served in the garden. Facilities are basic—there is an outdoor shower and toilet—but a stay here is an adventure.

✉ Mužilovčica 72 ☎ 044 710151
🕐 Closed Nov—end Mar 🛏 340kn;
breakfast 25kn per person. Discount for stays of more than three nights 🛈 2 🅿 On the main road through Mužilovčica, between Čigoć and Lonja

OSIJEK

HOTEL CENTRAL

www.hotel-central-os.hr

Next to the Church of SS Peter and Paul, Osijek's oldest hotel has become something of an institution over the past 120 years. Pass through the wonderful art deco entrance lobby to the superbly appointed rooms with every facility you could

Opposite *Stylish Korana hotel on the banks of the River Korana, Karlovac*

ever need. All in all, the hotel is good value for money.

✉ Trg A Starčevića 6 ☎ 031 283399
✋ 580kn 🛈 32

OSIJEK

www.hotelosijek.hr

This gleaming glass skyscraper beside the River Drava reopened in 2004 and is a symbol of post-war reconstruction. Rooms are equipped with all modern conveniences, including wireless internet access. The 14th-floor spa has Turkish baths and Jacuzzis with panoramic views.

✉ Šamačka 4, Osijek ☎ 031 230333
✋ From 1,050kn 🛈 147 🔵 📺

PLITVIČKA JEZERA
JEZERO

www.np plitvicka-jezera.hr

Of the three hotels within the Plitvice Lakes park, the Jezero, is the largest, with rooms overlooking Lake Kozjak. Its facilities include an indoor pool, tennis courts and gym. Five of the rooms are specially adapted for visitors with disabilities.

✉ Plitvička Jezera ☎ 053 751400
✋ From €106 (Jun and Sep); rates vary throughout the year 🛈 229 🏊 Indoor 📺

SAMOBAR
LIVADIĆ

www.hotel-livadic.hr

This family-run hotel in a 19th-century townhouse on the main square of Samobor is one of the most romantic, relaxing and characterful places to stay in Croatia. The spacious rooms have rugs, antiques and parquet floors, while the breakfast room is a riot of luxurious drapes and high-backed chairs. The attached coffee house, Kavana Livadić is the best in town. Parking is available behind the hotel.

✉ Trg Kralja Tomislava 1, Samobor ☎ 01 336 5850 ✋ 465kn 🛈 23 🔵

SLAVONSKI BROD
ZDJELAREVIĆ

www.zdjelarevic.hr

One of the top wineries in Slavonia

was extended in 2004 with the opening of Croatia's first wine hotel, surrounded by vineyards in the village of Brodski Stupnik. Rooms are decorated in traditional style, with large hand made wooden beds. Tours of the vineyards are available, or you can visit the winery, enjoy a tasting session in the cellar and sample the wines in the restaurant (▷ 111).

✉ Vinogradska 102, Brodski Stupnik
☎ 035 427040 ✋ 712kn 🛈 15
🔵 🚌 Take the road from Slavonski Brod to Nova Gradiska and turn right after 7km (4 miles) in Brodski Stupnik

TRAKOŠĆAN
HOTEL CONING

www.coning.hr

The Coning is set in beautiful surroundings just opposite the castle. The hotel's 2010 facelift should see rooms brought into the 21st century and a number of new guest facilities added. Check the website for details.

✉ Trakošćan 5 ☎ 042 796224 🚌 Bus from Varaždin

VARAŽDIN
MALTAR

This friendly family-run pension in the centre is the best place to stay in town. Rooms are small but adequate for a one-night stay.

✉ Ulica Prešernova 1, Varaždin ☎ 042 311100 ✋ €65 🛈 15 🚌 In the city centre

HOTEL VARAŽDIN

www.hotelvarazdin.com

This relative newcomer, opposite the railway station, opened in 2007. A modern, clean-cut hotel, the Varaždin makes the most of the old building in which it is housed, with lots of exposed brick and stone. Rooms are simple but modern and have everything you require for a comfortable stay. There's live music every Saturday in the cellar restaurant.

✉ Kolodvorska 19 ☎ 042 290720
✋ 600kn 🛈 27 🔵

ZAGORJE
LOJZEKOVA HIŽA

www.lojzekovahiza.com

One of the earliest examples of rural tourism in the Zagorje is still one of the best, with rooms in the attic of a picturesque traditional farmhouse complete with a stream running through the garden. The owners can arrange carriage rides in the forest, and there is a playground and football pitch to keep children entertained. The half-board option includes hearty farmhouse dinners.

✉ Gusakovec 116, Marija Bistrica ☎ 049 469325 ✋ 240kn 🛈 9 🚌 Signposted from the road between Marija Bistrica and Donja Stubica

Above *Lie back and relax in one of the region's comfortable hotels*

ISTRIA

From Pula's 2,000-year-old Roman ruins to the region's bilingual town and street names, centuries of Italian influence are in evidence on the triangular Istrian peninsula, producing a hybrid culture. Like their Adriatic neighbours, the people of Istria share an appreciation of fine food, and Croatia's best produce is grown here. Away from the markets and restaurant tables, sun lovers will enjoy the bustling resorts of Rovinj and Poreč, while the quieter hinterland is rich in historical hilltop towns, south-facing slopes laced with vineyards and shady oak woods.

From 42BC Istria was part of the Roman province of Dalmatia and it is the architecture bequeathed to the peninsula by the Romans that impresses visitors most. The most notable and striking site can be found in Pula, where a first century AD amphitheatre and a perfectly preserved mosaic have survived intact.

Istria is often described as Croatia's larder, and the cheese, ham, olives, wine and truffles produced on the peninsula are second to none. You can find produce from Istria in shops all over the country, but locals say it is best at source, fresh on your restaurant plate and in your glass from forest, farm and vineyard. Istrian truffles in particular are highly sought after.

Istria is one of the most popular tourist destinations in the Adriatic and one of the best locations for a beach getaway. The peninsula is lined with hidden coves, their white pebble beaches sloping gently into warm waters. High-rise tourist development has been kept to a minimum, meaning Istria perhaps best fulfils the Croatian Tourist Board's slogan, as it truly is 'the Mediterranean as it once was'.

BALE (VALLE)

www.istria-bale.com

Bale is a typical compact Istrian hilltop town lying on the road from Pula to Rovinj. It was built just inland from the sea on the site of an Illyrian and Roman fort, Castrum Vallis, though its history goes back much farther than that. Recent underwater excavations have discovered dinosaur fossils off the nearby coast; there are plans to build a museum of dinosaurs, but in the meantime the bones are on display inside the town hall (tel 052 824303; weekday mornings in summer). Facing the town hall across the square is the 15th-century Venetian Gothic palace of the Soardo-Bembo family, who were the lords of Bale during the period of Venetian rule. Beneath the tower, with its sundial and winged lion of St. Mark, an archway leads into the walled town. It takes less than five minutes to make a complete circuit of Castel, the main street of the old town, which is little more than a cobbled lane spanned by arches.

✚ 284 A5 🚹 Rovinjska 1 ☎ 052 024391 ⚙ Jun–end Sep Mon–Sat 8–8 🚌 From Pula and Rovinj

BRIJUNI (BRIONI)

▷ 118–119.

BUJE (BUIE)

www.tzg-buje.hr

The largest of Istria's hill towns occupies a strategic position, 5km (3 miles) from the Slovenian border, on the old trade route from Pula to Trieste. In medieval times it was known as 'the watchtower of Istria' and it is easy to see why when you stand on the terrace beside Trg Slobode, with views over the countryside and the Italian Alps visible across the sea. At the top of the main street is the Etnografski Muzej (Trg Slobode 4, tel 052 773075; Jun–end Sep Tue–Sun 9–12, 6–8), with rooms full of knick-knacks, in the style of a rural Istrian home. From here, a short climb leads to the church of Sveti Servula (St. Servolo), built on the site of a Roman temple within the medieval town walls. Note the Venetian winged lion on the bell tower, and the scallop-shell niche above the portal. Buje is also the capital of an important wine-growing area, with much of the best Istrian wine being produced in the nearby villages of Brtonigla and Momjan.

✚ 284 A4 🚹 Istarska 2 ☎ 052 773353 ⚙ Jun–end Sep Mon–Sat 8–8; Oct–end May Mon–Fri 8–3 🚌 From Pula, Poreč and Rovinj

BUZET (PINGUENTE)

www.istria-buzet.com

High on a bluff above the River Mirna, Buzet seems almost to grow out of the rock. From the heart of the modern town on Trg Fontana, a long staircase leads to the old town, entered through the 16th-century Vela Vrata (Large Gate) and still partly enclosed by its medieval walls. With its narrow streets, Venetian palaces and attractive baroque fountain, the old town makes an enjoyable place to stroll. The former Bigatto palace houses the Zavičajni Muzej (Trg Rašporskih Kapetana 1, tel 052 662792; Mon–Fri 11–3), a regional museum of archaeology, ethnology and crafts. From the walls behind the church of Sveti Juraj (St. George), there are views over the Čićarija mountains, which divide Istria from the rest of Croatia.

The Subotina festival is usually held on the first Saturday in September (▷ 141).

✚ 284 B4 🚹 Trg Fontana 7 ☎ 052 662343 ⚙ Easter–end Oct Mon–Fri 8–3, Sat 9–2; Nov–Easter Mon–Fri 8–3 🚌 From Pula

Opposite *A cobbled lane in the peaceful medieval hilltop town of Bale*
Below *Buzet, largest of the Istrian hill towns*

BRIJUNI (BRIONI)

INFORMATION

www.brijuni.hr

➕ 284 A5 ℹ️ Nacionalni Park Brijuni, Brijunska 10, Fažana ☎ 052 525883

✋ Boat trips: Jul–end Aug: adult 210kn, child 105kn; Jun, Sep: adult 200kn, child 100kn; Apr, May, Oct: adult 170kn, child 85kn; Nov–end Mar: adult 125kn, child 65kn

INTRODUCTION

These luxuriant islands off the west coast of Istria have long been a playground for the rich and famous. Wealthy Roman patricians built their summer villas here to take advantage of the mild climate. Centuries later, in 1893, Austrian magnate Paul Kupelweiser (1843–1919) bought the islands with the intention of turning them into a luxury resort. After hiring Nobel prize-winning bacteriologist Robert Koch (1843–1910) to successfully eradicate malaria on the islands, he set about building hotels, tennis courts, a golf course and heated seawater pool. For a while Brijuni was the favoured playground of the Austro-Hungarian aristocracy; visitors included Archduke Franz Ferdinand and the author James Joyce. During the Communist era, Tito used the islands as his private retreat. In 1983, Brijuni was declared a national park and it continues to attract celebrities; an Italian company has plans to redevelop Veli Brijun as a luxury spa resort, and a polo tournament last staged in the 1930s was reinstated in 2004.

Of 14 islands in the Brijuni archipelago, only the two largest, Veli Brijun and Mali Brijun, can be visited. They lie off the west coast of Istria, 3km (2 miles) from the port of Fažana. The best way of visiting is on one of the official Brijuni National Park boat trips which operate several times daily in summer and once or twice a week in winter. Included in the price is a three-hour guided tour of Veli Brijun by miniature safari train, with visits to the safari park, museums and Roman villa. It is best to book several days in advance. In summer, the national park also offers trips to Mali Brijun, including a visit to a fort. Tour operators on the dock at Fažana advertise boat trips to the islands, but most of these cruise around Veli Brijun rather than going ashore.

Above *Brijuni National Park, an archipelago of 14 luxuriant islands off the west coast of Istria*

WHAT TO SEE

TITO NA BRIJUNIMA (TITO ON BRIJUNI)

This fascinating photographic exhibition recalls the time from 1947 to 1979 when Tito used the Brijuni islands as his summer retreat, entertaining visitors at the Bijela Vila (White House). More than 60 heads of state visited Brijuni, including Emperor Haile Selassie of Ethiopia, Queen Elizabeth II of Great Britain and President Fidel Castro of Cuba. In 1956 Tito hosted the founding of the Non-Aligned Movement on Brijuni, accompanied by President Nasser of Egypt and President Nehru of India. As well as statesmen, he enjoyed the company of film stars, and there are pictures of Tito relaxing with glamorous actresses Elizabeth Taylor, Gina Lollobrigida and Sophia Loren.

SAFARI PARK

The safari park at the northern tip of Veli Brijun contains animals given to Tito by world leaders, including antelopes, zebras and a pair of Indian elephants donated by Indira Gandhi. Visitors can walk around a small ethno-park featuring rare breeds of farm animals, including the *boškarin* (long-horned Istrian cattle).

OTHER SIGHTS

Also featured on the tour are the remains of a first-century Roman villa and a 15th-century church. The safari train also crosses the golf course, where you can look out for wild mouflon and deer. Much of the island is covered in forests of laurel and holm oak, and there is a thousand-year-old olive tree in a meadow near the harbour.

If you are exploring on your own, Veli Brijun boasts around a hundred sites of archaeological interest from every era of human habitation. The two most obvious and interesting ruins, both reachable by bicycle, are a seventh-century Byzantine fortress, which lies around 2km (1.25 miles) southwest of Brijun harbour at Dobrika Cove, and the remains of an Austrian defence system dating from the 19th century just 500m (520 yards) south. Other Neolithic, Roman, Byzantine and medieval sites are less visible and you'll need a local guide to point them out.

TIPS

» If you want to explore the island of Veli Brijun on your own, you can rent bicycles or electric golf buggies (carts) or even take an expensive ride in Tito's 1953 Cadillac.
» Guests staying at the hotels on Veli Brijun have unlimited crossings to the mainland included in the price, and also receive discounts on golf, tennis and sailing excursions.

Below *The ruins of a first-century AD Roman villa at Veli Brijun*

REGIONS | ISTRIA • SIGHTS

DRAGUĆ (DRAGUCCIO)

www.draguc.com

The picturesque village of Draguć is little more than a single street of houses perched on a cliff. Under Venetian rule, this was a fortified town and some of the houses are built onto the medieval ramparts. From the terrace beside the main square, there are expansive views over central Istria. The 12th-century cemetery church at the entrance to Draguć contains poorly preserved frescoes, and the altar incorporates a Roman tombstone. At the other end of the village, the lovely little chapel of Sveti Roka (St. Roch) has 16th-century frescoes of the Annunciation and the Adoration of the Magi by Master Antonio of Padova. The chapel is usually locked but you can peer through the open window or ask for the key at the bar. If Draguć looks like a film set, that's because it is. During the 1980s, it was known as the Croatian Hollywood and it is currently experiencing a revival. Among movies shot in Draguć are *La Femme Musketeer* (2003) starring Gérard Départieu, and *Libertas* (2005), about the life of Dubrovnik playwright and libertine Marin Držić, in which Draguć takes the role of 16th-century Florence.

✚ 284 B4

Right and below *Once-deserted Grožnjan experienced a renaissance in the 1960s and today is a thriving cultural centre*

GRAČIŠĆE (GALLIGNANA)

Time seems to have stood still in Gračišće, a village of stone lanes and 15th-century houses. On a hilltop on the road from Pazin to Labin, this was once a fortress on the boundary of the Venetian and Habsburg empires. At one time, Gračišće had 15 churches and Venetian Gothic palaces and was the summer residence of the bishops of Pićan. The church of Sveta Marije na Placu (Our Lady on the Square), just inside the town gate, has a beautiful porch and 15th-century frescoes, which can be glimpsed through the window grille. Look carefully for the remains of nails hidden between the stones; this was a votive chapel where infertile women would leave gifts and prayers in the hope of being blessed with a child. From the terrace behind the parish church there are views over the Istrian countryside, with Mount Učka looming on the horizon.

✚ 284 B4

GROŽNJAN (GRISIGNANA)

www.tz-groznjan.hr

A few decades ago, Grožnjan was crumbling and deserted; now it is a thriving artistic and cultural centre. Surrounded by walls in the 12th century and ruled by Venice for over 400 years, it was part of Italy along with the rest of Istria from 1918 to 1945. When Istria joined Yugoslavia after World War II, Grožnjan was abandoned by its largely Italian population. In 1965, the decaying town was proclaimed a city of artists; and just four years later it hosted the first annual summer school of Jeunesses Musicales Croatia. Now the town has some 30 art galleries and studios, a film academy and concert hall and an active Italian association. On summer evenings concerts of jazz and classical music are held in the town's churches and squares. The best places to head to soak up the atmosphere are the Venetian loggia or the belvedere on the church terrace.

The 16th-century chapel of SS Cosmas and Damian, restored in 1989, is worth a visit. It was decorated with frescoes by the Croatian artist Ivan Lovrenčić (1917–2002) in 1990.

✚ 284 A4 🛈 Umberta Gorjana 3 ☎ 052 776131

HUM (COLMO)

www.hum.hr

The self-proclaimed smallest town in the world has fewer than 20 inhabitants and a handful of stone houses lining its two narrow streets. What makes it a town rather than a village is its annual election for mayor, when the judges of the parish gather around a stone table beneath the municipal loggia, carving notches in a wooden stick to make their choice. Hum still preserves its medieval town walls, though the original entrance gate now contains a pair of copper doors engraved with Glagolitic writing and a calendar of rural activities. This is the last monument in the Aleja Glagoljaša (Glagolitic Alley), a sculpture trail which follows the road for 7km (4.5 miles) from Roč to Hum. The sculptures, by Želimir Janeš (1916–96), reflect themes from Croatian and Istrian history, in particular the importance of the Glagolitic script (▷ 21) in this region. Some of the monuments are designed in the shape of Glagolitic characters; one is a large stone block depicting the letters of the Glagolitic, Cyrillic and Latin alphabets in juxtaposition.

The cemetery church of Sveti Jeronima (St. Hieronymus), outside the town gates, has 12th-century frescoes and Glagolitic graffiti.

✚ 284 B4

Above *From the hill town of Labin there are bird's-eye views over neighbouring Rabac*
Above left *The church tower in Hum, the smallest town in the world*

LABIN (ALBONA)

www.istria-rabac.com

Sitting above Rabac (▷ 123) on Istria's southeast coast, Labin is divided into two parts, its typical medieval hill town looking over the modern district of Podlabin. Until the mines closed in 1999 Labin was Croatia's coal-mining capital; in 1921 striking miners declared the town an independent socialist republic. These days it has a new lease of life as an art colony—at least 30 artists and potters have their studios here, and in summer the Labin Art Republic takes over the streets, with live theatre, outdoor concerts and open ateliers. From the main square, Titov Trg, with its Venetian loggia, steps lead up to the town gate. Beyond the gate is a delightful ensemble of Renaissance and baroque architecture, with the palaces of the Venetian nobility painted in bright orange, lemon and vanilla. The 18th-century Battiala-Lazzarini palace houses the Narodni Muzej (tel 052 852477; summer Mon–Fri 9–1, 5–8, Sat 10–1; winter Mon–Fri 7–3), where the most unusual exhibit is a reconstructed coal mine; be prepared to don a hard hat as you walk through the underground passages. Near here is the parish church of the Blessed Virgin Mary, with a rose window and a winged lion of St. Mark on the facade.

✚ 284 B4 🛈 Titov Trg 10 ☎ 052 852399 🕓 Easter–end Oct Mon–Sat 8am–9pm, Sun 10–1, 6–9, Nov–Easter Mon–Fri 9 4 🚍 From Pula and Rijeka

LIMSKI KANAL

This flooded karst valley forms a fjordlike inlet which flows for 10km (6 miles) beneath thickly wooded cliffs. Boat trips along the gorge are advertised at the harboursides in Poreč, Vrsar and Rovinj during the summer; it makes a popular excursion for families staying on the Istrian coast. The boats usually stop for lunch at the far end of the gorge, where restaurants serve fresh mussels and oysters from the fjord; on the way back you will probably visit the cave of Romuald, an 11th-century hermit who lived in the cliffs over the gorge.

✚ 284 A4

INFORMATION
www.istra.hr/motovun
🕂 284 A4 🛈 Trg Andrea Antico
1 ☎ 052 681642 ⊕ Jun—end Sep
Mon—Sat 8—4 🚌 From Pazin

TIP

» This is a good place to try Istrian
truffles, which grow in the nearby oak
woods. Restaurants in Motovun specialize
in truffle dishes, and shops sell truffles,
local wine and *biska* (mistletoe brandy).

MOTOVUN (MONTONA)

Perched atop a hill, some 277m (906ft) above the Mirna valley, and surrounded
by vineyards, Motovun is the most attractive inland Istrian town. Like so many
towns in Istria, it once had a large Italian population—the former Formula
One motor-racing champion Mario Andretti was born here in 1940—but was
depopulated after World War II when Istria joined Yugoslavia. Now tourists
crowd its narrow streets in summer and its lively international film festival
(▷ 141), established in 1999 and held annually in late July, has put the town
firmly on the European cultural map.

THE WAY IN

You can leave your car at the foot of the hill and walk up—a staggering 1,052
steps—or pay a toll in summer to drive up the twisting road to the town. If you
do drive, you will have to park outside the gates. Walk through the outer gate
to arrive at the Venetian loggia. A second gate leads to the square, Trg Andrea
Antico, named after a Renaissance composer from Motovun.

WHAT TO SEE

All of the main sights are found on or around the square. Notice the old well, the
crenellated bell tower of the parish church, and the sculptural relief of a winged
lion, symbol of the Venetian republic, dating from 1322. From here you can make
a short promenade around the ramparts, with views all the way.

Don't miss the lapidarium inside the outer gate, with a Roman sculpture on
one side, Venetian lions on the other, and a recent addition—a stone carving of
the Motovun Film Festival logo.

Above *Visible long before you reach it,*
Motovun is the perfect hill town

NOVIGRAD (CITTANOVA)

www.istria-novigrad.com

Built on an islet near the mouth of the River Mirna, Novigrad was originally a Greek and then a Roman colony and was joined to the mainland in the 18th century. Its name dates back to the sixth century, when it was called Neopolis (New Town). The main square, Veliki Trg, is dominated by the parish church, dedicated to local third-century martyrs St. Pelagius and St. Maximus. The present church dates mostly from the 18th century, with much baroque decoration adorning the interior, including a main altar by Picco of Palmanova. Below the church lies an 11th-century crypt containing the former cathedral pulpit and 12th-century confessional. The separate bell tower, added in 1883, is modelled on St. Mark's in Venice, though it is topped by a bronze statue of the town's patron, St. Pelagius. Until 1831 Novigrad was the seat of a bishop and people still refer to the church as the cathedral. Parts of the medieval walls remain intact. A delightful promenade starts at the town beach and continues to the inner harbour. It passes a 16th-century Venetian loggia, overlooking the sea.

➕ 284 A4 ℹ️ Porporella 1 ☎ 052 757075 🕐 Jun–end Sep daily 8–8; Apr, May daily 8–7; Oct–end Mar Mon–Fri 8–3, Sat 8–1 🚌 From Poreč and Umag

PAZIN (PISINO)

www.tzpazin.hr

Pazin was chosen as the capital of Istria in 1945, partly because of its central position and partly because it did not have the Italian associations of larger coastal towns like Pula. The result is that this small provincial town of 10,000 people has an importance far outweighing its size. On the first Tuesday every month it hosts the largest traditional fair in Istria, the Pazinski Samanj, which has been held here since 1574. The town is dominated by its castle, first mentioned in 983 in a deed of gift from Emperor Otto II to the Bishop of Poreč and later used as a prison in the days of the Austro-

Above *Pleasure craft moored at the harbour at Rabac. The resort is southeast Istria's largest but despite extensive tourist development retains a village-like feel*

Hungarian empire. It now houses the Etnografski Muzej Istre (tel 052 622220; mid-Apr to mid-Oct Tue–Sun 10–6; mid-Oct to mid-Apr Tue–Thu 10–3, Fri 11–4, Sat–Sun 10–4; adult 25kn, child 18kn; www.emi.hr), an enjoyable ethnographic museum with displays of folk costumes, musical instruments, household goods and children's toys. The square tower contains documents and maps on the history of the castle as well as instruments of torture in the old dungeon. The castle is on a cliff overlooking Pazin Pit, where the River Pazinčica enters an underground canyon. The canyon never runs dry, even in years of drought, and the cave system through which the water runs has never been fully explored. The hero of Jules Verne's novel *Mathias Sandorf* made a dramatic escape from the castle by throwing himself into the gorge and then swimming along the subterranean river to the sea.

➕ 284 B4 ℹ️ Franine i Jurine 14 ☎ 052 622460 🕐 Jun–end Aug Mon–Fri 9–7, Sat–Sun 9–1; Sep Mon–Fri 9–7; Oct–end

May Mon–Fri 9–4 🚌 From Poreč, Pula and Rovinj 🚆 From Buzet and Pula

POREČ (PARENZO)

▷ 124–125.

PULA (POLA)

▷ 126–129.

RABAC

www.rabac-labin.com

The largest resort on Istria's southeast coast lies 4km (2.5 miles) beneath the hill town of Labin (▷ 121). Rabac became popular in the late 19th and early 20th century when wealthy city folk began building villas here. Although it has since witnessed extensive tourist development and can accommodate up to 10,000 visitors in summer, Rabac still has the feel of a Mediterranean fishing village, with whitewashed houses, pebble beaches and pretty coves. The only sight of note is the chapel of St. Andrew, with its simple rectangular layout, Gothic portal and 15th-century statue of St. Andrew.

➕ 284 B4 ℹ️ Labin (▷ 121)

POREČ (PARENZO)

INFORMATION

www.istria-porec.com

🕂 284 A4 🛈 Zagrebačka 9 ☎ 052 451293 ⊕ Jun–end Sep daily 8am–9pm; Oct–end May Mon–Sat 8–3 🚌 From Pula and Rovinj

Above *Poreč's sixth-century basilica, Eufrazijeva Basilika, is famed for its beautiful Byzantine mosaics*

INTRODUCTION

Although it has become a busy, modern tourist resort, Poreč is at its heart a Roman town. Founded as Parentium in the first century BC, it has retained its original Roman grid plan, with two intersecting streets, Cardo and Decumanus, providing the main routes of the old town. In 1267 Poreč was the first town in Istria to be conquered by the Venetians. Tourism began in 1845 with the publication of the first guidebook; the first public beach opened on the island of Sveti Nikola in 1895, and during the 1970s Poreč was Yugoslavia's biggest resort. It is worth coming here just to see the sixth-century Basilica of Euphrasius, richly ornamented with Byzantine mosaics. In 1997, the basilica was designated a UNESCO World Heritage Site.

The oldest part of Poreč occupies a narrow peninsula, but it has expanded on all sides and is now swamped by the hotels, campsites and tourist villages of Lanterna and Zelena Laguna. Coastal footpaths, buses, boats and a miniature road train in summer link the resorts to the old town. The old town is small and easily explored on foot. In summer, you can catch a ferry from the harbourside promenade to the wooded isle of Sveti Nikola.

WHAT TO SEE

EUFRAZIJEVA BASILIKA (BASILICA OF EUPHRASIUS)

The one must-see sight in Poreč is this sixth-century church, built in honour of Bishop Euphrasius, Poreč's first bishop, who was martyred in the third century. The basilica, which stands on the site of a fourth-century oratory, has been under UNESCO's wing since 1997 and contains some of the finest examples of Byzantine art anywhere in the world.

You enter the complex through the colonnaded atrium; to your left is the octagonal baptistry, which gives access to the bell tower (Easter–end Oct 10–6; adult 10kn, child 5kn), which you can climb for views over the town. On the right is the basilica, with mosaics on the facade. A long nave, lined with Greek marble columns, leads to the altar, sheltered beneath a 13th-century ciborium (canopy). Behind here is the sanctuary, completely covered in mosaic and gold leaf. The central panel depicts the Madonna and Child; on her right is St. Maurus, and beyond him, Bishop Euphrasius holding a model of his church; the upper panel depicts Christ with his Apostles. The bishop's palace, off the atrium, contains a museum (tel 052 451711; Easter–end Oct 10–6; adult 10kn, child 5kn), with stone sculptures and remnants of the original fourth-century oratory, including a mosaic fish, a secret symbol of the underground Church in Roman times.
✉ Eufrazijeva ⏰ Summer daily 7am–8pm; winter 10–7 ✋ Free

ZAVIČAJNI MUZEJ (REGIONAL MUSEUM)

Housed in the 17th-century baroque Sinčić Palace, the museum contains archaeological artefacts and extensive collections mapping the history of Poreč from prehistoric times to the 20th century. There are also displays of 18th-century furniture, altar paintings and early Christian crucifixes.
✉ Dekumanska 9 ☎ 052 431585 ⏰ Jun–end Sep Mon–Sat 10–1, 6–9, Sun 10–1; Oct Mon–Sat 10–1; Nov–end May by appointment ✋ Adult 10kn, child 5kn

MORE TO SEE

SVETI NIKOLA

Ferries and other private craft leave regularly in the summer months for the very brief sailing to the tiny island of Sveti Nikola just 500m (545 yards) offshore, where there are sandy beaches, shady woodland and some very secluded but rocky bathing spots. The only building on the islet belongs to the Fortuna Island Hotel, a novel place to stay.

TIPS

» Look out for classical concerts in the basilica and jazz concerts in the lapidarium of the Regional Museum in summer.

» Mass is held in the basilica at 7.30am and 6pm on weekdays, and at 11am on Sundays.

» If you get too hot after all that sightseeing, take a boat to the island of Sveti Nikola for an afternoon on the beach.

Below left *Tour boats moored along Poreč's waterfront*
Below *Detail of an intricately carved column*

PULA (POLA)

INTRODUCTION

Pulu was built on the site of a Histrian hill fort, conquered by the Romans under Julius Caesar in the first century BC. It reached its peak under Emperor Augustus, when it was a city of 5,000 people, with temples, theatres, monumental walls and gates. Decline set in under Venetian rule, but Pula revived in the 19th century, when it became the chief naval base of the Austro-Hungarian fleet. During the 20th century it expanded due to industry and tourism and it is now the seventh-biggest city in Croatia.

Although Pula is now a sprawling city of 60,000 people, the Roman monuments are concentrated in a small area at its heart. Beginning at the Arena, the sixth-largest amphitheatre in the world, you can make a brief circuit of the main sights following the streets that wind around the base of a fortified hill. Downhill from the amphitheatre, Ulica Kandlerova leads to the Forum, from where Via Sergia continues to the Arch of Sergi; turn left beyond the arch to return to the Arena via Giardini and the Archaeological Museum. The big hotels and beaches are 5km (3 miles) south of the centre, on the Punta Verudela peninsula and around Pješčana Uvala.

WHAT TO SEE

ARENA

Built on a natural slope beside the harbour, the well-preserved Roman amphitheatre has two rows of arches on its seaward side, a single row on the landward side, and tiered stone seats climbing to a grassy hillock. Begun in the reign of Emperor Augustus, it was completed in the first century AD and once held more than 20,000 spectators for gladiatorial contests. Today it is a popular concert venue: artists who have played here include Sting, Michael Bolton and the late Luciano Pavarotti. Beyond the impressive scale of the building itself, there is not much for visitors to see, though you are free to wander at will. The underground gallery, where wild beasts were kept before fights, houses an exhibition on Roman Istria, with olive presses and amphorae. The gift shop sells models of the Arena as well as replica Roman items.

✉ Ulica Flavijevska ☎ 052 219028 ⑭ May–end Sep daily 8am–9pm; Oct–end Apr daily 9–7 💴 Adult 40kn, child 20kn 🅿 30kn ⌨ Audioguide 30kn (May–Sep only) ♿

FORUM

The old Roman forum is still Pula's central square, with open-air cafés, the tourist office and town hall. The Temple of Augustus, built between 2BC and AD14, has steps leading up to a porch supported by six Corinthian columns. Under Venetian rule, it was used as a church and a grain store, but it now houses a lapidarium of Roman sculpture (May–end Sep daily 9–8). The temple was destroyed by an Allied bomb during World War II and rebuilt in 1947. The arcaded building next door is the Renaissance town hall, which incorporates parts of the Roman Temple of Diana into its rear facade.

SLAVOLUK SERGIJEVACA (ARCH OF SERGI)

This triumphal arch was erected around 30BC by a wealthy widow to commemorate the role played by her husband and brothers in the Battle of Actium, when a fleet commanded by Octavian (later Emperor Augustus) was victorious over Mark Antony for control of the Roman empire. The arch was previously joined to the Porta Aurea (Golden Gate), part of the Roman walls; when the walls were torn down in the 19th century the arch remained. Inscribed in honour of Lucius Sergius Lepidus, it features reliefs of eagles, sphinxes, dolphins, acanthus leaves and bunches of grapes, along with chariots and the

INFORMATION

www.pulainfo.hr
www.mdc.hr/pula
✚ 284 A5 🈯 Forum 3 ☎ 052 212987 ⑭ Jun–end Sep daily 8am–10pm; Oct–end May daily 9–7 🚌 From Poreč, Rijeka and Rovinj

Opposite Slavoluk Sergijevaca, a Roman triumphal arch dating from 30BC, originally joined the city walls but now stands in isolation on Trg Portarata

REGIONS ISTRIA • SIGHTS

127

TIPS
» Tour boats at the harbour offer cruises to the Brijuni islands (▷ 118–119) in summer.
» The tables outside Cvajner Caffe on the Forum make a great venue for people-watching, but go inside to see the 16th-century frescoes uncovered during restoration of the building.

Roman goddess of victory. Just inside the arch is a bronze sculpture, by Mate Čvrljak (b.1934), of the Irish novelist James Joyce (1882–1941) sitting on a chair outside the Uliks bar. Joyce taught English for a few months in 1904–05 at the Berlitz school on this site.

ARHEOLOŠKI MUZEJ (ARCHAEOLOGICAL MUSEUM)
The twin arches of Porta Gemina, a surviving Roman gateway, lead to this museum, which displays artefacts from Roman Pula, including jewellery, coins, mosaics, glassware, pottery, oil lamps, sarcophagi and an extensive open-air lapidarium of sculpture. As well as Roman objects, the museum covers the prehistoric and early medieval periods—look for the pre-Roman tombstone depicting a horseman and goddess of fertility, and the carved stone altars with typically ornate braiding from medieval Croatian churches. Afterwards, climb the hill behind the museum to see a small semicircular Roman theatre, built in the second century AD.

✉ Ulica Carrarina 3 ☎ 052 218603 ⏰ May–end Sep Mon–Sat 9–8, Sun 10–3; Oct–end Apr Mon–Fri 9–2 🖐 Adult 20kn, child 10kn 🏛

MORE TO SEE
POVIJESNI MUZEJ ISTRE (ISTRIAN HISTORY MUSEUM)
Housed in a star-shaped Venetian fortress at the top of the town, this museum houses collections of naval uniforms and medals from the Austro-Hungarian empire and displays on Pula's shipbuilding history. Perhaps of greater interest than the exhibits are the views of the amphitheatre from the grassy ramparts and the building itself. Dating from 1630, it was commissioned by Istria's Venetian overlords to protect sea-going trade in the northern Adriatic, though it's thought that a Roman fortress once stood on the strategic site. The round tower was added in the 19th century. To get there, climb the steps from Via Sergia and enter across the drawbridge beside a row of cannon.

✉ Kaštel ☎ 052 211566 ⏰ Daily 8–7 🖐 Adult 10kn, child 5kn

Below *Pula's Roman amphitheatre, once the stage for gladiatorial contests, is now a popular concert venue*

RIMSKI MOZAIK (ROMAN MOSAIC)

Around 2m (6.5ft) below today's ground level and located behind a car park (parking lot) just off the Forum, this perfectly preserved second-century mosaic was discovered in 1959 as a result of bomb damage in World War II. It probably adorned the floor of a wealthy patrician's villa, and features fish, birds and flowers around a central panel depicting the legend of the punishment of Dirce, with the twins Amphion and Zethus seen tying their stepmother to the horns of a bull. The mosaic is quite difficult to find—follow the brown signs from the Forum.

KATEDRALA (CATHEDRAL)

Close to the Forum in a small square, Pula's cathedral has a 17th-century facade tacked onto an early Christian basilica, built on the site of a Roman temple with a third-century Roman sarcophagus for an altar. Fragments of fifth- and sixth-century floor mosaics can also be seen. The free-standing bell tower was added in the 17th century using stone from the arena. Services here are held in Italian and Croatian.

✉ Obala Maršala Tita ◷ Daily 8.30–2, 6–8

KAPELA SV. MARIJE FORMOZE (CHAPEL OF ST. MARY FORMOSA)

Near the Roman mosaic, this was one of two chapels built in stone in the sixth century as part of a Benedictine monastery. The complex was destroyed in the 16th century, but this chapel survived. Much of the mosaic work that adorned the building's walls and floors now forms part of the collection at the Archaeological Museum (▷ 128). Almost unchanged for 1,500 years, this is one of Pula's most precious pieces of architecture, but unlike most of the others it is still in use today as a venue for a temporary art exhibitions during the summer.

✉ Ulica Flaciusova ◷ During exhibitions only

Above left Distinctive mural close to the Roman amphitheatre
Above The Temple of Augustus, rebuilt in 1947 after its destruction by Allied bombing in World War II

ROVINJ (ROVIGNO)

Above *The bell tower of Svete Eufemije church dominates views of Rovinj*

INFORMATION

www.tzgrovinj.hr

✚ 284 A4 🛈 Obala Pina Budicina 12
☎ 052 811566 🕓 Jun–end Aug daily
8am–10pm; Sep daily 8–4; Oct–end May
Mon–Fri 8–3, Sat 8–1 🚍 From Poreč
and Pula

INTRODUCTION

With red-roofed houses crowded onto a peninsula, surrounded by the sea on three sides, Rovinj is as pretty as a picture. This is the most Italian place in Croatia, with a Mediterranean atmosphere. Originally a small Roman settlement, Rovinj was ruled by Venice from 1283 to 1797. For most of its history it was actually an island, which became joined to the mainland when engineers filled in the narrow channel in 1763. Like other towns in Istria, it had a large Italian community, but here the Italian influence lives on. The town council is officially bilingual; there is an Italian-language school, and in 2001 Rovinj elected an Italian-speaking mayor, Giovanni Sponzam, still in office today.

The best way to view Rovinj is from the sea, by taking the ferry to the islands of Sveta Katarina or Crveni Otok in summer. From here, Rovinj appears as a jumble of brightly coloured houses reflected in the water, crowned by the tall Venetian bell tower of St. Euphemia's church. Cars are not allowed in the centre, so leave your vehicle at the large car park by the jetty on Obala Parih Boraca, a short walk from the market square, Trg Valdibora, and the main square, Trg Maršala Tita, from where cobbled streets lead up into the heart of the old town. This is best explored on foot.

WHAT TO SEE

MUZEJ GRADA ROVINJA (ROVINJ HERITAGE MUSEUM)

www.muzej-rovinj.com

The town museum occupies a 17th-century palace on the harbour square, and has collections of archaeology, maritime history, Old Masters and contemporary art, with rotating exhibitions of each. Among the works is a Madonna and Child by Venetian artist Giovanni Bellini (1430–1516). One room is devoted to the seascapes of Alexandar Kircher (1867–1939), the official artist of the Austro-Hungarian Navy. In summer, the museum sponsors the annual Rovinj Art Colony and an outdoor exhibition on Grisia.

✉ Trg Maršala Tita 11 ☎ 052 816720 🕓 Mid-Jun to mid-Sep Tue–Fri 9–3, 7–10, Sat–Sun 9–2, 7–10; mid-Sep to mid-Jun Tue–Sat 10–1 💰 Adult 15kn, child 10kn 📷

BALBIJEV LUK (BALBI ARCH)

In medieval times, Rovinj was surrounded by walls and gates, demolished when the town expanded under Venetian rule. The main entrance to the old town is through Balbi Arch, a baroque archway erected in 1680 on the site of the outer town gate. Above the arch, beneath the winged lion of the Venetian republic and the coat of arms of the Balbi family, is the sculpted relief of a turbanned Turk's head. On the other side of the arch is a Venetian—a clear message that the town belonged to Venice and that Turks should keep out.

CRKVA SVETE EUFEMIJE (ST. EUPHEMIA'S CHURCH)

From the Balbi Arch, the narrow lanes of the old town thread their way up the hill. The main street is Grisia, where in summer artists display their work on the steps. Grisia ends at the parish church of St. Euphemia, dedicated to a third-century Turkish Christian martyred in Constantinople on the orders of Emperor Diocletian. According to legend, the sarcophagus containing her body was washed up in Rovinj in AD800 and she was immediately adopted as the town's patron saint. The tomb lies in an aisle to the right of the altar. Climb the 200 wooden steps of the campanile for views over the terracotta roofs and out to sea. Note the copper statue on top of the tower; it depicts St. Euphemia with the wheel on which she was tortured before being thrown to the lions.

🕐 Apr–end Oct daily 8–6; for services at other times. Campanile: Apr–end Oct daily 8–6
💰 Campanile: 10kn

ZLATNI RT (GOLDEN CAPE)

This attractive forest park was designed by the industrialist Baron Georg Huetterott (1852–1910) as part of an ambitious plan to develop Rovinj as a tourist resort at the beginning of the 20th century. With shady footpaths leading through cedar, pine and cypress plantations to rock and pebble beaches, it makes a lovely place for a walk (▷ 136–137). You can also explore the park by bicycle in summer. Just inside the entrance to Zlatni Rt, Lone is the popular town beach.

TIPS

» Young children will enjoy the Aquarium (▷ 139) and Mini Croatia (▷ 140).
» Watch the sunset from the wine bars along Ulica Svetog Križa, which follows the sea wall uphill from the harbour.
» If you want to swim in the heart of town, head for the popular bathing rocks, beneath the church at the top of Ulica Svetog Križa.

Left *Ruled by Venice for five centuries, Rovinj retains an Italian character*
Below *Detail of an Italianate fountain on Trg Maršala Tita, the main square*

THE ISLANDS

The Rovinj archipelago contains around 20 islands and islets, most of which are uninhabited. In summer, you can take a ferry from the harbour at Trg Maršala Tita to two of the larger islands. The nearest is Sveta Katarina, just 200m (220 yards) offshore, with magnificent views towards Rovinj. The biggest island, Crveni Otok (Red Island), is actually two islands linked by a causeway, which leads to a number of remote naturist beaches. Both islands have hotels if you want to enjoy them when the crowds have left, and are justifiably popular with day-trippers. Even if you do not want to spend a whole day on the beach, it is worth visiting for the views alone.

MORE TO SEE

KUĆA O BATANI (HOUSE OF BATANI)

www.batana.org

This interactive museum is dedicated to the *batana*, a flat-bottomed wooden fishing boat unique to Rovinj. The multimedia exhibits include a slide show on the two-month process required to build a *batana*, as well as tools, fishing nets and photographs of old Rovinj. In the 1960s, almost every family in town owned a motor-powered *batana* as they were used for fishing as well as leisure. *Batani* can still be seen bobbing in Rovinj harbour although they are less popular than they once were.

✉ Obala Pina Budicina 2 ☎ 052 812593 🕐 Jun–end Aug daily 10–1, 7–10; Sep Mon–Sat 10–1, 6–9; Oct–end Dec Tue–Sun 10–1 and by appointment; Mar–end May Tue–Sun 10–1, 3–5. Closed Jan, Feb 💺 Adult 10kn, child 5kn 🏛

GALERIJA ADRIS

Opened in 2001, this modern art gallery is inside Croatia's largest tobacco factory, which dominates the east side of the harbour. The star attraction is a ceramic mural by Edo Murtić (1921–2005), a leading Croatian expressionist artist who had a studio in nearby Vrsar.

✉ Obala Vladimira Nazora 1 ☎ 052 801122 🕐 For exhibitions only

Below *Head to one of the islands in the Rovinj archipelago to kick back and relax*

UMAG (UMAGO)

www.tz-umag.hr

Umag is the northernmost town on the Istrian coast, lying just 40km (25 miles) from the Italian city of Trieste. With easy access from Central Europe, it is a popular summer resort, particularly with visitors from Italy. The big hotels and tourist villages are to the north of town, leaving the historic area largely intact. Among the medieval streets and squares and surviving sections of wall, an old fortress is now the town museum (tel 052 741440; Apr–end Oct 10–1, 7–9; Nov–end Mar by appointment; free), with displays including amphorae and oil lamps from the Roman colony of Umacus.

A coast road leads 8km (5 miles) through the pine woods to Savudrija, where Croatia's oldest lighthouse, built in 1818, stands on a cape at the country's northwest tip.

✚ 284 A4 ⓘ Trgovačka 6 ☎ 052 741363 ◉ Jun–end Sep daily 8–8; Oct–end May Mon–Fri 8–3, Sat 9–12 🚌 From Novigrad and Poreč

Above *Boat trips for Limski Kanal depart from the jetty at Vrsar*

VODNJAN (DIGNANO)

www.istria-vodnjan.com

Until the mid-19th century Vodnjan was the largest settlement in southern Istria; these days it is a sleepy provincial town 10km (6 miles) north of Pula. There is still a significant Italian community, some of whom speak the Istriot dialect, which survives only here and in Rovinj.

The main square, Narodni Trg, is lined with Gothic and Renaissance palaces, including the Venetian Gothic town hall with its balconies and arcades. From the square, a narrow lane leads to the church of Sveti Blaža (St. Blaise), the largest parish church in Istria, with a 63m (206ft) bell tower. Inside the church, the Sacred Art Collection (tel 052 511420; Jul–end Aug Mon–Sat 9–7, Sun 2–7; Sep–end Jun by appointment; adult 35kn, child 30kn) contains the remains of three mummified saints, whose desiccated but perfectly preserved bodies were brought here from Venice in 1818.

As far as is known, the bodies were not embalmed, and there is no scientific explanation for their preservation. One of the saints is Leon Bembo, a 12th-century Venetian noble and ambassador to Syria whose body has been attributed with miraculous healing powers. Also on display is a casket said to contain the tongue of St. Mary of Egypt, a sixth-century prostitute who converted to Christianity and lived a life of solitude in the desert for 47 years in repentence for her former life. The mummies are kept behind glass cases and the display is poorly lit, but it is worth a visit for its macabre fascination.

✚ 284 B5 ⓘ Narodni Trg 3 ☎ 052 511700 ◉ Mon–Sat 8.30–1.30 🚌 From Pula

VRSAR (ORSERA)

www.istria-vrsar.com

Vrsar is a busy tourist resort at the mouth of the Limski Kanal (▷ 121). From a distance it looks like a smaller version of Rovinj, with red-roofed houses crowned by a Venetian campanile; in fact, the bell tower on the parish church dates from as recently as 1991. Vrsar's much-restored 12th-century castle was the summer residence of the bishops of Poreč.

Since the 1960s Vrsar has been known as the naturist capital of Croatia, with thousands of nudists flocking to its campsites and beaches. The resort hosted the 1972 International Nudist Congress and ever since authorities have continued to develop facilities on Koversada Island, south of Vrsar. The largest nudist camp in Europe, Koversada campsite is able to accommodate around 5,000 unclothed holidaymakers. It would be interesting to know what the Venetian playboy Giacomo Casanova (1725–98), whose memoirs record numerous conquests in Orsera, would have made of it.

✚ 284 A4 ⓘ Rade Končara 46 ☎ 052 441746 ◉ Jun–end Sep Mon–Sat 8am–10pm, Sun 9–1, 6–9; Oct–end May Mon–Fri 8–2 🚌 From Poreč and Rovinj

DRIVE

HILL TOWNS OF ISTRIA

Take a day out from the coast to explore the Istrian interior, with its vineyards, olive groves, oak woods and medieval hilltop towns. This gentle circuit forms a figure-of-eight around Motovun, so it is easy to divide it into two shorter loops.

THE DRIVE

Distance: 112km (70 miles)
Allow: 2.5 hours
Start/end: Buzet ✚ 284 B4

★ Buzet (▷ 117), perched on a hill above the River Mirna, is still partly surrounded by its medieval walls. Most residents live in the modern district of Fontana.

Begin by the roundabout in Trg Fontana, at the foot of the old town. With Hotel Fontana to your right, follow the road out of town and turn right towards Buje. Stay on this wide road as it winds through the Mirna valley, bypassing the spa town of Istarske Toplice. After 12km (7.5 miles) you get your first glimpse of hilltop Motovun. Continue for another 4km (2.5 miles) to a crossroads. For the shorter drive, turn left here.

❶ The oak forests around the Mirna valley are where Istria's truffles are found. The village of Livade, 1km (0.5 miles) to the right, is home to the celebrated Zigante restaurant (▷ 143).

For the longer drive, turn right at the crossroads, pass through Livade and stay on this road as it climbs high above the valley, with dizzying views as you ascend to Oprtalj.

❷ Oprtalj (Portole), first mentioned in 1102, was built on the ruins of a prehistoric fort. This small town occupies a spectacular position, with extensive views over the vineyards from the terrace and the rampart walk. The chapels at either end of the town are decorated with frescoes, which are sadly in a poor state of repair. The 17th-century loggia contains a lapidarium of ancient sculpture, including a winged lion of St. Mark.

Drive through Oprtalj and continue for 1km (0.5 mile), then turn left in Sveta Lucija and follow this minor road all the way to Buje.

❸ Buje (▷ 117) is Istria's largest hill town, occupying a strategic position 5km (3 miles) from the Slovenian border on a former trade route from Pula to Trieste. Under Venetian rule, the town was known as 'the watchtower of Istria'.

On the outskirts of Buje, turn left and left again to arrive at a crossroads. Turn right here if you want to visit the town; otherwise turn left and continue on this road for 7km (4.5 miles) to Grožnjan.

④ Grožnjan (▷ 120) is a lovely hilltop town with cobbled streets. Once deserted, it now has a thriving cultural scene.

Leaving Grožnjan, continue for 5km (3 miles) on a dirt track that drops back down to the main road. At the end of the track, turn left and shortly afterwards turn left again to return to the Motovun crossroads. Now turn right across the bridge over the Mirna. The road climbs in a series of bends to reach the car park at the foot of Motovun.

⑤ Leave your car here and climb to Motovun (▷ 122), or pay a toll in summer to drive up the hill.

Stay on this road as it crosses typical Istrian countryside. At a roundabout keep straight on in the direction of Pazin. About 12km (7.5 miles) out of Motovun, you skirt a crest and see the village of Beram below, with the slopes of Mount Učka rising in the distance. Reaching a main road, turn left towards Pazin to arrive at Beram.

⑥ Beram is known for the macabre 15th-century frescoes in the chapel of the Virgin Mary on Škriline, 1km (0.5 miles) outside the village. These depict a Dance of the Dead, with skeletons, musicians and medieval court jesters.

The road now continues to Pazin (▷ 123). Keep straight ahead at a roundabout and turn left at a junction to drive through the town. Leaving Pazin, keep left, following signs to Buzet to emerge on a straight road with Mount Učka ahead of you. After 8km (5 miles) you reach Cerovlje. Turn left just before the railway tracks and turn left again, signposted Buzet and Draguć. The road climbs to Kovačići, where a magnificent vista opens up, across the vineyards to Draguć with central Istria spread out beneath you. After another 2km (1.2 miles) you reach Draguć.

Opposite *The fortified hill town of Buzet*
Right *An old cart track lined with trees*

⑦ Draguć (▷ 120) is an attractive village, dramatically perched on a cliff. Walk to the far end of the village to see the frescoes in the tiny chapel of St. Roch.

Stay on this road as it rises and falls through a succession of rural villages, with views of the Čićarija mountain ridge to the right and glimpses of Lake Butoniga to your left on the way back to Buzet.

WHERE TO EAT
BARBACAN
▷ 143.

ZIGANTE
▷ 143.

PLACE TO VISIT
The chapel at Beram is usually kept locked. To see the frescoes, contact the keyholders (tel 052 622088 or 052 622444).

THE GOLDEN CAPE AT ROVINJ

This short, easy walk explores Rovinj's Zlatni Rt forest park, where shady paths lead along the shore to rocky coves and pebble beaches. To make a day of it, take a picnic and swimsuit, or rent bicycles to explore the park in depth.

THE WALK
Distance: 3km (2 miles)
Allow: 1 hour
Start/end: Zlatni Rt forest park (Park Šume Zlatni Rt), Rovinj ✚ 284 A4

HOW TO GET THERE
From the centre of Rovinj, follow the seafront path past the Delfin jetty and marina and continue walking along the shore. The entrance to Zlatni Rt is found beyond Uvala Lone, a small cove at the back of Hotel Eden.

★ Zlatni Rt (Golden Cape) forest park was laid out by Baron Georg Huetterott (1852–1910) after he purchased the peninsula and the nearby islands in 1890. A successful industrialist from Trieste, he was knighted by the Austrian emperor Franz Josef I in 1898. He planted the cape with trees such as holm

oak, cedar, cypress and Aleppo pine, and created paths and walkways for his visitors to enjoy. Huetterott had ambitious plans for this area. In a booklet published in 1908, he sang the praises of the Istrian coastline, which he called the Costa del Sole (Sunny Coast) and outlined his vision of a spa resort to match Brijuni (▷ 118–119). He set up a company to build hotels and villas on Zlatni Rt, but his death in 1910 meant that the plans were never carried out. Since 1948, the cape has been owned by the state as a protected nature reserve.

Walk through the entrance gates and keep to the right on a path which follows the shore. In summer, this area is crowded with visitors sunbathing on the popular Lone beach. Reaching the end of a long, flat section, the path divides at a

point where you have a fine view of Rovinj straight ahead. The right fork leads to a small beach and jetty; instead, keep left to climb to the top of a hill.

❶ This is Zlatni Rt (Golden Cape), also known in Italian as Punta Montauro. The cliffs to your left, part of a former Venetian stone quarry, are used for free climbing.

Walk over the hill and back down towards the sea, with views of Crveni Otok (Red Island) through the trees. The landscape becomes greener, with stone pine, tamarisk and cypress trees around a pretty garden. At a junction of paths beside a summer café, turn right to keep to the coast.

❷ The path now rounds Punta Corrente, the Italian name for all of Zlatni Rt. Just across the water, Crveni Otok (Red Island) was the summer home of Georg Huetterott, where his guests included Habsburg princes and princesses and the Austrian archduke Franz Ferdinand. The castle which he built on the site of an old monastery is now part of the Hotel Istra. The restaurant at Punta Corrente is housed in the old stone stables, formerly used by Georg Huetterott for his horses while he visited the island.

Stay on the seaside path beyond Punta Corrente as it passes a series of rocky coves. The beaches here are much less crowded than those nearer Rovinj and they tend to attract nudists. Reaching a viewpoint with a bench beneath the trees looking out to Crveni Otok, the path divides once again, with the right fork continuing along the shore to Škaraba Bay. Turn left here to leave the sea behind and follow the path uphill to reach a large meadow. Walk around the meadow, turn right at a junction of paths, then right again on a wide track through the forest to return to the entrance of the park.

❸ Shortly before leaving the park, you pass a small pink-painted cottage on your right. This is the Huetterott memorial room, opened in 2003 in the old forest ranger's house, containing memorabilia relating to Georg Huetterott.

From the entrance gates, it is an easy walk back to Rovinj.

WHERE TO EAT
The restaurant at Punta Corrente is open in summer. Alternatively, buy provisions from the market in Rovinj and make a picnic.

PLACE TO VISIT
HUETTEROTT MEMORIAL ROOM
🕐 Jun–end Sep daily 9–7 🖐 Free

IN MORE DEPTH
If you want to ride rather than walk, you can rent bicycles from Centractour (tel 052 813266) at the Delfin jetty and cycle into the forest park from there.

Opposite *Boats moored at Rovinj*
Below *Zlatni Rt forest park*

BRIJUNI
BRIJUNI GOLF
www.brijuni.hr

Play golf in beautiful surroundings on this unique island course, with deer strolling about the fairways and putting greens dusted with sand. Built in 1922, this was for many years the only golf course in Croatia and was at one stage exclusively reserved for Tito and his guests. It has been expanded to 18 holes. Make reservations through the national park office in Fažana and take the boat transfer to Brijuni.

✉ Veli Brijun ☎ 052 525888 🕐 All year 🖐 200kn, boat transfer 15kn 🚌 21 from Pula to Fažana 🚤 From Fažana

ULYSSES THEATRE
www.ulysses.hr

This Zagreb-based theatre company puts on performances of Shakespeare and other classics, as well as contemporary drama, at the old Austrian fort on Mali Brijun in July and August. Tickets are available in advance from the national park office in Fažana, or from 4pm until the departure of the boat.

✉ Mali Brijun ☎ 052 525581 🖐 150kn 🚤 From Fažana

BUJE
ZIGANTE TARTUFI
www.zigantetartufi.com

The Zigante Tartufi truffle shops were opened by local farmer Giancarlo Zigante after he earned a place in the *Guinness Book of World Records* by finding the world's biggest ever white truffle, weighing a massive 1.31kg (2.8lb), near Buje in 1999. During the autumn harvest from October to December, fresh white truffles can sell for over €3,000 per kg but more affordable products include minced black truffles and *tartufata* (truffle paste). Other Zigante Tartufi shops are in Buzet (▷ below), Grožnjan, Livade, Motovun and Pula.

✉ Trg J.B. Tita 12, Buje ☎ 052 772125 🕐 Daily 9–9 (to 8 in winter)

BUZET
ZIGANTE TARTUFI
www.zigantetartufi.com

The hill town of Buzet is known as the city of truffles, and this shop, part of a small chain (▷ above), sells the full range of products, together with a selection of Istrian wines, spirits and olive oil.

✉ Trg Fontana, Buzet ☎ 052 663340 🕐 Daily 9–9 (to 8 in winter)

GROŽNJAN
GALERIJA JEDAN PLUS
One of many galleries in this hilltop village, Mirjana Rajkovic is a potter specializing in hand-formed fruit, decorated with a variety of pretty coloured glazes.

✉ Vicenta iz Kastva 3 ☎ 052 776354 🕐 Jul–Aug daily 10–9; May–Jul, Sep to mid-Oct 10–1, 4–8. Call for winter opening times

MOTOVUN
ACTIVA TRAVEL
www.activa-istra.com

This company can organize truffle-hunting expeditions in the woods around Motovun between October and December for up to four people, with a guide and dogs. The price includes a farmhouse dinner.

✉ Scalierova 1, Pula ☎ 052 215497 🕐 Oct–Dec 🖐 From €50 per person

EVA
This small shop on the way up to the town gate sells local food and drink, including bottles of *biska* (mistletoe brandy) and *medenica* (honey brandy) in gift boxes.

✉ Prolaz Veli Jože 4, Motovun ☎ 052 681915 🕐 Mon–Sat 8–8, Sun 8–12

NOVIGRAD

VITRIOL

This trendy terrace bar is the best place to watch the sun go down over the sea, with a cool beer or a glass of the house cocktail.

✉ Ribarnička 6, Novigrad ☎ 052 758270
🕐 Daily 8am–midnight

POREČ

PER BACCO

This delicatessen has an extensive selection of Istrian wines, spirits, liqueurs, olive oil, truffles, honey and preserves, all tastefully displayed and reasonably priced.

✉ Trg Slobode 10, Poreč ☎ 052 451600
🕐 Mon–Fri 8–7, Sat 9–6, Sun 10–2

JAMA BAREDINE

www.baredine.com

Children and adults can explore the Baredine Cave on a 40-minute tour, seeing stalactites, stalagmites and subterranean chambers. Older children can try their hand at rope climbing or join a five-hour Speleo Adventure tour with a caving guide.

✉ Nova Vas, Poreč ☎ 052 421333
🕐 Jul, Aug daily 9.30–6; May, Jun, Sep, daily 10–5, Apr and Oct daily 10–4 👣 Adult 50kn, child 30kn 🚗 7km (4.5 miles) from Poreč on the road to Višnjan

RONILAČKI CENTAR PLAVA LAGUNA

www.plava-laguna-diving.hr

This diving centre can offer everything from shore diving and night diving from a wooden boat to longer trips to explore underwater caves and the wreck of the British Royal Navy warship *Coriolanus*, which sank near Poreč in 1945.

✉ Plava Laguna, Poreč ☎ 098 367619
🕐 Apr–end Oct 🚗 3km (2 miles) south of Poreč

TORRE ROTONDA

This 15th-century Venetian round tower houses a pleasant summer café, with a rooftop terrace that is an enjoyable place for a sunset drink.

✉ Narodni Trg, Poreč ☎ 098 255731
🕐 Apr–end Oct daily 10am–1am

VINOTEKA ARMAN

New-wave Istrian winemaker Marijan Arman has opened a shop in Poreč to showcase his award-winning Malvazija, Teran, Chardonnay and Cabernet Sauvignon.

✉ Ulica Marta 8, Poreč ☎ 052 446229
🕐 Mon–Sat 10–5

PULA

AQUARIUM PULA

www.aquarium.hr

Housed in an old Austro-Hungarian fort on Punta Verudela, a wooded peninsula surrounded by shingle beaches and hotels, Pula's aquarium makes an enjoyable day out with children. The ground floor is devoted to Adriatic marine life, the first floor has old fishing tools and underwater photography, while a tunnel leads to the moat, now containing fish from Croatia's rivers and lakes. The aquarium can also organize three-hour fishing expeditions.

✉ Fort Verudela, Pula ☎ 052 381402
🕐 From 9 or 10am daily. Closing times vary. 👣 Adult 40kn, child (7–18) 30kn, child (3–7) 20kn 🍴 🚌 🚗 2A, 3A from Pula

CVAJNER CAFFE

Soak up the atmosphere at the best people-watching spot in Pula, with outdoor tables on the old Roman forum. Be sure to go inside, though, to see the modern art and the frescoes uncovered during the restoration.

✉ Forum 2, Pula ☎ 052 216502
🕐 Daily 8am–midnight

MMC LUKA

www.mmcluka.hr

This multimedia outlet near the Roman arena is an art gallery, internet café and trendy bar in one. It hosts exhibitions of contemporary art and acts as an unofficial meeting place during the annual film festival.

✉ Istarska 30, Pula ☎ 052 224316
🕐 Mon–Fri 8am–midnight, Sat 8–3

ULIKS

The bar beside the Roman Arch of Sergi has become a shrine to Irish author James Joyce (1882–1941), who taught at the Berlitz school

on this site in 1904–05. A bronze sculpture of Joyce sits outside. The terrace tables are snapped up quickly, so go inside to enjoy the dark wood, marble counters, stained glass and cabinet of Joyce memorabilia. You can pick up a leaflet about Joyce's Pula links at the entrance.

✉ Trg Portarata 1, Pula ☎ 052 219158
🕐 Daily 6.30am–2am

WINDSURFING CENTAR PREMANTURA

www.windsurfing.hr

The best windsurfing in Istria is at Premantura, at the far southern tip of the peninsula beside Cape Kamenjak nature reserve. Spring and autumn are the best times for experienced surfers, while the calm winds of July and August are ideal for beginners. This friendly centre offers multilingual courses for adults and children, and rents out equipment.

✉ Premantura, Pula ☎ 091 512 3646
🕐 Apr–end Oct 🚌 26 from Pula 🚗 At Stupice campsite, 12km (7.5 miles) south of Pula

ROVINJ

AQUARIUM

Rovinj's aquarium is housed in a 19th-century building officially known as the Ruđer Bošković Institute Centre for Marine Research. Its old-fashioned approach appeals to small children, who can enjoy staring at tanks of starfish, scorpion fish, lobsters and other marine life.

✉ Obala Giordano Paliage 5, Rovinj
☎ 052 804712 🕐 Apr–end Oct daily 9–9 👣 Adult 20kn, child 10kn

BACCUS

Baccus doubles as a wine shop and wine bar with outdoor seating and harbour views. It sells a good range of Istrian wine, spirits, truffles and olive oils of consistently high quality.

✉ Via Carera 5, Rovinj ☎ 052 812154
🕐 Summer daily 8am–1am, winter daily 8am–10pm

DIVING CENTAR PETRA

www.divingpetra.hr

This diving outlet is open all year and offers courses for beginners.

✉ Ulica Svetog Križa 28, Rovinj ☎ 052 830683 🕐 Apr–end Oct daily 6pm–3am

ZELENA TRŽNICA (GREEN MARKET)

The open-air market in Rovinj is particularly attractive, with fresh produce laid out on stalls behind the harbour square. Farmers sell home-made wine, liqueurs and herb brandy, together with peppers and dried figs. You could make up a picnic here out of bread, tomatoes and local cheese. The nearby fish market sells freshly caught fish and seafood.

✉ Trg Valdibora, Rovinj 🕐 Daily 7–2

ZLATNI RT

You can rent bicycles to explore Zlatni Rt forest park (▷ 131–132) from this agency at the Delfin jetty. In summer, you can rent bicycles from stalls by the harbour and at the entrance to the park.

✉ Centractour, Ulica Vladimira Nazora, Rovinj ☎ 052 813266 🕐 All year ✋ 20kn per hour, 50kn per half day, 80kn per day

UMAG

ATP CROATIA OPEN

www.croatiaopen.hr

The leading professional men's tennis tournament in Croatia is held in Umag at the end of July.

✉ International Tennis Centre, Umag ☎ 052 741704 🕐 Late July

ISTRIAN FAIRS

There is a tradition of rural fairs in the towns of inland Istria. Originally livestock markets, today they attract a mixed crowd of locals and foreigners with food stalls, folk dancing and craft displays, and offer visitors the chance to experience true Istrian atmosphere. Markets take place once a month in the following towns on the days listed:

Vodnjan—first Saturday
Pazin—first Tuesday
Žminj—every other Wednesday
Motovun—third Monday
Buzet—third Thursday
Višnjan—last Thursday

For more experienced divers, it can organize dives to the *Baron Gautsch*, an Austrian navy steamship which sank after hitting a mine in 1914. It is known as the Titanic of the Adriatic.

✉ Matije Vlačića 22, Rovinj ☎ 052 812880 🕐 All year

DULCIS

Head to this delicatessen on Rovinj's main shopping thoroughfare for a lip-smacking array of olive oils, truffles, honey, Hvar biscuits and local wines, as well as Istrian grappa, chocolate and local pottery.

✉ Carera 45, Rovinj ☎ 052 813419 🕐 Summer 8am–10.30pm; winter 7.30am–8pm

HAVANA

Tap your feet to the Latino music beneath huge bamboo shades at this summer bar just a short walk from the harbour.

✉ Obala Alda Rismonda, Rovinj ☎ 052 813206 🕐 Apr to mid-Oct daily 10am–1am

LIMSKI KANAL

Boatmen by the harbour and Delfin jetty advertise cruises through the Lim Fjord (▷ 121) in summer, including trips on a mock 'pirate ship' with alcohol and soft drinks. The full-day excursions include a barbecue fish picnic or lunch at one of the restaurants in the fjord.

🕐 Apr–end Oct ✋ Adult 100kn, child 50kn

MINI CROATIA

This theme park has scaled-down models of Croatia's most famous monuments, buildings and landscapes.

✉ Milana Macana 5, Rovinj ☎ 091 206 8885 🕐 Jun–end Aug 9–8; Apr, May, Sep, Oct 10–6 ✋ Adult 25kn, child 10kn 🚗 Just outside Rovinj on the road to Pazin

LA PUNTULINA

This chic restaurant (▷ 143) is also a wine bar with the best sunset views in town, from terraces above the bathing rocks on the cliffs beneath the church.

✉ Ulica Svetog Križa 38, Rovinj ☎ 052 813186 🕐 Apr–end Oct daily 6pm–2am

VALENTINO

This cool cocktail bar is great for an evening drink, sitting on silk cushions on the rocks by candlelight, with your feet almost dangling in the water as you watch the sun go down.

FESTIVALS AND EVENTS

MAY

Z ARMONIK U ROČ (ROČ ACCORDION FESTIVAL)

The medieval village of Roč, near Hum, hosts traditional musicians who play the *triestina* (Istrian accordion) at an open-air stage on the square.
✉ Roč ☎ 052 662343 ⏰ Second weekend in May

JUNE–SEPTEMBER

GROŽNJAN MUSICAL SUMMER

www.hgm.hr
The beautiful hill town of Grožnjan comes alive each summer with the international summer school of Jeunesses Musicales Croatia. This stages workshops and concerts of chamber music, jazz and brass and recitals on harp, piano and violin in venues around the town.
✉ Grožnjan ☎ 01 611 1604 ⏰ Jun–end Sep

JULY

PULA FILM FESTIVAL

www.pulafilmfestival.hr
Not quite what it once was, the Pula Film Festival is still a prestigious event, with nightly film shows in the Roman arena and directors competing for the Golden Arena award.
✉ Pula ☎ 052 393321 ⏰ Mid- to late Jul

MOTOVUN FILM FESTIVAL

www.motovunfilmfestival.com
One of the liveliest events in the Croatian cultural calendar, this features more than 80 independent films from Croatia and abroad, with open-air screenings on the town's main square.
✉ Motovun ☎ 01 374 0708 ⏰ Late Jul

JULY AND AUGUST

HISTRIA FESTIVAL

www.histriafestival.com
Opera, ballet and music are performed in the spectacular setting of the Roman arena. Past performers at the festival have included Sting, José Carreras, Luciano Pavarotti and the Bolshoi Ballet.
✉ Kandlerova 14, Pula ☎ 052 522722 ⏰ Jul, Aug

NOVIGRAD CULTURAL SUMMER

www.laguna-novigrad.hr
Two months of outdoor concerts and events, including folk singers and classical music in the parish church, culminating with the festivities of town patron St. Pelagius over the final weekend in August
✉ Novigrad ☎ 052 758011 ⏰ Jul, Aug

KONCERTI U EUFRAZIJANI

www.concertsinbazilika.com
Classical, chamber music, choral and orchestral concerts are held in the lovely setting of the Basilica of Euphrasius in Poreč. The same organization puts on jazz concerts in the courtyard of the Regional Museum on Wednesday evenings throughout July and August.
✉ Poreč ☎ 052 887218 ⏰ Fri evenings in Jul and Aug

JULY–SEPTEMBER

ROVINJ SUMMER FESTIVAL

www.tzgrovinj.hr
Concerts of early music, piano recitals and string quartets take place in St. Euphemia's church and the cloisters of the Franciscan monastery in Rovinj.
✉ Rovinj ☎ 052 811566 ⏰ Mid-Jul to early Sep

AUGUST

TRKA NA PRSTENAC (TILTING AT THE RING)

This traditional festival in Barban, dating back to the 17th century, was revived in 1976. It features horsemen in medieval costume attempting to spear a metal ring with a lance while riding at full gallop.
✉ Barban ☎ 052 372113 ⏰ Mid-Aug

SEPTEMBER

SUBOTINA

On the evening of the second Saturday in September, a giant truffle omelette, cooked using 10kg (22lb) of truffles and more than 2,000 eggs, is served up on the main square in Buzet, forming the centrepiece of a weekend of festivities. Other activities include folk dancing and craft fairs.
✉ Buzet ☎ 052 662343 ⏰ Second weekend in Sep

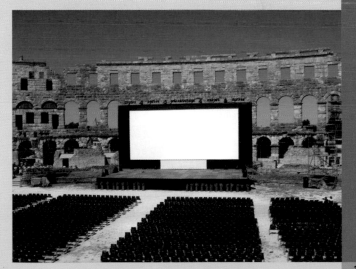

Right *In July, Pula's Roman arena is transformed into an open-air cinema for the city's annual film festival*

EATING

PRICES AND SYMBOLS

The restaurants are listed alphabetically. The prices given are the average for a two-course lunch (L) and a three-course dinner (D) for one person, without drinks. The wine price is for a litre of table wine followed by the least expensive bottle of quality wine. All the restaurants listed accept credit cards unless otherwise stated.

For a key to the symbols, ▷ 2.

BUJE
POD VOLTOM

This old-fashioned *konoba* is in a narrow alley off the main street. It serves classic Istrian fare such as sheep's cheese, pasta with truffles, scampi *na buzaru* (flash fried with tomatoes, onions, herbs and wine) and grilled fish. On warm days, dine on a terrace.

✉ Ulica Ante Babića, Buje ☎ 052 772232 🕐 Daily 10am–11pm 🍴 L 80kn, D 100kn, Wine 50/100kn

BUZET
STARA OŠTARIJA

The village inn was reopened in 2005 as a classy restaurant offering Istrian specialities such as *maneštra* (vegetable soup), *frittata* (truffle omelette) and steak with truffles. The stone-walled dining room juts out over the cliffs with views over the town below. Bread is served with olive oil from Oprtalj, and the wine list has Istrian wines.

✉ Ulica Petra Flega 5, Buzet ☎ 052 694003 🕐 Daily 12–8 🍴 L 100kn, D 150kn, Wine 60/90kn

TOKLARIJA

Set in a beautifully converted 14th-century olive mill in the village of Sovinjsko Polje, Toklarija has become a pilgrimage for food lovers from Italy, Slovenia and Zagreb. The eight-course tasting menu might include grilled vegetables, *maneštra* (vegetable soup), cured ham, ravioli, grilled beef and chocolate truffles. Reservations are essential.

✉ Sovinjsko Polje, Buzet ☎ 052 663031 🕐 Wed–Mon 1–10 🍴 Five-courses 370kn, eight-courses 550kn, Wine 70/90kn 🚗 Take the road from Buzet to Motovun and turn left through the village of Sovinjak to reach Sovinjsko Polje

GRAČIŠĆE
KONOBA MARINO

This traditional *konoba* inside the town gate has a summer terrace and serves delicious inexpensive Istrian cuisine, such as home-made sausages, *fuži* (pasta) with game and *maneštra* (vegetable soup). If you just want a snack, try a sandwich filled with sheep's cheese or Istrian ham. Wine is Malvazija and Teran from the local vineyards.

✉ Gračišće 75 ☎ 052 687081 🕐 Jul–Aug Thu–Tue 2–11; Sep–Jun Thu–Tue 2–10, Sun 2–11 🍴 L 50kn, D 70kn, Wine 60/90kn

GROŽNJAN
ENOTEKA ZIGANTE

www.zigantetartufi.com

In summer, this wine bar belonging to the Zigante Tartufi truffle empire (▷ 138) has tables under the Venetian loggia, where you can sip local Malvazija while feasting on Istrian ham, cheese and truffle-based canapés. On cooler days, sit inside the old stone house.

✉ Ulica Gorjana 5, Grožnjan ☎ 052 721998 🕐 Summer daily 10am–11pm, winter daily 10–8 🍴 Snacks from 20kn

HUM
HUMSKA KONOBA

A traditional stone cottage at the entrance to Hum hides this rustic *konoba*, offering simple dishes of ham, sheep's cheese and *fuži* (pasta) with truffles, served on wooden trays. The *maneštra* (vegetable soup) here is a meal itself, with sweetcorn and sausage. Start with a glass of home-made *biska* (mistletoe brandy), or try

Opposite Enoteka Zigante in Grožnjan, where you can enjoy local truffles

a jug of *supa*, warm red wine with olive oil, pepper and toast.
✉ Hum 2 ☎ 052 660005 🕐 Jun–end Oct daily 11–10; Nov–end May Sat–Sun 11–10 ✋ L 60kn, D 80kn, Wine 60/90kn

LIMSKI KANAL
FJORD

This is one of two popular restaurants beside the jetty where the tour boats stop after their journey along the Limski Kanal. It serves fresh oysters and mussels from the fjord. Other good options are seafood risotto and plain grilled fish.
✉ Sveti Lovreč ☎ 052 448222 🕐 Mar–end Dec daily 11–10 ✋ L 70kn, D 100kn, Wine 60/100kn

LIVADE
ZIGANTE

www.zigantetartufi.com

The flagship restaurant of truffle king Giancarlo Zigante offers a range of seasonal truffle-tasting menus. Dishes vary but might include octopus carpaccio with black truffles, *fuži* (pasta) with white truffles, and pancakes with white chocolate and truffle mousse. It is expensive, but worth it for an authentic Istrian treat.
✉ Livade 7 ☎ 052 664302 🕐 Daily 12–11 in summer; 11–10 in winter ✋ L 200kn, D 250kn, tasting menus 380–500kn, Wine from 120kn 🚗 Take the Buzet to Motovun road and turn right at the Motovun crossroads to reach Livade

MOTOVUN
BARBACAN

Art and food come together at this funky bistro, which serves inventive Istrian truffle dishes in a laid-back environment. Dishes include bruschetta with black truffles, saffron and truffle risotto, and polenta with truffles and sheep's cheese. It is just outside the outer town gate, in an old stone house with a summer terrace.
✉ Ulica Barbacan 1, Motovun ☎ 052 681791 🕐 Mid-Mar to end Nov Mon 12.30–3.30, Wed–Sun 12.30–3.30, 6.30–10.30 ✋ L 150kn, D 200kn, Wine from 70kn

POD VOLTOM

This brick-vaulted cellar beneath the arches leading up to Motovun's main square serves hearty dishes of Istrian home cooking, many using fresh truffles in season. Signature dishes include turkey escalope and veal medallions with truffles, as well as pasta and omelettes.
✉ Trg Josefa Ressela 6, Motovun ☎ 052 681923 🕐 Daily 12–11 ✋ L 100kn, D 120kn, Wine 60/90kn

NOVIGRAD
DAMIR I ORNELA

The trendiest spot in town is a stone cottage in one of the back streets. Owner-chef Damir Deletić is a Japanese-trained sashimi master, who offers fresh takes on Istrian seafood such as scampi marinated in salt, pepper and olive oil. It seats just 28 diners, so reservations are essential in summer.
✉ Ulica Zidine 5, Novigrad ☎ 052 758134 🕐 Tue–Sun 12–3.30, 6.30–11. Closed 2 weeks Oct ✋ L 100kn, D 120kn, Wine 70/110kn

PULA
VALSABBION

www.valsabbion.hr

Set in a bay on the outskirts of Pula, Valsabbion has been consistently voted one of the country's best restaurants. The emphasis is on simply prepared, seasonal ingredients such as truffles, asparagus, wild mushrooms and seafood. If you want to sample everything, choose from the six-course 'sea' or 'forest' menus or a tasting menu of 10 courses.
✉ Pješčana Uvala, Pula ☎ 052 218033 🕐 Daily 12–12. Closed Jan ✋ L 300kn, D 350kn, tasting menus 355–435kn, Wine from 135kn 🚗 Take the ring road around Pula and continue south, then turn left, following signs to Pješčana Uvala

VELA NERA

www.velanera.hr

This seafood restaurant overlooking the marina has a lovely boardwalk summer terrace. Specialities include salmon carpaccio in whisky and herbs and risotto Vela Nera, made with scampi, peaches and sparkling

wine. Take your pick from the great wine list.
✉ Marina Veruda, Pješčana Uvala, Pula ☎ 052 219209 🕐 Daily 8am–midnight ✋ L 150kn, D 200kn, Wine from 90kn 🚗 Take the ring road around Pula and continue south, then turn left, following the signs to Pješčana Uvala

ROVINJ
AL GASTALDO

With candles on the tables and wine bottles lining the walls, this trattoria is a cosy, intimate place; it is one of the few restaurants in Rovinj to stay open all year. It serves Italian fare such as grilled vegetables, carpaccio of beef, ravioli with spinach, sole with almonds and veal cutlet Milanese.
✉ Ulica Iza Kasarne 14, Rovinj ☎ 052 814109 🕐 Daily 11–3, 6–11 ✋ L 150kn, D 200kn, Wine 80/90kn

LA PUNTULINA

Perched at the tip of the old town, above the popular bathing rocks, La Puntulina is both a wine bar and a chic restaurant. Get here early to grab a table on the balcony to watch the sun set over the sea. The food combines Italian and Istrian influences, with an emphasis on seafood and fresh fish. There is also a four-course tasting menu, each course accompanied by a different Istrian wine.
✉ Ulica Svetog Križa 38, Rovinj ☎ 052 813186 🕐 Apr–end Oct daily 12–3, 6–11 ✋ L 200kn, D 250kn, tasting menu 350kn, Wine from 100kn

VELI JOŽE

With communal wooden benches and shelves cluttered with farm tools and antiques, this waterfront *konoba* is rustic in appearance in contrast to its neighbours. First-class Istrian ingredients create simple classics like *fuži* (pasta) with goulash, grilled vegetables, roast lamb with potatoes and steak with truffles. There are a few outdoor tables by the harbour, but these get snapped up quickly, so be prepared to wait or share.
✉ Ulica Svetog Križa 1, Rovinj ☎ 052 816337 🕐 Daily 11am–midnight. Closed Jan ✋ L 100kn, D 200kn, Wine 70/140kn

PRICES AND SYMBOLS

Prices are the lowest for a double room for one night. Breakfast is included unless noted otherwise. All the hotels listed accept credit cards unless otherwise stated. Note that rates vary widely throughout the year.

For a key to the symbols, ▷ 2.

BRIJUNI
NEPTUN-ISTRA

www.brijuni.hr

This quayside hotel on Veli Brijun offers the chance to remain in Brijuni National Park after the day-trippers have left, and enjoy golf, tennis, cycling and horseback-riding. Car parking and boat transfers are included in the price. The park also rents out seaside villas.

✉ Veli Brijun ☎ 052 525807 ⊙ Closed Jan ♨ From €101 ① 87 ⊟ National park boat from Fažana

BRTONIGLA
SAN ROCCO

www.san-rocco.hr

This small, family-run hotel in an old stone townhouse was voted best small hotel in Croatia in 2007 and 2008. The poolside terrace overlooks a garden of olive trees with distant sea views. The excellent restaurant specializes in fresh Istrian produce such as ham, cheese, seafood and truffle dishes, accompanied by local wines. Sauna, massage and bicycle rental are available.

✉ Srednja Ulica 2, Brtonigla ☎ 052 725000 ♨ From €119 ① 12 ⊙ ⊠ Outdoor ⊟ On the road from Buje to Novigrad

BUZET
FONTANA

On the square near steps leading up to the walled town, the Fontana offers plain, comfortable rooms. It is a good base for a night in inland Istria, with views of the old town and a chance to stock up on local delicacies from Zigante Tartufi (▷ 138) nearby.

✉ Trg Fontana 1, Buzet ☎ 052 662615 ♨ €60 ① 57

LABIN
PALAČA LAZZARINI-BATTIALA

www.sv-martin.com

The pink-painted baroque palace of the last Baron Labin, reached via a stone gateway and an avenue of chestnut trees, is now six apartments with kitchens, for two to five people. There is a restaurant in the palace walls, and a wine cellar and *konoba*. The palace is on a hillside, with large gardens.

✉ Sveti Martin, Nedešćina ☎ 052 856006 ♨ €45 ① 6 ⊟ Take the main road from

Opposite *Villa Angelo d'Oro, occupying a 17th-century palace in Rovinj's old town*

Labin to Rijeka and turn left at Vinež to reach Sveti Martin

MOTOVUN

KAŠTEL

www.hotel-kastel-motovun.hr

This stylish hotel on the main square is set in a Renaissance manor house. Its rooms, gardens and terraces offer tranquil views. The restaurant serves classic Istrian truffle dishes.

✉ Trg Andrea Antico 7, Motovun ☎ 052 681607 🖐 From 582kn 🛈 28

NOVIGRAD

VILLA CITTAR

www.cittar.hr

This family-run hotel beside the walls and near the marina was one of the first private hotels in Croatia. Rooms are spacious and tastefully decorated, and the airy breakfast room is a treat. There are tennis courts, and the marina and beach are a walk away.

✉ Prolaz Venecija 1, Novigrad ☎ 052 758780 🖐 €80 🛈 12 ⬡

POREČ

FILIPINI

www.istra.com/filipini

This small hotel in the woods, surrounded by olive groves and vineyards, has tennis courts and bicycles and makes a good base for an active holiday.

✉ Filipini, Poreč ☎ 052 463200 🖐 From €60 🛈 8 🚗 5km (3 miles) outside Poreč on the road to Pazin

PULA

HOTEL GALIJA

www.hotelgalija.hr

Basic, clean rooms and a convenient location just a short walk from the main sights make this a sound, no-frills option. Spartanly furnished rooms are air-conditioned and have satellite TV and modern bathrooms. It may not quite live up to its three-star rating but it is comfortable enough for a few nights.

✉ Epulonova 3, Porec ☎ 052 383802 🖐 600kn 🛈 21

HOTEL VALSABBION

www.valsabbion.net

Exclusive but not a wallet breaker, family-run but smart and clean-cut, this lovely hotel 6km (4 miles) south of Pula is the haunt of celebrities and those in the know. Rooms are stylishly hip and the superb hotel restaurant is regarded as one of the finest in the country.

✉ Pješčana Uvala 1X/26, Pula ☎ 052 218033 🖐 870kn 🛈 10 🏊 Indoor

SCALETTA

www.hotel-scaletta.com

With warm tones, soft furnishings and a bright, playful feel, this small hotel near the Roman arena is the nicest place to stay in central Pula. Rooms are decorated in yellow, with soft, angled lights, and the bathrooms have bright touches. The marine theme continues in the breakfast room, decorated in blue and yellow, where guests enjoy a good breakfast spread.

✉ Flavijevska 26, Pula ☎ 052 541599 🖐 718kn 🛈 12 ⬡

ROVINJ

HOTEL ADRIATIC

www.maistra.hr

Rovinj's most visible hotel is a good central option, so if you like to stay close to the hustle and bustle, this is the place for you. Rooms can be on the small side, but the amazing harbour views more than compensate for this. Be sure to request a room with a view as not all face the harbour.

✉ P. Budicin bb, Rovinj ☎ 052 815088 🖐 900kn 🛈 27 ⬡

VILA LILI

www.hotel-vilalili.hr

A family-run modern villa to the south of town, this hotel is popular with its guests. Rooms have everything you need for a comfortable stay (including air-conditioning) and the welcome is always friendly. Some guests complain that the mansard rooms are cramped and too hot in summer.

✉ A. Mohorovičića 16, Rovinj ☎ 052 840940 ⬡ 900kn 🖐 20 ⬡

VILLA ANGELO D'ORO

www.rovinj.at

This charming hotel, set in a 17th-century bishop's palace in Rovinj's pedestrian-only old town, is tastefully decorated with antique furniture and oil paintings. In summer, breakfast is served in a fountain garden. From the rooftop loggia there are views over the old town and out to sea. Facilities include a sauna, jacuzzi, and a private boat and yacht for rent. There is no vehicle access.

✉ Via Svalba 38-42, Rovinj ☎ 052 840502 ⬡ Closed Jan, Feb 🖐 From €106 🛈 24 ⬡

VODNJAN

STANCIJA NEGRIČANI

www.stancijanegricani.com

This rural hotel is a fine example of agrotourism, with rooms in an old stone farmhouse and excellent meals made from organic local produce. Bicycles are available and horse-riding can be arranged. The sea is just a short drive away.

✉ Stancija Negričani, Marčana ☎ 052 391084 🖐 €116–€132; breakfast 60kn per person 🛈 9 ⬡ 🏊 Outdoor 🚗 6km (4 miles) outside Vodnjan on road to Barban

Below *Many hotels offer rooms with fine sea views*

KVARNER

Basking in warm summer sun and battered by winter's raging *bora* wind, the landscapes of the Kvarner region are diverse, with mountain ranges, enticing Adriatic beaches and, in Kvarner Bay, the large islands of Krk, Cres and Rab. Elegant Opatija was once the resort of choice for the Austro-Hungarian well-to-do, but today the port of Rijeka, Croatia's third city, is the region's pulsating hub.

It could be said that the Habsburg era created modern mainland Kvarner; after the Treaty of Vienna handed the region to the Austrian Empire in 1815, Rijeka became a vital access point to the sea, a role it retains today as Croatia's biggest port. In contrast, Opatija, just up the road, became the stomping ground of the Empire's rich and famous, attracting a guest list that reads like a *Who's Who* of the age.

Away from bustling ports and elegant 19th-century guest houses, the Gorski Kotar, Učka and Velebit mountains provide ample opportunity to pull on hiking boots and experience Croatia's wild side. The northern Velebit mountains, an area declared a national park in 1999, form part of a wall of limestone that rises almost sheer from the sea.

Kvarner's main attractions, however, are the islands lying just offshore. These provide some of the best beach fun, prettiest medieval towns and most relaxing woodland. Croatia's largest island, Krk is closest to the mainland, separated from it by less than a kilometre (0.5 mile) of sea and connected to it with a bridge. Elongated and mountainous Cres comes a near second in size. Smaller Rab is a popular holiday destination with beautiful coves and beaches as well as a delightful Venetian-era capital. All the islands are easily reachable from the mainland, though poor connections between the islands make island-hopping difficult.

CRES

The second-largest Adriatic island combines wild beauty with a historic town. It is the largest of the Apsyrtides, a group of islands named after the mythical Greek hero Apsyrtus, killed by his sister Medea. According to legend, his body was chopped in pieces and thrown into the sea, and thus the islands were born. Cres is a long, narrow, mountainous island, 65km (40 miles) in length with a deep lake in the middle. A single main road follows a ridge across the island from Porozina to Osor.

THE NORTH

The northern part of the island is known as Tramuntana, whose main settlement is the ancient hill town of Beli. Here you will find the Caput Insulae eco-centre (▷ 164), with its griffon vulture reserve and waymarked walks (self-guided trails). South of Beli, Cres Town is the diminutive island capital, set in a sheltered bay. A 16th-century Venetian loggia stands guard over the harbour square, where an arch beneath the clock tower leads to the church of Sveta Marije Snježne (St. Mary of the Snows).

MUSEUM TOWN

Osor sits at the southern end of the island, where Cres is divided from Lošinj by a narrow canal, built by the Romans. Once a prosperous cathedral city with a population of 5,000, it is now a museum piece, with churches, monasteries and palaces scattered throughout the tiny village. The main square is on the site of the old Roman forum. The Archaeological Museum (Mon–Fri 10–12, also 7–9pm in summer), in the former town hall, has a scale model of Osor plus Roman finds.

INFORMATION

www.tzg-cres.hr

✚ 284 B5 🛈 Cons 10, Cres Town
☎ 051 571535 🕐 Jun–end Sep daily 8–8; Oct–end May Mon–Fri 8–1 🚌 From Rijeka 🚢 Car ferry from Brestova to Porozina and Valbiska (Krk) to Merag; catamaran from Rijeka to Cres

TIP

» Take a taxi boat across from Cres to Valun, whose church has the Valun Stone, an 11th-century tablet in Glagolitic and Latin recalling three generations of a family. A minor road from Valun climbs to Lubenice, a village of stone houses on a clifftop, with paths to a remote beach.

Above *The ancient hill town of Beli, in northern Cres*
Opposite *Visitors relax on one of the island's beaches*

149

INFORMATION

www.krk.hr

⊞ 284 C4 ℹ Vela Placa 1, Krk Town
☎ 051 221414 ⊕ Apr–May Mon–Fri
8–3, Sat 8–1, Sun 8–12; Jun–end Sep
daily 9–8 🚌 From Rijeka ⛴ Merag
(Cres) to Valbiska; also Lopar (Rab) to
Baška in summer

TIPS

» To explore the island in more detail,
follow the drive, ▷ 158–159.
» Baška, on the south coast, has a long
sand and pebble beach with shallow
water, which is perfect for children. The
nearby village of Jurandvor contains a
copy of the Baška Stone (▷ 158).

Above *Tour boats moored at Krk Town,
ready to do business*

KRK

There is intense rivalry between Cres and Krk for the title of Croatia's largest
island, though most experts agree that Krk just has the edge. What is not in
dispute is that Krk is the most populated and also the most accessible of the
Adriatic islands, linked to the mainland by a toll bridge. Founded as the Roman
colony of Curictum, Krk was the medieval stronghold of the powerful Frankopan
dynasty (▷ 21). Today it is a lively island, with large resorts at Omišalj, Njivice and
Malinska and one of Croatia's finest beaches at Baška.

POWER BASE

In summer, the capital, Krk Town, is buzzing with tourists from the nearby
beaches; in winter it is a drowsy island town, surrounded by the remnants of
Roman walls and a 12th-century Frankopan fortress. Ceramic plaques to Sveti
Kvirina (St. Quirinus), Krk's patron saint, adorn the gates into the old town, at the
heart of which the church of St. Quirinus shares its onion-dome campanile with
an 11th-century Romanesque cathedral. Nearby, a 15th-century hexagonal tower
stands over the harbour, with a Roman tombstone in its wall.

HOLY ISLAND

Punat, 4km (2.5 miles) east of Krk Town on the bay of Puntarska Draga, is home
to the oldest and one of the largest marinas in the Adriatic. Taxi boats by the
harbour ferry you to Košljun, a wooded isle, home to a Franciscan monastery
since the 15th century, where you can visit the library and museum of sacred art.

LOŠINJ

www.tz-malilosinj.hr

Separated from Cres by a swing bridge across the Kavuada canal at Osor, Lošinj is smaller but more developed than its neighbour. The capital, Mali Lošinj, is the largest town on the Adriatic islands. Ruled by Venice from 1409 to 1797, Mali Lošinj reached its heyday in the 19th century, when its tradition of shipbuilding and seafaring made it the second biggest port in the Adriatic. Set in a sheltered bay lined with pastel-painted houses, this is one of Croatia's most beguiling towns—it has lanes of handsome villas and gardens filled with exotic plants. Paths along the shore lead to the beaches and pine woods at Čikat and Sunčana Uvala (Sunny Bay). There is also a delightful seaside promenade connecting Mali Lošinj to Veli Lošinj (▷ 162–163), once the island's main town, now a pretty little harbourside village overlooked by a Venetian tower and church. The Blue World dolphin research centre here is well worth a visit (▷ 164).

The north of the island is dominated by Osorščica, a mountain ridge 10km (6 miles) long with views across Kvarner Bay from its 588m (1,929ft) summit, reached by footpaths from Nerezine and Osor. For an easier excursion, take the boat trip from Mali Lošinj to Susak,

a small traffic-free island. Susak is best known for the unusual folk costume of its women, featuring a brightly embroidered mini-skirt over pink tights.

🕂 284 C5 🛈 Riva Lošnjskih Kapetana 29, Mali Lošinj ☎ 051 231884 🕓 Jun–end Sep Mon–Sat 8–8, Sun 9–1; Oct Mon–Fri 8–5, Sat 8–1; Nov–end Feb Mon–Fri 8–3; Mar–end May Mon–Fri 8–5, Sat 8–1 🚌 From Rijeka and Cres 🚢 Car ferry from Pula and Zadar to Mali Lošinj in summer; daily catamaran from Rijeka to Mali Lošinj

LOVRAN

www.tz-lovran.hr

Lovran is named after the laurel trees which grow in abundance in the foothills of Mount Učka. At the southern end of the Lungomare promenade, it is the oldest town on the Opatija riviera. In the 12th century it was an important maritime trading port, but all that remains of the walls that surrounded the town are a tower and a drawbridge leading to Studica gate. The abiding image of Lovran is of its neo-Gothic and Viennese Secession villas, many designed by Austrian architect Carl Seidl (1858–1936) at the turn of the 20th

century, when Lovran was popular with the Habsburg aristocracy.

🕂 284 B4 🛈 Šetalište Maršala Tita 63 ☎ 051 291740 🕓 Jun–end Aug Mon–Sat 8–8, Sun 8–noon; Sep Mon–Sat 8–3; Oct–end May Mon–Fri 8–3 🚌 From Opatija and Rijeka

MOŠĆENIČKA DRAGA

www.tz-moscenicka.hr

This attractive old-style fishing village and low-key resort is the first place you come to when you cross from Istria into Kvarner along the southern coast. A long pebble beach leads to the harbour, with cafés and restaurants on a sunny promenade with views to Cres and the Velebit massif. A flight of more than 750 steps climbs to the medieval town of Mošćenice, built 173m (567ft) above the coast, with fine views over Kvarner Bay. There is a small ethnographic museum (tel 051 737551; Mar–end Dec daily from 10am, but variable), with an ancient olive oil mill on display.

🕂 284 B4 🛈 Aleja Slatina ☎ 051 739166 🕓 Jun–end Sep Mon–Sat 8–9; Oct–end May daily 8–noon 🚌 From Opatija and Rijeka

Below left *An ornate doorway at Lovran, the oldest town on the Opatija riviera*
Below *A pine-shaded bay near Veli Lošinj, on the eastern coast of the island of Lošinj*

INFORMATION
www.opatija-tourism.hr
➕ 284 B4 ℹ️ Ulica Vladimira Nazora
3 ☎ 051 271710 🕐 Jul–end Aug daily
8am–10pm; Sep–Oct and Easter–end Jul
daily 8–8; Oct–Easter Mon–Sat 8.30–3.30
🚌 From Pula and Rijeka

TIPS
» Take the bus to Lovran and walk back
along the Lungomare coast path.
» Look out for concerts in Villa Angiolina.
» For a taste of old Opatija, take tea in the
Hotel Kvarner (▷ 167) and peer into the
elegant Crystal Ballroom.

Below *Elegant Villa Angiolina, a remnant
from Opatija's 19th-century heyday*

OPATIJA

This elegant Habsburg resort is experiencing a second golden age as tourists
return to its villas, parks and promenades. Opatija is named after a 15th-century
abbey, built on the site of the chapel of Sveti Jakov (St. James). But the story of
Opatija really begins 400 years later, as the fashionable winter resort of Viennese
high society.

VIENNESE WHIRL

In 1844, Ignacio Scarpa, a wealthy businessman from Rijeka, bought a holiday
home in Opatija and named it Villa Angiolina after his late wife. He surrounded
the house with lush gardens of palm trees, and invited the cream of Austro-
Hungarian society to stay. This was the start of Opatija's golden age as the
Adriatic playground of the Habsburg aristocracy. Emperors and royals frequented
its belle époque villas and hotels; composers Mahler and Puccini and the
playwright Anton Chekhov all stayed here. Between the world wars Opatija went
into decline, annexed by Italy; only now is it returning to its former glory as the
faded elegance gives way to a new era of high-class tourism.

ON THE PROM

The one thing everyone does in Opatija is to walk the Lungomare, a seaside
promenade which runs north for 4km (2.5 miles) to the fishing village of Volosko
and south for 8km (5 miles) to Lovran (▷ 151). Begun in 1885 and officially
named Šetalište Franz Josef I after the Austrian emperor, this is a delightful walk
along a rocky shoreline, punctuated with gardens, villas and beaches and lighted
by old-fashioned lamps at night.

Above *Tranquil scene, Risnjak National Park*
Left *A bird's-eye view of the town of Senj*

RAB

▷ 154–155.

RIJEKA

▷ 156–157.

RISNJAK

www.risnjak.hr
Gorski Kotar is a mountainous region of primeval beech forests, limestone peaks and rushing rivers and streams, occupying a large area between Slovenia and Kvarner Bay. Around 64sq km (25sq miles) has been designated the Risnjak National Park, including two of the highest peaks, Veliki Risnjak (1,528m/5,013 ft) and Snježnik (1,506m/4,940 ft). The mountains are only a short distance from the sea, with views of the whole of Kvarner Bay; on clear days you can see the Italian Alps. At the information centre in Crni Lug you can pick up maps of hiking routes to the summits, each of which has a mountain hut for overnight stays. For a less challenging walk, follow the Staza Leska, an educational trail that winds for 4.2km (2.6 miles) through the forest, passing sinkholes, meadows and charcoal kilns. There is a feeding post for deer, with beds of hay that provide winter shelter for dormice, birds and squirrels. Among the large mammals roaming free in Gorski Kotar are brown bears and lynx. Winters in Gorski Kotar are long and harsh; the high ground is covered by snow for much of the year and even in summer temperatures are much lower than down on the coast.
✚ 284 C3 ✉ Nacionalni Park Risnjak, Crni Lug ☎ 051 836133 ✋ Adult 30kn, child 15kn ☐ Rijeka to Delnice, then Delnice to Crni Lug 🍴

SENJ

www.tz-senj.hr
This quiet town sits at the foot of a pass in the Velebit mountains; when the *bora* blows through the pass, it becomes the coldest and windiest place on the coast. From 1537 to 1617 this was the stronghold of the Uskoks, legendary warriors who fled the Balkan interior and used Senj as a base from which to attack the Turks with the tacit support of the Austrian rulers. High above the harbour, Nehaj fortress, built by an Uskok captain in 1558, dominates the town. The castle houses a museum about the Uskoks, complete with weapons and costumes (Jul, Aug Mon–Fri 7–3, 6–8, Sat 10–12, 6–8, Sun 10–12; Sep–end Jun Mon–Fri 7–3). Climb the battlements for views over the town.
✚ 285 C4 ℹ Stara Cesta 2 ☎ 053 881068 🕐 Mon–Fri 8–3 ☐ From Rab and Rijeka

SJEVERNI VELEBIT (NORTH VELEBIT)

www.np-sjeverni-velebit.hr
The Velebit mountain chain extends for over 100km (62 miles) from Senj to Zadar, rising from the coast like a sheer wall of limestone and shielding Kvarner Bay from the wind, rain and snow which fall on the far side. In 1999, the northern end of the range became Croatia's newest national park; it is also the least visited, attracting fewer than 6,000 visitors per year. The karst uplands make for superb walking, with jagged crags and remarkable caves. At a height of 1,480m (4,854ft), Velebitski Botanički Vrt (Velebit Botanical Garden) has rare plants, including mountain violets and the bright yellow *Degenia velebitica*, featured on the 50-lipa coin. The main entrance to the park is via the village of Krasno, on the road from Sveti Juraj to Otočac.
✚ 285 C5 ✉ Nacionalni Park Sjeverni Velebit, Krasno ☎ 053 665380 ✋ Adult 30kn, child 15kn ℹ Obala Kralja Zvonimira 6, Senj ☎ 053 884551

RAB

INFORMATION

www.tzg-rab.hr

✚ 284 C5 🛈 Trg Municipium Arbe, Rab Town ☎ 051 771111 🕓 Jun–end Aug daily 8am–10pm; Sep daily 8am–9pm; Oct–end May Mon–Fri 8–3 🚌 From Rijeka 🚢 Car ferry from Jablanac to Mišnjak; also from Baška (Krk) to Lopar in summer; passenger ferry from Rijeka to Rab

Above *Rab Town's skyline, characterized by its distinctive bell towers, remains virtually unchanged since the 12th century*

INTRODUCTION

Rab is the smallest of the Kvarner islands, noted for its sandy beaches and Rab Town, a medieval gem. The island was settled by the Romans in the first century BC. Later a self-governing city state, Rab subsequently alternated between Croatian and Venetian rule before coming under the Venetian republic in 1409. The well-preserved medieval town is virtually unchanged since the 12th century, when the cathedral, downgraded to a parish church in 1828, and three of the bell towers were built. Rab emerged unscathed from the Homeland War and even managed to keep its tourist industry going throughout the early 1990s.

Rab can be reached throughout the year by the short ferry crossing from Jablanac, some 100km (62 miles) south of Rijeka. In summer, there are also car ferries from Baška on the island of Krk. The island is small, just 96sq km (37sq miles), and easy to get around, with buses linking the main settlements of Rab, Kampor and Lopar. The east coast, facing the mainland and buffeted by the *bora* wind, is rocky and barren, while the west coast has pine woods, sheltered beaches and coves. The greatest attraction is Rab Town, a charming ensemble of churches and medieval lanes squeezed onto a narrow isthmus beside a natural harbour.

WHAT TO SEE

A WALK AROUND RAB

The oldest part of Rab is intersected by three parallel streets known as Gornja Ulica (Upper Street), Srednja Ulica (Middle Street) and Donja Ulica (Lower Street). To explore Rab in an hour, follow the tourist route around the old town, with informative panels in several languages. Start on Trg Sveti Kristofora, the large open piazza by the harbour, and climb the steps to the 15th-century Gagliardi tower. From here, follow Gornja Ulica to the cathedral. Drop down to the gardens behind the cathedral and return along the waterfront to Trg Muncipium Arbe, the main square. Note the Venetian Gothic Rector's Palace—now the town hall—which has a balcony supported by three stone lions.

THE BELL TOWERS

The most distinctive feature of Rab are its four campaniles standing on Gornja Ulica and silhouetted against the skyline like ships' masts. You can climb the tower of the church of St. John the Evangelist, in the ruins of a fifth-century basilica. It is also possible to climb the Great Bell Tower by the cathedral (May–end Sep daily 10–1, 6–10). For the best view, climb onto the remaining part of the medieval walls.

THE BEACHES

In summer, taxi boats shuttle across the bay to Kandarola, a rocky beach which is popular with naturists. The best sandy beaches are at Lopar, 15km (9 miles) north of Rab; the biggest is Rajska Plaža (Paradise Beach) by San Marino campsite. For more seclusion, footpaths from Lopar lead to remote bays and Sahara nudist beach.

TIPS

» Komrčar park, reached through an archway beneath the medieval walls, is a beautiful 19th-century landscaped park with shady paths and steps leading down to the town beach.

» Look carefully at the fountain on the harbourside square of Trg Sveti Kristofora in Rab Town. The modern sculpture is of Draga, a local shepherdess said to have been turned to stone rather than submit her chastity.

» In summer, take a boat excursion from Lopar to the island of Goli Otok, a notorious prison camp for Soviet sympathizers in Yugoslavia. The guides will show you around the prison buildings and relate its ugly history.

Left and below The ruins of the church of St. John the Evangelist, built on the site of an early Christian basilica. The bell tower, a 12th-century addition, has survived intact

INFORMATION
www.tz-rijeka.hr
➕ 284 B4 🛈 Korzo 33 ☎ 051 335882
🕐 Mid-Jun to mid-Sep Mon–Sat 8–8,
Sun 8–2; mid-Sep to mid-Jun Mon–Fri
8–8, Sat 8–2 🚌 From Opatija, Pula and
Zagreb 🚆 From Zagreb

INTRODUCTION
The capital of the Kvarner region is a busy industrial city and shipping port at the mouth of the River Rječina. It is a pleasant place, with a lively café culture and some interesting museums. The earliest inhabitants of Rijeka were a Liburnian hill tribe who settled at Trsat; later the Romans founded Tarsatica on the site of today's city centre. Unlike other Croatian coastal towns, Rijeka remained under Austro-Hungarian control from 1466 to 1918. It was occupied by Italy between the world wars and the River Rječina became the border between Italy and Yugoslavia. The late 20th century was a period of industrial decline, but Rijeka is following other Mediterranean port cities and turning warehouses and docks into exhibition and concert venues.

The city centre occupies a compact area behind the Riva, the busy road that runs along the quayside. Korzo is the central promenade, lined with cafés and shops, on the site of the old sea walls. From here, the Gradska Vrata (City Gate) leads into the oldest part of Rijeka, through a medieval archway topped by a baroque clock tower with busts of Habsburg emperors and a double-headed imperial eagle. To reach the castle and church at Trsat, take bus No. 1 or 1A from the Riva or climb the pilgrim stairway from Titov Trg, at the confluence of the Rječina and Mrtvi Kanal (Dead Canal).

WHAT TO SEE
IZLOŽBA GLAGOLJICA (GLAGOLITIC EXHIBITION)
Housed inside the university library, this fascinating collection of medieval art includes frescoes, manuscripts and stone carvings from Istria and the Kvarner islands, all using the Glagolitic script (▷ 21). Just as interesting as the showpiece exhibits are the examples of Glagolitic in everyday life.

Above *The Korzo, Rijeka's main promenade, lined with shops and cafés*

✉ Dolac 1 ☎ 051 336129 🕐 Mon–Fri 8–3 by appointment or ask at offices above ✋ 10kn

POMORSKI I POVIJESNI MUZEJ (MARITIME AND HISTORY MUSEUM)
www.ppmhp.hr

Rijeka's largest museum, in the former Habsburg governor's palace, has exhibits on seafaring and shipbuilding, including maps, charts and model ships, along with costumes and Austro-Hungarian furniture.

✉ Muzejski Trg 1 ☎ 051 213578 🕐 Jun–end Sep Tue–Fri 9–8; Oct–end May Tue–Fri 9–4, Sat 9–1 ✋ Adult 10kn, child 5kn

CRKVA SVETOG VIDA (ST. VITUS' CHURCH)

Walk through the City Gate and continue uphill past Rijeka's only surviving Roman arch to reach this round church, built in 1638 and dedicated to the city's patron. Its stern neoclassical lines are modelled on the church of Santa Maria della Salute in Venice.

✉ Grivica Trg

TRSAT CASTLE

Once the castle of the Frankopans of Krk (▷ 21), this fortress above the Rječina gorge was bought in 1824 by Irish-Austrian general Count Laval Nugent (1777–1862) and restored as a romantic folly. The former dungeons are now an exhibition gallery, along with the Classical-style temple designed as the Nugent family mausoleum. The nearby church of Our Lady of Trsat is built on the site where angels are said to have delivered the house of the Virgin Mary from Nazareth in 1291. A sculpture of Pope John Paul II stands outside in memory of his visit in 2003. The classic approach to Trsat is via a pilgrim path of more than 500 steps, beginning at a baroque archway on Titov Trg.

✉ Trsat ☎ 051 217714 🕐 Jun–end Sep daily 9–8; Oct–end May daily 9–5 ✋ Adult 10kn, child 5kn 🚌 Bus 1,1A, 8 💻

CRKVA GOSPE LURDSKE (LADY OF LOURDES CHURCH)

This striking building with an ornate neo-Gothic facade was begun in the early 20th century but wasn't finished until 1929. In an effort to raise money to complete the church, the Capuchin monks employed St. Johanca, who raised funds among local people by sweating blood (he was later arrested for fraud). Inside, the ceiling frescoes are by local artist Romulo Venucci.

✉ Trg Žabica ☎ 051 335233

TIPS

» If you are visiting in winter, try to be in Rijeka for the annual Carnival (▷ 165), the biggest and liveliest in Croatia.
» To save the long climb up to Trsat, take the bus instead and walk back down the pilgrim stairway to the city.
» There is free car parking at Trsat and a large pay car park (parking lot) at Delta, beside the River Rječina and a short walk from the sights.
» Look out for the headquarters of the Jadrolinija shipping company, a bright yellow building, dating from 1897, on the waterfront. The exterior is decorated with statues of ship captains and engineers, while the rear facade on Jadranski Trg has stylized female figures representing the continents.

REGIONS KVARNER • SIGHTS

Left The church of Crkva Svetog Vida, dedicated to St. Vitus, the city's patron
Below The 19th-century clock tower on the Korzo, a city landmark

AROUND KRK ISLAND

There is more to Croatia's largest island than an old Roman capital and a splendid beach. On this circuit of the island you will explore hilltop towns and villages and visit the site where the famous Baška Stone, inscribed with one of the earliest examples of the Glagolitic script, was discovered.

THE DRIVE

Distance: 77km (48 miles)
Allow: 2 hours
Start/end: Baška ✚ 284 C5

★ Baška is best known for its superb beach, which stretches for nearly 2km (1.2 miles) around the bay. In summer, this is a lively holiday resort, but in winter it is almost deserted and the coast is exposed to the biting *bora* wind. Alongside the modern hotels and apartments the old town survives virtually intact, with stone houses and narrow lanes set just back from the harbour.

Leave Baška by taking the main road across the island in the direction of Krk Town. After 2km (1.2 miles) you come to the village of Jurandvor.

❶ Jurandvor is the setting for the early Romanesque church of Sveta Lucije (St. Lucy), where the Bašćanska Ploča (Baška Stone) was discovered underneath the floor by the local priest in 1851. This limestone tablet, which dates from the 11th century and measures 2m (6.5ft) in length and 1m (3.3ft) in height, contains one of the oldest examples of the Glagolitic script (▷ 21). The inscription on the tablet records a donation of land from King Zvonimir to the parish. This is the earliest recorded mention of a Croatian king and the first known use of the word Croatian. The original stone is kept in the lobby of the Strossmayerova Galerija (▷ 62) in Zagreb, but a reproduction is on display inside the church.

Continue along the main road through the village of Draga Bašćanska before climbing through a part rocky, part forested landscape. Eventually you crest a summit with panoramic views of Krk and Cres spread out beneath you and the Gorski Kotar mountain range visible on the horizon. Shortly afterwards, there is a magnificent view of the monastery islet of Košljun (▷ 150) to your left, set in a sheltered bay. Turn right at the next junction, signposted Šilo and Vrbnik, and follow this road as it drops gently towards the coast before reaching the vineyards which signal the entrance to the wine town of Vrbnik.

❷ Vrbnik stands on a cliff, 48m (157ft) above the sea. You can park your car outside the centre and stroll through the cobbled streets before taking the steps down to the small harbour. Vrbnik is known throughout Croatia for its dry white Zlahtina wine, which you can buy at the Katunar winery at the entrance to the town (▷ 164).

Leaving Vrbnik, turn right, following signs to Dobrinj. The road soon leaves the vineyards behind and winds uphill through forest to Risika. Reaching a crossroads, turn left through the village of Sveti Vid to arrive at Dobrinj.

❸ Dobrinj is the only town on Krk to be located away from the sea. It is first mentioned in a Glagolitic script dated 1 January 1100. Although it has a population of just over 100, in summer this tiny village buzzes with visitors to its art galleries, concerts and museums of ethnography and sacred art. You can drive as far as the church square to explore the village on foot. From the garden above the square and from the terrace of the bell tower there are wide-ranging views of Rijeka, Opatija, Mount Učka and the Gorski Kotar mountains.

The road now crosses the island from east to west, passing over the main road from Krk to Rijeka and dropping down to the coast at Malinska.

❹ Malinska is a busy summer resort, set in a wide bay fringed with pine woods and beaches. The walk around the harbour makes a pleasant stroll, letting you admire the yachts and the chapel of Sveti Nikola (St. Nicholas), built in 2000 on the harbour square and with a striking stone-carved altar of Christ and his apostles.

Drive through the centre of Malinska, passing the harbour and climbing out of the village to return to the main road. Follow signs towards Krk until you reach a junction, where you should turn right towards the ferry port at Valbiska. After 8km (5 miles), you come to a crossroads. Turn left here, signposted to Bajčići and Vrh.

❺ To enjoy a meal in at Tri Maruna, in Poljica (▷ 166), one of the most atmospheric restaurants in Croatia, turn right at the crossroads. Return to the crossroads to continue the drive.

Stay on this minor road for 5km (3 miles) to Vrh. Turn right and then left, following signs to Krk. On the outskirts of Krk (▷ 150), turn right and drive down to the harbour if you want to explore the town, or turn left to return directly to Baška.

WHERE TO EAT
NADA
Enjoy excellent food and wine on a clifftop terrace in Vrbnik.
☎ 051 857065

TRI MARUNA
▷ 166.

PLACE TO VISIT
CRKVA SVETA LUCIJE, JURANDVOR
☎ 051 221018 ◷ Apr–end Oct daily 9.30–5.30 ✋ Adult 15kn, child (10–15) 7kn

Clockwise from below *The 15th-century Franciscan monastery on the islet of Košljun; Krk Town*

VULTURES ON CRES

Keep an eye out for griffon vultures and other birds of prey on a well-marked eco-trail through the landscapes of the Tramuntana region of northern Cres. The path is steep and rocky in places, so you will need good walking shoes.

THE WALK

Distance: 10km (6 miles)
Allow: 3–4 hours
Start/end: Caput Insulae eco-centre, Beli
✚ 284 B4

HOW TO GET THERE

Follow the signs to Beli and Caput Insulae from the main Porozina to Cres road, 13km (8 miles) north of Cres. The eco-centre is signposted up a hill to your left, just before you enter the village.

★ Caput Insulae eco-centre is housed in a former primary school, built in 1929 and closed in 1980 as a result of depopulation. There are two permanent exhibitions, one on the history of Beli and the other on the ecology of Cres and Lošinj. Behind the centre is a sanctuary for injured griffon vultures, including young birds who have fallen into

the sea while learning to fly. Around 60 pairs of griffon vultures nest on the nearby cliffs, along with golden eagles, buzzards, peregrines and eagle owls. Before doing the walk, pick up a copy of the excellent book *Tramuntana...through ancient forest... return to yourself* (100kn), which gives background information on fauna, flora, folklore and traditional architecture as well as maps and descriptions of the sculptures on the trail.

There are several marked trails around Beli but this follows the trail 'History and Art in Nature', which is waymarked with red and white circles. Walk downhill from the eco-centre and turn left onto a stony path between dry-stone walls.

❶ A stone sculpture beside the path portrays a *crkvica*, a small chapel similar to those once built

by shepherds. This is one of 20 sculptures along the trail by the artist Ljubo de Karina, engraved with verses by local poet Andro Vid Mihičić (1896–1992): 'When I arrived in Beli it was dark...gorges and glens full of ghosts, the sea full of stars and the sky full of deep secrets.'

Turn right at a junction, marked by a sculpture of a white stone cross, traditionally placed at a crossroads as a protection from evil fairies known as *kudlaci*. Reaching a road, turn left to the village. Almost immediately, follow the red and white waymarks to drop down to your right beside olive grove terraces. Turn right at the foot of the slope to cross a bridge across the Potok stream.

❷ The single-arched bridge dates from Roman times and was probably built in the first century AD. The name

Caput Insulae (Latin for 'head of the island') also dates from this time, when Beli was a fortified Roman settlement on the site of a Liburnian hilltop fortress.

Keep to the wide path as it climbs gently above the stream, at first with views of Beli to your left. Eventually you reach the old Roman road. Cross straight over the road and continue to climb through forests of oak, hornbeam and chestnut, with sea views opening up as you ascend. This is the steepest section of the walk. The track becomes less clear as you head into the woods, so use the waymarks as your guide.

❸ Reaching a plateau, you will see the Kirinići meadow to your right. The maze here was constructed out of 3,000 stones and is a larger version of a labyrinth at Chartres Cathedral in France. It is dedicated to Vesna, the pagan Slavic goddess of spring.

After passing a ruined cottage, bear right to join a wide track. Stay on this path for about 3km (2 miles) as it passes through oak woods, meadows, sheep pastures and dry-stone walls. When the blue route crosses the path, keep straight ahead, but at the next junction, where the two trails briefly join, turn right. After a few minutes, turn left to leave the blue route and head into the woods (signposted Jama Čampari).

❹ The karst scenery of the Tramuntana is riddled with sinkholes, fissures and caves. It is possible to go into the Čampari cave (known locally as Banic cave), which is 101m (331ft) deep, though access is only recommended for experienced potholers (cavers). A rope is provided at the entrance and a torch (flashlight) is essential. Skeletons of brown bears more than 12,000 years old have been discovered in the cave and there is also evidence of prehistoric humans in the form of pottery and the bones of domesticated dogs.

Follow the waymarks as the path drops steeply through the forest before turning right onto a clearly defined track which drops down towards Beli. The village appears beneath you as a jumble of brown and white houses perched on a cliff, overlooking a small harbour.

❺ Beli has been inhabited for about 4,000 years and probably takes its name from a Celtic god or king. In the Middle Ages, it was an independent commune that paid tribute to the Venetian doge in exchange for its freedom. Beli once had a population of more than 1,000 but now only 30 people live here.

Stay on this path to return to the eco-centre.

WHERE TO EAT
There are no facilities on the walk so take drinking water with you.

PANSION TRAMUNTANA
Beside the eco-centre, this *pansion* serves drinks and simple meals.
☎ 051 840519

PLACE TO VISIT
EKO-CENTAR CAPUT INSULAE
www.supovi.hr
☎ 051 840525 Ⓣ Mid-Jan to mid-Dec, daily 9–7 Ⓤ Adult 25kn, child 10kn, family 60kn

Clockwise from opposite *The hilltop village of Beli; a sign for the eco-centre in Beli, where there is a hospital for injured griffon vultures; griffon vulture*

LOŠINJ COAST PATH

The island of Lošinj has an extensive network of footpaths, including this delightful coastal promenade connecting the two main towns. If you are lucky, you may be able to spot dolphins playing in the clear waters just offshore.

THE WALK

Distance: 7km (4.5 miles)
Allow: 2 hours
Start: Mali Lošinj
⊞ 284 C6
End: Rovenska

HOW TO GET THERE

Trg Republike Hrvatske is the harbourside square at the heart of Mali Lošinj, a short walk from the bus stop and ferry port.

★ With a population of 7,000, Mali Lošinj is the biggest settlement on any of Croatia's Adriatic islands. Set in a sheltered bay surrounded by pastel-coloured houses, the town has a real buzz on summer evenings, when the people come out to stroll around the harbour and the promenade cafés are bursting with life. Mali Lošinj grew prosperous through the 18th-century shipping trade, with many of its sea captains returning to build grand villas by the sea. The first tourist society was formed here in 1866 and in the late 19th century the town promoted itself as a health resort for the Austro-Hungarian aristocracy.

Start at Trg Republike Hrvatske, the triangular piazza by the harbour, and walk along Riva Lošinjskih Kapetana, the promenade on the northern side of the bay. After passing the tourist office and ferry port, follow the road out of town as it climbs to a busy junction at Kadinj. Cross the main road and look for the start of the coast path—for most of its route it is an asphalted promenade clinging to the shore. Stay on this path as it makes a circuit of the Bojčić peninsula before arriving at pretty Sveti Martin.

❶ Sveti Martin is the original nucleus of Mali Lošinj, founded when farmers settled here in the 12th century. The church dates from 1450 and the town cemetery is also situated here. After visiting the church, leave the coast behind and climb uphill on Ulica Sveti Martin. Reaching the main road, turn left and walk for around 100m (110 yards) to arrive at a junction. When you see Veli Lošinj signposted to the left, take the steps down to Valdarke bay to rejoin the coast path.

❷ The path now follows the shore all the way to Veli Lošinj, passing the small cove of Valeškura and continuing as far as Hotel Punta. This is the best section of the route for observing the 150 or so bottlenose dolphins that inhabit the coastal waters around Cres and Lošinj, now the Lošinj Dolphin Reserve.

Walk through the grounds of Hotel Punta and follow the path downhill with views over Veli Lošinj.

❸ Veli Lošinj used to be the main town on the island (*veli* means large, *mali* means small) but it has long been eclipsed by its neighbour and now has a population of under a thousand. This is a charming spot, with pastel facades set around a narrow harbour guarded by the 18th-century baroque church of Sveti Antun (St. Antony). The bell tower is 15th-century Venetian, as is the circular defence tower above the harbour, which now houses a museum and art gallery. The star exhibit is a copy of *Apoxyomenos*, a fourth-century BC life-size bronze statue of a Greek athlete discovered in the sea at Veli Lošinj in 1999. Also at Veli Lošinj, you can visit the Blue World dolphin research centre (▷ 164) to learn about the lives of these remarkable creatures.

Arriving at the harbour in Veli Lošinj, take the steps down to the waterfront. From here, walk around the bay, climbing to St. Antony's Church. Behind the church is the graveyard, where you can pick up the coast path to Rovenska.

❹ Rovenska is a pretty fishing harbour sheltered by a breakwater, built to protect the boats from the effects of the harsh *bora* wind. The foundation stone was laid by the Austrian archduke Maximilian in 1856. These days, it is a popular spot for lunch, and a good place to end your walk, sitting by the harbour eating fresh fish and watching the fishermen mending their nets and repairing their boats.

You can return to Mali Lošinj the same way, or pick up a taxi or bus from the main road at Veli Lošinj. If you are walking, retrace your route as far as the steps above Valdarke bay, then cross over the main road and take Ulica Braće Vidulića downhill to return to Trg Republike Hrvatske.

WHEN TO GO

This walk is pleasant at any time of year, but you stand the best chance of seeing dolphins between October and May, as they are driven further out to sea during the busy summer

tourist season by excursion boats and yachts.

WHERE TO EAT
SIRIUS
Stop for a bite to eat at this fish restaurant by the harbour at Rovenska

☎ 051 236399) 🕐 Daily April–end Oct

TOURIST INFORMATION
www.tz-malilosinj.hr

✉ Riva Lošinjskih Kapetana, Mali Lošinj

☎ 051 231884

PLACE TO VISIT
BLUE WORLD
www.blue-world.org

☎ 051 604666 🕐 May, Oct Mon–Fri 9–4, Sat 9–2; Jun–Sep daily 9–1, 6–8; Jul, Aug daily 9–1, 6–10; Nov–Apr Mon–Fri 10–2

✋ Adult 15kn, child (6–10) 10kn

Opposite *Coastal path on the island of Lošinj*
Below *The sheltered harbour at Mali Lošinj, lined with pastel-coloured houses*

CRES

EKO-CENTAR CAPUT INSULAE

www.supovi.hr

Housed in an old school in the remote hamlet of Beli, this eco-centre includes a hospital for griffon vultures. There are exhibitions on the ecology of Cres and an enjoyable sculpture trail (▷ 160–161).

✉ Beli, Cres ☎ 051 840525 🕔 Mid-Jan to mid-Dec daily 9–8 ✋ Adult 25kn, child 10kn, family 60kn

GORSKI KOTAR

BJELOLASICA

www.bjelolasica.hr

The Croatian Olympic Centre at Bjelolasica is where the country's élite athletes train throughout the year. In winter it is home to Croatia's biggest ski resort. Ski rental is available and there is a ski and snowboard school.

✉ Vrelo, Jasenak ☎ 01 617 7707 🕔 Jan, Feb daily 9–4 ✋ Ski pass 100kn per day, 75kn per half-day 🚘 27km (17 miles) west of Ogulin; take A1 motorway to Split and follow signs from Ogulin exit

KRK

KATUNAR

www.katunar.com

This family-run winery at the entrance to Vrbnik sells the well-known

Žlahtina white wine from Krk, and also makes an unusual sparkling wine, Porin. Call in advance to arrange a visit to the winery and a tasting of wine, cheese and ham.

✉ Vrbnik, Krk ☎ 051 857393 🕔 Daily 8–4

LOŠINJ

BLUE WORLD

www.blue-world.org

This marine education facility is run by the Adriatic Dolphin Project, which monitors the bottlenose dolphin population off Cres and Lošinj. The multimedia visitor centre includes a film about the dolphins, as well as educational games and activities for younger children. Local tour companies offer boat trips to see dolphins in summer, but Blue World does not take part.

✉ Veli Lošinj ☎ 051 604666 🕔 Jun, Sep daily 9–1, 6–8; Jul, Aug daily 9–1, 6–10; May, Oct Mon–Fri 9–4, Sat 9–2; Nov–end Apr Mon–Fri 10–2 ✋ Adult 15kn, child (6–10) 10kn

OPATIJA

THALASSO WELLNESS CENTAR OPATIJA

www.thalassotherapia-opatija.hr

Thalassotherapy uses seawater to promote healing and relaxation. This

state-of-the-art facility has heated seawater pools, Finnish and Turkish saunas, plus a variety of beauty, wellness and massage packages from which to choose.

✉ Šetalište Maršala Tita 188, Opatija ☎ 051 202600 🕔 All year

RIJEKA

AROMATICA

The Rijeka branch of Aromatica, a chain selling natural cosmetics, is fragrant with soaps, shampoos and scented candles, all infused with essential oils compressed from the country's finest ingredients. The shop is just a few steps down from Crkva Svetog (St. Vitus' Church).

✉ Medulićeva 5a, Rijeka ☎ 051 321061 🕔 Mon–Sat 8.30–8

HEMINGWAY

www.hemingway.hr

Part of a chain of cocktail bars across Croatia, Hemingway occupies the ground floor of a grand Austro-Hungarian building on Rijeka's central, cafe-lined Korzo and doubles as a coffee house by day and trendy lounge bar at night, with a piano, art gallery, comfortable sofas and crystal chandeliers.

✉ Korzo 28, Rijeka ☎ 051 272887 🕔 Daily 7am–5am

FESTIVALS AND EVENTS

HRVATSKO NARODNO KAZALIŠTE (CROATIAN NATIONAL THEATRE)
www.hnk-zajc.hr

Designed in 1885 by Viennese architects Hermann Helmer and Ferdinand Fellner, who also designed the Croatian National Theatre in Zagreb, this is the city's home of Croatian and Italian drama, opera, ballet and classical music. A statue of composer Ivan Zajc (1832–1914) stands at the centre of the park, in front of the theatre.

✉ Uljarska 1, Rijeka ☎ 051 337114
🕐 Box office open Mon–Sat 9.30–12.30 and one hour before performance
✋ 30–150kn 💺

KRAŠ
www.kras.hr

The people of Rijeka must have a sweet tooth as there are two shops on the Korzo selling this well-known Croatian confectionary brand. Look out for Kraš 1911, a range of chocolates using original recipes.

✉ Korzo, Rijeka ☎ 051 214362
🕐 Mon–Fri 7am–8pm, Sat 7–2

MALA GALERIJA
www.mala-galerija.hr

The narrow street of Užarska was once lined with artisans making the *morčić* jewellery (▷ 257) for which Rijeka is renowned. You can buy *morčić* souvenirs at this arty gallery, along with figures of local folk heroine Karolina, who protected Rijeka from British troops during the Napoleonic wars.

✉ Užarska 25, Rijeka ☎ 051 335403
🕐 Mon–Fri 8.30–8, Sat 9–1

STEREO DVORANA
www.zabava.hr

There's something for everyone at this multifaceted club next to the Neboder Hotel, with regular live acts, all-night DJs and even heavy metal nights on the menu. Most of the action takes place on Fridays and Saturdays.

✉ Strossmayerova 1, Rijeka ☎ 051 315246 🕐 9pm–6am

JANUARY AND FEBRUARY
CARNIVAL
www.ri-karneval.com.hr

Rijeka hosts some of Europe's wildest Carnival festivities. The first big parade features the *zvončari*, dancers dressed in animal skins and masks who ring bells to frighten away the evil spirits of winter. For the next six weeks, the city is one big festival, with theatre performances, concerts, and a grand masked ball in the former governor's palace. A children's Carnival parade takes place a week before the main parade. What began in 1982 with a handful of revellers now has 10,000 participants from 12 countries and more than 100 floats. At the end of the parade, an effigy of Carnival is ritually burned in the harbour.

✉ Rijeka ☎ 051 315710 🕐 Dates vary according to Easter

JUNE–SEPTEMBER
OPATIJA SUMMER FESTIVAL
www.festivalopatija.hr

Performances of music, theatre and folk dance take place at an open-air theatre throughout the summer. The festival includes Liburnia Jazz, three days of jazz concerts on the outdoor stage and at Villa Angiolina.

✉ Opatija ☎ 051 271377 🕐 Jun–end Sep

RAPSKE GLAZBENE VEČERI (RAB MUSICAL EVENINGS)
www.tzg-rab.hr

Classical and chamber music concerts are held in Rab's churches.

✉ Rab ☎ 051 771111 🕐 Thu evenings Jun–end Sep

VELEBIT
REFUGIUM URSORUM
www.kuterevo-medvjedi.hr

Furry creatures don't come much more adorable than the bear cubs at this refuge in the mountains, founded to look after young bears orphaned

JULY
RAPSKA FJERA
www.tzg-rab.hr

Three days of festivities for the feast of Rab's patron, St. Christopher, include a medieval craft fair in the streets of the old town. On the evening of 27 July there is a re-enactment of a medieval tournament in which costumed knights fight each other. Similar events take place yearly on 9 May, 25 June and 15 August.

✉ Rab ☎ 051 771111 🕐 25–27 Jul

JULY AND AUGUST
LUBENIČKE GLAZBENE VEČERI (LUBENICE MUSICAL EVENINGS)
www.tzg-cres.hr

Open-air classical music concerts are held in a magical clifftop setting, on the main square of the usually deserted hilltop hamlet of Lebenice.

✉ Lubenice, Cres ☎ 051 571535
🕐 Fri evenings Jul, Aug

OSORSKE GLAZBENE VEČERI (OSOR MUSICAL EVENINGS)

This festival is mostly devoted to Croatian composers, with soloists and ensembles performing delightful chamber music in the old cathedral and on the town square.

✉ Osor, Cres ☎ 051 237110 🕐 Jul, Aug

KRK SUMMER FESTIVAL
www.krk.hr

Classical music, jazz, opera, ballet and drama are staged in the cathedral and Frankopan castle and at the Franciscan monastery on the islet of Košljun.

✉ Krk ☎ 051 221359 🕐 Mid-Jul to mid-Aug

as a result of hunting. There is an eco-trail around the village and you can see the bears at four feeding times a day. The centre is open all year but the bears hibernate in winter.

✉ Kuterevo ☎ 053 799222 🕐 Daily 9–6
🎫 Adult 20kn, child 10kn

EATING

PRICES AND SYMBOLS

The restaurants are listed alphabetically. The prices given are the average for a two-course lunch (L) and a three-course dinner (D) for one person, without drinks. The wine price is for a litre of table wine followed by the least expensive bottle of quality wine. All the restaurants listed accept credit cards unless otherwise stated.

For a key to the symbols, ▷ 2.

KRK
TRI MARUNA

Behind an unmarked wooden door on the edge of the church square in Poljica it's all stone walls and wooden tables. There is no menu, just whatever the cook suggests— perhaps a choice of *šurlice* (pasta tubes) with goulash, stuffed cabbage or roast lamb. The cooking is not sophisticated, but a visit here is a culinary experience.

✉ Poljica, Krk ☎ 051 861156 ⏰ Daily 1–10 🍴 L 40kn, D 60kn, Wine from 60kn 🚗 Take the road from Malinska to the ferry port at Valbiska and turn right at a crossroads opposite the road to Bajčići

OPATIJA
LE MANDRAĆ

An old fisherman's cottage on the Lungomare promenade houses an avant-garde restaurant whose conservatory and terrace provide harbourside dining all year. The menu is seasonal. The nine-course 'Exploring' menu includes small portions of everything from sashimi, soup and fish tempura to *foie gras* and truffle desserts. Or you can choose owner Deniz Zembo's signature dish—mussels and clams *buzara*, a shellfish soup with lemon foam and Istrian ham.

✉ Obala Frana Supila 10, Volosko ☎ 051 701357 ⏰ Daily 11–11 🍴 L 150kn, D 200kn, tasting menu 390kn, Wine from 150kn

RAB
KONOBA RAB

Cosy and aromatic with local flavour, this is a great choice in Rab town. Opt for lamb baked 'under the bell' and *Rabska Grota* (beef roll with cheese and cherry sauce) and you won't leave disappointed.

✉ Kneza Branimira 3, Rab ☎ 051 725666 ⏰ Mar–end Oct daily 10am–midnight 🍴 L 70kn, D 90kn, Wine from 90kn

RIJEKA
BRACERA

Just off the Korzo, Bracera serves delicious pizzas baked in a clay oven. It also does crispy salads that make a meal in themselves. The décor has a seafaring theme, with wooden planks, ropes, model ships and fishing nets on the walls and sails billowing from the ceiling.

✉ Ulica Kružna 12, Rijeka ☎ 051 322498 ⏰ Daily 11–11 🍴 L 70kn, D 100kn, Wine from 90kn

KONOBA BLATO 1902

If it's a bit of home cooking you are after, look no further than this traditional tavern, where the local food comes in generous portions. Simple fish and meat dishes, a lively atmosphere and low prices mean you'll probably be back before long.

✉ Titov Trg 8C ☎ 051 336970 ⏰ Mon–Sat 7am–10pm 🍴 L 70kn, D 100kn, Wine from 90kn

KONOBA NEBULOZA

This unassuming seafood tavern next to the River Rječina, one of only a handful of purely Croatian eateries in the town centre, offers a hearty welcome. The house specialities are black risotto, octopus and *šurlice* (pasta tubes) but leave room for a slice of superb home-made cake, too.

✉ Titov Trg 2b, Rijeka ☎ 051 372294 ⏰ Mon–Fri 10am–midnight, Sat 12–12 🍴 L100kn, D 130kn, Wine 80/110kn

Above *Le Mandrać restaurant, Opatija*

PRICES AND SYMBOLS

Prices are the lowest for a double room for one night. Breakfast is included unless noted otherwise. All the hotels listed accept credit cards unless otherwise stated. Note that rates vary widely throughout the year.

For a key to the symbols, ▷ 2.

KRK

ZVONIMIR

www.hotelibaska.hr

This large seaside hotel is separated by a promenade from the wide beach at Baška, with views across the water to the Velebit mountains. Completely renovated in 2003, it has indoor and outdoor pools and a number of interconnecting rooms which are suitable for families. Most rooms have a balcony with sea view.

✉ Emila Geistlicha 39, Baška, Krk ☎ 051 656810 ♨ From €114 or €120 (half-board) ⓘ 85 ✪ ≋ Indoor and outdoor

LOŠINJ

APOKSIOMEN

www.apoksiomen.com

Located in a harbourside villa on the promenade, Hotel Apoksiomen is typical of the new breed of townhouse hotels in Croatia, combining traditional ambience with modern comforts and standards of service. Rooms are decorated with paintings by modern Croatian artists, and the palm-lined terrace café has lovely waterfront views.

✉ Riva Lošinjskih Kapetana 1, Mali Lošinj ☎ 051 520820 ✪ Closed Nov–end Mar ♨ From €120 ⓘ 25 ✪

MANORA

www.manora-losinj.hr

Opened in 2005 by the Spišić family, the Manora is striking from the outside, with cubic-style Mediterranean villas painted in the bright primary colours that are a feature of Lošinj. The funky boutique atmosphere continues inside, with light, spacious rooms offering views

over the mountain or the sea. The restaurant serves some of the best food around, using island ingredients to produce creative dishes such as lamb cutlets with cream, steak with chocolate or ravioli with salmon, wild asparagus and ham.

✉ Mandalenska, Nerezine, Lošinj ☎ 051 237460 ♨ From €98 ⓘ 22 ✪ ≋ Outdoor ⌁ 🄴 Just outside Nerezine on the road to Mali Lošinj

LOVRAN

PARK

www.hotelparklovran.hr

This striking blue building by the harbour stands at the end of the Lungomare promenade. Fully restored and reopened in 2005, it features a wellness centre over two floors with pool, jacuzzi, massage, gym and beauty treatments. All of its facilities are accessible to visitors with disabilities.

✉ Šetalište Maršala Tita 60, Lovran ☎ 051 706200 ✪ All year ♨ From €124 ⓘ 46 ✪ ≋ Indoor ⌁

VILLA ASTRA

www.lovranske-vile.com

Villa Astra is a seafront villa on the road from Lovran to Opatija, commissioned in 1905 in Venetian Gothic style, with balustrades, stained glass, ornamental windows and gardens tumbling down towards the Lungomare promenade. Rooms are spacious and elegant, with rich fabrics and polished hardwood floors. The restaurant serves gourmet Istrian and Kvarner cuisine. During the winter Villa Astra offers themed weekend breaks.

✉ Viktora Cara Emina 11, Lovran ☎ 051 704276 ♨ From €225 ⓘ 6 ✪ ≋ Outdoor

OPATIJA

KVARNER

www.liburnia.hr

Built in 1884 as the first hotel on the Adriatic coast, the Kvarner symbolizes Opatija's belle époque

era. Although a little careworn, it is still the best place to recapture a bygone age. Tea and cakes are served at 5pm daily, and there are grand dances in the Crystal Ballroom and on the summer terrace. The lush gardens of Villa Angiolina are a short stroll away, and the hotel has its own private bathing platform and heated seawater pool.

✉ Pava Tomašića 1-4, Opatija ☎ 051 710444 ♨ From €90 ⓘ 87 ≋ Indoor and outdoor

RAB

ZLATNI ZALAZ

www.zlatnizalaz.com

This family run guesthouse on the cliffs is known as the 'Golden Sunset' because of the wonderful sunset views from the terrace. The location on the road from Rab to Lopar is perfect, with pine woods on one side and a shimmering bay on the other. Steps lead down to a beach and private mooring for boats. The award-winning restaurant serves creative meat and fish dishes, and you can dine on the terrace in summer.

✉ Supetarska Draga 379, Rab ☎ 051 775150 ✪ Closed Jan ♨ From €66 (half-board) ⓘ 21

RIJEKA

BONAVIA

www.bonavia.hr

Rijeka's best hotel occupies a sleek modern block just a few steps from the action on the Korzo. Tourists and businesspeople alike enjoy its good quality accommodation and room standards seem higher than the hotel's official four stars. One of the advantages of staying here if you have your own car is the ample parking—very handy in car-plagued Rijeka.

✉ Dolac 4, Rijeka ☎ 051 357100 ♨ From €97 ⓘ 121 ✪

SIGHTS 170
WALKS AND DRIVES 198
WHAT TO DO 204
EATING 208
STAYING 212

DALMATIA

This narrow ribbon of land wedged between towering grey mountains and the azure sea is the Croatia most people know, and for good reason. Roman Zadar and Split, Venetian Trogir, Hvar and Korčula, the glittering Adriatic and a mountainous hinterland combine to make this one of Europe's top destinations. Island-hopping adventures offer ancient sights, home-cooked food in family-run *konobas* (traditional taverns) and sun-drenched beach days by a balmy sea.

If it's sun-and-sand fun you are seeking, then Dalmatia, and especially its islands, is for you. The weather along this stretch of coast is noticeably warmer than further north, with the island of Hvar receiving more sunshine hours than any other place in Croatia. Warm currents from the south mean you can swim in the sea from early May to late September.

Many of the best beaches rim the islands that lie just offshore and further out in the Adriatic, and these form some of Dalmatia's main attractions. Hvar, Brač, Korčula and even distant Vis are popular for their beaches, water sports and historic sights, and are easily reached in summer by regular ferry from Split. Back on the mainland, the imposing wall of limestone that runs almost the entire length of the Dalmatian coast provides limitless opportunities for outdoor adventure, while the waterfalls and lakes of the Krka National Park are as dramatic as they are beautiful.

Split is the urban epicentre of Dalmatia and an essential halt on any tour. The ruins of Diocletian's Palace, a UNESCO World Heritage Site, are so huge that the core of the city fits into its halls and corridors. Zadar abounds in medieval and Roman stonework, and Šibenik is a popular stop for its Gothic and Renaissance architecture. For more recent history, head well off the beaten track to Knin, the capital of the Republic of Serbian Krajina during the Homeland War.

BRAČ

Brač is the largest and most accessible island off the Dalmatian coast, and in summer crowds of visitors flock here, attracted by the Golden Cape, Croatia's most famous beach.

As the island's glistening white houses and churches testify, Brač is the source of a fine white limestone, used in buildings from Diocletian's Palace in Split to the White House in Washington, DC. Limestone has been quarried here since Roman times, when the wealthy patricians of Salona and Split had summer villas on the island. Under Venetian rule, the capital was at Nerežišća, moving to Supetar in 1815. Tourism began in the 1920s with the building of the first hotels, and today Brač is once again a busy summer resort, popular with the people of Split and beyond.

Regular ferries make the crossing from Split to Supetar, on the north coast, throughout the year. Buses connect Supetar with the resort of Bol on the south coast, and there is also a direct catamaran service from Split to Bol. Although there is a good network of local buses, getting around Brač is easiest if you have your own transport. A rough track at the centre of the island leads to Vidova Gora, at 780m (2,552ft) the highest peak in the Adriatic.

ZLATNI RAT (GOLDEN CAPE)

This beautiful beach is the best-known feature of Brač and has become an iconic image of Croatia. Set on a shingle spit extending some 300m (330 yards) into the sea, its shape changes constantly with the wind and tides. The water is shallow, making it safe for children, and there are shady pine woods at the centre. Get there by following the 2km (1.2-mile) promenade from the harbour at Bol.

ZMAJEVA ŠPILJA (DRAGON'S CAVE)

This remarkable cave (tel 091 514 9787; guide Zoran Kojdić; 50kn per person) in the hills above Murvica, 4km (2.5 miles) west of Zlatni Rat, has dragons and mythical creatures carved into the rock. The climb up here is steep and not always clearly marked, so it is better to go with the guide, who has a key to the cave. Book by telephone one day in advance.

BRAČKI MUZEJ (MUSEUM OF BRAČ)

The village of Škrip is the oldest settlement on the island, with a fourth-century chapel and 16th-century castle. The fortified tower houses a small museum of local finds (tel 021 3.0033; Easter–end Sep daily 8–8; 1 Oct–Easter Mon–Sat 8–2; adult 10kn, child 5kn), including a Roman relief of Hercules. The nearby church of Sveta Helena is dedicated to St. Helen, the mother of Roman emperor Constantine the Great. Local legend suggests that she was born in Škrip.
🕇 287 F8 ✉ Škrip ☎ 021 630033 🕐 Easter–end Sep daily 8–8; Oct–Easter Mon–Sat 8–2 👋 Adult 10kn, child 5kn

SUPETAR

The capital since 1815, the biggest town on Brač is named after the sixth-century basilica of Sveti Petar (St. Peter), mosaic fragments of which can be seen in the floor outside the parish church. On a cape beside the harbour, the town cemetery contains numerous memorials by local sculptor Ivan Rendić (1849–1932). West of the town lie some superb beaches with warm, shallow water lapping over the sand.

PUSTINJA BLACA (BLACA MONASTERY)

Blaca Monastery, set high up on a cliffside, can be reached by a 6km (4-mile) hike from the village of Murvica. Established by Orthodox monks in 1552, the monastery operated until the last monk died here in 1963. It now houses a collection of astronomical instruments, weapons and a library.
🕐 Erratic opening hours 👋 Free

INFORMATION
BOL
www.bol.hr
🕇 287 F8 ℹ Porat Bolskih Pomoraca, Bol ☎ 021 635638 🕐 Jun–end Sep daily 8.30am–10pm; Oct–end May Mon–Fri 8.30–3 🚢 Car ferry from Split to Supetar and Makarska to Sumartin; catamaran from Split and Jelsa (Hvar) to Bol

SUPETAR
www.supetar.hr
🕇 287 F8 ℹ Porat 1 (by the harbour) ☎ 021 630551 🕐 Jun–end Sep daily 7.30am–10.30pm; Oct–end May Mon–Sat 8.30–3.30

TIPS
» To explore the island in more detail, follow the drive, ▷ 198–199.
» A steep path leads from Bol to the summit of Vidova Gora. The restaurant at the summit is open in summer.
» If the main beach at Zlatni Rat gets too crowded, try one of the quieter rocky coves further on.
» Take a boat trip in summer from Bol to Blaca, where you can hike up to a dramatic 16th-century hermitage, built into the cliff.
» Milna is a pretty harbourside fishing port around 20km (12.5 miles) southwest of Supetar.

Opposite A view of the coast between Bol and Murvica

HVAR

INFORMATION

www.tzhvar.hr

✚ 287 G8 ℹ Trg Svetog Stjepana, Hvar Town 16 ☎ 021 741059 ◷ Jun daily 8–2, 3–9; Jul–end Sep daily 8–2, 3–10; Oct daily 8–2, 4–8; Nov–end May daily 8–2 ⛴ Car ferry from Split to Stari Grad and Drvenik to Sućuraj; passenger ferry from Split to Hvar Town; catamaran from Split and Bol (Brač) to Jelsa; catamaran from Split and Korčula to Hvar Town

INTRODUCTION

Hvar, a long, thin island, stretching for 80km (50 miles) along a limestone ridge, is the sunniest island in the Adriatic. Its capital, Hvar Town, at its eastern tip, is Croatia's glitziest resort, the playground of the rich and fashionable.

Greek settlers from Vis established a colony at the site of modern-day Stari Grad in the fourth century BC. Its original name of Pharos possibly derives from their home island of Paros, or perhaps from the Greek word for a lighthouse. The Venetians moved the capital to Hvar Town after they conquered the island in the 13th century. Destroyed by Turkish raiders in 1571, Hvar was rebuilt in the Venetian Gothic style. In 1868 the Hvar Hygienic Society promoted Hvar as a health resort because of its 2,700 hours of sunshine a year. The climate is so reliable that hotels offer free board in the event of fog, snow or sub-zero temperatures—something that happened in 2005 for the first time in 10 years.

The most frequent ferry crossing to Hvar is from Drvenik on the Makarska riviera to Sućuraj, though you are then left with a long drive across the island to Hvar Town. There are also car ferries from Split to Stari Grad, and a passenger ferry to Hvar Town. This makes a lovely way to arrive on the island, with the view of Hvar Town from the sea. The best times to visit are in June, when the lavender is in full bloom, or in August to soak up the atmosphere of Croatia's answer to St. Tropez. Despite the year-round mild climate, Hvar virtually goes to sleep in winter, when most hotels, restaurants and museums are closed. Be aware that opening times at museums and other attractions are highly erratic on Hvar; if there are few tourists around, sights may be closed.

WHAT TO SEE

TRG SVETOG STJEPANA, HVAR TOWN

Hvar Town is built around a sheltered bay below a Venetian castle and medieval walls. From the ferry dock, a promenade lined with palm trees leads to Trg

Above The attractive main square, Trg Svetog Stjepana, is a focus for café life in Hvar Town

Svetog Stjepana, the town's main square. This flagstoned piazza, a focus for café life, is the largest in Dalmatia, with a 16th-century well at the centre and handsome Gothic buildings on three sides; the fourth side opens onto the inner harbour. On one side is the former Venetian governor's mansion, now Hotel Palace, with a clock tower and loggia bearing reliefs of the winged lion of St. Mark. Across the square, at its seaward end, is the Venetian arsenal— distinguished by the large archway through which galleys were brought in to be repaired—with the Hvar Community Theatre on its top floor (▷ below). The landward end is dominated by the 16th-century cathedral and its four-floor campanile, which employs the typical Venetian architectural device of having one arched window on the first floor, two on the second and so on. The bronze doors were sculpted by Kuzma Kovačić (b.1952), a local artist who also designed Croatia's coins. The attached bishop's palace contains a small museum of religious art (summer Mon–Sat 10–12, 5–7; winter by appointment).

FRANJEVAČKI SAMOSTAN (FRANCISCAN MONASTERY)
A short stroll from the ferry dock at Hvar Town brings you to this monastery complex overlooking a pebble cove. Inhabited by just two monks, the building has a lovely 15th-century cloister where concerts are held on some summer evenings. Inside you'll find a small museum, with displays of old oil jars and coins dating back to Roman times. The Venetian-era paintings are more interesting, with a large Last Supper by Matej Ponzoni Poncun taking up almost an entire wall. The church just off the cloisters is also worth a look for its altar and tombs.
☎ 021 741193 ⏰ May–end Oct Mon–Sat 10–12, 5–7 ✋ Adult 15kn, child 10kn

HVARSKO PUČKO KAZALIŠTE (HVAR COMMUNITY THEATRE)
The top floor of the Venetian arsenal houses one of Europe's oldest public theatres, which opened in 1612 and is still in use today. The interior is richly decorated in red velvet, with ceiling frescoes added in the early 19th century. In the lobby, look for the figurehead of a *zvir* (dragon), from the prow of a Venetian galleon which was built in Hvar and saw service at the Battle of Lepanto in 1571. In summer, look out for performances of plays by Hanibal Lučić (1485–1553), the leading Croatian Renaissance dramatist, who was born in Hvar.
✉ Trg Svetog Stjepana, Hvar ☎ 021 741009 ⏰ Closed for renovation at time of writing ✋ 15kn

TIPS
» Vehicles are not allowed in the centre of Hvar, so leave your car in the large car park (parking lot) on the edge of town (5kn/hour, 50kn/day) from where it is a short walk to the main square.
» If the crowds in Hvar Town get too much, escape to the unspoiled beaches of the south coast between Sveta Nedjelja and Zavala. Between the two is Ivan Dolac, a hilltop village overlooking the coast, which produces one of Croatia's best red wines.

Left *A panoramic view of Hvar Town and its sheltered harbour*
Below *A stone carving on the cathedral facade, Hvar Town*

PAKLENI OTOCI (PAKLENI ISLANDS)

Although there are pebble beaches to the west of Hvar Town, most people take a taxi-boat to this chain of wooded islands just offshore. In winter, the islands are uninhabited, but in summer they make a popular retreat, with yachts in the harbours and fish restaurants springing up beside remote beaches and coves. The best beach is at Palmižana, on the biggest island, Sveti Kliment; naturists head for the isle of Jerolim.

🚢 From Hvar Town

STARI GRAD

A touch quieter than bustling Hvar Town, Hvar's second town is built on the site of the original Greek settlement of Pharos, hence its name Stari Grad (Old Town). The ruins of Pharos can still be seen behind the 12th-century church of Sveti Ivana (St. John). The main sight, set back from the harbour, is Tvrdalj Petra Hektorovića (Jun–end Sep daily 10–1, 5–8), the fortified summer palace and gardens of the poet Petar Hektorović (1487–1572). His best-known work, *Ribanje i Ribarsko Prigovaranje (Fishing and Conversations with Fishermen)*, describing a three-day fishing trip to Brač and Šolta in the company of two fishermen, is a classic of Croatian folk literature. The residence itself, dating from 1520 but altered considerably since then, has a secluded cloister surrounding a pond and citations from Hektorović's works in Croatian, Latin and Italian on the walls.

Other attractions in Stari Grad include a Dominican Monastery (daily 10–12, 6–8). Displays at the monastery museum, which include Greek tombstones and other bits of masonry, hint at how the town may have looked in antiquity.

Below *The 16th-century cathedral and distinctive Venetian bell tower on Trg Svetog Stjepana, Hvar Town's main square*

The 19th-century monastery church contains a painting by Tintoretto called *The Interment of Christ*.

✚ 287 F8 🛈 Obala F. Tuđmana bb ☎ 021 765763 ◎ Jun–end Sep daily 8am–10pm; Oct–end May 8–2 🚢 From Hvar

Above *Detail of the cathedral façade, Hvar Town*
Above left *View of the Pakleni Otoci (Pakleni Islands) at sunset*

MORE TO SEE

FORTICA (FORTRESS)

Climb the steps from Trg Svetog Stjepana to the 16th-century fortress above Hvar Town. There is a small museum and you can visit the underground dungeons, but the main reason for coming is the view over the town, with the Pakleni Islands glistening offshore and Vis on the horizon.

☎ 021 742620 ◎ Summer daily 8am–midday, winter 9–7 🖑 Adult 15kn, child 10kn

MUZEJ HANIBAL LUČIĆ

In Hvar Town, the Benedictine convent in the former house of playwright Hanibal Lučić has a small museum of sacred art, and also sells lace made by the nuns.

✉ Groda, Hvar Town ☎ 021 741009 ◎ May–end Oct daily 9–1, 5–11; Nov–end Apr 10–12 by appointment 🖑 Adult 15kn, child 10kn

JELSA

This lively harbourside town faces Brač on the north coast, with regular taxi-boats making the excursion to Zlatni Rat (▷ 171) in summer. Look for the octagonal Crkva Sveti Ivana (Church of St. John) in a square behind the harbour. A Latin inscription on the lintel of a 1561 house in the same square declares *Dominus Chustodiat Introitum Tum et Exitum* (God protect your entrance and exit). Crkva Sv Fabijana i Sebastijana (Church of SS Fabian and Sebastian) is also interesting; slip in just before Mass begins to admire a magnificently carved altar by Antonio Porri and a statue of the Virgin brought here by refugees fleeing attack by the Ottoman Turks in the 16th century.

A footpath leads for 5km (3 miles) through pine woods to Vrboska, with beaches and a 16th-century crenellated church overlooking the bay. East of the village lies a sandy cove called Mina and the Soline public beach. The islet of Zečevo is popular with nudists and was one of the first places in Croatia where people bathed *au naturel*.

✚ 287 G8 🛈 Riva bb ☎ 021 761918 ◎ Jun–end Sep daily 8am–11pm; Oct–end May Mon–Fri 8–2 🚢 From Hvar

KORČULA

INTRODUCTION

Korčula, an island of vineyards, olive groves and oak forests, is best known for its capital of the same name, a perfectly preserved gem of a Venetian walled town.

Although humans have been living on the island for at least 10,000 years, its recorded history begins with the arrival of Greek settlers from Vis, who named it Korkyra Melaina (Black Corfu) because of its dark forests. Under the Venetian republic, which ruled Korčula for 700 years, the island was known for its shipbuilders and stonemasons; its fleet rivalled that of Dubrovnik and stone from Vrnik was used in buildings from Venice to Constantinople. The present layout of Korčula Town dates from the 13th to 15th centuries, when it was one of the finest cities in the Adriatic.

Ferries to Korčula arrive at Vela Luka and Korčula Town, linked by a road which runs for 45km (28 miles) across the island. The easiest approach from Split is to take a ferry to Vela Luka; from Dubrovnik and the south, drive across the Pelješac peninsula for the short crossing from Orebić. The ferry harbour for Korčula is actually 2km (1.2 miles) south of town at Dominče, though passenger boats and some car ferries arrive right on the dockside in Korčula Town. Of the two main towns, Vela Luka is the larger but almost everything of interest is in Korčula Town. Elsewhere, you will find the wine towns of Blato and Smokvica, pine and oak forests, sand and pebble beaches, offshore islands and hidden bays.

INFORMATION

www.korculainfo.com

🔡 287 G9 🛈 Obala Vinka Palentina, Korčula Town ☎ 020 715807 🕐 Mid-Jun to mid-Sep Mon–Fri 8–3, Sat 8–12, Sun 8–1; May to mid-Jun, mid-Sep to mid-Oct Mon–Fri 8–3, Sat 8–12; mid-Oct to end Apr Mon–Fri 8–2, Sat 8–12 🚢 From Dubrovnik 🚢 Car ferry from Split to Vela Luka and Orebić to Dominče; car ferry from Drvenik to Dominče in summer; passenger ferry from Orebić to Korčula Town; catamaran from Split and Hvar to Korčula Town; catamaran from Split to Vela Luka

WHAT TO SEE

KORČULA TOWN

The old town of Korčula is like an open-air museum, with churches, palaces, steep alleys and flagstoned piazzas crammed onto a tiny peninsula, partly surrounded by 13th-century walls, bastions and towers. A promenade follows the course of the old walls, offering fine views across the channel to the Pelješac mountains, just 2km (1.2 miles) away. Inside the walls, notice the herringbone pattern of the grid plan, ingeniously designed to allow sea breezes and views to penetrate the narrow streets while shielding the houses from the effects of strong winds in winter.

KOPNENA VRATA (LAND GATE)

A broad flight of steps leads up from Trg Kralja Tomislava to this archway, built in 1391 as the main entrance to the old town. The arch is crowned by the 15th-century Revelin Tower, whose outer wall features a relief of the winged lion of Venice and a plaque marking the 1,000th anniversary of the coronation of Tomislav, the first Croatian king. The tower now houses an exhibition on the *moreška* sword dance. This highly stylized dance, in which the Black King and his army battle with the White King and his followers (dressed in red) for the love of a Muslim maiden, dates to the 16th century and is a variation of the mock battles between Muslims and Christians found throughout the Mediterranean since the time of the Crusades. In summer, a special stage is erected outside the Land Gate, with *moreška* performances on Monday and Thursday evenings (▷ 204). You can climb onto the roof of the tower for views over the town (Jul–end Aug 9–9, Easter–end Jun and Sep–end Oct 9–1, 4–8).

KATEDRALA SVETOG MARKA (ST. MARK'S CATHEDRAL)

Korčula's cathedral has long been demoted to church status (though the name has remained) but this takes nothing away from this beautiful edifice. The Gothic-Renaissance structure stands on the main square of the old town, with a rose window looking down on the square and a portal flanked by sculptures of Adam and Eve and topped by a statue of St. Mark. Inside the church, look out for

Opposite *Korčula Town overlooks the mountains of the neighbouring Pelješac peninsula*

TIPS

» Cars are not allowed in the old town in Korčula and there is limited parking by the harbour, so leave your car at one of the car parks outside the town and walk in.

» Although the museums in Korčula Town are closed in winter, visits can be arranged through the tourist office.

» Try to catch a performance of the *moreška* sword dance (▷ 204); it is performed regularly on summer evenings at a stage by the Revelin Tower.

» Some excellent white wines are produced on Korčula, notably Grk from Lumbarda and Pošip from Čara and Smokvica.

Below *A number of pretty beaches and coves can be found near Vela Luka*

the altarpiece by Tintoretto (1518–94) beneath a 15th-century marble ciborium (canopy) by local stonemason Marko Andrijić. The bishop's palace beside the cathedral houses a Treasury of religious art, pottery and coins (Jul, Aug 9–9, May, Jun and Sep–end Oct 9–1, 4–8; closed rest of the year except for pre-booked groups).

GRADSKI MUZEJ (TOWN MUSEUM)

This museum occupies a 16th-century Renaissance palace opposite the cathedral and contains archaeological finds and displays on Korčula's shipbuilding history. In the atrium is a replica third-century BC stone tablet from Lumbarda, granting rights to Greek settlers to live inside the walled town and cultivate land outside. The original is kept in the Archaeological Museum in Zagreb (▷ 53). Another 16th-century palace on the same square houses a gallery of sculptures by local artist Frano Krsinić (1897–1982).

✉ Trg Svetog Marka ☎ 020 711420 ⊘ Mid-Jun to mid-Jul, Sep daily 9–2, 7–9; mid-Jul to end Aug daily 9–9; Apr to mid-Jun, Oct daily 9–2 ✋ Adult 10kn, child 5kn

KUĆA MARKA POLA (MARCO POLO'S HOUSE)

The traveller and writer Marco Polo (1254–1324) is believed to have been born in Korčula and the island claims him as its favourite son, although there is no firm evidence for the claim. He was captured in a naval battle off Lumbarda in 1298 while commanding a Venetian war galley against the Genoese fleet. Jailed in Genoa, he began dictating *Il Milione*, his memoirs of life at the imperial court in China, which became the best-known work of travel literature of all time. The historic home of the Depolo family was bought by Korčula Town Council in 2004 with the aim of opening it as a Marco Polo Museum; at present, only the tower is open. There are maps, manuscripts and the Depolo coat of arms on display, and

you can climb the wooden steps to the belvedere for views over the old town. There are also ambitious plans to build a replica of Marco Polo's galleon to put on permanent display in the harbour.

✉ Ulica Depolo ☎ 020 716529 🕐 Jul–end Aug daily 9–9; Apr–Jun and Sep–Oct 9–1, 4 8 👋 Adult 15kn, child 7kn

MORE TO SEE

GALERIJA IKONA (ICON GALLERY)

This small but worthwhile museum in Korčula Town houses a fascinating display of Greek Orthodox icons, painted on wood or gold and taken from Crete for safekeeping during a war between Venetian and Turkish troops. A covered bridge leads into the church of Svih Svetih (All Saints), with a beautiful 18th-century Pietà carved out of walnut wood. One of the highlights of the museum's collection is the huge candles, brought out and paraded around Korčula Town at important festivals.

✉ Trg Svih Svetih, Korčula Town ☎ 020 711306 🕐 Jul–end Aug daily 9–1, 5–7; May–end Jun and Sep 9–1 👋 Adult 10kn, child 5kn

VELA LUKA

www.tzvelaluka.hr

Korčula's biggest town is set around a long natural harbour, with several good beaches on nearby islands and bays. In a hill above the town, Vela Spila (Jun–end Sep daily 9–12, 5–8) is an enormous cave which was inhabited in the Stone Age. Concerts are held in the cave entrance in summer. Finds from the site are displayed at the Centar Za Kulturu (Jun–end Sep Mon–Sat 9–1, 8–11; Oct–end May Mon–Fri 9–1), in a building beside the church. The museum also contains a collection of wooden ships and an art gallery featuring two sculptures by Henry Moore, donated to Vela Luka after a high tide hit the town in 1978.

🛈 Ulica 3 ☎ 020 813619 🕐 Jun–end Sep Mon–Sat 8am–9pm; Oct–end May Mon–Fri 8–3 🚌 From Korčula

BEACHES AND ISLANDS

In summer, taxi-boats from Korčula Town will take you to Lumbarda, with its sandy Prižna beach. Or, take a boat to the isle of Badija, with its 14th-century monastery. There are also good beaches at Orebić on the Pelješac peninsula.

If you want solitude, head to almost deserted beaches on the tiny islands of Proizid and Ošjak, just off Korčula's western shore. Both can be reached by private or hired boat.

Above *Korčula Town's Gothic-Renaissance cathedral, Katedrala Svetog Marka*
Above left *The cathedral bell tower dominates Korčula Town's skyline*

KRKA

INFORMATION

www.npkrka.hr

✛ 286 E7 ℹ️ Nacionalni Park Krka, Trg Ivana Pavla II, Šibenik ☎ 022 201777
☎ Lozovac reception: 022 778702
🕐 Daily 9–6 💷 Jun–end Sep: adult 95kn, child 70kn; Oct: adult 80kn, child 60kn; Nov–end Feb: adult 30kn, child 20kn; Mar–end May: adult 80kn, child 60kn 🚌 From Šibenik 🍴 ☕ 🏧

INTRODUCTION

The stunning Krka river valley with its dramatic canyons and cascades rivals Plitvice Lakes for its beauty, and is much more accessible for visitors to the Dalmatian coast. The River Krka rises near Knin and flows for 72km (45 miles) to its mouth at Šibenik via the estuary at Skradin. Along the way it carves out a series of limestone gorges, forming travertine lakes and streams similar to those at Plitvice (▷ 91–93). Much of this area was declared a national park in 1985. Wildlife includes lizards, snakes and turtles, and flowers such as Adriatic violet and campanula (bell-flower).

The two main entrances to Krka National Park are at Skradin and Lozovac, both reached by regular buses from Šibenik. From Skradin, boats depart on the hour in summer along a wooded gorge to the foot of the Skradinski Buk waterfalls. From Lozovac, a shuttle bus takes you to the top of the falls, where you can buy tickets for the boat trips upstream to Visovac and Roški Slap. Between November and February, when the shuttle buses and boats do not operate, it is possible to drive to Skradinski Buk from Skradin or Lozovac. In summer, you should allow a full day for visiting the park; in winter, most people will be content with the two-hour circuit on foot around the falls.

Should you wish to stay longer and get well off the beaten track, pick up a map at the entrance gate and plan you own hikes to some of the many ruined medieval castles found within the park's boundaries. These include Trošenj, Kamičak, Nečven, Bogočin and Ključica castles.

WHAT TO SEE
SKRADINSKI BUK

Of seven sets of waterfalls, Skradinski Buk is the most spectacular, descending 45m (147ft) in a series of 17 cascades and ending in a clear pool where people swim in summer. The average flow over the falls is around 50 cubic metres (1,765 cubic feet) per second, rising to 350 cubic metres (12,360 cubic feet) after

Above *The town of Skradin, one of the two main entrances to Krka National Park*

rain. An easy network of footpaths and bridges leads around the falls, taking between one and two hours to complete. The best viewpoints are from the wooden footbridge at the base of the falls, and the Imperial Belvedere halfway up, built in 1875 for the visit of Austrian emperor Franz Josef I.

VISOVAC

From a jetty near the Lozovac entrance to Skradinski Buk, boats make the two-hour return journey (adult 70kn, child 40kn) to this Franciscan monastery on an island in the river at the point where it widens into a lake. The church was founded by Augustinian monks in the 14th century, though only the original cloisters remain. The monks here show visitors around the museum, which includes a 15th-century illustrated Croatian version of *Aesop's Fables*.

ROŠKI SLAP

A four-hour boat trip (adult 130kn, child 90kn) continues along the Krka canyon to the waterfalls at Roški Slap, where several old watermills, some recently brought back into use, and other water-powered workshops, line the banks. From here you can take a further trip (adult 100kn, child 70kn) along the quieter northern part of the river, to the Serbian Orthodox Krka monastery and the medieval Croatian fortress of Nečven.

MANOJLOVAC SLAP

While Roški Slap and Skradinski Buk receive most attention, some regard Manojlovac Slap as the most attractive waterfall on the River Krka. It is certainly the tallest, with water tumbling 32m (105ft) in some places. In summer, however, water is redirected to feed a nearby hydroelectric plant, leaving the rock face almost dry. There are more abandoned mills at the bottom of the waterfall.

KRKA MONASTERY

From Roški Slap you can take a further trip (adult 70kn, child 40kn) along the quieter northern part of the river to the Serbian Orthodox Krka Monastery, sometimes also known as the Holy Archangel Monastery, built on the site of an earlier hermitage at a broad part of the river. The main attractions here are the Byzantine church, the library and the tranquil location. Some of the monastery's collections were destroyed during the Homeland War.

Left *The secluded Franciscan monastery on a rocky island in Lake Visovac*
Below *Skradinski Buk waterfalls*

KLIS

www.tzo-klis.htnet.hr

Lying on a strategically important pass between the Kozjak and Mosor mountains, Klis has for centuries played a key role on the borders of the Venetian, Habsburg and Ottoman empires. The town is dominated by its Tvrđava fortress (Jun–end Sep Tue–Sun 9–7; Oct–end May Tue–Sun 10–4), which stands on a rocky bluff overlooking the coast. Built on the site of an Illyrian hill fort, this was the bulwark of the medieval Croatian kings. In the 16th century, the castle was taken over by the legendary Uskok warriors under their commander Petar Kružić, whose capture and execution by Turkish troops in 1537 forced the Uskoks to flee to Senj (▷ 153). After 111 years of Ottoman rule the fortress fell to Venice and later to the Austrian empire. Most of what you see today dates from the Venetian and Austrian eras, including the remains of the 17th-century church of St. Vitus, constructed over a Turkish mosque. Climb the ramparts for fine views of Split, just 10km (6 miles) to the southwest.

✚ 287 F7 ℹ Megdan 57 ☎ 021 240578 ◉ Jun–end Sep daily 8–3; Oct–end May Tue–Sun 10–4 🚌 From Split

KNIN

www.tz-knin.hr

The small town of Knin played a big part in Croatian history as the seat of the 10th-century kings and later the headquarters of the self-declared Republic of the Serbian Krajina (1990–95). At the start of the Homeland War the population of Knin was 90 per cent Serbian and it made an obvious base for the rebellion, allowing the Serbs to control road and rail links between Zagreb and Dalmatia. The capture of Knin by Croatian forces in August 1995 marked the effective end of the war; President Tuđman arrived the next day to hoist the Croatian flag on the castle. Standing on the Sveti Spas hill, the Tvrđava (Mar–end Oct daily 7–7; Nov–end Feb 7–3) was once the biggest fortress in Dalmatia and its fortunes mirror the region's history, changing hands between the Ottoman, Venetian and Austrian empires. A huge Croatian tricolour flies from the ramparts and it has become something of a nationalist shrine for Homeland War veterans.

✚ 286 F6 ℹ Ulica Tuđmana 24 ☎ 022 819822 ◉ Mon–Fri 8–3 🚌 From Šibenik

KORČULA

▷ 177–179.

KORNATI OTOCI (KORNATI ISLANDS)

www.kornati.hr

In this archipelago of 89 islands between Zadar and Šibenik the white rocky islands have a stark, ethereal beauty not seen elsewhere in the Adriatic. The easiest way to visit is on a day-trip from Murter, where boatmen by the quayside advertise tours in summer (these cost around 250kn including lunch and park entry). There are also organized excursions from Zadar and other coastal towns. Better still, take your own yacht, as the islands are a paradise for sailors. Swimming and snorkelling are allowed within the park but you need a permit for fishing, and diving must be within an organized group. If you want to extend your stay, travel agents in Murter offer stays in old fishermen's cottages, with well-water and your own fishing boat.

✚ 286 D7 ℹ Nacionalni Park Kornati, Ulica Butina 2, Murter ☎ 022 435740 ◉ Summer daily 7–3; winter Mon–Fri 7–3 🚌 From Šibenik to Murter 🚢 Organized excursions from Biograd-na-Moru, Murter, Šibenik and Zadar in summer 👋 National park entry fee: 150kn per boat if bought in advance, 250kn from mobile boat wardens within the park

KRKA
▷ 180–181.

LASTOVO
The remote island of Lastovo is one of the last untouched paradises in the Mediterranean. Closed to foreigners from 1976 to 1989 when it was used as a Yugoslav naval base, a visit here feels like a step back in time. A single paved road runs across the island, from the ferry port at Ubli to the main settlement at Lastovo Town and the beautiful Skrivena Luka (Hidden Bay), guarded by Struga lighthouse. The population of 800 lives by subsistence farming and fishing, working the fields by hand and producing their own wine and olive oil. In recent years tourism has started to make an impact, with fish restaurants springing up at remote beaches and coves to cater for visiting sailors in summer. There are plans to designate the entire Lastovo archipelago a nature park, with the aim of encouraging tourism but at the same time protecting its unique environment and beauty.
✚ 287 G9 ℹ Lastovo Town ☎ 020 801018 🚢 Car ferry and catamaran from Split, Hvar and Vela Luka (Korčula) to Ubli

MAKARSKA
www.makarska-info.hr
The Makarska Riviera is the name for a string of popular beach resorts that stretches for 60km (37 miles) from Brela to Gradac. The most attractive resorts are at either end, with long pebble beaches shaded by pine trees and the dark grey Biokovo massif looming behind. At the heart of the riviera, Makarska is a lively harbourside town set in a horseshoe bay protected by wooded peninsulas on both sides. Stroll around the palm-lined promenade to the town museum, Gradski Muzej Makarska (daily 9–1, 5–7), in a baroque palace on the waterfront, with displays of Bronze Age pottery, Dalmatian folk costumes and early tourist postcards.

The Malakološki Muzej (Mollusc Museum) has an extraordinary collection of seashells in an annex to the Franciscan monastery (May–end Oct daily 11–noon), painstakingly put together by Brother Jure Radić (1920–90).
✚ 287 G8 ℹ Obala Kralja Tomislava 16 ☎ 021 612002 🕐 Mid Jun to mid-Sep Mon–Sat 7–9, Sun 8–12, 5–8; mid-Sep to mid-Jun Mon–Sat 7–3 🚌 From Dubrovnik and Split

NIN
www.nin.hr
Nin has been called the cradle of Croatia. Between the 9th and 12th centuries, during the golden age of Croatian independence, this small island village was the ecclesiastical and royal capital of the country. Cross the stone bridge to enter through the 15th-century Donja Vrata (Lower Gate). From here, a single street runs through the town, ending at the Arheološki Muzej (daily Jun–end-Aug 9am–10pm; Sep–end May Mon–Sat 9–noon), behind which stand the remains of a first-century Roman temple. Not far from here is Nin's most famous sight, the beautiful whitewashed ninth-century Crkva Svetog Križa (Church of the Holy Cross).

The 11th-century Romanesque church of Sveti Nikole (St. Nicholas) stands on a hillock just outside Nin on the road to Zadar. According to tradition, this was where the medieval Croatian kings came to take an oath after their coronation.
✚ 285 D6 ℹ Trg Braće Radića ☎ 023 265247 🕐 May–end Sep daily 8–8; Oct–end Dec, Jan–end Apr daily 8–3 🚌 From Zadar

Clockwise from below *Pebble beach on the Makarska Riviera; Nin; Tvrdava fortress, Klis*

OMIŠ

www.tz-omis.hr

Omiš is situated where the River Cetina flows into the sea, 105km (66 miles) after beginning its journey at an underground spring in the small village of Cetina. From April to October this is Croatia's top rafting destination, as day-trippers flock here to ride the rapids of the dramatic Cetina gorge. Most people pass straight through Omiš on the road from Dubrovnik to Split, but it repays an hour or two of gentle strolling through the cobbled lanes of the old town and up to the Mirabela castle, whose tower you can climb in summer. There is also a long town beach, Gradska Plaža, with a mix of fine pebbles and sand.

✚ 287 G8 🛈 Trg Kneza Miroslava ☎ 021 861350 🕓 Jun–end Sep daily 8–8; Oct–end May Mon–Fri 8–3 🚌 From Dubrovnik, Makarska and Split

OTAVICE

www.mdc.hr/mestrovic

The pig-farming village of Otavice, 10km (6 miles) east of Drniš, was the childhood home of the sculptor Ivan Meštrović (▷ 23), who chose it as the setting for his family mausoleum in the crypt of the Crkva Presvetog Otkupitelja (Church of the Holy Redeemer). Built of local limestone to a Meštrović design between 1926 and 1931, the church stands at the top of a long flight of steps overlooking the village. The interior is decorated with reliefs by Meštrović, including the four evangelists and *Crucified Forever*. From 1991 to 1995 the church was occupied by Serbian soldiers who scrawled graffiti on the walls, desecrated the tombs and laid landmines in the nearby fields. Most of the resulting damage has now been repaired, but the bronze doors bearing portraits of Meštrović, his parents, wives and children were taken away and have never been returned.

✚ 286 F7 ☎ 022 872630 🕓 Jun–end Sep Tue–Sun 8–12, 5–8; Oct–end May Tue–Sun 10–2 💷 Adult 10kn, child 5kn

PAG

www.pag-tourism.hr

Arriving on Pag from the mainland—either across the bridge from Dalmatia or by ferry from the Kvarner coast—it seems surprising that it is able to support any life. Croatia's fifth-largest island resembles an arid desert or moonscape, with vegetation stripped bare by the sheep, who outnumber the human inhabitants by at least two to one. The main road from Pag Town to Novalja is lined with rocky slopes, dry-stone walls and sheep grazing on the salt marshes. Roadside stalls advertise *paški sir*, a mature sheep's cheese similar to Parmesan and flavoured with salt, herbs and olive oil. Pag's other claim to fame is *paški čipka* (Pag lace), which has been made here for centuries. You can buy it from old women in the streets and squares of Pag Town, or visit the small museum attached to the lace-making school.

Pag Town was rebuilt from scratch in the 15th century by Renaissance architect Juraj Dalmatinac, giving the old walled town a harmonious feel. The rose window on the facade of the parish church was designed to reflect the intricate patterns found in Pag lace.

One surprising fact about Pag is that it has the longest coastline of any Croatian island, with numerous pebble beaches and bays. Zrće beach, near Novalja, is Croatia's answer to Ibiza, with open-air clubs scattered around a wide arc of white pebbles and views of the Velebit mountains across the lagoon. The island has become the summer haunt of Zagreb's clubbers and Zrće is very busy on warm summer nights.

✚ 285 C6 🛈 Ulica Od Špitala 2, Pag Town ☎ 023 611301 🕓 Jul, Aug daily 8am–10pm; Apr–end Jun, Sep, Oct daily 8–7; Nov–end Mar daily 8–2 🚌 From Zadar 🚢 Car ferry from Prizna to Žigljen; catamaran from Rijeka and Rab to Novalja

Below Fortress on the barren island of Pag, where sheep outnumber human inhabitants

Above left to right *Rock climber in Paklenica National Park; the reed beds of Vransko Jezero*

PAKLENICA

www.paklenica.hr

Established in 1949, Paklenica National Park covers an area of 96sq km (38sq miles) at the southern end of the Velebit range. The lower slopes are forested with beech and black pine, while above are jagged limestone peaks. The park offers some of Croatia's best and most accessible mountain hiking and climbing. The most popular walk is along the Velika Paklenica canyon; from here, paths lead off to the summit of Anića Kuk (712m/2,335ft) and the Manita Peć cave, with its stalactites, stalagmites and columns (guided tours only; Jul, Aug daily 10–1; ask at entrance for other times). Serious hikers can climb Vaganski vrh (1,758m/ 5,766ft) for magnificent views over the islands and coast.

The underground bunkers in Velika Paklenica, secretly built during the Tito years, are currently closed for renovations.

✚ 285 D6 ℹ Nacionalni Park Paklenica, Ulica Tuđmana 14A, Starigrad Paklenica
☎ 023 369202; Park entrance: 023 369803
✋ Adult 40kn, child (7–18) 20kn; three-day ticket and climbing permit 80kn; cave 15kn
🚌 From Zadar

PAKOŠTANE

www.pakostane.hr

Pakoštane is a small beach resort 24km (15 miles) south of Zadar, on the shores of Vransko Jezero, Croatia's largest natural lake. A 30km (18-mile) cycle trail circles the lake, whose reed beds attract birds, including a rare colony of purple herons. Just up the coast, Biograd-na-Moru ('white town on sea') was a royal seat where Hungarian monarchs were crowned kings of Croatia; today it is a relaxed holiday resort, deserted in winter but lively in summer, with boats leaving for the peaceful island of Pašman and for cruises to the Kornati Islands (▷ 182).

✚ 286 D7 ℹ Trg Kraljice Jelene 78
☎ 023 381892 🚌 From Šibenik and Zadar

PRIMOŠTEN

www.summernet.hr/primosten

The old coast road from Šibenik to Trogir passes small beaches and coves with a relaxed holiday atmosphere. Around 20km (12.5 miles) south of Šibenik, Primošten is on an island that was joined to the mainland in the 15th century. It was founded by Bosnian refugees fleeing the Ottoman Turks and was fortified by the Venetians, who built town walls. From a distance, it resembles Rovinj in miniature (▷ 130–132), with a church tower rising above the rooftops and houses tumbling down the hills to the sea. Walk through an archway to enter the old town and climb the steps to the church of Sveti Juraj (St. George), with views of nearby islands from the terrace. There are good pebble beaches nearby as well as a large marina at Kremik. The vineyards around Primošten produce Babić, a full-bodied red wine.

To the south, Rogoznica is a busy summer resort on an island with a causeway to the mainland.

✚ 286 E7 ℹ Trg Biskupa Arnerića 2
☎ 022 571111 🕐 May–end Sep daily 8am–10pm 🚌 From Šibenik

Above *The ruined amphitheatre at Salona, captial of the Roman province of Dalmatia*
Above right *The Franciscan monastery at Sinj, a place of pilgrimage*

SALONA

www.mdc.hr

Built at the mouth of the Jadro river delta, the ancient city of Salona was the capital of the Roman province of Dalmatia, with a population of some 60,000 people. This is undoubtedly Croatia's most evocative archaeological site, with ruined basilicas, temples, cemeteries, theatres and baths standing amid fields on the edge of the modern town of Solin, within sight of Split. Salona flourished between the second century BC and seventh century AD, when its inhabitants fled to Split after the arrival of the Croats. The Roman emperor Diocletian was probably born here; so too was Domnius, the first Bishop of Salona, who was executed in the amphitheatre in AD304 during Diocletian's purge of Christians. His tomb is at Manastirine, just inside the entrance gate. Nearby Tusculum museum was built in 1898, incorporating Roman statuary in its walls; it now has an exhibition on the history of the site. From here, you can wander around the ruins of ancient Salona, tracing sections of Roman wall, exploring the amphitheatre and looking out for chariot tracks in the stones. It is fascinating to imagine a time when Salona was a thriving metropolis and Split a fishing village.

✚ 287 F7 ✉ Put Starina, Solin ☎ 021 211538 🕐 May–end Sep Mon–Fri 7–7, Sat 9–7, Sun 9–1; Oct–end Apr Mon–Fri 9–3.30, Sat 9–2 ✋ Adult 20kn, child 10kn 🚌 From Split 🚊 🏛

ŠIBENIK

▷ 187.

SINJ

www.tzsinj.hr

Set in the broad Cetina valley 34km (21 miles) inland from Split, Sinj is a potent mix of Catholicism, Croatian nationalism and military history which reaches its peak each August at the Sinjska Alka (▷ 207), a jousting tournament with riders in 18th-century costume. The festival is held to celebrate a famous victory in 1715, when a force of 60,000 Turkish soldiers attempting to storm the fortress was defeated by just 700 locals, with the help of a miracle-working 16th-century portrait of the Sinjska Gospa (Our Lady of Sinj). During the previous Turkish occupation, from 1513 to 1687, the painting was removed to Bosnia for safekeeping, where it was found to perform miracles. Topped with a golden crown, it is kept inside the parish church on the main square; the legend is repeated on the church's bronze doors, which depict the Virgin repelling the Turkish attack.

✚ 287 F7 ℹ Ulica Vrlička 41 ☎ 021 826352 🕐 Jul–end Aug daily 8–8; May–end Jun and Sep–end Oct Mon–Fri 8–3, Sat 8–1; Nov–end Apr Mon–Fri 8–3 🚌 From Split

ŠOLTA

www.solta.hr

Although it can be reached from Split in less than an hour, Šolta is the forgotten island of Central Dalmatia, attracting none of the summer crowds of neighbouring Brač and Hvar. Experience the relaxed atmosphere on this largely rural island of olives, figs and vines, with pebble beaches on the north coast and steep cliffs in the south. Ferries arrive at Rogač, the harbour for the main town of Grohote, though most people head west to Maslinica, a small village of fishermen's cottages around a sheltered bay, or east to Stomorska, a low-rise beach resort.

✚ 287 F8 ℹ Grohote ☎ 021 654151 🕐 Mon–Fri 8–4 🚢 Car ferry and catamaran from Split to Rogač; catamaran from Split to Stomorska

ŠIBENIK

Unlike other Dalmatian coastal towns, the busy port of Šibenik, at the mouth of the River Krka, was not occupied by the Romans but founded by Croatian settlers in 1066. The heart of the city is a labyrinth of narrow streets linking Trg Republike Hrvatske, the cathedral square, with Poljana, a large open piazza on the site of the original town gate.

THE CATHEDRAL

The highlight of Šibenik is Katedrala Svetog Jakova (St. James's Cathedral)—a fusion of Renaissance and Gothic styles. It is considered the masterpiece of Juraj Dalmatinac (c. 1400–73), a Venetian architect from Zadar, whose statue by Ivan Meštrović stands on the square. After his death, the work was continued by Nikola Firentinac (c. 1440–1505). The basic structure is a three-aisled basilica in the shape of a Latin cross, but the beauty is in the detail of the building. The main portal depicts the Last Judgment, while the side door is flanked by a pair of stone lions and statues of Adam and Eve with hands on their hearts. Don't miss the frieze around the outside of the apse; the 71 carved stone faces are thought to represent 15th-century Šibenik society.

THE FORTRESS

The Venetian fort Kaštel Svetog Mihovil (St. Michael's Castle) stands high above the town. Climb the steps from the cathedral square or follow the signs from Ulica Zagrebačka to reach the castle. It is currently undergoing restoration but you can walk around the ramparts for good views of the cathedral's unusual barrel-vaulted roof.

www.sibenik-tourism.hr
🕆 286 E7 🛈 Obala Franje Tuđmana 5
☎ 022 214411 🕓 Jul–end Aug daily 8–8; May–Jun and Oct daily 8am–9pm; Nov–end Apr Mon–Fri 8–3 🚍 From Split and Zadar

TIPS

» If arriving by car, park on the Riva (10kn/hr) or follow signs to the car park by the port (5kn/hr).
» For an easy circuit of the old town, walk along the waterfront promenade to the cathedral, then return along Ulica Kralja Tomislava and Ulica Zagrebačka.
» Children will enjoy Bunari (▷ 205), a multimedia exhibition in the old wells.

Above *Šibenik's cathedral, a triumph of Gothic and Renaissance architecture*

187

SPLIT

INTRODUCTION

Split is Croatia's second city, a bustling port, with ferries coming and going in the harbour and travellers passing through on their way to the Dalmatian islands. Its history begins in AD295, when the Roman emperor Gaius Aurelius Valerius Diocletianus (c.245–312), commonly known as Diocletian, ordered the building of a seafront palace near his childhood home. Born in Salona, the son of slaves, he rose through the army to become ruler of the Roman empire and is chiefly known for his vicious persecution and execution of Christians. In AD305 he became the first Roman emperor voluntarily to abdicate and retired to his palace at Split. In the seventh century refugees from Salona settled in the palace and it has been the core of the city ever since. During the 19th and 20th centuries Split experienced massive growth as an industrial port city and its population now exceeds 200,000.

The best way to arrive in Split is by sea, with the southern facade of Diocletian's palace at the heart of the city, seen on the waterfront against a backdrop of high-rise apartment blocks and distant mountains. A short stroll from the ferry dock leads to the Riva, a busy harbourside promenade with palm trees and terrace cafés. From here, you enter Diocletian's Palace through the Mjedena Vrata (Bronze Gate), which gives access to the underground galleries and central court. The main sights lie within the palace walls, though the city market is just outside the eastern Srebrena Vrata (Silver Gate) and the old town extends west through the Željezna Vrata (Iron Gate) to the shopping streets between Narodni Trg and Trg Republike. Beyond here, a pair of interesting museums lie at the foot of Marjan, the green hill overlooking the city.

INFORMATION

www.visitsplit.com

287 F8 Peristil ☎ 021 345606
 Jun–end Sep Mon–Sat 8–8, Sun 9–1; Oct–end May Mon–Fri 9–4, Sat 9–1
 From Dubrovnik, Šibenik, Zadar and Zagreb; local bus 37 from Trogir
 From Zagreb Ferry connections with Dubrovnik, Rijeka, Zadar, Brač, Hvar, Korcula, Lastovo, Šolta and Vis

Above The ruins of the Peristil courtyard of Diocletian's third-century AD palace are woven into the fabric of the modern city
Opposite The cathedral bell tower, built on the central Peristil courtyard

TIPS

» Guests staying for three nights receive a free Split Card, which gives free or discounted admission at museums and reductions on car rental, theatres and excursions. The card is also on sale at the tourist office (35kn for 72 hours).

» The city beach is at Bačvice, a crescent bay just beyond the ferry dock. There is also good bathing in summer from the rocky coves at the foot of the Marjan peninsula.

» Diocletian's Palace fills with tour groups from cruise ships during the day. For a more atmospheric and less crowded experience explore its narrow streets and underground spaces after dark.

Above *Split's palm-lined Riva and tranquil harbourfront*

WHAT TO SEE

DIOKLECIJANOVA PALAČA (DIOCLETIAN'S PALACE)

Designed as part imperial villa, part fortified garrison town, this is not a palace in the conventional sense; it is part of the fabric of the city. There is no need to buy a ticket, and instead of staring at Roman remains in respectful silence, you are just as likely to find yourself sitting on an ancient tombstone to eat your picnic. The original street plan largely survives, with its north–south and east–west axes, Cardo and Decumanus, meeting at the central Peristil courtyard. From here, steps lead up to the vestibule, a domed chamber now open to the sky. The rest of the palace has been dismantled over the centuries, with columns and arches recycled in other buildings, though parts of the old Roman walls survive, pierced by gates on their north, south, east and west sides. For a sense of the original palace layout, visit the Podrum or underground chambers (Jun–end Aug Mon–Sat 9–9, Sun 9–6; Sep and May Mon–Sat 9–8, Sun 9–6; Oct–end Apr Mon–Fri 8–3; adult 25kn, child 10kn), a former dungeon beneath the imperial quarters whose floor plan reflects the outline of the rooms above. Among the items discovered here is a marble dining table used by Diocletian.

KATEDRALA SVETI DUJE (CATHEDRAL OF ST. DOMNIUS)

In the Peristil courtyard, the octagonal mausoleum designed by Diocletian as his resting place is guarded by a black granite Egyptian sphinx from 1500BC. Originally this was one of a dozen sphinxes; the rest were destroyed by angry Christians after Diocletian's death. Ironically for an emperor renowned for his persecution of Christians, his mausoleum has become a cathedral, dedicated to one of his victims, the first Bishop of Salona. Note the elaborately sculpted altars to Domnius and Anastasius, another Christian martyr. Diocletian's tomb has long since disappeared, perhaps recycled in the stone pulpit, though traces of the emperor remain; portraits of him and his wife can be seen in the dome, together with scenes of chariot races and hunting. You can climb the adjoining bell tower (Apr–end Sep daily 8–8; Oct–end Mar 9–12, 4–7, 10kn) for views over the port. ✉ Peristil ⊕ Apr–end Sep daily 8–8; Oct–end Mar 8–12, 4–7 ✋ 15kn

JUPITEROV HRAM (TEMPLE OF JUPITER)

A narrow passage opposite the cathedral steps leads to the Roman Temple of Jupiter, now the cathedral baptistry, with images of the gods Jupiter and Hercules above the portal. The highlight is the 11th-century baptismal font, richly carved with the geometric braiding which was a feature of medieval Croatian art. The font also contains the earliest known portrait of a Croatian king, thought to be Petar Krešimir IV, seated on a throne with his crown and orb, with a citizen prostrated at his feet.

✉ Kraj Svetog Ivana ◷ Apr–end Sep daily 8–8; Oct–end Mar 9–12, 4–7; ask at cathedral at other times ✋ 5kn

MUZEJ GRADA SPLITA (CITY MUSEUM)

www.mgst.net

Housed in a Gothic mansion within the walls of Diocletian's Palace, this museum began in the 16th century when the owner, Dmine Papalić, collected monuments from the Roman ruins at Salona (▷ 186) and exhibited them in his courtyard. The museum provides a quick journey through the history of Split, from Roman coins bearing Diocletian's portrait to medieval manuscripts.

✉ Papalićeva 1 ☎ 021 344917 ◷ Jun–end Sep Tue–Fri 9–9, Sat–Mon 9–4; Oct–end May Tue–Fri 10–5, Sat–Mon 10–1 ✋ Adult 10kn, child 5kn 📖 75kn

ZLATNA VRATA (GOLDEN GATE)

The main entrance to Diocletian's Palace was through the monumental north gate, which stood at the start of the road to Salona. Outside the gate, a large bronze statue of Grgur Ninski (Gregory of Nin) by Ivan Meštrović recalls a 10th-century bishop who campaigned for the use of the Slavic script instead of Latin in Croatian churches. The statue was placed in the Peristil in 1929 to mark the thousandth anniversary of the Synod of Split, at which Gregory challenged the Pope, but was moved here under Italian occupation during World War II. There are copies in Varaždin (▷ 97–99) and Nin (▷ 183) but this is the original. If you are superstitious, touch the bishop's left toe, which has been worn to a bright gold sheen by generations of people.

Left *Detail of a stone lion at the foot of the cathedral bell tower*
Below *Hrvatsko Narodno Kazulište, the city's main venue for drama, ballet and opera*

ARHEOLOŠKI MUZEJ (ARCHAEOLOGICAL MUSEUM)

www.mdc.hr/split-arheoloski

Founded in 1820, Croatia's oldest museum displays Greek and Roman objects from across Dalmatia. Items from the Roman city of Salona (▷ 186), which flourished from the second century BC to the seventh century AD, include a second-century mosaic of Apollo, marble statues of the gods Bacchus, Diana and Venus, and everyday items such as jewellery, pottery, coins and dice. Also noteworthy is an ancient Greek clay oil lamp decorated with the gods Isis and Serapis from the island of Vis. The courtyard gallery has more examples of Roman art, with mosaics and sarcophagi featuring vivid scenes of chariot races and wild boar hunts.

✉ Ulica Zrinsko-Frankopanska 25 ☎ 021 329340 ⏰ Jun–end Sep Mon–Sat 9–2, 4–8; Oct–end May Mon–Fri 9–2, 4–8, Sat 9–2 ✋ Adult 20kn, child 10kn

MUZEJ HRVATSKIH ARHEOLOŠKIH SPOMENIKA (MUSEUM OF CROATIAN ARCHAEOLOGICAL MONUMENTS)

www.mhas-split.hr

This is one museum in Split where you will not find any Roman objects. In fact, it is the only museum in Croatia dedicated solely to the medieval Croatian state, which ruled from the 9th to 11th centuries. Considering the emotional attachment to Croatia's only previous period of independence, it is surprising that its history between the Roman and Venetian eras tends to be overlooked. Most of the exhibits are taken from medieval churches; they include several fine examples of delicately carved stonework, adorned with plaiting and Celtic-style geometric motifs typical of this period.

✉ Šetalište Ivana Meštrovića 18 ☎ 021 323901 ⏰ Mon–Fri 9–4, Sat 9–2 ✋ Adult 10kn, child 5kn; free on Mon and Thu 🚌 12

GALERIJA IVANA MEŠTROVIĆA

www.mdc.hr/mestrovic

The sculptor Ivan Meštrović (▷ 23) grew up in Dalmatia and planned to retire to this villa overlooking the coast, though in fact he only spent two years here after its completion in 1939 before moving to the USA.

The house and gardens contain a collection of his work, from female nudes and religious studies to a touching bronze portrait of his mother from 1909.

Below *Roman artefacts in the courtyard gallery of the Arheološki Muzej*

Left *The cathedral, which is built around Diocletian's octagonal mausoleum*
Above *The clocktower, Diocletian's Palace*

Look out too for monumental wooden sculptures of Adam and Eve (1941) and a rare Meštrović painting of the Last Supper (1945), as well as a portrait of a young Meštrović by the Cavtat artist Vlaho Bukovac (1855–1922). The ticket is also valid for the Kaštelet, a fortified 16th-century residence bought by Meštrović as a home for his *Life of Christ* cycle, a series of wood carvings completed between 1916 and 1950 and displayed in the simple, whitewashed Crkva Svetog Križa (Holy Cross Chapel), built for this purpose. From the Crucifixion produced during World War I to the Nativity and Last Supper completed in the USA, they represent a lifetime's work and are perhaps Meštrović's greatest achievement.
✉ Šetalište Ivana Meštrovića 46 ☎ 021 340800 🕐 May–end Sep Tue–Sun 9–7; Oct–end Apr Tue–Sat 9–4, Sun 10–3 ✋ Adult 30kn, child 15kn 🚌 12

MORE TO SEE
ETNOGRAFSKI MUZEJ (ETHNOGRAPHIC MUSEUM)
www.etnografski-muzej-split.hr
First opened in 1910 as a temporary exhibition of handicrafts, this museum is housed inside the vestibule of Diocletian's Palace. Exhibits include traditional Dalmatian folk costumes, including fur hats, boots, 10th-century military uniforms, and swords and lances used by riders at the annual festival in the nearby town of Sinjska Alka (▷ 207), in which a victory over Turkish troops in 1715 is commemorated.
✉ Ulica Severova 1 ☎ 021 343108 🕐 Jun Mon–Fri 9–2, 5–8, Sat 9–1; Jul to mid-Sep Mon–Fri 9–9, Sat 9–1; mid-Sep to end May Mon–Fri 9–3, Sat 9–1 ✋ Adult 10kn, child 5kn

MARJAN
The wooded Marjan peninsula, overlooking Split on its western side, is a popular weekend retreat, where Split's citizens come to escape the summer heat. The peninsula has long been considered a sacred place and on its southern slopes are hermits' caves and chapels dating from the 15th century. From Telegrin (178m/584ft), the highest point on the peninsula, there are wonderful views over the offshore islands of Šolta, Brač, Hvar and, on fine days, distant views of Vis. A leisurely walk is one of the best ways to explore the area (▷ 202–203).

STARI PAZAR (OLD BAZAAR)
Outside the eastern Silver Gate of Diocletian's Palace is one of the best open-air markets in Croatia, with farmers selling eggs, cheese, sausages, bacon, bread, vegetables, olives and dried fruit (▷ 205).

INFORMATION

www.tztrogir.hr

✚ 287 F8 ℹ Trg Ivana Pavla II ☎ 021 885628 🅲 Jun–end Aug daily 8am–9pm; Apr–end May, Sep–end Oct Mon–Fri 8–5, Sat 8–12; Nov–end Mar Mon–Fri 8–2 🚌 From Šibenik and Split

TIPS

» Make Trogir a base for visiting Split— the hotels are cheaper, the atmosphere is relaxed, and local bus 37 runs roughly every 20 minutes between Trogir and Split throughout the day.

» Make a complete circuit of the island on foot, following the old town walls, ending the day with a drink on the Riva.

Above *The Riva, Trogir's attractive harbourside promenade*

TROGIR

This lovely Venetian island town is delightful to explore, with Renaissance palaces and hidden courtyards in its narrow, cobbled streets. Founded in the third century BC by Greek settlers from Vis, Trogir is set on a small island, linked to the mainland and the larger island of Čiovo by a pair of bridges. You could easily visit as a day-trip from Split, but it is better to spend the night here, enjoying the atmosphere of one of Croatia's most seductive small towns.

ROMANESQUE MASTERPIECE

The classic entrance to Trogir is via the 17th-century Kopnena Vrata (Land Gate), crowned by a statue of St. John of Trogir, a 12th-century bishop. This leads into a maze of medieval lanes, converging on Trg Ivana Pavla II, the main square. On one side is the Venetian loggia; on the other is the cathedral. The cathedral's west door, carved in 1240 by stone-mason Radovan, is a triumph of Romanesque art, with details from rural life among the angels, saints and biblical scenes. The interior is almost equally impressive, especially the chapel of St. John of Trogir by the Florentine architect Nikola Firentinac (c.1440–1505). You can climb the bell tower in summer (mid-Jun to mid-Sep daily 9–12, 4–7).

ON THE WATERFRONT

Gradska, the main street of the old town, ends at the Gradska Vrata (Town Gate), beside the only surviving section of the 15th-century walls. From here, you can walk along the Riva, a harbourside promenade culminating in Kula Kamerlengo (Jun–end Sep daily 9–8), a Venetian fortress with fine views from the battlements. The terrace bars on the Riva are great spots to end the day.

REGIONS DALMATIA • SIGHTS

VIS

This remote Adriatic outpost, isolated from the outside world as a Yugoslav military base until 1989, now attracts a growing numbers of visitors, rivalling Hvar as a fashionable destination for sailors. It remains an unspoiled island of vineyards and fishing bays with a pretty harbourside town at either end. The islanders who left during the Tito years are returning and there is a new found feeling of prosperity.

ISLAND CAPITAL

Vis Town is set in a sheltered bay, watched over by a Franciscan monastery. It was founded as the Greek colony of Issa in the fourth century BC, the ruins of a Greek cemetery stand behind the tennis courts, not far from a Roman bathhouse with mosaic dolphins set into the floor. An Austrian battery by the harbour houses a branch of the Archaeological Museum in Split (Jul–end Aug Tue–Sat 10–1, 5–9, Sun 10–1), whose star exhibit is a beautiful bronze head of the Greek goddess Aphrodite.

THE BRITISH CONNECTION

British soldiers were stationed in Vis during both the Napoleonic Wars and World War II, when Tito briefly ran the Partisan operation from a cave in Mount Hum. A path above the harbour leads to the abandoned George III fortress, with a carved Union Jack (British flag) over the door. There is a small English cemetery on the other side of the bay, with a memorial to the 'comrades of Tito's liberation war'. Vis even has its own cricket club (www.viscricket.com), begun by winemaker Oliver Roki.

INFORMATION

www.tz-vis.hr

✚ 287 F9 🛈 Šetalište Stare Isse, Vis Town (opposite the ferry dock) ☎ 021 717017 🕘 Jun–end Sep 8.30–2.30, 5–8; Oct end May daily 8.30–2.30 🚢 Car ferry and catamaran from Split to Vis

TIPS

» Try the local wines—white Vugava and red Viški Plavac.
» Take the bus from Vis Town to Komiža, where boats depart in summer for the Modra Špilja (Blue Grotto) on Biševo, seen at its best at noon.
» Walk or drive to the summit of Mount Hum, the highest point on Vis, passing the cave which served as Tito's wartime hideout.

Above *The Franciscan monastery beside the harbour, Vis Town*

195

INFORMATION

www.zadar.hr

286 D6   Ilije Smiljanica 5   023 316166   Jun–end Sep daily 8am–midnight; Oct–end May Mon–Fri 8–8, Sat–Sun 9–1   From Šibenik and Split   From Dubrovnik, Pula, Rijeka and Split

INTRODUCTION

Zadar was first occupied by the Romans during the first century BC and became capital of the Byzantine province of Dalmatia in the seventh century AD. Much later, it became the Venetian capital of Dalmatia and a key trading port in the eastern Adriatic. From 1920 to 1944 the city was under Italian rule. During World War II the old town was largely destroyed by Allied bombing with the result that the city today is a diverse mix of architectural styles. Zadar came under attack again in 1991, when the surrounding villages were occupied by forces of the Republic of the Serbian Krajina.

The oldest part of the city is on a peninsula with the sea on three sides. On the northern side is the ferry port, along with some medieval walls and harbour gates. The southern side of the peninsula is open to the sea, with views from the waterfront promenade to the island of Ugljan. You enter the old town across the footbridge to the north, or through the Kopnena Vrata (Land Gate), a 16th-century Venetian triumphal arch. The old town is closed to traffic and is easily explored on foot. From Narodni Trg, the old town's main square, Široka Ulica, also known as Kalelarga, leads to the Roman Forum.

WHAT TO SEE

FORUM

The Forum has been at the heart of city life for more than 2,000 years. All that remains are a few columns and chunks of stone, but it is easy to imagine Roman colonnades and temples on this site. At the centre is St. Donat's Church, a Byzantine round church built by a ninth-century Irish bishop using stone from the Forum. The church is no longer used for worship but is open to visits (Apr–end Oct daily 9–8) and concerts are held here on summer evenings.

ARHEOLOŠKI MUZEJ (ARCHAEOLOGICAL MUSEUM)

Housed in a modern concrete building on the Forum, this is one of Croatia's oldest museums. The top floor is devoted to the prehistoric Liburnian culture, the first floor features Roman exhibits, while the ground floor has stone carvings and funeral goods from medieval Croatia.

✉ Forum ☎ 023 250516 🕓 Mon–Fri 9–1, 5–7, Sat 9–1 ✋ Adult 10kn, child 5kn

ZLATO I SREBRA ZADRA (GOLD AND SILVER OF ZADAR)

This stunning exhibition in the convent of St. Mary's Church features the work of medieval goldsmiths. The jewel-encrusted gold and silver reliquaries are said to contain the bones of saints. A separate wing contains the reconstructed chapel of Sveta Nediljica, with 11th-century carvings of biblical scenes adorned with medieval Croatian braiding.

✉ Forum ☎ 023 250496 🕓 Mon–Sat 10–1, 5–6.30, Sun 10–1 ✋ Adult 20kn, child 5kn

MORSKE ORGULJE (SEA ORGAN)

Zadar's latest attraction, and arguably its most popular, was built in 2005 at the end of the Riva promenade. The unique sea organ is 70m (230ft) long and consists of a series of steps descending into the sea, with underwater pipes creating an eerie symphony of nature, as sounds emerge and fade with the swell of the water. Join the crowds at dusk to witness one of Zadar's famous sunsets, described by film director Alfred Hitchcock (1899–1980) as the most beautiful in the world.

NARODNI MUZEJ ZADAR (NATIONAL MUSEUM ZADAR)

www.nmz.hr

Housed in a former Benedictine monastery, this undervisited museum traces the history of Zadar in models, paintings, stone carvings, period furniture, ceramics and other exhibits. Other interesting branches of the museum can be found at Narodni Trg (Ethnography) and Medulićeva 2 (art gallery and natural history).

✉ Poljana Pape Aleksandra III bb ☎ 023 251851 🕓 Mon–Fri 9–12, 5–8, Sat 9–1 ✋ Adult 10kn, child 5kn

TIPS

» Climb the 170 steps inside the bell tower of the cathedral (daily in summer, occasional weekends in winter; 10kn) for views over the city and port.

» The city beach is at Kolovare, within walking distance of the old town; leave via the Land Gate, walk around the Foša (inner harbour) and continue along the coastal path.

» Ferries leave from Zadar for the peaceful islands of Ugljan, Pašman and Dugi Otok.

» Most hotels are at Borik, 5km (3 miles) from the old town. You can get there by bus or by walking along the shore and taking a rowing-boat taxi from the northern breakwater to the ferry port.

Left *Kopnena Vrata, a Venetian triumphal arch, at the entrance to the old city*
Below *Dating from the ninth century, the circular church of St. Donat was built using stone from the ruins of the Forum*

DRIVE

OFF THE BEATEN TRACK IN BRAČ

See another side to this busy holiday island by renting a car for a circuit of its north and west. Along the way, you will pass beaches, bays, historic towns and villages, and the quarries that are the source of the famous Brač stone.

THE DRIVE
Distance: 68km (42 miles)
Allow: 1.5 hours
Start/end: Supetar ✚ 287 F8

★ Supetar is the largest town on Brač (although it is still quite small), and the administrative centre of the island, having taken over from the Venetian capital Nerežišća in 1815. It takes its name from a sixth-century early Christian basilica of Sveti Petar (St. Peter), though the modern town developed in the 16th century as the harbour for Nerežišća.

With hourly ferries to Split in the summer months and many people from the mainland having holiday homes here, Supetar feels much bigger than its population of 4,000 would suggest.

Leave Supetar in the direction of Sutivan and follow the coast road, with views across the water to Split. After 7km (4.5 miles) you will see Sutivan on the right, dominated by the onion dome of its church. The road now swings inland, passing between olive groves and dry-stone walls with the island of Šolta to your right. After another 6km (4 miles), you reach the pretty village of Ložišća, dramatically situated at the head of a gorge. Drive carefully through the narrow main street of the village.

❶ Ložišća has an onion-domed church, designed by Supetar artist Ivan Rendić (1849–1932) and typical of Brač. Beyond the church, the main road continues down into the

valley to the sheltered harbour at Milna, with stone houses on the Riva promenade. The marina is popular with yachtsmen in summer.

Turn left just beyond the church to climb a hill out of the village.

❷ The road from Ložišća to Nerežišća clings to a narrow ridge with heaps of stones piled up in the fields to either side. Some of these have been fashioned into sheep shelters or stone walls, but most have simply been moved to clear space for agriculture. Between Dračevica and Donji Humac you pass a limestone quarry where marble is still produced.

Continue to a junction, with Nerežišća visible on a hill to your right. Keep straight ahead and turn right at the next T-junction, remaining on the main road and skirting Nerežišća as the road bends left.

❸ Nerežišća was the island capital during the period of Venetian rule, superseded by Supetar only in the 19th century. The former governor's palace stands here, along with a Venetian loggia adorned with the winged lion of St. Mark, symbol of the Venetian republic.

The road now climbs in a dizzying series of bends to arrive at the access road for Vidova Gora.

❹ Vidova Gora (778m/2,552ft) is the highest peak on any of the Croatian islands. An easy detour of 5km (3 miles) on an asphalt road leads to the summit, marked by a white stone cross. On clear days, there are wonderful views over beautiful Zlatni Rat beach to the neighbouring island of Hvar and distant Korčula.

The main road continues across the island to Pražnica. Turn left here, signposted to Pučišća. Stay on this road for 7km (4.5 miles) as it drops down towards the sea before travelling through a fertile valley of vineyards to Pučišća.

❺ The harbourside village of Pučišća is the source of the best Brač stone and was once the chief export port for the marble used in Diocletian's Palace in Split. The houses here are even whiter than elsewhere on the island and the stone sculptures found in the village's public spaces are testimony to its long-standing stone-carving tradition. A stone-carving school stands on the bay, facing the Palača Dešković hotel (▷ 212).

Turn left at Pučišća and follow the coast road back to Supetar. The road climbs at first and clings to the cliffs high above the coast before dropping back down to sea level at Postira and Splitska.

❻ From Splitska it is possible to make a short detour inland to the village of Škrip, the oldest settlement on the island and home to the Museum of Brač (▷ 171), where local prehistoric and Roman archaeological finds are exhibited.

Stay on the coast road as it passes pine woods and shingle beaches on its way back to Supetar.

WHERE TO EAT
KONOBA VLADIMIR NAZOR
The restaurant on the summit of Vidova Gora serves hearty plates of Dalmatian ham and cheese and delicious roast Brač lamb. It is open in summer only.
☎ 021 549061 ⏰ Apr–Oct

BISTRO PALUTE
▷ 208.

WHEN TO GO
Brač is easily accessible by ferry from Split and by air from Zagreb and in summer can become very crowded. Out of season, however, it is a peaceful place.
  To enjoy the best views from Vida Gora, choose a clear day.

Clockwise from opposite *Zlatni Rat beach; cyclists on the road to Dragon Cave; a ruined building in the deserted village of Stipančići*

DRIVE

AROUND MOUNT BIOKOVO

This half-day tour begins on the coast before heading inland to make a circuit of Croatia's third-highest mountain. With pebble beaches, rugged limestone peaks and the dramatic Cetina gorge, it makes a good introduction to the varied landscapes of central Dalmatia.

THE DRIVE
Distance: 148km (92 miles)
Allow: 3–4 hours
Start/end: Omiš ✚ 287 G8

★ Omiš is at the mouth of the River Cetina, which rises near the Bosnian border in the foothills of Mount Dinara and carves a steep valley down to the coast before emptying into the sea through the Cetina gorge. In summer, there are rafting trips through the gorge (▷ 205), starting from the Slime waterfall, as well as canoe hire and fishing excursions.

From the bridge at the mouth of the Cetina, head south on the Magistrala coastal highway with views of the limestone massif of Mount Biokovo

up ahead. Shortly after Pisak, the final town on the Omiš riviera, the road rounds a huge bay and continues on the Makarska riviera to Brela.

❶ Brela is the most attractive of the Makarska riviera resorts. In 2003, the influential American business magazine *Forbes* rated Punta Rata as the most beautiful beach in Europe and one of the top 10 beaches in the world.

Turn right off Magistrala to drop down to Brela through the pine woods. Drive through the village and continue on a narrow road beside the beach to the neighbouring resort of Baška Voda, where you turn inland to rejoin the Magistrala. Turn right and drive towards Makarska.

❷ Makarska (▷ 183) is the main town of the Makarska riviera, set around a horseshoe bay at the foot of Mount Biokovo. It is also the departure port for ferries to Sumartin on Brač.

Continue on the coastal highway, bypassing Makarska, or follow signs to explore the town. When you reach the southern outskirts of Makarska, turn left on a road which is signposted to Vrgorac. The road climbs steeply through the village of Gornje Tučepi, offering spectacular views over the islands and coast. After 6km (4 miles) you reach the entrance to Biokovo Nature Park.

❸ The summit of Biokovo at Sveti Jure (1,762m/5,781ft) is the highest

Opposite The spectacular coastline of the Makarska riviera

point on the Croatian coast. From the park entrance, a road twists for 23km (14 miles) up to the TV tower at the summit. From April to October you pay a fee to visit the park. If you drive to the summit, allow at least an extra hour each way, and do not attempt it in winter or in difficult conditions. On a clear day, you can see Monte Gargano in Italy, more than 200km (125 miles) away.

The road to Vrgorac continues around the edge of the mountain, crossing a stark limestone landscape on its way to Ravča.

④ From Ravča you can make a detour of 6km (4 miles) each way to the wine town of Vrgorac.

Turn left at Ravča and stay on this road for 48km (30 miles) to arrive at Šestanovac.

⑤ The landward-facing slopes of Podbiokovo are much greener than the limestone face of Mount Biokovo as seen from the sea. On this side of the mountain, the greater snow and rainfall produces a gentler landscape, the karst fields interspersed with vineyards, strawberry plantations and rural villages.

Turn left at the crossroads in Šestanovac and drive through Zadvarje. Just beyond the village is a huge crucifix at a viewpoint overlooking the Cetina. Shortly after, take the right fork to drop down to the river beside the Kraljevac hydroelectric plant.

⑥ The nearby waterfall and village of Slime are the start point for rafting trips through the gorge.

Stay on this road as it climbs to Kučiće before returning to the river at Radmanove Mlinice. From here, the road clings to the banks of the river as it carves through a dramatic canyon on its way to Omiš.

Above *The ruined Mirabela fortress, high above the town of Omiš*

WHERE TO EAT
JENY
In the village of Gornje Tučepi, Jeny offers creative Dalmatian dishes on a summer terrace high above the sea.
✉ Gornje Tučepi 33 ☎ 021 623704 🕐 Apr–end Oct daily 6pm–midnight

RADMANOVE MLINICE
Enjoy local trout, frogs and eels as well as roast and grilled meat at this old mill beside the River Cetina.
☎ 021 862073 🕐 Apr–Oct daily 12–11

PLACE TO VISIT
PARK PRIRODE BIOKOVO (BIOKOVO NATURE PARK)
www.biokovo.com
☎ 021 625136 🕐 Apr to mid-May, Oct, Nov daily 8–4; mid-May to end Sep daily 7am–8pm ✋ 35kn

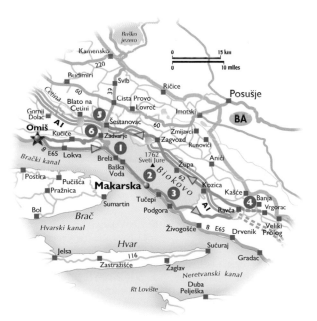

ON SPLIT'S GREEN HILL

A walk on the wooded Marjan peninsula offers wonderful views over Split, with the islands of Brač, Hvar and Šolta shimmering offshore. This is where the people of Split come on weekend afternoons to escape the bustle and traffic-filled streets of the city.

THE WALK

Distance: 5.5km (3.5 miles)
Allow: 2 hours
Start/end: Trg Franje Tuđmana, Split

HOW TO GET THERE

Walk west along the Riva, Split's café-lined waterfront esplanade, from Diocletian's Palace. Trg Franje Tuđmana is the small square with a fountain at the centre, situated at the western end of the Riva beneath the steps leading to Trg Republike.

★ The walk starts at the entrance to the Veli Varoš quarter, which was once a separate district of artisans and fishermen. One of Split's oldest neighbourhoods, it remains one of

the most attractive parts of the city, with its traditional stone houses and cobbled streets.

With the Riva behind you, begin by taking the road to the right of the Franciscan monastery church of Sveti Frane (St. Francis). The street is called Šperun at first but soon narrows and becomes Ulica Senjska. Climb the steps at the top of the lane to arrive at Café Vidilica.

❶ Café Vidilica is a popular meeting-point, particularly on summer evenings, when people gather here for drinks on the terrace overlooking the port and the city. A shady garden behind the café contains the remains of a 16th-century Jewish cemetery.

Cross over the parking area, walk through a gate and continue to climb. The steps end at a road in front of a small zoo: its poor record on animal welfare may deter some visitors. Turn left here, stay on the road and after 200m (220 yards) turn left again on the road to the summit. Look for a footpath beside the road to the left; this soon becomes a long flight of stone steps leading to Telegrin.

❷ Telegrin (178m/584ft) is the highest point on the Marjan peninsula and is marked by the inevitable Croatian flag flapping in the wind. From the raised terrace, there are stunning views out to sea and over the port. To one side, there is a bird's-eye view of the 35,000-seater Poljud stadium, home of soccer giants Hajduk Split and occasional venue for national matches (▷ 205), while to the north the views stretch along the coast as far as Trogir. The islands of Brač, Hvar and Šolta are clearly visible, and on fine days you should be able to make out the island of Vis in the distance.

Take the steps down on the far side of the terrace, passing some solar-powered lamps as you go. Keep straight ahead on Marjanski Put and look for a sign on the left pointing to *Špomenik Đirometa*. Take this path as it leads through woods of pine and holm oak, with glimpses of the sea through the trees.

❸ After 350m (385 yards) you pass a memorial to Professor Umberto Girometta (1883–1939), a distinguished archaeologist, speleologist and mountaineer.

Continue on this path as it climbs briefly to a summit then drops down to rejoin the road at a junction.

❹ The Marjan peninsula is believed to take its name from a Roman landowner, Marin. It has long been considered a sacred place; during the 15th century, hermits built caves and chapels on its southern slopes. Turn right at the junction to visit two of these hermitages. Keep to the shore road to arrive first at the 14th-century chapel of Betlem and then the 15th-century chapel of Sveti Jere (St. Hieronymus), with caves built into the cliff face above the church. It is reached by taking a path to the right at a 180-degree bend in the road. Return to the junction and keep straight ahead along Šetalište Alberta Marangunića, on a gravel path which clings to the shore, offering fine views out to sea.

❺ Towards the end of the walk, you pass the 13th-century chapel of Sveti Nikole (St. Nicholas), with its separate sloping belfry. Erratic opening hours mean that this is usually closed to passing walkers.

The path now becomes paved and drops steeply back down to Café Vidilica. Take the staircase to the right of the café terrace to reach the waterfront and turn left to return to Trg Franje Tuđmana.

WHERE TO EAT
There are no restaurants on Marjan peninsula, so save your appetite for a meal at a traditional restaurant in the Veli Varoš quarter near the end of the walk. Alternatively, Café Vidilica (▷ 210), near the start and end of the walk, is a great place to call a halt for drinks.

PLACE TO VISIT
SPLIT ZOO
✉ Kolombatićevo Šetalište 2 ☎ 021 394525 🕐 Daily 8–6 in summer, 8–4 in winter 💵 Adult 10kn, child 5kn

TOURIST INFORMATION
The tourist office on the Riva can issue a map of the city which includes the paths on the Marjan peninsula.
✉ Peristil ☎ 021 345606

WHEN TO GO
This walk is suitable for the relatively fit at any time of the year, but when temperatures soar in the summer months, you are strongly advised to take a bottle of water with you to avoid dehydration. The only place on the route to stop for a drink is Café Vidilica.

Below left to right *The emblem of Hadjuk Split; view of the harbour from Café Vidilica*

BRAČ

BIG BLUE SPORT
www.big-blue-sport.hr
Bol is a major base for watersports and this company near a beach offers windsurfing courses for all ages, rental of equipment, plus mountain bike excursions, scuba-diving courses and sea-kayaking.
✉ Podan Glavice 2, Bol ☎ 021 635614 ◷ Apr–end Oct

NATURE PARK SUTIVAN
Set among pine woods on the north-west coast of Brač, this enjoyable park has a small zoo of farm animals and birds, including ostriches, peacocks, donkeys, sheep and goats.
✉ Sutivan ☎ 098 133 7345 ◷ May–end Jun and Sep–end Oct 10–8; Jul–Aug daily 10am–midnight ✋ Free ⛽ 🚌 3km (2 miles) outside Sutivan on the road to Milna

YELLOW CAT
www.zutimacak.hr/kite
If you fancy trying your hand at kite-surfing, this outlet on the beach between Bol and Zlatni Rat offers five-day courses.
✉ Bol ☎ 098 288581 ◷ Apr–end Oct ✋ €290

Above *Island-hopping Dalmatian style*

ZMAJEVA ŠPILJA (DRAGON'S CAVE)
The best way to visit this remarkable cave (▷ 171) is with a guide, who can show you the way and has a key to the cave. The walk up here is steep and rocky in places, so take plenty of water and wear good shoes.
✉ Murvica, Bol ☎ 091 514 9787 ◷ Book by telephone one day in advance ✋ 50kn per person

HVAR

CARPE DIEM
www.carpe-diem-hvar.com
Carpe Diem has spawned a chain of bars across Croatia, but this hip cocktail bar and harbourside terrace is the original. In July and August the yachting set are in town and you need a reservation. There are resident DJs and music nights.
✉ Riva, Hvar ☎ 021 717234 ◷ Jun–end Sep 9am–3am

HVARSKO PUČKO KAZALIŠTE (HVAR COMMUNITY THEATRE)
This beautiful old Venetian theatre (▷ 173) closed for restoration in 2006, a process still on-going at the time of writing. It stages Croatian drama.
✉ Trg Svetog Stjepana, Hvar ☎ 021 741009 ◷ Call for details

KORČULA

MM-SUB
www.mm-sub.hr
This scuba-diving base in the village of Lumbarda runs diving courses for beginners and can also offer organized dives through caves, underwater cliffs and shipwrecks.
✉ Lumbarda ☎ 020 712288 ◷ Apr–end Sep

MOREŠKA SWORD DANCE
www.korculainfo.com
To the accompaniment of brass bands and clashing swords, the *moreška* dancers of Korčula battle over the love of a maiden. The dance is a feature of all the main festivals on Korčula and is performed twice a week in summer on an open-air stage outside the city walls.
✉ Tickets from Marko Polo Tours, Biline 5, Korčula ☎ 020 715400 ◷ Jun–end Sep Mon and Thu at 9pm ✋ 100kn

VINARIJA TORRETA
The Baničević family have a small wine museum at their vineyards in Smokvica. Tours and wine tastings are on offer, and you can buy local brandy and olive oil.
✉ Smokvica 165 ☎ 020 832100 ◷ Call for details 🚌 On main road across the island from Korčula to Vela Luka

OMIŠ

SLAP

www.hrslap.hr

This company offers half-day rafting trips through the River Cetina gorge, with all safety equipment provided. The trip starts at Slime waterfall near Kučiće, but a transfer from Omiš is included in the price.

✉ Poljički Trg, Omiš ☎ 021 757336 ⏰ Apr–end Oct daily at 9.30 and 2.30 ✋ Adult 160kn, child 80kn

PAG

AQUARIUS/KALYPSO/PAPAYA

On hot summer nights, Zrće beach is crowded with clubbers. The club scene on Pag started with Kalypso in the 1980s and now there are three open-air beach clubs on an arc of white pebbles. The Zagreb club Aquarius even opens a branch here in summer. All the clubs are open day and night so you can drift from one to the other. During the day, there are sports competitions, waterslides and beach parties; at night there are DJs, live bands and breakfast at 5am.

✉ Plaža Zrće, Novalja ⏰ Jun–end Aug 24 hours a day

PAŠKA SIRANA

www.paskasirana.com

The island of Pag is famous for its hard, salty sheep's cheese, which at its best is similar to Parmesan. You can buy it from markets and farm shops all over the island, but for a reliable selection of local cheeses, visit this shop on the main square of the old town.

✉ Trg Kralja Krešimira IV, Pag ☎ 023 612717 ⏰ Mon–Fri 8–8, Sat 8–2

ŠIBENIK

BUNARI—SECRETS OF ŠIBENIK

Undergoing extensive renovation at the time of writing (due for completion in 2010), this unusual attraction, in the vaults of the 15th-century wells, uses interactive multimedia to explore the city's history through themes such as seafaring and food. Children can race to build an ancient fort, or help Šibenik's patron St. Michael in his battle against the dragon. It is down steps opposite the cathedral.

✉ Trg Republike Hrvatske, Šibenik ☎ 099 681 5675 ⏰ Daily 9–1, 4–11 ✋ Free 💻

ŠIBENSKO KAZALIŠTE

This gorgeous theatre was started in 1864 by Trogir architect Josip Slade, with a Renaissance exterior, baroque interior and magnificent frescoed ceiling. In 1991, it took a direct hit from a grenade and was closed for 10 years, but it is once again showing plays and, in summer, hosts concerts of classical music.

✉ Ulica Kralja Zvonimira 1, Šibenik ☎ 022 213088 ⏰ Check posters for details

SPLIT

FILOMENA

www.filomena.hr

Unwind at this luxurious modern spa, fitness and relaxation centre east of central Split. Let off steam in the sauna, work out in the weights room or just kick back and relax over a fruit smoothie.

✉ Put Radoševca 39, Split ☎ 021 472777 ⏰ Daily 8–10 ✋ Full day €158, half-day €62.50

HRVATSKO NARODNO KAZALIŠTE (CROATIAN NATIONAL THEATRE)

www.hnk-split.hr

The Croatian National Theatre is the city's main venue for drama, ballet and opera, with a season from October to June. It is also the main organizer of the Split Summer Festival (▷ 207).

✉ Trg Gaje Bulata 1, Split ☎ 021 306908 or 021 363014 (box office) ⏰ Box office: Mon–Fri 8–2 and one hour before performance ✋ 30–150kn

HAJDUK SPLIT

www.hnkhajduk.hr

Founded in 1911, this soccer club has a passionate following across Dalmatia. A match at the Poljud stadium is an unforgettable experience, with fireworks, banners and colourful entertainment. The stadium seats 35,000 spectators and is sometimes used by the Croatian national soccer team. The season runs from August to May, with a break between December and February. Tickets are cheap and usually available on the gate.

✉ Mediteranskih Igara 2, Split ☎ 021 323650 ⏰ Call or check press for match times ✋ From 30kn 🚌 17

PRIRODOSLOVNI MUZEJ (NATURAL HISTORY MUSEUM)

The museum is down an alley off a square near the city market. It has displays of coral and shells from the Adriatic and Indian Ocean.

✉ Poljana Kneza Trpimira 3, Split ☎ 021 322988 ⏰ Mon–Fri 10–5, Sat 9–1 ✋ Adult 10kn, child 5kn

STARI PAZAR

The central market, known as the 'old bazaar', is on the eastern edge of Diocletian's Palace outside the Silver Gate. This is where the Dalmatian countryside comes to town, as farmers set up stalls selling eggs, cheese, sausages, bacon, bread, vegetables and wine.

✉ Stari Pazar, Split ⏰ Daily 7–2

TROGIR

GENA

www.gena-trogir.com

If you have always wanted an elegant handmade gentleman's suit, then visit tailor Boris Burić Gena in his atelier on the top floor of a Renaissance palace. His formal evening suits are in the style of the 19th century, complete with black silk collars and white bow-ties. The late opera singer Luciano Pavarotti was a client.

✉ Ribarska 6, Trogir ☎ 021 884329 ⏰ Call in advance

VIS

ISSA DIVING CENTER

www.scubadiving.hr

The waters around Vis are among the clearest in the Adriatic, providing excellent conditions for scuba-diving. The Issa Diving Center, based at Hotel Biševo, runs courses for all levels and can also arrange diving expeditions to the Modra Špilja (Blue

Cave) on Biševo or to see a US B17 bomber from World War II under the water.
✉ Komiža, Vis ☎ 021 713651
🕐 Apr–end Nov

VIS CRICKET CLUB
www.viscricket.com
The Sir William Hoste Cricket Club was founded in 2002 to restore the tradition of cricket on Vis, which began when British troops were stationed here during the Napoleonic Wars. The club's name comes from a British naval commander of the time. Matches take place in April and May against teams from Zagreb and Split. The club plays on an artificial pitch but there are plans to build a grass pitch.
☎ 021 714004 🕐 Contact: Oliver Roki. Call for details

ZADAR
ARSENAL
www.arsenalzadar.com
Opened in 2005 in the cathedral-like space of the 18th-century Venetian arsenal, this is a café, nightspot, bar, restaurant, art gallery and shopping arcade rolled into one. By day, you can relax on sofas or sip coffee beneath extraordinary Venetian architecture. At night, it turns into a trendy lounge bar, with DJs and live music ranging from Irish folk to modern jazz.
✉ Trg Tri Bunara 1, Zadar ☎ 023 253820
🕐 Daily 7am–3am; live music Sun–Thu from 8pm, Fri–Sat from 10.30pm

CRODELICE
This small deli sells tempting fare from small-scale producers in the Zadar area. The array of wines, cheeses, ham, truffles, almonds in honey and jams, many of which can be sampled before you buy, are hard to resist.
✉ Elizabete Kotromanić 5, Zadar ☎ 023 315566 🕐 Mon–Sat 8am–9pm

FORUM
If your idea of nightlife is a café terrace rather than a cocktail bar, you won't do better than this café on the Forum, with outdoor tables beneath St. Donat's Church bell tower. It serves good coffee and cakes, and on sunny days it is the busiest meeting place in town.
✉ Široka Ulica, Zadar ☎ 023 250537
🕐 Daily 7am–11pm

THE GARDEN
www.thegardenzadar.com
Opened in 2005 by British music producer Nick Colgan and James Brown, the drummer with reggae group UB40, The Garden has become the coolest place to be seen in Zadar. High up on the city walls with a beautiful garden terrace, it is open 'whenever the sun is shining or the stars are twinkling'. During the day people chill out on white sofas; after dark, there are DJs and visiting musicians. You can arrive in style—a rowing boat taxi will take you across the water from the jetty by the Maraska factory. The service

runs until midnight in summer and costs just 3kn.
✉ Liburnska Obala 6, Zadar ☎ 023 364739 🕐 May–end Sep 10am–1am

HRVATSKA KAZALIŠNA KUĆA
www.hkk-zadar.hr
Founded in 1945, the Croatian Theatre House is Zadar's biggest cultural institution, hosting a repertoire of classical music and drama all year and organizing the annual Zadar Summer Theatre festival.
✉ Široka Ulica 8, Zadar ☎ 023 301617
🕐 Box office open Mon–Fri 11–1, 6–8, Sat 11–1 ✋ Varies

PETITE CAFFE BAR
The belle époque furniture, gilt mirrors and luxurious armchairs make this an unexpected night spot, housed as it is in a modern complex at the southern end of town. It is a pleasant place to enjoy a morning coffee or an evening cocktail.
✉ Boškovića 4, Zadar ☎ No phone
🕐 7am–midnight, shorter hours winter

STUDIO LIK
Handmade lace from Pag, embroidered textiles from Dalmatia and traditional sheepskin slippers are sold at this folksy souvenir shop.
✉ Don Ive Prodana 7, Zadar ☎ 098 975 7661 🕐 Mon–Sat 9–3, 5–8

Below *Visitors on the road to Dragon Cave, on the island of Brač*

FESTIVALS AND EVENTS

FEBRUARY
POKLAD
www.lastovo.hr
An unusual Carnival celebration, dating back 600 years, takes place on Lastovo, when Poklad, a straw figure, is paraded through Lastovo and tied to a rope with fireworks attached to his boots. The ritual burning of Poklad starts a day of festivities marking the end of winter.
✉ Lastovo ☎ 020 801018 ⏰ Shrove Tuesday

JUNE–SEPTEMBER
HVAR SUMMER FESTIVAL
www.tzhvar.hr
Concerts of classical music, jazz and Dalmatian folk singing are held in the cloisters of the Franciscan monastery, and plays are staged in the old theatre throughout the summer months on Hvar.
✉ Hvar ☎ 021 741788 ⏰ Jun–end Sep

FESTIVAL DALMATINSKIH KLAPA
www.fdk.hr
The biggest festival of Dalmatian *klapa* (traditional *a cappella* singing) takes place in Omiš each July, with open-air concerts on the square in front of the parish church.
✉ Omiš ☎ 021 861015 ⏰ Three weeks in Jul

SVETI TODOR
Korcula's biggest festival, celebrating the feast of St. Theodor, features a performance of the traditional *moreška* sword dance (▷ 204). There are also regular *moreška* shows in summer on a stage near the Revelin tower and weekly performances of the *kumpanija* sword dance in the town of Vela Luka.
✉ Korčula ☎ 020 715701 ⏰ 29 Jul

SPLIT SUMMER FESTIVAL
www.splitsko-ljeto.hr
This festival has been going for more than 50 years and comprises four weeks of music, ballet and drama in spectacular settings including the underground chambers of Diocletian's Palace and Ivan Meštrović's Holy Cross Chapel. A highlight each year is the open-air opera performance in the Peristil of Diocletian's Palace. Tickets are available in advance from the tourist office and Croatian National Theatre (▷ 205).
✉ Split ☎ 021 363014 ⏰ Mid-Jul to mid-Aug

TROGIR SUMMER FESTIVAL
Concerts of classical, jazz and Dalmatian folk music are held in various venues including the cathedral, Kamerlengo fortress and outdoor stages.
✉ Trogir ☎ 021 881412 ⏰ Jul, Aug

ST. DONAT'S MUSICAL EVENINGS
www.donat-festival.com
This long-running festival features recitals of early music and orchestral concerts in churches. The main venue is the beautiful setting of St. Donat's Church, but other events take place in the cathedral and Roman Forum. Tickets are available in advance from the Croatian Theatre House (▷ 206).
✉ Zadar ☎ 023 300430 ⏰ Jul, Aug

SINJSKA ALKA
www.alka.hr
Dalmatia's most traditional festival takes place in the inland town of Sinj to commemorate a victory over Turkish troops in 1715. The climax is a jousting contest on the Sunday, with brass bands and galloping riders in 18th-century costume attempting to spear a metal ring suspended on a rope. The winner is crowned with the Croatian tricolour by the Duke of Sinjska Alka. Tickets are sold for the main event, but you can watch two days of rehearsals for free.
✉ Sinj ☎ 021 824833 ⏰ First Sun in Aug

MARCO POLO RE-ENACTMENT
A re-enactment of the naval battle of 1298 between the Venetian and Genoese fleets in which Marco Polo was captured takes place on the anniversary of the battle each year.
✉ Korčula ☎ 020 715701 ⏰ Early Sep

Below *A display of traditional* moreška *sword dancing, Korčula*

EATING

PRICES AND SYMBOLS

The restaurants are listed alphabetically. The prices given are the average for a two-course lunch (L) and a three-course dinner (D) for one person, without drinks. The wine price is for a litre of table wine followed by the least expensive bottle of quality wine. All the restaurants listed accept credit cards unless otherwise stated.

For a key to the symbols, ▷ 2.

BRAČ
BISTRO PALUTE

This harbourside restaurant is popular for its well-priced specials of roast veal, suckling pig and Brač lamb. It has tables by the water in summer. There is also a children's menu offering turkey, steak and fish.
✉ Porat 4, Supetar ☎ 021 631730
◷ Daily 10am–11pm 🖐 L 60kn, D 80kn, Wine 70/100kn

GRADAC
GUSTIRNA

There is only one thing on the menu at this quirky cellar restaurant set back from the seafront promenade:

thin, crusty pizza, cooked in a brick oven. Choose from small, medium or family sizes, then sit back to enjoy the musical décor, complete with antique accordions, fiddles and trumpets on the walls.
✉ Uz Kuk 6, Gradac ☎ 021 697561
◷ Summer daily 12–11, winter 6–11
🖐 Pizza from 25kn, Wine from 80kn

HVAR
BOUNTY

In contrast to some of the trendy bistros nearby, this waterfront restaurant serves classic Dalmatian fare such as grilled meat and fish, stuffed squid and *brodet* (fish stew). The tables on the quayside are perfectly placed to soak up the sun while enjoying the view of fishing boats and yachts.
✉ Mandrac, Hvar ☎ 021 742565
◷ Daily 11–11 🖐 L 60kn, D 80kn, Wine 70/100kn

KONOBA MENEGO

www.menego.hr
Hidden away in an old stone wine-cellar on the steps leading to

the castle, this family-run tavern serves tapas-style cold dishes accompanied by homemade wine. From Hvar goat's cheese with honey to marinated aubergines (eggplants) and peppers, and the selection of cold meats, almost everything served here is produced on the island. For dessert, try the delicious 'drunken figs', stuffed with almonds and soaked in brandy, followed by wild orange liqueur.
✉ Groda, Hvar ☎ 021 742036
◷ Apr–end Oct daily 12–2, 5–10
🖐 Dishes from 25kn, Wine from 50kn

LUCULLUS

Housed in a 16th-century palace (now the hotel Villa Nora) just off the main square in Hvar Town, Lucullus serves Italian-Mediterranean Slow Food such as *gregada* (fish stew with potatoes and wine), roast lamb and lobster. Start your meal with a selection of Hvar goat's and sheep's milk cheeses.
✉ Ulica Petra Hektorovića 7, Hvar ☎ 021 742498 ◷ Apr–end Oct daily 12–2, 6–11
🖐 L 200kn, D 250kn, Wine 70/150kn

PALAČA PALADINI

The 16th-century palace overlooking the harbour square was given to the Paladini family as a reward for their service in a sea battle between the Turkish and Venetian fleets. A meal here is a feast for all the senses, as you sit at a candlelit table in a courtyard with lavender and lemon trees, enjoying Luci and Antun Tudor's freshly prepared Dalmatian cooking. The specialities are grilled meat and fish, but there are good vegetarian dishes too.

✉ Ulica Petra Hektorovića 4, Hvar
☎ 021 742104 ⏰ Apr–end Oct daily 12–3, 6–12 ✋ L 150kn, D 200kn, Wine 60/100kn

ZLATNA ŠKOLJKA

One of several upscale eateries in Hvar's trendy restaurant quarter, the 'Golden Shell' is credited with introducing the Slow Food revolution to Hvar. Local ingredients are used in unexpected ways, such as gnocchi with octopus, 'drunken' fish in sweet wine, lamb in coconut sauce and rabbit with figs. Reservations are essential in summer.

✉ Ulica Petra Hektorovića 8, Hvar
☎ 098 168 8797 ⏰ Apr–end Oct daily 12–3, 7–12 ✋ L 150kn, D 200kn, Wine 60/100kn

KORČULA
ADIO MARE

You may need to wait for a table at this traditional fishermen's tavern, which serves some of the best food in Korčula at an old stone house beneath Marco Polo's tower. Steaks and kebabs are barbecued on an open fire in the corner, or you can have grilled fish, octopus or filling staples like *brodet* (fish soup with polenta) or *pašticada* (veal casserole with plums and sweet red wine). The menu and the décor have hardly changed in 30 years, but Adio Mare has built up a loyal following as a cheerful classic.

✉ Ulica Svetog Roka 2, Korčula
☎ 020 711253 ⏰ Apr–end Oct daily 6–12 ✋ D 100kn, Wine 60/100kn

MASLINA

This farmhouse restaurant, on the road to Lumbarda, is one of the few places on the island to stay open all year. Set among olive groves, it offers a simple menu of roast lamb, Dalmatian casseroles and home-made macaroni. The speciality is *pogača maslina*, a pizza-like dish of crusty bread topped with cheese, vegetables and olives.

✉ Lumbarajska Cesta, Korčula ☎ 020 711720 ⏰ Apr–end Oct daily 11am–midnight; Nov–end Mar daily 11–3, 5–12 ✋ L 60kn, D 90kn, Wine 70/80kn 🚌 Leave Korčula in the direction of Lumbarda, and Maslina is on your right

MORSKI KONJIĆ

This long terrace restaurant on the promenade around the outer walls is a lovely place to dine on a summer evening, with moonlit views across the water to the Pelješac peninsula. Its name means 'seahorse' and it duly specializes in seafood, from octopus salad to steamed mussels and plain grilled fish, accompanied by local Grk and Pošip wines.

✉ Šetalište Petra Kanavelića, Korčula
☎ 020 711878 ⏰ Apr–end Oct daily 8am–midnight ✋ L 100kn, D 150kn, Wine 60/100kn

MAKARSKA
RIVA

This fish restaurant with a summer courtyard behind the seafront promenade is the best place in town for a formal meal. The emphasis is on traditional seafood dishes, such as prawn cocktail, scampi soup and grilled scorpion fish. More adventurous choices include spaghetti with vodka and caviar, frogfish in vermouth sauce, and medallions of beef with cured ham in basil sauce.

✉ Obala Kralja Tomislava 6, Makarska
☎ 021 616829 ⏰ Daily 10am–1am
✋ L 150kn, D 200kn, Wine from 80kn

STARI MLIN

Set in an old stone mill with a vine-covered patio and modern art on the walls, this enjoyable bistro offers new variations on Dalmatian seafood

dishes, as well as a Thai menu that includes steamed mussels, prawn curry and grilled snapper with orange and chilli. There is also a simple children's menu.

✉ Ulica Prvosvibanjska 43, Makarska
☎ 021 611509 ⏰ Daily 10–2, 6–12
✋ L 150kn, D 200kn, Wine 70/120kn

MURTER
TIC-TAC

This trendy bistro in a quiet street behind the harbour offers alternatives to the standard menu of grilled fish available elsewhere. Among the Mediterranean-inspired dishes are grilled vegetables, octopus sushi, bouillabaisse, oven-baked monkfish and Greek salad.

✉ Ulica Hrokošina 5, Murter ☎ 022 435230 ⏰ Apr–end Oct daily 12–12
✋ L 120kn, D 170kn, Wine 60/80kn

OMIŠ
RADMANOVE MLINICE

www.radmanove-mlinice.hr
Set in an 18th-century stone mill on the banks of the River Cetina, this busy restaurant has a large riverside garden and play area. Meat and bread are cooked in the traditional style under a metal lid ('under the bell'). The menu also features frogs, eels and trout. Dalmatian folk dances are performed on Wednesdays at 0pm in July and August.

✉ Radmanove Mlinice, Omiš ☎ 021 862073 ⏰ Apr–end Oct daily 0am–10pm
✋ L 100kn, D 120kn, Wine 60/120kn
🚌 Start in Omiš and follow the Cetina for 6km (4 miles) upstream

ŠIBENIK
GRADSKA VIJEĆNICA

The highlight here is the setting, on the ground floor of the Venetian Gothic town hall, with tables under the loggia in summer offering views across a piazza to the cathedral. The menu is classic Dalmatian cuisine, including ham, sheep's cheese, octopus salad, steak and turkey in mustard sauce, with walnut pancakes for dessert.

✉ Trg Republike Hrvatske 3, Šibenik
☎ 022 213605 ⏰ Daily 8am–11pm
✋ L 120kn, D 150kn, Wine from 80kn

SKRADIN

CANTINETTA

It may look like a private house outside, but Cantinetta serves up excellent Dalmatian cuisine in a bright, arty atmosphere with low lighting, soft music and abstract art on the apricot- and mustard-coloured walls. Steak comes rare, topped with mustard and capers, surrounded by fries, bacon and roast peppers, with a basket of warm bread on the side. In summer you can dine in the garden.

✉ Skradinskih Svilara 7, Skradin ☎ 022 771183 ⏰ Daily 12–12 ✋ L 100kn, D 150kn, Wine 60/100kn

SPLIT

BOBAN

www.restaurant-boban.com

Buried deep in a residential district east of the city centre, this Split institution is worth seeking out for its top-notch Dalmatian cuisine. Fish dominates the menu, which gives a light, contemporary twist to many a Dalmatian favourite. The interior is modern and fresh without a checked tablecloth in sight.

✉ Hektorovićeva 49, Split ☎ 021 543300 ⏰ Mon–Fri 10am–midnight, Sat–Sun 12–12 ⏰ L 90kn, D140kn, Wine 90/120kn

CARDO

This chic restaurant belonging to the Hotel Atrium (▷ 213) is a place to see and be seen. You'll need to dress in your smartest clothes to install yourself at one of the elegantly laid tables and enjoy exquisitely crafted Mediterranean cuisine and Dalmatian specialities, all washed down with a red or white from the cream-of-the-crop wine list. Despite its luxurious ambience, prices are quite reasonable.

✉ Domovinskog rata 49a, Split ☎ 021 200000 ⏰ Daily 10am–11pm ✋ L 200kn, D 220kn, Wine from 150kn

KONOBA CETINA

This friendly, family-run inn tucked away in the narrow lanes just off Zagrebačka has been serving honestly prepared international and Croatian staples for over 20 years. Just given a major facelift,

it's a superb place to enjoy a meal of goulash or grilled meat, rounded off with some traditional pancakes. Lilting Dalmatian music on CD completes the atmosphere.

✉ Radunica 16, Split ☎ 021 482784 ⏰ Mon–Sat 10am–11pm, Sun 1–11 ✋ L 70kn, D100kn, Wine 60/70kn

KONOBA MARJAN

The six tables at this friendly, unpretentious eatery at the foot of Marjan hill fill quickly with those eager for hearty, home-cooked food. House specialities include seafood spaghetti, black risotto and goulash, and you should not refuse a shot of the Štulić family's home-distilled *rakija*.

✉ Senjska 1, Split ☎ 098 9346848 ⏰ 9am–midnight ✋ L 60kn, D100kn, Wine 60/120kn

LVXOR

Location is the winner here, for the Lvxor enjoys a highly visible spot right on the Peristil courtyard at the heart of Diocletian's Palace. This is a great place to take breakfast, catch up on the news back home (there's free international press available) and check your emails (free WiFi). The food is not its greatest asset, but it's a convenient place to rest tired feet mid-sightseeing.

✉ Kraj Svetog Ivana 11, Split ☎ 021 341082 ⏰ Daily 8am–late ✋ L 80kn, D 100kn, Wine from 100kn

MAKROVEGA

This vegetarian-macrobiotic restaurant just a short stroll east of Diocletian's Palace is a good advertisement for a meat-free lifestyle. Choose from tofu dishes, whole-wheat pastas and sandwiches, all made using organic or home-grown ingredients. With mains costing around 35kn and lunch menus for 55kn, this is an inexpensive lunch or dinner spot. The extensive menu of imaginative desserts also makes this a good place to stop for coffee and a sweet treat.

✉ Leština 2, Split ☎ 021 394440 ⏰ Mon–Fri 9–8, Sat 9–5 ✋ L 55kn, D 70kn, No wine

VIDILICA

High above Split, this café is best in the evening when locals gather on the terrace to sip wine and enjoy the views of the palm-lined Riva, islands and the harbour. It's also a handy refreshment stop on walks around the wooded Marjan peninsula (▷ 202–203). It may be a bit of a climb to reach the Vidilica, but it is well worth the effort.

✉ Nazorov Prilaz 1, Split ☎ 021 589550 ⏰ Daily 9am–11pm ✋ L 100kn, D120kn, Wine from 110kn

TROGIR

KONOBA ŠKRAPA

Chaotic, friendly and great fun, Škrapa is an unforgettable experience. The small, stone-walled dining room is cluttered with everything from hanging vines and dried flowers to vegetables in vases of water and wine bottles dripping with candle wax. Waiters bring steaming bowls of vegetable soup and *fažol* (bacon and bean stew), or plates of ham, cheese, sausages and sardines. The wine comes out of a tap in the wall.

✉ Ulica Hrvatskih Mučenika 9, Trogir ☎ 021 885313 ⏰ Mon–Sat 11–11, Sun 4–11. Closed Sun in winter ✋ L 50kn, D 70kn, Wine from 60kn

VIS

BAKO

www.konobabako.hr

This charming *konoba* (tavern) in the fishing village of Komiža has wine barrels, fishing nets and tables on the terrace beside a pebble beach. It serves traditional local dishes, such as octopus in wine, lobster soup and yellowtail fish with capers, laurel, rosemary and olive oil.

✉ Gundulićeva 1, Komiža ☎ 021 713742 ⏰ Apr–end Oct daily 4pm–2am; Nov–end Mar 5pm–midnight ✋ D 140kn, Wine 60/100kn

DORUČAK KOD TIHANE

An art nouveau hotel has been restored as a waterfront fish restaurant, whose name means 'Breakfast at Tiffany's'. On summer nights you can dine on the terrace, with dreamy views across the bay. The emphasis is on fresh fish and seafood, served as pâté, shrimp risotto or simply grilled fish, accompanied by the local Vugava wine. Round off your meal with a plate of *hruštule*, traditional biscuits from Vis.

✉ Obala Sveti Jurja 5, Vis ☎ 021 718472 🕐 Apr–end Oct daily 8am–midnight ✋ L 120kn, D 150kn, Wine 60/100kn

VILLA KALIOPA

There are few more romantic settings for a summer evening than the walled garden of the 16th-century Garibaldi palace, with its fountains, statues and palm trees. Dine by candlelight on fabulous fresh fish, choosing from a menu that changes seasonally. A meal here is an extravagant treat, but it is worth it for a special occasion. Reservations are essential.

✉ Ulica Vladimira Nazora 32, Vis ☎ 021 711/55 🕐 Apr–end Oct daily 5–12 ✋ D 300kn, Wine from 70/130kn

ZADAR
PET BUNARA

www.petbunara.hr

There are few traditional pizzerias in Zadar, but if you have got a craving for some crisp crust and hot, stringy cheese, then Pet Bunara is the place to head. The restaurant also serves some tasty gnocchi, meat dishes, pasta and salads, all of which can be enjoyed in engaging surroundings festooned with pictures of yesteryear Zadar.

✉ Trg Pet Bunara bb, Zadar ☎ 023 224010 🕐 Daily 8am–11pm ✋ L 90kn, D 120kn, Wine from 90kn

SKOBLAR

Zadar's oldest *konoba* (traditional tavern), just off the Trg Pet Bunara, serves grilled meat and fish (mainly using the 'under the bell' cooking method) to hungry locals and tourists. Enjoy honestly prepared dishes in unpretentious surroundings, washed down with a glass of Croatian wine, then relax to the tones of some Dalmatian folk music (weekends only).

✉ Trg Petra Zoranića bb, Zadar ☎ 023 213236 🕐 Daily 7am–midnight ✋ L 90kn, D 120kn, Wine from 80kn

TAMARIS

The restaurant belonging to the mid-range Tamaris Hotel is a sound choice in neutral surroundings. Locals and incomers alike flock here to sample the spit-roasted lamb, the most traditional of Dalmatian dishes and the house speciality. The wine list includes some exceptional Croatian red and white wines and the service is always prompt and pleasant. There is an indoor terrace for summer dining.

✉ Zagrebačka 5, Zadar ☎ 023 318700 🕐 Daily 7am–midnight ✋ L 150kn, D 170kn, Wine from 110kn

Below *Konoba Škrapa, a traditional tavern serving local specialities in Trogir*

PRICES AND SYMBOLS

Prices are the lowest for a double room for one night. Breakfast is included unless noted otherwise. All the hotels listed accept credit cards unless otherwise stated. Note that rates vary widely throughout the year.

For a key to the symbols, ▷ 2.

BRAČ
PALAČA DEŠKOVIĆ

www.palaca-deskovic.com

A 15th-century Renaissance mansion by the harbour in Pučišća has been converted into a small luxury hotel that makes an original place to stay. Rooms and suites are filled with antique furniture and decorated with Countess Dešković's own paintings. If you want to do it in style, arrive by yacht—the hotel has its own private moorings for guests.

✉ Pučišća, Brač ☎ 021 778240 ✋ From €150 ① 15 ⊙

GRADAC
MARCO POLO

www.hotel-marcopolo.com

Unlike most hotels on the Makarska riviera, this chic family-run boutique hotel at the end of the promenade in Gradac stays open all year. From the rooftop terrace, there are views across the water to the Pelješac mountains, and the top-floor fitness centre has a jacuzzi and looks out to sea. The restaurant serves dishes 'inspired by Marco Polo's travels'. A short walk along the promenade crosses a headland on its way to the long horseshoe beach at Brist.

✉ Obala 15, Gradac ☎ 021 697502 ✋ From €64 ① 25 ⊙ ▽

HVAR
RIVA YACHT HARBOUR

www.suncanihvar.com

The former Hotel Slavija was completely overhauled in 2006 and reopened as the Riva Yacht Harbour Hotel, the first Croatian member of Small Luxury Hotels of the World. The position is perfect, on the palm-lined promenade. Take advantage of the free WiFi to check your email on the terrace while enjoying the views. Roots restaurant serves creative Hvar-Mediterranean cuisine. There is no vehicle access.

✉ Riva, Hvar ☎ 021 750100 ✋ From €186 ① 54 ⊙

PAG
BOŠKINAC

www.boskinac.com

This small, luxury country house hotel lies on the fringes of a vineyard and olive grove in the wild, rocky scenery of northern Pag. The large bedrooms are decorated in bold colours and natural materials, and there is a restaurant and wine cellar offering tastings of Pag cheese and Dalmatian ham. Bicycle rental and horse-riding lessons are available.

Opposite A room with a view: picturesque Hvar harbour

✉ Novalja, Pag ☎ 053 663500
🌐 Closed Jan and Feb 🛏 From €120
ⓘ 11 ♿ 🚌 Signposted off the road from Novalja to Stara Novalja

SKRADIN
SKRADINSKI BUK
www.skradinskibuk.hr
If you want to explore the Krka National Park in depth, stay at this small townhouse hotel on the central square, a short walk from the harbour and the national park boats. Rooms are simply furnished and decorated in warm pastel shades, and the top-floor terrace has canyon views.
✉ Burinovac, Skradin ☎ 022 771771
🛏 From €56 ⓘ 28 ♿

SPLIT
HOTEL ATRIUM
www.hotel-atrium.hr
The classy new Atrium hotel, one of a kind in Split, is just a 10-minute walk from Diocletian's Palace and is suitable for both a business trip or a romantic weekend. Behind its glass-and-steel facade, you'll find top-notch guest rooms that are a study in understated luxury. The Atrium was built on top of Diocletian's aqueduct, a section of which can be seen in a special gallery within the hotel.
✉ Domovinskog rata 49a, Split ☎ 021 200000 🛏 1,170kn ⓘ 99 ♿ 🚌 Indoor
♨

HOTEL PERISTIL
www.hotelperistil.com
Sleep within the walls of Diocletian's Palace at this beautiful hotel in central Split. Impeccable guest rooms face out across the Peristil courtyard or are part constructed from the original Roman walls. All have wonderfully romantic antique touches and the ancient walls buzz with free WiFi and satellite TV.
✉ Poljana kraljice Jelene 5, Split ☎ 021 329070 🛏 1,200kn ⓘ 12 ♿

VESTIBUL PALACE
www.vestibulpalace.com
This stylish hotel inside Diocletian's Palace opened in 2005. Minimalism is the rule here, with sleek lines, glass ceilings, polished wood floors and plain black and white furniture blending in with ancient Roman walls. The hotel may be a little too self-consciously trendy for some people's tastes, but it is an oasis of calm and contemporary chic at the heart of the city. There is no vehicle access.
✉ Iza Vestibula 4, Split ☎ 021 329329
🛏 From €147 ⓘ 7 ♿

TROGIR
CONCORDIA
www.concordia-hotel.net
This small, family-run hotel in an 18th-century townhouse near the Kamerlengo fortress fronts the Riva, the town's attractive promenade, with views across to the island of Čiovo. All rooms have showers and are air-conditioned, and there is parking for guests. In summer, make the most of the sea views with breakfast on the hotel terrace. The Concordia also makes a good base from which to visit Split.
✉ Obala Bana Berislavica 22, Trogir
☎ 021 885400 🛏 500kn ⓘ 14 ♿

TRAGOS
www.tragos.hr
The first hotel within the walls of the old town was opened by the Žunić family in 2005. It is set in an 18th-century baroque palace a few steps from Trg Ivana Pavla II, the town's main square. Rooms are decorated in warm colours with original stone walls, and there is an attractive garden restaurant where guests can relax in the summer.
✉ Budislavićeva 3, Trogir ☎ 021 884729
🛏 600kn ⓘ 12 ♿

VIS
TAMARIS
This elegant Habsburg villa on the quayside is one of the few places in Vis that opens year-round. Some rooms have balconies and shutters with views across the bay to the Franciscan monastery on the far side. The terrace café is a good place to sip a glass of Vugava, the local white wine, while watching the sailors tying up their yachts and the sun setting over the sea.
✉ Obala Sveti Jurja 30, Vis ☎ 021 711350
🛏 600kn ⓘ 27

ZADAR
FUNIMATION
www.falkensteiner.com
The Austrian Falkensteiner chain has brought its concept to Croatia with the opening of this all-inclusive family resort. Tennis, beach volleyball and an adventure playground for kids are all included in the price, along with swimming pools, waterslides and a large aquapark by the beach. Meals, drinks and even ice creams are included too. Accommodation ranges from single rooms to large family suites.
✉ Majstora Radovana 7, Zadar ☎ 023 206636 🛏 From €160 (all-inclusive)
ⓘ 258 ♿ 🚌 Indoor and outdoor
♨

HOTEL PRESIDENT
www.hotel-president.hr
Plush, well-appointed rooms, a great location near the beach, superb service and an environmentally friendly approach ensure that a stay at this luxury hotel is a real treat. The President prides itself on the standard of its furnishings and fittings, which include cherry wood furniture and silver cutlery in the restaurant. The hotel's Vivaldi restaurant sets the ideal mood for a romantic dinner.
✉ Vladana Desnice 16, Zadar ☎ 023 333696 🛏 1,220kn ⓘ 27 ♿

PANSION ALBIN
www.albin.hr
Run by the same family for over 30 years and situated in the Borik area north of the historical heart of Zadar, Pansion Albin is the place to stay if you are looking for home comforts and a personal approach. The rooms are as good as at any hotel and immaculately tended by polite staff. If you can tear yourself away from the garden pool, the restaurant is as good as the rest of the *pansion*.
✉ Put Dikla 47, Zadar ☎ 023 331137
🛏 440kn ⓘ 16 ♿ 🚌 Outdoor

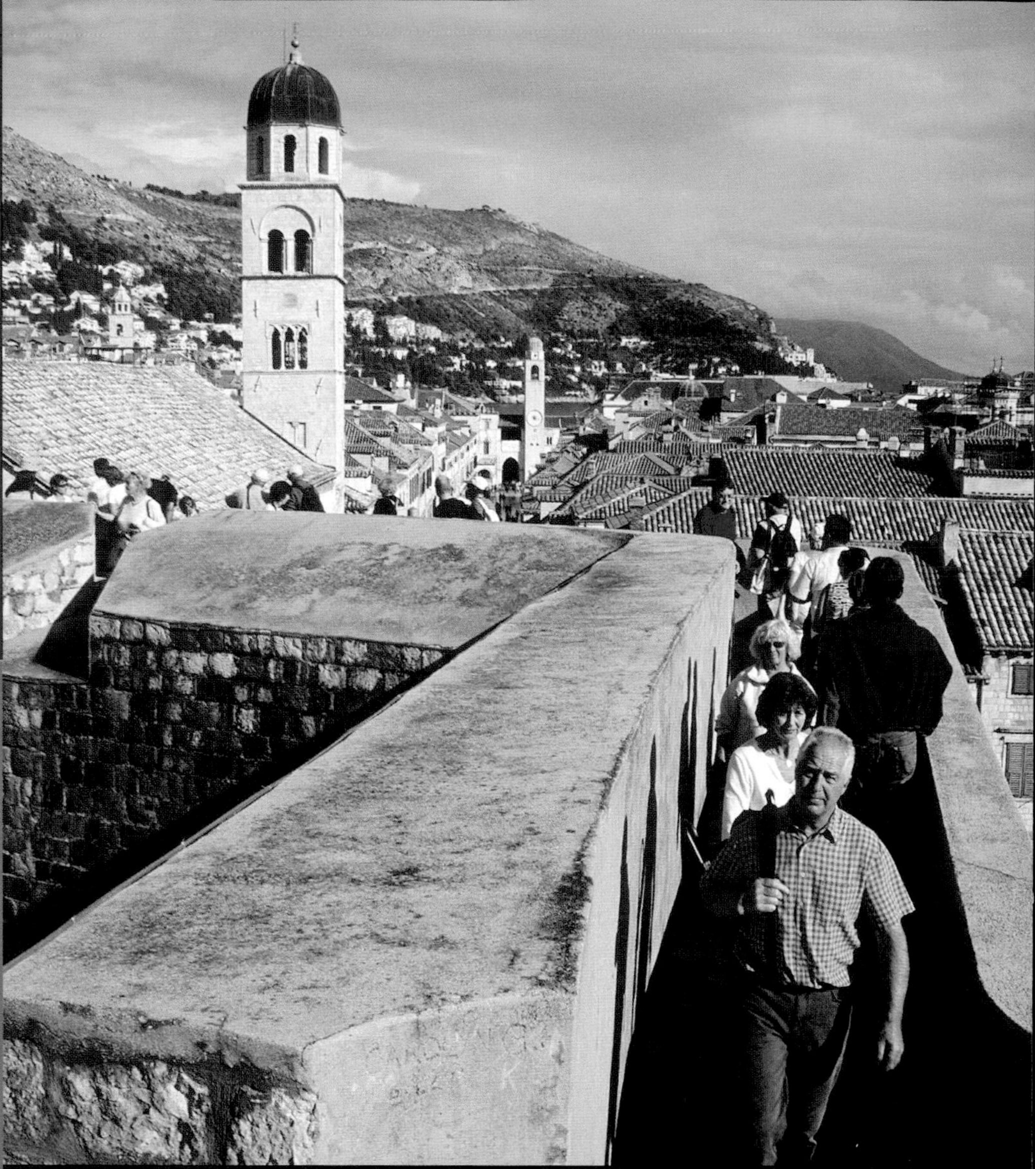

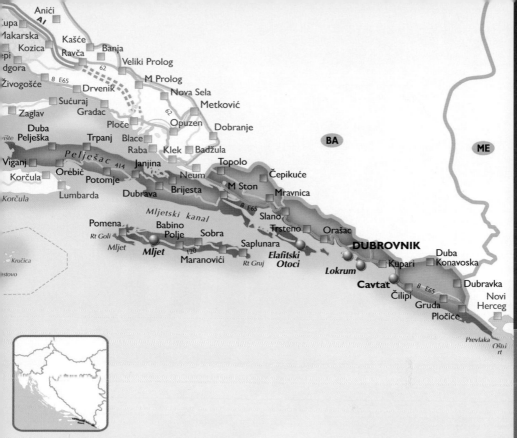

DUBROVNIK AND BEYOND

Dubbed the 'pearl of the Adriatic' by poet Lord Byron, Dubrovnik is the unrivalled focus of visitor activity in Croatia's far south, its gleaming marble pavements (sidewalks) polished by the feet of visitors from all over the world. Indeed, over the last decade this exceptional place has become one of Europe's top city-break destinations. Every tile and block of stone is steeped in history and thanks to strict conservation rules the city retains its original character. Sheer visitor numbers are an issue, but if you want to avoid the tourist crush, come in late September or October when it is quieter but the weather is still good and most sights and restaurants are open.

Only faint reminders of the damage that the city sustained during the Homeland War remain. In 1991 and 1992, the Yugoslav army bombarded Dubrovnik from high ground above the city. Shells damaged 80 per cent of the old town's historical buildings and the airport was completely devastated. The city's recovery has been remarkable, and wandering its streets, visiting its churches and looking across the city from the walls, you would never guess that this historical gem had been the focus of such an intense assault.

Away from Dubrovnik, Southern Dalmatia's islands are interesting diversions for those who have acquired a taste for island-hopping further north. Lokrum and the Elefati islands make interesting day trips from Dubrovnik, while Mljet and Korčula warrant longer exploration.

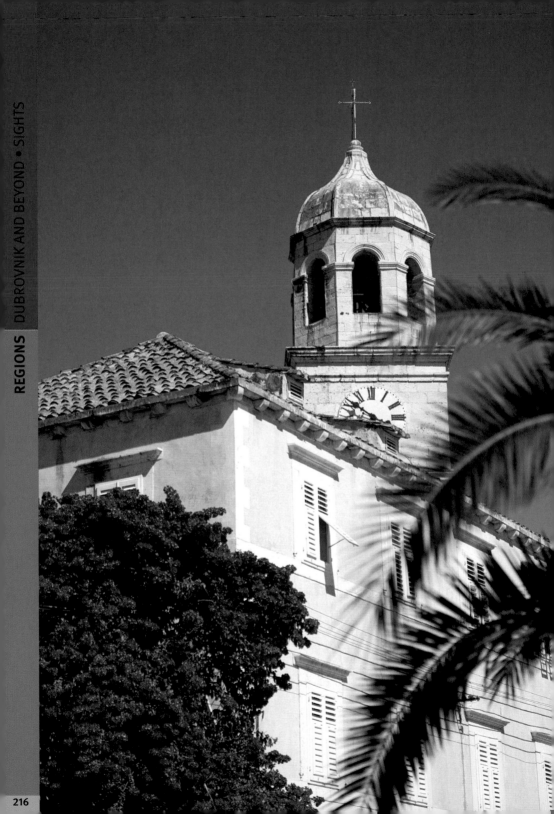

CAVTAT

Croatia's southernmost town is an attractive summer resort, with a lively harbourside promenade. Lying 16km (10 miles) south of Dubrovnik, close to Čilipi airport, Cavtat makes a good base for combining a beach holiday with excursions to the city. A palm-lined promenade looks out over a pretty bay, and seafront paths follow the shore to pine woods and beaches on the forested Rat and Sustjepan peninsulas. Boards by the harbour advertise boat trips to the offshore island of Supetar, and taxi-boats make the 45-minute journey to Dubrovnik throughout the day.

GREEKS AND ROMANS

Cavtat was founded as the Greek colony of Epidaurum in the third century BC, a thousand years before refugees from Epidaurum founded Dubrovnik. The original Greek and Roman settlement was situated on the Rat promontory, where today you will find the cemetery. Climb the path from the Franciscan church at the north end of the harbour to reach the summit, where tombstones are laid out in a peaceful garden overlooking the sea. The white marble mausoleum at the centre was built by Ivan Meštrović (▷ 23) for the wealthy Račić family.

LOCAL PAINTER

Cavtat was the birthplace of one of Croatia's finest artists, Vlaho Bukovac (1855–1922). He is best known for his realistic and charming portraits, though he also dabbled with Impressionism. His 19th century home and garden, set just back from the harbour, are now a gallery dedicated to his work. You can see more paintings by Bukovac in the museum in the Rector's Palace.

INFORMATION

www.tzcavtat-konavle.hr
✚ 286 J9 ⓘ Tiha 3 ☎ 020 478025
🕐 Apr–end Oct daily 8–8; Nov–end Mar Mon–Fri 8–3 🚌 10 from Dubrovnik
🚢 From Dubrovnik

TIPS

» Cavtat is the main town of Konavle, a fertile and narrow strip of land between the mountains of Bosnia and the Bay of Kotor. Local tour operators offer jeep safaris and bicycle rides across Konavle.
» The nearby village of Čilipi has folklore performances on the church square on Sunday mornings in summer.

Opposite *St. Nicholas Church, Cavtat*
Below *Aerial view over Cavtat*

DUBROVNIK

INFORMATION

www.tzdubrovnik.hr
www.visitdubrovnik.hr
✚ 286 J9 🛈 Stradun; other offices at
Gruž and Lapad ☎ 020 427591 🕓 Daily
8–7 ✈ Čilipi airport, 20km (12 miles)
south of city, with regular shuttle buses
to Pile Gate 🚌 The bus station is at Gruž
harbour, 4km (2.5 miles) west of the old
town; bus 1A,1B to Pile Gate 🚢 Car ferry
from Rijeka, Zadar, Split, Hvar and Korčula
to Gruž; taxi-boats from Cavtat to Old Port
in summer

INTRODUCTION

Dubrovnik was founded as the town of Ragusium by refugees from Roman Epidaurum (Cavtat) in the seventh century AD. The Venetians took over the city in 1202, introducing the system of government by nobility which was to be a hallmark of medieval Ragusa (▷ 21). From 1358 to 1808 this was a wealthy mercantile city state to rival Venice, nominally governed by a rector and paying tribute to Hungarian and Turkish rulers in exchange for its freedom. An earthquake in 1667 destroyed half of the city and left over 4,000 people dead. Occupied by Napoleon's troops in 1808, Ragusa later came under Austro-Hungarian and Yugoslav rule, officially adopting its Slavic name of Dubrovnik in 1918. During the siege of Dubrovnik (▷ 25) in 1991–92 the airport and port were destroyed and the majority of houses in the old town were shelled by the Yugoslav army. Dubrovnik today has risen from the ashes and is once again a self-confident, cultured city with a great sense of pride in its much-cherished motto, Libertas (Freedom).

Dubrovnik is a historic city, shipping port and modern holiday resort rolled into one. The main sights are located within Stari Grad (Old Town), a rocky outcrop enclosed by medieval walls which form an elevated promenade around the city. Inside the walls traffic is banned; walking is the only option. The classic approach is through Vrata od Pile (Pile Gate), conveniently reached by local bus from the bus station and Gruž harbour. From here, Stradun, the main street of the old town, leads to the Gradska Luka (Old Port), where boats depart for Lokrum and Cavtat in summer. Steep and narrow lanes to either side of Stradun climb up to the atmospheric districts beneath the walls. At the opposite end from Pile, Vrata od Ploča (Ploče Gate) leads to the city beach and some of the smartest hotels. Most hotels are situated on the Lapad and Babin Kuk peninsulas, 5km (3 miles) west of the old town, with regular buses to Pile Gate. Looming over the city is Mount Srđ, which has a snaking path that leads to the summit.

Above *Dubrovnik's Stari Grad (Old Town) is set on a rocky promontory and enclosed by thick walls*

WHAT TO SEE

GRADSKE ZIDINE (CITY WALLS)

The 2km (1.2-mile) walkway around the ramparts offers unrivalled views over Dubrovnik and is a must for first-time visitors to the city. The best place to begin is just inside Pile Gate (▷ below). Other entry points are inside Ploče Gate on Ulica Svetog Dominika, and near the entrance to Tvrđava Sveti Ivana (▷ below). Between these two is a section of free access around the Old Port, so keep your ticket to show at checkpoints. Starting from Pile Gate, an anticlockwise (counterclockwise) circuit passes along the cliffs, continues to the Old Port, returning to Minčeta Tower. Generally speaking, the views over the old town are better from the landward side, while the seaward side offers scenic views across the water to Lokrum. The audiotour, starting at Pile Gate, assumes you are walking in an anticlockwise (counterclockwise) direction, which is advisable anyway to avoid going against the flow.

The walls that you see today date from the 15th century, when Ragusa felt threatened by the rise of the Ottoman Turks. Up to 25m (82ft) high and 12m (40ft) wide in places, with over 20 bastions and towers, they protected Ragusa's freedom for centuries. Each of the gates and bastions is guarded by an effigy of St. Blaise, the city's patron saint.

Vrata od Pile (Pile Gate)

The historic entrance to the city is protected by a drawbridge and fortified double gate, Pile Gate. The outer portal, added in 1537, is topped by the city's oldest statue of St. Blaise. Inside the gate, a map records the locations of the shells which fell on the old town during the siege of 1991–92. The original gateway, with a figure of St. Blaise by renowned Croatian sculptor Ivan Meštrović (▷ 23), leads to Stradun and the entrance to the city walls on your left.

In summer, costumed guards in the military uniform of the Ragusan republic stand outside Pile and Ploče gates, as they did in medieval times. A ceremonial Changing of the Guard takes place each day between May and October from 10am to noon and 8 to 10pm at the entrances to the walled town.

Tvrđava Minčeta

The crenellated round tower (Trđava Minčeta) was designed by Michelozzo Michelozzi (1396–1472), chief architect to the Medici family of Florence, and completed by Juraj Dalmatinac, architect of Šibenik Cathedral. The rooftop has great views across the old town and out to sea.

Tvrđava Lovrijenac (St. Lawrence's Fort)

The ticket to the walls also gives access to St. Lawrence's Fort, built on a rocky promontory outside Pile Gate (Apr–end Oct daily 8–6.30; adult 20kn, child 10kn if visited separately). The sunsets from the roof terrace are magnificent, and there are theatre performances staged here during the prestigious annual Summer Festival (▷ 235).

Tvrđava Sveti Ivana (St. John's Fort)

The 16th-century St. John's Fort stands guard over the Old Port, facing across the harbour to Revelin Fort on the far side. The upper floors now house a maritime museum, Pomorski Muzej (Apr–end Oct Tue–Sun 9–6; Nov–end Mar Tue–Sun 9–4; adult 40kn, child 20kn), with maps and charts, and displays on Dubrovnik's nautical history. The ground floor makes an unusual setting for the city's aquarium (tel: 020 323978; May–end Oct daily 9–9; Nov–end Apr Mon–Sat 9–1; adult 25kn, child 15kn). Here Adriatic sea creatures ranging from starfish to loggerhead turtles swim in seawater tanks built into the city walls.

221 D2 | 020 324641 | Kneza Damjana Jude | City walls: Apr–end May and Sep–end Oct daily 8–6; Jun–end Aug 8–7.30; Nov–end Mar daily 10–3 | City Walls: Adult 50kn, child 20kn | Audioguide to city walls: 40kn (Apr–Oct only)

GRADSKE ZIDINE TIPS

» There are cafés and stalls selling cold drinks in summer, but it is advisable to take water as the walk can be hot and tiring.

» Make an early start to beat the crowds and do the hardest part of the walk before it gets too hot.

» As you look down over the rooftops, the war damage is clearly visible—note the difference in colour between the surviving original roof tiles and the shiny new post-war replacements.

» For a different perspective on the walls, take a boat trip around the base of the ramparts from the Old Port in summer.

» Buža (▷ 234), set on a cliff beneath the walls, makes a lovely place to relax after your walk.

Below *Vrata od Pile, the historic entrance to the Old Town and access point for the city walls*

TIPS
» Pick up a copy of the monthly *Dubrovnik* guide from tourist offices, with bus maps, ferry timetables and listings of concerts and events.
» Book accommodation well in advance for the Dubrovnik Summer Festival (▷ 235), when the entire city is turned into an open-air stage.
» Between November and February hotel guests receive a Dubrovnik Winter Card, giving discounts at museums and restaurants and free entry to special concerts.
» Buy bus tickets from news kiosks in advance—fares cost more on the bus and the drivers do not give change.

KNEŽEV DVOR (RECTOR'S PALACE)
www.mdc.hr/dubrovnik

The historic heart of Dubrovnik government is now a museum recalling the golden age of the city state of Ragusa. Ragusa was ruled by a rector, elected by adult male nobles with a mandate of just one month. Throughout his term of office he was confined to the palace, forbidden to see his family and only allowed to leave on official state business. The rector's palace was not only the seat of government; it was also a courtroom, prison and gunpowder store.

You enter the palace through the loggia, with columns carved from Korčula marble and a long stone bench. The main doorway leads to the atrium; at the centre is a bust of Miho Pracat (1528–1607), a wealthy shipowner from Lopud who left his fortune to the Ragusan republic. The former courtroom and prison cells house exhibitions of coins, weapons and Ragusan portraits.

A ceremonial staircase, used once a month for the inauguration of a new rector, leads to the state rooms on the upper floor. The salons have been re-created with aristocratic furniture, and the rector's study contains the original keys to the city gates. The Latin inscription above the door to the Great Council chambers reminds the rector of his duty: *Obliti privatorum publica curate* (Forget private concerns, think of the public good).

Go to a concert here if you can as the acoustics are superb. The Dubrovnik Symphony Orchestra gives recitals throughout the year and the atrium is used for concerts during the Summer Festival.

✚ 221 C2 ✉ Knežev Dvor 1 ☎ 020 321422 🕐 May–end Oct Mon–Sat 9–1, 4–5, Sun 9–1; Nov–end Apr Mon–Sat 9–1 ✋ Adult 40kn, child 20kn 🎁

STRADUN
www.zod.hr

Stradun, also known as Plaća, is the central thoroughfare of the old town, running for 300m (330 yards) in an ever widening straight line from Pile Gate to Luža square. With its souvenir shops and pavement (sidewalk) cafés, this is a popular meeting point and the venue for the evening *korzo* (promenade). A walk along Stradun is an essential Dubrovnik experience and is especially atmospheric at night, when street lamps bathe the stone in a golden glow.

Below *Knežev Dvor, heart of government for the medieval city state of Ragusa*

Stradun was originally a narrow channel separating the Roman island of Ragusium from the Slavic settlement of Dubrovnik; it was only when the channel silted up during the 12th century that the two sides came together to form a single city. The flagstones were laid down in the 15th century and Stradun has been the city's main promenade ever since. With the exception of Palača Sponza (▷ 224), the grand Gothic and Renaissance palaces which once lined the street were destroyed in the earthquake of 1667. Rebuilding from scratch, Roman architect Giulio Cerruti created a street of identical three-storey stone houses, with arched doorways and windows at street level. During the siege of 1991–92 Stradun suffered 45 direct hits from mortar shells and was for a time deserted.

Velika Onofrijeva Fontana (Onofrio's Large Fountain)
The large domed fountain inside Pile Gate was built in 1444 as part of a complex system of plumbing which provided Ragusa's first water supply. Severely damaged in the Great Earthquake of 1667 and again in 1991–92, the fountain has been restored and continues to supply fresh water to the city. There is also a smaller fountain by Onofrio della Cava beneath the clock tower in Luža.

Luža
The broad square where Stradun meets the Old Port has St. Blaise's Church (▷ 222) on one side and Palača Sponza (▷ 224) on the other. At the centre is Orlandov Stup (Orlando Column), with a figure of a knight at its base, erected in 1418 and believed to represent the French epic hero Roland, who legend says defended Dubrovnik against the Moors. Under the Ragusan republic, new laws were proclaimed from the column, criminals were executed here and Orlando's forearm was used as an official unit of measurement. The nearby clock tower dates from the 15th century; look out for the 'little green men' Maro and Baro, bronze figures who strike the hour by hitting the bell with their hammers. The originals are kept in the Sponza Palace.

✚ 221 C2 ❶ Širnka 1 ☎ 020 323587 ◷ Sep–end Jun Mon–Fri 8–7, Sat–Sun 9–2

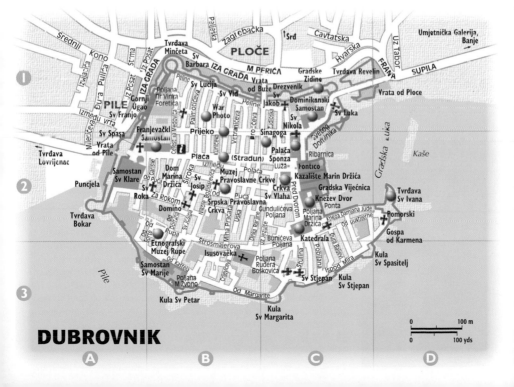

Above A narrow, café-lined street in central Dubrovnik

DUBROVNIK

Above *Visitors congregate on the Stradun by Vrata od Pile, gateway to the Old Town*
Below *The statue of St. Blaise, Dubrovnik's patron saint, above Crkva Svetog Vlaha*

FRANJEVAČKI SAMOSTAN (FRANCISCAN MONASTERY)

www.malabraca.hr

In the 14th century Franciscan monks were given permission to build their church inside the city walls and granted a plot close to Pile Gate. The original church was gutted by fire following the Great Earthquake and all that remains is the Gothic pietà over the south door. To visit the cloisters and museum enter via the narrow passage beside the neighbouring church of Sveti Spas (Holy Saviour).

With their twin columns, gardens of palm trees and bougainvillaea, a fountain at the centre and views of the bell tower, the Franciscan cloisters are a beautiful place to visit. A stone tablet records that they were built by Mihoje Brajkov of Montenegro, who died of plague in 1348. Among the capitals, carved with images of humans, animals and plants, look for the man with a swollen cheek, believed to be a self-portrait of Brajkov suffering from toothache. Just off the cloisters is the pharmacy (Mon–Sat 9–6), which has been in operation since 1317 and still sells herbal remedies and lotions made from original recipes.

The museum contains items from the old pharmacy and a 15th-century portrait of St. Blaise. The monastery suffered serious damage during the siege of Dubrovnik, receiving over 50 direct hits despite being used by the Red Cross. As a powerful memorial, two shells which fell on 'Black Friday' (6 December 1991) are on display.

Look out for candlelit concerts and recitals of chamber music in the lovely Gothic chapel of Sveti Spas.

✚ 221 B2 ✉ Stradun 2 ☎ 020 321410 🕐 Daily 9–6 ✋ Church: free. Museum and cloisters: Adult 30kn, child 15kn 🏛

CRKVA SVETOG VLAHA (CHURCH OF ST. BLAISE)

Dubrovnik's favourite church is dedicated to Sveti Vlaha (St. Blaise), the city's protector and patron saint. Wherever you go in Dubrovnik you will come across statues of St. Blaise. Not much is known about this third-century Armenian bishop, martyred by the Romans because of his Christianity by being flayed to death with an iron comb. Several centuries later, according to tradition, he appeared in a dream to a priest in Dubrovnik, warning of a Venetian attack. The invasion was repelled and the city adopted St. Blaise as its patron. The current baroque church was completed in 1715, replacing an earlier church destroyed by fire. Miraculously, the only object to survive was a 15th-century silver statue of St. Blaise, kept in a niche above the altar. The church is the focal point for the annual festival of St. Blaise (▷ 235), when the faithful line up to have their throats blessed by a priest. The reason for this custom is that St. Blaise is also the patron saint of throat ailments.

✚ 221 C2 ✉ Luža ☎ 020 323462 🕐 Daily 8–8 ✋ Free

DOMINIKANSKI SAMOSTAN (DOMINICAN MONASTERY)

The Dominican order of friars were given land inside Ploče Gate in the 14th century, on condition that they helped to protect the city as the Franciscans did at Pile Gate. The 15th-century monastery complex largely survived the Great Earthquake and today includes a church, cloisters and museum. The tranquil cloisters with their orange and lemon trees make a delightfully shady retreat from the city streets in summer. The church is dominated by a large gilded crucifix by 14th-century artist Paolo Veneziano, and also contains works by leading 20th-century Croatian artists, including a portrait of St. Dominic by Vlaho Bukovac and a sculpture of the Virgin and Child by Ivan Meštrović (▷ 23). Highlights of the museum are an 11th-century Bible and an altarpiece by Titian depicting Mary Magdalene and St. Blaise. Look out for the Gothic staircase leading up to the monastery. Its walled-in balustrade was designed to prevent views of women's ankles as they climbed the steps to the church.

✚ 221 C1 ✉ Ulica Svetog Dominika 4 ☎ 020 321423 🕐 Daily 9–6 ✋ Adult 20kn, child 10kn

ETNOGRAFSKI MUZEJ RUPE (ETHNOGRAPHIC MUSEUM)

This 16th-century granary is the only survivor of the grain stores built to preserve food for the citizens of Ragusa in the event of a siege. The grain was stored in deep circular wells hewn out of the rock, which still make a dramatic sight. Roman numerals carved into the wall record the capacity of each pit. On the top two floors, where the grain was dried, there is now a diverting exhibition of rural costumes and crafts, including the richly embroidered waistcoats and skirts of the Konavle villagers, dyed red Easter eggs and 19th-century jewel-encrusted Turkish daggers and pistols.

✚ 221 B2 ✉ Od Rupa 3 ☎ 020 412545 ◷ Tue–Sun 9–6 ✋ Adult 40kn, child 20kn ▣

KATEDRALA (CATHEDRAL)

Legend states that Dubrovnik's first cathedral was built by English king Richard the Lionheart (1157–99) in thanks for being rescued from a shipwreck at Lokrum on his return from the Crusades. Whatever the truth, the cathedral was destroyed in the Great Earthquake and the current baroque church dates from 1713. With its clean white walls and arches, the cathedral has a pleasing simplicity in contrast to so many overblown Croatian Catholic churches. The main attraction is the bizarre Riznica (Treasury), situated behind the altar and containing numerous examples of the gold and silver filigree work of Ragusa's medieval craftsmen. Many of the exhibits are reliquaries for the body parts of saints, with pride of place going to the relics of St. Blaise, acquired from Constantinople after he became Dubrovnik's patron saint in the 10th century. They include an 11th-century skull cap in the form of a Byzantine crown, and bejewelled and filigreed reliquaries containing the saint's arms, feet and throat. During the festival of St. Blaise (▷ 235), the relics are taken out of the cathedral and paraded around the city, with the faithful reaching out to touch them.

✚ 221 C2 ✉ Pred Dvorom ☎ 020 323459 ◷ Apr–end Oct Mon–Sat 9–5, Sun 11–5; Nov–end Mar Mon–Sat 10–12, 3–5, Sun 11–12, 3–5 ✋ Treasury: Adult 15kn, child 5kn

Below *The bell tower of the Franciscan monastery rises high above the roofs of the surrounding buildings*

Above *Dubrovnik's baroque cathedral, built in the 18th century*

UMJETNIČKA GALERIJA (MODERN ART MUSEUM)

www.ugdubrovnik.hr

Dubrovnik's modern art museum occupies an elegant Renaissance villa in Ploče, outside the eastern walls. Leave the old town via Ploče Gate and cross the drawbridge to Revelin Fort, then continue uphill past the Lazareti (a former quarantine hospital) and Banje beach to reach the museum. Inside, look out for portraits by Cavtat painter Vlaho Bukovac (1855–1922) and an abstract *Crveni Otok* (Red Island) by Dubrovnik artist Ivo Dulčić (1916–75), who also designed the stained glass windows in St. Blaise's Church. Climb the stairs from the courtyard to the sculpture terrace, with works by Ivan Meštrović (▷ 23) and views over the Old Port. The ticket includes entry to the Ronald Brown Memorial House (daily 10–8), which is opposite the main door to the cathedral.

✚ Off map 221 D1 ✉ Put Frana Supila 23 ☎ 020 426590 ⏰ Tue–Sun 10–8 ✋ Adult 30kn, child free

MORE TO SEE

MUZEJ PRAVOSLAVNE CRKVE (ORTHODOX CHURCH MUSEUM)

The Ragusan republic had a reputation for religious diversity which continues to this day: in addition to numerous Catholic churches there are Baptist and Orthodox churches, a synagogue and a mosque within the city walls. The Serbian Orthodox church of the Annunciation, completed in 1877, is the focus for Dubrovnik's Serb community. Rich in icons, incense and candle wax, it is typically Byzantine in style. A few doors along, climb the stairs of an ordinary-looking house and ring the doorbell to enter the Orthodox museum, containing icons from the 15th to 19th centuries and dark portraits of local Serbs by Cavtat artist Vlaho Bukovac (1855–1922).

✚ 221 B2 ✉ Od Puča 8 ☎ 020 323283 ⏰ Mon–Sat 9–2 ✋ Adult 10kn, child 5kn

PALAČA SPONZA

This elegant 16th-century palace, with its Venetian Gothic windows and Renaissance portico, was one of the few buildings to survive the Great Earthquake and was once used as Ragusa's customs house and mint. A Latin inscription in the courtyard cautions traders against cheating, warning that 'the scales we use to weigh your goods are used by God to weigh us'. During the Communist era, the palace became the Museum of the Socialist Revolution, but it now houses the Ragusa state archives and is used as a gallery hosting temporary exhibitions. Be sure to visit the Memorial Room to the Defenders of Dubrovnik, a moving tribute to the victims of the 1991–92 siege, with photos of the dead and images of Stradun in flames.

✚ 221 C2 ✉ Luža ☎ 020 321032 ⏰ May–end Oct 9am–10pm; Nov–end Apr 10–3 ✋ Free

SINAGOGA (SYNAGOGUE)

Dubrovnik's small synagogue is the oldest Sephardic synagogue in the world and the second-oldest surviving synagogue in Europe, after Prague. It was founded in the 15th century by Jews expelled from Spain, and was situated on the main street of the Jewish ghetto, whose gates were locked each night. It was reconsecrated in 1997 after years of Communist neglect and war damage. Brass lamps hang from the ceiling and wooden lattice screens hide an area previously reserved for women. A museum contains religious artefacts and records of the early Jewish community; more recent items include a list of Holocaust victims.

✚ 221 C2 ✉ Ulica Žudioska 3 ☎ 020 321028 ⏰ Jun–end Sep daily 10–8; Oct–end May Mon–Fri 10–3 ✋ Adult 15kn, child (under 14) free

SRĐ

The limestone bulk of Mount Srđ keeps a watchful eye over Dubrovnik, sheltering the city from the wind and rain which fall on the far side. Until 1991 you could take a cable car to the summit, but it was destroyed during the war and the only way up now is on foot. Leave the old town by Buža gate near the highest point of the walls and follow the road uphill. Climb the steps on Ulica Od Srđa to reach the Adriatic highway, then turn left and look for the path on your right. The climb to the summit takes about an hour—take plenty of water as there is little shade, and stick to the path in case of unexploded mines. The old French fort at the summit is in ruins, but the views over Dubrovnik are superb. The tall white cross is illuminated at night.

✚ Off map 221 C1

WAR PHOTO

www.warphotoltd.com

This thought-provoking gallery just off Stradun has exhibitions of war photography from the conflicts in the Balkans and around the world.

✚ 221 B1 ✉ Ulica Antuninska 6 ☎ 020 322166 🕒 Jun–end Sep daily 9–9; May, Oct Tue–Sat 9–3, Sun 10–2 ✋ Adult 30kn, child free

PRIJEKO

North of Stradun, narrow alleys and steep steps lined with potted plants lead uphill through the atmospheric districts beneath the city walls. Prijeko, an attractive street with restaurant tables on the pavement (sidewalk) in summer, lies halfway up, parallel to Stradun.

✚ 221 B1

BEACHES

The nearest beach to the old town is Banje, just outside Ploče Gate, where you can swim or sunbathe with a fabulous view of the Old Port. In summer Banje is crowded with locals who hang out both day and night at the fashionable East-West beach club (▷ 234). There are pebble beaches on the Lapad peninsula and a nudist beach at Lokrum, but for a real sandy beach, take the ferry to Lopud (▷ 226) and walk across the island to Šunj.

✚ 221 D1

Above left *Detail of elegant Palača Sponza*
Above right *The entrance to Dubrovnik's historic synagogue*

INFORMATION

www.visitdubrovnik.hr

✚ 286 J9 🛈 On the harbour at Lopud
☎ 020 759086 🕐 May to mid-Oct
Sat–Thu 8–1, 5–7; there is also an office
by the harbour at Šipanska Luka in
summer 🚢 From Dubrovnik

TIPS

» The islands virtually shut down between
November and April, so make sure you
bring your own food and drink.
» The sandy beach at Šunj is one of the
finest in Croatia and has a beach bar in
summer.
» Look out for the summer houses of
the Ragusan nobility on the waterfront
at Lopud.

Below *A sheltered bay on the peaceful
island of Lopud*

ELAFITSKI OTOCI (ELAFITI ISLANDS)

Enjoy the relaxed pace of life on these traffic-free isles, a short ferry ride from
the bustle of the city. When the people of Dubrovnik need to escape, they head
for the Elafiti Islands. Of 13 isles in the archipelago only three are inhabited, with
a combined population of under a thousand. There are no cars on Koločep and
Lopud and only a handful on Šipan, so the islands are perfect for walking. Three
ferries a day make the journey from Dubrovnik; in summer there are additional
fast shuttle boats from the Old Port and Cavtat, making it possible to visit all
three islands in a day.

KOLOČEP AND LOPUD

The ferry arrives first at Koločep, the smallest inhabited island, which is
covered in dense pine forest, vineyards, orchards and olive groves. A walled
lane connects the twin settlements of Gornje and Donje Čelo, with their sand
and pebble beaches. The ferry docks next at Lopud, whose only village is set
around a sheltered bay beneath a fortified 15th-century Franciscan monastery. A
footpath behind the harbour climbs to a 10th-century church and ruined castle at
the summit of the island, offering views as far as Dubrovnik. From here you can
continue to the sandy beach at Šunj.

ŠIPAN

The largest island, Šipan, is also the least visited. Ferries dock at the two main
towns of Suđurađ and Šipanska Luka, each based around a pretty harbour. A
minibus connects the two, or you can walk the 7km (4.5 miles), passing the
church of Sveti Duh (Holy Spirit).

LOKRUM

As you walk around the city walls in Dubrovnik, your eyes are drawn to the offshore island of Lokrum, a green pearl rising out of a shimmering blue sea. The nearest island to the city, Lokrum is a tranquil place of dense woods, gardens, and coves that has long been famed for its beauty. In summer, it makes a pleasant retreat from the hot and crowded city streets, with opportunities to walk and swim. Boats depart regularly from the Old Port in Dubrovnik, taking just 15 minutes to reach Lokrum; the price of the boat ticket includes entry to the Lokrum nature reserve.

SHADY WALKS

As you step ashore at the harbour, you see the old forest ranger's cottage, abandoned since its shelling in 1991. A map details the network of footpaths around the island, beginning with a walk along the northern shore. It takes around two hours to make a complete circuit of the island, including the climb to Fort Royal, a ruined French fort, whose rooftop offers panoramic views of Dubrovnik. From here, a processional route lined with cypress trees leads to the botanical garden.

SUN AND SEA

A short path from the harbour leads to an 11th-century Benedictine monastery, abandoned in the 19th century and later used as a summer villa by Archduke Maximilian von Habsburg, brother of the Austrian emperor. Nearby is the Mrtvo More (Dead Sea), a natural saltwater swimming pool fed by the sea. If you just want to swim and sunbathe, follow the crowds to the FKK (nudist) beach, which has views as far as Cavtat (▷ 217).

INFORMATION

www.lokrum.hr

✚ 286 J9 ☎ 020 427242 🕐 Apr–end Oct and at weekends in winter: boats depart from Dubrovnik's Old Port every half hour from 9am–6pm, weather permitting 💶 Adult 50kn, child 25kn 🔲

TIPS

» Smoking is not permitted on the island because of the risk of fire.
» Make sure you check the time of the last boat back to Dubrovnik—usually 7pm.
» There is a snack bar near the harbour and a restaurant in the monastery cloisters in summer, but it is a good idea to take food and water to the island just in case.

Above *Mrtvo More, a natural saltwater swimming pool on Lokrum island*

MLJET

INFORMATION

www.np-mljet.hr

286 H9 Nacionalni Park Mljet, Pristanište 2 020 744041 National park entry fee: Apr–end Oct 90kn, including minibus from Polače and boat trip to St. Mary's island; Nov–end Mar 30kn; child under 6 free Car ferry from Dubrovnik and Prapratno to Sobra; car ferry from Trstenik (Pelješac) to Polače in summer; catamaran from Dubrovnik to Sobra and Polače Details of *Nona Ana* sailing schedules from Atlantagent 020 313355

Above *The picturesque inland village of Korita, eastern Mljet*

INTRODUCTION

Mljet is the eighth-largest island in Croatia and a place of outstanding beauty, with unspoiled green forests and saltwater lakes. It holds a mythical appeal to visitors, as the legendary home of Calypso, the beautiful nymph who seduced the Greek hero Odysseus and imprisoned him for seven years after he was shipwrecked on the island. The story is told by Homer in his epic poem *Odyssey*.

The main sights are at the island's western end, which has been designated a national park, Nacionalni Park Miljet (Miljet National Park). It is possible to spend days here, walking, cycling, sailing and swimming in crystal-clear waters, but most people come on day trips as accommodation is limited. Tour operators in Dubrovnik and on the Dalmatian coast offer day excursions to Mljet in summer, including the national park entry fee and the boat trip to St. Mary's Island. Alternatively, the *Nona Ana* catamaran leaves Gruž harbour in Dubrovnik each morning, taking around an hour to reach Mljet. From June to the end of September it departs at 8 or 9.15am, with tickets (120kn return) going on sale at the quayside at 8am. It then sails to Polače within the national park, allowing plenty of time to explore before the return voyage at 4.55pm. From October to May, the boat leaves Dubrovnik at 10am, sailing to the main port of Sobra and continuing to Polače three times a week, though the early return to Dubrovnik gives you little time on the island. On arriving in Polače, buy a national park ticket from the harbourside kiosk before walking or taking the free minibus to the shores of Veliko Jezero. For more information on getting to Mljet, ▷ 229.

WHAT TO SEE

POLAČE

This pretty harbour village within Mljet National Park is many people's first view of the island as they approach by catamaran. Behind the port are the remains of a fourth-century Roman villa; from here, paths lead to the lakeshore at Pristanište (where the park headquarters are situated) and the abandoned hilltop village of Goveđari. Other ruins around Polače include a fort dating from late antiquity and, to the northwest, the remains of an early Christian basilica and church.

VELIKO JEZERO AND MALO JEZERO (BIG AND SMALL LAKES)

These two saltwater lakes are fed by the sea through the narrow Solinski channel. A footpath leads around the shore of both lakes, though it is not possible to make a complete circuit as the bridge spanning the seaward end of Veliko Jezero was destroyed in 1960. The two lakes meet at Stari Most (Old Bridge), where you can rent bicycles, rowing boats and canoes in summer. A pleasant cycle path around Veliko Jezero passes St. Mary's Island, with fine views of the monastery before you reach the open sea.

A signposted footpath from the shores of Veliko Jezero climbs to Montokuc, at 253m (830ft) the highest summit in the national park. From here, there are fine views of the island.

OTOK SVETA MARIJA (ST. MARY'S ISLAND)

This monastery on an islet on a lake on an island is one of the most photographed images of Croatia. Used as a hotel in the Communist era, it has now been returned to the Church and is currently being restored. Between April and the end of October shuttle boats ferry you across from Pristanište or Stari Most. You can explore the monastery's 12th-century cloisters, have lunch in the café, and stroll around the island, looking out for votive shrines built by shipwrecked sailors.

MORE TO SEE

SAPLUNARA

If you are staying longer, rent a car or bike to explore the rest of the island, including the beautiful sandy beach at Saplunara, on Mljet's southeastern tip. Hotels as such are non-existent here but local families rent out rooms during the high season.

TIPS

» If you are visiting Mljet in autumn, winter or spring, go on a Sunday. Between October and May, the *Nona Ana* sails from Dubrovnik at 10am and returns from Sobra at 5.30pm on Sundays, giving you enough time to explore the national park. The boat trips to St. Mary's Island do not operate in winter, but you can still walk around the lakes.

» There are restaurants at Polače and Pomena, and summer restaurants on St. Mary's Island and on the shores of Veliko Jezero.

» Hotel Odisej (www.hotelodisej.hr) at the seaside village of Pomena is Mljet's only hotel. It can organize boat trips into the cave where Calypso is said to have enchanted Odysseus.

» Smoking is allowed only at designated places within the national park because of the risk of forest fires.

Left *An aerial view of Mljet's beautiful lakes and dense green forests*
Below *Pretty waterside Hotel Odisej*

PELJEŠAC

This long, mountainous peninsula is virtually an island, joined to the mainland by a slender isthmus at Ston and separated from Korčula by a narrow channel at Orebić. The twin towns of Ston and Mali Ston, guarding the entrance to Pelješac, were second only to Dubrovnik in the days of the Ragusan republic, protected by a complex system of 14th-century fortifications that can still be climbed today. Mali Ston is famed for its oysters and mussels, which you can try at the waterfront restaurants. A single road runs for 90km (56 miles) across Pelješac, passing idyllic bays and offering magnificent views to the islands of Korčula, Lastovo and Mljet. Highlights include the vineyards at Potomje, source of Croatia's finest red wine, Dingač (▷ 267), and the laid-back beach resort of Orebić.

✚ 287 H9 🚹 Trg Mimbeli, Orebić ☎ 020 713718 ⏰ Jun–end Sep daily 8am–9pm; Oct–end May Mon–Fri 8–1 🚌 From Dubrovnik and Korčula 🚢 From Korčula

PREVLAKA

www.prevlaka.hr

At the southern tip of Croatia, facing Montenegro across the water, the rugged Prevlaka peninsula dips its toes into the Bay of Kotor. Acquired by the Ragusan republic from Bosnian rulers in 1441, this lonely spit of land has long had strategic significance. The Austrians built a fort here in the 19th century, which survives at the very edge of the peninsula, and there was a military base here in Yugoslav times. In 1991–92 Prevlaka was occupied by the Yugoslav army during the assault on Dubrovnik. After being guarded by UN peacekeepers for 10 years, it was returned to Croatia in 2001. The far end of Oštro cape is now an adventure and nature park, with activities ranging from kayaking and bicycle trails to a climbing wall, children's farm and sightseeing tour by miniature train. You can wander around the old fort and the labyrinth of underground tunnels, or relax on the beach. Just up the coast, the fishing village of Molunat has become a pleasantly low key resort, with campsites, private accommodation and clear waters.

✚ 286 K10 ☎ 020 791555 ⏰ Hours vary throughout the year 💷 Adult 15kn, child free including unlimited rides on sightseeing train 🚌 From Dubrovnik and Cavtat to Molunat 🍴 🛍 🏛

TRSTENO

In its heyday, the ruling class of the medieval city-state of Ragusa built their summer houses on the coast, where they gathered to discuss politics and state affairs. The botanic garden at Trsteno, 18km (11 miles) north of Dubrovnik, was originally part of a Renaissance villa belonging to wealthy patrician Ivan Gučetić. The small village of Trsteno was home to many sailors, and sea captains brought back cuttings and seeds from their travels to create a rich garden of exotic species. The gardens were nationalized in 1948 and turned into an arboretum. With shady avenues of pine trees and the scent of pomegranate, orange and lemon blossom hanging in the air, the garden makes a lovely place to take a stroll. Look out in particular for the romantic 18th-century water garden and grotto. A path leads to the harbour, with views of the Elafiti islands.

✚ Trsteno Arboretum 286 J9 ✉ Trsteno ☎ 020 751019 ⏰ May–end Oct daily 7–7; Nov–end Apr daily 8–4 💷 Adult 30kn, child 15kn 🚌 From Dubrovnik

Below *A view of the island of Korčula from the mountainous Pelješac peninsula*

Opposite *Statue of Neptune in the grotto of Trsteno Aboretum*
Below *Fortifications at Ston*

IN AND OUT OF DUBROVNIK

Lying outside the city walls in the shadow of Lovrijenac fortress, Pile is the forgotten corner of Dubrovnik. This short walk explores the sights of Pile, including its peaceful park, before passing through Pile Gate to wander the narrow streets of the old town.

THE WALK

Distance: 3km (2 miles)
Allow: 1–2 hours
Start/end: Vrata od Pile (Pile Gate)
✚ 221 A2

HOW TO GET THERE

Pile is the arrival point for buses to the old town from the bus station, Gruž harbour and Lapad peninsula.

★ Pile Gate is the main entrance to the walled city, topped by a statue of Sveti Vlaha (St. Blaise). Most people arrive here by bus and head straight into the old town, but this walk begins by exploring the district of Pile itself.

With Pile Gate behind you, look for the gravel park, with a fountain at the centre, outside Café Dubravka. Take the steps down from the park to arrive on Ulica Svetog Đurđa, following signs to Lovrijenac. Walk along this street, passing a small church with an upturned boat on

the pavement and turn left into Ulica Od Tabakarije to emerge at Orhan (▷ 237), a restaurant overlooking a small beach on the site of Dubrovnik's first harbour.

❶ Tvrđava Lovrijenac (▷ 219) can be visited (summer only) using the same ticket as for the city walls. The quickest route is to take the steps behind the restaurant; afterwards you can go down the main path to rejoin the walk.

Continue to the end of Ulica Od Tabakarije, passing the main path to Lovrijenac, then climb the steps to Dubrovnik Inter-University Centre. Walk up a steep slope and take a sharp left around the building to climb to a gravel car park on a cliff between two coves.

❷ From the car park, you can divert briefly down the hill to Danče. Here you will find the church of Our Lady

of Danče and a beautifully kept cemetery and garden, tended by the nuns from the Franciscan convent. The nuns still maintain the tradition of ringing the church bells whenever a ship passes at sea. Beneath the church, the bathing rocks offer views across the bay to Lapad.

Return to the car park and enter Gradac, the leafy park on your left, with a clifftop promenade and views stretching from Mount Srđ to Lokrum. Take the steps leading up into the park and continue to climb on a pine-shaded path to the summit. When you see another flight of steps coming up from your left, turn right through a narrow gateway and walk down the steps between stone walls.

❸ On your right is the stately mansion and garden of the Pucić family, now home to the Dubrovnik Symphony Orchestra.

Opposite *Boats moored in Dubrovnik's picturesque Old Port*

Turn right at the foot of the steps and follow busy Ulica Branitelja Dubrovnika to return to Pile Gate. Now it is time to enter the old town. Cross the moat and drawbridge to pass through the outer gate, then continue beneath a second arch to arrive on Stradun (▷ 220–221) beside the Onofrio fountain. Bear right around the fountain to Ulica Od Puča, the main shopping street of the old town.

4 The street ends in Poljana Gundulićeva, where a market is held on weekday mornings.

Bear right across the market square and look for a lane in the opposite corner leading to Bunićeva Poljana, a lively café-filled plaza which is animated on summer evenings. Keep left alongside the cathedral and go through the small archway

ahead of you to arrive at the old harbour, passing the fish market and Lokanda Peskarija (▷ 236). Keep left to walk around the harbour, then turn left to return to the walled town through Ribarnica gate. Turn right here to climb the steps towards the Dominican monastery (▷ 222). At the top of the steps, turn left through an archway to enter Prijeko along a narrow alley beside the church of Sveti Nikola (St. Nicholas). Walk straight ahead along Prijeko and take the second right up Ulica Žudioska.

5 Ulica Žudioska was the main street of the 16th-century Jewish ghetto. The synagogue used by Dubrovnik's Jewish community is a few steps downhill to your right.

Turn left at the top of Ulica Žudioska into Peline, the highest street of the old town. Pass the Buža gate and pass beneath the city walls with the Minčeta tower (▷ 219) visible up ahead. Turn left down Ulica Kunićeva

or any of the steep, narrow lanes of stone steps to return to Stradun and Pile Gate.

WHERE TO EAT
KAMENICE
▷ 236.

LOKANDA PESKARIJA
▷ 236.

ORHAN
▷ 237.

ROZARIJ
▷ 237.

SESAME
▷ 237.

PLACE TO VISIT
TVRDAVA LOVRIJENAC
▷ 219.

Below *The dome of Crkva Svetog Vlaha, rising above the city's rooftops*

WHAT TO DO

DUBROVNIK

ADRIATIC KAYAK TOURS
www.adriatickayaktours.com
This American-owned company offers half-day tours of Lokrum and full-day visits to the Elafiti Islands by kayak. The tours are suitable for beginners as instruction and safety equipment are provided. Accompanied children are welcome.
✉ Zrinsko Frankopanska 6, Dubrovnik ☎ 020 312770 ◉ May–end Oct

ALGORITAM
www.algoritam.hr
This branch of Croatia's biggest bookstore sells a wide range of English-language titles, including guidebooks and maps to Dubrovnik and Croatia.
✉ Stradun 8, Dubrovnik ☎ 020 322044 ◉ Jun–end Sep Mon–Sat 9am–11pm, Sun 10–1, 6–10; Oct–end May Mon–Fri 9–8.30, Sat 9–3, Sun 10–1

BUŽA
Pass through a hole in the city wall beneath a wooden sign saying 'Cold Drinks', walk down the steps and you come to this bar, perched on the rocks in a cliff face with views across to Lokrum. It is easy to spend hours here, relaxing to mellow music and occasionally diving into the sea. It serves only cold drinks (beer, wine and soft drinks in plastic cups) but the view cannot be bettered.
✉ Access from Ulica Od Margarite, Dubrovnik ☎ No tel ◉ Hours vary depending on the weather

DUBROVAČKA KUĆA
This attractive gallery on the square opposite the Dominican Monastery sells Dalmatian wines and liqueurs, candied fruits from the Elafiti islands, aromatic oils, natural cosmetics and work by local artists. On the same square is a small unnamed workshop selling stone and marble sculptures of St. Blaise.
✉ Ulica Svetog Dominika 4, Dubrovnik ☎ 020 322092 ◉ Jun–end Sep daily 9am–11pm; Oct–end May Mon–Sat 9–8

EAST-WEST BEACH CLUB
Just outside of the Ploče Gate, this trendy restaurant, with attached strip of beach, is a pleasant spot for a cooling swim following a hike round Dubrovnik's walls.
✉ Frana Supila bb, Dubrovnik ☎ 020 412220 ◉ Daily12–12

FOLK MUSIC
Look out for free displays of folk music and dance in Dubrovnik and nearby towns throughout the summer. Between May and October concerts take place on Sunday mornings at 11am outside St. Blaise's Church, with performances ranging from majorettes to traditional sword dancers from Korčula. The other popular event is the Sunday morning folk dance display in the church square at Čilipi, with dancers in traditional Dalmatian costume.

FRANJA
This upmarket delicatessen on the main shopping street of the old town sells a wide variety of Croatian wines and spirits plus olive oil, Pag cheese, gingerbread, honey, truffles, chocolates and coffee, as well as attractively presented gift baskets of lavender oils and soaps.
✉ Od Puča 9, Dubrovnik ☎ 020 324818 ◉ Daily 8am–9pm

KARAKA
www.karaka.info
This fine replica of a 16th-century Dubrovnik merchant galleon can accommodate 200 passengers. In winter, it is moored in Gruž harbour but in summer it moves to the Old Port, where it is open every night as a bar unless it is operating cruises.
✉ Gradska Luka, Dubrovnik ☎ 020 358108 ◉ Jun–end Sep daily 8pm–midnight

Opposite *Traditional folk dancing, Dubrovnik*

KAZALIŠTE MARINA DRŽIĆA

www.kazaliste-dubrovnik.hr

This lovely 19th-century theatre is named after Renaissance playwright Marin Držić (1508–67). It mostly performs serious Croatian drama, with occasional shows in English by visiting companies.

✉ Pred Dvorom 3, Dubrovnik ☎ 020 321088 ⓘ Box office: Mon–Sat 9–2 (9–2, 6–8 on performance days) 🎭 Varies

LINDA

A small stretch of Od Puča is lined with jewellery shops selling the gold and silver filigree work that has been produced in Dubrovnik since medieval times. This one also has chunky silver necklaces and Ottoman-inspired pieces.

✉ Od Puča 18, Dubrovnik ☎ 020 324082 ⓘ Mon–Sat 9am–11pm, Sun 9–9

LINĐO

In summer, this well-known folklore ensemble performs Croatian songs and dances twice a week on an outdoor stage at Lazareti, outside Ploče Gate. It also puts on regular concerts during the Dubrovnik Summer Festival.

☎ 020 324023 ⓘ Jun–end Sep Mon, Fri 9.30pm 🎟 80kn

MILIČIĆ

This wine shop on a corner of Stradun offers you the chance to taste Miličić wines from the Pelješac peninsula. It also sells various fruit brandies and liqueurs.

✉ Ulica Od Sigurate 2, Dubrovnik ☎ 020 321777 ⓘ Jun–end Sep daily 9am–10pm; Oct–end May Mon–Sat 9–12, 5–8, Sun 9–1

RONCHI

This traditional family-run hat shop was founded in 1858 and continues to make both men's and women's hats, using the same antique tools and blocks that have survived for over a century.

✉ Ulica Lučarica 2, Dubrovnik ☎ 020 323699 ⓘ Mon–Fri 9–1, 5–7, Sat 9.30–1

FEBRUARY
FESTA SVETOGA VLAHA (FEAST OF ST. BLAISE)

Festivities start on the afternoon of 2 February when the bishop releases white doves as a symbol of the city's freedom, the flag of St. Blaise is raised outside St. Blaise's Church and *trumbunjeri* (musketeers) fire their guns in the Old Port. Throughout this day and the next the faithful queue at St. Blaise's Church for the *grličanje* (blessing of the throat) ceremony. Early on 3 February the people of the surrounding villages gather at the city gates, dressed in traditional costume. They process down Stradun to the accompaniment of marching bands and gunpowder explosions from the *trumbunjeri*. After an open-air Mass outside the cathedral, the bishop leads a procession along Stradun carrying the holy relics of St. Blaise. The festival ends with the lowering of the flag and the singing of the hymn of St. Blaise, followed by the national anthem as the Croatian flag is raised.

✉ Dubrovnik ⓘ 2–3 Feb

JULY AND AUGUST
DUBROVNIK SUMMER FESTIVAL

www.dubrovnik-festival.hr

This is Croatia's biggest and most prestigious cultural event, with performances of music, drama and folk dance at venues around the city. It begins on 10 July, with fireworks and the raising of the Libertas flag on Luža square to the recital of *Ode to Liberty*, a celebration of Dubrovnik's freedom by Renaissance poet Ivan Gundulić (1589–1638). For the next six weeks, the city turns itself into an open-air stage. A highlight of the festival is the performance of Shakespeare's *Hamlet* at Lovrijenac fort. Tickets for events can be bought at the festival office on Stradun or the kiosk outside Pile Gate.

☎ 020 326100 ⓘ 10 Jul–25 Aug

TRINITY

Housed in a splendid 17th-century palace on the corner of Stradun and Palmotićeva, this jewellery boutique sells exquisite handcrafted traditional pieces. Silver filigree, coral and semi-precious stones dominate the display.

✉ Palmotićeva 2, Dubrovnik ☎ 020 322350 ⓘ Daily 9am–10pm

TROUBADOUR

Almost everyone in Dubrovnik ends up at the Troubadour, owned by Marko Brešković, a former Eurovision Song Contest contestant. There is live jazz every night from 10pm in summer, spilling out of doors on the square. In winter, the bar has a more intimate atmosphere as visitors and locals gather around the piano. Drinks are not cheap but you are paying for the atmosphere.

✉ Bunićeva Poljana 2, Dubrovnik ☎ 020 323476 ⓘ May–end Oct daily 9am–3am; Nov–end Apr daily 5–11

PELJEŠAC
INDIJAN

This family-run winery in the village of Potomje has a giant wine-barrel in the garden where you can help yourself and leave your money in the cash box. Ring on the doorbell to buy bottled wines and home-made spirits.

✉ Potomje, Pelješac ☎ 020 742235

MATUŠKO

One of the better producers of Pelješac wine sells direct from the cellar. Products range from Rukatac and Pošip whites to vintage Dingač.

✉ Potomje, Pelješac ☎ 020 742393 ⓘ Ring bell

VINARIJA DINGAČ

The most famous name in Croatian wine has a modern winery in Potomje. The showroom offers sales and tastings of Dingač, Postup and Plavac Mali wines.

✉ Potomje, Pelješac ☎ 020 742010

PRICES AND SYMBOLS

The restaurants are listed alphabetically. The prices given are the average for a two-course lunch (L) and a three-course dinner (D) for one person, without drinks. The wine price is for a litre of table wine followed by the least expensive bottle of quality wine. All the restaurants listed accept credit cards unless otherwise stated.

For a key to the symbols, ▷ 2.

CAVTAT

GALIJA

www.galija.hr

With tables under the pine trees at the end of the harbourside promenade, this restaurant is a delightful place to spend a summer evening. The food is a mix of traditional and modern, including grilled fish, steaks, prawns with honey, carpaccio of grouper with Parmesan, and oven-baked octopus. Reservations are essential in summer.
✉ Vuličevićeva 1, Cavtat ☎ 020 478566 ☉ Daily 11am–midnight ✋ L 150kn, D 200kn, Wine 90/120kn

DUBROVNIK

BUFET ŠKOLA

If you fancy a snack, this tiny bar in an alley off Stradun serves great sandwiches, with thick crusty bread filled with Dalmatian ham and cheese in olive oil. Other choices are salted sardines and green salad.
✉ Antuninska 1, Dubrovnik ☎ 020 321096 ☉ Daily 8am–midnight ✋ Sandwiches from 21kn, Wine from 60kn

DUBROVAČKI KANTUN

The restaurant is bedecked in old knick-knacks such as yesteryear telephones and nostalgia-inducing radios. The chef-owner has also revived the past in some of his recipes, a few of which date back to the 15th century. Enjoy tasty dishes such as beef stew, lentil soup, scampi in tomato sauce, and cuttlefish, in an intimate dining space.
✉ Boskovićeva 5, Dubrovnik ☎ 020 321123 ☉ 11am–midnight ✋ L 100kn, D 120kn, Wine 90/140kn

GILS

www.gilsdubrovnik.com

Make sure your wallet is up to the job at this chic, mainly open-air place set within the battlements of Dubrovnik's defensive walls near the Ploče Gate. Dishes are Dalmatian and French-influenced, the wine list is second to none and the service impeccable.
✉ Svetog Dominika bb, Dubrovnik ☎ 020 322222 ☉ 12–11 ✋ L 350kn, D 400kn, Wine from 150kn

KAMENICE

This lively café on the market square is popular with locals at lunchtime. Its name means 'oyster' and it makes a great place for a fishy snack of oysters, scampi *na buzaru* (in a tomato, wine and garlic sauce) mussel risotto, octopus salad or *girice* (small fried fish).
✉ Gundulićeva Poljana 8, Dubrovnik ☎ 020 323682 ☉ Apr–end Oct daily 7am–11pm; Nov–end Mar daily 7am–8pm ✋ L 65kn, D 90kn, Wine from 120kn

LOKANDA PESKARIJA

With simple, wooden tables outside the fish market and views over the Old Port, Lokanda is the perfect setting in which to enjoy simply prepared but delicious seafood dishes. The menu is limited but everything on it is first-class, from tasty fish pâté to seafood risotto and fried sardines to grilled squid. The only accompaniments you need order are a crisp green salad and a glass of chilled Pošip—a white wine from Korčula.
✉ Ribarnica, Dubrovnik ☎ 020 324750 ☉ Daily 8am–midnight ✋ L 80kn, D 100kn, Wine 80/120kn

Above *Taking a break at a quayside café in Cavtat*

NISHTA

www.nishtarestaurant.com

Vegetarian restaurants are scarce in Croatia so non-meat eaters should make the most of this celebrated eatery a few steps up from Stradun, the main street. The menu is firmly international (chow mein, falafel, fajitas), the service mellow and the atmosphere relaxed. It's a great place either for a full-blown meal or just a cooling, freshly squeezed fruit juice.

✉ Prijeko bb, Dubrovnik ☎ 098 186 7440 ◷ Tue–Sat 12–3, 6–10, Mon 6pm–10pm. Closed Jan to mid-Feb ✋ L 90kn, D 120kn, Wine 90/100kn

ORHAN

Hidden away beside a pebble cove outside Pile Gate, Orhan is one of Dubrovnik's best-kept secrets. On summer evenings, you can dine on a covered terrace beside the sea, with views of Lovrijenac fortress on one side and the city walls on the other. Fresh grilled fish is the speciality –the waiter will bring a tray to your table to help you make your choice—but less expensive options include risotto and Dalmatian steak dishes.

✉ Ulica Od Tabakarije 1, Dubrovnik ☎ 020 414183 ◷ Feb–end Oct daily 11am–midnight ✋ L 150kn, D 200kn, Wine 80/150kn

ROZARIJ

The best of the restaurants off Prijeko is tucked away off a narrow passage between St. Nicholas's church and the Dominican Monastery. With just a handful of tables, it serves good Dalmatian classics like mussels, *brodet* (fish stew) and *crni rižot* (black cuttlefish risotto).

✉ Prijeko 2, Dubrovnik ☎ 020 321257 ◷ Mar–end Jan daily 11am–midnight ✋ L 100kn, D 120kn, Wine 100/150k

SESAME

www.sesame.hr

Popular with artists, musicians and students, this bistro outside the Pile Gate offers a wide-ranging menu of Mediterranean fare, with plenty of vegetarian choices. The cook's specialities are *gregada* (Hvar fish stew with potatoes and white wine) and Poporela-style fish, baked in egg white and sea salt. The wine list is extensive.

✉ Ulica Dante Alighierija, Dubrovnik ☎ 020 412910 ◷ 8am–midnight ✋ L 150kn, D 200kn, Wine from 90kn

TAJ MAHAL

With a name like 'Taj Mahal', you'd be forgiven for thinking you'd stumbled on a rare Indian takeaway in the heart of Dubrovnik. The incongruous name, however, belongs to the city's only Bosnian eatery, which has a dark, aromatic interior, a peaceful outdoor seating area and friendly service. Grilled meats, kebabs, salads and baklava abound on the menu, and giving one of the world's least known cuisines a try is half the fun.

✉ Nikole Gučetica 2, Dubrovnik ☎ 020 323221 ◷ 10am–midnight ✋ L 110kn, D150kn, Wine from 90kn

TONI

If you feel like going Italian, it's hard to beat this spaghetteria in the old town, the pick of the restaurants south of the Stradun. Home-made pasta dishes such as spaghetti carbonara and tortellini with walnuts and Gorgonzola along with bruschetta, salads and pizzas make for an inexpensive and filling lunch or dinner. Get here early to bag one of the few outdoor tables.

✉ Ulica Nikole Božidarevića 14, Dubrovnik ☎ 020 323134 ◷ 12–11 ✋ L 70kn, D 90kn, Wine 100/150kn

PELJEŠAC
KAPETANOVA KUĆA

www.ostrea.hr

Gourmets head out to Mali Ston on the Peljašac peninsula to eat fresh oysters at this famous restaurant, whose glass conservatory offers sea views. The waiter will bring you a complimentary starter of fish pâté while you look at the menu. Oysters are served raw, fried or in soup, or you might prefer beef in oyster sauce. The house special is black risotto, made with cuttlefish, squid and local mussels.

✉ Mali Ston ☎ 020 754555 ◷ Daily 9am–10pm ✋ L 120kn, D 170kn, Wine 80/130kn 🚌 Take the Magistrala coast road north from Dubrovnik and turn left after around 40km (25 miles) to reach Mali Ston

Below *Head to the fishing village of Mali Ston on the Peljašac peninsula to enjoy some of Croatia's best seafood*

PRICES AND SYMBOLS

Prices are the lowest for a double room for one night. Breakfast is included unless noted otherwise. All the hotels listed accept credit cards unless otherwise stated. Note that rates vary widely throughout the year.

For a key to the symbols, ▷ 2.

CAVTAT

CROATIA

www.hoteli-croatia.hr

This enormous beach hotel, surrounded by pine woods and gardens on the Sustjepan peninsula, has now been renovated and reopened as a five-star resort and one of the top seaside hotels in Croatia. Sports facilities include tennis, volleyball, watersports and an outdoor pool.

✉ Frankopanska 10, Cavtat ☎ 020 475555 ✋ From €150 ⓘ 480 ♻ ≋ Indoor and outdoor ▼ 🚌 10 to Cavtat 🚗 Fork left at the entrance to Cavtat

VILLA KVATERNIK

This small, attractive boutique hotel is owned by Croatian Australians. It is set in a 400-year-old stone house in the back streets of Cavtat, a short climb from the end of the seafront promenade. The owners can also offer eight rooms in the former Franciscan monastery, with simpler accommodation and breakfast served in the hotel.

✉ Kvaternikova 3, Cavtat ☎ 020 479800 ✋ From €85 ⓘ 6 ♻ 🚌 10 to Cavtat

DUBROVNIK

AQUARIUS

www.hotel-aquarius.net

Deep in the Lapad district about 3km (2 miles) from the historical heart of Dubrovnik, this modern, very comfortable, small-scale hotel has recently undergone renovation. It's a short walk from a popular beach and regular bus services link Lapad to the Pile Gate. The restaurant is

surprisingly plush but dishes are reasonably priced.

✉ Mata Vodopića 8, Dubrovnik ☎ 020 456112 ✋ 580kn ⓘ 24 ♻

DUBROVNIK PALACE

www.dubrovnikpalace.hr

The flagship of Goran Štrok's Adriatic Luxury Hotels lies at the southwestern tip of the Lapad peninsula. The lobby sets the tone, all sleek interior design in glass, wood and stone, and the Sunset Bar has panoramic views of the Elafiti Islands. Spread over 10 floors cascading towards the beach, all the rooms have sea-facing balconies. There are jogging paths and footpaths in the nearby pine woods.

✉ Masarykov Put 20, Lapad, Dubrovnik ☎ 020 430000 ✋ From €220 ⓘ 308 ♻ ≋ Indoor and outdoor ▼ 🚌 4

Above *The stately Zagreb Hotel in Dubrovnik dates from the 1930s*

EXCELSIOR
www.hotel-excelsior.hr

If you're feeling flush or want to impress someone special, this ultra-sophisticated luxury hotel, fresh from a total refit, is the place for you. Some 112 of the modern rooms have Adriatic views, there's a private beach, and extras such as free WiFi and 24-hour room service come as standard. Despite its plush facilities, superb location by the sea and glowing name, the hotel receives mixed reviews from guests.

✉ Frana Supila 12, Dubrovnik ☎ 020 353353 💰 1,400kn 🛈 158 🏋 🏊 Indoor 🚌 5, 8

GRAND VILLA ARGENTINA
www.gva.hr

Just outside Ploče Gate with magnificent views of the old town, the Argentina is the grandest address in town, with a guest list that has included Richard Burton, Elizabeth Taylor, Tito and Margaret Thatcher. As well as the main hotel building, there are four villas in the grounds, including the oriental-style folly, Villa Shcherozade, which can be hired by groups of 10 people for €6,000 a day. Terraced gardens lead down to a private beach with views of the Old Port, while the Energy Clinic offers expensive spa and beauty treatments.

✉ Frana Supila 14, Dubrovnik ☎ 020 440555 💰 From €193 🛈 186 🏊 Indoor and outdoor 🏋 🚌 5, 8

HILTON IMPERIAL
www.dubrovnik.hilton.com

The first Hilton in Croatia opened in 2005 in this art nouveau classic just outside Pile Gate. The rooms on the top floors have views of Lovrijenac fortress and the sea. Although it has local character, with prints of old Ragusan argosies (merchant ships) on the walls, the hotel also has all the hallmarks of the Hilton brand, including its popular breakfast buffet.

✉ Ulica Marijana Blažića 2, Dubrovnik ☎ 020 320320 💰 From €250 🛈 147 🏊 Indoor 🏋 🚌 1, 2, 3, 4, 5, 6, 8, 9 to Pile

HOTEL ADRIATIC
www.hotelimaestral.com

This no-frills but clean and well equipped hotel lies in the Lapad district about 3km (2 miles) from the city walls. With its fitness centre, clay tennis courts and sandy beach, it is geared towards sporty guests. Rooms serve their purpose well and if you can get one with a sea view, all the better. Hop on local city buses to reach the sights.

✉ Masarykov Put 9, Dubrovnik ☎ 020 433520 💰 600kn 🛈 133 🚌 4

HOTEL SUMRATIN
www.hotels-sumratin.com

Another Lapad establishment and belonging to the same mini-chain as the Zagreb (▷ 240), this attractive three-storey 1920s villa has slightly dated rooms and facilities, but is well situated. It is a good budget choice.

✉ Šetalište Kralja Zvonimira 27, Dubrovnik ☎ 020 436333 💰 600kn 🛈 44 🚌 5

KARMEN
www.karmendu.tk

These spacious apartments beside the Old Port are among the most attractive places to stay in the old city. Each has a kitchen, and some have a balcony or terrace overlooking the port. Breakfast is not included.

✉ Bandureva 1, Dubrovnik ☎ 020 323433 💰 €75–€120 🛈 4 🚌 1, 2, 3, 4, 5, 6, 8, 9 to Pile

PETKA
www.hotelpetka.hr

This high-rise hotel by Gruž harbour is a good base for early-morning departures to the Elafiti Islands and Mljet. It is worth paying extra for a room with a balcony and a view of the harbour and the Lapad peninsula.

✉ Obala Stjepana Radića 38, Gruž, Dubrovnik ☎ 020 410500 💰 From €70 🛈 104 🚌 1A, 1B, 3, 7, 8

PUCIĆ PALACE
www.thepucicpalace.com

With stone walls, dark oak floors, original artworks and handwoven rugs, this stylish hotel in a baroque palace on the market square combines modern comforts and

antique style. This was the first hotel to open within the walled city and its informal luxury continues to set the standard for boutique townhouse hotels throughout Croatia. All rooms have DVD players and WiFi, with Bulgari toiletries in the bathrooms. There is even a private yacht for guests to hire.

✉ Od Puča 1, Dubrovnik ☎ 020 326200 💰 €515 🛈 19 🚌 1, 2, 3, 4, 5, 6, 8, 9 to Pile

SESAME INN
www.sesame.hr

The friendly owner of the Sesame restaurant (▷ 237) has four rooms available on the ground floor of a 200-year-old family home in the Pile district. Accommodation is simple but comfortable, with windows over a pretty garden. For visitors on a budget, this is among the most affordable accommodation within a short walk of the old city.

✉ Don Frana Bulića 5, Dubrovnik ☎ 020 412910 💰 390kn 🛈 4 🚌 1, 2, 3, 4, 5, 6, 8, 9 to Pile

Below *Dubrovnik's Hilton Imperial occupies a beautiful art nouveau building*

STARI GRAD

www.hotelstarigrad.com

This delightful small hotel is in an 18th-century townhouse, whose antique furniture and handsome salons recreate the atmosphere of Ragusa's golden age. Wicker chairs and sofas on the tiny rooftop terrace make a lovely spot to enjoy the view across to the island of Lokrum.

✉ Od Sigurate 4, Dubrovnik ☎ 020 322244 ✋ From 920kn ① 8 🛠 🚍 1, 2, 3, 4, 5, 6, 8, 9 to Pile

VILLA DUBROVNIK

www.villa-dubrovnik.hr

Known simply as 'the villa' by its fans, this hotel has acquired a cult following across the Mediterranean. Built as a rest home for Communist officials in 1958, it was used to house refugees during the 1991–92 war and then later as a military headquarters. The villa is showing its age and is scheduled for a major renovation in the next few years. Nothing, however, can detract from its setting, a bright white villa on a cliff, surrounded by rich gardens and terraces with views to the Old Port. Every room has a balcony with sea view. From the landing stage a private boat travels to the old city several times a day.

✉ Vlaha Bukovca 6, Dubrovnik ☎ 020 422933 ③ Closed Nov–end Mar ✋ From €220; Mid-Jul to mid-Sep half-board only ① 40 🛠 🍷 🚍 5, 8 🚗 Take Frana Supila uphill from Ploče Gate and fork right beyond Grand Villa Argentina

VILLA WOLFF

www.villa-wolff.hr

You'd better reserve early to bag one of the rooms at this exclusive boutique villa with just 6 deluxe doubles and suites. Rooms are named after Greek gods and the views are simply heavenly. The hotel's Casa Restaurant is right on the waterfront and provides a romantic setting for both guests and non-residents to enjoy a meal.

✉ Nika i Meda Pucića 1, Dubrovnik ☎ 020 438710 ✋ 1,350kn ① 6 🛠 🚍 5

Right *Enjoy luxurious surroundings in some of Croatia's most exclusive hotels*

VIS

www.hotelimaestral.com

Its location, next to a pebbly beach in Lapad, makes this an attractive choice for families with children, who may appreciate access to the sea more than proximity to the city's historical core. Rooms are standard issue and there are a snack bar, restaurant and bar on the premises. A frequent public bus service links the area with Pile Gate.

✉ Masarykov Put 4, Dubrovnik ☎ 020 433555 ✋ 700kn ① 152 🛠 🚍 4

ZAGREB

First opened as a hotel in 1932, this 19th-century villa guarded by stately palm trees stands at the start of the promenade that leads to Lapad bay and beach. The Zagreb is the best choice for mid-price comfort and is only a short bus ride from the old city.

✉ Šetalište Kralja Zvonimira 27, Lapad, Dubrovnik ☎ 020 436333 ✋ From €70 ① 23 🛠 🚍 2, 4, 5, 6, 7, 9

ELAFITSKI OTOCI
VILLA VILINA

www.villa-vilina.hr

This stone house by the harbour

at Lopud is owned by the Vilina family and offers comfortable accommodation in a peaceful setting, a short ferry ride from Dubrovnik. There are lovely walks along the promenade and over the summit of the island to Šunj. You can also sample the owner's home-made rose-petal brandy.

✉ Obala Iva Kuljevana 5, Lopud ☎ 020 759333 ③ Closed Nov–end Apr ✋ From €119 ① 18 🛠 ⛱ Outdoor 🚢 Lopud

PELJEŠAC
OSTREA

www.ostrea.hr

Owned by the same family as the famous Kapetanova Kuća restaurant (▷ 237), this stone house by the harbour in the village of Mali Ston makes a romantic place to stay, and is popular with honeymooners, who come here to test the aphrodisiac qualities of the oysters. The waterside terrace is a lovely spot to sit and admire the views.

✉ Ante Starčevića 9, Mali Ston ☎ 020 754555 ✋ From 900kn ① 10 🛠 🚍 Take the Magistrala coast road north from Dubrovnik and turn left after around 40km (25 miles) to reach Mali Ston

PRACTICALITIES

Practicalities gives you all the important practical information you will need during your visit, from money matters to emergency phone numbers.

Adriatic coast regularly exceed 25°C (77°F) in summer and rarely drop below 5°C (41°F) in winter. The inland regions have a more extreme continental climate, characterized by hot summers and cold winters. In January, the temperature averages 0°C (32°F) in Zagreb and can reach as low as –10°C (14°F) in some highland areas. Snow is usual in the mountains.

» The *bora*, a fierce north-easterly wind, blows out to sea, striking fear into the hearts of sailors. At its strongest, it can force the closure of roads and ferries. It is most powerful in the Kvarner region in winter. Other winds are the *maestral*, a north-westerly sea breeze, and the *jugo*, a southerly wind bringing clouds and rain in winter.

» Long and short-range weather forecasts are available on the internet from the BBC, CNN, Weather Online and Yahoo. The Croatian Meteorological Office posts forecasts on its website (http://meteo.hr). Within Croatia, you can get forecasts

from local media, tourist offices and hotels or the weather forecast information line, tel 060 520520.

WHEN TO GO
» July and August are the peak holiday months. Hotel prices are at their highest and rooms are hard to find unless reserved. Roads are crowded and there are long waits for island ferries. On the plus side, the weather is reliable, and the sea

WEATHER
CLIMATE
» Croatia has two distinct climatic zones. The coast and islands have a Mediterranean climate, with warm, dry summers and mild, wet winters. Temperatures on the

TIME ZONES		
CITY	**TIME DIFFERENCE**	**TIME AT 12 NOON ZAGREB**
Auckland	+9	9pm
Dublin	-1	11am
London	-1	11am
New York	-6	6am
Sydney	+9	9pm

Croatia is on Central European Time (CET), one hour ahead of Greenwich Mean Time (GMT+1). Daylight saving time (GMT+2) operates from late March to late October. Clocks are put forward one hour on the last Sunday in March and put back one hour on the last Sunday in October.

DUBROVNIK
TEMPERATURE

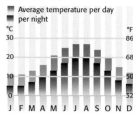

OSIJEK
TEMPERATURE

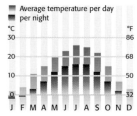

RIJEKA
TEMPERATURE

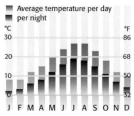

RAINFALL

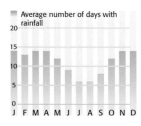

RAINFALL

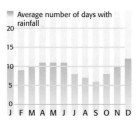

RAINFALL

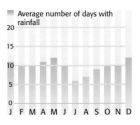

is warm and the coastal towns are buzzing with life.

» Spring (May and June) and autumn (September and October) are pleasant, with mild weather but without the crowds. The sea is usually still warm for swimming, and these are good months for walking, cycling and sailing.

» Between November and April many hotels are shut and the islands virtually close. The weather can be cold, wet and windy and ferry services are minimal. This can be a good time for a break in Zagreb, with its cosy cafés and Christmas markets. On sunny days the coastal towns can be mild, but only Dubrovnik and Opatija are geared up for tourists year-round.

DOCUMENTS
PASSPORTS AND VISAS

» Citizens of the UK, US, Canada, Australia and New Zealand need a valid passport to enter Croatia.

» Citizens of European Union countries require a passport or national identity card.

» Passport holders from the EU, US, Canada, Australia and New Zealand do not need a visa for stays of up to three months.

» Citizens of South Africa and most other countries require a visa, available in advance from the nearest Croatian embassy or consulate. For up-to-date details of visa requirements by country and a full list of Croatian embassies, see the Ministry of Foreign Affairs website at www.mfa.hr

» All foreign nationals must register with the police within 24 hours of arrival in Croatia. In practice this will usually be done for you by hotels, using a photocopy of your passport.

» Those passing through the Neum corridor on their way to southern Dalmatia should check the visa requirements for Bosnia-Herzegovina as they may differ for some nationalities. Check the situation in advance at www.mvp.gov.ba

INSURANCE AND HEALTH

» Even if your country has a reciprocal health care agreement with Croatia (▷ 245), it is advisable to take out travel insurance covering medical emergencies as well as accidents, theft and personal liability. Not all costs are covered by the reciprocal agreement and some treatment may only be available privately.

» There are no compulsory vaccinations for Croatia but check that your anti-tetanus inoculations are up to date before you go and consult your doctor or clinic to see whether any further vaccinations are recommended. Visitors to rural and forest areas of inland Croatia, particularly those visiting between April and October, should seek advice on inoculation against tick-borne encephalitis.

CUSTOMS
FROM AN EU COUNTRY

The following maximum customs allowances apply to all travellers entering Croatia:

» 200 cigarettes or 50 cigars or 250g of tobacco
» 1 litre of spirits
» 2 litres of table wine
» 250ml of toilet water
» 2 litres of fortified wine or sparkling wine or liqueurs
» 50ml of perfume
» The alcohol and tobacco allowances cannot be used by travellers under 18 years of age.
» Boats are subject to a temporary importation procedure provided they are registered with customs at the nearest Port Authority on arrival.
» Valuable photographic and computer equipment should be declared on arrival.
» Pets may only be brought into Croatia if accompanied by an International Vaccination Certificate.
» The full customs regulations can be seen at www.carina.hr

CROATIAN EMBASSIES AND CONSULATES ABROAD

EMBASSY	CONTACT DETAILS
Australia	Embassy of the Republic of Croatia, 14 Jindalee Crescent, O'Malley, Canberra, ACT 2606; tel 02 6286 6988
Canada	Embassy of the Republic of Croatia, 229 Chapel St, Ottawa, Ontario K1N 7Y6; tel 613 562 7820
Ireland	Embassy of the Republic of Croatia, Adelaide Chambers, Peter St, Dublin 8; tel 01 476 7181
New Zealand	Consulate General of the Republic of Croatia, 291 Lincoln Road, Edmonton, Auckland; tel 09 836 5581
South Africa	1160 Church St, 0083 Colbyn, Pretoria; tel 012 342 1206
UK	Embassy of the Republic of Croatia, 21 Conway St, London W1T 6BN; tel 020 7387 2022
US	Embassy of the Republic of Croatia, 2343 Massachusetts Ave NW, Washington DC, 20008; tel 202 588 5899

MONEY

Croatia's official currency is the kuna, abbreviated to HRK or kn. It takes its name from the pine marten, whose pelts were used for trading in medieval times. Banknotes are issued in denominations from 10kn to 1,000kn, with portraits of aristocratic poets and statesmen on one side and Croatian landmarks on the other. The kuna is divided into 100 lipa, though these are rarely used. Coins have a flowering linden tree *(lipa)* or pine marten *(kuna)* on one side, with native animals, birds and plants on the reverse. The only coins that are widely in circulation are 10 lipa, 20 lipa, 50 lipa, 1kn, 2kn and 5kn.

The euro (€), which is used by the majority of visitors to Croatia, is increasingly being adopted as a parallel currency and is expected to become the official currency by 2012. Prices for hotels and excursions are often quoted in euros but you can pay in either euros or Croatian kuna. Exchange rates vary from day to day but are usually around 7.50 kuna to the euro, 8 kuna to the British pound and 5 kuna to the US dollar.

CHANGING MONEY

» Cash and travellers' cheques can be exchanged at banks, post (mail) offices, exchange bureaux, travel agents, hotels, campsites and marinas.
» Commission charges vary from around 1 to 5 per cent.
» Euros are the most widely accepted foreign currency, but US dollars and sterling are also acceptable.
» Travellers' cheques bought in advance provide an extra degree of security but the commission for exchanging them is likely to be higher than for changing foreign currency.
» The post office beside Zagreb railway station has currency exchange facilities and is open 24 hours a day.

ATMS

» The easiest, if not necessarily the most cost effective, way of getting Croatian kuna is by using your credit or debit card to withdraw cash from an ATM. These are found in all the main towns and resorts, as well as at railway and bus stations. Even on the islands, there is usually at least one ATM *(bankomat)* in all but the smallest villages.
» Most ATMs accept credit cards, including Visa, Mastercard and Eurocard, and debit cards bearing the Cirrus, Maestro and Plus logos. American Express cards are less widely accepted.
» Instructions on how to withdraw money from the ATM are given in a choice of languages.
» Before leaving home, make sure that you know your PIN (personal identification number). Never write it down in a way which could identify it, and never let anyone see you entering it into the machine.
» Your bank will probably make a charge for debit card withdrawals and levy interest payments for credit card cash advances. Find out what the charges are likely to be before setting off to avoid any unpleasant surprises when you see your next bank statement.

CREDIT AND DEBIT CARDS

» Credit cards such as Visa, Mastercard, Diner's Club and American Express are widely accepted at hotels, shops, restaurants, petrol (gas) stations and car rental agencies.
» You can also pay using a debit card such as Cirrus or Maestro, which will debit the funds directly from your bank account.
» Chip-and-pin technology is becoming more widespread, so make sure that you know your PIN as you may have to enter it onto a keypad rather than using your signature as identification.
» Never rely on being able to use a credit or debit card, except in the bigger cities and international hotels. Croatia is still a largely cash-based economy, and you should always carry enough cash to pay for everyday purchases such as food, drink and fuel. Many restaurants do not accept credit cards, and

private accommodation (private rooms) should always be paid for in cash. Even where credit cards are accepted, you may find that there is a discount for paying in cash.

WIRING MONEY

In an emergency, money can be wired from your home country by friends or relatives using a money transfer service such as Western Union (www.westernunion.com) or MoneyGram (www.moneygram.com). Payments can be made in person, by telephone or online, and collected as little as 10 minutes later in Croatia. Post offices across Croatia act as agents for Western Union, while major branches of Atlas Travel act as agents for MoneyGram. This is a very expensive way of acquiring money and should only be used as a last resort.

SALES TAX REFUNDS

Foreign visitors can reclaim up to 17 per cent VAT (sales tax) on purchases over 500kn at shops displaying the Tax Free Shopping sign. For details of how to claim ▷ 256.

PRICES OF EVERYDAY ITEMS	
ITEM	PRICE
Coffee with milk	10kn
Ice cream scoop	5kn
0.5 litre of beer	15kn
Litre of house wine	80kn
Litre of mineral water (in café)	15kn
Litre of mineral water (in shop)	7kn
Litre of unleaded fuel	8kn
10-minute telephone call to UK	36kn
Taxi from airport to Zagreb	200kn
Zagreb tram ticket	8kn

HEALTH

Public health services in Croatia are of a similar standard to those elsewhere in Europe. There are hospitals in all the main cities, and clinics on the islands and in smaller towns. There are also many private doctors and health centres. Most doctors speak English.

BEFORE YOU GO

» Make sure that you have a comprehensive travel insurance policy, including emergency medical assistance and repatriation. If you plan on doing any potentially hazardous sports and activities such as scuba-diving or skiing, ensure that these are covered by your insurance.
» EU citizens receive free medical care and hospital treatment on production of a passport or European Health Insurance Card (EHIC). However, you should still take out travel insurance as not all costs are covered and some treatment may only be available privately.

WHAT TO TAKE

» If you are taking any regular medication, bring enough for your stay. It is also a good idea to take a copy of the prescription.
» If you wear glasses or contact lenses, pack a spare set and bring your prescription in case you lose or break them.
» Pack a small first-aid kit including plasters (Band Aids), cotton wool, pain relief tablets, antihistamine tablets, anti-diarrhoea tablets and sea-sickness pills.

IF YOU NEED TREATMENT

» In an emergency, call an ambulance by dialling 94 from a public phone or 112 from a mobile phone.
» Alternatively, ask at your hotel or ask a taxi driver to take you to the nearest hospital (bolnica) or clinic (klinika).
» EU citizens should show the doctor their passport or EHIC card to receive free treatment. Travellers from non-European countries must pay according to a fixed scale of charges and keep the receipt to claim

the money back from their insurers. Contact your insurance company as soon as you can, preferably before you receive any treatment.

HEALTHY FLYING

» Visitors to Croatia from as far as the US, Australia or New Zealand may be concerned about the effect of long-haul flights on their health. The most widely publicized concern is Deep Vein Thrombosis, or DVT. Misleadingly called 'economy class syndrome', DVT is the forming of a blood clot in the body's deep veins, particularly in the legs. The clot can move around the bloodstream and could be fatal.
» Those most at risk include the elderly, pregnant women and those using the contraceptive pill, smokers and the overweight. If you are at increased risk of DVT see your doctor before departing. Flying increases the likelihood of DVT because passengers are often seated in a cramped position for long periods of time and may become dehydrated.
» To minimize risk:
Drink water (not alcohol)
Don't stay immobile for hours at a time
Stretch and exercise your legs periodically
Wear elastic flight socks, which support veins and reduce the chances of a clot forming

EXERCISES

1. Ankle Rotations
Lift feet off the floor. Draw a circle with the toes, moving one foot clockwise and the other counterclockwise

2. Calf Stretches
Start with heel on the floor and point foot upward as high as you can. Then lift heels high, keeping balls of feet on the floor

3. Knee Lifts
Lift leg with knee bent while contracting your thigh muscle. Then straighten leg, pressing foot flat to the floor

Other health hazards for flyers are airborne diseases and bugs spread by the plane's air-conditioning system. These are largely unavoidable but if you have a serious medical condition seek advice from a doctor before flying.

PHARMACIES IN CROATIA		
CITY	PHARMACY	CONTACT DETAILS
Zagreb	Gradska Ljekarna	Trg Bana Jelačića 3, tel 01 481 6198
		Open 24 hours a day
	Gradska Ljekarna	Ilica 301, tel 01 375 0321
		Open 24 hours a day
Dubrovnik	Gruž	Gruška Obala 9, tel 020 418990
	Ljekarna Dubrovnik	Stradun 4, tel 020 321133
One of the above pharmacies will always be on duty		

PHARMACIES

» Pharmacies are indicated by the word *ljekarna* and a green cross, which is illuminated when they are open. In the larger towns and cities, there will always be at least one pharmacist on duty according to a rota system. The name of the duty chemist outside usual hours can be found on pharmacy doors.

» Pharmacies sell prescription and non-prescription medicines and drugs. The brand names of common products may vary, so it helps to take along the original packaging listing the active ingredients.

DENTAL TREATMENT

» EU citizens receive free emergency dental treatment, but other treatment has to be paid for. Most travel insurance policies cover only emergency treatment.

» The standard of dental care is high and costs are low in comparison with the European average.

» To find a dentist *(stomatološka klinika)*, ask at your hotel or contact the Croatian Dental Chamber, Kurelčeva 3, Zagreb (tel 01 488 6710).

» The emergency dental clinic at Perkovčeva 3, Zagreb is open throughout the night and weekends (tel 01 482 8488).

HEALTH HAZARDS

» The sun can be very hot in summer, and skin burns easily despite the deceptively cooling sea breezes. Apply a high-factor sun cream (sunscreen) regularly, especially after swimming. Other sensible precautions are to wear a sun hat and sunglasses, lightweight, long-sleeved clothes and drink plenty of water and non-alcoholic drinks.

» Look out for sea urchins, and wear plastic sandals to avoid getting the spikes in your feet.

» Snakes are frequently encountered when walking in the mountains. Most are harmless, but there are also venomous species such as the horn-nosed viper. Wear boots, thick socks and long trousers and seek medical advice immediately if you are bitten.

» Mosquitoes can be a nuisance in summer. Use an insect repellent and cover up with long-sleeved clothing and long trousers.

» More seriously, ticks are found in rural and forest areas between April and October. Some of these carry tick-borne encephalitis, a potentially fatal viral disease. The precautions are the same as those for mosquitoes, so use an insect repellent and cover up bare skin. If you plan to walk, cycle or camp in forest regions seek advice on inoculation before travelling.

» Landmines are still a potential hazard in remote areas of Croatia close to the borders with Serbia and Bosnia-Herzegovina. If you are travelling in former war zones, stick to main roads and marked footpaths and pay attention to warning signs. The usual sign is a red skull and crossbones accompanied by the words 'PAZI MINE'.

WATER

» Tap water in Croatia is safe to drink, but bottled mineral water is widely available.

KEEPING CHILDREN SAFE

» Small children need to be well protected from the sun.

» A pair of inexpensive plastic sandals provides protection on the beach against rocks, pebbles, sea urchins and jellyfish.

» Children under the age of 16 must wear a cycle helmet when riding a bicycle.

BASICS

WHAT TO PACK

» Electrical adaptor

» First-aid kit

» Insect repellent

» Plastic sandals or flip-flops are a good idea on Croatian beaches, especially for children whose small feet can easily be hurt by pebbles or rocks. You can also buy waterproof swimming shoes for adults and children.

» Prescription drugs and medication, plus a copy of the prescription.

» Spare sets of glasses and contact lenses in case of loss or damage.

» Sun cream (sunscreen) and sunglasses.

» Swimwear and beach towel.

» Walking shoes, trainers (sneakers) or sandals. Even if you do not plan on trekking in the mountains, a good pair of shoes is useful for negotiating cobbled streets and uneven surfaces in towns.

» Warm and waterproof clothing. In summer on the coast a light sweater or jacket for the evenings should suffice, but in the mountains it can get cold at any time of year.

» Take photocopies of documents such as your passport, driver's licence and travel insurance certificate, or send scanned copies to an email account that you can access while you are away. Make a separate note of your passport number, credit card numbers and emergency telephone numbers in the case of loss or theft.

ELECTRICITY

The electric power supply is 220V AC, 50Hz. Plugs have two round pins, in common with most of Continental Europe. Visitors from the UK will need an adaptor and visitors from the US will need a transformer for appliances operating on 100–120V.

PUBLIC TOILETS

Public toilets (restrooms) exist in most towns and cities. There is usually a small charge for use, or you should leave some coins as a tip for the attendant. There are also public toilets at rail and bus stations. In an emergency, it is always possible to use the toilet in a bar or café, but it is polite to buy a drink first.

LOCAL CUSTOMS AND ETIQUETTE

Talking to strangers

Croatians are very sociable, and it is generally easy to strike up a conversation with strangers. Many young people speak excellent English and other foreign languages. It is best to avoid controversial topics such as politics, nationalism, the Homeland War and the trials of alleged war criminals at The Hague. You might find that people want to talk about these subjects, but it is often better to listen sensitively than to express strong opinions. Like everywhere else, football and sport always make good topics for conversation, especially among men.

Dress

Formal clothing is rarely necessary in Croatia except for business, and casual dress is acceptable at all but the smartest restaurants. However, Croatians do like to dress up and look their best, and young women in particular can often be seen in the latest fashions. If you want to join in, put on your best casuals for the evening *korzo*, the Croatian equivalent of the ritual promenade common all over the Mediterranean, when everyone strolls around in their latest outfit hoping to see and be seen. Do not wear beachwear or revealing clothing when visiting churches.

Nudism

Naturism has a long tradition in Croatia, and many beaches are officially designated FKK (free body culture). It is generally acceptable to take your clothes off at secluded beaches and bays. Non-naturists are welcome to use naturist beaches, but you should behave sensitively and avoid taking photographs. Elsewhere, topless sunbathing is acceptable for both men and women on the majority of Croatian beaches.

Smoking

Cigarette smoking is widespread in Croatia, with few areas set aside for non-smokers. It is quite normal to see people smoking at restaurants. Smoking is banned on all forms of public transport, apart from in dedicated smoking carriages on long-distance trains.

What's in a name?

In towns and cities, especially Zagreb, you may notice that the names marked on street signs and addresses bear little resemblance to those used in conversation and on the map. For example, Ulica Gaja becomes Gajeva, Ulica Tesle becomes Teslina and Trg Maršala Tita becomes Titov Trg. This variation is due to the complexity of Croatian grammar, which changes word endings according to the case. Once you have grown accustomed to this, you can usually work out where you are by using a combination of logic, guesswork and common sense.

PLACES OF WORSHIP

» Croatia is predominantly Roman Catholic. There are Catholic churches in every town and village, but many of them are open only for Mass on Sunday mornings.

» Mass is held in English at 10.30am and Anglican services at noon on Sundays during term time at the Jesuit Seminary, Jordanovac 110, Zagreb.

» The Anglican Church in Vienna holds monthly services at the Jesuit Seminary in Zagreb. For details, see www.europe.anglican.org

PLACE OF WORSHIP	ADDRESS	TELEPHONE
Baptist Church	Radićeva 30, Zagreb	01 481 3167
Evangelical Lutheran Church	Gundulićeva 28, Zagreb	01 485 5622
Serbian Orthodox Church	Ilica 7, Zagreb	01 481 7531
Islamic Centre	Gavellina 40, Zagreb	01 613 7162
Jewish Community	Palmotićeva 16, Zagreb	01 492 2692

FINDING HELP
PERSONAL SECURITY

» Crime rates are low in Croatia but you should still take the same precautions as you would anywhere else to avoid becoming a victim of theft or petty crime.

» Keep money, credit cards and valuables in a hotel safe and avoid carrying around large amounts of cash.

» Keep a passport or identity card on you at all times, with a photocopy in your hotel safe. The police have the power to ask for your passport at any time, and it will also help to identify you in the case of an accident.

» Make a note of the serial numbers of travellers' cheques and keep it separate from the cheques in case of loss or theft.

» Never let anyone see you entering your PIN when withdrawing cash from an ATM, or when using a chip-and-pin device.

» Beware of pickpockets on crowded buses and trams in cities such as Zagreb, Split, Rijeka and Dubrovnik.

» Never leave money or valuables unattended on a beach or poolside.

» Always make sure that your car is locked and keep all valuables out of sight in the boot (trunk), or better still take them with you.

» If you are driving a rental car, take the rental documents out of the car whenever it is left unattended.

» Avoid discussing the war in sensitive areas, particularly in the former war zones close to the Bosnian and Serbian borders.

IF YOU NEED HELP

» In an emergency you can call the police by dialling 92 from a public phone or 112 from a mobile phone.

» If something is stolen you must report the theft to the police and obtain a crime report to pass to your insurance company when you file your claim.

» If your passport is lost or stolen, contact your embassy or consulate to arrange a replacement.

» If you are arrested, ask to speak to your embassy or consulate.

EMBASSIES AND CONSULATES IN ZAGREB		
COUNTRY	ADDRESS	TELEPHONE NUMBER
Australia	Centar Kaptol III, Nova Ves 11	01 489 1200
Canada	Prilaz Gjure Deželića 4	01 488 1200
France	Hebrangova 2	01 489 3600
Germany	Ulica Grada Vukovara 64	01 630 0100
Ireland	Miramarska 23	01 631 0025
Italy	Medulićeva 22	01 484 6386
New Zealand	Trg Stjepana Radi 3	01 615 1382
UK	Ulica Ivana Lučića 4	01 600 9100
US	Ulica Thomasa Jeffersona 2	01 661 2200

COMMUNICATION

TELEPHONES

» Telephone services are provided by Hrvatski Telekom, a subsidiary of T-Mobile.

» To call Croatia from abroad, dial the international access code (011 from the US and Canada, 00 from most other countries) followed by Croatia's country code 385. This should be followed by the full local number, omitting the initial 0 from the area code. For example, the number for Zagreb tourist information is 01 481 4051. To call this number from the UK/Europe you should dial 00 385 1 481 4051 or from the US/Canada you should dial 011 385 1 481 4051. See panel below for Croatian area codes.

» To call the UK from Croatia, dial 00 44 followed by the local number, omitting the first 0 from the area code; to call the US, dial 00 1 followed by the full 10-figure number

» To call other countries from Croatia, dial the international dialling code (▷ below), followed by the number.

» For calls within Croatia, dial the area code and local number For calls within the same area, omit the area code and simply dial the seven-figure local number in Zagreb or six-figure number elsewhere.

» Numbers beginning 06 are charged at national rate, 08 are freephone numbers, and 09 are mobile phones.

PUBLIC TELEPHONES

» Public phone booths are a common sight in towns and cities, and there is usually at least one public phone even in small villages.

» Phones are blue, and instructions are given in a choice of languages. To change language, press the button

marked with a flag and the letter L

» Calls cost 0.8kn per minute within Croatia, 3kn to most countries of Europe, 3.5kn to the UK and Ireland, and 5kn to the US, Canada and Australia. Calls to Croatian mobile numbers cost 2kn per minute.

» To use a public phone you must buy a phonecard *(telekarta)*, from newsagents, kiosks or post offices. Cards are sold in denominations of 30, 50, 100kn and 200kn, and usually contain a bonus amount. For example, a 30kn card gives 33kn worth of calls and a 100kn card gives 115kn worth of calls.

» You can also make international calls from main post offices. Calls are metered and you pay afterwards.

MOBILE PHONES

» Mobile phone use is widespread in Croatia, with over 60 per cent of the population owning a mobile phone. The two main networks are VIPnet, a partner of Vodafone, and T-Com, owned by T-Mobile and Hrvatski Telekom. VIP numbers begin 091 and 092 and T-Com numbers begin 098 and 099.

» If you have a GSM phone, it will work in Croatia provided you have set it up for international roaming with your network operator before you leave home. Calls within Croatia could be expensive as they

AREA CODES WITHIN CROATIA	
Dubrovnik	020
Osijek	031
Pula	052
Rijeka	051
Split	021
Varaždin	042
Zadar	023
Zagreb	01

INTERNATIONAL DIALLING CODES	
Australia	00 61
Canada	00 1
Germany	00 49
Ireland	00 353
Italy	00 39
New Zealand	00 64
UK	00 44
US	00 1

USEFUL TELEPHONE NUMBERS	
Directory enquiries	988
International directory enquiries	902
Police	92
Fire	93
Ambulance	94
All emergencies	112

The European emergency number 112 has been adopted in Croatia, but the old numbers still work. You can dial 112 free of charge from any GSM mobile phone to be connected to the emergency operator.

will be routed through your home country. You may also be charged international rates for receiving calls and for sending and receiving text messages.

» For longer stays, consider buying a Croatian SIM card for your mobile phone. This will give you a local number and access to one of the networks within Croatia. SIM cards are available from phone shops and post offices with prices starting from around 300kn. You can buy top-up cards from news kiosks and post offices, or top up your phone at ATMs. If you do not have a GSM-enabled phone, you can buy mobile phone and pre-paid card packages for around 700kn.

INTERNET

» Internet access is widely available in Croatia. Bigger cities such as Zagreb and Dubrovnik have large internet cafés and computer centres, but even on the islands and in smaller inland towns you can usually find a travel agent or bar with a computer terminal to check your email.

» Most places offer high-speed internet access for around 20–30kn per hour. Internet cafés also offer printing, scanning and the option of burning your digital photos onto a CD.

» Larger hotels have business centres with high-speed internet connections and some of the more upscale hotels provide WiFi in the rooms. Smaller hotels often have a computer in the lobby, which is sometimes coin-operated and sometimes free for hotel guests.

» Croatian keyboards differ from those in other countries, so ask staff if you are not sure how to find characters. Croatian website and email addresses do not require accents.

USING A LAPTOP

» A number of hotels offer modem points for high-speed internet access from your room.

» Visitors from the UK will need an electricity adaptor and visitors from the US may need a transformer and surge protector for their laptop.

» If you need to use a dial-up connection, it is cheaper to dial up a local service provider than to make calls to your home network. You should also set your modem to

ignore dial tones as these vary from country to country.

» WiFi is becoming more common at airports, hotels and marinas. Rijeka was the first city in Croatia to offer free WiFi, with a free wireless 'hot spot' along the Korzo.

POST

» Post offices (pošta) are open Monday to Friday 7–7 and Saturday 7–1. In villages and on the islands they may open mornings only. Main post offices in larger towns and cities are open longer hours, with some remaining open until 10pm.

» The post office beside the railway station in Zagreb is open 24 hours.

» Stamps can also be bought at news kiosks and tobacconists as well as in post offices.

» Post boxes are yellow.

» Letters and postcards typically take 3–5 days to arrive in EU countries and 7–10 days to reach North America. See panel below for postal rates for mail to UK/Europe, US/Canada and Australia.

MAILING RATES		
DESTINATION	**LETTER**	**POSTCARD**
UK/Europe	8kn	3.50kn
US/Canada	11kn	6kn
Australia	12kn	8kn

OPENING TIMES AND NATIONAL HOLIDAYS

BUSINESS HOURS

» Office hours are Monday to Friday 8–4.

» Working hours vary throughout the year, especially on the coast. During the summer months some shops and offices close for a few hours during the afternoon and reopen in the evening until 10pm.

» Tourist offices and private travel agencies (▷ 252) have widely varying opening hours depending on the season. In winter, many are open only on weekday mornings from 8 to 2. In summer, tourist offices in the major cities and coastal resorts operate for very long hours, typically 8am–10pm daily between June and the end of September.

» Churches in main towns and cities are open from around 7am to 7pm daily, but village churches are usually kept closed except for times of Mass.

» Museums are usually closed on Sunday afternoons and Mondays, but this varies around the country so check individual opening hours.

» Meal times are typically around 12–3 for lunch and 7–10 for dinner, but many restaurants stay open throughout the day from noon to midnight.

» The Croatian attitude to time is quite flexible and you should not rely on fixed opening hours. Although most museums, restaurants and tourist offices have official opening hours they vary from season to season and are always liable to change at short notice due to weather, local festivals or unexpected circumstances. If you are going out of your way, it is always best to check in advance by telephone.

NATIONAL HOLIDAYS

1 January	New Year's Day
6 January	Epiphany
March/April	Easter Sunday and Monday
1 May	Labour Day
May/June	Corpus Christi (60 days after Easter)
22 June	Anti-Fascist Resistance Day
25 June	Croatian National Day
5 August	Victory Day
15 August	Feast of the Assumption
8 October	Independence Day
1 November	All Saints' Day
25–26 December	Christmas

In addition, there are numerous local and regional festivals and saints' days, when museums, shops and offices will be closed to coincide with local festivities.

OPENING TIMES

Banks	Mon–Fri 7–7, Sat 7–1
	Outside these hours money can be changed at exchange bureaux, travel agents and hotels, or you can withdraw cash at ATMs.
Pharmacies	Mon–Fri 8–8, Sat 8–2
	In larger towns and cities there will always be at least one pharmacist on duty at night and weekends.
Post offices	Mon–Fri 7–7, Sat 7–1
	In villages and on the islands many post offices are only open in the morning. Main post offices in the bigger cities operate longer hours, with some staying open until 10pm.
Shops	Mon–Fri 8–8, Sat 8–2
	Supermarkets and department stores in Zagreb and Split may open on Saturday afternoons and Sundays. Some smaller shops close for a siesta on weekday afternoons. Shops in tourist resorts on the islands and coast work long hours in summer, with some staying open from 8am–10pm daily to meet demand. Markets are busiest early in the morning, from 8am to noon Monday to Saturday, and sometimes on Sunday as well.

TOURIST OFFICES

Croatia has a network of tourist information offices, together with private travel agencies offering places to stay, excursions and information.

BEFORE YOU GO

The Croatian National Tourist Board has offices in Europe and the US that will send out information and maps to help you plan your visit. As well as general tourist information, the CNTB publishes an annual hotel directory and brochures in various languages on camping, diving, fishing, sailing and adventure travel. Visit their website www.croatia.hr

TOURIST OFFICES IN CROATIA

» You will find official tourist offices in all towns and cities, operated by the local tourist board (turistiška zajednica). In major cities such as Zagreb and Dubrovnik, these open for long hours all year, but on the coast and islands they operate reduced hours or close down altogether in winter. Between June and September tourist offices in coastal towns and resorts are open daily from around 8am to 10pm.

» The quality of information varies widely from place to place, but most tourist offices can provide maps and leaflets. Staff can usually speak some English and German.

» Travel agents in the main towns and resorts are also good sources of tourist information. Although these are private businesses, they are usually happy to provide advice. Staff generally speak English and German, and have knowledge of local attractions and events. Most travel agencies also offer excursions, private accommodation, souvenirs and currency exchange. The biggest agency is Atlas (www.atlas.hr).

CROATIAN NATIONAL TOURIST BOARD OFFICES

Croatia	Iblerov Trg 10/4, Zagreb
	Tel 01 469 9333
France	Avenue Victor Hugo 48, 75116 Paris
	Tel 01 45 00 99 55
Germany	Kaiserstrasse 23, 60311 Frankfurt
	Tel 069 238 5350
Italy	Via dell'Oca 48, 00186 Roma
	Tel 06 3211 0396
Netherlands	Nijenburg 2F, 1081 Amsterdam
	Tel 020 661 6422
Spain	Calle Claudio Coello 22/Ese B/IoC, 28001 Madrid
	Tel 91 781 5514
Sweden	Kungsgatan 24, 11135 Stockholm
	Tel 08 5348 2080
UK and Ireland	2 The Lanchesters, 162–164 Fulham Palace Rd, London W6 9ER
	Tel 020 8563 7979
US	350 Fifth Avenue, Suite 4003, New York, NY 10118
	Tel 212 279 8672

TOURIST INFORMATION OFFICES IN CROATIA

Dubrovnik	Široka 1, Dubrovnik
	Tel 020 427591; www.tzdubrovnik.hr
Hvar	Trg Svetog Stjepana, Hvar Town
	Tel 021 741059; www.tzhvar.hr
Korčula	Obala Franje Tuđmana, Korčula Town
	Tel 020 715701; www.visitkorcula.net
Osijek	Županijska 2, Osijek
	Tel 031 203755; www.tzosijek.hr
Pula	Forum 3, Pula
	Tel 052 219197; www.pulainfo.hr
Rab	Trg Municipium Arbe, Rab Town
	Tel 051 771111; www.tzg-rab.hr
Rijeka	Korzo 33, Rijeka
	Tel 051 335882; www.tz-rijeka.hr
Šibenik	Obala Franje Tuđmana 5, Šibenik
	Tel 022 214411; www.sibenik-tourism.hr
Split	Peristil, Split
	Tel 021 345606; www.visitsplit.com
Varaždin	Ulica Padovca 3, Varaždin
	Tel 042 210987; www.tourism-varazdin.hr
Zadar	Ilije Smiljanića, Zadar
	Tel 023 316166; www.tzzadar.hr
Zagreb	Trg Bana Jelačića 11, Zagreb
	Tel 01 481 4051; www.zagreb-touristinfo.hr

WEBSITES

GENERAL INFORMATION

www.croatia.hr
Information in Croatian, English and German, with links to national tourist board sites in other languages.

www.hr
Croatian Homepage, with over 17,000 links in 700 categories. Croatian and English.

www.croatiatraveller.com
English only.

www.visit-croatia.co.uk
Information, advice and readers' tips. English only.

www.inyourpocket.com
Savvy advice and listings for urban travellers. English only.

NEWS

www.hina.hr
Official Croatian news agency. Croatian and English.

www.hic.hr
English and Spanish.

www.setimes.com
News and comment. English and nine Balkan languages.

TRAVEL AND WEATHER

www.autobusni-kolodvor.com
Everything you need to know about Croatia's bus network, including timetables.

www.croatiaairlines.hr
Croatian, English and German.

www.hznet.hr
Croatian Railways. Croatian, English and German.

www.jadrolinija.hr
Ferry travel. Croatian, English, German and Italian.

www.hak.hr
Croatian Auto Club. Croatian, English, German and Italian.

www.hac.hr
Croatian Motorways site. Croatian and English.

www.dhmz.htnet.hr or **meteo.hr**
Weather forecasts. Croatian and English.

MISCELLANEOUS

www.dubrovnik-festival.hr
Croatian and English.

www.mdc.hr
Museums. Croatian and English.

REGIONAL TOURIST BOARDS

Zagreb	www.zagreb-touristinfo.hr
Zagreb County	www.tzzz.hr
Istria	www.istra.hr
Kvarner	www.kvarner.hr
Zadar and northern Dalmatia	www.zadar.hr
Split and central Dalmatia	www.dalmatia.hr
Dubrovnik	www.tzdubrovnik.hr
Dubrovnik County	www.visitdubrovnik.hr

KEY SIGHTS QUICK WEBSITE FINDER

SIGHT/TOWN	WEBSITE	PAGE
Brač	www.bol.hr	171
Brijuni	www.brijuni.hr	118–119
Cavtat	www.tzcavtat-konavle.hr	217
Cres	www.tzg-cres.hr	149
Dubrovnik	www.tzdubrovnik.hr	218–225
Hvar	www.tzhvar.hr	172–175
Kopački Rit	www.kopacki-rit.com	84
Korčula	www.korculainfo.com	177–179
Krk	www.krk.hr	150
Krka	www.npkrka.hr	180–181
Kumrovec	www.mdc.hr/kumrovec	85
Lokrum	www.lokrum.hr	227
Lonjsko Polje	www.pp-lonjsko-polje.hr	86–87
Mljet	www.np-mljet.hr	228–229
Opatija	www.opatija-tourism.hr	152
Osijek	www.tzosijek.hr	88–89
Plitvička Jezera	www.np-plitvicka-jezera.hr	91–93
Poreč	www.istra.porec.com	124–125
Pula	www.pulainfo.hr	126–127
Rab	www.tzg-rab.hr	154 155
Rijeka	www.tz-rijeka.hr	156–157
Rovinj	www.tzgrovinj.hr	130–132
Samobor	www.tz-samobor.hr	94
Šibenik	www.sibenik-tourism.hr	187
Split	www.visitsplit.com	188–193
Trogir	www.tztrogir.hr	194
Varaždin	www.tourism-varazdin.hr	97–99
Vis	www.tz-vis.hr	195
Zadar	www.zadar.hr	196–197
Zagorje	www.tz-zagorje.hr	100–103
Zagreb	www.zagreb-touristinfo.hr	46–77

MEDIA

For decades the press in Croatia was used as a political mouthpiece. It is only since the election of President Mesić in 2000 that press freedom has been encouraged in Croatia, and the country now has a lively and independent media expressing a wide range of views and styles.

NEWSPAPERS AND MAGAZINES

» Newspapers can be bought at kiosks, or read for free in cafés and bars. The most popular dailies are *24 Sata, Jutarnji List* and *Večernji List*, all of which combine news, sport and weather with the latest showbiz gossip.

» *Globus* and *Nacional* are weekly glossy news magazines, similar to *Time* or *Newsweek* in the US. Nacional also publishes an online edition in English, available by subscription (www.nacional.hr).

» *Feral Tribune* is a popular satirical weekly in Split.

» Foreign newspapers and magazines are sold at bookshops in Zagreb and Dubrovnik, and also in coastal resorts during the summer.

DAILY NEWSPAPERS

Glas Istre In Istria
Glas Slavonije In Slavonia
Jutarnji List The most popular Croatian national daily
La Voce del Popolo Italian-language paper for Istria and Kvarner
Novi List In Rijeka
Slobodna Dalmacije In Split
Sportske Novosti National daily sports paper
Vecernji List Popular national evening paper
24 Sata News and gossip.

TOURIST PUBLICATIONS

» The *In Your Pocket* series of city guides have attracted a cult following throughout Eastern Europe for their irreverent, no-nonsense approach and opinionated reviews of restaurants, nightlife and shops. Published every two months for Zagreb and annually for Dubrovnik, Osijek, Rijeka, Split and Zadar, the guides are an excellent source of up-to-date information on everything from concert listings to public transport maps. The guides fit easily in your pocket and can be picked up free of charge from tourist offices, cafés and hotels. Copies can also be downloaded from www.inyourpocket.com

» *Welcome to Zagreb* and *Welcome to Dubrovnik* are full-size free magazines produced three or four times a year by the city tourist boards, with articles on city life and traditions, in Croatian and English.

TELEVISION

» The main national TV and radio stations are operated by public service broadcaster Hrvatski Radiotelevizija (HRT).

» HRT1 broadcasts news, chat and game shows, including Croatian versions of popular programmes such as *The Weakest Link* and *Who Wants to be a Millionaire?*

» HRT2 programming includes sport, soap operas and foreign drama and films, many of which are broadcast in their original English-language version with Croatian subtitles.

» RTL and Nova are nationwide commercial channels.

» A range of cable, digital and satellite channels are available on subscription. Most hotel rooms have access to satellite TV channels such as BBC and CNN.

RADIO

» HRT operates three national and eight regional radio channels. HR1 broadcasts news and talk, HR2 popular music and entertainment, and HR3 broadcasts classical music.

» There are daily news bulletins broadcast in English on HR1 (92.1 FM) at 8.05pm Monday to Saturday. Between July and the end of September, HR2 (98.5 FM) broadcasts regular updates on traffic and sailing conditions in English, German and Italian.

HISTORY AND WAR

» *Croatia: A Nation Forged in War* (1997) by Marcus Tanner is a comprehensive and highly readable account of 2,000 years of Croatian history by a journalist who covered the Balkan wars for the London-based *Independent*.

» *The Fall of Yugoslavia* (1996) by Misha Glenny is an eyewitness account written by a former BBC correspondent.

» *Madness Visible* (2004) by Janine di Giovanni is a powerful portrait of the Balkan wars by a writer for the London-based *Times*. Although it focuses on Bosnia and Kosovo and there is little on Croatia, it is a harrowing, compelling account of the horrors of war.

» *They Would Never Hurt A Fly* (2005) by Croatian exile Slavenka Drakulić tells the stories of some of the people charged with war crimes in The Hague, and asks how war can turn ordinary people into monsters. The same author became known for her books of essays on everyday life in Eastern Europe, including *How We Survived Communism And Even Laughed* (1991), *Balkan Express* (1993) and *Café Europa. Life After Communism* (1996).

» *Dubrovnik. A History* (2003) by Robin Harris is a scholarly account, from the medieval origins of Ragusa to the 1991 siege.

TRAVELOGUES

» *Black Lamb And Grey Falcon* (1942) by Rebecca West is a 1,000-page epic volume describing a series of journeys through Yugoslavia in the 1930s, beginning with Croatia. Outdated and prejudiced in places, it is still worth reading for its quirky observations, entertaining character sketches and understanding of Balkan history and culture.

» *Through The Embers Of Chaos: Balkan Journeys* (2002) by veteran travel writer Dervla Murphy is an enjoyable account of a journey by bicycle through the newly independent states of former Yugoslavia.

» *Another Fool In The Balkans: In The Footsteps of Rebecca West* (2005) by Tony White describes a series of visits to Zagreb, Belgrade and Istria by a young British writer.

FICTION

» *The Bridge Over The Drina* (1959) is the masterpiece by Nobel prizewinning author Ivo Andrić (1892–1975). Born in Bosnia to Croatian parents and writing in the Serbian language, Andrić embodies the contradictions of the Balkans. Set in the Bosnian town of Višegrad over a period of 500 years, the novel tells the story of Balkan and Ottoman history through a series of sketches set on the bridge of the title.

» *The Ministry of Pain* (2005) by Dubravka Ugrešić is a novel set in Amsterdam among a group of ex-Yugoslav exiles, by a Croatian author who left during the war. Her earlier books include *The Culture of Lies* (1998), a set of essays attacking the rise of nationalism in Croatia.

MUSIC

» Bookstores and souvenir shops sell CDs of Croatian folk music, including the *tamburica* (mandolin) music of Slavonia and the *klapa* (male voice choirs) of Dalmatia. Reliable names to look out for include the Lado ensemble from Zagreb and the Linđo ensemble from Dubrovnik.

» *The Rough Guide to the Music of the Balkans* (2003) is a good introduction to the region, featuring two Croatian groups alongside brass bands and gypsy music.

» Tamara Obrovac is a singer and flautist who combines jazz with traditional Istrian folk songs, including some in the Istriot dialect, on her albums *Transhistria* (2001), *Sve Pasiva* (2003) and *Daleko je...* (2005).

» Darko Rundek is a singer and actor from Zagreb who blends Balkan rhythms, jazz and cabaret sounds with his Cargo Orkestar on albums such as *La Comedie des Sens* (2004) and the more recent *Mhm A-Ha Oh Yeah Da-Da: Migration Stories and Love Songs* (2006).

» US jazz siren Helen Merrill was born Jelena Ana Milčetić to Croatian immigrants. She explores her Croatian roots on the autobiographical *Jelena Ana Milčetić aka Helen Merrill* (2000).

WHAT TO DO

SHOPPING

Though not generally regarded as a particularly exciting shopping destination, Croatia has come a long way since the days of state-run Yugoslav department stores with their dowdy displays of dusty bottles and bulky electrical goods. Now price rather than availability has become the greatest obstacle to a happy shopping experience, and those hunting for bargains are likely to be disappointed by Croatia's hefty mark-ups.

Young Croats are pretty fashion-conscious and cities like Zagreb and Split have boutiques offering the latest trends, usually heavily influenced by the fashion houses of nearby Italy. Most big cities in Croatia now have large shopping complexes outside their historical centres. Shops in the coastal resorts sell everything from mass-produced souvenirs to local arts and crafts. For local colour, pay a visit to one of the farmers' markets, which take place each morning in all the major towns.

When it comes to day-to-day grocery shopping, visitors to Croatia may be surprised to find that a single supermarket (Konzum) completely dominates the supermarket sector.

Very few foreign chains have gained a foothold in the country.

PRACTICALITIES
» Most shops open Monday to Friday 8–8, and Saturday 8–2. Smaller shops may close for a siesta during the afternoon. Many shops on the coast keep longer hours in summer, opening from 8am to 10pm daily. Markets are busiest on weekdays between 8 and noon.
» Payment by credit and debit card is increasingly accepted, though some smaller shops accept only cash.
» Goods are generally fixed price and bargaining is not acceptable, though you may be able to haggle at markets and open-air stalls.

» Foreign visitors can reclaim up to 17 per cent VAT (sales tax) on transactions over 500kn at shops displaying the Tax Free Shopping logo. Ask for a tax refund form PDV-P and get it filled in and stamped at the time of purchase. You must leave the country within three months and present the receipt, tax refund form and unwrapped goods at the border for authorization of your refund.

WHAT TO BUY
Arts and Crafts
Artists sell their paintings at open-air street stalls in summer, and studios and galleries in Dubrovnik and the Istrian towns of Grožnjan, Labin, Poreč and Rovinj. Much of the work

on offer consists of standard tourist landscapes, but look carefully and you will discover some work of real quality. The village of Hlebine (▷ 82), near Koprivnica, has painters and sculptors specializing in naïve art. Popular handicrafts include embroidery, ceramics, woodwork, stonework, model boats and intricate lacework from the island of Pag. In Istria and Dalmatia, shops sell miniature stone houses which are typical of the region, while a reproduction of the Vučedol Dove makes a powerful souvenir of Vukovar.

Cosmetics

The pure air and water of the Adriatic coast create perfect conditions for the wild flowers, herbs and fruit that grow on Croatia's islands. These include rosemary, sage, thyme, mint and wild tangerines, but best known is Hvar lavender. Some are made into natural cosmetics and toiletries, which you can buy in Zagreb or at open-air markets on Hvar and the Dalmatian islands in summer.

Cravats and Ties

Few people realize that the necktie, the uniform of businessmen the world over, has its origins in Croatia. The red silk scarves worn by Croatian officers during the Thirty Years' War (1618–48) attracted the attention of the French and were soon adopted in fashionable Parisian society, where the custom of dressing with a necktie became known as *à la croate*, later adapted to *cravate*. Silk scarves, cravats and ties are still manufactured in Croatia by the Croata company, many adorned with typical Croatian designs such as medieval braiding or the red and white check of the Croatian flag.

Food, Wine and Spirits

Foodstuffs to take home include Pag cheese, Dalmatian ham, fig jam, Samobor mustard, lavender honey, Istrian truffles and olive oil. Before buying, check the customs regulations of your home country as there may be restrictions on some food items. Croatia produces a wide variety of wines and spirits (▷ 267)

which make great souvenirs. It is best to buy from the vineyard or a market, where you can usually taste before you buy.

Jewellery

Probably the best place to pick up handcrafted jewellery is Dubrovnik, where numerous tiny shops sell silver filigree items, sometimes inlaid with coral and semi-precious stones. All coral sold in Dubrovnik is harvested from sustainable sources, so you can buy with a free conscience, knowing that your purchase will not harm the environment.

One item that is unique to Croatia is the *morčić*, an enamel figure of a turbanned Moor attached to earrings and gold jewellery. Its origins as a good-luck charm worn by the citizens of Rijeka are said to date back to the Ottoman empire.

Music

Bookstores and record shops sell CDs of contemporary folk music, including the *tamburica* (mandolin) music of Slavonia and *klapa* (male voice choirs) from Dalmatia. For traditional Croatian folk music, the best groups to listen to are the Lado and Linđo ensembles.

ENTERTAINMENT AND NIGHTLIFE

Croatia has a rich tradition of performance arts, from classical music and opera in grand Habsburg-era theatres to the many open-air festivals which take place across the country. Cities such as Zagreb and Dubrovnik have an active cultural scene throughout the year, while smaller towns on the islands and coast come alive for a few weeks each summer. Nightlife for most Croatians means sitting out of doors on a summer evening sharing a drink with friends. Few people can afford the cost of clubbing, so café terraces and ice-cream parlours make the perfect venues for drinking, chatting and flirting beneath the stars.

PRACTICALITIES
» Tourist offices and travel agents are good sources of information about local events. You can find out what's on by looking in newspapers or checking out the billboards you can find in most towns. *Zagreb In Your Pocket* magazine is published every two months with full listings of concerts and theatre performances. It is available from tourist offices, cafés and hotels or can be downloaded from www.inyourpocket.com. Tourist boards in Zagreb and Dubrovnik also publish monthly events guides.
» It is generally best to make ticket reservations at least a day or two in advance, though it is usually possible to buy tickets just before the performance. The easiest way to book in advance is to go to the theatre box office. Some venues, including the Croatian National Theatre (www.hnk.hr), take online

and phone bookings. Most seats are in the *parter* (stalls) or *balkon* (balcony), but if you want a special experience, choose a reasonably priced seat in a *loža* (box).
» There is no strict dress code, but most people dress up to go to the theatre or opera and you would look out of place if you wore a T-shirt, shorts or jeans. However, for outdoor events in summer, more casual clothing is acceptable.

BARS
There can be few greater pleasures in Croatia than sitting at a harbourside bar sipping chilled wine or beer on a balmy night. From Istria to Dalmatia, if you want to find the best bars, just head for the Riva or waterfront promenade to be found in all coastal and island towns. The in-crowd congregates at chic cocktail bars like Valentino in Rovinj and Carpe Diem

in Hvar, but thousands of ordinary bars and pubs offer outdoor seating and sea views. The most popular spots in Zagreb are in the traffic-free streets around Trg Bana Jelačića: Tkalčićeva, Bogovićeva and Trg Petra Preradovića.

CINEMA
The latest international movies are shown in the original language with Croatian subtitles. Widescreen multiplexes such as Broadway Tkalča and Cinestar in Zagreb are just like those in any other big city. Almost every town has at least one cinema.

CLUBS
As the only big city in Croatia, Zagreb is the centre of the club scene, though Osijek, Rijeka and Zadar are catching up fast. The biggest club in Zagreb is the vast Aquarius (▷ 68), founded in 1992, which plays

electronic music to some 2,000 clubbers on the shores of Lake Jarun. There are others on the banks of the River Sava. For the lowdown on the hottest clubs in Zagreb, check out the latest edition of *Zagreb In Your Pocket*. During the warm summer months, the club scene shifts to Pag, with open-air nightclubs spread around the wide arc of Zrće beach.

GAY AND LESBIAN SCENE

Although same-sex relationships have been legal since 1977, attitudes to gay and lesbian people have been slow to change in Croatia and it is still very unusual to see overt displays of homosexuality in public. Zagreb is the only place with gay clubs and bars, though resorts such as Hvar, Rovinj and Dubrovnik are generally gay-friendly. The website www.friendlycroatia.com has information in English on the gay and lesbian scene in Croatia, including gay-friendly clubs, bars and beaches. In Zagreb, Queer Zagreb (www.queerzagreb.org) is an annual festival of gay culture. The same organization hosts film nights at the Tuškanac cinema on the third Friday and Saturday of the month. The Pride march (www.zagreb-pride.net) is in mid-June and has been held in Zagreb each year since 2002.

LIVE MUSIC

Keep an eye out for posters advertising live music, especially in summer when many coastal towns host open-air performances of pop, jazz and traditional folk music. Live music can also be heard in pubs, bars and jazz clubs in the bigger cities. Two of the best are the BP Club in Zagreb (▷ 70), owned by vibraphoneplayer Boško Petrović, and the legendary Troubadour (▷ 235) in Dubrovnik, where former Eurovision Song contestant Marko Brešković plays his double-bass some nights.

MUSIC

Performances of classical music take place throughout the year at the Croatian National Theatre and Vatroslav Lisinski concert hall in Zagreb. The Dubrovnik Symphony Orchestra has year-round events. For many, the most memorable musical experiences are the open-air concerts that take place in summer at venues such as the Roman arena at Pula, Trsat castle at Rijeka and the island of Lokrum. The country's biggest, most prestigious event is the Dubrovnik Summer Festival (▷ 235), with big-name international artists such as jazz musician Dizzy Gillespie and British flautist Sir James Galway. During this six-week event performances of music, drama and folk dance are held in venues around the city, including the Rector's Palace, Sponza Palace and on the island of Lokrum.

THEATRE, OPERA AND BALLET

The most prestigious venue is the Croatian National Theatre, which has branches in Zagreb, Split, Rijeka, Osijek and Varaždin. Most of these are based in magnificent Austro-Hungarian opera houses that are worth visiting for the buildings alone. Plays are performed in Croatian, but opera is sung in the original language. The National Theatre in Zagreb is also home to the National Ballet and National Opera. Other good venues are the Marin Držić Theatre in Dubrovnik and the community theatre at Hvar (closed for renovation).

SPORTS AND ACTIVITIES

Croatia's mountains, rivers, lakes and sea are a paradise for outdoor sports enthusiasts. Walking, cycling and fishing are all popular, while extreme sports such as climbing and rafting attract adventurous visitors. The crystal-clear Adriatic waters provide perfect conditions for sailing, diving and swimming. Croatians are passionate about spectator sports, and the country has enjoyed huge success in soccer, handball and tennis.

BASKETBALL
There are top teams in Split and Zadar but the biggest basketball team is Cibona of Zagreb. The season runs from September to April and matches are held at the Dražen Petrović stadium in Zagreb.

CANOEING, KAYAKING AND RAFTING
Extreme sports enthusiasts can get their thrills on Croatia's rivers, enjoying canoeing, kayaking and rafting between April and October. Canoeing takes place on the River Dobra near Karlovac and the River Neretva north of Dubrovnik. The top rafting destination is the River Cetina near Omiš, though there is also good rafting on the River Korana and River Una. Sea-kayaking is on offer at Dubrovnik and the Elafiti Islands. It is important to book with a reputable operator and to check that full safety equipment, including helmets and

lifejackets, is provided. Huck Finn Adventure Travel (tel 01 618 3333, www.huck-finn.hr) offers canoeing, kayaking and rafting in Dalmatia and the Plitvice Lakes National Park.

CYCLING
Bicycle trails have been established in Istria, Kvarner, Dalmatia and Zagreb. In summer, it is possible to rent bicycles in most coastal resorts. For information, ▷ 43.

DIVING
The clear Adriatic waters provide excellent conditions for scuba-diving, with underwater cliffs, caves, reefs and shipwrecks to explore. All divers must buy an official diving card issued by the Croatian Diving Federation, which costs 100kn for a year. Diving is not permitted in the Brijuni and Krka national parks, and is allowed in the Kornati Islands and Mljet only in organized groups.

Diving centres in Istria, Kvarner and Dalmatia offer lessons and equipment; for a full list go to www.diving.hr

FISHING
Croatia's rivers, lakes and sea are teeming with fish. Freshwater fish include trout, perch, pike, carp and catfish, while sea fishermen can catch grouper, bass and bream. To fish in Croatia you need a licence, available from harbourmasters and travel agencies. Tour operators on the coast organize deep-sea fishing trips.

GOLF
Golf has been slow to develop in Croatia, and until recently there was only one 9-hole course, on Brijuni. There are now courses at Zagreb and Krašić, with others under construction at Zaprešić, Motovun and Dubrovnik. New courses are planned in Istria, Dalmatia and Hvar.

HANDBALL

Croatia won Olympic gold medals in 1996 and 2004. Sixteen teams play in the national league and the season is from September to May.

HIKING AND CLIMBING

There is good walking in the mountains and national parks, especially the Gorski Kotar and Velebit ranges. Conditions in the mountains can change quickly even in summer, so take warm and waterproof clothing as well as food, water, map, compass and a phone. Paths, mountain huts and refuges are managed by the Croatian Mountaineering Association (tel 01 482 4142, www.plsavez.hr). Footpaths are marked with a white dot inside a red circle. Serious hikers should obtain a copy of *Walking in Croatia* by Rudolf Abraham (Cicerone Press), a collection of day- and multi-day routes, while *Landscapes of Croatia* by Sandra Bardwell (Sunflower Books) is more suitable for families, with a wide range of graded walks aimed at varied abilities. Rock-climbers can tackle the challenging faces of the North Velebit and Paklenica national parks.

SAILING

You can charter your own motorboat or yacht to explore the Croatian islands, but novices must take a skippered boat. Most marinas offer boat charter and some run learn-to-sail courses. The biggest operator of marinas is ACI Club (tel 051 271288, www.aci-club.hr). Useful websites for yacht charter are www.charter.hr and www.ayc.hr, while complete sailing holidays can be booked through Sail Croatia (www. sailcroatia. net) and Sailing Holidays (www. sailingholidays.com).

SKIING

Croatia has a small number of ski slopes. The most accessible is Sljeme, at the summit of Medvednica in Zagreb while Bejelolasica is the highest and biggest ski resort in Croatia. There is skiing and ski-jumping at Delnice, and skiing with a view of the sea at Platak near Rijeka.

SOCCER

Soccer is Croatia's most popular spectator sport. There is fierce rivalry between the two biggest teams, Dinamo Zagreb and Hajduk Split. Most matches take place at weekends between August and May, with a two-month break between December and February. It is generally easy to buy tickets on the gate. The national team plays at Dinamo's Maksimir stadium.

SWIMMING

The Adriatic is enticing for bathers, but most beaches have either pebbles or rocks, while private hotel beaches are often concrete bathing platforms above the water. Take plastic sandals or waterproof shoes to protect your feet. Most large hotels have outdoor pools open in summer, and there are public swimming pools in most seaside towns.

TENNIS

Tennis is growing in popularity, thanks to the success of players like Goran Ivanišević, Mario Ančić and Ivan Ljubičić. Many hotels and campsites have courts with equipment for hire, and there are public courts in most towns.

WINDSURFING

Boards and equipment can be rented at sailing schools and windsurf centres on the coast.

HEALTH AND BEAUTY

Health tourism has a long tradition in Croatia, going back to the days of the Austro-Hungarian empire, when the cream of Viennese high society would take the waters in Croatia's thermal spas. In recent years there has been a revival of interest in health and beauty treatments, and many hotels now offer state-of-the-art spa and wellness facilities.

SPA RESORTS

Croatia has a number of traditional spa resorts, based on thermal springs with curative waters rich in sulphur, magnesium, calcium and other minerals. They include Istarske Toplice in Istria, Varaždinske Toplice near Varaždin, and Krapinske Toplice, Stubičke Toplice and Tuheljske Toplice in the Zagorje. Many date back to the 18th and 19th centuries. Although most have been modernized, they retain an old-fashioned sanatorium feel and most visitors come for the medicinal benefits rather than relaxation.

Hotels in Opatija offer spa treatments, and there is a state-of-the-art thalassotherapy centre (tel 051 202600; www.thalassotherapia-opatija.hr) with heated seawater pools.

HOTELS

Many top hotels offer spa and wellness centres with Turkish baths, saunas, beauty treatments and massage. The Energy Clinic (www.energyclinic.com) uses treatments based on traditional Chinese medicines, natural remedies and aromatherapy. It has various branches including in Dubrovnik and on the island of Mljet.

FOR CHILDREN

Croatia is a very welcoming country for families with children. Although there are few attractions aimed specifically at children, they are welcome almost everywhere and given a lot of attention. Most large hotels and campsites have children's pools and playgrounds, and activities such as mini-golf and table-tennis. Many also run children's clubs in summer, with organized sports and entertainment. Children love splashing about in the water, whether it is playing on the beach or taking a ride in a pedal-boat or canoe. There are few sandy beaches, so bring plastic sandals to help protect children's feet.

ATTRACTIONS

The biggest attraction for children is probably the Adriatic, which provides hours of water-based fun. Boat trips are always popular, whether it is taking a ferry to one of the islands or a pirate cruise on the Limski Kanal. Inland, the Plitvice Lakes and Krka national parks also offer boat trips, though smaller children might find the walking difficult. Children usually love animals and there are zoos in Zagreb and Osijek, a brown bear sanctuary in the Velebit mountains, a vulture reserve on Cres, a dolphin research centre at Veli Lošinj, a safari park on Brijuni and aquariums at Poreč, Pula, Rovinj, Rijeka and Dubrovnik. With a bit of imagination, many sights can be turned into children's attractions, as they play gladiators in the arena at Pula or climb over the ramparts of Dubrovnik's walls.

FESTIVALS AND EVENTS

Hardly a day goes by in Croatia without a traditional festival taking place. Every town and village has its own saint's day, celebrated with music, dancing, fireworks and religious processions. Most festivals are Catholic in origin but also include elements of pagan ritual and a large dose of Croatian patriotism, particularly those held to commemorate a historic victory over the Turks. On top of this are the numerous summer festivals, with open-air concerts and folk performances taking place along the Adriatic coast. Full details of all these events can be found at the end of the Entertainment pages in the regional chapters.

RELIGIOUS FESTIVALS

The biggest religious festival is the feast of St. Blaise in Dubrovnik at the beginning of February. Large crowds gather at pilgrimage sites such as Marija Bistrica and Trsat on holy days in the Catholic calendar, particularly Assumption (15 Aug) and the Birth of the Virgin (8 Sep). Across Croatia, local saints' days are a good excuse for a party even in the smallest towns and villages. Local tourist offices will have details.

CARNIVAL

The pre-Lenten Carnival in February is traditionally a time to abandon inhibitions before the fasting and denial of Lent. The biggest celebrations take place in Rijeka, which has balls and parades to rival Venice. Carnival parades also take place in Dubrovnik, Samobor and on the Dalmatian island of Lastovo.

FOLK FESTIVALS

The region of Slavonia has a rich folk heritage, which is celebrated at several traditional festivals each summer. Highlights include the Brodsko Kolo at Slavonski Brod in June and Đakovački Vezovi at Đakovo in July. The biggest folk festival is the International Folklore Festival held in Zagreb in July. Harvest festivals such as the wine fair in Ilok are accompanied by Slavonian folk music and dancers in traditional costume performing the *kolo* (circle dance).

TRADITIONAL FESTIVALS

Some of Croatia's festivals have their origins in the historic battles between the Venetian, Austrian and Turkish empires. The best-known example is Sinjska Alka, held in the Dalmatian town of Sinj in August, which features jousting competitions and riders in 18th-century cavalry uniform. A similar event is held in the Istrian town of Barban. In Rab there are annual re-enactments of medieval tournaments by costumed knights fighting with crossbows.

CULTURAL FESTIVALS

The summer months are filled with outdoor music and arts festivals taking place in atmospheric venues across the country. The biggest event is the Dubrovnik Summer Festival, which lasts for six weeks in July and August. Similar events take place in Split, Zadar and other coastal towns. In Pula, concerts are held in the Roman arena, while in Zagreb there are promenade concerts in the bandstand of Zrinjevac park. Another annual event is the summer school of Jeunesses Musicales Croatia in the Istrian hill town of Grožnjan, offering musical workshops and classical and jazz concerts.

EATING

Croatian food is an intriguing blend of Central European and Mediterranean influences, with the Italian-style cuisine of the coastal regions contrasting with the heavier Balkan fare of the interior. The range of fresh produce is superb and the modern generation of chefs is discovering a lighter touch, influenced by the Slow Food movement from Italy. The best restaurants serve simple, fresh, local food.

PRACTICALITIES

» Mealtimes are around 7–10am for breakfast *(doručak)*, 12–3pm for lunch *(ručak)* and 7–10pm for dinner *(večera)*, but many restaurants stay open throughout the day.

» It is not necessary to make a reservation at the vast majority of restaurants. However, opening times vary throughout the year and many restaurants close their doors or reduce their hours in winter, so it is always a good idea to check before you go. It is also sensible to book in advance if you want to eat out at a popular restaurant in July or August or at weekends.

» Casual dress is acceptable in all but a handful of restaurants, though

Croatians do like to look smart; you will look like a tourist if you are dressed in T-shirt and shorts.

» Non-smokers should note that smoking is allowed in restaurants at the owner's discretion.

» Some restaurants accept credit cards but many do not, so it is always best to carry enough cash.

PRICES

» The cost of eating out in Croatia is fairly reasonable by European standards, but much higher on the coast than inland.

» There is usually a small cover charge for bread.

» Fresh fish is sold by weight, which makes it appear very expensive

on the menu, as it is priced by the kilogram. A portion of around 150–250g (6–10oz) should be sufficient for one person.

» House wine is sold by the litre. It is perfectly acceptable to ask for a 0.5l or 0.3l carafe, or a glass of 0.2l. More expensive wines are sold by the bottle.

» If you have received good service, round up your bill (check) to the nearest 10kn or leave a larger tip if you wish.

WHAT TO EAT
Breakfast

Hotels offer a buffet of bread, pastries, yogurt, fruit, omelettes and cold meats. Alternatively, head for a café for continental-style croissants or pastries.

Brunch
Many restaurants serve *merenda* or *gableci* between around 10am and 2pm—cheap, filling snacks such as sausages, tripe, goulash and bean stew.

Starters
The most popular cold starters are *pršut* (cured ham), salami and cheese. A less expensive, but equally tasty, option is soup.

Warm starters
Pasta and risotto dishes are listed as 'warm starters' on the menu, but are usually enough for a main course.

Meat dishes
Croatians love eating meat. The most common meats are lamb, pork, chicken and veal, served either roasted, grilled or as a breaded schnitzel. A mixed grill is a popular standby.

Fish dishes
Fresh fish is usually served simply grilled, with olive oil and lemon, accompanied by *blitva* (Swiss chard) with potatoes, garlic and olive oil. Other favourites include shrimps, oysters, octopus and a rich fish stew.

Salads and side dishes
These are ordered separately. The most common are green salad, cabbage salad, beetroot salad, mixed salad, boiled potatoes, chips (fries), rice and pasta.

Desserts
The national dessert is pancakes, which are served with chocolate, jam, walnuts or cream. The only other choice is usually ice cream.

Fast food
Street stalls sell grilled meats such as *ćevapčići*, *pljeskavica* and *ražnjići*. Another popular snack is *burek*, filo pastry stuffed with meat or cheese.

REGIONAL SPECIALTIES
» Istria is the gourmet capital of Croatia and the centre of its Slow Food movement. Look for dishes containing local truffles, particularly in Buzet and Buje.

» Along the Adriatic coast, meat is roasted *ispod peka* (under the bell), cooked slowly in a metal dish which is placed in the embers of a fire.

» Dalmatian specialities include *pašticada* (sweet veal casserole), *brodet* (fish stew) and Dalmatian-style steak with garlic and red wine.

» The cooking of inland Croatia is heavy and spicy. Barbecued meat, game dishes and stews predominate in the mountains. Slavonia specializes in Hungarian-style casseroles such as goulash.

VEGETARIANS
Vegetarians are not well catered for in Croatia. There are a handful of vegetarian restaurants in Zagreb and other major cities, but the concept is not readily understood. Vegetarian-sounding dishes may contain bacon, sausage or pork, or be cooked in meat stock.

WHERE TO EAT	
gostionica	rustic-style inn offering cheap, filling local food
kavana	café serving drinks, pastries and snacks
konoba	traditional tavern specializing in local dishes and wine
pekara	bakery selling bread and snacks
pivnica	pub or beer hall, sometimes attached to a brewery, offering beer and simple fare such as sausages and stews
pizzeria	pizzeria serving wood-fired, Italian-style pizza
restoran	formal restaurant with waiter service and a range of Croatian and international dishes
slastičarnica	pastry shop specializing in ice cream and cakes

Menus are divided into appetizers or cold starters, warm starters, meat dishes, fish dishes, salads, side dishes and desserts.

Ajvar Spicy aubergine (eggplant) and pepper relish to accompany grilled meats.

Bečki odrezak Wiener schnitzel (veal cutlet in breadcrumbs).
Blitva Swiss chard, usually fried in olive oil with potatoes as the standard accompaniment to fish, especially in Dalmatia.
Brodet Dalmatian-style fish stew.
Burek sa mesom Filo pastry stuffed with minced meat.
Burek sa sirom Filo pastry stuffed with cottage cheese.

Ćevapčići Minced-meat rissoles or meatballs, grilled and served with raw onions, bread and *ajvar*.
Češnjovke Garlic pork sausage, a speciality of Samobor, served with mustard and sauerkraut.
Čobanac Hot, spicy meat stew from Slavonia.
Crni rižot Black cuttlefish risotto.

Dalmatinski pržolica Dalmatian-style rib-eye steak with garlic and red wine.

Fiš paprikaš Spicy, peppery fish stew from Slavonia.
Fuži Istrian-style pasta twirls, served with truffles or goulash.

Grah Bean stew, sometimes with sausage added.
Gregada Hvar-style fish casserole with potatoes and white wine.
Gulaš Goulash (spicy meat casserole), usually served with gnocchi or pasta.

Ispod peka Meat roasted 'under the bell'.

Janjetina na ražnju Spit-roast lamb.

Kiseli kupus Sauerkraut.
Kobasica Sausages.
Kulen Spicy salami from Slavonia, flavoured with paprika.

Maneštra Istrian-style vegetable soup, with bacon or sweetcorn added.
Mješana salata Mixed salad of lettuce, tomatoes, cabbage, carrot and beetroot.
Mješano meso Mixed grill of lamb and pork chops, *ćevapčići* and other grilled meats.

Na buzaru Seafood flash-fried with tomatoes, onions, herbs and wine.
Na žaru Barbecued or grilled.
Njoki Gnocchi A kind of pasta dumplings.

Palačinke Pancakes, served with chocolate, jam, walnuts or cream.
Paški sir Hard, salty sheep's cheese from Pag.
Pašticada Dalmatian casserole of veal stewed in sweet wine, served with gnocchi.
Pljeskavica Croatian-style burger or minced-meat patty.
Pogača Vis-style pizza or focaccia bread topped with anchovies, tomatoes, vegetables and cheese.
Pomfrit Chips (French fries).
Pršut Cured, air-dried ham from Istria or Dalmatia.
Punjene lignje Stuffed squid.
Punjene paprike Peppers (capsicums) stuffed with minced meat and rice.
Purica z mlincima Roast turkey with thin sheets of Zagorje-style pasta.

Ražnjići Grilled pork kebabs on a skewer.
Riblja juha Fish soup.
Rožata Dubrovnik-style dessert, similar to crème caramel.

Salata od hobotnice Octopus salad with potatoes, onions, olive oil and vinegar.
Samoborska kremšnita Flaky custard tart, a speciality of Samobor.
Sarma Cabbage leaves stuffed with minced meat and rice.
Sladoled Ice cream, sold in a huge variety of flavours.
Štrukli Cottage cheese parcels, a speciality of Zagorje.
Šurlice Pasta tubes from the island of Krk.

Tartufi Istrian truffles.

Zagrebački odrezak Zagreb-style veal steak, stuffed with ham and cheese and fried in breadcrumbs, similar to *cordon bleu*.
Zelena salata Green salad.

WINE, BEER AND SPIRITS

Wine has been produced in Croatia ever since Greek settlers planted the first vineyards on the Dalmatian islands of Korčula, Hvar and Vis. Today, Croatia is attracting a growing reputation for its quality wines.

WHITE WINE
» Malvazija is a straw-coloured dry white wine from Istria, where some of the best wines in Croatia are being produced by a new generation of winemakers such as Marijan Arman, Gianfranco Kozlovic and Ivica Matošević.
» Graševina is a dry white wine from Slavonia. The same region produces classic white wine varieties such as Chardonnay, Rizling (Riesling) and Fume (Sauvignon Blanc).
» Traminac is the local name for Gewürztraminer, a delicate floral white wine produced in the cellars of Ilok.
» White wines on the islands include Žlahtina from Krk, Vugava from Vis, and Grk and Pošip from Korčula.

RED WINE
» Dingač is the finest and most expensive red wine in Croatia. It is produced from Plavac Mali grapes grown on the southern sea-facing slopes of the Pelješac peninsula. Closely related to Californian Zinfandel, Plavac Mali produces a powerful, heavy wine. Cheaper wines labelled Plavac Mali rather than Dingač use the same grapes, but are grown on the landward side.
» Other Dalmatian red wines include Postup from Peljošac, Viški Plavac from Vis, Ivan Dolac from Hvar and Babić from Primošten.
» Teran is a light fruity red wine produced in Istria. In winter, it is heated with olive oil, pepper and toast and served as supa.
» Portugizac is a red wine from the Samobor region which is drunk immediately after the harvest in autumn, rather like Beaujolais Nouveau.

APERITIFS AND DESSERT WINES
» Bermet is an aromatic vermouth from Samobor, introduced by French troops during the Napoleonic occupation and still produced today.
» Muškat Momjanski is a semi-sweet white wine made from the Muškat grape near Buje in Istria.

» Prošek is a sweet red wine, usually made from the Plavac Mali grape in Dalmatia and best served chilled.

MIXED DRINKS
bambus red wine and cola
bevanda red wine and water
gemišt white wine and sparkling mineral water
miš-maš red wine and lemonade

BEER
» Most beer produced in Croatia is European lager-type beer. Popular brands include Karlovačko from Karlovac, Ožujsko from Zagreb, Osječko from Osijek, Pan from Koprivnica and Laško, imported from Slovenia.
» Tomislav is a dark beer from the Ožujsko brewery in Zagreb.
» If you prefer draught to bottled beer, ask for *pivo točeno*.

SPIRITS AND LIQUEURS
Croatia produces a vast range of brandies, spirits and liqueurs, using everything from blueberries to figs. At markets you will be greeted by a kaleidoscopic array of bottles, containing home-made brandy or eau-de-vie with the addition of various preserved fruits and herbs. Most of these come under the broad heading of *rakija*, a generic term similar to brandy or Italian grappa. *Rakija* is an essential aspect of Croatian culture and hospitality, and you can expect to be offered a glass at any time of day.

RAKIJA READER
biska mistletoe brandy from Istria
kruškovac pear brandy
lozovača grape brandy
maraschino sour cherry brandy
medenica honey brandy
orahovica walnut brandy
pelinkovac bitter wormwood and herbal liqueur
šljivovica plum brandy
travarica herb brandy

STAYING

Accommodation in Croatia ranges from practical to palatial, from stone cottages and lighthouses to campsites and five-star hotels. Since independence from Yugoslavia, standards have risen and soulless Communist-era hotels have been upgraded or replaced by smaller establishments emphasizing character and service. Hotels in Zagreb and the bigger cities open all year, but on the islands most places close in winter and it can be difficult to find rooms between November and March.

PRACTICALITIES

» The Croatian National Tourist Board publishes an annual hotel directory and guides to camping, marinas and private accommodation. The guides are available free from tourist offices or can be downloaded from www.croatia.hr. You can also use the website to search for accommodation by region.

» It is always a good idea to reserve ahead, particularly between June and September.

» The cost of accommodation varies significantly throughout the year. The most expensive months are July and August, followed by June and September. Mid-season prices usually apply in April, May and October. For hotels that remain open in winter, low season is November to March, with exceptions for busy periods like Christmas and New Year.

» All visitors over 12 must pay a tourist tax which varies according to season, locality and class of accommodation. A typical cost is 5kn per person per day in a mid-range hotel, with children aged 12–18 paying half price.

HOTELS

» Most large hotels on the coast were built during the 1960s and are lacking in architectural character. They are frequently situated out of town, in purpose-built resort areas a few kilometres from the centre. Many were damaged or used to house refugees during the war but these former state-run hotels have now been privatized and upgraded with the help of foreign investment. Most offer comfortable accommodation together with facilities such as swimming pools, tennis courts, playgrounds, wellness centres, spas, watersports and private beaches.

» A recent trend has been the opening of small, family-run hotels, often in buildings of historic interest.

Many of these are members of the Association of Small and Family Hotels (tel 021 317880, www.omh.hr), which publishes an annual directory of over 100 hotels.

» Hotel prices are usually quoted in euros, though you can pay in either euros or Croatian kuna. Where prices are quoted in euros, they are given in euros in this book. Most hotels accept credit cards but there is occasionally a discount for paying in cash.

» The price of a single room is typically 60–80 per cent of the cost of a double.

» A buffet breakfast is usually included in the price.

PRIVATE ACCOMMODATION

» Private accommodation ranges from a spare room with shared bathroom in a family home to self-contained studios and apartments. Although it can be basic, it is usually good value, and staying with a Croatian family gives you a taste of local life.

» The cheapest rooms are available by negotiating with owners who meet buses and ferries arriving in popular resorts. However, you should be aware that these rooms may not be officially licensed or inspected and you should ask to see the room before you commit yourself.

» Private rooms *(sobe)* and apartments *(apartmani)* can also be booked through local accommodation agencies, though you will probably pay a small supplement as commission. Agencies can be found in all main towns and resorts, usually close to the bus station, ferry port or tourist office. The accommodation has been licensed and graded according to standards. If you want to make a reservation in advance, there is a searchable database of private accommodation available online at www.croatia.hr

» Prices start from around 100kn per person per night. Breakfast is not included. There is usually a supplement for stays of less than three nights.

SELF-CATERING

» Self-catering properties include everything from stylish city apartments to restored stone cottages. Staying in self-catering accommodation can make a good option for families or larger groups. A number of UK tour operators (▷ 270) offer self-catering villas and cottages, mostly in Istria and Dalmatia, some with private pools.

» In Zagreb, NEST (tel 01 487 3225, www.nest.hr) offers modern city centre apartments for short-term rentals, with a minimum stay of three nights.

» Apartments in Dubrovnik can be booked through www.dubrovnik-apartments.com and www.dubrovnik-online.com

AGROTOURISM

» Rural tourism (www.seoski-turizam.net) is growing in popularity in Croatia, from accommodation on working farms to upmarket rural hotels. It is particularly developed in Istria and areas of inland Croatia such as Zagorje and the Plitvice Lakes.

» Look out for signs advertising *agroturizam* or *seoski turizam* (rural tourism).

» In addition to accommodation, many places offer farmhouse cooking using local produce and home-made wine. Some of the best examples are given in the regional listings.

» A directory of rural accommodation in Istria can be found at www.istra.com/agroturizam or www.istra.hr/en/agritourism

YOUTH HOSTELS

» There are youth hostels in Zagreb, Pula, Rijeka, Krk, Zadar and Dubrovnik which are open throughout the year. The youth hostels at Punat (Krk) and Veli Lošinj (Lošinj) are open from May to September only.

» Some hostels are located in modern settings, while others are in historic buildings or places of interest. The hostel at Rijeka is in a 19th-century villa, the hostel at Krk is in the island's first tourist hotel, and the hostel at Pula is on a beach with its own campsite.

» Accommodation is generally in multi-bedded dormitories, though

the hostel at Rijeka has double rooms and Zagreb also offers single and double rooms with adjoining bathrooms. Prices range from around 85kn for a bed in a six-bed dorm to 250kn for a double room with private shower. Breakfast is an extra charge.

» To stay in a youth hostel, you must hold a membership card of an IYHF (International Youth Hostels Federation) affiliated organization. Non-members can join by paying a supplement for the first night's stay and will receive a membership card entitling them to stay at youth hostels in over 100 countries for one year.

» Bookings and information from the Croatian Youth Hostels Association (tel 01 482 9294, www.hfhs.hr).

» Most Croatian cities now have one or more privately run hostels for budget travellers of all ages. Accommodation usually consists of several dorms positioned around a common room, and there's normally a kitchen, internet access and laundry facilities. Book online at www.hostelworld.com or www.hostelbookers.com.

LIGHTHOUSES AND FISHING COTTAGES

If you really want to get away from it all with a back-to-nature experience, there are two adventurous options:

» Eleven of Croatia's lighthouses

have been converted into self-catering apartments for between two and eight people. Three are on the mainland at Umag, Poreč and Makarska, while the others are on islands with varying degrees of remoteness. The most remote is on the tiny island of Palagruža, 70km (44 miles) from Vis. In most cases, there is a resident lighthouse keeper. Prices start from around €150 per person per week. Contact Adriatica (tel 01 241 5611, UK tel 020 7183 0437, www.adriatica.net).

» Travel agents in Murter offer 'Robinson Crusoe' fishermen's cottages for rent on the Kornati Islands in summer. These are old stone cottages, a few metres from the sea, with no electricity and water from a well. Conditions are basic, but you can rent your own fishing boat and supplies are delivered by boat twice a week. If you are seeking solitude in a beautiful setting, this could be the experience of a lifetime. Contact Kornatturist (tel 022 435854, www.kornatturist.hr).

CAMPING AND CARAVANNING

» Camping is the most popular form of tourist accommodation in Croatia, accounting for over a third of all visitors. The majority of campsites are situated on the coast in Istria, Kvarner and Dalmatia. An exception is Camping Korana, in the Plitvice Lakes National Park.

» There are over 150 registered campsites, which are graded from two to five stars according to facilities. Some consist mainly of tent pitches, while others are

sprawling camping villages with bungalows, chalets, mobile homes and accommodation for over 5,000 people. There are also a large number of mini-camps with up to 30 pitches. Most campsites have hot and cold water, showers and laundry facilities, and most large campsites also have pools, tennis courts, boat and bicycle hire and access to a beach. Around 12 campsites, mainly in Istria, cater exclusively for naturists, while many others have nudist beaches.

» Most campsites are open from May to September, though a small number stay open throughout the year.

» You can make a complete search of campsites by region at www.camping.hr and www.croatia.hr

» Camping outside official campsites and caravan (RV) parks is forbidden in Croatia.

MARINAS

» There are 50 marinas along the Adriatic coast, with a total of over 13,000 berths at sea. The largest operator of marinas is ACI Club (tel 051 271288, www.aci-club.hr). Many are open throughout the year, with facilities including yacht charter, parking, petrol and repairs, plus showers, shops, restaurants, laundry service, internet access and currency exchange. A few also offer accommodation on land. Smaller marinas are open in summer only. In addition, sailors can moor their boats at some 350 natural harbours along the Adriatic coast and islands.

» You can search for marinas at www.croatia.hr

UK TOUR OPERATORS TO CROATIA		
NAME	**TELEPHONE**	**WEBSITE**
Alabaster & Clarke Wine Tours	01730 263111	www.winetours.co.uk
Bond Tours	01372 745300	www.bondtours.com
Bosmere Travel	01473 834094	www.bosmeretravel.co.uk
Croatian Affair	020 7385 7111	www.croatianaffair.com
Croatian Villas	020 8888 6655	www.croatianvillas.com
Hidden Croatia	0800 021 7771	www.hiddencroatia.com
My Croatia	0118 961 1554	www.mycroatia.co.uk
Sailing Holidays	020 8459 8787	www.sailingholidays.com
Simply Travel	0871 231 4050	www.simplytravel.co.uk
Vintage Travel	0845 344 0460	www.vintagetravel.co.uk

Croatian is one of the most phonetic of all European languages and, unlike English, particular combinations of letters are nearly always pronounced the same way.

Vowels are pronounced as follows:

a	as in	c**a**r, but shorter
e	as in	v**e**t
i	as in	b**i**t
o	as in	n**o**t
u	as in	b**oo**k

Note also these combinations:

aj	'ai' as in h**igh**	
ej	'ei' as in m**ay**	
oj	'oi' as in t**oy**	

Consonants as in English except:

c	as **ts** in ma**ts**
č	as **ch** in **ch**at
ć	as **t** in over**t**ure
dž	as **g** in ca**g**e
đ	as **d** in **d**uration
h	in the back of the throat like the Scottish lo**ch**
j	as **y** in **y**es
lj	as **ll** in mi**ll**ion
nj	as **ny** in ca**ny**on
r	harder than the English **r**, more similar to the Scottish **r**
š	as **sh** in **sh**are
ž	as **s** in plea**s**ure

All Croatian nouns are either masculine, feminine or neuter. They also have case endings that change according to how the noun is used in a sentence. An adjective's ending changes to match the ending of the noun. Verbs are also marked masculine, feminine or neuter as well as singular or plural. It is therefore easier to treat basic phrases as a whole, but different options of a basic form are given when necessary (e.g. masculine or feminine verb endings, marked as 'masc/fem').

Personal pronouns (e.g. I, you, they) are usually omitted from the beginning of the sentence, unless it is important to stress who the subject

is. The personal pronoun 'you' has two forms, polite 'vi' and informal 'ti' and the verb endings change according to which form is used. The context requires the use of the polite form in most of the phrases here, but the informal option is also given when appropriate (marked as 'pol/inf' following the phrase).

CONVERSATION

I don't speak Croatian
Ne govorim hrvatski

I only speak a little Croatian
Govorim samo malo hrvatski

Do you speak English?
Govorite li engleski?

I don't understand
Ne razumijem

Please repeat that
Molim vas ponovite

Please speak more slowly
Govorite sporije, molim vas

What does this mean?
Što to znači?

Write that down for me, please
Napišite mi to, molim

My name is
Zovem se

What's your name?
Kako se zovete/zoveš? (pol/inf)

Hello, pleased to meet you
Zdravo, drago mi je da smo se upoznali

This is my friend
Ovo je moj prijatelj/moja prijateljica (male/female)

This is my wife/husband/ daughter/son
Ovo je moja supruga/moj muž/moja kći/moj sin

Where do you live?
Gdje živite/živiš? (pol/inf)

I live in...
Živim u...

What is the time?
Koliko je sati?

When do you open/close?
Kad otvarate/zatvarate?

Good morning/afternoon/evening
Dobro jutro/dobar dan/dobra večer

Goodbye/Bye-bye
Doviđenja/Ćao

See you tomorrow
Vidimo se sutra

How are you?
Kako ste/si? (pol/inf)

Fine, thank you
Dobro, hvala

That's alright
U redu je

USEFUL WORDS

yes	da
no	ne
please	molim
thank you	hvala
you're welcome	nema na čemu
excuse me/sorry!	oprostite!
where	gdje
here	ovdje
there	tamo
when	kad
now	sad
later	kasnije
why	zašto
who	tko
may I/can I	smijem li/mogu li

SHOPPING

Could you help me, please?
Možete li mi pomoći, molim?

How much is this?
Koliko stoji?

I'm looking for...
Tražim...

Where can I buy...?
Gdje mogu kupiti...?

How much is this/that?
Koliko stoji ovo/to?

When does the shop open/close?
Kad se prodavaonica otvara/zatvara?

I'm just looking, thank you
Samo razgledam, hvala

This isn't what I want
To nije ono što želim

I'll take this
Uzet ću ovo

Do you have anything less expensive/smaller/larger?
Imate li što jeftinije/manje/veće?

Are the instructions included?
Jesu li upute priložene?

Do you have a bag for this?
Imate li vrećicu za ovo?

I'm looking for a present
Tražim poklon

Can you gift wrap this, please?
Možete li mi ovo umotati, molim?

Do you accept credit cards?
Prihvaćate li kreditne kartice?

I'd like a kilo of...
Molim kilu...

Do you have shoes to match this?
Imate li cipele koje idu s ovim?

This is the right size
Ovo je prava veličina

Can you measure me, please?
Možete li me izmjeriti molim?

Do you have this in...?
Imate li ovo u...?

Is there a market?
Ima li ovdje tržnica?

SHOPS

baker's
pekarnica

bookshop
knjižara

butcher's
mesnica

cake shop
slastičarna

clothes shop
prodavaonica odjeće

delicatessen
prodavaonica delikatesne robe

dry-cleaner's
kemijska čistionica

fishmonger's
ribarnica

florist
cvjećarna

gift shop
prodavaonica suvenira

grocer's
trgovina mješovitom robom

hairdresser's
frizerski salon

jeweller's
prodavaonica nakita

launderette
praonica rublja

newsagent's
trafika

photographic shop
fotografska radionica

shoe shop
prodavaonica obuće

sports shop
prodavaonica sportske robe

tobacconist's
prodavaonica duhana

POST AND TELEPHONES

Where is the nearest post office/ mail box?
Gdje je najbliža pošta/najbliži poštanski sandučić?

What is the postage to...?
Koliko je poštarina za...?

One stamp, please
Jednu marku, molim

I'd like to send this by air mail/ registered mail
Želim ovo poslati zrakoplovom/ preporučeno

Can you direct me to a public phone?
Možete li me uputiti k najbližoj telefonskoj govornici?

Where can I buy a phone card?
Gdje mogu kupiti telefonsku karticu?

What is the charge per minute?
Koliko stoji jedna minuta?

Can I dial direct to...?
Mogu li direktno zvati...?

Do I need to dial 0 first?
Moram li prvo okrenuti nulu?

Where can I find a phone directory?
Gdje mogu naći telefonski imenik?

What is the number for directory enquiries?
Koji je broj službe za telefonske informacije?

Please put me through to...
Molim spojite me s...

Have there been any calls for me?
Je li bilo telefonskih poziva za mene?

Hello, this is...
Halo, ovdje...

Who is this speaking, please?
Tko je na telefonu molim?

I'd like to speak to...
Htio/htjela (masc/fem) bih govoriti s...

Extension ... please
Interni broj ... molim

Please ask him/her to call me back
Molim vas recite mu/joj da me nazove

NUMBERS

0	nula
1	jedan
2	dva
3	tri
4	četiri
5	pet
6	šest
7	sedam
8	osam
9	devet
10	deset
11	jedanest
12	dvanaest
13	trinaest
14	četrnaest
15	petnaest
16	šesnaest
17	sedamnaest
18	osamnaest
19	devetnaest
20	dvadeset
21	dvadeset jedan
22	dvadeset dva
30	trideset
40	četrdeset
50	pedeset
60	šezdeset
70	sedamdeset
80	osamdeset
90	devedeset
100	sto
1,000	tisuću

million	milijun
quarter	četvrt
half	po

MONEY

Is there a bank/currency exchange office nearby?
Ima li u blizini banka/mjenjačnica?

What is the exchange rate today?
Koji je današnji tečaj?

I'd like to change sterling/dollars into kunas (Croatian currency)
Želim promijeniti britanske funte / američke dolare u hrvatske kune

Can I use my credit card to withdraw cash?
Mogu li podići gotovinu svojom kreditnom karticom?

I'd like to cash this traveller's cheque
Želim unovčiti ovaj putnički ček

GETTING AROUND

Where is the train/bus station?
Gdje je željeznički/autobusni kolodvor?

Does this train/bus stop at...?
Staje li ovaj vlak/autobus u...?

Please stop at the next stop
Molim zaustavite na sljedećem stajalištu

Where are we?
Gdje smo?

Do I have to get off here?
Moram li sići ovdje?

Where can I buy a ticket?
Gdje mogu kupiti kartu?

Where can I reserve a seat?
Gdje mogu rezervirati mjesto?

Please can I have a single/return (one-way/round-trip) ticket to...
Molim vas jednosmjernu/ povratnu kartu za...

When is the first/last bus to...?
Kad ide prvi/zadnji autobus za...?

I would like a standard/first-class ticket to...
Molim jednu kartu za drugi/prvi razred za...

Where is the information desk?
Gdje su informacije?

Where is the timetable?
Gdje je vozni red?

Do you have a metro/bus map?
Imate li kartu podzemne željeznice/ autobusa?

Where can I find a taxi (rank)?
Gdje mogu naći taksi (stajalište)?

Please take me to...
...(address), molim

How much is the journey?
Koliko stoji ova vožnja?

Please turn on the meter
Molim vas uključite taksimetar

I'd like to get out here, please
Želim ovdje izaći, molim vas

Could you wait for me, please?
Možete li me pričekati, molim vas?

Excuse me, I think I am lost
Oprostite, mislim da sam se izgubio/ izgubila (masc/fem)

IN THE TOWN

on/to the right
na desno/ desno

on/to the left
na lijevo/lijevo

opposite
nasuprot

straight on
ravno

near
blizu

in front of pred	**town hall** gradska vijećnica	**What is the admission price?** Koliko stoji ulaz?
behind iza	**square** trg	**Is there a discount for senior citizens/students?** Imate li popust za starije osobe/ studente?
north sjever	**street** ulica	
south jug	**island** otok	**Are there guided tours?** Imate li ekskurzije s vodičem?
east istok	**river** rijeka	**Are there boat trips?** Imate li izlete brodicom?
west zapad	**lake** jezero	**Is there an English-speaking guide?** Imate li engleskog vodiča?
free besplatno	**bridge** most	**Are there organized excursions?** Imate li organizirane ekskurzije
donation prilog	**no entry** zabranjen pristup	**Can we make reservations here?** Možemo li ovdje napraviti rezervaciju?
open otvoreno	**entrance** ulaz	**What time does it open/close?** U koliko sati otvarate/zatvarate?
closed zatvoreno	**exit** izlaz	**Is photography allowed?** Smije li se fotografirati?
daily dnevno	**lavatories** zahodi (WC)	**Do you have a brochure in English?** Imate li brošuru na engleskom?
cathedral katedrala	**men/women** muški/ženski	**Where can I find a good nightclub?** Gdje mogu naći dobar noćni klub?
church crkva	**Theatre** Kazalište	**What time does the show start?** U koliko sati počinje predstava?
castle tvrđava	**Garden** Vrt	**Could you reserve tickets for me?** Možete li mi rezervirati karte?
museum muzej	**TOURIST INFORMATION**	**How much is a ticket?** Koliko stoji jedna karta?
monument spomenik	**Where is the tourist information office/tourist information desk, please?** Gdje je ured za turističke informacije / gdje su turističke informacije, molim?	**Should we dress smartly?** Trebamo li se odjenuti elegantno?
palace palača		
gallery galerija	**Do you have a city map?** Imate li plan grada?	**DAYS**
town/old town grad/stari grad	**Can you give me some information about...?** Možete li mi dati informacije o ...?	Monday...................... ponedjeljak Tuesday................................utorak Wednesday .... srijeda Thursday .... četvrtak

Friday	petak
Saturday	subota
Sunday	nedjelja

TIMES

morning (until about 10am)	ujutro
(the rest of the morning)	prije podne
afternoon	poslije podne
evening	večer
night	noć
day	dan
month	mjesec
year	godina
today	danas
yesterday	jučer
tomorrow	sutra

MONTHS

January	siječanj
February	veljača
March	ožujak
April	travanj
May	svibanj
June	lipanj
July	srpanj
August	kolovoz
September	rujan
October	listopad
November	studeni
December	prosinac

SEASONS

spring	proljeće
summer	ljeto
autumn	jesen
winter	zima

HOLIDAYS

Easter	Uskrs
National Holiday	državni blagdan
Christmas	Božić
26 December	Sveti Stjepan
New Year's Eve	Novogodišnja noć/ Silvestrovo
New Year's Day	Nova godina

IN TROUBLE

Help!
Upomoć!

Stop, thief!
Stani, lopov!

Can you help me, please?
Možete li mi pomoći, molim vas?

Call the fire brigade/police/an ambulance
Zovite vatrogasce/policiju/hitnu pomoć

I have lost my passport/wallet/ purse/handbag
Izgubio/izgubila (masc/fem) samputovnicu/lisnicu/novčanik/tašnu

Is there a lost property office?
Ima li ovdje ured za izgubljeno-nađeno?

Where is the police station?
Gdje je policijska postaja?

I have been robbed
Pokraden/pokradena (masc/fem) sam

I have had an accident
Imao/imala (masc/fem) sam nezgodu

Here is my name and address
Ovdje su moje ime i adresa

Did you see the accident?
Jeste li vidjeli nezgodu?

Are you insured?
Jeste li osigurani?

Please can I have your name and address?
Mogu li dobiti Vaše ime i adresu molim?

I need information for my insurance company
Trebam informacije za moje osiguranje

ILLNESS

I don't feel well
Ne osjećam se dobro

Is there a doctor/pharmacist on duty?
Ima li ovdje dežurnog liječnika/ ljekarnika?

I need to see a doctor/dentist
Trebam liječnika/zubara

Where is the hospital?
Gdje je bolnica?

When is the surgery open?
Kad je ordinacija otvorena?

I need to make an emergency appointment
Trebam hitno vidjeti liječnika

I feel sick
Zlo mi je

I am allergic to...
Alergičan/alergična (masc/fem) sam na...

I have a heart condition
Imam slabo srce

I am diabetic
Imam dijabetes

I'm asthmatic
Imam astmu

I've been stung by a wasp/bee
Ubola me osa/pčela

Can I have a painkiller?
Mogu li dobiti tabletu protiv bolova?

How many tablets a day should I take?
Koliko tableta dnevno trebam uzeti?

How long will I have to stay in bed/hospital?
Koliko dugo moram ostati u krevetu/ bolnici?

I have bad toothache
Jako me boli zub

I have broken my tooth/crown
Slomio mi se zub/slomila mi se krunica

A filling has come out
Ispala mi je plomba

Can you repair my dentures?
Možete li mi popraviti zubnu protezu?

RESTAURANTS

I'd like to reserve a table for ... people at ...
Želim rezervirati stol za ... osoba u ... sati

A table for ..., please
Stol za ..., molim

Could we sit there?
Možemo li sjesti tamo?

We would like to wait for a table
Htjeli bismo sačekati slobodan stol

Could we see the menu/drinks list?
Možemo li pogledati jelovnik/cjenik pića?

Is there a dish of the day?
Imate li specijalitet dana?

Do you have the menu in English?
Imate li jelovnik na engleskom?

Where are the lavatories?
Gdje su zahodi?

I can't eat wheat/sugar/salt/ pork/ beef/dairy
Ne smijem jesti pšenicu/ šećer/sol/ svinjetinu/govedinu/mlijeko i mliječne proizvode

I am a vegetarian
Ja sam vegetarijanac

Could I have bottled still/ sparkling water?
Molim bocu negazirane/ mineralne vode

The food is cold
Jelo je hladno

The meat is overcooked/too rare
Meso je prepečeno/nedovoljno pečeno

I ordered...
Naručio/naručila (masc/fem) sam...

This is not what I ordered
Ovo nisam naručio/naručila (masc/ fem)

Can I have the bill, please?
Račun, molim

Is service included?
Je li napojnica uključena u cijenu?

HOTELS

I have made a reservation for ... nights
Imam rezervaciju za ... noći

Do you have a room?
Imate li sobu?

How much per night?
Koliko stoji jedna noć?

Double/single room
Dvokrevetna/jednokrevetna soba

Twin room
Soba s dva odvojena kreveta

With bath/shower
S kupaonicom/tušem

May I see the room?
Mogu li vidjeti sobu?

Could I have another room?
Mogu li dobiti drugu sobu?

Is there a lift in the hotel?
Ima li u hotelu dizalo?

Are the rooms air-conditioned/ heated?
Jesu li sobe klimatizirane/s grijanjem?

Is breakfast included in the price?
Je li zajutrak uključen u cijenu?

Do you have room service?
Imate li sobno posluživanje?

I need an alarm call at...
Trebam naručiti buđenje u ... sati

The room is too hot/too cold/ dirty
U sobi je prevruće/ prehladno/soba je prljava

Please can I pay my bill?
Mogu li platiti račun, molim?

Please order a taxi for me
Naručite mi taksi, molim

COLOURS

black	crna
brown	smeđa
pink	ružičasta
red	crvena
orange	narančasta
yellow	žuta
green	zelena
blue	plava
purple	grimizna
white	bijela
gold	zlatna
silver	srebrna
grey	siva
turquoise	tirkizna

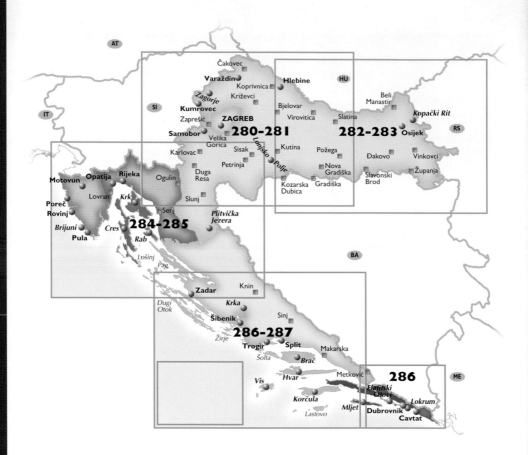

Čakovec

Varaždin
Koprivnica
Zagorje
Križevci

Kumrovec
Zaprešić
ZAGREB
Samobor
Velika
Gorica
Karlovac
Sisak
Petrinja

Hlebine

Bjelovar
Virovitica
Slatina

Beli
Manastir

Kopački Rit

280-281

282-283
Osijek

Kutina
Požega
Đakovo
Vinkovci

Nova
Gradiška
Slavonski
Brod
Županja

Kozarska
Dubica
Gradiška

Motovun
Opatija
Rijeka
Lovran
Krk
Poreč
Rovinj
Ogulin
Duga
Resa

Brijuni
Cres
Rab
Slunj

Pula

Senj
Plitvička
Jezera

284-285

Lošinj

Pag

Dugi
Otok
Zadar
Knin

Krka
Sinj

Šibenik

Žirje

286-287
Trogir
Split
Šolta
Makarska

Vis
Brač

Hvar
Metković

286

Korčula
Mljet
Elafitski
Otoci
Lokrum
Lastovo
Dubrovnik
Cavtat

AT
HU
SI
IT
RS
BA
ME

Zagorje
Longsko
Polje

280-287
0   20 km
0   10 miles

▬▬▬	Motorway
▬◄	National road
◄▬	Regional road
▬▬	Local road
····	Railway
▬▬▬	International boundary

●	Featured place of interest
■	City / Town / Village
▬	Built-up area
▬	National park
✈	Airport
621 ▲	Height in metres

MAPS | CROATIA

MAPS

Map references for the sights refer to the atlas pages within this section or to the individual town plans within the regions. For example, Split has the reference ✚ 287 F7, indicating the page on which the map is found (287) and the grid square in which Split sits (F7).

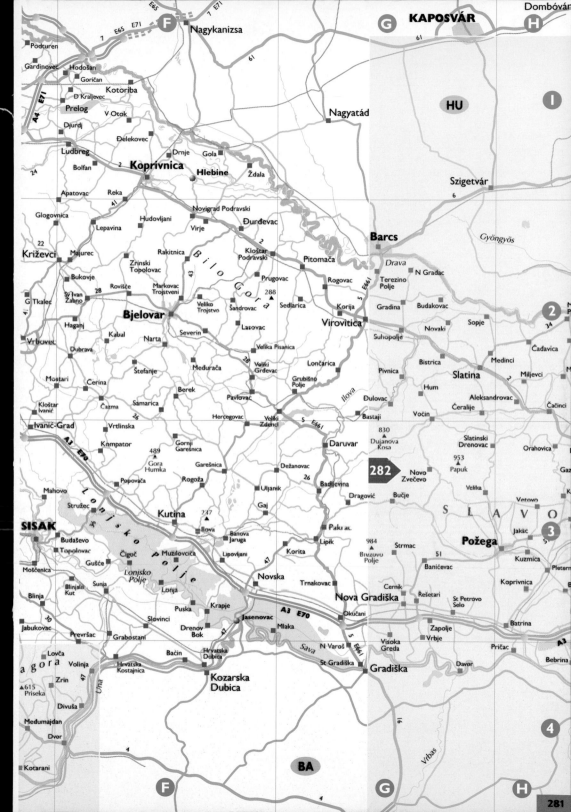

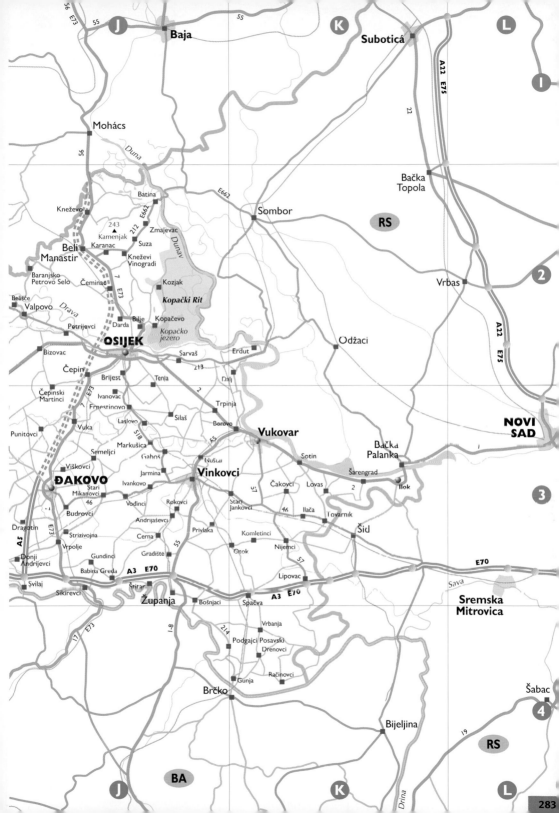

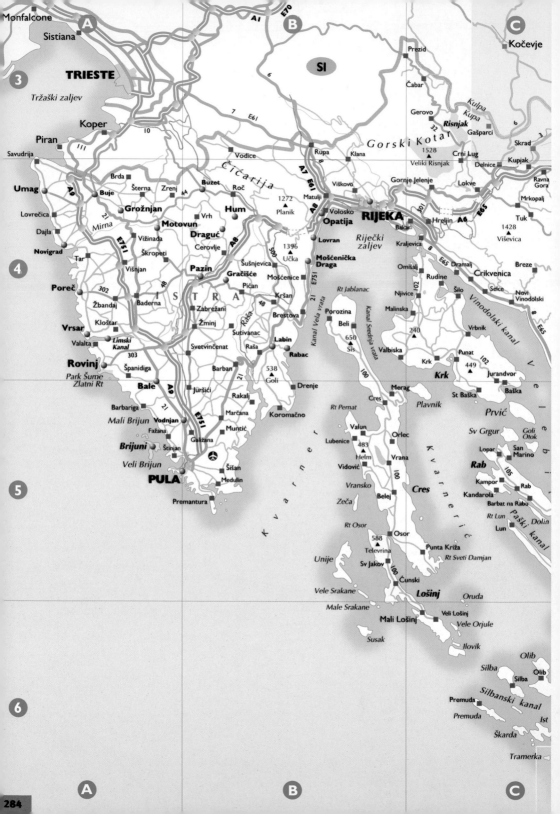

C · D · E

Starigrad
Vlašići · Ražanac · Paklenica · Suçevici
Lozice · Rt · Duboki Dol · Zrmanja Vrelo
Vir · Vrsi · G Slivnica · Jasenice · Krupa · Strmica
Porat · Privlaka · Nin · Poljica · Jovići · Posedarje · Novigrad · Obrovac · 285 · Kaštel Žegarski · Kom · Plavno
Molat · Petrčane · Poličnik · Pridraga · 502 · Bukovica · Pađene · Knin
Tun Veli · Sestrunj · Rivanj · Murvica · E65 · Donji Zemunik · D Biljane · 674 · Orljak · Biovičino Selo · Radučić · Orlić
Sestrunj · Ugljan · ZADAR · Bibinje · Galovac · Raštević · Benkovac · Dobropoljci · Kistanje · Zvjerinac · 1148
Veli Rat · Zverinac · Dragove · Ugljan · Kali · Gorica · Polača · Vukšić · Bribirske Mostine · 509 · Oklaj · Promina Tepljuh
Brbinj · Rava · Veli Iž · Ždrelac · 274 · Sukošan · Sv Filip Jakov · Vransko Jezero · Mala Čista · Krka · Drniš · Kričke
Dugi Otok · Iž · Mali Iž · Pašman · Biograd · Skradin · 33
V Straža · Luka · Pašman · Sit · Tkon · Pakoštane · E65 · Pirovac · Raslina · Lozovac · Planjane
Zaglav · Lavdara · Žut · Vrgada · Murter · Vodice · Cera
Lučica · Kornat · Murter · Tisno · Šibenik · A1
Levrnaka · Vrulje · Kaprije · Tijat · Zlarin · Brodarica · Vrpolje
Kornati Otoci · Jadra · Lavsa · Vela Smokvica · Kakan · Zmajan · Boraja · 58
Kurba Vela · Žirje · Žirje · Primošten · Široke · 738
Podorljak · Marina
Ražanj · Vinišće
Mali Drvenik · Veliki Drvenik

108 · Nova Sela · Metković
62 · BA
8 · 9 · E73 · Dobranje · Bileća · ME
Raba · Opuzen · Badžula
564 · Klek · Badžula
Neum · Topolo · Trebinje
Dubrava · Brijesta · M Ston · Mravnica · Rt Stupišće
Ston · 332 · E65 · Slano · 20
Mljetski kanal · Šipan · Trsteno · Orašac · Visočnik · Biševo
Babino Polje · Sobra · Jakljan · Koločep · 909 · Duba Konavoska
Maranovići · Saplunara · Lopud · Dubrovnik · Kupari · 1234 · Dubravka
Mljet · Rt Gruj · Lokrum · Cavtat · Čilipi · E65
Gruda · Novi Herceg
Pločice
Prevlaka

H · J · K

286

Bosansko
Grahovo **F**

G

H

6

Vrbas

Bugojno

1831
Dinara

1851
V Bat

BA

16

Kupres

Polača

Cetina

1913
Troglav

Suica

7

1207
Bat

Vrlika

Koljane

Perućko
jezero

Livno

Buško
jezero

Posušje

Štikovo

Otavice

Buzovi

Dabar

56

Maljkovo

1508
Svilaja

Hrvace

219

1855
Konj

16

Umljanović

G Ogorje

Sinj

Glavice

D Korita

Ričice

Vrba

G Muć

Brnaze

Otok

E71

Kamensko

Zmijavci

Posušje

Kladnice

Prugovo

Bisko

Trilj

60

220

Svib

Cista Provo

Lovreč

Imotski

Al

Dugopolje

1340

Budimiri

60

39

Šestanovac

60

Runovići

Aniči

Kaštel Sućurac
Kaštel Stari

Salona

Klis
Žrnovnica

Gornji
Dolac

Blato na
Cetini

Zagvozd

Al

Kozica

Kašće

Banja

Trogir

Split

Jesenice
Dugi Rat

Omiš

Zadvarje

Biokovo

1762
Sveti Jure

Župa

62

Vrgorac

Veliki Prolog

8

Clovo

Splitski kanal

Rogač

Sutivan

Supetar

Postira

Kučiće

Lokva

Brela

Baška
Voda

Biokovo

Kozica

Ravča

M Prolog

Maslinica

Šolta

G Selo

Ložišća

Milna

Blaca

780

Pražnica

Pučišća

Makarska

Sumartin

Tučepi

Podgora

Drvenik

Gradac

108

Nova Se

Brač

Murvica

Bol

Hvarski kanal

Živogošće

8

E65

Ploče

62

Rt Pelegrin

Brusje

Stari
Grad

Vrboska

Hvar

Sućuraj

Neretvanski kanal

Blace

Hvar

626

Jelsa

Zastražišće

Zaglav

Trpanj

Raba

Pakleni Otoci

Sv
Nedjelja

Zavala

Šćedro

Rt Lovište

Duba
Pelješka

961

Pelješac

Janjina

Kiek

56

Viški kanal

Korčulanski kanal

Viganj

Korčula

Orebić

Potomje

414

Vis

Komiža

Podstražje

Proizd

Korčula

Lumbarda

Rt Ražnjić

Dubrava

B

Podhumlje

Vis

117

Vela Luka

Blato

Smokvica

Brna

568

118

Rt Velo Dance

Lastovski kanal

Mlje

Pomena

Rt Goli

Polače

Babin
Pol

Sušac

Prežba
Mrčara

Lastovo

415

Kopište

Ubli

Kručica

Lastovo

Mljet

9

Mlje

MAPS INDEX

MAPS INDEX

PICTURES

The Automobile Association would like to thank the following photographers, companies and picture libraries for their assistance in the preparation of this book.

Abbreviations for the picture credits are as follows: (t) top; (b) bottom; (l) left; (r) right; (c) centre; (AA) AA World Travel Library.

134 AA/P Bennett;
135 AA/P Bennett;
136 AA/P Bennett;
137 AA/P Bennett;
138 Franco Cogoli/4Corners Images;
140 AA/P Bennett;
141 Dubravko Grakalic/Alamy;
142 AA/T Kelly;
144 allOver Photography/Alamy;
145 JR Stock/Alamy;
146 Damir Fabijanic /4Corners Images;
148 Franco Cogoli/4Corners Images;
149 AA/P Bennett;
150 AA/P Bennett;
151l AA/P Bennett;
151r Ellen Rooney/Robert Harding;
152 AA/P Bennett;
153l AA/J Smith;
153r AA/P Bennett;
154 AA/P Bennett;
155l Franco Cogoli/4Corners Images;
155r AA/P Bennett;
156 AA/J Smith;
157l AA/J Smith;
157r AA/J Smith;
158 Art Kowalsky/Alamy;
159 AA/P Bennett;
160 Woodystock/Alamy;
161l AA/P Bennett;
161r AA/P Bennett;
162 Arco Images GmbH/Alamy;
163 AA/P Bennett;
164 Wolfgang Pölzer/Alamy;
166 AA/T Kelly;
168 TTL Images/Alamy;
170 AA/P Bennett;
172 Ian Cumming/Axiom;
173l Croatian National Tourist Board;
173r AA/P Bennett;
174 AA/P Bennett;
175l AA/P Bennett;
175r AA/P Bennett;
176 David Noton/The Travel Library;
178 AA/J Smith;
179l AA/J Smith;
179r AA/J Smith;
180 AA/P Bennett;
181l AA/P Bennett;
181r AA/P Bennett;
182 AA/J Smith;
183l AA/J Smith;
183r AA/P Bennett;
184 AA/P Bennett;

184l AA/P Bennett;
184r AA/P Bennett;
186l AA/P Bennett;
186r AA/J Smith;
187 AA/P Bennett;
188 Ellen McKnight/Alamy;
189 AA/J Smith;
190 Frank Fell/The Travel Library;
191l AA/J Smith;
191r AA/J Smith;
192 AA/J Smith;
193l Angus McComiskey/Alamy;
193r AA/J Smith;
194 AA/P Bennett;
195 AA/J Smith;
196 AA/J Smith;
197l AA/J Smith;
197r AA/J Smith;
198 AA/P Bennett;
199l AA/P Bennett;
199r AA/P Bennett;
200 LOOK Die Bildagentur de Fotografen GmbH/Alamy;
201 AA/J Smith;
202 AA/P Bennett;
203l AA/P Bennett;
203r Frank Fell/The Travel Library;
204 AA/P Bennett;
205 AA/P Bennett;
207 Franco Cogoli/4Corners Images;
208 Ian Cumming/Axiom;
211 AA/T Kelly;
212 Alison Jones/Danita Delimont/Alamy;
214 AA/P.Bennett;
216 Gavin Hellier/Robert Harding;
217 Bertrand Gardel/Hemis/Corbis;
218 AA/P Bennett;
219 AA/P Bennett;
220 AA/J Smith;
221t AA/P Bennett;
221b AA/P Bennett;
222t AA/P Bennett;
222b AA/P Bennett;
223 AA/J Smith;
224 AA/P Bennett;
225l AA/J Smith;
225r AA/J Smith;
226 AA/J Smith;
227 AA/P Bennett;
228 Wayne Walton/Lonely Planet Images;
229l courtesy of Mljet Tourist Office;
229r courtesy of Mljet Tourist Office;

230 AA/P Bennett;
231l Angus McComiskey/Alamy;
231r AA/P Bennett;
232 AA/P Bennett;
233 AA/P Bennett;
234 International Photobank/Alamy;
236 AA/P Bennett;
237 Images & Stories/Alamy;
238 AA/T Kelly;
239 AA/T Kelly;
240 AA/Karl Blackwell
241 World Pictures/Photoshot;
242 AA/P Bennett;
243 Strauss/Curtis/Corbis;
245 AA/J Smith;
246 Food Collection/Photolibrary;
248 AA/J Smith;
249 AA/J Smith;
250 PCL/Alamy;
251 PCL/Alamy;
254 AA/J Smith;
255 Hemis/Photoshot;
256 AA/P Bennett;
257l AA/J Smith;
257r AA/J Smith;
258 Ellen Rooney/Axiom;
259 Digitalvision;
260 AA/P Bennett;
261l Ian Cumming/Axiom;
261r Corbis
262 Image 100
263 AA/M Lynch;
264 AA/N Setchfield;
265 AA/J Smith;
266 AA/P Bennett;
267 John Frumm/Hemis/Axiom;
268 AA/T Kelly;
269 AA/T Kelly;
270 AA/T Kelly;
271 Johanna Huber/4Corners Images;
279 AA/P Bennett

CREDITS

Managing editor
Marie-Claire Jefferies

Project editor
Laura Linder

Design
Drew Jones, pentacorbig

Picture research
Clare Limpus

Image retouching and repro
Sarah Montgomery

Mapping
Maps produced by the Mapping Services Department of AA Publishing

Main contributors
Lindsay Bennett, Marc Di Duca, Tony Kelly

Updater
Marc Di Duca

Indexer
Marie Lorimer

Production
Lorraine Taylor

Published by AA Publishing, a trading name of AA Media Limited, whose registered office is Fanum House, Basing View, Basingstoke, RG21 4EA. Registered number 06112600.
A CIP catalogue record for this book is available from the British Library.

ISBN 978-0-7495-6757-6

KeyGuide is a registered trademark in Australia and is used under license.
Colour separation by AA Digital Department
Printed and bound by Leo Paper Products, China

We believe the contents of this book are correct at the time of printing. However, some details, particularly prices, opening times and telephone numbers do change. We do not accept responsibility for any consequences arising from the use of this book.
This does not affect your statutory rights. We would be grateful if readers would advise us of any inaccuracies they may encounter, or any suggestions they might like to make to improve the book. There is a form provided at the back of the book for this purpose, or you can email us at travelguides@theaa.com

A04201
Maps in this title produced from data supplied by Global Mapping, Brackley, UK.
Copyright © Global Mapping/Hibernia
Weather chart statistics supplied by Weatherbase © Copyright (2005) Canty and Associates, LLC
Transport map © Communicarta Ltd, UK

Find out more about AA Publishing and the wide range of travel publications and services the AA provides by visiting our website at
theAA.com/shop

Thank you for buying this KeyGuide. Your comments and opinions are very important to us, so please help us to improve our travel guides by taking a few minutes to complete this questionnaire.

You do not need a stamp (unless posted outside the UK). If you do not want to cut this page from your guide, then photocopy it or write your answers on a plain sheet of paper.

Send to: **KeyGuide Editor, AA World Travel Guides**
FREEPOST SCE 4598, Basingstoke RG21 4GY
Email: **travelguides@theaa.com**

Find out more about AA Publishing and the wide range of travel publications the AA provides by visiting our website at theAA.com/shop

ABOUT THIS GUIDE

Which KeyGuide did you buy? ....

Where did you buy it? ....

When? .... month .... year

Why did you choose this AA KeyGuide?
☐ Price ☐ AA Publication
☐ Used this series before; title
☐ Cover ☐ Other (please state)

Please let us know how helpful the following features of the guide were to you by circling the appropriate category: very helpful (VH), helpful (H) or little help (I H)

Size	VH	H	LH
Layout	VH	H	LH
Photos	VH	H	I H
Excursions	VH	H	LH
Entertainment	VH	H	LH
Hotels	VH	H	LH
Maps	VH	H	LH
Practical info	VH	H	LH
Restaurants	VH	H	LH
Shopping	VH	H	LH
Walks	VH	H	LH
Sights	VH	H	LH
Transport info	VH	H	LH

What was your favourite sight, attraction or feature listed in the guide?

Page.................Please give your reason ....
....

Which features in the guide could be changed or improved? Or are there any other comments you would like to make?

....

ABOUT YOU

Name (Mr/Mrs/Ms)...

Address ....
....
....
Postcode.. Daytime tel nos ....

Email...
Please only give us your mobile phone number/email if you wish to hear from us about other products and services from the AA and partners by text or mms.

Which age group are you in?
Under 25 ☐   25–34 ☐   35–44 ☐   45–54 ☐   55+ ☐

How many trips do you make a year?
Less than1 ☐   1 ☐   2 ☐   3 or more ☐

ABOUT YOUR TRIP

Are you an AA member?   Yes ☐ No ☐

When did you book? .... month .... year

When did you travel?...............month .... year

Reason for your trip?   Business ☐ Leisure ☐

How many nights did you stay? ....

How did you travel?   Individual ☐ Couple ☐ Family ☐ Group ☐

Did you buy any other travel guides for your trip? ....

If yes, which ones?...

Thank you for taking the time to complete this questionnaire. Please send it to us as soon as possible, and remember, you do not need a stamp (unless posted outside the UK).
AA Travel Insurance call 0800 072 4168 or visit www.theaa.com

Titles in the KeyGuide series:
Australia, Barcelona, Berlin, Britain, Brittany, Canada, China, Costa Rica, Croatia, Florence and Tuscany, France, Germany, Ireland, Italy, London, Mallorca, Mexico, New York, New Zealand, Normandy, Paris, Portugal, Prague, Provence and the Côte d'Azur, Rome, Scotland, South Africa, Spain, Thailand, Venice, Vietnam, Western European Cities.

The information we hold about you will be used to provide the products and services requested and for identification, account administration, analysis, and fraud/loss prevention purposes. More details about how that information is used is in our privacy statement, which you'll find under the heading "Personal Information" in our terms and conditions and on our website: www.theAA.com. Copies are also available from us by post, by contacting the Data Protection Manager at AA, Fanum House, Basing View, Basingstoke, Hampshire RG21 4EA.

We may want to contact you about other products and services provided by us, or our partners (by mail, telephone, email) but please tick the box if you DO NOT wish to hear about such products and services from us. ☐

AA Travel Insurance call 0800 072 4168 or visit www.theaa.com

Entrepreneurial Intensity

Entrepreneurial Intensity

Sustainable Advantages for
Individuals, Organizations,
and Societies

Michael H. Morris

Foreword by Leyland Pitt

QUORUM BOOKS
Westport, Connecticut • London

Library of Congress Cataloging-in-Publication Data

Morris, Michael H.
   Entrepreneurial intensity : sustainable advantages for
individuals, organizations, and societies / Michael H. Morris; foreword
by Leyland Pitt.
      p.   cm.
   Includes bibliographical references and index.
   ISBN 0–89930–975–5 (alk. paper)
   1. Entrepreneurship.   I. Title.
HB615.M674   1998
338'.04—dc21   97–31518

British Library Cataloguing in Publication Data is available.

Library of Congress Catalog Card Number: 97–31518
ISBN: 0–89930–975–5

First published in 1998

Quorum Books, 88 Post Road West, Westport, CT 06881
An imprint of Greenwood Publishing Group, Inc.

Printed in the United States of America

The paper used in this book complies with the
Permanent Paper Standard issued by the National
Information Standards Organization (Z39.48–1984).

10 9

Copyright Acknowledgments

The author and publisher are grateful for permission to reproduce portions of the following copyrighted material:

Table 3.1, "Criteria for Evaluating Opportunities," from J.A. Timmons, *New Venture Creation: Entrepreneurship in the 1990s* (Homewood, IL: Irwin, 1990). Copyright 1990. Reprinted with permission of The McGraw-Hill Companies.

Figure 4.2, " 'Missing the Boat' and 'Sinking the Boat' Risk," from "Missing the Boat and Sinking the Boat: A Conceptual Model of Entrepreneurial Risk." Reprinted with permission from *Journal of Marketing,* published by the American Marketing Association, Peter R. Dickson and Joseph J. Giglierano, Vol. 50 (July 1986), 64.

Table 5.1, "Selected Findings on the Role of Environmental Conditions in Facilitating Entrepreneurship," from D.R. Gnyawali and D.S. Fogel, "Environments for Entrepreneurship Development: Key Dimensions and Research Implications," *Entrepreneurship: Theory and Practice,* 18(4) (1994), 47–49. Reprinted with permission.

Figure 7.1, "Key Business Dimensions and Entrepreneurship," from H. Stevenson, M.J. Roberts, and H.I. Grousbeck, *New Business Ventures and the Entrepreneur,* 4th ed. (Burr Ridge, IL: Irwin, 1994). Permission to reproduce granted by Harvard Business School Publishing, August 1997.

To Minet

Entrepreneur, Scholar, Partner, Friend

Contents

Illustrations

TABLES

FIGURES

Foreword

In a recent *Harvard Business Review* article, Amar Bhide writes lucidly about the questions every entrepreneur must answer. These include

- What kind of enterprise do I need to build?
- What risks and sacrifices does such an enterprise demand?
- Can I accept those risks and sacrifices?
- Is the strategy well defined?
- Can the strategy generate sufficient profits and growth?
- Is the strategy sustainable?
- Are my goals for growth too conservative or too aggressive?
- Do I have the right resources and relationships?
- How strong is the organization?

He goes on to emphasize that the problems entrepreneurs confront every day would overwhelm most managers. Not least among these problems, in my opinion, would be how to answer the questions Bhide poses. While they seem quite straightforward and simple, they lie at the very heart of entrepreneurship itself.

This book will facilitate the answering of these questions by scholars, teachers, researchers, and managers, and most importantly, by entrepreneurs themselves. In it, Michael Morris demonstrates conclusively that entrepreneurship is a process characterized by innovation, proactive behavior, and the willingness to assume risk. All of these attributes are critical to the well-being of our societies today, yet in so many aspects of everyday life they are sorely lacking. In my opinion, the most important contribution of the book is that Morris convinces the reader that entrepreneurship is not just something that small start-up business firms do, but rather that it should be a pervasive facet of our lives. In large and small firms, in for-profit and nonprofit organizations, and in government itself, the entrepreneurial spirit lives, unstifled by bureaucracy, indifference, and comfort.

Entrepreneurship is in danger of becoming another popular "buzzword," loosely applied by consultants, government officials, managers, and others to describe all manner of activity. People use the term "entrepreneurial" to describe potential they see in their children, a job category, departments in their companies, an approach to solving a problem, the strategies their competitors are using, great leaders they admire, countries they have visited, and many other things. Morris moves us beyond the vague conceptualizations and the popular myths. He demonstrates that entrepreneurship is a measurable phenomenon, and that people, companies, and nations should have strategies for managing the role that entrepreneurship will play in their futures. His concept of entrepreneurial intensity (EI) enables us to apply entrepreneurship in specific contexts and to continually enhance the levels of EI that are achieved.

The text is written with all the scholarly rigor one would expect from an outstanding researcher, scholar, and teacher. Yet the spirit of the entrepreneur shines through, and the book is eminently readable. If you are a manager in a large or small organization, I know that you will find a whole host of practical ideas to apply. If you are a researcher in the general field of management, or in entrepreneurship particularly, I expect that you will exploit this text as a valuable scholarly resource. If you are an entrepreneur, I trust that you will find yourself constantly testing ideas against the contents of the book. And if you are a student of entrepreneurship, I hope that you will learn both passively and actively from it.

Michael Morris is a researcher whose work has appeared in the premier journals of his various disciplines. He is a teacher who has classes with students ranging from undergraduates through MBAs to hardened executives on the edges of their seats with his enthusiasm and style. He is also an entrepreneur. He brings these talents to life once more in the pages of this book.

Leyland Pitt
Professor of Marketing and Strategy
Cardiff Business School
University of Wales
Cardiff, United Kingdom

Preface

It has been said that we live in the "age of entrepreneurship." One tends to wonder exactly what this means. Entrepreneurship has actually been with us for a very long time. History is filled with stories of great entrepreneurs who created significant change and built sizable empires. Economists have focused on the concept for well over 200 years. Many courses have been offered and books published that address the subject. So, what is different today?

Obviously, one difference is that the amount of entrepreneurial activity the world over is at unprecedented levels. The number of business start-ups, patents granted, new products and services, technological process improvements, and new organizational forms being introduced is clearly at an all-time high, with reason to believe it will only get higher. And this activity knows no geographic boundaries. With the fall of communism and the opening up of free trade around the world, there is an explosion of entrepreneurship in country after country. The beauty of the current entrepreneurship is that it is also quite democratic. It knows no limitations in terms of the age, race, gender, IQ, cultural background, or politics of the people who make it happen. We find it coming from the most unusual quarters, with everyone from 80-year-old grandmothers to formerly virulent anti-capitalists creating new ventures. And we find entrepreneurial behavior applied in firms small and large, as well as in non-profit organizations, political movements, and even government agencies.

But the age of entrepreneurship is defined by much more than an increase in activity. It represents a fundamental change in our way of thinking about business, life, and the environments in which we find ourselves. This new way of thinking centers around the concepts of individual responsibility and personal choice.

Let's first consider the individual. The age of entrepreneurship is one in which we focus on the microcosm before the macrocosm, where approaches are bottom-up not top-down, and small units in alliance consistently outdo large organizations that rely on scale and control. Words like devolution, downsizing, decentralization, and empowerment attempt to capture this movement away from the concentrated center to the diverse individual. Entrepreneurship today involves a recognition that people can affect change in their environments and are ultimately responsible for the course that their lives take. Each of us has innate entrepreneurial potential, and each of us can make a meaningful difference in our neighborhoods, schools, workplaces, volunteer efforts, and social encounters. However, we can only do so by taking personal responsibility for change, contribution, and improvement.

Just as critical is the need to recognize that, while the individual is both a valued and respected player in the entrepreneurial age, he/she represents the means rather than the ends. Entrepreneurship is not about self-aggrandizement, hero worship, or greed. It is about individuals who are able to build, share with, motivate, and grow teams of other individuals. Jointly, they create value where there was none. They do so by putting together resources in a slightly (and sometimes significantly) different way than anyone before them. Their willingness to dream and to act on those dreams is not limited by the resources they currently control.

The age of entrepreneurship is also an age of choice. Entrepreneurs have created many of these choices, and their survival today depends on their ability to continually expand and enhance these choices for society's members. Any choice in life (e.g., products, schools, jobs, partners, social encounters, religions) involves a risk-reward trade-off. Entrepreneurship is about recognizing choices for what they are, finding the opportunity in the choices that come along, creating choices where there appear to be none to make, and learning from each and every choice that we make, regardless of the outcome.

This means that entrepreneurship is no longer something that we do at a point in time. It represents a guiding philosophy as well as a behavioral process that can be managed throughout our lives. As a philosophy, the concern is with a consciousness of, and respect for, opportunity, innovation, calculated risk-taking, and tolerance of failure. Behaviorally, there is a need for each of us to develop a personal strategy for determining how much entrepreneurship should be demonstrated at different points in time and in different settings or situations.

The title of this book, *Entrepreneurial Intensity*, is meant to capture this new age of entrepreneurship. The word ''intensity'' refers to something that is highly concentrated; has a high degree of strength, force or energy; or is strongly emphasized. Entrepreneurial intensity (EI) refers to strength or force of entrepreneurship at three levels: in our individual lives, in the lives of the organizations that we create or join, and throughout our societies. The central thesis of this book is that entrepreneurship occurs in varying degrees and amounts, and that environments can be created in ways that heighten EI at all three levels. It is my sincere wish that in these pages the reader discovers a new relevance for entrepreneurial thinking, dreaming, acting, doing, and being. Further, I hope that the framework, models, and concepts proposed herein provide a kind of broad blueprint for applying that entrepreneurial thinking and doing to the entire panorama of life's experiences.

1

Common Myths Regarding Entrepreneurship

INTRODUCTION

This book is about entrepreneurship, a subject that has certainly come into vogue in recent years. Governments are trying to foster it, individuals are attempting to practice it in unprecedented numbers, and large organizations are desperately seeking to recapture it. In response, there has been a dramatic increase in the number of schools and universities around the world that are teaching courses in entrepreneurship, with many of them establishing entire programs on the subject. Similarly, the number of books, academic journals, and magazines devoted to the topic has exploded in the past decade.

In the pages that follow, we will attempt to explore various aspects of entrepreneurship, establish why entrepreneurship matters, and discuss how it can be encouraged. As will become apparent, entrepreneurship is a field containing many open controversies and unresolved issues. Considerable disagreement surrounds even such basic questions as the definition of the word "entrepreneurship." This might seem surprising, given that entrepreneurship as an academic or intellectual concept has been around for well over two hundred years. We will put forward a number of perspectives and ideas regarding these issues, while also inviting the reader to develop his/her own opinions.

As a beginning point, it may be helpful to address some of the many misconceptions that people seem to have about entrepreneurship. A number of myths continue to influence the way people think about the topic. These misunderstandings can lead to serious mistakes on the part of would-be entrepreneurs, executives attempting to stimulate the spirit of entreprenurship within established companies, and public policy makers seeking to facilitate entrepreneurial behavior at the societal level. Below, we have identified thirteen key myths or misconceptions and attempted to explain the reality that lies behind each of them.

MYTH 1: ENTREPRENEURSHIP IS ABOUT STARTING AND RUNNING A SMALL BUSINESS

Not necessarily. Entrepreneurship represents a *growth-oriented* outlook. It implies an *innovative* and *proactive* approach to challenges, tasks, needs, obstacles, and opportunities. Many small firms are not very entrepreneurial and can be considered "mom and pop" type operations. For most of these businesses, the only entrepreneurial thing they ever do is open up in the first place. They then become fairly stagnant, complacent, status quo operations. While they do serve an important purpose in the economy, they do not provide much dynamism.

Consider the owner of a dry cleaners located within a strip shopping center in a local suburb. If you ask this individual where he will be in five years, the honest answer is, "I'll be right here. I'm not getting rich but we get by. I don't have to work for anyone else; I employ a family member or two; my boy works here during his summer breaks; and we take a vacation every couple of years." Now, consider the person in the same circumstances who is asked the same question but produces a strategic plan that lays out an inventive franchising and financing concept that he/she has come up with. This person explains, "I have streamlined and standardized my operations and plan to have fifteen of these dry cleaners around the local area in two years, and 150 of them located throughout the region within five years." It is this second person who more closely reflects the entrepreneurial spirit.

Table 1.1 represents a summary of key differences between conventional small businesses and more highly entrepreneurial firms. At the same time, it is dangerous to draw this distinction too finely, for reasons expounded upon in misconception three, below.

Instead, our perspective in this book is that entrepreneurship is a universal construct that is applicable to any person, organization (private or public, large or small), or nation. A growing body of evidence suggests that an entrepreneurial orientation is critical for the survival and growth of companies as well as for the economic prosperity of nations. The need for entrepreneurship is greatest where there are diminishing opportunity streams, as well as rapid changes in technology, consumer needs, industry and market structures, social values, and political roles. In addition, where decision-makers are confronted with short decision windows, unpredictable resource needs, and a lack of long-term control over the environment, entrepreneurship becomes vital.

MYTH 2: ENTREPRENEURSHIP IS A DISCRETE EVENT THAT JUST "HAPPENS"

Entrepreneurship is not a fixed event that occurs at a particular point in time. There is a dynamic process involved, and this process takes time to unfold. The

Table 1.1

Differences between Typical Small Businesses and Entrepreneurial Ventures

Characteristics of Many Small Businesses	*Characteristics of Entrepreneurial Ventures*
Stable	Unstable
Status quo-oriented	Change-oriented
Not aggressive	More aggressive
Socially-oriented	Commercially-oriented
Interaction between personal and professional activities	Clear separation of personal and professional activities
Involvement of family members	Involvement of professionals
More informal	More formal
Tactical	Strategic
Present-oriented	Future-oriented
Preference for low-risk/low-return activities	Preference for high-risk/high-return activities
Internally oriented	Externally oriented
Steady number of employees	Growing employee base with high potential for conflicts
Level resource needs	Expanding resource needs with ongoing cash shortages
Resource driven	Opportunity-driven
Concerned with personal profit, income substitution	Concerned with growth and appreciation of business value

process has specific, identifiable stages, starting with the identification of an opportunity and ending with the ultimate success or failure of an implemented concept. As a process, entrepreneurship can be managed. This is a critical point, for the more we recognize that the steps, or stages, are manageable, the more the mystique surrounding entrepreneurship begins to disappear. Further, the process nature of entrepreneurship means that it can be applied in organizations of all sizes and types. The typical entrepreneurial idea undergoes significant modification as it evolves through the process. Getting it through the process requires persistence and patience, aggressiveness, and adaptability.

MYTH 3: ENTREPRENEURSHIP IS AN "EITHER/OR" THING

People seem to approach entrepreneurship in "black and white" terms. Someone is either an entrepreneur, or they are not. Similarly, a company is either thought to be entrepreneurial or not. We place people and organizations into boxes, drawing absolute distinctions between a manager and an entrepreneur, between an entrepreneurial enterprise and a bureaucratic company.

In the real world, entrepreneurship happens in different amounts, and in varying degrees. Every person and every organization does entrepreneurial things at one time or another. Some do them more (versus less) often, and some do things that are more (versus less) innovative. The key is to recognize that entrepreneurship is a *variable* phenomenon.

MYTH 4: ENTREPRENEURSHIP IS ABOUT TAKING WILD RISKS

It is popular to think of entrepreneurs as "gamblers," who are willing to "bet the farm." They seize an opportunity and passionately go after it, throwing caution to the wind. The truth is entrepreneurs are *not* wild-eyed risk-takers. They are willing to assume risks but not unnecessary ones. In fact, their risk profile does not tend to differ statistically all that much from society at large. The difference is, they are *calculated* risk-takers. They will carefully analyze and evaluate a situation. They systematically identify the key financial, technical, market, and other specific risk factors. They then go about identifying ways to manage and minimize the likelihood of any of the underlying risk factors occurring.

Successful entrepreneurs are also good at sharing risks by involving partners, leveraging resources, leasing instead of owning, borrowing instead of buying, and contracting instead of hiring. The entrepreneur is not preoccupied with controlling lots of assets or using only his/her own resources. He/she is not into status or power but only wants to do what is necessary to turn a dream, or vision, into reality.

MYTH 5: ENTREPRENEURS ARE BORN

People also get caught up in the personality cult that surrounds entrepreneurship. We think of the Richard Bransons, Ted Turners, Akio Moritos, and Bill Gateses of the world and associate entrepreneurship with some superhuman class of individuals who are somehow different from the rest of us. After literally hundreds of studies on the psychological and sociological makeup of the entrepreneur, one conclusion emerges—entrepreneurs are not a unique and separate group that is somehow genetically predisposed to be entrepreneurial. They are not born. Rather, we all have some degree of entrepreneurial potential within us. The ability to develop and realize that potential is very much a function of one's environment.

One has only to consider the finding that children who have entrepreneurial role models earlier in life are more likely to do something entrepreneurial than are those who do not have such role models. Similarly, why is there so much more entrepreneurship per capita in some countries (e.g., the United States, Taiwan) than right next door in neighboring countries (e.g., Mexico, China)? The truth is that entrepreneurs are made by learning and experience. Entrepreneurship has much less to do with the gene pool, and much more to do with the family, school, social, and work environments to which individuals are exposed. The making of an entrepreneur depends on the accumulation of activities, skills, and knowledge over time and includes large doses of self-development.

MYTH 6: ENTREPRENEURSHIP IS ABOUT GREED

We've all heard about the entrepreneur who wants to be a millionaire by age 30 and retired by age 40, but it just doesn't work that way. Even for those few who are rich and retired at 40, the probability is quite high that, at 41, they are right back at it, pursuing some new opportunity. The real motivator behind entrepreneurial behavior is not money, and it certainly is not power or position. Entrepreneurial individuals tend to be driven by a desire to achieve, to make a difference, to do what others said could not be done, to overcome all the obstacles and naysayers.

This is not to suggest that they don't like money. At least for entrepreneurs in the private sector, financial returns play an important role. They serve as a source of feedback, letting the entrepreneur know that progress is being made. Entrepreneurial events are ambiguous and take time to unfold. The tremendous uncertainty, especially in the early stages, can lead the entrepreneur to question himself/herself, the validity of the concept, and whether it is all worth it. Rewards are like road markers, letting the entrepreneur know that he/she is on the right path and is moving towards his/her destination.

MYTH 7: ENTREPRENEURSHIP IS ABOUT INDIVIDUALS

Entrepreneurial events usually have a driving force behind them in the form of a visionary individual, who assumes risk and persists in making change happen. Even in corporate settings, there must be a champion who keeps a new concept alive and sells the organization on it. By definition, entrepreneurship implies a degree of individual autonomy and a sense of personal ownership of an innovative concept. Innovation rarely involves a democratic process.

But entrepreneurship does not happen without teams. Not only is the existence of a team critical, but so too is the quality of the team. Too much must be done to bring a concept to reality, and no one individual has either the time or the talent to do it all well. The obstacles are formidable and the technical, legal, financial, marketing, managerial and administrative requirements are complex.

The challenge is to balance the need for individual initiative with the spirit of cooperation and group ownership of innovation. This balance occurs over the stages of the entrepreneurial process. Individuals are needed to provide the vision, unwavering commitment, and internal salesmanship without which nothing could be accomplished. But as the process unfolds, the entrepreneur requires teams of people with unique skills and resources. These teams may be formal or ad hoc, and their membership is likely to be fluid as people join or depart depending on the venture's requirements. Moreover, the members of the team do more than provide functional expertise or perform specific tasks. They modify and adapt the innovation as new and unanticipated obstacles arise, all the while being kept on track and spurred on by the entrepreneurial champion. They bring to the task a spirit of camaraderie and a sense of being a part of something important. In the final analysis, it is important that this amorphous group take ownership of, and credit for, the end-product.

MYTH 8: THERE IS ONLY ONE TYPE OF ENTREPRENEUR

There is no single prototype of the entrepreneur. They come from all walks of life and represent a diverse mix of age groups, races, religions, cultures, genders, and occupational backgrounds. Some do entrepreneurial things all of their lives, while others pursue some highly entrepreneurial opportunity only after spending a relatively conservative career in some large bureaucratic company.

At the same time, researchers have noted the existence of general categories of entrepreneurs (see Table 1.2). For instance, a distinction has been drawn between *craftsmen* entrepreneurs, who tend to have a fairly narrow educational background, limited social awareness, a limited time orientation, and demonstrate a tendency to create fairly rigid ventures, and *opportunistic* entrepreneurs, who often have a broader educational and social background, are more socially confident and future-oriented, and tend to create more adaptive, growth-oriented enterprises (Smith and Miner, 1983). Another identified category consists of

Table 1.2
Different Categories of Entrepreneurs Identified by Researchers

Author	Categories
Smith (1967)	Craftsmen Entrepreneurs
	Opportunistic Entrepreneurs
Smith (1967) and Kets de Vries (1977)	R&D/Technical/Inventor Entrepreneurs
Vesper (1980)	Solo Self-Employed
	Team Builders
	Independent Innovators
	Pattern Multipliers
	Economy of Scale Exploiters
	Acquirers
	Buy-Sell Artists
	Conglomerators
	Apparent Value Manipulators
Kao (1991)	Creative/Charismatic Entrepreneurs
	Conventional Entrepreneurs
Miner (1996)	Personal Achievers
	Supersalespeople
	Real Managers
	Expert Idea Generators

technical/inventor entrepreneurs. These are people with strong technical backgrounds, who often have worked in a research and development or related position within a large organization and start a venture based on some invention, technology application, or new process that they have designed.

More recently, in a landmark study by Miner (1996), four major types of entrepreneurs were identified based on extensive research: the *personal achiever*, the *supersalesperson*, the *real manager*, and the *expert idea generator*. Personal achievers are classic entrepreneurs, with lots of initiative, strong commitment, and a strong internal locus of control (sense of their ability to affect change in their external environment). They like feedback about their performance and enjoy planning and goal setting for future achievements. Supersalespeople demonstrate a great deal of feeling for, and a desire to help, other people. They are very good at the soft sell and external relationship building, while letting others handle the administrative details of running the business. Real managers like power and taking charge. They often come from a large corporate background, are competitive and decisive, employ the hard sell, and are good at building an existing business into something much larger. Expert idea generators build a venture around new products, niches, or processes that they have been involved with inventing. They are often involved with high-tech companies.

MYTH 9: ENTREPRENEURSHIP REQUIRES LOTS OF MONEY

Entrepreneurial individuals are opportunity-driven, not resource-driven. They do not limit the scope of their vision by how much money, time, staff, or related resources they own. Rather, they go after their dream by leveraging resources— by borrowing, begging, partnering, sharing, leasing and recycling resources. And it's not just financial resources. Studies of entrepreneurial failure suggest that the problem far more often is related not to money, but to other resources, such as poorly prepared managers, inadequate distribution channels, or ill-conceived marketing efforts.

While people tend to associate entrepreneurship with coming up with creative business concepts, the reality is that lots of us come up with novel ideas for a new product or service but never do anything about it. In many instances, the truly entrepreneurial behavior comes into play in identifying usable resources and finding ways to acquire them without necessarily buying them outright. Also, good entrepreneurs manage to get more out of less when it comes to resources. They often move ahead without all of the requisite resources and fill in the gaps as opportunities arise.

MYTH 10: ENTREPRENEURSHIP IS ABOUT LUCK

No, entrepreneurs tend to create their own "luck." It's much more about hard work, creative insight, in-depth analysis, adaptability, and an openness to opportunity when it comes along. The evidence suggests there is no best way to generate new ideas and concepts. However, entrepreneurs are more externally-than internally-focused, more opportunity- than resource-driven. In addition, experience is a vital factor.

The entrepreneurial individual recognizes a pattern—a trend, a possibility, an incongruity, an unmet need—when it is still taking shape. These patterns consist of recognizable pieces that can be adapted from one context to another and then put together. They are rooted in the market, and more specifically, in such factors as customer needs, customer problems, buying behavior, limitations of current products, and assumptions made by competitors. Further, the ability to link knowledge of technology, familiarity with distribution channels, awareness of regulatory and legal restrictions, and an understanding of the capabilities of suppliers to these aspects of the market is what typically produces brilliant and successful entrepreneurship. Entrepreneurs come up with unique concepts for capitalizing on a trend or need and do so while the window of opportunity is open. They put themselves in the right place at the right time and are fully aware of the downside chances of failure.

MYTH 11: ENTREPRENEURSHIP STARTS WITH A NEW PRODUCT OR SERVICE

This is one of the great mistakes many would-be entrepreneurs make. They come up with a novel product concept without ever determining whether a need exists, how extensive that need actually is, how satisfied customers are with current products, what their switching costs would be, and whether they will be able to see meaningful advantages in the new product. Entrepreneurship does not start with the product or service one would like to sell. It starts with an opportunity, and opportunities are rooted in the external environment.

There is an old adage, "If you build a better mousetrap, the world will beat a path to your door." The greater likelihood is that the grass will grow tall on the pathway to your door unless

- the mousetrap is targeted to the right audience,
- that audience is sufficiently large,
- the audience is sufficiently unhappy with, and not loyal to, the product they are using now,
- distributors exist who are willing to carry the mousetrap given their current product assortment and supplier agreements,
- the technology used in making the mousetrap is not likely to become outdated any time soon,
- competitors are not likely to introduce a better or cheaper version of the mousetrap a month from now,

- economic conditions do not exist that make, or will make, the mousetrap unaffordable, and

- new safety regulations are not on the horizon that will force a redesign in the mousetrap to bring it into compliance.

This is but a sample of environmental factors that can spell defeat for even the most innovative new products or services.

It is easy to get very excited about any new concept. The problem is that the people who come up with these ideas often suffer from a kind of "entrepreneurial myopia." They are preoccupied with the product (and keeping it a secret), as well as with all the start-up obstacles and issues that they face. As a result, they just assume that a market need exists, that suppliers and distributors are readily available, and that environmental conditions will remain as they are now.

MYTH 12: ENTREPRENEURSHIP IS UNSTRUCTURED AND CHAOTIC

There is also a tendency to think of entrepreneurs as gunslingers—as people who shoot from the hip and ask questions later. They are assumed by some to be disorganized and unstructured, leaving it to others to keep things on track. The reality is that entrepreneurs are heavily involved in all facets of their venture, and they usually have a number of balls in the air at the same time. As a result, they are typically well-organized individuals. They tend to have a system, perhaps elaborate, perhaps not, but personally designed to keep things straight and maintain priorities. In fact, their system may seem strange to the casual observer, but it works.

When doing something entrepreneurial, one is dealing with the unknown, and there is a need to be tolerant of ambiguity. Unanticipated developments arise all the time. Success is often a function of how prepared one is for the unknown, and how much one is in a position to capitalize on the unanticipated. The entrepreneur's ability to meet daily and weekly obligations, while also growing the venture, and while also being able to move quickly when novel events occur, is strongly affected by his/her organizing capabilities. Plans, outlines, forecasts, checklists, timetables, budgets, databases, and pert charts are examples of tools that the contemporary entrepreneur always keeps close at hand.

MYTH 13: MOST ENTREPRENEURIAL VENTURES FAIL

Many do, but many do not. Failure rates differ widely by industry, ranging from as low as 10% to as high as 90%. Further, they drop off significantly after the first few years of operation. And yet, entrepreneurship is about making change happen. People (customers, managers in established companies, bankers, suppliers, distributors, regulators) naturally resist change. Thus, in any entrepreneurial effort, there will be all of the natural obstacles, plus all of the arbitrary obstacles that people throw in one's path. Failure becomes a normal by-product of entrepreneurial effort. It is the number-one way in which an entrepreneur learns what works and does not work. He/she then determines the reasons why and makes the adjustments necessary to fight another day.

It is also important to keep in mind that failure rates rise as the amount of entrepreneurial activity rises. One has only to consider the high failure rates experienced by new restaurants. Many of these fail because they are not well-positioned, the target market is not well-defined, or the restaurant fails to adequately differentiate itself. However, the failure rate is especially high because the number of start-ups is high. The same goes for bankruptcy. Some observers read a newspaper headline that says the bankruptcy rate is at an all-time high and interpret this as bad news. But bankruptcy rates are high because the new business start-up rate is also at an all-time high.

So, failure rates are likely to go up in the coming years as the number of new products introduced and new businesses started goes up. The likelihood of failure can be significantly reduced, however, by planning for, and systematically managing, the stages in the entrepreneurial process.

CONCLUSIONS

One might wonder why myths such as the ones outlined in this chapter continue to persist. The answer is that, while we tend to encounter entrepreneurship all around us, brushing up against it in all facets of our lives, there really is no "discipline of entrepreneurship." That is, unlike chemistry or physics or accounting, entrepreneurship is not really a formal discipline. It is a cross-disciplinary pursuit, involving bits of psychology, finance, engineering, sociology, marketing, physics, management, mathematics, and economics.

As an area of serious intellectual endeavor, most of the substantive research on entrepreneurship has been done during this century, and much of it in the past 30 years. As a result, there is no universal theory of entrepreneurship, and most of the theories one does find in the research are borrowed from other disciplines. It is difficult to talk of "paradigm shifts" in the field, for the paradigms themselves have yet to be clearly defined. Few laws, principles, or established concepts exist to guide the efforts of academics or practitioners who are attempting to better understand the phenomenon of entrepreneurship. Further, much of the published research is qualitative in nature, which makes it very difficult to draw generalizable conclusions.

Yet, entrepreneurship makes great headlines. The success stories of people like Ray Kroc of MacDonald's, Sochiro Honda of Honda Motors, or Herb Kelleher of Southwest Airlines are nothing short of inspirational. And when some entrepreneur gets into serious ethical or legal trouble, as John Delorean and his controversial automobile did a few years back, that also receives a lot of attention. As stories are told and retold regarding these heroes and anti-heroes, a mythology is created.

However, entrepreneurship is mostly about simple people with simple dreams. As we have seen, the practical requirements of turning these dreams into realities are quite far removed from many of the myths and misconceptions. In the chapters that follow, we will examine a number of these issues in much more detail. We begin first by exploring the controversies surrounding the definition of entrepreneurship.

REFERENCES

Kao, J.J. 1991. *The Entrepreneur*. Englewood Cliffs, N.J.: Prentice-Hall.

Kets de Vries, M.F.R. 1977. "The Entrepeneurial Personality: A Person at the Crossroads." *Journal of Management Studies*, 14 (1), 34–57.

Miner, J.B. 1996. *The 4 Routes to Entrepreneurial Success*. San Francisco: Berrett-Koehler Publishers.

Ronstadt, R.C. 1985. *Entrepreneurship: Text, Cases and Notes*. Dover: Lord Publishing.

Smith, N.R. 1967. *The Entrepreneur and His Firm: The Relationship between Type of Man and Type of Company*. East Lansing: Bureau of Business and Economic Research, Graduate School of Business Administration, Michigan State University.

Smith, N.R., and Miner, J.B. 1983. "Type of Entrepreneur, Type of Firm, and Managerial Motivation: Implications for Organizational Life Cycle Theory." *Strategic Management Journal*, 4 (4), 325–340.

Stevenson, H.H., Roberts, M.J., and Grousbeck, H.I. 1994. *New Business Venture and the Entrepreneur*. Homewood, IL: Irwin.

Timmons, J.A. 1990. *New Venture Creation: Entrepreneurship in the 1990s*. Homewood, IL: Irwin.

2

Understanding Entrepreneurship

INTRODUCTION

The significant amount of attention devoted to entrepreneurship in recent years has resulted in a keen awareness of the limitations of current knowledge on the subject. For instance, various critiques of the available literature note the lack of a well-defined research agenda or set of research programs in the entrepreneurship field and conclude that most of the contemporary research lacks clarity and consensus regarding purpose, theoretical perspective, focus, level of analysis, time frame, and methodology.

A more fundamental concern is the general lack of agreement among scholars and practitioners regarding the nature of entrepreneurship itself. A wide variety of definitions can be found in even the most recent literature, and conflicting schools of thought continue to debate the relative importance of various underlying dimensions and to disagree about the distinction between a small business and an entrepreneurial venture.

In this chapter, we attempt to provide a unified conceptualization regarding the nature and scope of entrepreneurship. A distinction is drawn between inputs to, and outputs from, the entrepreneurial process. It is argued that entrepreneurship is a variable phenomenon that can be characterized in terms of its intensity. An integrative model is presented that relates entrepreneurial input, process, intensity, and output. It is argued that the model can be applied at the level of the individual, the organization, or society.

THE DEFINITION OF ENTREPRENEURSHIP

Historical Perspectives

Although the term "entrepreneurship" has been used in a business context for well over 200 years, there is still considerable disagreement about its meaning. While there have been literally hundreds of perspectives, seven of the most prevalent themes are summarized in Table 2.1.

Early definitions, which were formulated principally by economists, tended to emphasize assumption of risk, supply of financial capital, arbitrage, and coordination of the factors of production. While the entrepreneur was clearly involved in the initiation of a business, these early perspectives saw entrepreneurship as an ongoing function in companies, and profit as a return for addressing uncertainty and coordinating resources. Economists historically failed to make a distinction between management and entrepreneurship or to address the differences between small and large firms. In fact, distinctions like these were not well established until the 1930's. Even so, the prevalent tendency has been to associate entrepreneurship with small business start-up and management. As such, the entrepreneur has been viewed as someone who assumes the social, psychological, and financial risks necessary to start and run a small business (Hisrich and Peters, 1992).

Based on the work of Schumpeter and others in the first half of the twentieth century, the central focus shifted to innovation, or carrying out unique combi-

Table 2.1

Seven Perspectives on the Nature of Entrepreneurship

Creation of Wealth	Entrepreneurship involves assuming the risks associated with the facilitation of production in exchange for profit.
Creation of Enterprise	Entrepreneurship entails the founding of a new business venture where none existed before.
Creation of Innovation	Entrepreneurship is concerned with unique combinations of resources that make existing methods or products obsolete.
Creation of Change	Entrepreneurship involves creating change by adjusting, adapting, and modifying one's personal repertoire, approaches, and skills to meet different opportunities available in the environment.
Creation of Employment	Entrepreneurship is concerned with employing, managing, and developing the factors of production, including the labor force.
Creation of Value	Entrepreneurship is a process of creating value for customers by exploiting untapped opportunities.
Creation of Growth	Entrepreneurship is defined as a strong and positive orientation towards growth in sales, income, assets, and employment.

nations of resources in order to create new products, services, processes, organizational structures, sources of supply, and markets (Schumpeter, 1934). Entrepreneurs were engaged in an activity labelled "creative destruction," where they continually made existing methods and products obsolete by successfully introducing innovations. An extension of the Schumpeterian perspective is to identify entrepreneurship as a principal agent of change in society (Tropman and Morningstar, 1989).

More recently, there has been an attempt to distinguish the entrepreneur from entrepreneurship. The traits and characteristics that distinguish entrepreneurs from both managers and society-at-large was a favored research topic in the late 1970's and early 1980's (e.g., Brockhaus and Horwitz, 1985). The entrepreneur has been characterized in terms of such psychological traits as achievement motivation, internal locus of control, calculated risk-taking, tolerance of ambiguity, and persistence. Similarly, sociological characteristics, such as being first in the family birth order, being an immigrant, and having early role models, have been associated with the entrepreneurial personality. While the findings and implications of this stream of research remain controversial, attention has moved from examining the person to examining the process.

Conceptualizing entrepreneurship as a process that occurs in an organizational setting has significantly advanced the field, with considerable attention devoted to describing the steps or stages involved and identifying factors that both constrain and facilitate the process. Although the process has been described in various ways, it generally consists of the stages involved in moving from identifying opportunity to defining a business concept, assessing resource requirements, acquiring those resources, and managing and harvesting the venture (Stevenson et al., 1989).

Approached as a process, entrepreneurship could be applied to organizations of all sizes and types, according to a number of researchers in the 1980's (Brandt, 1986; Kao, 1989; Pinchot, 1985). In fact, a number of the benchmarking studies of corporate excellence suggested that the best-run companies tended to be more entrepreneurial than their competitors in the same or other industries. To the extent that this is true, the distinction between management and entrepreneurship again became unclear. Moreover, some observers began to distinguish entrepreneurial from nonentrepreneurial firms, concluding that many small firms were not especially entrepreneurial.

There has also been a tendency to associate entrepreneurship with the creation of employment (Hornaday and Aboud, 1971). Studies by Birch (1979) and others have demonstrated that entrepreneurial firms are responsible for creating a disproportionate number of the new jobs in the economy. Recent years have witnessed a related conceptualization, in this case emphasizing growth. Growth in this context refers to a significant increase in sales, profits, assets, employees, and sometimes locations. The entrepreneurial firm is defined as one that proactively seeks to grow and is not constrained by the resources currently under its control.

Contemporary Perspectives

While these perspectives suggest an evolution of thought regarding entrepreneurship, elements of all of them can be found in contemporary thinking. This assertion is based on a critical review of 77 definitions found in journal articles and leading textbooks published over a five-year period. We performed a content analysis of key words on definitions appearing in journal articles from *Entrepreneurship: Theory and Practice*, the *Journal of Business Venturing*, the *Journal of Small Business Management*, and the *American Journal of Small Business*, as well as textbooks from major publishing houses that have achieved widespread adoption.

The results are summarized in Table 2.2. As can be seen, fifteen key terms appear at least five times in the sample. The most common terms include starting or creating a new venture; innovating or creating new combinations of resources; pursuing opportunity; the marshaling of necessary resources; risk-taking; profit-seeking; and creating value. These findings are consistent with the results of a delphi study by Gartner (1990), in which he surveyed 36 scholars and 8 business leaders. Based on a set of 90 attributes, Gartner found the greatest emphasis was placed on creating a new venture, adding value, capitalizing on opportunity, bringing resources to bear, and implementing innovations.

Synthesizing the Different Perspectives

Gartner (1990) concludes that a universal definition has yet to emerge but suggests we are talking about a single phenomenon. It is, further, a phenomenon with multiple components. The relative importance of these different components can differ based on the environmental context within which an entrepreneurial event occurs.

And yet, it would seem that the available perspectives can be synthesized into a unified framework. First, the focus should be on the process rather than the (entrepreneurial) person, while recognizing the indispensable role played by the person. Second, it is helpful to distinguish components that are inputs during the entrepreneurial process from those that are outcomes. For instance, the entrepreneurial person represents an input, while economic growth is an outcome. Third, it should be recognized that the set of necessary inputs is fairly definite, while the set of possible outcomes may or may not happen.

Accordingly, the following is proposed as a synthesis of contemporary thought:

Entrepreneurship is the process through which individuals and teams create value by bringing together unique packages of resource inputs to exploit opportunities in the environment. It can occur in any organizational context and results in a variety of possible outcomes, including new ventures, products, services, processes, markets, and technologies.

Table 2.2
Key Terms Identified in Content Analysis of 75 Contemporary Definitions of Entrepreneurship*

		# of Mentions
1.	Starting/founding/creating	41
2.	New business/new venture	40
3.	Innovation/new products/new market	39
4.	Pursuit of opportunity	31
5.	Risk-taking/risk management/uncertainty	25
6.	Profit-seeking/personal benefit	25
7.	New combinations of resources, means of production	22
8.	Management	22
9.	Marshalling resources	18
10.	Value creation	13
11.	Pursuit of growth	12
12.	A process activity	12
13.	Existing enterprise	12
14.	Initiative-taking/getting things done/proactiveness	12
15.	Create change	9
16.	Ownership	9
17.	Responsibility/source of authority	8
18.	Strategy formulation	6

*Terms receiving five or more mentions.

THE VARIABLE NATURE OF ENTREPRENEURSHIP

Entrepreneurship has attitudinal and behavioral components. Attitudinally, it refers to the willingness of an individual or organization to embrace new opportunities and take responsibility for effecting creative change. This willingness is sometimes referred to as an "entrepreneurial orientation." Behaviorally, it includes the set of activities required to move a concept or idea through the key stages in the entrepreneurial process to implementation.

Underlying entrepreneurial attitudes and behaviors are three key dimensions:

innovativeness, risk-taking, and proactiveness (Covin and Slevin, 1989; Miller, 1983; Morris and Sexton, 1996). These dimensions are illustrated in Figure 2.1 and will be explored in further detail in Chapter Four. Innovativeness refers to the seeking of creative, unusual, or novel solutions to problems and needs. These solutions take the form of new technologies and processes, as well as new products and services. Risk-taking involves the willingness to commit significant resources to opportunities having a reasonable chance of failure. These risks are typically moderate and calculated. Proactiveness is concerned with implementation, with doing whatever is necessary to bring an entrepreneurial concept to fruition. It usually involves considerable perseverance, adaptability, and a willingness to assume some responsibility for failure.

To the extent that an undertaking demonstrates some amount of innovativeness, it can be considered an entrepreneurial event and the person behind it an entrepreneur. Further, any number of entrepreneurial events can be produced in a given time period. Accordingly, entrepreneurship is not an either-or determination but a question of ''how often'' and ''how much.''

The variable nature of entrepreneurship is illustrated in Figure 2.2. The vertical axis represents the ''how often'' aspect or the *frequency* of entrepreneurship (number of entrepreneurial events), while the horizontal axis captures the ''how much'' dimension or the *degree* of entrepreneurship (the extent to which such events are innovative, risky, and proactive). Further, as illustrated in the model, the concept of *entrepreneurial intensity* (EI) is introduced to capture the combined effects of both the frequency and degree of entrepreneurial behaviors. Importantly, this framework describes the phenomenon of entrepreneurship at both the micro (i.e., the individual entrepreneur or organization) and the macro (i.e., the national or global region) levels. In later chapters, we shall elaborate on this concept and its application on various levels.

AN INTEGRATIVE MODEL OF ENTREPRENEURSHIP

Now let us try to bring all of these ideas together to provide an integrative model regarding the nature of entrepreneurship. Figure 2.3 illustrates such a model. The input-output approach to the definition of entrepreneurship has been expounded upon to include the process perspective and to incorporate the variable nature of entrepreneurship (i.e., intensity). Moreover, the proposed model

Figure 2.1
Underlying Dimensions of Entrepreneurship

Figure 2.2
The Variable Nature of Entrepreneurship

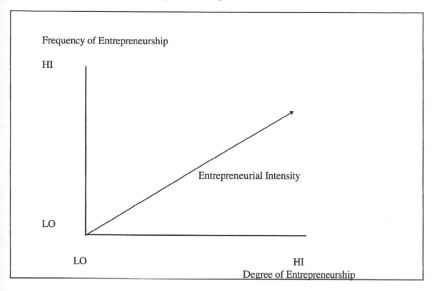

Frequency of Entrepreneurship

HI

Entrepreneurial Intensity

LO

LO   HI
Degree of Entrepreneurship

Figure 2.3
An Integrative Model of Entrepreneurial Inputs and Outcomes

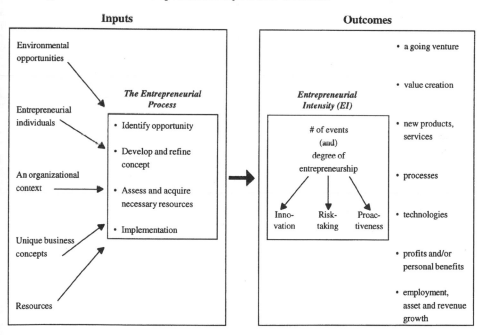

Inputs   Outcomes

Environmental opportunities

The Entrepreneurial Process

Entrepreneurial individuals

- Identify opportunity

- Develop and refine concept

An organizational context

- Assess and acquire necessary resources

Unique business concepts

- Implementation

Resources

Entrepreneurial Intensity (EI)

# of events
(and)
degree of entrepreneurship

Inno-vation   Risk-taking   Proac-tiveness

- a going venture

- value creation

- new products, services

- processes

- technologies

- profits and/or personal benefits

- employment, asset and revenue growth

reflects the arguments in the literature regarding the importance of innovation and growth orientation by acknowledging that both are possible outcomes of the entrepreneurial process.

The input component of Figure 2.3 focuses on the entrepreneurial process itself and identifies five key elements that contribute to that process. The first is environmental opportunities, such as a demographic change, the development of a new technology, or a modification to current regulations. Next is the individual entrepreneur, the person who assumes personal responsibility for conceptualizing and implementing a new venture. The entrepreneur develops some type of business concept to capitalize on the opportunity (e.g., a creative approach to solving a particular customer need). Implementing this business concept typically requires some type of organizational context, which could range from a sole proprietorship run out of the entrepreneur's home, or a franchise of some national chain, to an autonomous business unit within a large corporation. Finally, a wide variety of financial and non-financial resources are required on an ongoing basis. These key elements are then combined over the stages of the entrepreneurial process. Stated differently, the process provides a logical framework for organizing entrepreneurial inputs.

The output component of Figure 2.3 first includes EI. Thus, the process can result in any number of entrepreneurial events and can produce events that vary considerably in terms of how entrepreneurial they are. Based on this level of intensity, final outcomes can include one or more going ventures, value creation, new products and processes, profit, and economic growth. Moreover, the final outcome is often failure, and the economic, psychic, and social costs associated with failure.

The model not only provides a fairly comprehensive picture regarding the nature of entrepreneurship, it can also be applied at different levels. For example, at the organizational level, the model describes the phenomenon of entrepreneurship in both the independent start-up company and the venture that is developed within a strategic business unit of a large corporation. Similarly, the input-output perspective is descriptive of entrepreneurship in not-for-profit organizations, with the outputs taking on slightly different interpretations, such as the creation of social value or growth measured in number of volunteers or dollars of contributions.

It is also possible to examine the input-output framework at the societal level. Much like organizations, countries would appear to differ in terms of their EI (e.g., Hughes, 1986; Wilken, 1979). These differences can be traced to the relative availability of the inputs described in Figure 2.3. Moreover, outputs such as the overall rate of new product introduction, national value added, economic growth rates, and societal wealth appear to be related to the relative emphasis on the entrepreneurial process within a society (Birch, 1981; Morris and Lewis, 1991).

CONCLUSIONS

In this chapter, we have attempted to clarify the nature of entrepreneurship by adopting an input-output perspective. The input component enables us to focus on the process nature of entrepreneurship and distinguishes the entrepreneur from the entrepreneurial process. The output component stresses the variable nature of entrepreneurship and recognizes the variety of possible consequences that can result when the inputs are combined.

Arguably, the inputs cited in Figure 2.1 are prerequisites for successful entrepreneurship. That is, without an opportunity, or absent the key resources, the entrepreneurial process is likely to result in failure with little in the way of positive outcomes. Alternatively, even with the right set of inputs, the likelihood of any particular outcome is highly uncertain. For instance, a going concern might result, but it may not be especially profitable.

Importantly, the framework is descriptive of entrepreneurial efforts in organizations of all sizes and types. Consequently, significant implications can be drawn for both prospective entrepreneurs and practicing managers. For the entrepreneur pursuing a start-up venture, the input component of the framework is perhaps more problematic, as the organizational context must be created and critical resources are much more difficult to obtain. While the entrepreneur is able to exercise considerable latitude, he/she must be wary of overcommitting to ill-defined business concepts or pushing concepts before (or after) the strategic window of opportunity opens (or closes).

For established firms, the inputs are more readily available, since the organizational context and many of the needed resources are in place. However, the entrepreneurial individual is hard to find and keep, and the organizational environment in these firms poses numerous obstacles, such as bureaucratic structures and restrictive control systems. Managers must ensure that mechanisms exist for identifying environmental opportunities, and that there is an organizational mind-set to capitalize on such opportunities whenever possible. Further, an organizational environment that supports the activities of entrepreneurial individuals or work groups is essential for the success of the process. The culture and reward system of the enterprise must be one that encourages innovative thinking, fosters proactive behaviors, and perhaps most important, tolerates failure when appropriate. Finally, managers must be willing to allocate the resources necessary to ensure that entrepreneurial initiatives have a reasonable chance of success, despite the potential risks that must be assumed.

It is also important for entrepreneurs and managers to appreciate the varying nature of entrepreneurship. Entrepreneurial behaviors need not be revolutionary nor must they occur continuously. Rather, entrepreneurial activity can vary in accordance with the industry and environmental conditions. One might expect EI to be higher in small start-up firms, as large public corporations may be less willing to pursue ventures that effectively represent "betting the farm." Ultimately, however, managers must be sensitive to the level of EI exhibited by their firms and the appropriateness of that level in relation to the competitive environment in which they operate.

Finally, the outcomes of the entrepreneurial process will also vary across firms. While growth and profitability will typically be among the set of desired outcomes, the relative importance of each may vary significantly from firm to firm. Independent start-ups may be more concerned with cash flow and profits (which flow more directly to the entrepreneur), while established firms may focus on a variety of strategic outcomes. For instance, organizations that operate in highly volatile and rapidly changing environments may direct their entrepreneurial efforts toward achieving a competitive edge that will build the company's market share. Firms that operate in more stable or mature industries may look toward entrepreneurial initiatives to lower costs, improve efficiency, or otherwise improve organizational profitability. Under certain conditions, entrepreneurial efforts may be directed toward achieving some blend of both kinds of objectives. Regardless of the specific outcomes desired, it is important for the manager to have a clear understanding of the potential strategic benefits of the outcomes of the entrepreneurial process.

REFERENCES

Birch, D.L. 1979. *The Job Generation Process*. Washington, DC: U.S. Department of Commerce.

Birch, D.L. 1981. "Who Creates Jobs." *The Public Interest*, 65 (Fall), 62–82.

Brandt, S.C. 1986. *Entrepreneuring in Established Companies*. Homewood, IL: Irwin.

Brockhaus, R., and Horwitz, P.S. 1985. "The Psychology of the Entrepreneur." In D. Sexton and R. Smilor (eds.), *The Art and Science of Entrepreneurship*. Cambridge, MA: Ballinger Publishing, 25–48.

Carland, J.W., Hoy, F., Boulton, W.R., and Carland, J.C. 1984. "Differentiating Entrepreneurs from Small Business Owners." *Academy of Management Review*, 9, 354–359.

Covin, J.G., and Slevin, D.P. 1989. "Strategic Management of Small Firms in Hostile and Benign Environments." *Strategic Management Journal*, 10 (January), 75–87.

Gartner, W.B. 1985. "A Conceptual Framework for Describing the Phenomenon of New Venture Creation," *Academy of Mangement Review*, 10 (4), 696–706.

Gartner, W.B. 1990. "What Are We Talking About When We Talk About Entrepreneurship?" *Journal of Business Venturing*, 5, 15–28.

Hisrich, R.D., and Peters, M.P. 1992. *Entrepreneurship: Starting, Developing, and Managing a New Enterprise*, 2nd ed. Homewood, IL: Irwin.

Hornaday, J.A., and Aboud, J. 1971. "Characteristics of Successful Entrepreneurs." *Personal Psychology*, 24, 141–153.

Hughes, J. 1986. *The Vital Few: The Entrepreneur and American Economic Progress*. New York: Oxford University Press.

Kao, J.J. 1989. *Entrepreneurship, Creativity and Organization*. Englewood Cliffs, NJ: Prentice-Hall.

Low, M., and MacMillan, I. 1988. "Entrepreneurship: Past Research and Future Challenges." *Journal of Management*, 14 (2), 139–161.

Miller, D. 1983. "The Correlates of Entrepreneurship in Three Types of Firms." *Management Science*, 29 (July), 770–791.

Morris, M.H., and Lewis, P.S. 1991. "Entrepreneurship as a Significant Factor in Societal Quality of Life." *Journal of Business Research*, 13 (1) (August), 21–36.

Morris, M.H., and Paul, G.W. 1987. "Innovation in Conservative and Entrepreneurship Firms." *Journal of Business Venturing*, 2, 247–259.

Morris, M.H., and Sexton, D.L. 1996. "The Concept of Entrpreneurial Intensity: Implications for Company Performance." *Journal of Business Research*, 36 (1), 5–14.

Pinchot, G., III. 1985. *Intrapreneuring*. New York: Harper & Row.

Schumpeter, J.A. 1934. *The Theory of Economic Development*, trans. R. Opie from the 2nd German ed. (1926). Cambridge: Harvard University Press.

Sexton, D.L., and Bowman-Upton, N.B. 1991. *Entrepreneurship Creativity and Growth*. New York: MacMillan Publishing Company.

Stevenson, H.H., Roberts, M.J., and Grousbeck, D.E. 1989. *Business Ventures and the Entrepreneur*. Homewood, IL: Irwin.

Tropman, J.E., and Morningstar, G. 1989. *Entrepreneurship Systems for the 1990's*. New York: Quorum Books.

Wilken, P.H. 1979. *Entrepreneurship: A Comparative and Historical Study*. Norwood, NJ: Ablex Publishing Corporation.

3

The Process of
Entrepreneurship

INTRODUCTION

Considerable uncertainty and ambiguity surround any entrepreneurial event.
Both to the outsider and the entrepreneur, things may seem disorderly on a good
day, and chaotic on most days. By definition, the entrepreneur is attempting to
do something that has not been done before. And so, one is tempted to conclude
that entrepreneurship cannot really be managed. Innovation implies something
new, something unknown, something that has not happened yet. Management
implies control, structure, and systems. But how does one control the unknown?

The reality is that one does not. There is a real need for flexibility and adaptability in any entrepreneurial venture. Successful entrepreneurs are able to combine adaptability with persistence in adjusting their concept when confronted
with the obstacles, both natural and arbitrary, that arise along the way.

At the same time, entrepreneurial events are not only easier to understand,
but they tend to achieve better results, when approached as a process. The
benefits of a process approach are many. The first, and most obvious, is that the
entrepreneurial effort can be broken down into specific stages, or steps. Although
these stages will tend to overlap, and one may have to periodically revisit an
earlier stage, they tend to evolve in a logical progression. Further, approached
as a process, entrepreneurship is not some mystical or chance event pursued
only by those who are genetically endowed to be entrepreneurs. Rather, it is a
manageable event that can be pursued by literally anyone. In addition, the entrepreneurial process can be applied in any organizational context, from the start-
up venture to the large corporation to the public enterprise. Finally, processes
are sustainable. They can be ongoing or continuous. As such, entrepreneurship
can become a normal, ongoing activity in any organization.

Numerous attempts to conceptualize the entrepreneurial process have appeared in the literature. For our purposes, we will rely and expand upon the version of the process introduced in Chapter 2 and illustrated in Figure 3.1. Here, a number of the major options that are available to the entrepreneur in each of the stages have also been identified. Let us further explore each of the stages.

IDENTIFY AN OPPORTUNITY

Entrepreneurship does not start with products (or services or other innovations). The beginning point is an opportunity, which can be defined as a favorable set of circumstances creating a need or an opening for a new business concept.

The reality is that many new concepts fail not because of the concept itself, but because there was no opportunity. An example is the so-called "better mousetrap that nobody wanted." Arguably the largest single category of new product failures, these are products that are state-of-the-art advances, ones the casual observer might find quite interesting. And yet, when the test of the marketplace is applied, not enough customers are willing to buy, either because they are already satisfied, the concept is too complex or difficult to understand, the perceived switching costs are too high, or they don't have a need.

Unfortunately, a lot of would-be entrepreneurs, both in start-up and established companies, adhere to the *Field of Dreams* philosophy. In that popular film, Kevin Costner was repeatedly told, "If you build it, they will come." All too often, new products, services, and processes are developed in isolation, where the sole focus is overcoming technical, financial, and human challenges. The market opportunity is simply assumed. The next lesson learned by many companies is that having a better product at a better price with better product availability and better customer service means nothing if the market does not exist, is too small, or is unwilling to change; if competitors are completely entrenched; or if any other components of the opportunity are inadequate.

The entrepreneur must specify exactly what the opportunity consists of and quantify its size and scope to the extent possible. What is the source of the opportunity? Is it a new market segment, a demographic change, an opening that has resulted from deregulation, or some other factor? In an attempt to systematically identify where opportunities originate, Peter Drucker (1985) proposes seven major sources:

- The unexpected—events or developments that produce successes or failures that were not expected, often because of limitations in our own assumptions, vision, knowledge, or understanding.
- An incongruity—discrepancies between what is and what "ought" to be, or between what is and what everyone assumes to be, or between efforts and expectations, or in the logic of a process.

Figure 3.1
Examples of Alternatives Available at Each Stage in the Entrepreneurial Process

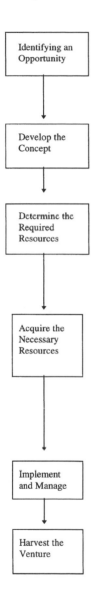

Changing Demographics
Emergence of New Market Segments
Process Needs
New Technologies
Incongruities
Regulatory Change
Social Change

New Products
New Services
New Processes
New Markets
New Organizational Structures/Forms
New Technologies
New Sales or Distribution Channels

Need for Skilled Employees
Need for General Management Expertise
Need for Marketing and Sales Expertise
Need for Technical Expertise
Need for Financing
Need for Distribution Channels
Need for Sources of Supply
Need for Production Facilities
Need for Licenses, Patents, and Related Legal Protection

Debt
Equity
Leveraging Schemes
Outsourcing
Leading
Contract Labour
Temporary Staff
Supplier Financing
Joint Ventures
Partnerships
Barter
Gifts

Implementation of Concept
Monitoring of Performance
Payback to Resource Providers
Reinvestment
Expansion
Achievement of Performance Goals

Absorption of New Concept into Mainstream Operation
Licensing of Rights
Sell Venture
Go Public
Shut Down Venture

- Process needs—unmet needs or requirements within the process of a business, an industry, or a service. These needs are based on some task or job that is not currently being adequately performed or accomplished.
- Changes in industry or market structures—substantive changes in regulation, competitive entrants, power in distribution channels, technology, or market requirements that lead to industry or market restructuring.
- Demographic changes—emerging developments in the size, age, structure, composition, employment, income, or educational status of the population.
- Changes in perception, mood, or meaning—regardless of realities, general change in outlook, perception, or interpretation of the facts, which in turn influences the needs, wants, and expectations of people.
- New knowledge—development of new information, insights, technological advances, or theories.

Implicit in Drucker's analysis is the need to attack the conventional wisdom or the popular assumptions regarding a potential opportunity. Procter & Gamble's successful introduction of Depends disposable diapers represents a case in point. Introduced many years after their successful Pampers brand, which effectively created the plastic/paper diaper market for babies, Depends was targeted to senior citizens who experienced diminished bladder control or incontinence. Procter & Gamble's success was directly attributable to its defiance of the traditional assumptions that senior citizens had no money (as a group they are fairly well off), lived shut-in lives (today they tend to live active, rich lifestyles), and were too few in number (they are the fastest growing demographic segment in the United States).

A related concern is the need to recognize the existence of a "window of opportunity." For every new concept, there is an optimal time period during which it can be implemented with a reasonable chance of success. Alternatively, one can introduce something too early: for instance, before the actual number of people with a need is sufficiently large, or people are sufficiently dissatisfied with the current solution, or the necessary support infrastructure is in place. Similarly, one can introduce a concept too late: for instance, when competitors are well-entrenched, distribution channels are saturated, growth in demand has leveled off, and new technologies are emerging. In one interesting study across a number of decades, researchers found product failure was most often related to entering the market too early in the 1960's and too late in the 1980's (Bruno and Leidecker, 1988).

A good opportunity has certain characteristics. In Table 3.1, a set of criteria are presented for evaluating an opportunity, including some possible benchmarks for distinguishing attractive from unattractive opportunities. While some of these may be somewhat arbitrary, they provide some general guidelines.

DEVELOP THE CONCEPT

With an opportunity clearly in mind, the entrepreneur specifies a business concept. This could be a new product or service, a new process or method for

Table 3.1
Criteria for Evaluating Opportunities

Criterion	Stronger Opportunity ─────────── Weaker Opportunity	
Market Issues		
Need	Identified	Unclear
Customers	Reachable; receptive	Unreachable or loyalties established
Payback to user/customer	Less than one year	Three years or more
Potential for value added or Created	High	Low
Likely product life	Long; beyond time to recover investment plus profit	Short; less than time to recover investment
Industry structure	Disorganized competition or emerging industry	Aggressively competitive or highly concentrated or mature industry or declining industry
Potential market size	$100 million sales	Unknown or less than $10 million sales
Market growth rate	Growing at 30% to 50% or more	Contracting or less than 10%
Gross margins	40% to 50% or more; sustainable	Less than 20%; volatile
Market share attainable (year 5)	20% or more; leader	Less than 5%
Economic/Harvest Issues		
Profits after tax	10% to 15% or more; durable	Less than 5%; fragile
Time to:		
Break even	Under 2 years	More than 3 years
Positive Cash Flow	Under 2 years	More than 3 years
ROI potential	25% or more/year; high value	Less than 15% - 20%/year; low value
Value	High strategic value	Low strategic value
Capital requirements	Low to moderate; fundable	Very high; unfundable
Exit mechanism	Present or envisioned harvest options	Undefined; illiquid investment
Competitive Advantage Issues		
Fixed and Variable Costs		
Production	Lowest	Highest
Marketing	Lowest	Highest
Distribution	Lowest	Highest
Degree of Control		
Prices	Moderate to strong	Weak
Costs	Moderate to strong	Weak
Channels of supply/ resources	Moderate to strong	Weak
Channels of distribution	Moderate to strong	Weak
Barriers to Entry		
Proprietary protection/ Regulation advantage	Have or can gain	None
Response/lead time advantage in technology; product, market innovation, people, location, resources, or capacity	Resilient and responsive; have or can gain	None
Legal, contractual advantage	Proprietary or Exclusivity	None
Sources of differentiation	Numerous, substantive, sustainable	Few or none, nominal, replicable
Competitor's mindset and Strategies	Live and let live; not self-destructive;	Defensive and strongly reactive
Other Issues		
Management team	Existing, strong, proven performance	Weak, inexperienced, lacking key skills
Contacts and networks	Well-developed; high quality; accessible	Crude; limited; inaccessible
Risk	Low	High
Fatal flaws	None	One or More

Source: Adapted from Timmons (1990). Reprinted with permission of The McGraw-Hill Companies.

accomplishing a task, or a new application of an existing product, among other possibilities. As outlined in Table 3.2, there are at least seven major categories of innovative concepts, and within the process category, ten additional subcategories.

There is a tendency to confuse the opportunity with the business concept. This mistake is one of the leading causes of product and business failure. Entrepreneurs frequently have highly innovative ideas for new product concepts, but no opportunity exists. Or, the opportunity is real, but the business concept

Table 3.2
Classifying Types of Innovations

-   New to the world product or service
-   New to the country and/or market product or service
-   New product or service line (new to the company)
-   Addition to a company's existing product or service line
-   Product/service improvement, revision, including addition of new feature or option or change
-   New application of existing product or service, including application to a new market segment
-   Repositioning of an existing product or service
-   Process improvement that leads to customer value creation, productivity enhancement, and/or cost reduction
    *   new administrative system or procedure
    *   new production method
    *   new marketing or sales approach
    *   new customer support program
    *   new distribution channel or method
    *   new logistical approach
    *   new financing method
    *   new pricing approach
    *   new purchasing technique
    *   new organizational form or structure

---

is too vague or unclear. Sometimes what one is calling a business concept is little more than a loosely defined opportunity, while at other times the business concept is assumed to be the opportunity.

Opportunities represent potential—potential customers, potential users, potential revenue, potential cost savings. Business concepts represent ways to capitalize on that potential with new products or services or processes. Any one opportunity could conceivably be capitalized upon with a variety of different business concepts.

Consider the social environment, and specifically, the changing nature of women's participation in the labor force. In the past 20 years, women have not only entered the workplace in larger numbers but have also tended to pursue full-time instead of part-time employment, careers instead of jobs, and senior managerial positions rather than lower-level or clerical jobs. This represents an opportunity. Successful business concepts that have capitalized on this opportunity range from L'eggs panty hose to La Petite Daycare Centers, Lean Cuisine microwaveable dinners, and Bally's Health and Racquet Clubs.

Additional examples of opportunities and related business concepts are summarized in Table 3.3. Each demonstrates the point that, while one must have a well-conceptualized business concept, success demands that the concept be clearly targeted to an untapped or inadequately tapped opportunity.

What then, is a well-conceptualized business concept? Criteria for rating a concept as good, average or weak include the need for it to be

Table 3.3
Linking the Business Concept to the Opportunity

The Opportunity	The Business Concept
Decline of demographic segmentation and emergence of youthful, lifestyle-based, market segment	Ford Mustang automobile--"affordable" sports car
Large numbers of people interested in computer possibilities but intimidated by the complexities and rigors involved in the available products	Apple personal computer with simple icons and a playful mouse
Baby boomers reaching late 30's-early 40's, with successful careers and families	Taurus automobile with state-of-art design and positioning both in terms of quality and function
Working women with active lifestyle and no time to spare	L'eggs panty hose packaged distinctively, positioned and promoted as "convenience" and distributed through grocery stores
Fast pace of change and information overload experienced by many consumers	Cable News Network (CNN) with ability to provide instant information, any time, from anywhere
Perception by many that we are generally overweight, out of shape, and/or afflicted with various health ailments	General Nutrition Centers (GNC)--national chain of health foods, vitamins, and diet products
Growing numbers of women employed full-time and/or female heads of households	La Petite Daycare Centers franchised nationally
Emergence of senior citizen market with disposable income and desire for active lifestyles	Depends disposable plastic/paper diapers
Growing need for business resources from professionals and students away from or without an office of their own	Kinko's self-help copy, computer, and communications centers

- unique
- comprehensive
- internally consistent
- feasible
- sustainable

Uniqueness refers to the need for a degree of novelty or innovativeness in a new concept. Failure commonly results from initiative, me-too new products, services, or processes, as the customer or user sees little net advantage and refuses to switch from something with which he/she is already familiar. Without sufficient uniqueness, differentiation becomes problematic. *Comprehensiveness* concerns the extent to which the new concept addresses all of the relevant strategic variables that make up the user's total value proposition. Thus, the entrepreneur must look beyond the product itself and consider such issues as packaging, pricing, distribution channels, location, and logistics. *Internal consistency* involves an assessment of how well the components above (product, location, price, distribution) work together. For instance, is the proposed distribution channel inconsistent with the target market and the product attributes being emphasized? *Feasibility* addresses the question of realism. Can the concept be developed and implemented in a timely manner and at an acceptable cost? Is our market size estimate reasonably conservative, and have we properly acknowledged the prospective customer's loyalty to, or satisfaction with, current products? Lastly, *sustainability* has to do with whether the concept, once implemented, is likely to endure in the face of competition or alternative solutions, changing costs, new technologies, or related subsequent developments. Sustainability is also a function of the entrepreneur's ability to create barriers to entry.

DETERMINE RESOURCE REQUIREMENTS

The natural tendency is to assume that the principal resource required for any entrepreneurial event is money. Money certainly matters, and entrepreneurs are notorious for over- or under-estimating their financial requirements. However, a careful review of success and failure stories makes it clear that money is only occasionally the defining factor in explaining the performance of a given entrepreneurial project. Moreover, the persistent entrepreneur with a good idea will find the money.

No, the critical resources are typically non-financial, and identifying them requires insight, judgement, and patience. For instance, creative technical skills, a loyal distributor, a permit/license or patent, well-established customer contacts, a competent manager, or a great location might prove to be determinant factors in explaining the ultimate success of a concept. The self-confidence of entrepreneurs can lead them to believe that resources such as these are secondary, or that they can do most of these things themselves. This is a recipe for failure. Entrepreneurship is about individuals who can construct, inspire, and reinforce teams, and the shrewd entrepreneur attempts to staff teams with talent to match his/her own.

ACQUIRE THE NEEDED RESOURCES

Entrepreneurship is mostly associated with the ability to come up with inventive concepts (Stage Two in the process), but the greatest amounts of entrepreneurial behavior are actually required when attempting to obtain resources and implement the concept (Stages Four and Five). Howard Stevenson (1994, p. 5) of the Harvard Business School has suggested that entrepreneurship is concerned with ''the pursuit of opportunity without regard to resources currently controlled.'' In most cases, at the time an entrepreneur develops a concept, he/

she not only does not have the requisite resources on hand but also does not know where to get them.

Resource acquisition typically requires creative interpretation of rules. It entails begging, borrowing, and "stealing" resources from conventional and nonconventional sources. The entrepreneur in effect becomes a trader, bargainer, politician, negotiator, networker, and borrower. He/she may need to make currently owned resources appear greater than they actually are. Not surprisingly, it is in this stage that the entrepreneur also encounters a number of ethical dilemmas.

At the same time, not all resources have to be owned or directly controlled by the entrepreneur. A key concept in this regard is "leveraging." According to the dictionary, leveraging involves the mechanical advantage obtained by use of a lever, where the lever is some physical object, such as a metal rod or piece of wood. However, if we replace a few words, the concept becomes quite meaningful in a business context. Specifically, it becomes "the achievement of economic or competitive advantage through the use of resources not owned or controlled by the company."

Basically, leveraging is about renting, borrowing, leasing, chartering, contracting, or temporarily employing assets or resources instead of purchasing, employing, or owning them. It means the firm is not permanently committed to assets, which creates more flexibility and enables the firm to move more quickly in the marketplace.

Consider an example of an entrepreneur who builds a business using the leveraging concept:

- She rents her office space
- She finances the business through commercial loans
- She leases her copier, computer, company vehicle, and cell phone
- She employs only contract labor
- She outsources her production process, warehousing, accounting function, delivery service, and janitorial service
- She sells on consignment through a local retailer or through independent representatives
- She uses a plant and flower service to keep the offices looking green

And this is just a beginning. The reality is that today there are billion-dollar companies with fewer than 100 employees—everything is leveraged. Take the case of the rented or leased copier. Not only does leasing not require a large up-front capital expenditure, but copier technology is changing so fast that products are obsolete before their useful life has expired. Further, resources aren't tied up in fixed assets. Or, consider taking a loan from a bank instead of using one's own funds or attracting equity funding. The lender is the one who is tying up his/her funds, not you. Moreover, the lender is the one assuming risks for you, and the lender requires a relatively fixed return regardless of future circumstances. Finally, why would a firm choose to outsource its maintenance or information technology function? Perhaps an external vendor can do it better or cheaper because they specialize, but not always. In some cases, the firm simply determines that a certain function does not fit with its core competencies, and it can get a better return by freeing up the resources dedicated to a particular activity.

There is an even bigger benefit. Leveraging allows the firm to do more than it otherwise would. The entrepreneur can employ resources quickly and temporarily; this enables him/her to perform tasks beyond the capabilities of currently owned fixed assets and staff. It can also enhance the firm's image, while getting the staff to be more externally and opportunity focused rather than internally and resource focused.

IMPLEMENT THE CONCEPT AND MANAGE THE OPERATION

No matter how well-planned, implementation of the business concept is likely to be hectic and stressful. Tremendous learning is taking place, everyone involved in the venture is busy "doing," and the entrepreneur is faced every day with myriad decisions that must be resolved quickly. Problems and obstacles arise that were not anticipated, and a number of assumptions made when planning the concept prove to be unfounded.

Keys at this stage of the process are adaptability, tolerance of ambiguity, and a balanced internal-external focus. On the one hand, the entrepreneur must not lose sight of his/her dream or overall vision. On the other hand, he/she must be capable of adapting, modifying, and adjusting the concept, the resource requirements, the approach to acquiring resources, and the operating methods as circumstances develop. Further, given the time it takes for an entrepreneurial concept to unfold, the entrepreneur must set intermediate targets to ensure steady progress is being made along an inherently ambiguous path. In addition, the significant number of internal crises that occur, given the fact that so much learning is taking place, often creates a "fire-fighting" mentality, where the entrepreneur loses sight of external developments (e.g., with customers and suppliers).

Many entrepreneurs, brilliant as they are at putting the venture together and making things happen, are poor managers. They attempt to do too many tasks themselves and never learn to properly delegate. They tend to overcontrol employees and micro-manage the enterprise. Fear of having someone steal their innovative ideas makes them hesitant to seek advice or assistance. Further, they lead by the power of their personality. Once the venture starts to take off, they fail to bring in professional managers or institute the kinds of systems and controls necessary for sustainable growth.

HARVEST THE VENTURE

These days, opportunity windows and product life cycles are getting shorter, resources are becoming more quickly obsolete, and customer loyalties are more fleeting. Akio Morito of Sony once explained that his company's fundamental task was to make its own products obsolete. The message to the entrepreneur is not simply that he/she must be quick and nimble. Just as critical is the need for the entrepreneur to have a model regarding both how to get into the venture and how to get out.

Many possible models exist. One example might involve looking at the business as an investment in a blue chip stock versus a high-tech stock. In the blue chip stock scenario, the entrepreneur is looking for a steady, acceptable dividend each year. He/she uses the venture as a source of income into the forseeable future. With a high-tech stock, the entrepreneur expects no income as all the money is plowed back into growth and development of the business. However, he/she expects a significant capital gain in five or six years.

The model one adopts effectively defines how the concept will be harvested. One possibility is that the venture will be held onto and passed to one's heirs. Others include taking the company public, being acquired, selling the venture to a third party, licensing the rights to the concept, franchising the business, or liquidating the operation and selling off the assets.

CONCLUSIONS

In this chapter, we have explored the central notion that entrepreneurship involves a logical process. The process can be applied in literally any organizational context. The six major steps or stages in the process have been examined, and key tools and concepts for addressing each stage have been identified.

It is important to keep in mind the dynamic nature of the process. Not only do the stages overlap, but there are likely to be feedback loops between them. For instance, as an entrepreneur is developing the business concept, he/she may learn new information about the opportunity, which in turn leads to a refinement of the concept. Similarly, a change in technology or regulation may make a given resource much more affordable, which leads not only to greater reliance on that resource but also results in further modification to the concept and a change in how one plans to harvest the venture.

A related point is that opportunity tends to beget opportunity. Once an entrepreneur takes the plunge and goes after an opportunity, he/she tends to become more "opportunity aware." Moving through the stages in the entrepreneurial process is sort of like walking down a corridor, to paraphrase Ronstadt (1985). The entrepreneur suddenly becomes aware of a number of doors along the corridor that he/she never noticed before. Each door represents new or additional opportunities, and the entrepreneur, having done it once, is more likely to open some of these other doors. The danger, of course, is that everything starts to look like an opportunity, and the entrepreneur gets overcommitted or is spread too thin. Under such circumstances, one failure can bring down the entrepreneur's entire operation.

REFERENCES

Bruno, A.V., and Leidecker, J.K. 1988. "Causes of New Venture Failure 1960s vs 1980s." *Business Horizons* (November–December).

Drucker, P. 1985. *Innovation and Entrepreneurship: Practices and Principles.* New York: Harper & Row.

Ronstadt, R.C. 1985. *Entrepreneurship: Text, Cases and Notes.* Dover: Lord Publishing.

Stevenson, H., Roberts, M.J., and Grousbeck, H.I. 1994. *New Business Ventures and The Entrepeneur*, 4th ed. Burr Ridge, IL: Irwin.

Timmons, J.A. 1990. *New Venture Creation: Entrepreneurship in the 1990s.* Homewood, IL: Irwin.

4

The Concept of
Entrepreneurial Intensity

INTRODUCTION

What does it mean to say that a venture is "entrepreneurial"? As was suggested in Chapter 2, entrepreneurship is not an either-or phenomenon, it is a variable. There is some level of entrepreneurship in every person, organization, and nation. Even in the most oppressive days of communist rule in the former Soviet Union, one could find a variety of examples of people doing entrepreneurial things. Similarly, within the most bureaucratic government organizations in the United States, people such as Hyman Rickover, J. Edgar Hoover, and Robert Moses have produced significant entrepreneurship. The question then becomes one of determining how entrepreneurial a given person or event is. Again, entrepreneurship has three underlying dimensions: innovativeness, risk-taking, and proactiveness. Let us explore each of these dimensions in greater detail.

EXPLORING THE UNDERLYING DIMENSIONS OF ENTREPRENEURSHIP

Innovativeness

The first dimension that defines an entrepreneurial orientation is innovativeness. Here, the concern is with how much an entrepreneurial concept represents a departure from what is currently available. To what extent is it more (or less) novel, unique, or creative?

A range, or continuum, of possibilities exists. Does the concept address a need that has not previously been addressed, such as the first laser surgical tool? Does it change the way one goes about addressing a need, such as the fax machine or the microwave oven? Is it a dramatic improvement over conventional solutions, such as the cellular telephone or the electric automobile? Does it represent a minor modification or improvement to an existing product, such as a longer lasting lightbulb or a less fattening dessert product? Is it really just the geographic transfer of a proven product, such as the sale of frozen yogurt in a country where it is unknown?

The examples above are all products. Innovation can also take the form of new or improved services. The tremendous growth of the service sector is a testimonial to the entrepreneurial spirit at work. America Online (AOL), The Discovery Zone, and La Petite Daycare Centers represent just a few of the thousands of successful entrepreneurial service concepts. In fact, given their intangible nature and the ease with which they can be replicated, services lend themselves to continuous innovation and improvement.

The third innovation frontier is in processes, or finding new and better ways to accomplish a task or function. Many entrepreneurial ventures produce products that are fairly standard and certainly not all that unique. However, they have come up with highly innovative process innovations that are a major source of competitive advantage (i.e., they result in lower costs, faster delivery, improved quality, or better customer service). Examples include innovative production techniques, distribution approaches, selling methods, purchasing programs or administrative systems. Consider the novel hub-and-spoke transport system used by Federal Express to provide quick and dependable overnight parcel delivery service, or the highly inventive production techniques mastered by Nucor that resulted in speciality grade quality steel produced in a mini-mill.

Risk-Taking

Anything new involves risk, or some likelihood that actual results will differ from expectations. Risk-taking involves a willingness to pursue opportunities that have a reasonable likelihood of producing losses or significant performance discrepancies. Our emphasis is not on extreme, uncontrollable risks, but instead on the risks that are moderate and calculated. Entrepreneurship does not entail reckless decision making, but rather, a reasonable awareness of the risks involved—including financial, technical, market, and personal—and an attempt to manage these risks. Also referred to as "riskiness" by Venkatraman (1989), these risks are reflected in the various resource allocation decisions made by an individual or organization, as well as in the choice of products, services, and markets to be emphasized. It can thus be viewed as both an individual-level trait, as well as an organization-level construct.

An interesting perspective on calculated risk-taking is provided by Hamel and Prahalad (1993). They use the analogy of the baseball player who comes to bat concentrating hard on perfecting his swing and hitting a home run. Further, the batter is preoccupied with his batting average. Obviously, if he comes to bat only twice and gets a hit on one of those occasions, the result is a .500 batting average. Unfortunately, companies often approach the development of new products, services, and technologies as does our baseball player. They pursue few projects, rely on cautious, go-slow strategies that aim to perfect the concept, and hold off on introduction until they are certain they have a winner. Meanwhile, scrappier competitors beat them to the punch.

Successful hits are a function of both one's batting average and the number of times one comes to bat. The message is that entrepreneurs and entrepreneurial companies need to come to bat more often. Risks are better managed by focusing on frequent, lower-risk market incursions with a variety of new product and service options targeted to different segments and niches. By engaging in lots of experiments, test markets and trial runs, the entrepreneur is better able to determine what works and what does not. Such quickened learning may come at the expense of minor failures, but it is also likely to ensure more sustainable long-term success.

One might be tempted to assume that innovativeness and risk-taking are directly correlated: that doing more innovative things means taking higher risks and vice versa. In reality, the relationship may be more complex. In Figure 4.1, this relationship is pictured as a curvilinear function. As can be seen, risk is high when the company ignores new product and service opportunities, and when it pursues truly innovative opportunities. Companies that do not innovate are faced with higher risk of market and technology shifts that go unperceived and are capitalized on by competitors.

At the same time, firms that engage in breakthrough innovation are often

Figure 4.1
Relating Innovativeness to Risk

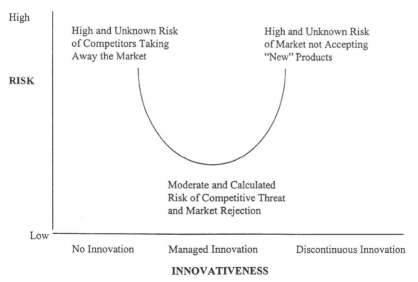

moving into uncharted waters where no one has been before. Consequently, there is high risk of market failure through improper market analysis, mismatch of technology to market needs, or inadequate design of marketing programs. In the middle of the continuum, risks are moderate, while success rates are the highest.

It is also critical to note that, from an entrepreneurial standpoint, there are actually two sides to the risk equation. Discussions of risk generally focus on what happens if the entrepreneur pursues a concept and it does not work out. This side of the equation has been labeled "sinking the boat" risk by Dickson and Giglierano (1986). It is reflected in such factors as a poorly conceptualized concept, bad timing, an already well-satisfied market, inadequate marketing and distribution approaches, and inappropriate price levels. The other side of the equation is called "missing the boat" risk, or the risk in *not* pursuing a course of action that would have proven profitable. It occurs when the entrepreneur delays acting on a concept for too long and is pre-empted by competitors or changing market requirements. Here, the entrepreneur is being too cautious or conservative and often seeks more security in the form of additional market research, financial data, or inputs from consultants.

Figure 4.2 illustrates the relationship between these two types of risk. With more planning time, sinking the boat risk steadily declines, as the entrepreneur is able to refine his/her concept, put together a better resource package, and identify more effective approaches to production, marketing and other operational concerns. Meanwhile, missing the boat risk initially falls, as the entrepreneur identifies fatal flaws that represent reasons to rethink or shelve the concept.

Figure 4.2
"Missing the Boat" and "Sinking the Boat" Risk

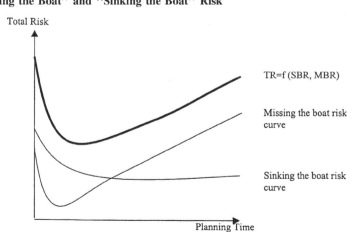

Source: Dickson and Giglierano (1986). Reprinted with permission.

He/she may let competitors be the first to the market, let them make the mistakes from which he/she can learn, then enter with a much better market solution. However, the longer the delay in action, the more likely that competitors will move quickly and lock up the market opportunity, or that the market opportunity itself will disappear. Total risk, then, becomes a function of the outcomes if one acts and if one does not.

Proactiveness

The third dimension of entrepreneurship, proactiveness, is less easy to define. The opposite of reactiveness, it is not found in the dictionary. Nonetheless, it has come into popular usage as a term to describe an action orientation. The essence of proactiveness is captured in the well-known Nike slogan "Just do it." Miller (1987) sees it as a facet of assertiveness, which he in turn views as a dimension of strategy making. He sees entrepreneurial firms as *acting on rather than reacting to* their environments. His short scale to operationalize proactiveness includes three items: following or leading competitors in innovation; favoring the tried and true versus emphasizing growth, innovation, and development; and trying to cooperate with competitors versus trying to undo them.

Proactiveness is also concerned with implementation, with taking responsibility and doing whatever is necessary to bring an entrepreneurial concept to fruition. It usually involves considerable perseverance, adaptability, and a willingness to assume some responsibility for failure. In his study of the strategic orientation of business enterprises, Venkatraman (1989) uses the term to refer to a continuous search for market opportunities and experimentation with potential responses to changing environmental trends. He suggests it is manifested and, indeed, could be operationalized in terms of

- seeking new opportunities that may or may not be related to the present line of operations;
- introduction of new products and brands ahead of competition; and
- strategically eliminating operations that are in the mature or declining stages of the life cycle.

Bateman and Crant (1993) introduce "proactive behavior" as a dispositional construct that identifies differences between people in the extent to which they take action to influence their environments. This construct holds that behavior is both internally and externally controlled, and that situations are as much a function of individuals as individuals are themselves functions of their environments. As Buss (1987) has put it, people are not "passive recipients of environmental pressures": they influence their own environments. Bateman and Crant's (1993) perspective on the essential characteristic of proactive behavior is one which fits the entrepreneurial construction very well—namely that people can intentionally and directly change their current circumstances, social or non-social.

To illustrate the proactiveness dimension, consider the engineer who works for a firm that delivers engineering services to customer sites, many of which are in remote locations. Routinely, crews must drive company trucks loaded with sensitive technical equipment to these customer sites. Traveling along bumpy, poor roads, and often dirt roads in the countryside, the equipment is often damaged or knocked out of calibration. The field crews often have to wait at a site while more equipment is sent out from the head office, or they must return another day. Our engineer takes it upon himself to fix the problem in his free time, and using resources he begs, borrows, and "steals" from the organization. Lo and behold, he comes up with a design for the truck bed that would allow the truck to be driven through a veritable hurricane, and the equipment would not come out of calibration or otherwise be damaged. Is this proactive? Yes and no. He certainly has done much more than analyze a problem; he has produced a solution. But proactiveness is more than this. He has to sell his solution to his boss, who likely will not have the time or money to support the engineer. He then has to persist in selling it to the organization, which will entail overcoming large numbers of obstacles and playing politics. If, in the end, the company's truck fleet is converted to his design, successful entrepreneurship has occurred. Even better than this would be the subsequent licensing of his design to other companies.

ENTREPRENEURIAL INTENSITY—DEGREE AND FREQUENCY OF ENTREPRENEURSHIP

The variable nature of each of these dimensions suggests that degrees of entrepreneurship are possible. Thus, a given event might be highly or nominally innovative, entail significant or limited risk, and require varying degrees of proactiveness. Further, entrepreneurship occurs in varying amounts. A given person, organization, or society might produce a steady stream of entrepreneurial events over time or generate no entrepreneurial behavior beyond the initial start-up. Organizations can be characterized, then, based on both the degree and amount of entrepreneurship they produce, or on their entrepreneurial intensity (EI).

Entrepreneurial intensity is thus a linear combination of "degree of entrepreneurship," or the extent to which events are innovative, risky, and proactive, and "amount of entrepreneurship," or the frequency with which entrepreneurial events occur. This does not mean that more of each of the three dimensions of entrepreneurship is necessarily ideal. Rather, entrepreneurship is ideally a balanced process, but the appropriate degree depends on the situation.

To visualize this, entrepreneurship might be conceived of as a vector in three-dimensional space, as shown in Figure 4.3. Three situations (E1, E2, and E3)

Figure 4.3
Entrepreneurship as a Vector

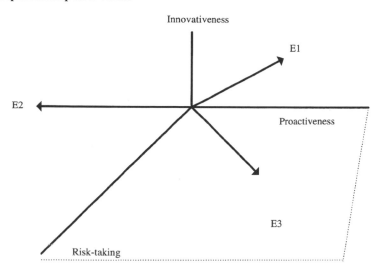

are portrayed in Figure 4.3. The first situation (E1) represents a firm, or group of managers/entrepreneurs, that is highly innovative or proactive but highly risk averse. The second situation (E2) finds another firm, or group of managers/entrepreneurs, that is highly innovative and risk-taking to the point of gambling but lacking in proactiveness—the persistence and ability to implement entrepreneurial concepts. The third firm, or group of managers/entrepreneurs (E3), has a more or less balanced entrepreneurial orientation. Two observations can be made. First, while the discussion in the figure applies to firms or groups of managers/entrepreneurs, it could just as well apply to departments or functions within firms, such as sales management or selling, and obviously the vector could be applied to an individual. Thus, there could be individuals who are indeed too innovative and not proactive enough, or who attempt to overcome personal limitations in innovativeness by taking disproportionate risks—perhaps to the extent of gambling on products, customers, or sources of supply. Second, the entrepreneurial mix, or the magnitude and direction of the vector, is obviously not standard or easy to calculate and specify. Rather, it depends on situations within industries or sales environments. Thus for example, high-tech markets might require greater levels of innovative input for success than would fast moving consumer goods markets, and real estate sales situations might reward greater risk-seeking than would situations in telemarketing.

Another worthwhile approach would be to examine the position of an organization, a department within an organization, or an individual on a matrix formed by any two of the three dimensions, and to consider the implications of this.

For example, consider a sales department within a company. The sales department might find itself in one of four positions on the risk-taking and innovativeness dimensions of entrepreneurial behavior, as illustrated in Figure 4.4. The "stuck-in-the-mud" sales manager would seldom innovate or be willing to assume the risks that such innovation would require. The "dreamer" would be highly innovative in thinking but unwilling to take risks to give the innovations a chance of success. Taking risks would be all the "wild-eyed gambler" did—the concepts on which risks were taken would not be innovative or creative but would merely be risky "bets." The entrepreneurial sales manager would balance risk-taking and innovativeness, realizing that innovative ideas also necessitate some risk-taking. Similarly, two-by-two grids can also be used to examine the dichotomies of innovativeness and proactiveness, and risk-taking and proactiveness.

THE ENTREPRENEURIAL GRID

To better understand the concept of EI, consider Figure 4.5. Here, a two-dimensional matrix has been created with the number, or frequency, of entrepreneurial events on the vertical axis, and the extent or degree to which these events are innovative, risky, and proactive on the horizontal axis. This matrix shall be referred to as the entrepreneurial grid. For purposes of illustration, five sample scenarios have been identified in Figure 4.5, and these have been labeled

Figure 4.4
Dichotomizing the Entrepreneurial Dimensions of Risk-Taking and Innovativeness

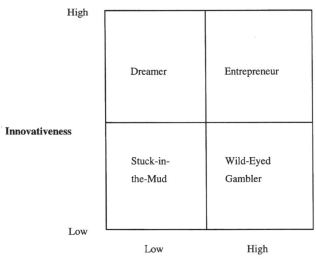

Figure 4.5

The Entrepreneurial Grid: Degree of Entrepreneurship (Innovativeness, risk-taking, proactiveness)

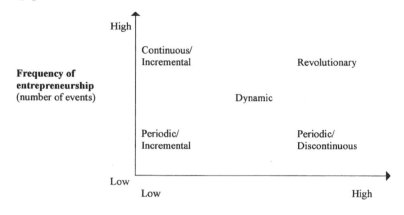

Periodic/Incremental, Continuous/Incremental, Periodic/Discontinuous, Dynamic, and Revolutionary. Each of these reflects the variable nature of entrepreneurial intensity.

For example, where few entrepreneurial events are produced, and these events are only nominally innovative, risky, and proactive, the society, organization, or individual can be described as Periodic/Incremental in terms of its (modest) level of EI. Similarly, a society, organization, or individual that is responsible for numerous entrepreneurial events that are highly innovative, risky, or proactive will fit into the Revolutionary segment of the entrepreneurship matrix and will exhibit the highest levels of EI.

While Figure 4.5 depicts five discrete segments, it is important to note that these segments have been arbitrarily defined to provide an example of how EI may vary. Amounts and degrees of entrepreneurship are relative; absolute standards do not exist. Further, any given person, organization, or nation could be highly entrepreneurial at some times and not very entrepreneurial at others. Consequently, they could occupy different segments of the matrix at different points in time.

APPLYING THE GRID AT THE LEVEL OF THE INDIVIDUAL

As noted elsewhere in this book, entrepreneurs tend to have certain characteristics in common. They are committed, determined, and opportunity-driven. They tolerate risk and ambiguity and are achievement-motivated. They tend to learn from experience. Yet, in spite of such commonalities, there is no single prototype of the entrepreneur. Some are technically-oriented, some are aggressive promoters of a concept, and others are good managers.

Some people do entrepreneurial things early in life, some do them late in life, and others do them throughout their lifetime. Similarly, the entrepreneurial events pursued by entrepreneurs will vary from being nominally innovative, risky, and proactive (e.g., the first dry cleaners to have a drive-up window, stay open twenty-four hours a day, and specialize only in cleaning men's suits) to highly innovative, risky, and proactive (e.g., Ted Turner and Cable News Network [CNN]).

Entrepreneurs can fall into different areas on the entrepreneurial grid. Figure 4.6 provides some hypothetical examples. If we consider someone like Richard DeVos, founder of Amway Products, his profile probably falls into the Continuous/Incremental segment, as his orientation has been a steady stream of complementary lines and product improvements. Bill Gates of Microsoft might be characterized as a Dynamic entrepreneur, as he has championed a substantial number of significant software innovations. Howard Head, who personally drove the development of the metal ski in the 1950's and the oversize Prince tennis racket in the 1970's, most likely falls into the Periodic/Discontinuous area of the grid. Finally, someone like Herb Kelleher, of Southwest Airlines fame, has built his very service-oriented company around a clearly defined strategy and a people-oriented management style. He probably would fall more in the Continuous/Incremental section of the grid.

Figure 4.6
Levels of Entrepreneurial Intensity among Individuals (Entrepreneurs)

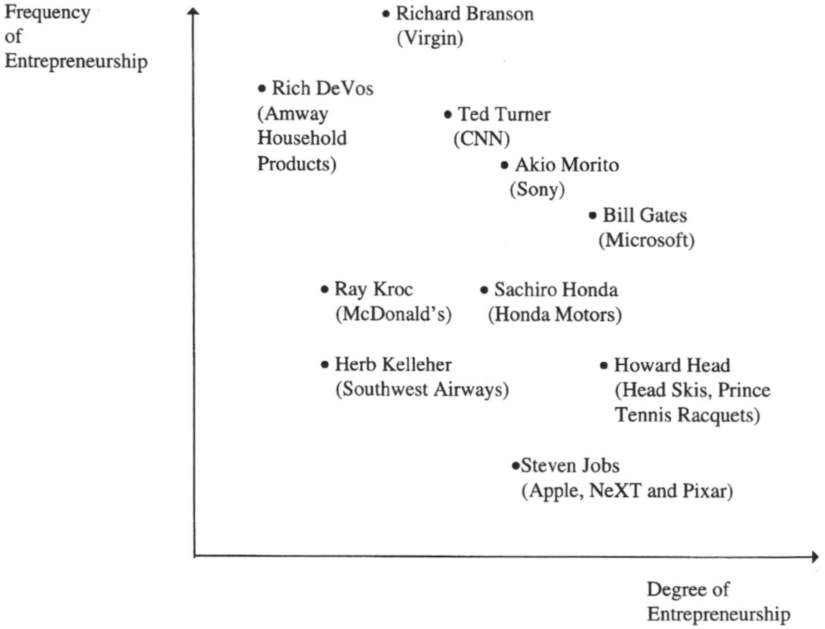

Another way in which the grid might be applied to individuals would involve characterizing how the entrepreneur approaches the external environment. Many individuals achieve success by quickly adapting to environmental change. Others base their efforts on actually creating major change in the environment. Ray Kroc was a great adapter, while Steven Jobs is more of a change agent. If we drew a vertical line at the mid-point of the horizontal, or "degree," axis, the former group would fall on the left-hand side of the grid, while the latter group would fall on the right-hand side.

Environmental circumstances are apt to influence the personal strategy one pursues in terms of where they fall in the grid. Not only might industry and market conditions influence one's personal strategy, but so too might such factors as the perceived cost of failure at different time periods, developments in one's personal life, one's past record of entrepreneurial success or failure, and the extent to which one is acting alone or in concert with others. In addition, positioning in the grid is probably influenced by other psychological traits, such as need for achievement, locus of control, risk-taking profile, and tolerance of ambiguity. The position of individuals in the grid in terms of their professional or business life is apt to differ from their entrepreneurial orientation in other domains, such as in the managment of their personal financial affairs and social relationships.

APPLYING THE GRID AT THE LEVEL OF THE ORGANIZATION

Organizations can also be characterized in terms of their entrepreneurial orientation. In fact, entrepreneurship can be an integral part of the mission, objectives, overall strategy, structure, and culture of organizations, large and small, private and public.

Consider an application of the entrepreneurial grid at the organizational level, specifically, to five successful companies (Figure 4.7). These are firms that exhibit varying degrees of EI, and as a consequence, are representative of different spaces or scenarios within the model. They include

- *Wendy's*. Started in 1969, this highly successful fast-food chain rapidly captured third place in the industry by developing an innovative product/service delivery system and by targeting a relatively untapped market consisting of young adults with a desire for higher-quality food. Throughout the years, it has maintained a competitive advantage by responding to changing environmental trends. For example, an increasing demand for convenience led Wendy's to pioneer drive-up window service, and shifting consumer preferences for lighter, low-calorie meals were met through the introduction of salads and baked potatoes. Responding to saturated demand and heightened competitive intensity, a "value menu" was added. While none of these activities can be considered highly innovative, Wendy's can be credited with introducing a few creative changes to the fast-food industry. As such, Wendy's is representative of the Periodic/Incremental segment of the entrepreneurial grid.

Figure 4.7
Entrepreneurial Grid at the Organizational Level

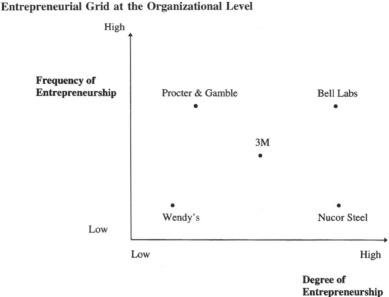

- *Procter & Gamble (P&G)*. With the leading brand in 22 of the 40 product categories in which it competes, P&G has remained on top in the highly competitive consumer packaged goods industry by placing priority on research and development. The result has been a continuous stream of product improvements, with an occasional new product entry. P&G excels at evolutionary adaptations to, and improvements in, existing product concepts. Therefore, this company is representative of the Continuous/Incremental segment of the grid.

- *Nucor*. Founded in 1968 as a mini-mill that produced steel construction joints, Nucor introduced a radically new technical process for producing sheet metal in small electric arc furnaces. It mastered the ability to produce a ton of sheet steel in three-quarters of a man-hour versus the conventional three man-hours. In addition to transforming the competitive and economic structure of the steel industry, this innovation has affected the cost structure of firms in many other industries (e.g., automobile, construction). Therefore, while Nucor has been responsible for few entrepreneurial initiatives, its efforts have had a relatively dramatic effect on several industries. As such, Nucor represents Periodic/Discontinuous entrepreneurship.

- *Minnesota Mining and Manufacturing Company (3M)*. 3M's unique talent is finding commercial uses for new product technology, developing that technology into dozens of marketable forms, and finding novel applications for these products. Today the firm has over 6,800 different consumer and industrial products. An example is Scotch cellophane tape, from which many successful products were derived. 3M sets a goal of achieving 25% of annual sales from products that have been developed in the last five years. The stream of innovative products that comes from this firm suggest that it is representative of the Dynamic segment of the entrepreneurial grid.

• *Bell Laboratories.* Credited with breakthrough advances in both basic and applied research, Bell Labs has earned a reputation as one of the most innovative and productive industrial research laboratories in the world. Among the labs' most notable achievements are the transistor, the laser, the solar cell, and fiber-optic transmission. The primary emphasis at Bell Labs today is developing products and processes with commercial applicability. For example, it recently developed a solution to the overcrowding of airwaves that was resulting from the increased use of cellular phones. The activities of Bell Laboratories represent the highest level of EI and, consequently, appear to fit the Revolutionary segment of the entrepreneurial grid.

These companies represent a study in contrasts. Consider a comparison of Nucor's major technological advancement in the production of steel to the constant flow of new products and processes that come from cross-functional ranks of 3M, or the development of the drive-up window concept to the development of laser technology. Yet, each firm has refined a strategy for EI that has proven to fit with its internal and external environments and to be profitable.

A company's EI score will vary depending on a number of internal and external factors. Internally, entrepreneurship is more evidenced where company structures are flat, control systems contain a measure of slack, appraisal systems include innovation and risk-taking criteria, jobs are broad in scope, and reward systems encourage a balance of individualism and group orientation. Externally, industries that are highly concentrated; and have little direct competition, demand that is captive, technologies that rarely change, and margins that are comfortable, will likely contain companies with low EI scores. Frequency of entrepreneurship may be directly related to the intensity of competition and amount of market heterogeneity, while degree of entrepreneurship is likely to be related to the rate of technological change in an industry and amount of product heterogeneity

APPLYING THE GRID AT THE SOCIETAL LEVEL

Countries can also be described in terms of their entrepreneurial profiles. Regardless of its political, cultural, social, religious, or economic orientations, every nation produces some level of entrepreneurship. Whether measured by business start-ups, patents issued, licenses granted, significant improvements in worker productivity, or some other proxy indicator, the amount of entrepreneurship evidenced in different societies (e.g., entrepreneurship per capita) is likely to vary.

Figure 4.8 represents an attempt to categorize countries within the entrepreneurial grid. As with the applications at the individual and organizational levels, this illustration is not based on empirical evidence. Rather, it is based on subjective judgement and is only for illustrative purposes.

Figure 4.8
Entrepreneurial Grid at the Societal Level

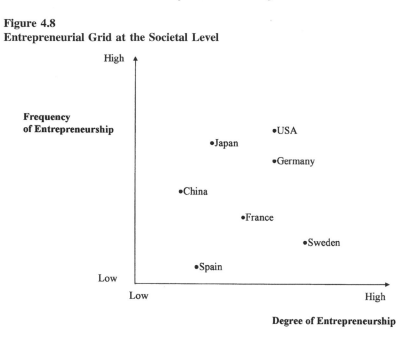

Baumol (1990) has persuasively argued that the level of entrepreneurship in a society is a direct function of society's rules (regulations and policies) governing the allocation of rewards. Further, he suggests that entrepreneurial potential is rich in every nation, but that the rules of the game determine where this potential gets channeled. In many cases, it gets channeled into unproductive or dysfunctional behaviors, such as criminal activity, speculative financial transactions that make no contribution to the productive capacity of the economy, take-overs, tax evasion, military ventures, and litigation that seeks to produce windfalls.

Entrepreneurship would also appear to be more compatible with certain countries' cultures than with others. In his landmark work on national culture, Hofstede (1980) demonstrates meaningful differences among countries on such cultural variables as individualism-collectivism, power distance, masculinity-femininity, and uncertainty avoidance. He further demonstrates linkages between certain of these variables and other variables (e.g. Confucianism, dynamism) and national wealth and economic growth.

Other findings demonstrating relationships between entrepreneurial activity, on the one hand, and both national wealth and economic growth, on the other, would suggest that certain cultural values and norms directly conflict with innovative, risk-taking, proactive behaviors.

MEASURING ENTREPRENEURIAL INTENSITY

The discussion up to this point has implied that EI can be measured. While reliable and valid measures have yet to be developed at the individual and societal levels, progress has been made at the organizational level. Building on the work of Miller and Friesen (1983), a number of researchers have reported success both in measuring a company's entrepreneurial orientation and in linking that orientation to various strategic and performance variables.

One adaptation of these measures is presented in Table 4.1. The items in this questionnaire capture both the degree and frequency of entrepreneurship, as well as the underlying dimensions of innovativeness, risk-taking, and proactiveness. In addition, both product or service and process innovation are covered. Various studies in which these measures have been employed have reported more than satisfactory statistics for their reliability and validity.

Using measures such as those in Table 4.1, researchers have demonstrated statistically significant relationships between EI and a number of indicators of company performance. Examples of such indicators include profits, the income-to-sales ratio, the rate of growth in revenue, the rate of growth in assets, the rate of growth in employment, and a composite measure of twelve financial and non-financial criteria (Covin and Slevin, 1989, 1990; Davis, Morris and Allen, 1991; Miller and Friesen, 1983; Morris and Sexton, 1996; Peters and Waterman, 1982; Zahra, 1986). This linkage between EI and performance appears to be especially strong for companies that operate in increasingly turbulent environments.

The measurement of EI also provides numerous opportunities for further research. For example, the relative importance of degree and frequency when measuring EI may actually vary depending on certain strategic factors, such as the pace of technological change in an industry, the levels of competitive intensity, or the heterogeneity of market demand. Research is needed to identify the conditions under which degree or frequency is the strongest contributor to performance. It is also necessary to determine if frequency and degree contribute equally to short-term as opposed to long-term performance. It may be that frequency has more of a short-term impact, whereas degree is better able to impact long-term outcomes. Although hypothetical, such a possibility is implicit in the work of Hamel and Prahalad (1991). Using a baseball analogy of hitting many singles versus attempting to hit a home run, they emphasize the value of companies pursuing multiple smaller projects at a time as opposed to pursuing a potentially breakthrough project. A risk-reward trade-off is involved in which the former are thought to generate short- and intermediate-term profits, whereas the latter significantly impact long-term profitability.

Research might also be directed toward identifying realistic time lags between a decrease or increase in EI within a firm and changes in organizational performance. This would require the development of longitudinal databases. The lag may vary depending on where the organization finds itself on the EI con-

Table 4.1
The Entrepreneurial Performance Index (applied to South African companies)

I. New Product Introduction

1. What is the number of new products your company introduced during the past two years? _____

	Significantly less		Same		Significantly more
2. How does the number of new product introductions your company made compare with those of your major competitors?	1	2	3	4	5
3. To what degree did these new product introductions include products that had not previously existed anywhere before ("new to the world")?	1	2	3	4	5
4. To what degree did these new product introductions include products that did not previously exist in your markets ("new to the South African market")?	1	2	3	4	5
5. To what degree did these new product introductions represent modifications to current products or extensions of current product lines?	1	2	3	4	5

II. New Service Introduction

1. What is the number of new services your company introduced during the past two years? _____

	Significantly less		Same		Significantly more
2. How does the number of new service introductions your company made compare with those of your major competitors?	1	2	3	4	5

	Not at all			To a great extent	
3. To what degree did these new service introductions include services that had not previously existed anywhere before ("new to the world")?	1	2	3	4	5
4. To what degree did these new service introductions include services that did not previously exist in your markets ("new to the South African market")?	1	2	3	4	5
5. To what degree did these new service introductions represent modifications to current services or an extension of your current service line?	1	2	3	4	5

Table 4.1 (continued)

III. New Process Introduction

1. Please estimate the number of new production or operational processes your company implemented during the past two years. Examples of process innovations include: new systems for managing inventories, an improved process for collecting unpaid accounts, major new sales or distribution approaches, etc. _____

	Significantly less		Same	Significantly more	
2. How does the number of new production or operational process introductions your company made compare with those of your major competitors?	1	2	3	4	5

	Minor				Major
3. To what extent did these new process improvements represent a minor or major modification of existing processes?	1	2	3	4	5

IV. Company Orientation

For the following statements, please circle a number that best corresponds to your level of agreement with each statement.

Our company is characterized by:	Strongly agree				Strongly disagree
1. a high rate of new product/service introduction, compared to our competitors (including new features and improvements);	1	2	3	4	5
2. an emphasis on continuous improvement in methods of production and/or service delivery;	1	2	3	4	5
3. risk-taking by key executives in seizing and exploring chancy growth opportunities;	1	2	3	4	5
4. a "live and let live" philosophy in dealing with competitors;	1	2	3	4	5
5. seeking of unusual, novel solutions by senior executives to problems via the use of "idea people," brainstorming, etc.;	1	2	3	4	5
6. a top management philosophy that emphasizes proven products and services, and the avoidance of heavy new product development costs;	1	2	3	4	5
7. a charismatic leader at the top.	1	2	3	4	5

At our company, top level decision making is characterized by:	Strongly agree				Strongly disagree
8. cautious, pragmatic, step-at-a-time adjustments to problems;	1	2	3	4	5

53

Table 4.1 (continued)

9. active searches for big opportunities;	1	2	3	4	5
10. rapid growth as the dominant goal;	1	2	3	4	5
11. large, bold decisions despite uncertainties of the outcomes;	1	2	3	4	5
12. compromises among the conflicting demands of owners, government, management, customers, employees, suppliers, etc.;	1	2	3	4	5
13. steady growth and stability as primary concerns.	1	2	3	4	5

V. Key Business Behavioral Dimensions

The following questions relate to the situational factors that face individuals in your organization on a day-to-day basis. Please circle the number that best represents the emphasis your company places on the two criteria given. The number 1 means more emphasis is placed on the left and number 5 more emphasis on the right.

1. When it comes to our company's current strategic orientation, we are:

Influenced primarily by the resources we currently control.	1	2	3	4	5	Influenced primarily by the perception of untapped opportunity.

2. When it comes to our company's approach to new opportunities, we tend to:

Commit fairly quickly, capitalize and move to the next opportunity.	1	2	3	4	5	Approach with an evolution- ary commitment that tends to be of long duration,

3. Our company's approach to investing resources in new opportunities tends to involve:

Multiple stages with minimal commitment at each stage.	1	2	3	4	5	A single stage with complete commitment upon decision.

4. When it comes to the way in which we manage or control resources, we prefer:

Episodic use, renting, leasing, contracting, and outsourcing of resources.	1	2	3	4	5	Ownership, purchase, control, and employment of the resources we use.

5. Our company's management structure can be characterized as:

A flat structure with multiple informal networks.	1	2	3	4	5	A hierarchical structure with clearly defined authority and responsibility.

6. Our company's compensation and reward system is:

Value based and team based with unlimited earnings potential for employees.	1	2	3	4	5	Resource based, driven by short-term performance data, with limited earning potential for employees.

tinuum, as well as on the relative emphasis placed on the degree versus the frequency components of EI.

Research should also be directed toward establishing the types and amounts of costs associated with EI. Resource requirements are likely to vary considerably at different levels of EI within a given industry, and the shape of the cost curve should be estimated. A related question concerns the failures that result from EI. Product and service failure rates are likely to be positively associated with both the frequency and degree components of EI, and research is needed to determine which is greater and why.

Another fertile area for researchers involves the role of EI in determining environment-strategy-structure relationships. It would seem that EI serves a potentially critical role in integrating these three variables. As a case in point, firms experiencing higher levels of environmental turbulence may require higher levels of EI to survive and grow, which in turn generates corporate strategies that are more aggressive (e.g., prospecting, acquisition) as well as structures that are more flexible, decentralized, and open.

Finally, the robustness of the EI concept and the EI measures presented here must be established. Whereas a wide variety of organizational contexts should be explored, it might be especially worthwhile to examine the application of EI to non-profit and government organizations. Progress in these areas is likely to require additional work in defining what constitutes a new product, service, or process and in establishing the strategically meaningful measures of performance.

CONCLUSIONS

There is a growing research foundation to support the concept of EI. Keats and Bracker (1988) use the term in characterizing different types of entrepreneurs and suggest that organizational performance is affected by intensity. Stuart and Abetti (1987), in a study of factors contributing to venture success, examined a variable they termed ''organic emphasis'' to describe the extent to which a firm's internal environment and culture are innovative, opportunistic, and risk-taking, as well as a variable labeled ''entrepreneurship level'' to reflect the degree to which a firm's leaders demonstrated characteristics associated with the entrepreneurial personality. Schaefer (1990) assesses ''levels of entrepreneurship'' in an organizational context. Jennings and Seaman (1990) discuss the ''entrepreneurial aggressiveness'' of savings and loan institutions, as reflected behaviorally in their financial portfolios. Cheah (1990) proposes a continuum of entrepreneurial possibilities based on the extent to which the entrepreneur is creating significant new profit opportunities (disturbing the equilibrium) versus capitalizing on available opportunities (bringing disequilibrium into equilibrium). Covin and Slevin (1991) refer to the ''entrepreneurial posture'' of firms.

Although both frequency and degree are implicit in much of the available research, the distinction between the two has not been sufficiently emphasized.

For instance, Cheah's conceptual argument appears to emphasize degree, whereas the measures used by Jennings and Seaman seem to focus more on frequency. Alternatively, Covin and Slevin mention the "extensiveness and frequency of product innovation," and Schaeffer examines how entrepreneurial decision making is in general, as well as the number of new services introduced by the firms she studied.

This distinction is clearly delineated in the entrepreneurial grid and the sample measures presented in this chapter. A central thesis of this book is that EI should be used as a key activity ratio that is monitored and measured on an ongoing basis. Measurement at the level of the individual can be useful in helping managers and others to examine and refine their own leadership styles, as well as in characterizing employee behavior over time. At the organizational level, measures can be used to benchmark and track entrepreneurial performance, establish norms and draw industry comparisons, establish entrepreneurship goals, develop strategies, and assess relationships between EI and company performance variables over time. Societal measurement of EI can be valuable in benchmarking and making cross-national comparisons. Measures of EI can be correlated with national wealth, economic growth rates, and various measures of societal quality-of-life dimensions. Such measures also represent a focal point of public policy effort, as public officials attempt to establish "rules of the game" that determine the relative emphasis on the frequency versus degree of entrepreneurial effort in society.

REFERENCES

Bateman, T.S., and Crant, J.M. 1993. "The Proactive Component of Organizational Behavior: A Measure and Correlates." *Journal of Organizational Behavior*, 14 (March), 103–118.

Baumol, W.J. 1990. "Entrepreneurship: Productive, Unproductive, and Destructive." *Journal of Political Economy*, 98 (5), 893–921.

Buss, D.M. 1987. "Selection, Evocation and Manipulation." *Journal of Personality and Social Psychology*, 53 (4), 1214–1221.

Cheah, H.B. 1990. "Schumpeterian and Austrian Entrepreneurship: Unity within Duality." *Journal of Business Venturing*, 5 (December), 341–347.

Covin, J.G., and Slevin, D.P. 1989. "Strategic Management of Small Firms in Hostile and Benign Environments." *Strategic Management Journal*, 10 (1), 75–87.

Covin, J.G., and Slevin, D.P. 1991. "A Conceptual Model of Entrepreneurship as Firm Behavior." *Entrepreneurship Theory and Practice*, 16 (Fall), 7–25.

Davis, D., Morris, M., and Allen, J. 1991. "Perceived Environmental Turbulence and Its Effect on Selected Entrepreneurship, Marketing and Organizational Characteristics in Industrial Firms." *Journal of the Academy of Marketing Science*, 19 (Spring), 43–51.

Dickson, P.R., and Giglierano, J.J. 1986. "Missing the Boat and Sinking the Boat: A Conceptual Model of Entrepreneurial Risk." *Journal of Marketing*, 50, 43–51.

Hamel, G., and Prahalad, C.E. 1991. "Corporate Imagination and Expeditionary Marketing." *Harvard Business Review*, 69 (4) (July–August), 31–93.

Hofstede, G. 1980. "Motivation, Leadership and Organization: Do American Theories Apply Abroad?" *Organizational Dynamics*, 9 (3), 42–63.

Jennings, D.F., and Seaman, S.L. 1990. "Aggressiveness of Response to New Business Opportunities Following Deregulation: An Empirical Study of Established Financial Firms." *Journal of Business Venturing*, 5 (October), 177–189.

Keats, B.W., and Bracker, J.S. 1988. "Toward a Theory of Small Business Performance: A Conceptual Model." *American Journal of Small Business*, 13 (Spring), 14–58.

Miller, D., and Friesen, P.H. 1983. "Innovation in Conservative and Entrepreneurial Firms: Two Models of Strategic Momentum." *Strategic Management Journal*, 3 (1), 1–25.

Miller, D. 1987. "Strategy Making and Structure: Analysis and Implications for Performance." *Academy of Management Journal*, 30 (1), 7–32.

Morris, M.H., Sexton, D., and Lewis, P. 1994. "Reconceptualizing Entrepreneurship: An Input-Output Perspective." *SAM Advanced Management Journal*, 59 (1) (Winter), 21–31.

Morris, M.H., and Sexton, D.L. 1996. "The Concept of Entrepreneurial Intensity." *Journal of Business Research*, 36 (1), 5–14.

Peters, T., and Waterman, R. 1982. *In Search of Excellence*. New York: Harper & Row.

Schaefer, D.S. 1990. "Level of Entrepreneurship and Scanning Source Usage in Very Small Businesses." *Entrepreneurship Theory and Practice*, 15 (1), 19–31.

Stuart, R., and Abetti, P.A. 1989. "Start-up Ventures: Towards the Prediction of Initial Success." *Journal of Business Venturing*, 2 (3), 215–230.

Venkatraman, N. 1989. "Strategic Orientation of Business Enterprises: The Construct, Dimensionality, and Measurement." *Management Science*, 35 (August), 942–962.

Zahra, S.A. 1986. "A Canonical Analysis of Corporate Entrepreneurship Antecedents and Impact on Performance." In *Best Paper Proceedings*, Pearce and Robinson (eds.), 46th Annual Meeting, Academy of Management, 71–75.

5

The Environment for Entrepreneurship

INTRODUCTION

Based on the discussion in Chapter 4, the level of entrepreneurial intensity (EI) can be expected to vary considerably among persons, companies, industries, geographic regions, and nations. In the United States, for instance, entrepreneurial efforts resulted in sizeable contributions to the gross national product and the standard of living in the second halves of the nineteenth and the twentieth centuries. But such efforts were much less significant in Mexico during the same period.

The question is, Why? Americans are not inherently any more entrepreneurial than are Mexicans. Nor are people in Taiwan inherently more entrepreneurial than those in China, although there are probably differences between the two in what Davidsson (1992) calls their "entrepreneurial culture scores," a measure of mental preparedness and drive to exhibit entrepreneurial behavior. In the same vein, there must be some logical reason why immigrant populations produce more entrepreneurship per capita than non-immigrant populations, and why some think that first-born children pursue an entrepreneurial path more often than second- or third-born children.

Such situational differences can be traced to the context within which entrepreneurship occurs. It is important that we dispense once and for all with the notion that entrepreneurship is a function of genetics, luck, cyclical patterns, uncontrollable circumstances, or just being in the right place at the right time. Entrepreneurship is neither innate to certain people and societies nor a random or chance event. Rather, it is determined by environmental conditions operating at a number of levels.

There are, of course, hundreds of variables operating in a given environment that could inhibit or facilitate entrepreneurial behavior. In Figure 5.1, we attempt to capture these environmental variables by grouping them into three general categories. These include

- the environmental infrastructure which characterizes a society;
- the degree of environmental turbulence present in a society; and
- the personal life experiences of a society's members.

The combined effect of these three environmental influences is the level of EI in a society. Although these environmental influences are admittedly inter-dependent, each represents a relatively distinct construct that has a differential impact on societal entrepreneurship. Let us examine all three in more detail.

ENVIRONMENTAL INFRASTRUCTURE

We use the term "environmental infrastructure" loosely to capture the economic, political, legal, financial, logistical, educational, and social structures that characterize a society. As proposed in Figure 5.2, certain structures would appear to facilitate entrepreneurial attitudes and behaviors. For instance, in places like

Figure 5.1
A Model of the Environmental Determinants of Entrepreneurship

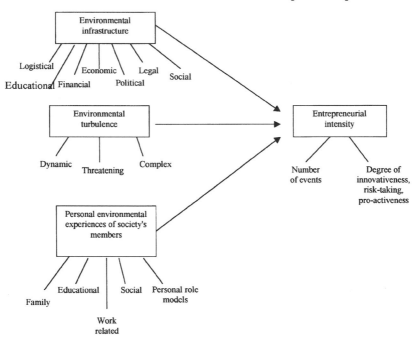

Figure 5.2
Infrastructure and Entrepreneurship

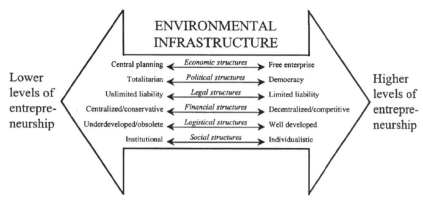

Hong Kong that have had relatively free, competitive market economies, available pools of capital, limited regulation, and political freedom, entrepreneurship is more in evidence.

Certain aspects of the economic system can act as incentives for individuals and help ensure that scarce economic resources are allocated to value-creating activities. They include freely fluctuating prices, private ownership, strong profit incentives, limited taxation, and a limited role for government. Governments can play a role in ensuring that these market mechanisms function more efficiently by removing conditions that create entry barriers, market imperfections, and administrative rigidities. Economic policies that encourage low levels of inflation without excessive interest rates also play a role.

Similarly, a political system fosters entrepreneurship when it is built around freedom of choice, individual rights, democratic rule, and a series of checks and balances among the executive, legislative, and judicial branches of government (Friedman, 1982; Schumpeter, 1950). Such designs are apt to be more accepting of innovation in all walks of life. Further, policy initiatives that facilitate or incentivize entrepreneurial activity (e.g., incubator programs, tax incentives) play a meaningful role in reinforcing an entrepreneurial ethic (Willis, 1985).

Legal and regulatory structures are significant positive factors to the extent that they recognize the corporate form of enterprise, permit limited liability, ensure contract enforcement and intellectual property protection, allow liberal treatment of bankruptcy, encourage competition, and impose fairly strong restrictions on monopolistic (restraint of trade) practices. These encourage risk-taking and pre-empt many of the obstacles to new product and process development. Alternatively, entrepreneurs are clearly discouraged from starting ventures where they are forced to comply with many rules and procedural requirements, must report to an array of institutions, and have to spend extensive time and money in fulfilling the documentation requirements. The evidence also suggests that regions with corrupt governments, and a concentration of parastatals or government-run industries, find the development of new ventures with growth potential to be highly problematic.

Financial systems are more encouraging of entrepreneurship when they are developed around institutional autonomy, competition among sources of capital, competitive interest rates, stable currencies, partial reserve requirements, well-backed deposit insurance, and large private investment pools (Birch, 1981; Brophy, 1982; Kent, 1986). These characteristics give rise to more diverse investment strategies by the mainstream financial institutions, novel types of investment organizations, and creative financing mechanisms. Further, research has shown that the establishment rates for new businesses are associated with the creation of investment companies, provision of low interest loans, and availability of credit guarantee schemes. As a result, individuals and organizations wishing to engage in entrepreneurial activity find the supply of financial resources is greater, and there are more choices in the trade-offs that must be made to obtain funding (Brophy, 1982; Eisenhardt and Forbes, 1984).

This is important, given that entrepreneurs require financial assistance for at least one of three different purposes: to diversify or spread start-up risk, to generate start-up capital, and to finance growth and expansion. Moreover, traditional bankers tend to lack both the inclination and the expertise necessary to support a wide range of entrepreneurial activity (Vesper, 1994).

Educational structures also play a role. Low levels of technical and business skills are a major deterrent to the starting of new ventures (Vesper, 1990; Davidsson, 1991). In addition, the skills and knowledge required for entrepreneurial success tend to vary across the different stages of business development. It is also noteworthy that evidence from the developed economies suggests that the educational background of start-up entrepreneurs has increased substantially in recent decades. Both government-sponsored and private training courses can positively impact entrepreneurship (Management Systems International, 1990). Other evidence suggests the presence of colleges and universities for training and research is an important facilitator. In one noteworthy U.S. study, Phillips (1993) demonstrated that every 1% increase in a state's college-educated population was associated with an 11.2% increase in jobs created by small firms.

Logistical arrangements include the development of roads, power grids, waterways, airports, efficient communication systems, and well-integrated channels of distribution. When these are highly developed, entrepreneurs are better able to identify and serve marketplace needs quickly and to capitalize on new methods and technologies (Aldrich, 1990; Stevenson and Sahlman, 1986). Markets themselves become more sophisticated.

Social structures that foster attitudes of individual freedom and an orientation toward self-direction and personal achievement are conducive to entrepreneurial initiatives (Birch, 1987; Tropman and Morningstar, 1989). In societies where the main concern is for the individual rather than the group, reward systems are more likely to encourage risk-taking, proactivity, and innovation. Individual goal-setting, independence, and personal ambition are recognized and encouraged in societies with individualistic social structures. Further, social systems that facilitate the development of networks to share information, identify opportunities, and marshal resources are conducive to entrepreneurial activity (Aldrich and Zimmer, 1986; Carsrud and Johnson, 1989).

Several researchers have stressed the importance of prevailing attitudes, values, beliefs and social norms—the so-called "mental software"—for explaining variations in entrepreneurship and economic development (Carsrud and Johnson, 1989; Davidsson, 1992; Etzioni, 1987; Shapero and Sokol, 1982). Alternatively, entrepreneurship will suffer if most of the members of society view it with suspicion. Both a favorable attitude on the part of society toward entrepreneurship and widespread public support for entrepreneurial activities are needed to motivate people to confront the risks, frustrations, stress, lengthy development cycles, and related hardships that are inherent in any entrepreneurial endeavor. Programs that create social awareness and social reinforcement of entrepreneurship are important. Awards programs and public recognition for entrepreneurs, news features on entrepreneurial role models, and business start-up competitions in schools are examples of vehicles that have helped create more social emphasis on entrepreneurship as a desirable path to pursue.

Further insights into ways in which entrepreneurship is impacted by the environmental infrastructure are provided by Gnyawali and Fogel (1994). In a comprehensive review, they examine empirical findings from research studies performed in a variety of countries around the world. Many of these studies are summarized below in Table 5.1.

ENVIRONMENTAL TURBULENCE

Environmental turbulence is the second component of our model. Turbulence has three components. These include the rate of change in key components of the environment, the extent to which the environment is hostile or threatening, and the degree of complexity in the environment. Turbulence in the technological, economic, customer, supplier, competitive, legal/regulatory, and social environments produces both threats and opportunities. It means the rules of the game may well be changing, and that the current assumptions may no longer hold. It suggests that certain needs no longer exist, others are changing, and new needs are appearing.

Turbulence is a major trigger, or catalyst, for entrepreneurial activity (see Figure 5.3). Consider the boom in entrepreneurial activity that occurred with the demise of the communist state in Poland. In South Africa under the former apartheid regime, the imposition of economic sanctions against the country led to extremely entrepreneurial activity as companies sought new sources of supply. The subsequent demise of apartheid has also produced a substantial increase in entrepreneurial activity. In the United States and Europe, deregulation of the telecommunications industry has produced a general lowering of prices, the ap-

Table 5.1
Selected Findings on the Role of Environmental Conditions in Facilitating
Entrepreneurship

Environmental Conditions and Research Findings	Source
Government Policies and Procedures	
In the Cayman Islands, entrepreneurship was facilitated by keeping paperwork and procedural requirements at a minimum.	Dana, 1987
In Malaysia, concentration of power in the business development agency established by the government and too many procedural requirements discouraged entrepreneurship.	Dana, 1990
In Saint Martin, excessive regulation of business suppressed growth and entrepreneurship; conversely, in Sint Maarten, minimum regulation and procedural requirements encouraged entrepreneurship.	Dana, 1990
In Mexico, key barriers to start-up included excessive government regulation, high tax rates, and increasing inflation.	Young & Welsch, 1993
Socioeconomic Conditions	
In Sweden, tax and other incentives had a greater impact on persons who were strongly motivated to start a business than on persons who were less motivated.	Davidsson, 1991
In the Czech and Slovak Republics, negative public attitudes toward entrepreneurs discouraged entrepreneurs.	Swanson and Webster, 1992
Cities having a larger number of economic development programs achieved a higher growth in the number of new firm establishments than cities having a smaller number of such programs.	Feiock, 1987
The greater the percentage of small firms in a growing sector, the greater the share of jobs created by small firms in that sector.	Phillips, 1993
Entrepreneurial and Business Skills	
In Sweden, both business-related experiences and business education were highly correlated with entrepreneurs' ability to start and manage a business.	Davidsson, 1991
In the region of Sub-Saharan Africa, entrepreneurs suffered from barriers such as the need for following societal stereotypes and traditions, a general lack of realization of the importance of thrift, and lack of perseverance.	Takyi-Asiedu, 1993
Every 1% increase in a state's college-educated population led to an 11.2% increase in jobs created by small firms.	Phillips, 1993
Financial Support	
In the Cayman Islands, creation of investment companies facilitated entrepreneurship.	Dana, 1987

Table 5.1 (continued)

Environmental Conditions and Research Findings	Source
In Singapore, provision of low-interest loans and government grants facilitated entrepreneurship development.	Dana, 1987
In the United States, availability of financial resources was an important contributor to organizational birth rate.	Pennings, 1982
In Michigan, investment by the State Pension Fund in venture capital investment attracted large venture capital companies to invest in small businesses.	Kleiman and Bygrave, 1998
In Japan, 52 credit guarantee associations exist to guarantee loans to small and medium-sized enterprises (SMEs); local governments have special funds that serve as a reserve for loans to SMEs. Consequently, most entrepreneurs got loans for start-up business.	Hawkins, 1993
In the United Kingdom, private investors are attracted to invest in new companies because the government provides tax relief for new equity investment by individuals in unquoted companies.	Harrison and Mason, 1988
In Mexico, key barriers for start-up included lack of working capital, difficulty in obtaining loans, and seasonal fluctuations in cash.	Young and Welsch, 1993

Non-Financial Support

In Australia, the provision of nationwide management training programs and the supply of textbooks and information materials on business start-up issues encouraged new business start-ups.	Dana, 1987
In the Virgin Islands, a tax concession on all businesses for 10 years, a tax concession for hotels for 20 years, and exemption from custom duty on imports of capital equipment facilitated the development of entrepreneurship.	Dana, 1987
In the Cayman Islands, a government guarantee not to tax businesses for 20 years attracted entrepreneurs.	Dana, 1987
In the United States, entrepreneurs spent nearly half of their time during business start-ups in making contacts.	Aldrich, 1986
In Japan, regional information centers gather, analyze, and disseminate technical and market information and offer free access to computers; local business development centers provide free consulting and training services; government purchases a certain quantity of the products of small enterprises every year. All of these have facilitated entrepreneurship development.	Hawkins, 1993
In Canada, the government procurement program helped firms to grow faster and to develop competence in marketing and export-related activities.	Doutriaux, 1988

Table 5.1 (continued)

Environmental Conditions and Research Findings	Source
In the United States, large urban areas and the presence of universities for training and research assistance were important factors contributing to the birth of new firms.	Pennings, 1982
Presence of business development assistance was significantly correlated with the share of jobs created by small firms.	Phillips, 1993

Source: Gnyawali and Fogel (1994). Reprinted with permission.

pearance of a number of new entrepreneurial firms, and many new product and service innovations.

Historically, environmental turbulence has been a factor in a large percentage of new product and technological innovations (Myers and Marquis, 1969; Wright, 1947). More recently, it has been demonstrated that the more dynamic, hostile, and heterogeneous the environment, the higher the level of innovation, risk-taking, and proactivity among the most successful firms (Covin and Slevin, 1989; Miller and Friesen, 1983). Brittain and Freeman (1980) have demonstrated that technological and demographic changes create opportunities for those positioned well to capitalize on them. Similarly, Tushman and Anderson (1986) have illustrated that technological change, whether competence-enhancing or competence-destroying, creates opportunities to be exploited through entrepreneurial behaviors.

The relatively stable, predictable business environment of the 1950's and

Figure 5.3
Environmental Turbulence and Entrepreneurship

1960's led to the development of many large mechanistic organizations. Such an organizational design may be quite appropriate where customers are captive, technology rarely changes, economic conditions are favorable, and competition is passive (or the competitive rules are fixed). Static environments create less need for creative responses to changing conditions, fewer rewards for innovative behavior, and most importantly, fewer penalties for failing to innovate. But the mechanistic type of structure is inappropriate for responding effectively to dynamic, threatening, complex change. Burdened by excessive layers of management, red tape, and inflexible policies and rules, large organizations are often incapable of adapting to changes in the environment in a timely fashion. The hard lesson is that, faced with conditions where survival depends on an effective response to market variations, innovation and entrepreneurship must occur.

Today, we find ourselves experiencing historically high levels of turbulence, and environments are likely to become even more turbulent in the next few decades. As a by-product, entrepreneurs and managers are confronted with shortened decision windows, diminishing opportunity streams, changing decision constituencies, increased resource specialization, lack of predictable resource needs, fragmented markets, greater risk of resource and product obsolescence, and a general lack of long-term control. The result has been intensified pressure for innovation and a dramatic increase in societal entrepreneurship over the past two decades.

Flexible, organic structures and managerial styles are more capable of identifying potential opportunities, reallocating resources, shifting managerial commitment quickly, and developing products, services, or processes to capitalize on strategic opportunities resulting from changing conditions. Successful adaptation to environmental change requires quick, thorough, and frequent internal and external analysis, short planning horizons, and the development of flexible plans that can be adjusted as necessary. Entrepreneurial efforts and behaviors become virtually a necessity for coping with such environmental change.

These efforts, in turn, create additional environmental turbulence by bringing product and process innovations to markets and changing the way business is done (see Figure 5.4). The implication is that entrepreneurship is a response to environmental turbulence as well as a source of institutionalized societal change, where firms initiate changes in technology, marketing, or organizational design

Figure 5.4
Entrepreneurship as Result and Cause of Environmental Turbulence

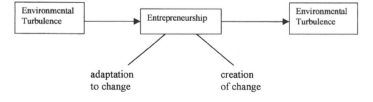

and strive to maintain the lead in changes over competitors. As the degree of entrepreneurial effort intensifies, so too does the rate of environmental change.

PERSONAL LIFE EXPERIENCES

The third and final component of our model is the personal life experiences of society's members. In addition to the influences of the infrastructure and the level of turbulence, the tendency to do entrepreneurial things is very much affected by the specific twists and turns in a given person's life.

There has been a significant amount of research into identifying the personal traits and characteristics of entrepreneurs (e.g., Collins and Moore, 1964; Brockhaus, 1980, 1982; Brockhaus and Horwitz, 1986; Birch, 1987; McClelland, 1987; Sexton and Bowman-Upton, 1990). However, attempts to develop a unique psychological profile of the entrepreneur have met with only marginal success because of the significant degree of variation among entrepreneurial types (Gartner, 1985). Most recent research has focused on the more relevant question of why the entrepreneur develops such characteristics (Delacroix and Carroll, 1983). The answer to this question is pretty clear-cut: family background, childhood experiences, exposure to role models, previous job experiences, and educational experiences all have a strong influence on the development of the entrepreneur.

Figure 5.5 is a summary of some of the types of personal life experiences thought to be associated with higher levels of entrepreneurship. Relevant aspects of family background that have been examined include parental relationships, order of birth, family income, and immigrant status. Parents instill an early sense of independence and desire for control in future entrepreneurs (Bird, 1989; Hisrich and Brush, 1984). Entrepreneurs often experience turbulent and disruptive childhoods. Particularly important is their relationship with their fathers. Several researchers have found that many entrepreneurs experienced relatively negative relationships with their fathers (e.g., Zaleznik and Kets de Vries, 1985; Silver, 1983), ranging from neglect as a result of career demands to actual physical or

Figure 5.5
Life Experiences and Entrepreneurship

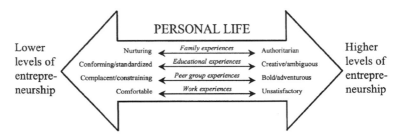

emotional abuse or abandonment. To compensate for paternal deficiencies, mothers devote themselves to helping their children succeed by instilling in them a need to excel. Having been raised with distant or uninvolved father figures, entrepreneurs develop a need for independence, self-reliance, and control. Consequently, in an effort to avoid authoritarian relationships and loss of control, and to fulfill their needs for success and achievement, individuals turn toward developing entrepreneurial ventures.

It is also argued that entrepreneurs are more often first-born children than second- or third-born, although little consensus exists on this issue. Others suggest that entrepreneurs are frequently from poorer families, and are often immigrants, or the children of immigrants (Collins and Moore, 1964; Gilder, 1984). It appears that those whose lives contain an extra degree of struggle to fit into society will more frequently develop their entrepreneurial potential.

Another important determinant of entrepreneurial behavior is the individual's exposure to successful role models (Kent, 1986; Eisenhardt and Forbes, 1984; Scherer, Adams and Wiebe, 1989; Bird, 1989; Vesper, 1990). Studies have shown that many entrepreneurs have parents who were self-employed (Hisrich and Brush, 1984; Ronstadt, 1984; Shapero and Sokol, 1982). Others find themselves working for or with an entrepreneur who becomes a role model. Another form of vicarious experience involves watching a friend develop a business. Such role models demonstrate to prospective entrepreneurs that risk-taking, tolerance for ambiguity, proactiveness, and innovation lead to independence and self-control.

Previous work experience also shapes the entrepreneur. Brockhaus (1980) found that job dissatisfaction "pushes" entrepreneurs out of established organizations and toward developing entrepreneurial ventures. In fact, the majority of entrepreneurs (59%) in Brockhaus's study indicated a desire to start their own business before they had a product or service in mind; only a small percentage (14%) were drawn away from a traditional job by the desire to market a particular product or service. Brockhaus also found that the greater the job dissatisfaction, the greater the likelihood of entrepreneurial success.

Personal experience with entrepreneurship is another factor in explaining the current or future performance of specific entrepreneurs. Whether the experience comes from ventures started on the side while in school, jobs taken on during summer breaks, or work in the family business, once a potential entrepreneur sees opportunity being capitalized upon, he/she often becomes more opportunity-aware. One of the interesting side-effects of pursuing an entrepreneurial path is the tendency to subsequently recognize additional opportunities for other ventures. Ronstadt (1984) has labeled this the "corridor principle."

Finally, educational experiences influence entrepreneurship. Some years ago, Brockhaus and Nord (1979) found that entrepreneurs had, on average, a lower level of education than managers. This tendency could lead entrepreneurs to feel limited in traditional organizations. Frustrated by an inability to achieve their desired level of success in established organizations, they choose to pursue a venture in which their own assessment of their abilities is more relevant. Some would suggest that the "school of hard knocks" prepares one better than colleges, universities, seminars, and books (Bird, 1989).

More recent evidence suggests that formal education helps entrepreneurs to succeed, and that median education levels among successful entrepreneurs have increased in the past few decades (Robinett, 1985; Ronstadt, 1985). In fact, today's entrepreneur is most likely a college graduate, and many have advanced degrees.

However, traditional teaching methods used in schools may actually stifle entrepreneurship. By stressing conformity and standardization and penalizing creative or novel approaches to problem solving, educators discourage the development of an entrepreneurial orientation in young people. Business schools and management consultants also tend to perpetuate resistance to entrepreneurship through their emphasis on structured organizational processes and decision making.

CONCLUSIONS: SPECIFYING THE PROPOSED RELATIONSHIPS

Figures 5.2, 5.3, and 5.5 each represent attempts to capture relationships between environmental variables and EI. They provide a foundation for developing clearly specified variables and formulating specific hypotheses concerning cause-and-effect relationships. Each component of the infrastructure, turbulence, and life experiences is pictured as a continuum on some characteristic. For example, political structure varies from totalitarianism to democracy, and the customer or market environment ranges from homogeneous to heterogeneous.

Two caveats should be kept in mind. First, the anchor points on each dimension are not necessarily opposites. Instead, they represent mutually exclusive alternatives that exist in varying degrees. Second, each dimension can be described in terms of a number of characteristics beyond those identified in Figures 5.2, 5.3, and 5.5. For instance, work environments could be characterized as comfortable or dissatisfactory but also as challenging, complex, stressful, or mundane. The particular characteristics cited in these figures were selected because they appear to have the most salient entrepreneurial implications.

While the relationships proposed in Figures 5.2, 5.3, and 5.5 are pictured as linear, this is not likely to be the case in actual practice. For example, financial or logistical infrastructures can discourage entrepreneurship when they are undeveloped, but also when they become overdeveloped and bureaucratic. Similarly, entrepreneurship may be fostered as environmental turbulence increases, but extreme levels of turbulence may make successful innovation impossible or remove the incentive for it.

In sum, the environmental determinants of entrepreneurship can be viewed as a set of characteristics that describe interdependent conditions of infrastructure, turbulence, and life experiences. Their effect on EI is both direct and nonlinear.

Although entrepreneurship certainly can occur under virtually any set of conditions, the relationships proposed here provide guidance for establishing conditions that foster (or suppress) the aggregate level of entrepreneurship that occurs in a given community, region, or society.

REFERENCES

Aldrich, H. 1990. "Using an Ecological Perspective to Study Organizational Founding Rates." *Entrepreneurship: Theory and Practice* (Spring), 7–24.

Aldrich, H. 1986. "Social Behavior and Entrepreneurial Networks." In R. Ronstadt, J.A. Hornaday, R. Peterson, and K.H. Vesper (eds.), *Frontiers of Entrepreneurship Research*. Wellesley, MA: Babson College, 239–40.

Aldrich, H. and Zimmer, C. 1986. "Entrepreneurship through Social Networks." In D.L. Sexton and R.W. Smilor (eds.), *The Art and Science of Entrepreneurship*. Cambridge, MA: Ballinger; 2–23.

Birch, D.L. 1987. *Job Creation in America.* New York: The Free Press.

Birch, D.L. 1981. "Who Creates Jobs?" *The Public Interest*, 65 (Fall), 62–82.

Bird, B. 1989. *Entrepreneurial Behavior.* London: Scott, Foresman and Co.

Brittain, J. and Freeman, J. 1980. "Organizational Proliferation and Density Dependent Selection." In J. Kimberly and R. Miles (eds.), *The Organizational Life Cycle*. San Francisco: Jossey-Bass, 291–338.

Brockhaus, R.H. 1982. "The Psychology of the Entrepreneur." In C. Kent, D. Sexton and K. Vesper (eds.), *Encyclopedia of Entrepreneurship*. Englewood Cliffs, NJ: Prentice-Hall.

Brockhaus, R.H. 1980. "Risk Taking Propensity of Entrepreneurs." *Academy of Management*, 23, 509–520.

Brockhaus, R.H. and Horwitz, P.S. 1986. "The Psychology of the Entrepreneur." In D.L. Sexton and R.W. Smilor (eds.), *The Art and Science of Entrepreneurship*. Cambridge, MA: Ballinger, 25–48.

Brockhaus, R.H., and Nord, W.R. 1979. "An Exploration of Factors Affecting the Entrepreneurial Decision: Personal Characteristics vs. Environmental Conditions." *Proceedings*, Annual Conference, Academy of Management.

Brophy, D.J. 1982. "Venture Capital Research." In C.A. Kent, D.L. Sexton, and K.H. Vesper (eds.), *Encyclopedia of Entrepreneurship*. Englewood Cliffs, NJ: Prentice-Hall, 165–192.

Carsrud, A.L. and Johnson, R.W. 1989. "Entrepreneurship: A Social Psychological Perspective." *Entrepreneurship and Regional Development*, 1 (1), 21–31.

Collins, O.F., and Moore, D.G. 1964. *The Enterprising Man.* East Lansing, MI: MSU Business Studies.

Covin, J.G., and Slevin, D.P. 1989. "Strategic Management of Small Firms in Hostile and Benign Environments." *Strategic Management Journal*, 10 (1), 75–87.

Dana, L.P. 1990. "Saint Martin/Sint Maarten: A Case Study of the Effects of Culture on Economic Development." *Journal of Small Business Management*, 28 (4), 91–98.

Dana, L.P. 1988. "The Spirit of Entrepreneurship and the Commonwealth Government of Australia." *Journal of Small Business Management*, 26 (1), 63–65.

Dana, L.P. 1987. "Entrepreneurship and Venture Creation—An International Comparison of Five Commonwealth Nations." In N.C. Chruchill, J.A. Hornaday, B.A. Kirchhoff, O.J. Krasner, and K. H. Vesper (eds.), *Frontiers of Entrepreneurship Research*. Wellesley: MA: Babson College, 573–583.

Davidsson, P. 1991. "Continued Entrepreneurship: Ability, Need, and Opportunity as Determinants of Small Firm Growth." *Journal of Business Venturing*, 6, 405–429.

Davidsson, P. 1992. *Entrepreneurship and Small Business Research: How Do We Get Further?* BA-Publications 126. Umeå: Umeå Business School, Sweden.

Delacroix, J., and Carroll, G. 1983. "Organizational Foundings: An Ecological Study of the Newspaper Industries of Argentina and Ireland." *Administrative Science Quarterly*, 28 (June), 274–291.

Doutriaux, J.A. 1988. "Government Procurement and Research Contracts at Start-up and Success of Canadian High-Tech Entrepreneurial Firms." In B.A. Kirchhoff, W.A. Long, W.E. McMullan, K.H. Vesper, and W.E. Wetzel (eds.), *Frontiers of Entrepreneurship Research*. Wellesley, MA: Babson College, 582–594.

Eisenhardt, K.M., and Forbes, N. 1984. "Technical Entrepreneurship: An International Perspective." *Columbia Journal of World Business*, 19 (Winter), 31–37.

Etzioni, A. 1987. "Entrepreneurship, Adaption, and Legitimation." *Journal of Economic Behavior and Organization*, 8, 175–189.

Feiock, R. 1987. "Urban Economic Development: Local Government Strategies and Their Effects." In S. Nagel (ed.), *Research in Public Policy Analysis and Management*. London: JAI Press.

Friedman, M. 1982. *Capitalism and Freedom*. Chicago, IL: University of Chicago Press.

Gartner, W.B. 1985. "A Conceptual Framework for Describing the Phenomenon of New Venture Creation." *Academy of Management Review*, 10 (4), 696–706.

Gilder, G. 1984. *The Spirit of Enterprise*. New York: Simon & Schuster.

Gnyawali, D.R., and Fogel, D.S. 1994. "Environments for Entrepreneurship Development: Key Dimensions and Research Implications." *Entrepreneurship: Theory and Practice*, 18 (4), 43–62.

Harrison, R.T., and Mason, C.M. 1988. "Risk Finance, the Equity Gap, and New Venture Formation in the United Kingdom: The Impact of the Business Expansion Scheme." In B.A. Kirchhoff, W.A. Long, W.E. McMullan, K.H. Vesper, and W.E. Wetzel (eds.), *Frontiers of Entrepreneurship Research*. Wellesley, MA: Babson College, 570–581.

Hawkins, D.L. 1993. "New Business Entrepreneurship in the Japanese Economy." *Journal of Business Venturing*, 8 (3), 137–150.

Hisrich, R.D., and Brush, C.G. 1984. "The Woman Entrepreneur: Management Skills and Business Problems." *Journal of Small Business Management*, 22, 31–37.

Kent, C.A. 1986. *The Environment for Entrepreneurship*. Lexington, MA: D.C. Heath & Company.

Kets de Vries, Manfred F.R. 1985. "The Dark Side of Entrepreneurship." *Harvard Business Review*, 63 (November–December), 160–167.

Kleiman, R.T., and Bygrave, W. 1988. "Public Sector Involvement in Venture Capital Finance: The Case of Michigan." In D.A. Kirchhoff, W.A. Long, W.E. McMullan, K.H. Vesper, and W.E. Wetzel (eds.), *Frontiers of Entrepreneurship Research*. Wellesley, MA: Babson College, 610–611.

Management Systems International. 1990. *Entrepreneurship Training and Strengthening*

Entrepreneurship Performance. Washington, DC: United States Agency for International Development.

McClelland, D.C. 1987. "Characteristics of Successful Entrepreneurs." *Journal of Creative Behavior*, 21 (2), 219–233.

Miller, D., and Friesen, P.H. 1983. "Innovation in Conservation and Entrepreneurial Firms: Two Models of Strategic Momentum." *Strategic Management Journal*, 31 (3), 1–25.

Myers, S., and Marquis, D.G. 1969. *Successful Industrial Innovation.* Washington, DC: National Science Foundation.

Pennings, J.M. 1982. "Organizational Birth Frequencies: An Empirical Investigation." *Administrative Science Quarterly*, 27 (2), 120–44.

Phillips, B. 1993. "The Growth of Small Firm Jobs by State, 1984–1988." *Business Economics*, 12 (April), 48–53.

Robinett, S. 1985. "What Schools Can Teach Entrepreneurs." *Inc.* (February), 50, 54, 58.

Ronstadt, R. 1985. "The Educated Entrepreneurs: A New Era of Entrepreneurial Education Is Beginning." *American Journal of Small Business* (Summer), 7–23.

Ronstadt, R. 1984. "Ex-entrepreneurs and the Decision to Start an Entrepreneurial Career." In J. Hornaday et al. (eds.), *Frontiers of Entrepreneurship Research.* Wellesley, MA: Babson College, 112–115.

Schumpeter, J., 1950. *Capitalism, Socialism, and Democracy.* New York: Harper & Row.

Sexton, D.L., and Bowman-Upton, N.B. 1990. "Female and Male Entrepreneurs: Psychological Characteristics and Their Role in Gender Related Discrimination." *Journal of Business Venturing*, 5 (1), 29–36.

Shapero, A., and Sokol, L. 1982. "The Social Dimensions of Entrepreneurship." In C. Kent, D.L. Sexton, and K.H. Vesper (eds.), *Encyclopedia of Entrepreneurship.* Engelwood Cliffs, NJ: Prentice-Hall, 72–90.

Scherer, R., Adams, J., and Wiebe, F. 1989. "Developing Entrepreneurial Behaviors: A Social Learning Theory Perspective." *Journal of Organizational Change Management*, 2 (3), 16–27.

Silver, A.D. 1983. *The Entrepreneurial Life.* New York: John Wiley.

Stevenson, H.H., and Sahlman, W.A. 1986. "Importance of Entrepreneurship in Economic Development." In D.C. Heath (ed.), *Entrepreneurship, Intrapreneurship and Venture Capital.* Lexington, MA: Lexington Books, 3–26.

Swanson, D., and Webster, L. 1992. *Private Sector Manufacturing in the Czech and Slovak Republic: A Survey of Firms*, Washington DC: The World Bank.

Takyi-Asiedu, S. 1993. "Some Socio-Cultural Factors Retarding Entrepreneurial Activity in Sub-Saharan Africa." *Journal of Business Venturing*, 8 (1), 91–98.

Tropman, J.E., and Morningstar, G. 1989. *Entrepreneurial Systems for the 1990s.* Westport, CT: Quorum Books.

Tushman, M., and Anderson, P. 1986. "Technological Discontinuities and Organizational Environments." *Administrative Science Quarterly,* 31, 439–465.

Vesper, K.H., 1990. *New Venture Strategies.* Englewood Cliffs, NJ: Prentice-Hall.

Vesper, K.H. 1994. *New Venture Experience.* Seattle: Vector Books.

Willis, R. 1985. "What Should Be the Federal Role in Startups?" *Management Review* (November), 11–13.

Wright, D.M., 1947. *The Economics of Disturbance.* New York: Macmillan.

Young, E.C., and Welsch, H.P. 1993. "Major Elements in Entrepreneurial Developments in Central Mexico." *Journal of Small Business Management*, 31 (3), 80–85.

Zaleznik, A., and Kets de Vries, Manfred F.R. 1985. *Power and the Corporate Mind*. Chicago: Bonus Books.

6

The Entrepreneurial Individual

INTRODUCTION

Entrepreneurship does not happen without entrepreneurs. Of all the elements necessary for successful entrepreneurship, the individual entrepreneur is the most critical. Without the visionary leadership and persistence demonstrated by this individual, little would be accomplished. As we shall discuss later in this chapter, entrepreneurship requires a team, and successful entrepreneurs tend to rely on extended networks. However, someone must come up with a concept, a vision, a dream. They must translate this dream into products and people within some sort of organizational context. They must champion the concept to a wide range of publics and partners. They must adapt the concept to reflect the realities encountered within the environment. And they must persevere in overcoming the normal and the arbitrary obstacles that are thrown into their paths.

The central role of the entrepreneur in driving the entrepreneurial process is illustrated in Figure 6.1. An individual is needed who can both dream and do. He/she must be able to fill multiple roles and demonstrate multiple characteristics. These include visionary, leader, promoter, risk-taker, leverager of resources, networker, and adapter. This individual is responsible for developing, adapting, or adopting a business concept. As discussed in Chapters 3 and 4, concepts can take any number of shapes or forms and will vary in terms of their innovativeness, riskiness, and level of proactiveness required. He/she implements the business concept within some type of organizational context. It might be a sole proprietorship run out of the person's garage at home, a franchise, or a venture team operating within a billion-dollar corporation. Finally, he/she must ensure that there is a fit between the business concept and the opportunity. The opportunity is defined by forces in the environment (e.g., the market, competi-

Figure 6.1
The Entrepreneur as Driving Force

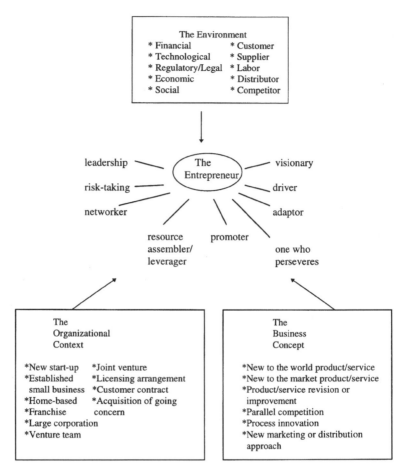

tion, technology). The environment is also a source of various threats and obstacles, which the entrepreneur must be prepared to address (see Chapter 5).

The characteristics and skills that determine the successfulness of the entrepreneurial venture will differ, depending upon the nature of the business concept, the organizational context, and the environment. Willingness and ability to assume and manage risks are more critical with truly new-to-the-world products. Political skills become crucial in large corporate settings. Adaptability and tenacity may be bigger factors in highly turbulent environments. At the same time, certain traits are fairly consistently associated with entrepreneurial personality. Let us further explore this controversial issue.

THE ENTREPRENEURIAL PERSONALITY

The single most researched question within the field of entrepreneurship is, "Who is the entrepreneur?" A variety of sometimes conflicting findings exist regarding the sociology and psychology of the entrepreneurial prototype. Many of these studies suffer from significant methodological problems. Samples are often small or unrepresentative. The validity and reliability of the measures employed are frequently not apparent, measures are applied long after the individual has done anything entrepreneurial, and it is often not clear if the researchers are focusing only on successful entrepreneurs, on people who have started small businesses, on people who identify themselves as entrepreneurs, or on some other delimiter.

Nonetheless, there do appear to be some characteristics around which a consensus has emerged. On the sociological side, immigrant populations appear to produce more entrepreneurship per capita than non-immigrant populations, perhaps because they face a greater struggle to fit into society. Of course, the very fact that they immigrated suggests an opportunistic mind-set. Another finding concerns birth order within families. While it is a controversial issue, some have argued that first-born children more frequently pursue an entrepreneurial path, than do second- or third-born children, possibly because they are given more responsibility, confront more discipline, and deal with more ambiguity than their siblings (Bird, 1989). Other research suggests age is a factor, with some people arguing that successful entrepreneurs tend to be younger (Sexton and Van Auken, 1982), and others indicating that milestone years (e.g., ages 20, 25, 30, 35) exist, when individuals are more likely to do something entrepreneurial (Ronstadt, 1984). Age is, of course, correlated with education and experience. The average education level of entrepreneurs has increased over the past two decades, although disagreement exists as to whether entrepreneurs differ significantly from managers in terms of their educational backgrounds. Nonetheless, successful entrepreneurs tend to have more education than their less successful counterparts (Sexton and Van Auken, 1982). Work experience, also, has more to do with predicting entrepreneurial success than with distinguishing entrepreneurs from non-entrepreneurs (Bird, 1989).

On the psychological side, there is some agreement on at least six characteristics (see Table 6.1 for a more comprehensive list of psychological traits associated with the entrepreneurial personality). Let us start with motivation. Entrepreneurs are driven by a variety of factors, ranging from necessity (I need to survive!) to dissatisfaction (I can't stand my present job) to curiosity (What if . . . ?) to material gain (We could make a killing!) to happenstance (Here's an opportunity if you want it). Yet, based on the classic studies of motivation done by McClelland, in which he assessed three fundamental types of motivators (power, affiliation, and achievement), the research evidence identifies entrepreneurs as being more achievement-motivated than anything else. They are driven

Table 6.1
Seventeen Common Traits and Characteristics Associated with the
Entrepreneurial Individual

Achievement Motivation
Internal Locus of Control
Calculated Risk-taking
Tolerance of Ambiguity
Persistence/Perseverance/Tenacity
Independence
Self-confidence
Dedication/Strong Work Ethic
Organizational Skills
Opportunistic
Adaptability/Versatility
Initiative/Energetic
Resourcefulness
Creativity
Perceptiveness
Assertiveness
Persuasiveness

by the task, the challenge, the opportunity to accomplish what others said could not, would not, or should not be done. Money certainly counts, but it is a by-product. Money serves as a score card, telling the entrepreneur that he or she is making progress.

Second, entrepreneurial individuals demonstrate a strong internal locus of control. Unlike those who believe that external events control their lives and dictate what happens around them, entrepreneurs are change agents. They fundamentally believe that, with enough time and effort and their own involvement, they can change their workplace, their markets, their industries—in short, their environments.

Third, entrepreneurial individuals are calculated risk-takers. The entrepreneur tends to be about a 5.5 on a 10-point scale, where 1 = "risk avoidant" and 10 = "bold gambler." Calculated risk-taking can be defined as pursuit of a course of action that has a reasonable chance of costly failure, where failure is a significant negative difference between anticipated and actual results. It is calculated in the sense that (a) the individual has considered and attempted to estimate (at least conceptually) the likelihood and magnitude of the key risk factors; and

(b) he/she has attempted to manage or mitigate the key risk factors through good planning and managerial decision making.

Fourth, the very nature of the entrepreneurial process demands that the entrepreneur demonstrate a high "tolerance of ambiguity." Things do not have to be precise, fit a precast mold or follow an exact process. The process will inherently be loose, messy, and can abruptly move in new and unanticipated directions. Few entrepreneurs find that their successful business concept is an exact replica of their original idea. Few ventures unfold in the manner described in the original business plan. This is not because of poor conceptualizing or planning; it is the fundamental nature of the game. Even in the case of a franchise purchase, where there may be less risk-taking and innovativeness, ambiguities are likely in dealings with financiers, suppliers and service providers, and in the marketplace.

Fifth, entrepreneurs tend to prize their independence. They are self-motivated, self-reliant, and prefer a degree of autonomy when accomplishing a task. The perception that they have room to maneuver in affecting their own destiny is highly valued. Finally, it is generally agreed that entrepreneurs are tenacious and demonstrate significant perseverance.

Other common findings, about which there is less consensus, suggest that entrepreneurs are versatile, persuasive, creative, well-organized, extremely hardworking, and competitive (need to win).

According to some observers, there is also a "dark side" to entrepreneurs. Kets de Vries (1984) argues that many entrepreneurs have an excessive need for control, which may produce a tendency to micro-manage or do other people's jobs for them. They can also demonstrate a tendency toward suspicious thinking that goes beyond thinking someone will steal their concept. Other characteristics include impatience, a need for applause, seeing the world in terms of black and white, defensiveness, and the externalizing of internal problems.

As indicated earlier, our position is that entrepreneurs are not born, nor can someone simply be taught to be entrepreneurial. Although filled with controversy, the research on entrepreneurial characteristics makes one thing clear. The traits associated with entrepreneurial behavior are strongly influenced by the environment (see Chapter Five) and are developed over time. The list of traits and characteristics in Table 6.1 does not contain items that are clearly genetic, such as intelligence, physical prowess, or artistic talent. The tendencies to be self-confident, to have an internal locus of control, and to be achievement motivated, and similar attributes are the result of family, educational, social, and work experiences. Further, there is some entrepreneurial potential in each and every one of us.

Bird (1989) has provided an excellent illustration of the environmental perspective applied at the level of the individual. She synthesizes a wide array of findings from the literature to demonstrate how the prototypical entrepreneur is the product of specific developments in his/her social, economic, and family environments. This synthesis appears in Table 6.2. At the same time, Bird's perspective, and the perspective presented up to this point, implies the existence of a single prototype of the entrepreneur. As we shall see, there are, in fact, different types of entrepreneurs.

CATEGORIES OF ENTREPRENEURS

One of the earliest attempts to identify types or categories of entrepreneurs involved distinguishing "craftsmen" from "opportunists" (Smith, 1967). Craftsmen are characterized by narrowness in education and training, blue-collar origins, low social awareness and involvement, a feeling of inadequacy in dealing with the social environment, and a limited time orientation. They create businesses of a more rigid nature. Alternatively, opportunistic entrepreneurs exhibit breadth in education and training, middle-class origins, a variety of work experiences, high social awareness and involvement, confidence in their ability to deal with the social environment, and an awareness of, and orientation towards, the future. They are more likely to create organizations that are adaptable to change and growth-oriented.

Kets de Vries (1977) adds a third category of entrepreneur, the Research and Development (R + D) or technical entrepreneur. These individuals often, but not always, come up with their own inventions or product modifications. They typically have work experience in a high technology environment, have a more formal technical education, and make greater use of teams.

A distinction somewhat similar to the one above is made by Kao (1991), who discusses "creative or charismatic" and "conventional" entrepreneurs. The former tend to do something that is more innovative and has a higher risk profile, while the latter build a venture around existing (or slightly improved) products or services. As well, the former are often more growth-oriented than the latter.

In examining why some entrepreneurs succeed in one type of venture and fail in another, and why some succeed initially but fail once a venture reaches a certain size, Miner (1996) concludes that four different types of entrepreneurs exist, each of which achieves success by approaching entrepreneurship from a different route. These include:

The Personal Achiever (the classic entrepreneur):

- high need for achievement
- need for performance feedback
- desire to plan and set goals
- strong individual initiative
- strong personal commitment and identification with their organization
- internal locus of control
- belief that work should be guided by personal goals, not those of others

Table 6.2

A Psychoanalytic Model of Entrepreneurship

Social, cultural, historic, economic context
Society that supports the development of authoritarian personality Family poverty
AND
Childhood family dynamics

Father's: Absence   Mother's: Dominance
               Remoteness   Nurturance
               Villainy
               Role-model

RESULT IN
Disrupted, deprived childhood Conflicts in identification (love-hate) Splitting the good and bad (either-or thinking, closed-mindedness) Persistent feelings of dissatisfaction, rejection, powerlessness, low self-esteem, distrust
THAT DEVELOP INTO
Young adulthood characterized by
Disorientation, goal-lessness, testing Non-conformity, rebelliousness Enjoying setbacks (martyrdom, masochism) High need for control Suspicious thinking Fear of being victimized Scanning the environment
THROUGH A SERIES OF CONSCIOUS CHOICES A PERSON ENDS UP AS AN ENTREPRENEUR
Adulthood creation of an organization that is
Authoritarian Centralized Lacking trust and delegation Lacking planning, impulsive A work environment of high dependency and power that is a function of centrality or closeness to the entrepreneur Unresolved regarding succession: Rivalry with sons   Coping with loss or losing control

Source: Bird (1989).

The Super-Salesperson (follows the selling route to success, caters to the needs of customers)

- capacity to understand and feel with another, to empathize
- desire to help others
- belief that social processes are important; social interaction and relationships are important
- need to have strong positive relationships with others
- belief that the salesforce is crucial to carrying out company strategy
- background of fewer years of education and more years of business experience, and especially selling experience, than other entrepreneurs

The Real Manager (unless he/she overmanages the early stage venture, is able to grow the venture significantly)

- desire to be a corporate leader
- desire to compete
- decisiveness
- desire for power
- positive attitudes to authority
- desire to stand out from the crowd

The Expert Idea Generator (expertise plus creativity = innovator)

- desire to innovate
- love of ideas, curious, open-minded
- belief that new product development is crucial component of company strategy
- good intelligence; thinking is at center of their entrepreneurial approach; intelligence as a source of competitive advantage
- desire to avoid taking risks

Some people are likely to demonstrate patterns that fit into more than one of these categories. Miner (1996) argues that these individuals can succeed by pursuing more than one route. For others, however, their success is dependent on pursuing an approach to entrepreneurship consistent with the dominant pattern into which they fall.

An alternative typology, proposed by Vesper (1980), looks not at the characteristics of the person, but instead, at the method they rely upon to build their venture. He identifies ten types of entrepreneurs:

1. *Solo self-employed*: Includes Mom and Pop stores, professionals, and trades people who work alone or with very few people, and who do most of the work themselves.
2. *Team builders*: People who build an organization through incremental hiring.

3. *Independent innovators*: Inventors who build an organization to produce and sell an invention; they may build a high-technology organization.

4. *Pattern multipliers*: People who expand a business concept through franchises or chains of similar stores.

5. *Economy of scale exploiters*: People who increase volume and lower price by large-scale production or sales.

6. *Acquirers*: People who purchase or inherit a going concern.

7. *Buy-sell artists*: Those who buy companies to later resell them at a profit: turnaround artists, corporate raiders, and take-over experts.

8. *Conglomerators*: Variation of acquirers: those who use the assets of one company to buy control of others not necessarily related to the first business.

9. *Speculators*: People who purchase an asset such as land to leverage the purchase of other assets (more land, construction); resell later at a profit.

10. *Apparent value manipulators*: The "buy low, sell high entrepreneur," the classic "arbitrageur": those who repackage, redefine, or restructure to add apparent value.

In conclusion, there has been little research on the identification of categories of entrepreneurs, and the research that has been done suffers from methodological limitations. Even so, there is strong reason to believe that multiple types exist, and that entrepreneurs can differ in terms of their relative risk profiles, sources of motivation, managerial capabilities, and other characteristics.

THE PATHS TO ENTREPRENEURSHIP: TRIGGERING EVENTS

The term "entrepreneur" is a label. It has been applied fairly indiscriminately to describe small business owners, industry pioneers, inventors, corporate turn-around artists, dynamic leaders, those who creatively engineer take-overs or buyouts, and builders of large conglomerates. These days, it is applied to people who start political and religious movements, instigate major social changes, or remake nations. To be designated an entrepreneur is usually considered a positive attribution, suggesting one has successfully built something more from something less. However, success is not a necessary ingredient, for many entrepreneurs fail.

Yet most of those individuals that we think of as entrepreneurs did not wake up one morning and say to themselves, "I think I'll be an entrepreneur." (Ironically, many of them do not consider themselves entrepreneurs even after they have achieved great success.) The paths that they take are as different as the stars in the sky. They may start early or late in life or do entrepreneurial things throughout their lives. Some pursue the path deliberately; others find themselves there due to circumstances. Some begin with a vision; others develop one along the way. One may start with a single goal and, once it is accomplished, aim for a bigger goal. Another begins with a grand objective and will settle for nothing less. Some are luckier than others, and some work much harder than others.

While there is no formula or recipe that entrepreneurs follow, many start down the path because of some "triggering event." Table 6.3 provides thirteen examples of entrepreneurial triggers. This is not an exhaustive list but does highlight most of the major factors that ultimately cause the individual to "go for it" at a particular point in time. It is interesting to note that all of the triggers in Table 6.3 except "deliberate search" are the result of circumstances or developments in the environment.

Table 6.3
Thirteen Entrepreneurial Triggers

Negative Triggers	Illustration
Survival	"My current situation does not pay the rent"
Job dissatisfaction	"I hate my boss, my work, my environment"
Lay-off or retrenchment	"My employer no longer needs me"
Business in trouble	"We lost a key account, technology has made us obsolete, costs are through the roof, our major supplier dropped us . . . we've got to do something"
Divorce	"I'm suddenly on my own with no source of support"
Death	"Dad died unexpectedly and left me with a troubled business that I had to turn around"
Positive Triggers	
Fresh start	"I just graduated from school, or just moved to a new place, and am ready to do something different
Opportunity knocks	"My employer offered to finance me if I would become his outsourced supplier" (or) "A customer promised me a huge order if I could develop a widget for him"
Curiosity	"What if . . . I saw something that intrigued me and just decided to give it a go"
Desire to improve one's lot	"I wanted to take control of my life and put myself in a situation where my own efforts determined my returns"
Now or never	"I turned forty, realized I'm not getting any younger and decided to go for it"
Windfall	"I won the lottery or inherited a bundle from Aunt Betty, and decided to do something positive with it"
Deliberate Search	"I've always known I would do something entrepreneurial, I just needed to find the right opportunity"

Consider Dino Cortopassi, a farmer in Northern California. Dino, whose father was also a farmer, found that he had no strategic leverage when it came to marketing his cherries, tomatoes, and other farm products. He was a price taker, and could basically sell whatever he produced at going market rates, which fluctuated considerably based on aggregate supply and demand conditions. No matter how large or efficient he got, margins were uncontrollable, and returns on a sizable fixed investment were often dismal. Faced with these circumstances, he decided to move downstream and get into food processing. Dino pioneered the branding of what many considered to be a commodity—the tomato. Today, his San Tomo Group is a leading marketer of high quality, branded tomato by-products, such as tomato paste and tomato sauces. San Tomo products are used in many of the best restaurants in North America.

Consider the list of triggers in Table 6.3. Dino wanted room to maneuver in determining his own destiny. He would therefore be an example of "desire to improve one's lot," although some of the other triggers may also have been operating.

While we have grouped the triggering factors in Table 6.3 into positive and negative, another perspective is to distinguish between "push" and "pull" factors (Phillips and Brice, 1988). One is pushed into entrepreneurship by unemployment or job dissatisfaction. One is pulled by the perception of market opportunities, the receipt of an economic windfall, or the desire to mimic some role model. Unfortunately, the available research findings regarding whether success rates differ based on whether one is pushed or pulled are mixed.

THE ROLE OF TEAMS

Up to this point, we have argued that entrepreneurship does not happen without entrepreneurs. Just as important is the need to recognize that successful entrepreneurship does not happen without teams.

In the contemporary environment, new ventures are frequently built around a mix of technologies; interdependent methods of production, inventory management, supplier relationships, and logistics; relatively complicated financing schemes; leveraged assets that are not easy to control; customization of products and communications to different market segments or individual clients; and a mix of regular and contract employees as well as full- and part-time employees. Getting things done properly and on a timely basis is dependent on a skilled and well-integrated team. Further, the entrepreneurial process is lengthy and filled with obstacles, suggesting the need for a motivated, coordinated group of individuals, each having his/her own contributions to make.

It becomes necessary to reconcile the concept of individualism, which we intimately associate with entrepreneurial behavior, with the concept of the team, group, or collective, which is also a necessity. Individualism refers to a self-orientation, an emphasis on self-sufficiency and control, the pursuit of individual goals that may or may not be consistent with those of one's colleagues or associates, and a value system where people derive pride from their own accomplishments. A group or collective orientation involves the subordination of personal interests to the goals of the larger work group, an emphasis on sharing, cooperation, and group harmony, a concern with group welfare, and antipathy towards those outside the group.

In a work context, there are positive and negative aspects to both individualism and a group or collective orientation. Table 6.4 provides a summary of these pros and cons. In essence, an individualistic ethic may foster development of an individual's self-confidence, lead to a greater sense of personal responsibility, create more of a competitive spirit, and produce higher-risk, breakthrough innovations. It can also produce selfishness, high levels of stress, and interper-

Table 6.4
Individualism versus a Group or Collective Orientation

Individualism	Group or Collective Orientation
Pros: • Employee develops stronger self-concept, more self-confidence • Consistent with achievement motivation • Competition among individuals encourages greater numbers of novel concepts and ideas; breakthrough innovations • Stronger sense of personal responsibility for performance outcomes • Linkage between personal effort and rewards creates greater sense of equity Cons: • Emphasis on personal gain at expense of others, selfishness, materialism • Individuals have less commitment/loyalty, are more "up for sale" • Differences among individuals are emphasized • Interpersonal conflicts are encouraged • Greater levels of personal stress, pressure for individual performance • Insecurity can result from overdependence on oneself • Greater feelings of loneliness, alienation, and anomie • Stronger incentive for unethical behaviour, expediency • Onus of failure falls on the individual	Pros: • Greater synergies from combined efforts of people with differing skills • Ability to incorporate diverse perspectives and achieve comprehensive view • Individuals treated as equals • Relationships more personalized, synchronized, harmonious, while interpersonal conflicts are discouraged • Greater concern for welfare of others, network of social support available • More consensus regarding direction and priorities • Credit for failures and successes equally shared • Teamwork produces steady, incremental progress on projects Cons: • Loss of personal and professional self to group/collective • Greater emotional dependence on individuals in the group or organization • Less personal responsibility for outcomes • Individuals "free ride" on efforts of others, rewards not commensurate with effort • Tendency toward "group think" • Outcomes can represent compromises among diverse interests, reflecting need to get along more than need for performance • Collectives can take more time to reach consensus, may miss opportunities

sonal conflict. A group orientation offers the advantages of more harmonious relationships between individuals, greater synergies, more social support, and can result in a steady stream of incremental improvements and innovations. On the downside, the team or group focus can entail the loss of individual identity, greater emotional dependency, a tendency to "free ride" on the efforts of others, compromises rather than optimizing behavior, and "group think," in which individuals get locked into a singular shared way of viewing or approaching a problem.

The ability to start, grow, and sustain any entrepreneurial venture requires a balance between the need for individual initiative and the spirit of cooperation and group ownership of innovation. This balance is pictured in Figure 6.2. As the entrepreneurial process unfolds, the individual champion requires not just specialist expertise, but teams of people, some of whom can fill multiple roles. Members of these teams are able to collaborate in meeting tight timelines, identifying and overcoming unanticipated obstacles, and finding angles and opportunities that often redefine the entrepreneur's concept, putting it on a more successful path. Sometimes it is the entrepreneur who keeps the team on track, and other times it is the team that is the voice of reason and consistency.

NETWORKS AND THE ENTREPRENEUR

In addition to internal teams, every entrepreneur is dependent on external networks (corporate entrepreneurs actually have a network that consists of both

Figure 6.2
The Relationship between Entrepreneurship and an Emphasis on the Individual versus the Group or Collective

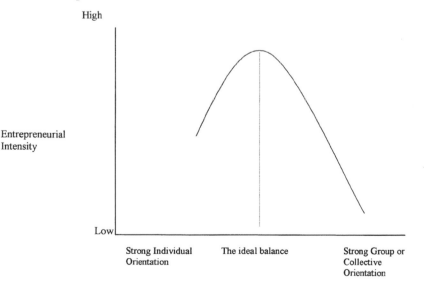

internal and external elements). The entrepreneur's networking abilities and the quality of the network he/she builds often define the ultimate level of success achieved by the venture.

The term "network" is used to describe a number of people and organizations that are connected. They are formed for a variety of purposes but, in this case, to facilitate some form of economic exchange. The network approach emphasizes the dynamic ability of the entrepreneur to shift and switch among the resources used in the venture. Three major benefits result from a good network:

- Empowerment—through the network, the entrepreneur is able to gain access to resources that he/she would not otherwise have; the entrepreneur can achieve reach, power, and economies of scale.

- Predictability—networks result in long-term relationships that reduce the uncertainty surrounding whether and when the entrepreneur can obtain assistance and where to go for that assistance.

- Expanded scope and focus—in addition to providing resources for current operations, the network is a vehicle for recognizing and capitalizing on opportunities the entrepreneur would otherwise have missed.

Networks can be characterized in terms of their diversity, density, reachability, and the value of each member (Dubini and Aldrich, 1991). *Diversity* is a reflection of the variety of those who make up the network. A non-diverse network might consist only of one's close acquaintances. A diverse network might include casual and close acquaintances, strangers, company representatives, government officials, an interactive Internet site, and much more. *Density* refers to the extensiveness of ties between the various network members. These ties can be absent or present, weak or strong. In dense networks, individuals are all aware of one another, and information and resources are rapidly and efficiently transferred within the network. *Reachability* is concerned with the path between two persons or organizations. Can a given member of the network be reached directly, only through an intermediary or perhaps two intermediaries, or is the person fairly isolated? *Value* is a reflection of a member's contribution to the entrepreneur's network. It attempts to capture how useful or critical a role the member plays. A member generates value through the information he/she provides, through non-informational resources (e.g., money, office space, advice), or through the linkages he/she provides to other members of the network.

A valuable component of any network is the presence of brokers. These are people that enable the entrepreneur to leverage his/her effectiveness by using available knowledge to access more effective resource providers. Thus, brokers do not provide resources directly, they provide access. Brokers essentially facilitate the interests of entrepreneurs who are not directly connected to the best resource providers.

To see a network in action, let's consider an example of an entrepreneur and the start-up process she went through (Figure 6.3). Her firm operates tours for

Figure 6.3
An Illustration of an Entrepreneur's Network: The Case of a Tour Operator

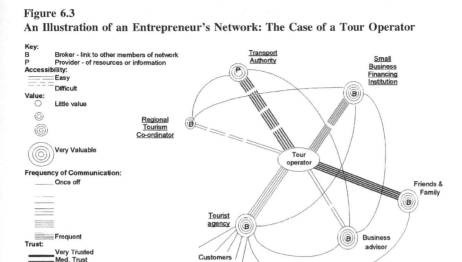

international and local visitors into black townships in South Africa. She has a technical diploma and previous work experience related to the venture she was starting up. At the start-up of her venture, she had only her house and a small personal savings account at the bank. So at face value, her resources appear extremely limited.

Our entrepreneur's original job was with a tourist agency, and through her strong relationship with them, and their knowledge of the industry, she was able to establish her company with very few resources of her own. She even got the telephone company to install her telephone without any down payment required. The links in the network she developed represent sets of relationships. These relationships can be characterized not only by their of accessibility, value, and the frequency of communication, but also by the level of trust that develops between her and the other party. Trust is the key underlying variable that de termines how solid and permanent a given link in the network is. In effect, a network allows our entrepreneur to expand her circle of trust.

Her network formation efforts are graphically represented in the diagram above. Her previous employer acted as a broker in her network formation efforts, by connecting her with a sophisticated business advisor, as well as referring her services to potential customers. This advisor, with whom she had a short, ex tremely valuable, one time, but trusting connection, put her in contact with a small business financing institution as well as a transport authority. From the finance institution she received funds, and from the transport authority she man aged to negotiate to use the local public transport vehicles and their drivers during off-peak hours. This relationship with the transport authority enabled her to provide a service to her customers in authentic local transport without having to make any long-term commitment.

The density of her network implies that a high level of trust runs throughout her entire set of relationships and indicates how she was able to quickly arrive at effective sources of resources to capitalize on her opportunity. The network also facilitated rapid information and resource transfer. The presence of valuable members indicates that each was used to his/her fullest potential with the highest level of cooperation and the greatest possible economic benefit derived. A possible limitation to her network is its reachability; her network has essentially not extended beyond that which she had developed at start-up. This should be the focus of future development efforts.

Entrepreneurs should keep in mind that the ultimate goal of all the members of a network is to achieve common goals. Emphasizing mutually beneficial relationships can lead the entrepreneur to recognize new opportunities as well as improve the quality of day-to-day business decisions. Entrepreneurs can better conceptualize their positions within a network and seek ways to harness potential benefits and opportunities that arise out of network cooperation. Individuals with limited resources can use their networks to significantly leverage their positions by tapping into the resources of others.

In the final analysis, by forming strategic alliances and broadening the reach of their network during the start-up phase of a new venture, entrepreneurs significantly increase the likelihood of survival and growth. In fact, advice on creating and managing external networks may actually prove more valuable in the long run than advice on how to run the business itself.

CONCLUSIONS

Entrepreneurship is a bottom-up process. It does not start with government policy or corporate strategy. It begins with people. The modern history of the entrepreneur has focused on special people who stand out from the crowd. Our argument is that the focus should actually be on ordinary people who do special things. Stated differently, everybody has some level of entrepreneurial potential.

A related conclusion is that there is no single prototype of the entrepreneur. There may be some general traits that entrepreneurs tend to have more in common than do corporate managers, government administrators, blue-collar workers, or other groups. Yet, entrepreneurs vary in terms of these traits, and some are strong on other traits that are not generally associated with the "classic" entrepreneur. As a result, four or five general categories of entrepreneurs emerge.

Finally, the culture of entrepreneurship is assumed to be rooted in a tradition of individualism. We believe individualism is vital and question those who would abandon the individual in favor of the group or collective. Even so, rarely does the entrepreneurial concept succeed without a devoted team and a supportive network. Teams will vary in their nature and scope, but they are indispensable. Some play more of a strategic role, and others are more operational. In some organizations, the entrepreneur is a co-equal team participant, while in others he/she is dictatorial and the team follows and implements. Similarly, networks provide a vehicle for entrepreneurs to do more, do it faster, and achieve higher quality levels. There is a need in most entrepreneurial ventures for an explicit "networking strategy," which should cover such issues as the size and membership of one's network, the roles to be played, the frequency and types of communication with members, the types of mutual benefits to be created, and the methods of building trust.

In deciding what is an appropriate level of entrepreneurial intensity in one's life, individuals must balance frequency of entrepreneurial activity against degree. Further, they must balance their own risk-taking profile and innovativeness against their personal responsibilities and lifestyle choices, as well as against their personal abilities to build, motivate, and work with teams and networks.

REFERENCES

Bird, B.J. 1989. *Entrepreneurial Behavior*. London: Scott, Foresman.

Dubini, P., and Aldrich, H. 1991. "Personal and Extended Networks are Central to the Entrepreneurial Process." *Journal of Business Venturing*, 6, 305–313.

Kao, J.J. 1991. *The Entrepreneur*. Englewood Cliffs, NJ: Prentice-Hall.

Kets de Vries, M.F.R. 1977. "The Entrepreneurial Personality: A Person at the Crossroads." *Journal of Management Studies*, 14, 34–57.

Kets de Vries, M.F.R. 1984. *Can You Survive an Entrepreneur?* Boston: HBS Case Services.

McClelland, D. 1987. "Characteristics of Successful Entrepreneurs." *Journal of Creative Behavior*, 21, 219–233.

Miner, J.B. 1996. *The 4 Routes to Entrepreneurial Success*. San Francisco: Berrett-Koehler Publishers.

Phillips, B., and Brice, H. 1988. "Black Business in South Africa: A Challenge to Enterprise." *International Journal of Small Business*, 6 (3), 42–58.

Ronstadt, R.C. 1984. *Entrepreneurship: Text, Cases and Notes*. Dover, MA: Lord Publishing.

Sexton, D.L., and Van Auken, P.M. 1982. *Successful vs. Unsuccessful Entrepreneurs: A Comparative Study*. Paper presented at the Babson College Entrepreneurship Research Conference.

Smith, N.R. 1967. *The Entrepreneur and His Firm: The Relationship between Type of Man and Type of Company*. Lansing, MI: Bureau of Business and Economic Research, Graduate School of Business Administration, Michigan State University.

Vesper, K. 1980. *New Venture Strategies*. Englewood Cliffs, NJ: Prentice-Hall.

7

The Entrepreneurial Organization

INTRODUCTION

Organizations can be characterized in terms of their overall strategic orientation. A key aspect of this orientation concerns entrepreneurship. As we saw in Chapter 4, organizations differ significantly in terms of the level of entrepreneurial intensity (EI) that they demonstrate. The entrepreneurial organization is one in which managers are more inclined to take business-related risks, to favor innovation and change in advancing the organization's interests, and to anticipate and preemptorily respond to the actions of suppliers, competitors, customers, and other publics.

Achieving an entrepreneurial orientation is not something that management can simply decide to do. It requires considerable time and investment, and there must be continual reinforcement. As we shall see, the typical organization imposes significant constraints on entrepreneurial behavior. To be sustainable, the entrepreneurial spirit must be integrated into the mission, goals, strategies, structure, processes, and values of the organization.

The importance of entrepreneurship in a corporate context is primarily environmentally determined. Where the external environments of corporations are characterized as increasingly dynamic, threatening, or complex, managers find themselves losing control over these environments. The appropriate strategies for addressing such environmental turbulence can be generally grouped into two categories: adaptive and entrepreneurial.

The adaptive approach is to anticipate environmental change, and then quickly adjust to the changing conditions, or buffer the firm to limit its vulnerability. Organizational survival is a function both of a firm's speed in responding to change and of its ability to establish defensive barriers to moderate the impact of significant environmental developments.

Although widely accepted, this is an overly passive and reactive point of view. The survival of firms as we move into the twenty-first century may well depend on their ability to manage the environment and to serve as agents of change. Such firms will seek to continually rewrite the rules of the competitive game. This is the entrepreneurial approach.

MANAGERS AS PROMOTERS VERSUS TRUSTEES

An extremely useful perspective that can be applied to organizational entrepreneurship is provided by Stevenson and colleagues (1994). As summarized in Figure 7.1, they suggest that a business can be characterized in terms of six key dimensions: the company's strategic orientation, commitment to opportunity, methods for making resource commitments, strategies for controlling resources, organizational structure, and approach to rewards. A further distinction can be drawn between the manager as "promoter" and the manager as "trustee." A promoter adopts an entrepreneurial approach to management, focuses on the pursuit of opportunity, and promotes change. A trustee is at the other end of the continuum, and is someone primarily concerned with efficient utilization of the resources under his/her control. A more complete comparison of promoters and trustees can be found in Table 7.1.

In essence, the entrepreneurial organization has managers who wear the "promoter" hat far more often than the "trustee" hat. These organizations design strategies that are opportunity-driven rather than resource-driven; they make revolutionary commitments to new opportunities, capitalize on a given opportunity, and then move on to the next one. Their resource commitments are multi-staged, with minimal exposure at each stage; these resources are leveraged, leased, rented, or contracted; the organizational structure is flat with informal networks; and the reward system is based on value created with no limits on what a person or team can potentially earn.

The other significant contribution of the Stevenson framework concerns the identification of factors creating a need for more entrepreneurial (promoter) versus administrative (trustee) approaches to managing the organization. The authors imply that EI becomes more critical as organizations find their opportunity streams diminishing and external environments changing faster. Further, short decision windows, limited decision constituencies, lack of predictable resource needs, an inability to control internal and external developments, pressures for more opportunity per resource unit, and employee demands for more independence are all factors that force organizations to become more entrepreneurial.

For many large, established firms, the pressures from each of these can be expected to magnify in the foreseeable future. In fact, much of the current interest in facilitating corporate entrepreneurship originates from companies facing these very pressures. Furthermore, there is a small but growing volume of

Figure 7.1
Key Business Dimensions and Entrepreneurship

Pressures toward this side	Promoter	Key Business Dimension	Trustee	Pressures toward this side
Diminished opportunity streams Rapidly changing: technology, consumer economics, social values	Driven by perception of opportunity	**Strategic orientation** ← Entrepreneurial domain → Administrative domain	Driven by resources currently controlled	Social contracts Performance-measurement criteria Planning systems and cycle
Action orientation Short decision windows Risk management Limited decision constituencies	Revolutionary with short duration	**Commitment to opportunity** ← Entrepreneurial domain → Administrative domain	Evolutionary of long duration	Acknowledgement of multiple constituencies Negotiation of strategy Risk reduction Management of fit
Lack of predictable resource needs Lack of long-term control Social need for more opportunity per resource unit Interpersonal pressure for more efficient resource use	Multi-staged with minimal exposure at each stage	**Commitment of Resources** ← Entrepreneurial domain → Administrative domain	Single-staged with complete commitment upon decision	Personal risk reduction Incentive compensation Managerial turnover Capital allocation systems Formal planning systems
Increased resource specialization Long resource life compared to need Risk obsolescence Risk inherent in any new venture Inflexibility of permanent commitment to resources	Episodic use or rent of required resources	**Control of Resources** ← Entrepreneurial domain → Administrative domain	Ownership or employment of required resources	Power, status and financial rewards Coordination Efficiency measures Inertia and cost of change Industry structures
Coordination of key non-controlled resources Challenge to legitimacy of owner's control Employees' desire for independence	Flat with multiple informal networks	**Management Structure** ← Entrepreneurial domain → Administrative domain	Formalized hierarchy	Need for clearly defined authority and responsibility Organizational culture Reward systems Management theory
Individual expectations Competition Increased perception of personal wealth-creation possibilities	Value-based Team-based Unlimited	**Compensation/ Reward Policy** ← Entrepreneurial domain → Administrative domain	Resource-based Driven by short-term data Promotion Limited amount	Societal norms Tax regulations Impacted information Search for simple solutions for complex problems Demands on public shareholders

Source: Stevenson et al. (1994). Reprinted with permission.

Table 7.1
Promoters and Trustees

The Manager as PROMOTER (entrepreneur)
• Confident of his/her ability to seize opportunity
• Expects surprises
• Adjusts to and capitalizes on change
• Flexible -- can move from project to project, team to team, division to division
• Proactive, makes things happen; believes in own ability to effect change
• Opportunity-driven rather than resource-driven; pursues opportunity regardless of resources currently controlled
• Calculated risk-taker
• Externally-focused
• Views failure as valuable learning experience
• Less concerned with long-term job security -- more concerned with autonomy and freedom
The Manager as TRUSTEE (administrator)
• Threatened by change
• Cautious, emphasizes maintenance of status quo
• Stresses predictability, relies on conventional wisdom and rules of thumb
• Concentrates on efficiency in utilizing resources
• Resource-driven, not opportunity-driven
• Risk-aversive
• Reactive
• Internally-focused
• Concerned with job security, power, position

empirical research supporting the need for more entrepreneurial management. Miller and Friesen (1983), for instance, have found a significant positive relationship between the degree of environmental dynamism, hostility, and heterogeneity present and the amount of proactive, risk-taking, and innovative behavior in successful firms. They found no such relationship, however, in unsuccessful firms (see also Morris and Sexton, 1996).

EFFECTING CHANGE: WHERE TO FOCUS ATTENTION

Organizations tend to evolve through different stages as they grow and mature (Adizes, 1978; Griener, 1972). The requirements of size are such that developing firms go through a metamorphosis in moving from start-up venture to large diversified corporation. Stated differently, large companies are not simply scaled-up versions of small companies. While many small enterprises fail to demonstrate significant entrepreneurship, the constraints on entrepreneurship in such firms are comparatively limited. However, the changes instituted or experienced by larger companies to accommodate growth also tend to undermine the potential for ongoing entrepreneurship in these firms (Knight, 1987; Stefflre, 1985).

While the actual constraints on corporate entrepreneurship derive from many sources, they can be generally classified into six groups: systems, structure, strategic direction, policies, people, and culture. This framework is proposed based on an extensive review of the limited literature on corporate entrepreneurship, surveys of a number of medium-size and large industrial organizations, and in-depth assessments of three Fortune 500 companies.

Examples of the specific constraints found within each group are provided in Table 7.2. This set of items is not an exhaustive list but instead includes some of the more pervasive problem areas. Also, the groups are not mutually exclusive or independent. For instance, systems overlap with policies, while people problems may be highly correlated with cultural problems. Keeping this interdependence in mind, let us examine each of the categories.

Systems

Maturing organizations are typically dependent upon a number of formal managerial systems that have evolved over the years. These systems seek to provide stability, order, and coordination to an increasingly complex internal corporate environment. The trade-off, however, is a strong disincentive for entrepreneurship.

For example, employee reward and measurement systems often encourage safe, conservative behavior and actions that produce short-term payoffs. Other

Table 7.2
Six Categories of Organizational Constraints on Entrepreneurship

Systems	Structures	Strategic Direction	Policies and Procedures	People	Culture
• Misdirected reward and evaluation systems • Oppressive control systems • Inflexible budgeting systems • Arbitrary cost allocation systems • Overly rigid, formal planning systems	• Too many hierarchical levels • Overly narrow span of control • Responsibility without authority • Top-down management • Restricted communication channels • Lack of accountability • Bloated staff functions	• Absence of innovation goals • No formal strategy for entrepreneurship • No vision from the top • Lack of commitment from senior executives • No entrepreneurial role models at the top	• Long, complex approval cycles • Extensive documentation requirements • Overreliance on established rules of thumb • Unrealistic performance criteria	• Fear of failure • Resistance to change • Parochial bias • "Turf" protection • Complacency • Short-term orientation • Inappropriate skills/talents	• Ill-defined values • Lack of consensus over priorities • Lack of fit • Values that conflict with entrepreneurial requirements

times, they are vague, inconsistent, or perceived as inequitable. Steven Kerr (1975) explains that many managers are guilty of the "folly of rewarding A, while hoping for B." They tend to ask for or expect innovative behavior, but actually measure and reward non-innovative behaviors. Control systems encourage managers to micro-manage the expenditure of every dollar and to establish quantifiable performance benchmarks in as many activity areas as possible. These benchmarks become ends in themselves. They also convey a lack of trust in employee discretion. Budgeting systems provide no flexibility for the funding of bootleg projects or experimentation and tend to reward the politically powerful. Costing systems are frequently based on arbitrary allocation schemes, where any product or project can be made to look untenable simply as a function of the indirect fixed costs that must be recovered.

Planning, although critical for successful entrepreneurship, often serves as an obstacle. This occurs because of an overemphasis on superfluous analysis, on form instead of content, on the document instead of the process, and on professional planners instead of having those charged with implementing the plan actually prepare the plan. The result is an overly rigid process that is incapable of quickly responding to new opportunities with short decision windows.

Structure

As a firm designs more hierarchical levels into the organizational structure, the ability to identify market opportunities, achieve management commitment, reallocate resources, take risks, or implement effective marketplace moves becomes problematic. Moreover, hierarchies tend to be accompanied by two other entrepreneurial barriers, top-down management and restrictive channels of communication. The result is frequently intransigence and a lack of commitment to innovation and change at all levels of the organization.

There is also a tendency to narrow the span of control of managers and to overdepartmentalize as firms mature. The result is oversupervised employees with little room to be creative or improvise. Furthermore, as employees become more segmented and compartmentalized, frames of reference become quite narrow. The ability to integrate perspectives and methods across boundaries is stifled. Meanwhile, accountability for effective change efforts is sufficiently diffused such that no one has a positive stake in ensuring that change occurs.

Structures that assign responsibility for entrepreneurial activities to managers, without commensurate authority, represent an additional constraint. Lacking the authority to try new methods or approaches to addressing obstacles, or to expend required resources, the manager is likely to become frustrated and perhaps cynical.

Strategic Direction

While the desire may be to achieve entrepreneurship throughout the firm, little can be accomplished without meaningful direction from the top. Established firms frequently have sophisticated planning systems that produce comprehensive strategies for marketing, production, and corporate finance but ignore the subject of innovation altogether. In the absence of specific goals for product and process innovation, and a strategy for accomplishing such goals, entrepreneurship will only result from happenstance.

More fundamental, however, is the lack of commitment from senior executives to the principle of institutionalized entrepreneurship. This requires leaders who are visionaries, seeing the firm and its people for what they can be, not what they have been. Instead, senior management is more typically cautious, suspicious, or completely unaware of efforts to break with tradition and capitalize on opportunity. Middle- and lower-level employees are strongly influenced by the role models found at the top of the organization. What they often find are politicians and technocrats, well-versed in the art of corporate survival.

Policies and Procedures

Those involved in entrepreneurial endeavours are, by definition, addressing the unknown. Their efforts are often undermined by organizational policies and procedures that were established to bring order and consistency to the everyday operational requirements of the firm. These requirements tend to be relatively well-known. Operating guidelines are established based on the rules of experience, with a premium placed on conservatism. The corporate entrepreneur comes to view these policies and procedures as burdensome red tape, and many find success to be unattainable unless rules are bent or broken.

Two of the most costly side-effects of detailed operating policies and procedures are complex approval cycles for new ventures and elaborate documentation requirements. These obstacles not only consume an inordinate amount of the entrepreneur's time and energy but frequently serve as well-designed mechanisms for incrementally dismantling an innovative concept.

A related problem is the tendency for existing policies and procedures to impose unrealistic timetables and performance benchmarks on entrepreneurial programs. This creates an incentive to compromise on truly novel ideas. The entrepreneur finds it necessary to tailor innovations to performance criteria that do not reflect changing competitive conditions.

People

Our research suggests that people are the greatest obstacle of all. The number-one priority in any attempt to increase the entrepreneurial intensity of an organization must be to change people, and specifically, to get them to be accepting of change and tolerant of failure in their own work. Entrepreneurship is concerned with change and the management of change efforts. There is, however, a natural tendency for people to resist change. Given the opportunity, employees become comfortable with established ways of doing things. They value predictability and stability and are frequently skeptical of the need for change.

Change is viewed as threatening and is met with a defensive, parochial attitude. This is especially the case where employees have no role in the change program.

There is, furthermore, a preoccupation among workers with the demands of the present, not the future. Correspondingly, it is unrealistic to expect them to adopt a long-term perspective or to recognize the need for continual adaptation.

The entrepreneurial spirit is additionally stifled by a pervading fear of failure that is prevalent in most companies. People come to believe it is better to avoid failure than to risk success. They apparently perceive there is more to lose than to gain. Not that failure must be congratulated; rather, it should be personally detested. But failure is an important medium for learning; it should be embraced as such. The reality is that a majority of new ventures (companies, products, services, processes) fail, suggesting the need for a realistic appraisal of the outcome of any entrepreneurial effort.

People motivation is also a problem, especially for those driven by a need for power and status. Such individuals approach questions of innovation from the standpoint of "turf protection." They hoard resources, especially information. They resist open communication and are suspicious of collaborative efforts.

One additional people-related issue concerns a general lack of skills and talents in the entrepreneurial area. While there is ample creative potential in every employee of the firm, many have never learned to develop or channel their creative energies. Some convince themselves that they are incapable of creative thinking. Others refuse to look beyond their current field of reference for ideas and solutions. Still others, on finding a creative solution, lack the skills necessary to bend the rules, build the coalitions, and work through or around the system to achieve successful implementation. Such problems are compounded by the apparent inability of many of those in supervisory positions to motivate and manage creative individuals.

Culture

Companies noted as successful innovators tend to foster a strong organizational culture. This culture is built around a central set of values that pervades every aspect of company operations. Employees are indoctrinated to internalize these values, and those who do not rarely last. These values are the lifeblood of the firm, creating the standards and providing the direction for growth and development.

Where companies fail to clearly define what they stand for, or do not achieve a consensus over value priorities (e.g., customer needs, quality, efficiency, service, reliability), entrepreneurship will have no focus. Even when priorities exist, values can be inconsistent with current competitive requirements. For instance, the company that stresses reliability or efficiency may find the marketplace puts a much higher premium on flexibility and value for the dollar.

Furthermore, entrepreneurship must itself become part of the organizational value system. This means company-wide commitment to innovation, calculated risk-taking, and proactiveness. Such a commitment becomes impossible when the pervading emphasis is on imitation of competitors, conservation, and self-aggrandizement.

HUMAN RESOURCE MANAGEMENT POLICIES AND ENTREPRENEURSHIP

Of all the managerial decision areas that can affect corporate entrepreneurship, human resource management (HRM) would seem to be one of the more vital. Indeed, the HRM field appears to be experiencing a fundamental transformation from a micro-oriented, bureaucracy-based, tool-driven discipline to one centered around the congruence of the various aspects of the HRM system with business strategies. The argument of Balkin and Logan (1988) that poorly designed compensation and performance appraisal systems may constrain entrepreneurial behavior in established firms is reflective of this transformation. Similarly, Schuler (1986) has suggested that organization-level entrepreneurship can be influenced by a large number of HRM-related policies.

The set of HRM policies and procedures available to managers includes numerous and varied choice alternatives. Schuler and Jackson (1987) have presented a typology of these alternatives that identifies key decision options in each of six areas: planning, staffing, appraising, compensating, training and development, and labor-management relations. Underlying the various decision options are a number of bipolar dimensions, such as the extent to which a given policy reflects an open versus closed, structured versus unstructured, or short-term versus long-term orientation. It would seem that particular organizational strategies, such as entrepreneurship, can be furthered by putting together consistent sets of HRM practices.

Entrepreneurial activities require employees to act and think in ways not normally associated with non-entrepreneurial or bureaucratic organizations. Based on his review of the literature, Schuler (1986) suggested the following employee characteristics were associated with successful entrepreneurial efforts: creative and innovative behavior, risk-taking, a long-term orientation, a focus on results, flexibility to change, cooperation, independent behavior, tolerance of ambiguity, and a preference to assume responsibility. He also notes that HRM practices are a reflection of a firm's culture, and others (Brandt, 1986; Cornwall and Perlman, 1990; Peters, 1987; Tropman and Morningstar, 1989) have suggested corporate entrepreneurship requires a culture built around emotional commitment, autonomy, empowerment, earned respect, and a strong work ethic. Using these desired employee and cultural characteristics, it becomes possible to identify the HRM policy combinations most conducive to fostering entrepreneurial behavior.

Let us now consider specific linkages. Beginning with job planning, innovation and risk-taking behaviors would seem more consistent with a long-term orientation and an emphasis on formal planning with high employee involvement. Job-related tasks would need to be broadly defined, with more decision-making discretion. Also, greater emphasis would have to be placed on results over process or procedure. Jobs are likely to be less structured or constrained by rigid organizational policies. Multiple policies and procedures, along with centralized decision making, tend to constrain action alternatives and inhibit the proactive decision-making necessary for successful entrepreneurial events.

Turning to the staffing choices of the firm, entrepreneurial behavior implies unpredictable external environments and internal requirements. The fit between company direction and available internal resources may be poor. Therefore, firms may be forced to rely on external sources for job candidates. The need to create and maintain an entrepreneurial culture, combined with a reliance on external sources of employees, would in turn increase the need for extensive orientation and socialization programs. Further, rapid environmental change and continuous product and market innovation can be expected to produce time pressures as well as variable job demands and requirements. The result in entrepreneurial organizations is likely to be a reliance on more general, more implicit, and less formalized selection criteria (Olian and Rynes, 1984; Roberts and Fusfeld, 1981).

Once a person is selected into the organization, staffing practices are likely to be designed around broad career paths and multiple ladders (Pearson, 1989). Broad paths and multiple ladders provide exposure to more areas of the organization and different ways of thinking. This exposure in turn enhances idea generation and problem solving and encourages cooperative activities. Staffing procedures in these organizations are apt to be fairly open. Entrepreneurial individuals are goal- and action-oriented. Thus, an employee should not be selected for, or assigned to, entrepreneurial tasks simply on the basis of past performance on other tasks or because they have the basic knowledge and skills the job requires. Open selection procedures allow for more self-selection into entrepreneurial positions and hence a better match between the entrepreneurial requirements of the organization and the individual's needs.

Training and development practices can promote entrepreneurial behavior to the extent that they are applicable to a broad range of job situations and encourage high employee participation. Changing job demands and the need to keep abreast of the newest technologies suggest a need for continuous, ongoing training, as well as training activities that are less structured or standardized and that focus on individualized knowledge requirements. This type of training approach enables employees to respond in unique ways to new challenges, adapt to dynamic environmental conditions, and feel comfortable with ambiguity. Training programs may also include an attitudinal component, wherein acceptance of change, a willingness to take risks and assume responsibility, and reliance on teamwork and shared achievements are central themes. Finally, it may be necessary to teach political skills to prospective entrepreneurs, including ways to obtain sponsors, build resource networks, and avoid early publicity of new concepts and ventures.

Organizations communicate performance expectations and reinforce desired employee behaviors through their performance appraisal and reward practices, both of which should be designed around specific criteria. Entrepreneurship can be fostered where performance evaluations and discretionary compensation are based on long-term results and a balance between individual and group performance (Balkin and Logan, 1988; Maidique, 1980; Morris, Avila and Allen, 1993). Moreover, given that risk implies failure, the appraisal and reward systems should reflect a tolerance of failure and offer some employment security. Because entrepreneurial individuals tend to demonstrate a high need for achievement but are also reward conscious, it is important that they be active participants both in setting high performance standards and in designing customized reward systems.

Appraisals should be conducted at intermittent and irregular time intervals in entrepreneurial organizations, rather than at uniform or fixed intervals. They should be tailored to the life cycle of a project. This is because entrepreneurial events require time to evolve, with each one encountering unique sets of obstacles and with various projects typically at different stages of development. In addition, entrepreneurial success often depends on the ability of employees to obtain resources from novel sources or in non-traditional ways and occasionally to violate or ignore standard company policies and procedures. Accordingly, performance appraisals will need to emphasize end results, or outcomes, rather than the methods employed to achieve those results. The evaluation of employees will need to include explicit measures of innovativeness and risk assumption, which implies some use of qualitative and subjective measures of performance (e.g., Jennings and Seaman, 1990).

With regard to rewards, personal incentives (financial and non-financial) are necessary to reinforce the risk-taking and persistence required to implement an entrepreneurial concept. To retain entrepreneurial employees, these incentives must be significant. Individual incentives must be balanced by rewards linked to group performance over periods of time longer than the typical semi-annual or annual review periods to encourage cooperative, interdependent behavior (Kanter, 1983; Reich, 1987; Stewart, 1989). Taking responsibility for innovation and achieving a long-term commitment can be furthered by compensation practices that emphasize external pay equity and incentives such as stock options and profit sharing. The customized nature of these reward systems also suggests that responsibility for their design and implementation be decentralized, or delegated to the divisional or departmental level. Table 7.3 represents a summary of HRM practices that are believed to be facilitators of entrepreneurship. This list is not intended to be comprehensive, but rather, captures a set of key strategic relationships based on the extant literature. Morris and Jones (1993) have provided some initial empirical evidence to support a number of the proposed relationships.

WHAT ABOUT PUBLIC SECTOR ORGANIZATIONS?

Entrepreneurship also has the same underlying dimensions when applied in a public sector context. Thus, entrepreneurial events can be characterized in terms

Table 7.3
Summary of the HRM Policies Proposed to Be Consistent with Entrepreneurial Behavior

General area	Practices encouraging entrepreneurship
Planning/overall job design	Reliance on formal planning Long-term orientation in planning and job design Implicit job analysis Jobs that are broad in scope Jobs with significant discretion Jobs that are less structured Integrative job design Results-oriented job design High employee involvement
Recruitment and selection	Reliance on external sources for candidates Broad career paths Multiple career ladders General, implicit, less formalized selection criteria Extensive job socialization Open recruitment and selective procedures
Training and development	Long-term career orientation Training with broad applications Individualized training High employee participation Unsystematic training Emphasis on managerial skills Continuous/ongoing training
Performance appraisal	High employee involvement Balanced individual-group orientation Emphasis on effectiveness over efficiency Results oriented (vs. process) Based on subjective criteria Emphasis on long-term performance Includes innovation and risk criteria Reflects tolerance of failure Appraisals based on project life cycle
Compensation/rewards	Emphasizes long-term performance Decentralized/customized at division or departmental levels Tailored to individuals Emphasizes individual performance with incentives for group efforts Merit and incentive-based Significant financial rewards Based on external equity

of their innovativeness, risk-taking, and proactiveness. Innovativeness will tend to be more concerned with novel process improvements, new services, and new organizational forms. Examples might include a drive-in window for voter registration, day care service for welfare mothers in job training programs, or a public/private joint venture to address AIDS awareness. Risk-taking involves pursuing initiatives that have a calculated likelihood of resulting in loss or failure. While public sector organizations cannot incur bankruptcy, failure can result in non-delivered services, cutbacks in service levels, programs or organizational unit closures, staff reassignments, and budget cuts. Although high visibility in the public sector typically means risk-taking is moderate to low, the public sector does undertake highly risky ventures, such as the controversial luggage handling system at the Denver, Colorado airport. There is also career-related risk in the public sector, for while it is difficult to fire people, advancement can be influenced by visible failures. Proactiveness entails an action-orientation, and an emphasis on anticipating and preventing public sector problems before they occur. This action-orientation includes creative interpretation of rules, skills at networking and leveraging of resources, and a high level of persistence and patience in effecting change.

Public sector entrepreneurship is much closer to entrepreneurship in a large corporation than to a new venture start-up. Both public and large private organizations typically have formalized hierarchies, established stakeholder groups with competing demands, deeply entrenched cultures, detailed rules and procedures to guide operations; a desire on the part of managers for power and security; and fairly rigid systems governing financial controls, cost allocations, budgeting, and employee rewards. Managers in both types of organizations are often more concerned with internal than external developments and tend to focus more on considerations of process than on outcomes. Public sector entrepreneurs, like those in large corporations, and unlike those in a start-up context, are not independent, do not "own" the innovations that they develop, and confront very finite limits on the rewards that they can receive; alternatively, they have more job security, are not personally assuming the financial risks associated with a project, and have access to an established pool of resources.

Arguments For and Against Public Sector Entrepreneurship

A number of arguments can be raised that challenge the role of entrepreneurial behavior in public sector organizations. Public employees are not in a position to put taxpayer monies at significant risk, and this combined with the difficulties in measuring risk-return trade-offs in the public sector usually makes high-risk pursuits inappropriate. In addition, high visibility and a need for consensus in decision making suggest that incremental change is more realistic than bold innovation. Also, the lengthy periods of time required for an entrepreneurial event to unfold are inconsistent with public sector budgeting and re-election cycles. Moreover, bureaucracy and the civil service system serve to protect the status quo, ostensibly from the arbitrary or politically influenced behavior of political leaders and public executives. As entrepreneurship is fundamentally about disrupting the status quo and affecting organizational change, again there would seem to be an inherent inconsistency.

At a more fundamental level, some would argue that entrepreneurship can result in innovative measures (e.g., user fees, redevelopment agencies, off-budget enterprises, investment revenues, tax-increment financing, and development fees) that enable public officials and public administrators to avoid voter approval and increase their autonomy, thereby undermining democracy. Further, entrepreneurship entails the pursuit of opportunity regardless of resources currently controlled, while public sector managers are often limited by legislative or regulatory statute to using only those resources formally assigned to their organizations. Finally, the mission, structure, and major initiatives of the public organization are dictated from outside sources (legislative bodies, councils, authorities). Public managers are expected to implement these dictates in a reasonably effective and efficient manner. Entrepreneurship, alternatively, represents an internal dynamic that can serve to change the strategic direction of an organization, potentially putting it in conflict with its stated mission or mandate. Similarly, entrepreneurial efforts can lead public enterprises to generate new services or fundraising schemes that effectively put them in competition with private sector enterprises, which the private sector might argue is a form of unfair competition.

The counter argument is that there have always been elements of innovation and entrepreneurship in public sector organizations, and that the issue is more one of formally defining the entrepreneurial role and then determining appropriate degrees and frequencies of entrepreneurship for a given organization, department, or unit. Creating value for customers, putting resources together in unique ways, and being opportunity-driven are not inherently in conflict with the mission or purpose of public agencies. This is why there does not appear to be any shortage of examples of successful innovations that originate in mainstream public organizations (e.g., Jordan, 1990; Moore, 1983).

There is, one could further suggest, a growing need for entrepreneurial approaches in public administration. The contemporary environment confronting public sector managers is far more complex, threatening, and dynamic than in years past. One has only to consider a public school. A few decades ago, the school was principally accountable for providing a sound, well-rounded basic education. Today, teachers and administrators are responsible for increasing computer literacy, deterring sexual harassment, detecting child abuse, discouraging drug consumption, ensuring the physical safety of students, facilitating bilingualism, providing aftercare, assisting those with learning disabilities, and accommodating those with physical handicaps. The ability to recognize and adequately respond to such changing circumstances is severely limited. Quite simply, the more turbulent the environment in which public managers must operate, the less effective is the traditional bureaucratic model.

Bureaucracy has many advantages and can be quite effective when operating in a relatively stable and predictable environment. However, when faced with highly turbulent environments where funding is not dependable, client demographics and needs are in flux, technology is rapidly changing, social and environmental pressures are increasing, skilled labor shortages are the norm, citizens are calling for privatization, litigation is rampant, and a host of other discontinuities continue to present themselves, the bureaucratic framework fails to provide the flexibility, adaptability, speed, or incentives for innovation that are critical for effectively carrying out the mission of the public enterprise.

There are, of course, different degrees of bureaucratization, and the higher the degree, the greater the conflict with entrepreneurship. Morris, Schindehutte, and Pitt (1996) review fourteen key characteristics of the highly bureaucratic organization that make it incompatible with higher levels of EI. This is not to suggest entrepreneurship as a comprehensive alternative to the bureaucratic model. However, it is proposed as a core component of any post-bureaucracy conceptualization of public sector management.

Bellone and Goerl (1992) agree that potential conflicts do exist between public entrepreneurship and democracy but suggest that these can be bridged with what they refer to as a "civic-regarding entrepreneurship." This conceptualization emphasizes accountability to the extent that the principles of democratic theory are incorporated into the design of entrepreneurial initiatives. In noting (p. 133) that "a strong theory of public entrepreneurship requires a strong theory of citizenship," they argue that such initiatives should be developed in ways that facilitate citizen education and participation. They cite as examples of ways to accomplish such participation, citizen budget committees, advisory boards, vehicles for elevating citizen choice (e.g., vouchers), and volunteerism.

Turning Obstacles into Facilitators

The distinct nature of the public sector operating environment creates significant obstacles to entrepreneurial behavior. While a number of these obstacles are the same as those faced by corporate entrepreneurs (e.g. elaborate control systems, long approval cycles, top-down management, closed communication channels, rules and procedures, fear of failure), some of them are unique to the public sector.

Ramamurti (1986) has identified six major barriers to entrepreneurship in the public sector work environment: multiplicity and ambiguity of goals (which is related to difficulties in defining one's customer); limited managerial autonomy and high potential interference; high visibility; skewed reward systems (i.e., penalizing failure); a short-term orientation (reinforced by budget and election cycles); and restrictive personnel policies (e.g., hiring, firing, promoting). To these we would add a lack of competitive incentives for improved performance, difficulties in segmenting or discriminating among users (i.e., services must be available to all), and a lack of accountability among managers for innovation and change.

Approached differently, however, obstacles such as these can be used to facilitate entrepreneurial behavior. For instance, Ramamurti (1986) proposes that goal ambiguity is a potential source of discretion to the entrepreneurial manager, that the media can be used as a source of power, and that outsiders can be co-opted to enable one to take organizational risks without taking personal risks.

There is no formal blueprint or model regarding how entrepreneurship can be accomplished in large established companies, and the same conclusion would seem to apply in the public sector. The key appears to be experimentation. While public sector managers do not have the luxury of being able to experiment freely with structures, control systems, rewards, communication systems, or budgeting methods, there is typically more room for flexibility than is acknowledged by so-called bureaucracy bashers. At the same time, and as noted earlier, the greatest obstacle to entrepreneurship is people themselves—managers and employees who fear failure and resist change. The individual who believes in his/her own ability to affect change, and who is in fact change oriented, will find ways around many of the other obstacles.

This brings us to the final question: Who is the public entrepreneur? Like their private sector counterparts, public sector entrepreneurs are not born. Work environments can be designed that accommodate the tendency to be entrepreneurial. Further, and in spite of the inherent obstacles, the public sector work environment may contain sufficient ambiguity, flexibility, and contradictions in values to leave room for the entrepreneur to operate.

Pinchot (1985) has done some interesting work attempting to conceptualize the corporate entrepreneur (which he calls the ''intrapreneur'') and contrast him/her with the start-up entrepreneur. In Figure 7.2 we have attempted to extend Pinchot's efforts to incorporate the public sector entrepreneur. The key characteristics being proposed include a mix of power and achievement motivation, an ability to work strategically—which depends on small steps, strong political and external networking skills, calculated risk-taking, and self-confidence—and an ability to tolerate and use ambiguity as a source of discretion.

CONCLUSIONS

Organizations tend to evolve through a number of stages while moving from relatively open and loosely structured start-up enterprises to large conglomerates with complex integrating mechanisms and extensive administrative bureaucracies. Along the way, the role of entrepreneurship changes, while the level of EI generally declines. For very logical reasons, managers put systems and structures in place that have the (usually unintended) side effect of constraining or discouraging entrepreneurial behavior.

In this chapter, we have provided a framework for identifying the obstacles or constraints on entrepreneurial intensity in organizations. They consist of systems, structures, strategic direction, policies and procedures, people and culture. This framework actually represents a blueprint for facilitating entrepreneurship if it is just turned upside down. That is, by doing such things as explicitly evaluating employees on innovative performance, creating slack in the control

Figure 7.2
Comparing Independent, Corporate, and Public Entrepreneurs

	Independent Entrepreneur	Corporate Entrepreneur	Public Sector Entrepreneur
PRIMARY MOTIVE	Wants freedom; goal oriented and self-reliant; achievement-motivated	Wants freedom and access to corporate resources; goal-oriented and self-motivated, but also responds to corporate rewards and recognition	Power motivated and achievement motivated; may think in grandiose terms; not constrained by profit motive
TIME ORIENTATION	End goals of 5-10 year growth of business	End goals of 3-15 years depending on type of venture	End goals of 10-15 years; begins with impressive short-term success, then implements long-term plan as series of short-term programs
SKILLS	Knows business intimately; more business acumen than managerial or political skill	Strong technical skills or product knowledge; good managerial skills; weak political skills	Strong political skills; able to develop power sources beyond those formally assigned; adept at using public relations and the media to advantage
ATTITUDE TOWARD SYSTEM	Frustrated by system so rejects it and starts his/her own	Dislikes system but learns to work within it and manipulate it	Tends to redesign or restructure the system to accomplish his/her own ends
FOCUS	External; markets and technology	Internal and external; builds internal networks and finds mentors or sponsors	Learns to co-opt or use external forces to accomplish internal change; builds constituencies of support among politicians, unions, the private sector, the media and the community
RISKS AND FAILURES	Assumes considerable financial and personal risk; identifies key risk factors and tries to minimize them; sees failure as learning experience	Likes moderate risks; principal risks are career-related, sensitive to need to appear orderly within corporation; hides risky projects so can learn from mistakes without political cost of public failure	Calculated risk-taker; takes big organizational risks without taking big personal risks by managing the process by which risky decisions are made; tends to deviate from rules only slightly at first, then progressively more; since failure is harder to define, will manage events to promote positive outcomes
COURAGE AND DESTINY	Self-confident, optimistic, bold	Self-confident, optimistic, bold; cynical about the system but believes he/she can manipulate it	Self-confident, optimistic, bold; high tolerance for ambiguity; uses ambiguity as a source of managerial discretion

Source: adapted from Pinchot (1985).

Figure 7.3
Integrating Entrepreneurship throughout the Organization

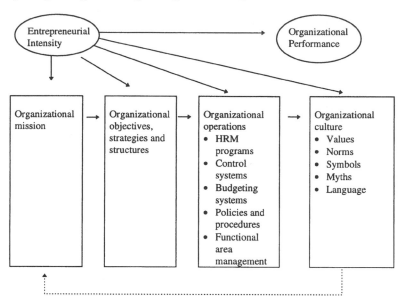

system, flattening the organizational structure, broadening spans of control, setting innovation objectives, shortening approval cycles, removing documentation requirements, and reducing the perceived costs of failure, management can create entrepreneurial work environments.

In the final analysis, EI represents an attitudinal and behavioral orientation that should pervade all aspects of an organization. As demonstrated in Figure 7.3, there is a direct positive link between EI and company performance. Further, the effectiveness of this linkage depends on how well integrated entrepreneurship is into the mission, objectives, strategies, structures, operations, and culture of the enterprise. The basic responsibility of management becomes one of determining the appropriate degree and amount of EI for the organization overall, and for each major functional area within the organization's operations.

REFERENCES

Adizes, I. 1978. ''Organizational Passages—Diagnosing and Treating Lifecycle Problems of Organizations.'' *Organizational Dynamics* (Summer), 2–25.

Balkin, D.B., and Logan, J.W. 1988. ''Reward Policies that Support Entrepreneurship.'' *Compensation and Benefits Review*, 20, 18–25.

Bellone, Carl J., and George, F.G. 1992. ''Reconciling Public Entrepreneurship and Democracy.'' *Public Administration Review*, 52 (2) (March–April), 130–134.

Bird, B.J. 1989. *Entrepreneurial Behavior*. Glenview, IL: Scott, Foresman and Co.

Brandt, S.C. 1986. *Entrepreneuring in Established Companies*. Homewood, IL: Dow Jones–Irwin.

Cornwall, J.R., and Perlman, B. 1990. *Organizational Entrepreneurship*. Homewood, IL: Irwin Publishing.

Griener, L.E. 1972. "Evolution and Revolution as Organizations Grow." *Harvard Business Review* (July–August), 37–46.

Jennings, D.F., and Lumpkin, J.R. 1989. "Functional Modeling Corporate Entrepreneurship: An Empirical Integrative Analysis." *Journal of Management*, 15 (2), 485–502.

Jennings, D.F., and Seaman, S.L. 1990. "Aggressiveness of Response to New Business Opportunities Following Deregulation: An Empirical Study of Established Financial Firms." *Journal of Business Venturing*, 5 (October), 177–189.

Jordan, F. 1990. *Innovating America*. New York: The Ford Foundation.

Kanter, R.M. 1983. *The Change Masters*. New York: Simon & Schuster.

Kao, J. 1989. *Entrepreneurship, Creativity and Organization*. Englewood Cliffs, NJ: Prentice-Hall.

Kerr, S. 1975. "On the Folly of Rewarding A, While Hoping for B." *Academy of Management Journal*, 18 (December), 769–783.

Knight, R.M. 1987. "Corporate Innovation and Entrepreneurship: A Canadian Study." *Journal of Product Innovation Management*, 4 (4), 284–297.

Maidique, M.A. 1980. "Entrepreneurs, Champions and Technological Innovation." *Sloan Management Review*, 21, 59–76.

Miller, D., and Friesen, P.H. 1983. "Strategy-Making and Environment: The Third Link." *Strategic Management Journal*, 4, 221–235.

Moore, B.H. (ed.) 1983. *The Entrepreneur in Local Government*. Washington, DC: International City Management Association.

Morris, M.H., Avila, R., and Allen, J. 1993. "Individualism and the Modern Corporation: Implications for Innovations and Entrepreneurship." *Journal of Management*, 19, 3.

Morris, H.H., and Jones, F. 1993. "Human Resource Management Practices and Corporate Entrepreneurship: An Empirical Assessment." *International Journal of Human Resources Management*, 4 (3), 28–43.

Morris, M.H., Schindehutte, M., and Pitt, L.F. 1996. "Sustaining the Entrepreneurial Society." *Small Business Foundation of America: The Research Institute for Emerging Enterprise*. Working Paper, 1 (March).

Morris, M.H., and Sexton, D.L. 1996. "The Concept of Entrepreneurial Intensity: Implications for Company Performance." *Journal of Business Research*, 36 (1), 5–14.

Olian, J.D. and Rynes, S.L. 1984. "Organizational Staffing: Integrating Practice with Strategy." *Industrial Relations*, 23, 170–183.

Pearson, G.J. 1989. "Promoting Entrepreneurship in Large Companies." *Long Range Planning*, 22 (3), 87–97.

Peters, T.J. 1987. *Thriving on Chaos*. New York: Alfred A. Knopf.

Pinchot, G. 1985. *Intrapreneuring*. New York: Harper and Row.

Ramamurti, R. 1986. "Public Entrepreneurs: Who They Are and How They Operate." *California Management Review*, 28 (3) (Spring), 142–158.

Reich, R. 1987. "Entrepreneurship Reconsidered: The Team as Hero." *Harvard Business Review*, 65 (May–June), 77–83.

Roberts, E.B., and Fusfeld, A.R. 1981. "Staffing the Innovative Technology Based Organization." *Sloan Management Review* (Spring), 19–34.

Schuler, R.S. 1986. "Entrepreneurship in Organizations." *Human Resource Management* (Winter), 614–629.

Schuler, R.S., and Jackson, S.E. 1987. "Linking Competitive Strategies with Human Resource Management Practices." *Academy of Management Executive*, 1, 207–219.

Souder, W. 1987. *Managing New Product Innovations*. Lexington, MA: D.C. Heath & Co.

Stefflre, V. 1985. "Organizational Obstacles to Innovation: A Formulation of the Problem." *Journal of Product Innovation Management*, 2, 3–11.

Stevenson, H., Roberts, M.J., and Grousbeck, H.I. 1994. *New Business Ventures and the Entrepreneur*, 4th ed. Burr Ridge, IL: Irwin.

Stewart, A. 1989. *Team Entrepreneurship*. Newbury Park, CA: Sage.

Tropman, J.E., and Morningstar, G. 1989. *Entrepreneurial Systems for the 1990's*. New York: Quorum Books.

Zeithaml, C.D., and Zeithaml, V.A. 1984. "Environmental Management: Revising the Marketing Perspective." *Journal of Marketing*, 18 (Spring).

8

Entrepreneurship at the Societal Level

INTRODUCTION

As the millennium draws to a close, the world is witnessing an unprecedented movement toward free enterprise. The end of the Cold War, the passing of Soviet client state linkages, and the market reforms that the International Monetary Fund and the World Bank impose with increasing vigor on financially wayward nations contribute to this movement. The emergence of the North American, South American, European Community, and Pacific Rim trading blocks is testimony to a multilateral desire to radically reduce trade barriers. The General Agreement on Tariffs and Trade (GATT) agreements are an expression of this goal worldwide.

Such developments are much more than a sign that the West won the Cold War. Even in traditionally capitalistic countries, fundamental questions are being raised about the nature and scope of government's role in the economy and in facilitating societal quality of life. Hence, one finds that the public agenda has shifted toward consideration of such issues as privatization, devolution of federal power, voucher programs, tax reductions, and restructuring of taxation systems. Recognition is growing that markets work and that they work best when left to their own devices.

And yet, it is not enough to simply install or enhance market mechanisms. Entrepreneurship is the engine that drives market-based economies. It is the entrepreneurial individual or team that identifies and capitalizes on opportunity, puts together unique combinations of resources, assumes risks, and manages and harvests a venture. The problem, then, becomes one of not simply encouraging competition, the profit motive, the price mechanism, private property, and the freely interacting forces of supply and demand, but one of creating infrastructures and facilitating environments conducive to entrepreneurial behavior.

THREE EXAMPLES OF ENTREPRENEURIAL ECONOMIES

Nations vary in terms of their levels of entrepreneurial intensity (EI). Some are good at breakthrough innovation, others at imitation. Ultimately, though, the question is one of how dynamic and growth-oriented the country is. Unfortunately, there currently is no measure available of EI at a national level. One could look at new business start-up rates, patents issued, new product announcements, or other such indicators, but the availability of reliable data is inconsistent across nations. Nonetheless, it is possible to identify countries that have achieved high rates of sustained growth and that continue to demonstrate a strong growth orientation.

Three such countries are Singapore, South Korea, and Chile. Each is a modern, or relatively recent, success story. Each has moved from being a poor third-world debtor nation to having economies that are rapidly growing and that have produced dramatic improvements in per capita gross domestic product (GDP). Their paths to success have been different, with one emphasizing the attraction of multinationals and the development of a domestic technological base, another stressing the development of capital-intensive industry with a strong export focus, and the third concentrating on fiscal conservatism and the unleashing of free market capitalism internally. Government has played critical, but very different, roles in each case. In all three countries, however, the ultimate focus has been to create domestic environments that are conducive to entrepreneurial behavior on the part of individuals and organizations.

Let us briefly look at each of these case studies.

Singapore

Singapore is one of the great success stories of the twentieth century. Since achieving autonomy (1959) and independence (1965), it has achieved remarkable growth, especially in the post–1980 period. It has evolved from an economy based on plentiful low-cost labor (i.e., a factor-driven economy) to one that is investment-driven and innovation-driven. It is an important secondary home base to multinationals, while boasting a growing number of successful indigenous companies.

Tang and Yeo (1995) compare the national development of Singapore to the development of an entrepreneurial firm. They argue that "technopreneurship," or the mix of technological competence and entrepreneurship, has played a key role in Singapore's progress. According to these authors, Singapore has evolved through three stages: start-up, competence building, and selective pioneering. At start-up, the nation had limited resources and technological competence and had to leverage resources (expertise, finance) by attracting multinationals. Government played a leadership role in building infrastructures, developing human resources, and gaining the confidence of investors with innovative and pragmatic policies. In stage two, and now with a sufficient quantity of technically-qualified members of the workforce, two things occurred. The government convinced multinational investors to increase levels of investment to cover more sophisticated means of production and emphasize high-value-added, upstream activities and products. At the same time, local entrepreneurs and indigenous companies began to enter into technology businesses on a notable scale. The government instituted policies that encouraged a symbiotic relationship between foreign multinationals and growing local companies. In stage three, Singapore began to target selective technological fields in which it could be among the world's leaders. The government helps detect trends but defers to the private sector in actually pioneering new ventures. The focus is on initiatives with the least controlled uncertainty, and especially the development or adoption of new and emerging technologies. By now, lower-end production operations have been relocated to lower-cost countries.

In Singapore, this evolution occurred because of what Tang and Yeo (1995) call "government entrepreneurship." The government has developed strategic policies and programs and then demonstrated consistency and perseverance in following the planned course of action. It has been opportunity-oriented, detecting and moving on new opportunities as they arose. Daring investments have been made when they had to be. Most importantly, the government created an infrastructure and environment that helped entrepreneurs prepare themselves, get on their feet, and grow, but then the government got out of their way.

South Korea

South Korea is also a story of dramatic turnaround and success. Constrained during this century by 35 years of repressive colonization by Japan, and a devastating civil war that resulted in the partitioning of North Korea from the south, the country has experienced dramatic economic growth over the past three decades. Average incomes have risen from $100 to $8,500 per year, while annual growth has averaged between 5 and 10% in real terms (Mallaby, 1995).

The so-called Korean model of economic development is a growth-obsessed model. While there is some debate as to the exact nature of this model, it can be characterized by a strong export orientation (including the need to meet international standards), an emphasis on heavy manufacturing, and a mix of private enterprise, competition, educational investment, and stable macroeconomic policy. Just as important, though, were draconian labor policies, the squeezing of savers (with negative real returns) to spur investment, political repression, and the achievement of growth by sacrifice. Building on a well-educated labor force in the 1960's, the government both subsidized and coordinated investment decisions. Export industries were pushed, and the government directed companies on what to produce, what to charge, and how much to borrow. All of this was complemented by an internal investment boom, with significant demand for imported capital goods.

However, growth from squeezing more and more savings and labor out of the citizenry is not sustainable. Further, the government maintained a heavy hand in far too many facets of the economy long after it was necessary, while its policies have resulted in the domination of the economy by relatively inefficient "chaebol" (e.g., Hyundai, Daewoo, Samsung), or large industry groups.

A major backlash by workers and the public at large led to significant democratic reforms beginning in the late 1980's. Also, various policies have attempted to rein in the power of the "chaebol," subsidies to major industries have been cut, and companies are now freer to make their own strategic decisions. And, while the "chaebol" remain dominant and there is much more to be done in terms of meaningful deregulation, South Korea has maintained its amazing growth rate. Much of this is due to the momentum from years of sacrifice, but perhaps more critical is a culture that emphasizes an external focus, learning, flexibility, and aggressiveness.

Chile

A third example of a more entrepreneurial economy is Chile, easily the star performer of South America in recent decades. Relatively low inflation, high foreign reserves, government budget surpluses, low unemployment, a stable institutional investment base, and significant foreign investment (over $1 billion per year in recent years) all characterize Chile today. Annual growth in GDP has exceeded 6% since 1985.

If there is a "Chilean model," its three tenets are macro-economic stability, a vigorous private sector, and a liberal export-oriented trading environment ("The Miracle Unmasked," 1995). At the root of it all is a 25-year period of experimentation with radical free market initiatives. Tight fiscal and monetary policies, privatization, elimination of trade barriers, deregulation of the labor market, a private pension system (in which nearly the entire working population was enrolled in private pension fund management companies), and a general reduction in the size of government have been pursued aggressively. Importantly, structural reform followed macroeconomic stabilization, as the latter proved to be a prerequisite for the success of the former (Bosworth et al., 1994).

Chile also witnessed a transfer to democratic government in 1990. Both the military government under Pinochet and the subsequent democratic government have been less susceptible to the influence of pressure groups and lobbies. While the new leadership has invested in social programs and much-needed infrastructure, they have generally stuck to a course of economic liberalization. For example, capital controls have been partially loosened in recent years. Alternatively, the indexing of prices continues to be a problem that works against further reductions in inflation.

Although the Chilean economy boasts a number of large enterprises, most notably in copper and mining, small and medium-size firms play a major role in producing growth (Pilling, 1994). The strategic focus in Chile today continues to be on export businesses, which account for nearly two-thirds of GDP, on achieving more diversity in the export base, on major infrastructural investment, and on social upliftment (Beerman, 1996).

SUSTAINING THE ENTREPRENEURIAL SOCIETY: THE RULES OF THE GAME

It becomes clear from these examples that, even at the societal level, entrepreneurship is a manageable phenomenon. If entrepreneurship were viewed as a societal resource, with each country having a rich potential reserve of this resource, then societal-level efforts should address two questions:

1. How can this resource be most effectively allocated?
2. Are there things we can do to grow the amount of this resource residing within the people and organizations that make up the society?

These are not independent questions, as entrepreneurship can be allocated in ways that actually serve to increase the amount of entrepreneurship. Consider, for instance, a change in regulation involving the creation or removal of rules so as to permit or incentivize the establishment of innovative financing sources, such as venture capital firms (of which some countries have few or none). This rule change is, in effect, a decision to reallocate society's entrepreneurial resources towards more high-risk activities (given the typical investment profile of a venture capital firm compared, say, to a commercial bank). When those with financial resources take advantage of the rule change or incentive and set up a venture capital firm, this development represents an entrepreneurial event. This event in turn makes it possible for other individuals to get funding they otherwise might go without. They then start firms with innovative new products and services, which also represent entrepreneurial events. Each of these firms then serves as a training ground within which some employees learn how entrepreneurship works, only to subsequently break away and start their own ventures.

The allocation issue is also more than a question of whether people choose to do or not to do entrepreneurial things. Just as important is what they do. Decisions to commercialize a product invention, introduce a new method of production, open a new market for an existing product, implement a new franchising approach, or tap a new source of supply represent alternative courses of action that are more or less attractive depending on society's rewards and sanctions. Baumol (1990) makes a convincing case that other (what he terms "unproductive") options exist for the channeling of entrepreneurial energies, such as the discovery of a previously unused legal gambit that is effective in diverting returns to those who are first in exploiting it.

The rules determine the perceived costs and benefits of different types of entrepreneurial activity. Thus one could argue that the lucrative drug or auto-mobile highjacking trades in an urban ghetto represent a very logical channeling of entrepreneurial energy given the opportunity costs. Both the upside and down-side potentials of such activities are a function of the rules of the game that define opportunities, or the lack thereof, open to ghetto youth. Examples of "unproductive" entrepreneurship such as these, or the legal gambit mentioned above, have led Baumol (1990) to conclude that the net level of innovativeness and growth in society is strongly affected by the extent to which society's rules and rewards result in more value being placed on productive versus unproductive entrepreneurial behavior.

The rules and rewards of the game are many, as we shall see in the next chapter. They range from tax structures and health and safety regulation to the treatment of bankruptcy, intellectual property protection, licensing rules, and antitrust legislation. These rules also serve to reflect and reinforce the social and cultural values of society, such as whether those who succeed in commercial enterprise are held in higher or lower esteem than, say, those who succeed in politics, the arts, the military, or academe.

Sustainable entrepreneurship at the societal level is also a matter of the model used in writing the rules of the game. One model involves trying to identify the people and organizations in society with more entrepreneurial potential and then targeting society's resources to those individuals. This is what can be termed the "picking the winners" approach and is analogous to a banker deciding who does and does not receive a business loan. A second model concentrates on creating a supportive environment that allows entrepreneurial people and organ-izations to self-identify themselves and "step up to the plate." The second model, which we can label the "building the infrastructure" approach, assumes that environments can be created that help people and organizations develop their own entrepreneurial potential over time. It could be argued that the South Korean model was, at least initially, closer to "picking the winners," while the Chilean example is reflective of "building the infrastructure." As a generali-zation, we believe the "building the infrastructure" model is much more con-ducive to sustainable entrepreneurship (see also Davidsson, 1992).

THE IMPLICATIONS OF SOCIETAL ENTREPRENEURSHIP: IMPACT ON QUALITY OF LIFE

We have addressed the ideas that some countries can be more entrepreneurial than others, and that countries can improve their own levels of entrepreneurship. One might conclude from this discussion that a fundamental value judgement is being made: namely that, all other things being equal, more entrepreneurship is better than less at the societal level. But is it? What are the implications of higher levels of entrepreneurship for societal well-being or quality of life (QOL)? Clearly, where countries have experienced dramatic growth in a relatively short period of time, such as in South Korea, there is a quality of life price to be paid. But even in more stable economies, such as the United States, entrepreneurship has both short-term and long-term impacts on QOL.

Although there are as many definitions of societal QOL as there are people, issues such as "well-being" and "life satisfaction" are discussed by most who have studied the topic. For example, Sirgy et al. (1985) described societal QOL as a composite of both psychological (i.e., life satisfaction) and physical (i.e., life expectancy) well-being. Granzin (1987) suggests that perceived QOL is a function of the degree of satisfaction that one finds in a certain state of affairs as compared with a desired state of affairs. In addition, QOL has been approached using need satisfaction theories (e.g., those of Maslow, 1970). For instance, Sirgy et al. (1985) discusses improvements in QOL as a movement from satisfaction of lower-order needs (i.e., physiological needs, safety needs) towards higher-order needs (i.e., self-actualization).

For our purposes, societal QOL can be defined as the general state of well-being experienced by society's members. It is comprised of both objective (material conditions of life) and subjective (perceptions or evaluations of well-being) components (Campbell, 1976). While these components appear distinct, they are, in fact, very closely interrelated (Withey, 1972).

Although the overall concern is society's general well-being, the specific dimensions that constitute societal QOL are less apparent. The totality of life has been defined by Rice et al. (1985, p. 296) as a "mosaic field consisting of many specific domains of life in which an individual participates." Many observers have attempted to define specific domains, but no consensus has been reached. Day (1987) provided a summary listing of thirteen life-experience domains. However, his focus was at the level of the individual. When applied at a societal level, these experiences can be collapsed into seven domains:

Economic. the general state of the economy as reflected by economic vitality, economic stability, the position of the economy within the world economy, and the availability and quality of goods and services.

Health. the general state of mental and physical well-being of the society and the quality and availability of medical products, services, and facilities.

Social. the general state of security, values, attitudes, lifestyles, and norms as related to human development and need satisfaction.

Technological. the general state of effectiveness/efficiency of techniques and processes for converting resource inputs to goods and services.

Work. the general state of well-being in the work/organizational environment in terms of such issues as job satisfaction, job security, and job safety.

Institutional. the general state of societal institutions such as governmental (national security, welfare services, taxes, etc.), educational, religious, business, and family units in terms of their ability to meet societal needs.

Ecological. the general state of the natural environment in terms of such issues as resource preservation and conservation.

These domains are reasonably comprehensive, given their broad definitions, but not mutually exclusive. To assess the net impact of entrepreneurship on societal QOL, we must draw implications for each.

Impact of Entrepreneurship on Societal QOL

Whereas entrepreneurship produces a variety of both functional and dysfunctional effects in each of the domains, some of the more salient implications are summarized in Table 8.1. Each is discussed in more detail below.

Economic

Entrepreneurship increases economic vitality through the creation of new products and services. Additional jobs are generated to support the production and delivery of these goods and services. For instance, it is estimated that 80% of new jobs created in the past two decades resulted from entrepreneurial efforts (e.g., Birch, 1981). The economic activity that results from these new products and additional jobs results in greater overall societal wealth and a higher standard of living.

Schumpeter (1950) has suggested that entrepreneurship, not price competition, is the driving force behind development in market economies. Specifically, entrepreneurs produce the dynamic innovations that keep the capitalist engine in motion. These innovations serve to continually revolutionize the economy, at the same time making existing products and methods obsolete. Hence, entrepreneurs are involved in a process of "creative destruction." Foster (1986) has echoed this argument in claiming that successful companies are those willing to replace profitable product lines with potentially more profitable lines.

There is an alternative perspective that emphasizes negative economic outcomes resulting from entrepreneurship. Critics argue that increases in wealth resulting from entrepreneurial efforts are at an individual level and of little benefit to the aggregate economy. Optimization of wealth at an individual level may be suboptimal for society. Marx (in Tucker, 1978) went further, in arguing that entrepreneurship is predicated on private property, individualism, and greed, and that entrepreneurs are in an endless race with one another to "accumulate or be accumulated." They exploit the surplus value of labor in the form of profits, pay artificially low wages, and are forced over time to replace labor with capital.

In addition, entrepreneurship has been criticized for its reliance on high-risk resource utilization, as evidenced in the high rate of new product and service failures. As a result, entrepreneurship has the potential to magnify the peaks and troughs of business cycle activity. Discontinuous innovation not only makes existing products and processes obsolete but generates significant investment as other firms seek to imitate the innovations. Expectations can be raised beyond

Table 8.1

Positive and Negative Effects of Entrepreneurship on Societal QOL

QOL Dimensions	Effects of Entrepreneurship	
	Functional	Dysfunctional
Economic	Greater economic vitality via increases in GDP and the creation of jobs Increased societal wealth and higher standards of living	Creation of individual wealth versus societal wealth Higher risk use of resources More pronounced cyclical swings in the economy Loss in the competitive position of large established firms
Health	Medical product, service, and process innovations	Greater stress levels as a result of greater incidence of change
Social	Improvements in material affluence leading to increased emphasis on the higher-order needs of society Greater societal confidence in the state of progress and security	Disruptions of existing attitudes and lifestyles Unethical and/or immoral business behaviors in an attempt to quickly capitalize on profit opportunities becomes an acceptable standard
Technological	Proactive, cutting edge technological innovations and transfers Greater resource productivity as a result of improved production techniques Improved competitive position within a global business environment	Acceleration of technology life cycles resulting in higher product and business failure rate Dynamic, unpredictable, competitive environment Disruptive technostructural organizational change
Work life	Organizational behavioral benefits due to entrepreneurial cultures Superior organizational performance due to improved productivity, quality, and the development of new products, services, and processes	Job dissatisfaction on the part of employees with high resistance both to idiosyncratic behavior of the entrepreneurial personality and to organizational change Rapid obsolescence of employee work skills Greater emphasis on individual rather than group or division
Institutional	Increased tax base and lower costs of government services Increased opportunities and greater ability to meet consumer/societal needs	Challenges to the structure, roles, and missions of many societal institutions Need for new rules and procedures which complicate administrative processes Anti-managerial biases may develop
Ecological	Creative solutions to resource scarcity and environmental crises	Wasted resources as a result of unneeded innovation and rapid product obsolescence Depleted resources due to rapid economic growth Damage to natural environment from unfettered economic growth

the levels justified by the nature of the innovation, ultimately resulting in over-production and recession.

Further, as the criticism of Ferguson (1988) and Reich (1987) illustrate, an economic system that facilitates small entrepreneurial companies at the expense of large established firms may weaken the global competitiveness of a nation by fragmenting industries. Entrepreneurs capitalize on the huge investments and technological developments of established firms to create profitable ventures. However, in an attempt to remain competitive, they undermine the larger firms and society as a whole by selling the technology (or themselves) to the highest bidder—often an offshore competitor. Moreover, entrepreneurial firms stress breakthrough innovations to the exception of more incremental product and process improvements necessary for companies to sustain a competitive edge over time.

Health

Entrepreneurial societies produce high rates of innovation in medical proc-esses, products, and services, which leads to greater physical and mental well-being for most societal groups. Many historically terminal diseases now have cures or treatments, and there is optimism that most disease will one day be remedied. The development of advanced pharmaceutical and medical products has extended average life spans and reduced physical suffering in most societies.

On the dysfunctional side, entrepreneurship often leads to greater levels of stress for those affected by the significant and sometimes dramatic change that results from the entrepreneurial process. Current medical beliefs suggest that stress is associated with a substantial portion of all physical and mental illnesses. In addition, an inability to cope with the societal pressures that accompany entrepreneurial change can result in heightened levels of alcoholism and drug abuse.

Social

In societies where the functional aspects of entrepreneurship are evident, ma-terial affluence leads to the satisfaction of lower-order needs (i.e., physiological and security). As a result, societal goals can be focused on the fulfilment of higher-order needs. In addition, confidence in the state of societal progress and security may improve as a result of entrepreneurial advancements. The end result is that human development is enhanced.

At the same time, entrepreneurship can lead to the disruption of societal at-titudes, norms, and lifestyles. New products and services have the potential not only to speed the pace of life but also to change the way it is lived. An example is the development over the past 25 years of a "disposable society" in the United States. In addition, new innovations can create ethical dilemmas, such as medical advances that have the ability to perpetuate human life for longer and longer time periods.

A different perspective was provided by Veblen (1967), who criticized entrepreneurs for purposely disrupting or undermining the established social order and reaping profits from the resulting confusion. In his view, entrepreneurs are saboteurs who create chaos for self-gain.

The preoccupation of some entrepreneurs with immediate profits also has dysfunctional social implications. Unbridled entrepreneurship can lead to a preoccupation with doing whatever is necessary to achieve success. The entrepreneur's obsession with making it happen, combined with the primacy placed on individualism and independence and a disdain for the rules and constraints of societal institutions, can encourage more than rule-bending. Tacitly unethical or illegal behavior is sometimes a by-product, and where the entrepreneur is held in high esteem, society may come to believe that such behavior is acceptable. Similarly, the entrepreneurial quest for material gain may produce a societal focus on materialism.

Technological

Entrepreneurship is a major factor behind the increased pace of technological progress today. Entrepreneurs have been responsible for both technological innovations (the development of new processes and methods) and technological transfers (the application of new processes and methods to the development and delivery of products and services). Also, where resources are scarce, entrepreneurial efforts that result in new production techniques can lead to greater productivity per resource unit. As a consequence, successful entrepreneurial efforts result in greater satisfaction of consumer needs via the efficient production of more high quality products and services.

In addition, through major technological advances, a society can significantly enhance its competitive position within world markets. As Young (1985) has noted, successful challenges to the dominant global competitive position of the United States can be substantially attributed to inadequate investment in the development and application of new technologies. Drucker (1985) concludes that no country can have a viable high-tech sector without having an entrepreneurial economy.

Yet, rapid technological advancements give rise to greater environmental turbulence and complexity. As entrepreneurship spawns new and better technologies for delivering products and services, a higher rate of business failure is likely to occur. Functionally useful products are made obsolete. The competitive arena for the organizations affected becomes more dynamic and less predictable. Technological forecasting becomes critical. Firms are forced to implement technostructural changes that may be highly disruptive to the operations of the organization in the short-term, and sometimes permanently.

Work

Quality of work life is affected in a variety of ways by entrepreneurship. Firms that encourage and support entrepreneurial efforts typically develop cultures that focus on identifying, and capitalizing on, new opportunities. Employees find ample rewards for innovative and creative ideas that facilitate the exploitation of such opportunities. Employee independence is encouraged; flat management structures with multiple informal networks typically prevail. Employees retain greater individual freedom to make the decisions necessary to accomplish their work goals. Where employees appreciate and desire relative independence, significant organizational behavioral benefits can occur. Higher productivity, improved quality, and a faster rate of new product and service introduction are the end result.

Such freedoms are not always perceived as positive, however. As many industries have matured, associated organizations have evolved into relatively bureaucratic institutions with well-defined work rules and procedures. Employees of organizations such as these have become comfortable with the level of predictability and stability in their work routine. For such employees, the challenges of being involved in a truly entrepreneurial firm may not be appealing.

Entrepreneurs create change, make new rules, demand resource support, and set new standards of performance. Their charisma, while inspiring, may also be perceived as threatening. Further, entrepreneurial managers can alienate subordinates with behaviors that reflect their personal need for control, sense of distrust, need for applause, and overall defensiveness (Kets de Vries, 1984). Employees can also find that the organizational changes brought about by the entrepreneurial process lead to rapid obsolescence of work skills. For individual employees who feel secure in stable and predictable work environments, the organizational instabilities that result from entrepreneurial efforts can lead to deteriorating job satisfaction and job security.

Reich (1987) posited that entrepreneurship suffers from a preoccupation with the individual. The entrepreneur is glorified, whereas the critical others who contribute to his/her success are assumed to be replaceable. As a result, entrepreneurship tends to produce major new breakthroughs and cutting-edge scientific discoveries but not the incremental improvements and cost reductions that result from collective action over time. Reich suggested that the latter type of progress can best be achieved by an emphasis on collective entrepreneurship or the "team as hero."

Institutional

In any society, institutions (e.g., governmental, educational, religious) exist to serve specific needs of the aggregate population. Institutional QOL is improved to the extent that entrepreneurship has a positive effect on the functioning of such institutions. For example, entrepreneurial ventures create an enhanced tax base that can be used by governmental bodies to support social services. Further, entrepreneurial attempts at privatization have the potential to reduce the cost of many government functions. Innovations in technology make it possible to provide more universal educational opportunities, including opportunities for the economically disadvantaged and the handicapped. Religious institutions find that they are able to communicate and tailor their services to larger numbers of people. Businesses are able to employ more people and produce a wider array of goods and services.

At the same time, entrepreneurial efforts challenge the structure, mission, and roles of many institutions. For instance, advances in medical technology have created challenges to the role of organized religion in family planning, while opportunities for female entrepreneurship have challenged the role and functioning of the family unit. Unions have found their power undermined by the rapid growth in entrepreneurial start-up ventures. Moreover, the need for new rules and procedures to facilitate entrepreneurship complicates the administrative processes in established institutions and may lead to ineffective performance.

In a related vein, Kaplan (1987) claimed that entrepreneurship produces an anti-managerial bias, wherein large firms and corporate managers are denigrated. He believes that entrepreneurship would not be possible in modern society without the stability provided by huge private conglomerates, public utilities, and charitable institutions.

Ecological

Environmentalists speak of ecological problems that will eventually invade the daily lives of people in all societies. Concerns are voiced about population crises, pollution crises, resource scarcities, and related problems that form the basis of the limited growth thesis. And yet, where entrepreneurship has led to more rapid increases in production than in consumption, the arguments of the limited growth proponents are weakened. Entrepreneurial ideas have spurred important and unique mechanisms for conserving, and in some cases, creating additional resources. For example, Enis (1987) discussed the impact of the development of a heavy manufacturing industry in outer space on the ecological position of this planet. Innovations have permitted more to be produced with less, eliminated sources of pollution, and replaced natural resources with synthetic substitutes.

In contrast, entrepreneurship can aggravate ecological problems when failed ideas and efforts lead to wasted resources. Even entrepreneurial successes can lead to wasted resources when new products and services cause perfectly functional goods and services to become obsolete. Additionally, the fast pace of economic growth resulting from entrepreneurial efforts can lead to rapid depletion of societal resources. Where entrepreneurship is intense, growth becomes more uncontrolled, and the assets of the environment can be damaged and destroyed.

QUALITY OF LIFE, GROWTH, AND THE
ENTREPRENEURIAL DYNAMIC

Entrepreneurship has a significant long-term impact on all QOL dimensions (see Table 8.2). This impact is greatest on the economic dimension. While there is little conclusive evidence, economic QOL would seem to account for a larger proportion of total QOL than does any other dimension (e.g., Pennings, 1982). For instance, an economically prosperous society is more able to develop technology or improve work conditions.

Entrepreneurship is fundamentally a celebration of growth. But growth has been a source of considerable controversy over the centuries. In contemporary times, a no-growth school argues that continued growth has only resulted in a population explosion and consequent malnutrition, depletion of critical natural resources, pollution and its ill effects on the environment and on personal health, an ethic of materialism and greed, and modernism (e.g., Schumacher, 1973; Meadows et al., 1972). Growth critics predict that the future will bring the exponential growth of population and capital, followed by social and economic collapse, as well as a stop to industrial growth, exacerbated levels of economic inequality, and a dismal, depleted existence. Proposed solutions have included deliberate restrictions on growth, learning to live with less, redistribution of income, and a radical transformation of moral values.

The response from growth proponents emphasizes that QOL is better today for more people than at any time in history, that the projective facts and meth-

Table 8.2
Net Impacts of Entrepreneurial Intensity on QOL

Major QOL Domain*	Dominant Impact of Entrepreneurship	Net Impact
E, W	Extensive Job Creation	Positive
E	Sizable Income/Wealth Creation	Positive
E, H, T	Most New Innovation	Positive
E, T, Ec	Rapid Product Obsolescence	Negative
Ec	More Efficient Resource Utilization	Positive
Ec	Rapid Depletion of Existing Resources	Negative
Ec	High-Risk Use of Resources	Negative
W	Greater Opportunities for Employee Development/Advancement	Positive
W, I	Less Concern for Family Relationships	Negative
S, Ec	Pressure for Expediency/Unethical Behavior	Negative
H, W, I	High Levels of Personal Stress	Negative
I	More Personal Freedom	Positive

*Key: E = Economic, H = Health, S = Social, T = Technological, W = Work Life, I = Institutional, EC = Ecological.

odologies used by the growth critics are fundamentally flawed, and that although real and severe problems exist, human ingenuity will produce creative solutions. They cite doomsayers of the past whose predictions were proven wrong because of technological change, and they note more recent research indicating some of the resource and environmental problems are less severe than previously thought or are not as directly related to economic growth.

Caught between these two positions are entrepreneurship and the question of how it affects QOL. Entrepreneurship is not only the major source of economic growth, it is also the major source of solutions to the dysfunctional outcomes growth produces. Stated differently, entrepreneurship is both the problem and the solution. Entrepreneurship enhances QOL (principally through the economic dimension) but in the process contributes to problems that detract from QOL (e.g., through the social and ecological dimensions). Yet it represents the best hope for addressing the problems that it helped create (e.g., through the technological dimension). By letting this state of affairs persist in the United States, societal QOL has continually improved. Figure 8.1 captures the relationships suggested here. Also included is a feedback loop, as there is some evidence that suggests entrepreneurship is fostered where QOL is better (Pennings,1982).

Conversely, if entrepreneurship is eliminated, or severely constrained, will growth be substantially reduced? If so, will environmental problems, such as pollution and resource depletion, either resolve themselves or become less serious? The answer to the first question is clearly yes. Considerable evidence exists that economic growth rates are slower in societies with a limited or nonexistent entrepreneurial sector, and higher in those with more entrepreneurship (Gilder, 1984; Hofstede, 1980; Hoselitz, 1960; Hughes, 1986; Wilken, 1979).

With regard to the second question, the answer would appear to be no. Populations will continue to grow, scarce resources will be consumed, pollution will be produced, and the haves will continue to want more and be unwilling to give to the have-nots. Revelations regarding the status of various QOL dimen-

Figure 8.1
A Dynamic Model of Entrepreneurship and QOL

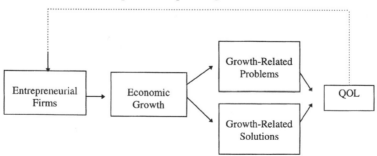

sions following the demise of communist regimes in the countries that once formed the Soviet Union and its Eastern European satellites (where entrepreneurial sectors were severely limited) would seem to support this conclusion.

Under these circumstances, where will the solutions come from? The non-entrepreneurial segments of the business community will not produce solutions, nor will the non-profit institutions of society, which would find themselves in an increasingly underfunded state. The remaining source of solutions would be the government, whose policies have often tended to magnify rather than resolve such problems (Maurice and Smithson, 1984; see also Chapter Nine). Moreover, governments are highly inefficient at developing and manufacturing products and services that eliminate pollution, slow birth rates, or replace natural resources. As we saw, especially in the cases of Chile and Singapore, enlightened government's principal contribution is to facilitate coherent growth strategies built around a dynamic entrepreneurial sector.

CONCLUSIONS

The ability of a nation to achieve and sustain economic prosperity is dependent upon how well it supports the development and allocation of the innate entrepreneurial potential of its people and organizations. We believe in a bottom-up perspective, wherein the vast majority of entrepreneurial behavior derives from individual action and free choice by society's members.

However, there must also be a vision from the top. A country's leaders must espouse a clear philosophy regarding entrepreneurship. They must delineate where the country seeks to be in terms of the entrepreneurial grid (see Chapter 4) and formulate a national strategy for accomplishing this position. Such a strategy provides a long-term guide to determining the desired rates of growth, levels of risk exposure, and degrees of innovativeness in the economy.

This is not an argument for government to plan or control the economy. Actually, just the opposite is needed. Enlightened government consists of leaders who know how to provide a vision, and who can design rules and rewards that reinforce that vision, while getting out of the way by letting individuals and organizations act on their own entrepreneurial potential in their own way. The purpose of government becomes one of steering, not rowing, and of building an enabling infrastructure.

Determining the appropriate level of EI at the societal level also requires an understanding of the linkages between entrepreneurship and societal well-being or QOL. As we have argued, each of the dimensions, or domains, of the QOL experienced by members of a society is affected both positively and negatively by entrepreneurship. The relative importance of these dimensions is likely to vary depending on the values and the stage of economic development of a nation. Correspondingly, the saliency placed on a given functional or dysfunctional outcome of entrepreneurship can be expected to differ across countries.

In the final analysis, it is not a question of whether to emphasize entrepreneurial intensity, but how strongly. This conclusion is based on a dynamic model of societal entrepreneurship, in which EI is recognized as the source of growth and dynamism, as the creator of growth-related problems, and as a source of the solutions to these problems.

REFERENCES

Birch, D.L. 1981. "Who Creates Jobs?" *The Public Interest*, 65 (Fall), 62–82.

Baumol, W.J. 1990. "Entrepreneurship: Productive, Unproductive, and Destructive." *Journal of Political Economy*, 98 (5), Part 1: 893–921.

Beerman, K. 1996. "Moving On—Chile's Alternatives to NAFTA." *Harvard International Review*, 18 (3), 64–69.

Bosworth, B.P. et al. 1994. *The Chilean Economy: Policy Lessons and Challenges*. Washington, DC: Brookings Institution.

Campbell, A. et al. 1976. *The Quality of American Life: Perceptions, Evaluations and Satisfactions*. New York: Russell Sage Foundation.

Davidsson, P. 1992. *Environment and Entrepreneurship: Culture, Structure, and New Firm Formation Rates in Sweden*. Paper presented at ENDEC World Conference on Entrepreneurship, Singapore (August).

Day, R.L. 1987. "Relationships Between Life Satisfaction and Consumer Satisfaction." In A.C. Samli (ed.), *Marketing and the Quality-of-Life Interface*. Westport, CT: Quorum Books, 289–311.

Drucker, P. 1985. *Innovation and Entrepreneurship: Practices and Principles*. New York: Harper and Row.

Enis, B.M. 1987. "Growth Without Limits: A Marketing Perspective on Twenty-First Century Quality of Life." In A.C. Samli (ed.), *Marketing and the Quality-of-Life Interface*. Westport, CT: Quorum Books, 139–152.

Ferguson, C.H. 1988. "From the People Who Brought You Voodoo Economics." *Harvard Business Review*, 66 (May–June), 55–62.

Foster, R. 1986. *Innovation: The Attacker's Advantage*. New York: Summit.

Gilder, G. 1984. *The Spirit of Enterprise*. New York: Simon and Schuster.

Granzin, K.L. 1987. " A General Systems Framework for Quality of Life." In A.C. Samli (ed.), *Marketing and the Quality of Life Interface*. Westport, CT: Quorum Books, 15–46.

Hofstede, G. 1980. "Motivation, Leadership, and Organizations: Do American Theories Apply Abroad?" *Organizational Dynamics*, 9 (Summer), 42–63.

Hoselitz, B.F. 1960. "The Early History of Entrepreneurial Theory." In J.J. Spengler and W.R. Allen (eds.), *Essays in Economic Thought: Aristotle to Marshall*. Chicago: Rand McNally, 234–258.

Hughes, J. 1986. *The Vital Few: The Entrepreneur and American Economic Progress*. New York: Oxford University Press.

Kaplan, R. 1987. "Entrepreneurship Reconsidered: The Antimanagement Bias." *Harvard Business Review*, 65 (May–June), 84–89.

Kets de Vries, Manfred, F.R. 1984. "The Dark Side of Entrepreneurship." *Harvard Business Review*, 63 (November–December), 160–7.

Mallaby, S. 1995. "South Korea: Quick, Quick, Quick." *Economist*, 335 (7917) (June), SS3–SS5.

Maslow, A.H. 1970. *Motivation and Personality*, 2nd ed. New York: Harper and Row.

Maurice, C., and Smithson, C.W. 1984. *The Doomsday Myth*. Palo Alto, CA: Hoover Institution Press.

Meadows, D.H. et al. 1972. *The Limits to Growth*. New York: Universe Books.

"The Miracle Unmasked." 1995. *The Economist* (December), 4–6.

Pennings, J.M. 1982. "The Urban Quality of Life and Entrepreneurship." *Academy of Management Journal*, 25, 63–79.

Pilling, D. 1994. "Chile's Champion of Stability." *Euromoney*, 305 (September), 286–287.

Reich, R.B. 1987. "Entrepreneurship Reconsidered: The Team as Hero." *Harvard Business Review*, 65 (May–June), 77–83.

Rice, R.W. et al. 1985. "Organizational Work and The Perceived Quality of Life: Toward A Conceptual Model." *Academy of Management Review*, 10, 296–310.

Schumacher, E.F. 1973. *Small Is Beautiful: Economics As If People Mattered*. New York: Harper and Row.

Schumpeter, J. 1950. *Capitalism, Socialism, and Democracy*. New York: Harper and Row.

Sirgy, M.J. et al. 1985. "The Question of Value in Social Marketing: Use of a Quality of Life Theory to Achieve Long-Term Life Satisfaction." *The American Journal of Economics and Sociology*, 44 (April), 215–228.

Tang, H.K. and Yeo, K.T. 1995. "Technology, Entrepreneurship and National Development: Lessons from Singapore." *International Journal of Technology Management*, 10 (7–8), 797–814.

Tucker, R.C. 1978. *The Marx-Engels Reader*, 2nd ed. New York: Norton Publishing.

Veblen, T. 1967. *The Theory of the Leisure Class*. New York: Viking Press.

Wilken, P.H. 1979. *Entrepreneurship: A Comparative and Historical Study*. Norwood, NJ: Ablex.

Withey, S.B. 1972. "Values and Social Change." In B. Strumpel (ed.), *Subjective Elements of Well-Being*. Paris: Organization for Economic Cooperation and Development.

Young, J. 1985. "Global Competition: The New Reality." *California Management Review*, 28 (Spring), 11–25.

9

Government and
Entrepreneurship

INTRODUCTION

The major theme of this book concerns the need for public policy makers, education officials, business executives, and community leaders to create environments that facilitate entrepreneurial intensity at the individual, organizational, and societal levels. Government policy is especially critical here, for as Baumol (1990, p. 894) notes, "How the entrepreneur acts at a given time and place depends heavily on the rules of the game—the reward structure in the economy—that happen to prevail." Unfortunately, the orientation of current public policy is to create a pernicious set of rules that effectively discourages entrepreneurship while tacitly supporting small business start-ups.

IN FAVORING SMALL BUSINESS, GOVERNMENT
IGNORES ENTREPRENEURSHIP

Small business owners and lobbyists have maintained for many years that most social regulations, antitrust laws, securities regulations, and intellectual property laws have a detrimental effect on small businesses. Many of the regulations in environmental protection, labor standards, and tax policy have extremely negative implications for the competitive abilities of small firms.

Weidenbaum (1992) calculated that regulation adds over $400 billion to private-sector costs, and Susbauer (1981) has estimated that regulatory paperwork alone adds as much as $20 billion to small business costs. Singh et al. (1987) demonstrated that small businesses pay the highest effective corporate tax rates. Others point out that small businesses also suffer because they can ill afford litigation when accused of a potential regulatory violation.

There is no question that regulatory policies create significant hardships for small businesses. However, it is the growth-oriented business that is most heavily penalized. The reality is that regulatory constraints serve only to inflate the costs associated with growth. These costs fall into two major categories: compliance costs and innovation costs.

The costs of regulatory compliance include legal fees for interpretation of regulations, consultant fees for recommendations on meeting regulatory requirements, costs associated with actually complying with applicable regulations (e.g., labor, material, equipment), costs of generating and maintaining documentation of compliance, and costs of staff for reporting and filing compliance documents. While compliance costs are potentially high for any firm, such regulations are often regressive in nature and thus of greater consequence to the bottom line of small businesses. Thus, Sommers and Cole (1981) have provided empirical evidence that the cost of compliance per unit sold or service provided is higher in small businesses than in mid-size or large organizations. The Batelle Human Affairs Research Center estimates that it costs businesses with fewer than 50 employees seven to ten times as much to comply as it does larger firms. As a result, compliance costs may reduce the small firm's ability to compete effectively, and the long-term effect of this can range from lost business to the demise of the firm (Berney and Swanson, 1982; McKee, 1992).

While these arguments are quite compelling, extensive lobbying efforts by small business advocates have helped protect most small businesses from mandatory compliance with many regulatory requirements. Although the definition of small varies among regulatory agencies, a perusal of the Environmental Protection Agency (EPA), Occupational Safety and Health Administration (OSHA), Equal Employment Opportunity Commission (EEOC), Labor Department, and Internal Revenue Service (IRS) rules suggests that many small firms are exempt or otherwise receive favorable treatment. Many special exemptions exist for particular industries or firms faced with certain prescribed circumstances.

Few would dispute that compliance exclusions for small businesses are essential for their competitive viability and for incubating certain infant industries. But these exclusions may have an unintended consequence: they can be a disincentive for growth. Entrepreneurial firms with a growth orientation find that to grow means to be subjected to costly regulations that significantly reduce their profitability while exacerbating what is typically already a critical cash-flow shortage.

A growth-oriented small business must at some point surpass the upper limits of the regulatory exclusions as it increases its sales, the number of its employees, the payroll deductions it processes, or the waste that it generates. The firm thus becomes exposed to regulatory policy from which it was protected before it grew. Compliance often requires excessive expenditures that seem unjustifiable in the face of other costs associated with growth. The entrepreneurial firm must balance the perceived benefits of growth against the perceived risks and also factor in the very tangible costs imposed via public policy. While small firms are able to pursue a strategy of partial compliance (Sommers and Cole, 1981), entrepreneurial firms are not. Because their violations are more difficult to detect, small firms may simply choose not to comply. This option is less realistic for growth-oriented firms, for growth itself serves to heighten their visibility.

Less tangible but equally important, are innovation costs. These are the opportunity costs of foregoing new technologies, products, and services that would require compliance with regulations. Burdened by excessive and sometimes incomprehensible policies regulating the entry into new industry or product categories, many growth-oriented businesses simply choose not to innovate.

Even large growth-oriented firms may be stifled by excessive government regulation. Consider, for example, how the FDA's complicated process for approving new biotechnology has hindered advances in agriculture. Further, regulatory restrictions on the telecommunications industry were faulted for the U.S.'s lag in developing fiber optics and high-definition television (Warner, 1992). In the final analysis, while the tangible monetary costs of regulatory compliance are quite high, the costs of lost opportunities for economic growth and innovation are probably the most significant, especially in terms of the long-term impact on societal quality of life (see Chapter 8).

THE DANGEROUS DIRECTION OF PUBLIC POLICY

Of perhaps even greater concern is the overall trend in regulation. Quite simply, the creation of government rules and tax constraints represents a growth industry. Consider a few examples.

In recent years, government policy has effectively placed employers in the health-care business. This has come at a time when health-care costs have increased at a relentless pace far exceeding the annual rate of inflation. As the burden of health insurance continues to grow, enterprises are forced to compromise on their growth ambitions because new employees become artificially overpriced.

Product liability has also shifted dramatically away from consumers and toward manufacturers. Legal remedies for injured consumers have broadened, and the scope of manufacturer culpability has expanded. As a result, companies today are held liable for damages regardless of how much the consumer misuses or abuses the product, fails to follow clearly visible instructions, or otherwise does not exercise common sense. Not surprisingly, the number of suits filed in federal and state courts is increasing at a double-digit annual pace. As a result, Begley (1995) notes that 47% of surveyed companies withdrew products from markets because of fears of litigation, and 25% discontinued a line of research. Obviously, the companies that innovate more are the most vulnerable to such a total liability philosophy. This creates an incentive for firms to concentrate instead on imitative, "me-too," innovation, where established products are changed incrementally.

Another example concerns affirmative action requirements. A significant move away from the original intentions of affirmative action has occurred as government has sought not only to monitor but to direct the private discretionary and voluntary actions of individuals and organizations. Thus, the focus today is on effective quotas (with companies subject to litigation on the grounds of de facto underrepresentation of a given minority class proportional to the population). Diluted, race-normed examinations, gender-normed selection criteria, and racial and gender set-asides that guarantee an increasingly disproportionate percentage of government contracts for protected classes have been introduced. The result is a spoils system that promotes group rights over individual merit. Such programs foster bitter resentment and heightened polarization of the citizenry, leading to accusations that relatively under-qualified employees are being hired, which undermines the principles of merit, efficiency, and cost-effectiveness. Further, beneficiaries of these programs are often stereotyped as not having earned their positions; as a result, they may be ostracized and placed on a slow promotion track.

Growing constraints on entrepreneurial behavior can also be seen in the environmental area. In 1994, Americans were spending over $125 billion or 2.5% of the gross national product (GNP) to comply with environmental statutes and regulations (Bowermaster and Gest, 1995). The EPA, with a staff of 18,000 and a yearly budget of $6.7 billion, consumes one-third of the federal regulatory budget. Such key environmental programs as the Clean Air Act, the Clean Water Act, and the Resource Conservation and Recovery Act are all top-down, command-and-control regulations (i.e., inflexible approaches that ignore market-based incentives or marketplace solutions). They tend to involve slow-moving and ill-informed processes, highly adversarial confrontations, inefficiencies (in that uniform standards fail to account for unique difficulties that arise in satisfying the requirements of different industries and regions of the country), and politicized decisions regarding whom to penalize when violations occur. The result is explosive litigation costs, deceptive increases in the price of goods, and overt bars against competition.

Antitrust regulation represents one final example of how regulation has come to serve as a mechanism to create barriers to market entry or to confer other special privileges. Antitrust essentially represents an effort not to expand but to suppress an objectively competitive market while restraining output and growth in productivity. In today's globally competitive marketplace, it is a severe impediment to innovation. These regulations assume a naive micro-economic analysis that ensures a "perfectly" competitive static paradigm, when it is *dynamic* competition that is relevant (Jorden and Teece, 1990). Dynamic competition issues from the development of new products, services, or processes. Antitrust negatively affects the ability of innovating firms to cooperate in their development and communication efforts and limits business strategies or inter-firm agreements to keep "me too" competitors at bay. In fact, antitrust has become much more favorable towards mergers than towards inter-firm agreements.

As government constraints on entrepreneurial growth continue to escalate, significant concerns should be raised about the long-term competitive viability of the U.S. economy, and by extension, the societal quality of life (QOL).

BUREAUCRACY AND THE ANTI-ENTREPRENEURIAL BIAS OF GOVERNMENT

Government at all levels is inherently anti-entrepreneurial. Fundamental conflicts exist between the way government does business and the requirements of the start-up or the corporate entrepreneur. In fact, these conflicts undermine the very essence of entrepreneurship. Table 9.1 summarizes twelve of these conflicts.

While this bias can be traced to a number of factors (e.g., value systems of those attracted to public service), the endemic nature of this bias is related to government's continued reliance on a bureaucratic model of organization.

Numerous theoretical perspectives on bureaucracy have been offered over the years (see Etzioni-Halevey, 1983; Wiggs, 1994; and Wittergreen 1988, for a more detailed treatment of these perspectives). Regardless of the perspective, bureaucracy as a form of government organization is threatened by an entrepreneurial person or firm that acts as an agent of change. While the entrepreneur as a start-up or mom-and-pop business proprietor can typically be ignored, the entrepreneur as a growth-oriented innovator cannot be.

Modern bureaucracy has developed at least fourteen key characteristics that make it incompatible with high levels of entrepreneurial intensity (EI) (Averch, 1990; Howard, 1968; Stein, 1995). These can be summarized as follows:

Pluralism. Administrative agencies are boxed in by intricately related and often strongly opposing interests. To survive, they must take into account, and be responsive to, all politically effective groups, any number of which may have problems with the change wrought by an entrepreneurial enterprise. The bureaucracy becomes a contending and offsetting collection of fiefdoms.

Overload. The revolution in entitlements over the past 50 years has produced an expectation by dependent groups that the government is the first resort for their well-being. Increasing demands have made the government increasingly unable to cope. The more decisions it must handle, the more it becomes hostage to political and governmental influences.

Rational Limited Search. Bureaucracies fail to seek the most effective solutions and concentrate on precedent and standard operating procedures. Unlike entrepreneurs, they do not seek the greatest level of performance for the least cost. Similarly, faced with uncertainty, they do not estimate the relevant probability distribution of various outcomes and apply the appropriate discount rates to maximize rates of return to society.

Multiple Objectives and Constituencies. Bureaucrats rarely ask, "Who is our market?" Enabling legislation for the programs they administer often contains vague and conflicting objectives because of the necessity to achieve consensus. Moreover, growth-oriented enterprises are rarely included on any list of possible constituencies to be served.

Table 9.1
Summary of Twelve Conflicts between the Orientation of Government and
Requirements of Entrepreneurship

	Government Orientation	Entrepreneurial Requirement
1	Standardized approaches and operating procedures	Need for flexible approaches to reflect novel circumstances
2	Compromise among the conflicting objectives of multiple constituencies	Sole focus on growth and innovation as the means to other societal ends
3	Focus on process, how things are done	Concerned with outcomes, what gets done
4	Approaches tied to short-term budget cycles (1-2 years)	Concern is life of a project or opportunity
5	Largely unconcerned about costs of compliance with its decisions	Costs of compliance detract from competitiveness and ability to create value for customers
6	Absolutist approach to remedying a societal ill	Need for trade-offs in flexibly developing innovative solutions
7	Risk-aversive	Calculated risk-taking
8	Side-effects of innovation must be minimized	Net benefits of innovation should outweigh costs of the innovation and its side-effects
9	Slow, ponderous decision process involving extensive consultation and transparency	Quick decisions to reflect short windows of opportunity
10	Growth as disruptive and a source of problems	Growth as the objective
11	Resource-driven	Opportunity-driven
12	Adversarial approach to dealing with private sector	Willingness to partner with government in addressing opportunities

Uncertain Production Functions. It is very difficult to measure the efficiency or effectiveness of bureaucratic performance. The production function is only partially known. A bureaucracy rarely knows what would happen if it employed alternative combinations of inputs. There is little incentive to experiment to see if the organizational design, the staff, and the technology used can be varied to increase, let alone maximize, output.

Input-Output Measures. Because performance tends to be measured by the amount of inputs from sponsors or publics, not by indicators of output or government impact, bureaucracies design programs, and conspire with clients and constituents, to achieve more staff and budget. Should the bureaucracy request fewer inputs, its client groups are apt to accuse it of dishonoring its mandate, while lower budget requests (e.g., due to productivity gains or problem resolution) invite even greater cuts the next time around.

Need for Symbols. Besides their stated objectives, bureaucracies have symbolic and "signaling" objectives. Since a bureaucracy's sponsor faces conflicting claims and limited resources, bureaucracies will seek the most visible programs to justify their budget requests. Even though effectiveness may depend on concentrating resource expenditures, political pressures may dilute how expenditures are actually allocated.

Equity vs. Effectiveness. Bureaucracies must make program trade-offs between effectiveness and equity. They tend to start a new program or initiative with an ostensibly effective design and rational criteria, but soon pressure is exerted to expand eligibility or entitlement. Unlike in the marketplace, those excluded from benefits find that bureaucracy itself becomes the vehicle for redress. So perverse is the syndrome that equity per se becomes the objective of most government programs. By emphasizing equity, flexible solutions that differentiate and reinforce the contributions of growth-oriented enterprises are not possible.

Budget Cycles and Floors. Bureaucracies operate with one- or two-year budget cycles that compress the need to justify the level of resources they receive and amplify the need to expand those resources. There is a built-in incentive to allocate resources to marginal projects. Unspent or unobligated funds cannot be rationalized. Attempts to cut budgets will only make the bureaucracies seek new constituencies that must be served. Staff reduction will result in potentially more money being spent on temporary personnel or outsourcing.

Tenure of Senior Decision-Makers. High-level managers, especially political appointees, have short tenure and no ownership claims on the organization. Perceived short-term success (e.g., expanding the budget) is often more important than long-term success (solving the problem).

Sunk Costs. In the private sector, sunk costs are not allocated to current operations but are recovered over a product's life cycle. In a bureaucracy, when sunk costs do not generate positive outcomes over time, the problem is explained not as too much money expended, but as too little.

Random Agenda Solution. Bureaucrats are driven by a combination of publicity concerns, pressure from and reporting requirements of funding bodies, agitation by public-interest organizations, and random developments. The agenda emphasized at a given time will vary depending upon the overriding source of influence.

Tunnel Vision. Bureaucracies bring an extreme perspective to risk-taking. Unable to see how any particular risk fits into the overall range of risks in the world, they fail to consider trade-off possibilities. Instead, they are obsessed with the last 10%. They insist not on reasonableness but on complete solutions to a given societal problem.

Inconsistency. Regulations do not deal with risks of similar magnitude in similar ways. At one extreme, the EPA's ban on asbestos might cost $250 million to save eight lives over thirteen years. At the other extreme, disease screening and vaccination programs may save lives at a cost of $50,000 to $70,000 each. Bureaucratic rules allow little leeway to adjust procedures to specific cases.

These fourteen characteristics make it impossible for bureaucracies to do anything but hinder entrepreneurship efforts; therefore, greater EI is met with more bureaucratic resistance. Entrepreneurship threatens bureaucracy to the extent that it represents a significant reallocation of resources, makes existing rules (and government jobs) irrelevant and obsolete, and demands novel public-sector solutions. From a QOL perspective (see Chapter 8), government bureaucracies focus only on the dysfunctional aspects of growth that result from entrepreneurial efforts, even at the expense of functional aspects.

TOWARD ENTREPRENEURIAL GOVERNMENT

In these chapters, we have argued that entrepreneurship is an environmentally driven phenomenon and that it is the major force for improvements in societal QOL. While there are other influences, government has a lead role in affecting the environment for entrepreneurship. Unfortunately, its actual role tends to be problematic. Mired in process, driven by often conflicting goals, resistant to change, and defining success by inputs rather than results, government bodies inevitably adopt "one size fits all" policies, and this places tremendous costs on entrepreneurial individuals and organizations.

What is needed is a fairly radical redefinition of the role of government in the economy. The neoclassical or laissez-faire conceptualization of government's role emphasized limiting interference to activities that fostered competitiveness or made the free market operate more efficiently, and to those necessary functions that the private marketplace could not be expected to adequately carry out. The significant expansion of government involvement during the twentieth century has come in response to a number of concerns, many of which have little to do with enhancing economic freedom or improving the economic dimension of QOL. In fact, the explicit focus appears to be on the non-economic QOL dimensions. Examples of such concerns include controlling the spillover costs that result from normal business operations, redistribution of income from haves to have-nots, redressing employment-related civil rights violations, and improving workers' safety, health, and family lifestyles.

While the regulated areas are fairly similar in most advanced industrial societies, the U.S. is unique in the way regulation is accomplished. Compared to other developed nations, U.S. regulatory authorities impose more detailed rules and interpretations, more paperwork, more formal inspections and reports, and significantly higher compliance costs. Thus, Puryear and Wiggins (1981) observed that some 90 federal agencies issue about 7,000 new rules each year. Weidenbaum (1992) noted funding for 122,400 regulators in the 1992 federal budget. Consistent with our earlier argument, Kristol (1978) suggests that regulatory agencies are staffed with career employees who share an antipathy toward business and the free market system. They bring zeal and aggressiveness to the regulatory task, while trying to redistribute power from the private to the public sector.

It is our position that government efforts to facilitate the non-economic dimensions of QOL actually come at the expense of both the economic as well as the non-economic QOL dimensions to the extent that these efforts hinder entrepreneurial behavior. The fact that many governmental actions have mixed and seemingly contradictory effects may reflect the absence of a consistent philosophy or ideological foundation on which to base these actions. Ironically, as its involvement level has expanded, the role and objectives of government in the private sector have become more obscure.

Several modern schools of thought exist regarding the role of government. One of the more prominent contemporary perspectives that is noticeably anti-entrepreneurial has been put forward by a number of scholars from the Massachusetts Institute of Technology (MIT) and Harvard University (Ferguson, 1988; Lawrence and Dyer, 1983; Reich, 1987). They argue for more collaboration between government and big business, ostensibly to generate national industrial plans and policies. Centralization and standardization are cornerstones of this philosophy. Entrepreneurial firms are viewed as counterproductive entities responsible for selling off America's public assets and undermining the competitiveness of mainstream industries.

We believe the opposite course must be pursued. The central objective of public policies directed at the private sector should be to facilitate entrepreneurial behavior. It is not a big business or small business issue, but instead, one of singling out entrepreneurs and entrepreneurial firms as focal points for regulatory support. As such, the central tenets of government policy should be decentralization, flexibility, and specialization or customization.

Decentralization refers to the need to move administrative decision making closer to the entrepreneur. In many decision areas, federal responsibility should be reassigned to states and locales. Within the organizational structures at each level, greater discretionary freedom should be extended to mid-level and even low-level bureaucrats so they can waive regulations if they deem them inappropriate for a given situation. Such *flexibility* must also be applied to the entire question of risk. Total risk to society must be considered when constraining entrepreneurial efforts, and reasonable trade-offs must be made (1) among categories or types of risks, and (2) between societal benefits and costs. *Specialization* implies a need for government to segment its markets and tailor unique programs and solutions to differing markets. It also suggests that government bodies should take on fewer and more fundamental tasks and return as many questions relative to risk-taking to the marketplace, where, as von Mises (1944) argued, decision-makers are not free from the economic consequences of their policies and must act accordingly.

This approach means developing programs of incentives and limited restraints for business segments that accomplish growth, regardless of the industry they are in. It also means customized programs that give incentives to entrepreneurs to concentrate on products and services that address the dysfunctional aspects of conventional entrepreneurship (e.g., pollution, resource depletion). In both cases, policies favoring proactive competition, innovation, risk-sharing, organizational autonomy, and the search for long-term profits are critical. Regulatory agencies must also be free to select from among competing regulatory solutions while favoring entrepreneurial incentives over penalties. Moreover, they must be held accountable for demonstrating that benefits of a given regulatory solution exceed costs.

More fundamentally, the bureaucratic model itself must be abandoned in favor of an entrepreneurial model of governance. The prescriptions of the recent literature on reinventing government represent a good first step in this direction (see Chapter 7). The essence of these proposals is that a number of free-market principles can and should be applied to public-sector management, including competition, the price mechanism, management of the forces of supply and demand, a customer orientation, and the leveraging of resources. But our position is that things should be taken even further.

The culture of public organizations must be changed to emphasize the values of innovation, calculated risk-taking, and proactive behavior. The goal should be to creatively respond to targeted customer segments, and entrepreneurial enterprises should be the priority. Entrepreneurial enterprises should also be considered as partners, not adversaries. By removing all obstacles to entrepreneurial growth, while concentrating resource deployment on further developing the educational, financial, social, legal, and logistical structures so as to enable entrepreneurial intensity, government will contribute significantly to the enhancement of societal QOL. Since QOL is a moving target, public policy must be able to rapidly adapt to emerging societal opportunities. Perhaps the key to accomplishing such an orientation lies in getting public-policy administrators to view themselves as entrepreneurs, and the process of regulation as an entrepreneurial undertaking.

CONCLUSIONS

Government policy-makers would appear to distinguish small organizations from large ones, and profit-seeking from not-for-profit ones. They make a distinction among organizations based on whether they are capital- or labor-intensive, and what industry grouping they fall into. However, when it comes to growth and innovation, there is a noticeable silence. Government targets little in the way of incentives, rewards, or regulatory support to organizations that achieve or sustain high rates of growth or contribute significant innovations. Actually, just the opposite is the case.

Overcoming the anti-entrepreneurial bias of government requires a revolution in the public sector no different from the one that is underway in the private sector. Corporations are unbundling, restructuring, reengineering, downsizing, empowering, and outsourcing. But more than this, fundamental questions are being raised about their relationships with suppliers, competitors, and customers. Traditional theory is under assault.

The same challenges confront government. Traditional structures and roles are being challenged. Bureaucracy as a model for governing is obsolete. We are not suggesting a need for less bureaucracy but instead, for a new model based on partnerships, decentralization, flexibility, and specialization or customization. Government as regulator and watchdog must be replaced by government as facilitator of entrepreneurial solutions to such problems as product safety, crime, environmental protection (enhancement), and labor market discrimination. The tax and regulator penalties should be targeted at those who fail to innovate, while protective support must be taken away from those who fail to create growth or find new sources of value.

REFERENCES

Averch, H. 1990. *Private Markets and Public Intervention: A Primer for Policy Designers.* Pittsburgh, PA: University of Pittsburgh Press.

Baumol, W.J. 1990. "Entrepreneurship: Productive, Unproductive, and Destructive." *Journal of Political Economy*, 98 (5), Part 1, 893–921.

Begley, R. 1995. "Product Liability: Reform at Last." *Chemical Week*, 2 (August), 5.

Berney, R. and Swanson, J. 1982. "The Regressive Impact of Governmental Regulations: Some Theoretical and Empirical Evidence." *American Journal of Small Business*, 51 (3), 16–25.

Bowermaster, D., and Gest, T. 1995. "Say You Want a Revolution." *U.S. News and World Report*, 119 (14), 38–41.

Etzioni-Halevy, E. 1983. *Bureaucracy and Democracy: A Political Dilemma.* London: Routledge and Kegan Paul.

Ferguson, C.H. 1988. "From the People Who Brought You Voodoo Economics." *Harvard Business Review*, 66 (May–June), 55–62.

Howard, P.K. 1968. *The Death of Common Sense: How Law Is Suffocating America.* New York: Random House.

Jorden, T.M., and Teece, D.J. 1990. "Innovation, Dynamic Competition, and Antitrust Policy." *CATO Review of Business and Government* (Fall), 35–44.

Kristol, I. 1978. *Two Cheers for Capitalism.* New York: Basic Books.

Lawrence, P., and Dyer, D. 1983. *Renewing American Industry: Organizing for Efficiency and Innovation.* New York: The Free Press.

Litan, R., and Nordhaus, W. 1983. *Reforming Federal Regulation.* New Haven, CT: Yale University Press.

McKee, B. 1992. "Environmental Price Tags." *Nation's Business* (April), 36–38.

Puryear, A.N., and Wiggins, C.P. 1981. "The Impact of Federal Regulations." In *The Environment for Entrepreneurship and Small Business: Summary Analysis of the Regional Research Reports.* Washington, DC: U.S. Small Business Administration, Office of Advocacy, 50–51.

Reich, R.B. 1987. "Entrepreneurship Reconsidered: The Team as Hero." *Harvard Business Review*, 65 (May–June), 77–83.

Singh, D., Wilder, R.P., and Chan, K.P. 1987. "Tax Rates in Small and Large Firms." *American Journal of Small Business* (Fall), 41–51.

Sommers, P., and Cole, R. 1981. "Costs of Compliance in Small and Medium-Sized Businesses." *American Journal of Small Business*, 51 (1), 25–29.

Stein, J. 1995. "Building a Better Bureaucrat." *Regulation*, 3, 24–33.

Susbauer, J.C. 1981. "The Impact of Federal Regulations." In *The Environment for*

Entrepreneurship and Small Business: Summary Analysis of the Regional Research Reports. Washington, DC: U.S. Small Business Administration, Office of Advocacy, 108–109.

Von Mises, L. 1944. *Bureaucracy.* New Haven, CT: Yale University Press.

Warner, D. 1992. "Regulations, Staggering Costs." *Nation's Business* (June), 50–54.

Weidenbaum, M. 1992. "Return of the 'R' Word." *Policy Review* (Winter), 40–53.

Wiggs, F.W. 1994. "Bureaucracy and the Constitution." *Public Administration Review*, (January–February), 65–72.

Wittergreen, J.A. 1988. "The Regulatory Revolution and the New Bureaucratic State." *The Heritage Lectures*, 10 (August), 1–13.

10

A Braver New World: Entrepreneurship and the Future

INTRODUCTION

What does the future hold? Obviously, no one knows for sure. Even those who specialize in spotting trends and extrapolating them have very different views on what will happen, much less when, where, and how it will happen. Yet, there are some areas of general agreement, and we will explore those, and their implications for entrepreneurial behavior, in this chapter.

As a beginning point, we believe one thing is certain: turbulence. The environments surrounding individuals, organizations, and societies are only likely to become more turbulent in the next two decades. Specifically, it would seem reasonable to expect that:

- technological change will *not* slow down and *will not* become less complex as existing and emerging technologies are integrated;
- markets will *not* become more homogeneous with fewer segments or niches;
- competition is *unlikely* to become more passive or predictable;
- governments will *not* impose fewer regulations on business;
- social values are *not* likely to be challenged less; social diversity is *not* apt to diminish;
- employees will *not* become more passive, and critical skills needed by companies will *not* be in greater abundance;
- resource prices and availability will *not* fluctuate less.

In fact, dramatic change is probably going to be the case in each of these areas. The implications for the entrepreneur are two-fold. First, turbulence creates disturbances or threats to the existing approach, the status quo, and the conventional wisdom. The fundamental need becomes greater for entrepreneurs who can find opportunity within these threats or develop innovative solutions that address these threats. More succinctly, in the future we shall all have to be entrepreneurs or at least tap much more of the entrepreneurial potential that resides within us. Secondly, threats will not only become more numerous, they will come more quickly and be of less predictable duration. This means entrepreneurs will have to be able to move quicker and adapt more readily to capitalize on emerging opportunities.

THE PROGNOSTICATORS

There are many trend spotters and predictors of the future, or futurists, who try to bring order to the turbulence. In fact, given the sales of such books as *Megatrends* (Naisbitt and Aburdene, 1990), *The Popcorn Report* (Popcorn, 1991), and *The Age of Unreason* (Handy, 1989), it would seem that futurism is an entrepreneurial growth industry (which is not surprising in turbulent times). Let us examine the work of four of the leading prognosticators.

One of the most popular of the futurists is Charles Handy. He has written a series of books that attempt to prepare us for a new way of life that is, in many ways, already upon us. One of his premises is that we live in an era of increasing paradox, where we are confronted with seemingly contradictory circumstances (Handy, 1994). Table 10.1 summarizes these paradoxes, each of which has important implications for entrepreneurship.

For example, entrepreneurs will increasingly find that their intellect and openness to continuous learning are not only competitive weapons but represent the fundamental source of value creation in any venture. Their most critical (ongoing) investment will be in people, who themselves will prove to be less permanent or loyal, and the skills and intellectual capital of these employees will become "obsolete" more quickly. The growth of the do-it-yourself and informal markets present a host of entrepreneurial opportunities. Examples include businesses targeting the "self" concept (e.g., self-publishing, self-training, do-it-yourself (d-i-y) home repair) and those that sell support services to this market (e.g., telephone answering services, office rentals by the day, temporary computer access services). Perceived time shortages suggest opportunities for those who can operate on a real-time basis, with shortened order cycle times and a willingness to be accessible 24 hours a day. Further, organizational paradoxes suggest that entrepreneurial companies will take hybrid forms, with extremely flat structures, organizational charts with curves and circles instead of lines or boxes, and extended external networks. As discussed in Chapter 6, a key objective will be to balance individual drive and vision against the need for cooperative teams of generalists and specialists.

To the paradoxes in Table 10.1, Naisbitt (1994, p. 1) adds one more. He argues that "the bigger the world economy, the more powerful its smallest players." In a mass production era, economies of scale, standardization, and

Table 10.1
Handy's Nine Paradoxes

Paradox 1:
Intelligence, which has none of the characteristics typically associated with property (cannot be redistributed, owned or taken away by someone else, valued on balance sheets, is owned by everyone) is property. The ability to acquire and apply knowledge becomes the source of value creation and wealth.

Paradox 2:
People either have work and money but no time, or no work or money but plenty of time. Those without jobs or time do not have the tools to create their own employment opportunities. A divided society results from the dilemma of choosing between fewer, better-paid, better-educated, better-protected workers, or more but cheaper ones.

Paradox 3:
Productivity concerns find more people forced into the do-it-yourself (d-i-y), informal or black market, where much of their economic contribution is not counted. The formal market no longer values their economic contributions, although the d-i-y, informal and black markets may represent the major source of economic growth in society.

Paradox 4:
Technology and productivity improvements mean we leave longer and it takes less time to accomplish most tasks, and yet people seem to have less free time.

Paradox 5:
Growing wealth in developed countries has produced a decline in births, which means fewer customers domestically. Growth can only come from exporting to less developed countries who cannot afford to buy from, and instead need to sell to, the developed countries. Thus, one must invest in one's potential competitors.

Paradox 6:
Companies must, at one and the same time, be global yet local, small yet large, centralized yet decentralized, planned yet flexible, differentiated yet integrated, standardized yet customized, with workers who are autonomous but team players.

Paradox 7:
Society's current generation sees itself as different from its predecessor, but plans for its children's generation to not differ from itself. Yet, the next generation will start work later, quit working earlier, will not be as scarred by war or nuclear threat, with children being planned and women's roles redefined.

Paradox 8:
Individualism requires teamwork, and teamwork requires individualism.

Paradox 9:
People must have an equal chance to achieve unequal rewards. Those who work hard and smart deserve to achieve more than others, but only if everyone has an equal opportunity to work hard and smart.

Source: Adapted from Handy (1994).

control typically defined success. But in the future, it will be networks of entrepreneurs that drive the system.

"Bigger is better" as a philosophy has already been replaced with an ethic
that emphasizes flexibility, nimbleness, speed, and focus. Thus, the global economy will increasingly be dominated by small and medium-size enterprises, acting as part of cooperative networks. Many of these enterprises may be affiliates
of multinational conglomerates, but traditionally large organizations will have
"deconstructed" or downsized and reengineered themselves into confederations
of smaller autonomous and highly aggressive units.

A very different perspective can be found in the work of Faith Popcorn and
her Brain Reserve colleagues (1996). They identify sixteen trends that drive the
consumer world. The trends are presented as a landscape, or framework, within
which individuals can find where they and their ideas might fit or not fit. The
authors demonstrate how an awareness of particular trends can serve as a launch-
ing point for a new venture. Table 10.2 illustrates a few of their trends and
related business concepts that have been, or might be, successful.

Consider, as a case in point, Popcorn's concept of "anchoring." If people
are looking for sources of stability and consistency, they might turn to religion.
Pat Robertson (1996) foresees the decline of secular humanism and a growing
role for God in our lives. This creates opportunities not only for churches (especially those who, understanding the 99 lives (see Table 10.2) trend, will sched-
ule services and activities at flexible times) but for commercial entrepreneurs.
Whether it is the mainstreaming of gospel music artists, sales of t-shirts with
the pope's image on them, the marketing of weekend religious retreats at nature
preserves, or the growth of the Family Channel (formerly the Christian Broadcast Network) on cable television, we find entrepreneurs at work capitalizing on
the trend.

A third perspective is offered by Alvin Toffler (1990) and John Naisbitt
(1990), who separately examine large societal shifts resulting from the transition
to an information technology base from a manufacturing and industrial base. As
illustrated in Table 10.3, these observers talk of dramatic developments in literally every walk of life. They argue that these are not idiosyncratic or random
developments, but reflect an entirely new set of rules and assumptions (many
of which are still being written or require continuous updating) in the post-
industrial age.

As an example of the entrepreneurial potential that results from this transition,
one has only to consider education. The move to an information-based society
in which knowledge is power suggests a large growth in expenditures for employee training. Combining this with other trends, one can anticipate the privatization of training providers, the customization of training programs, training
that focuses on the holistic individual, innovations so that training can be done
at non-traditional times (e.g., in the middle of the night, or while driving), a
speeding up of the delivery of training, new vehicles for training (e.g., interactive
video), and training materials that more rapidly incorporate the newest insights

Table 10.2

A Sample of Popcorn's Trends and Their Application to Entrepreneurship

The Trend	Sample Entrepreneurial Concepts
"Cocooning" - stay at home more, build comfortable, secure environment in which can escape or be buffered and protected from a crazy world	• smart appliances • innovative lawn and garden tools • service providers (e.g., travel agents, medical testing companies) who come to your home • personal protection stun devices • home collect and deliver services • home security systems
"Anchoring" - desire for linkages to things stable, consistent, and secure from one's past; a guest for spiritual roots, religious ties, and self-identity	• genealogy-related products • meditation retreats • yoga centers • books, films, music focusing on miracles and angels • nature and gospel music • family networks and programming
"99 lives" - pace of life is so accelerated that each of us must increasingly fill multiple roles, work at multiple jobs, and undergo multiple changes at the same time	• beepers, pagers, cell phones, voice recorders, voicemail • instant news from anywhere available anytime • software to manage time, organize activities, manage personal finances • on-line banking, shopping, and schooling • e-mail
"Icon Toppling" - tendency to challenge or question our leaders, role models, pillars of society, authority figures, parents, police, and others	• alternative religious groups • private security services • anti-establishment designs in clothing, architecture, packaging • expose-all, tabloid TV, radio, newspapers, and books • anti-heroes featured in movies and as basis for new products and product endorsements
"Vigilante Consumer" - lack of trust in corporations, government and other institutions; general skepticism of advertising and sales claims; consumerism and a demand for better service, better products, better treatment, and more value for the money	• magazines telling people which products or vendors to boycott • devices to detect traces of (ostensibly illegal) drugs • systems to measure customer service levels • products/designs to reduce queuing or waiting times • new product labeling systems • interactive, on-line complaint handling systems
"Save Our Society" - a concern with environmentalism, including the depletion of natural resources, the extinction and abuse of animals and other species, air/water/noise/smoke pollution, overpopulation	• recycled products • natural products • biodegradable materials • noiseless dishwashers, vacuum cleaners, hand tools • paperless restaurants • ecotourism

Source: Adapted from Popcorn and Marigold (1996).

Table 10.3
Some of Naisbitt's "Megatrends" and Toffler's "Power Shifts"

- Booming global economy, free trade and trading blocks, growing economic interdependence
- Privatization and decline of the welfare state, devolution of state power
- Rise of the Pacific Rim and eastern values
- Advancement of democracy and democratic values
- Women in leadership, women as role models, emphasis on values of caring and sharing
- Age of biology/biotechnology
- Global lifestyles and cultural nationalism
- Renaissance of the arts, leisure, and escapism
- Multiple jobs, multiple careers, and part-time work
- Knowledge as power, serving as essence of financial or military power
- Decentralization, deconstruction, downsizing
- Fusion of producer and consumer
- Small runs of customized goods aimed at niche markets
- Higher levels of speed in everything; real-time simultaneity rather than sequential stages
- Electronic money, electronic transactions, electronic information
- Higher level of diversity combined with more complex forms of integration
- Shift in power within distribution channels from manufacturers to wholesalers and retailers
- Transparency, openness, availability of information
- Flexible manufacturing, inventory, logistical, and purchasing systems
- Speech-driven machines and products
- Value that derives from relationships, networks, extended alliances, and mosaics
- Interactivity, mobility, convertibility, connectivity, ubiquity, and globalization in communications

---

Source: Adaped from Naisbitt and Aburdene (1990) and Toffler (1990).

from anywhere in the world. Similarly, while companies can be expected to outsource all of their educational requirements, traditional public educational institutions may outsource most of their basic operations (including teaching, information technology, marketing, food service, janitorial service, grounds maintenance, fundraising). Opportunities for the entrepreneur abound.

CHANGING MARKETS, MARKETING, AND THE ENTREPRENEUR

Of all the changes underway, perhaps the most significant from the entrepreneur's point of view concern customers and markets. The entrepreneur's ultimate accountability is to the customer, without whom there is no venture (start-up or corporate). Creating value for a customer and developing a sustainable relationship are the building blocks to achieving competitive advantage.

Developments in technology, demographics, standards of living, information availability, deregulation, social mores, and the intensity of competition have all combined to dramatically affect how markets must be defined and approached. The future success of entrepreneurs will depend on their ability to capitalize on the revolution taking place in markets and, by extension, in marketing.

Only a few years ago, the core problem in many organizations was to move from thinking of marketing as selling to approaching marketing as a set of value-creating activities that are captured in the so-called marketing mix (product, price, promotion, and distribution). Today, the problem is much more complicated. Figure 10.1 illustrates three related trends in the ongoing evolution of marketing practice.

In essence, the left-hand column in Figure 10.1 suggests that the mass market is dead. From hotels to beers to publishing to financial services to structural steel, market after market is fragmented, segmented, and niched. Consider ath-

Figure 10.1
Three Different Ways in Which Markets and Marketing Approaches Are Evolving

Approach to the Marketing Mix	Approach to the Customer	Performance Objectives
MASS MARKETING "Rely on one size fits all marketing"	DISCRETE TRANSACTIONS "The customer is a fish to be caught"	SALES "Close the deal"
SEGMENTED MARKETING "Find groups of customers with homogeneous needs/buying behaviors"	REPEAT TRANSACTIONS "Let's tie the customer in"	MARKET SHARE "Own the market or capture all you can"
	BRAND/SOURCE LOYALTY "Create a sustainable attitudinal preference"	
NICHE MARKETING "Specialize in a segment"		OPERATING PROFIT "Generate an acceptable rate of return on product/segment/ channel investments"
RELATIONSHIP MARKETING "Invest in a two-way, mutually beneficial and ongoing exchange"	RELATIONSHIPS "Invest in a two-way mutually beneficial and ongoing exchange"	
ONE-TO-ONE MARKETING "Customize to the level of the individual customer"	PARTNERSHIPS "Develop products, processes, services, channels, technologies jointly with customers"	CUSTOMER EQUITY "Focus on our desired proportion of the buyers' total expenditures on a product class over a number of years"

letic shoes (once called sneakers or tennis shoes). In times past, a consumer went to the shoe department in a department store, or to a shoe store, and had a choice between black and white, high-top or low-top. Today, he/she goes to an athletic shoe store and has 60 or 70 shoe types to select from, one for every type of athletic activity and type of foot, with numerous features to choose from as well (e.g., color, air pump, lace versus velcro).

Increasingly, the entrepreneur must segment the market, prioritize one or two key segments to be targeted, and tailor the marketing mix (i.e., the product or service offering, the price charged, the communications approach, and the distribution channel or method) to each segment. Further, entrepreneurs will often specialize in serving a single segment, or niche. Beyond this is relationship marketing, where the firm makes unique investments in individual customer accounts, interacts closely with them, and tailors aspects of the marketing mix. The ultimate step is where the firm engages in one-to-one marketing and tailors the entire marketing mix to individual accounts. Business-to-business marketers have done this for years (e.g., IBM when it deals with NASA or Ford Motor Company), but increasingly innovative consumer marketers are engaging in one-to-one marketing. A case in point is Lands End, the highly successful and very entrepreneurial direct marketing company. It is able to customize aspects of the product (e.g., a man's shirt with a personal monogram), quote a unique price, have highly personalized communication, and quickly deliver the product to the customer's front door using express delivery services.

A second evolution involves what one is trying to achieve vis-à-vis the customer. The traditional concern has been the "one-time or single occasion" transaction. Increasingly, however, survival requires that firms develop groups of attitudinally and behaviorally loyal customers, or that they establish formal relationships, or perhaps even that they partner with customers in developing new technologies, products, or logistical approaches.

The third evolution concerns how the entrepreneur measures performance. Sales revenue and market share were the old gods. Today, however, the concern is more with the profitability of individual segments and customers. The move is on, though, to focusing on the "lifetime value" of a customer and setting a goal for how much of their expenditure in a particular product category the entrepreneur wants to capture over that lifetime (or a strategically relevant time period). This is called customer equity. Thus, Land's End might set a goal of capturing 40% of your total clothing expenditures over the next ten years.

Let's consider the entrepreneur who has purchased a gas station and upgraded it to also include a quick lube and quick tune service center. Significant opportunity can be discovered by doing an assessment of the current customer base. Assume that two of the major sub-groups identified include (1) passing tourists who stop in for gas, but who are not from the area and are unlikely to return; and (2) local residents on the way to or from work. The first group are managed as one-off transactions, where quality service is the rule, but the ultimate goal is to maximize revenue per transaction. The second group is typified by Ms.

Jones, a local accountant who is well-established in the community. In her case, the entrepreneur has a potential relationship. The question becomes What proportion of Ms. Jones's total gasoline and auto maintenance expenditures over the next seven years do I want to capture? Our entrepreneur might get creative, offering Ms. Jones a special attractively-priced package. Suppose he offers to pick her car up at her place of work on the first Wednesday of every other month, bring it to the station, change all the lubricants, do a quick tune-up, wash and wax the car, and return it before the end of the workday? He also offers her credit, regular specials, and a log that includes detailed information on her car, its condition, what he has done to it, and when. Finally, he communicates with her personally through monthly mailings that cover such topics as when to use which fuels, how to use less gas when driving, future price trends, and when to start looking for a new car.

Movement along each of the evolutionary paths pictured in Figure 10.1 results in the entrepreneur's marketing efforts becoming:

- more intense,
- more focused,
- more expensive,
- more complex, and
- requiring more hard work.

Essentially, we are saying that the entrepreneur will have to become more of a marketer, and as a marketer, he/she will have to be more of an entrepreneurial marketer.

What then, is meant by the term "entrepreneurial marketing"? It is an opportunistic perspective wherein the marketer is not simply responsible for communication activities but instead, must continually discover new sources of value for customers. Value is created through unique combinations within the marketing mix. The entrepreneurial marketer challenges the assumptions and conventional wisdom that prevail in a given industry. He/she strives to lead customers rather than follow them.

As markets and marketing approaches evolve, the challenge to the entrepreneur will be to uncover distinct market segments and niches, while finding ways to customize the marketing mix down to the level of the market segment and the individual account. He/she must also learn to estimate the lifetime value of a customer and then determine the appropriate levels and types of investments to be made in individual accounts. All of this implies the need for keen insight into customer lifestyles or operations and (often unstated or unperceived) customer needs, and into the changing trade-offs that customers are willing to make among core product, service, and vendor attributes. The entrepreneurial marketer becomes a creative consultant, helping customers adapt to a discontinuous future.

It also suggests that entrepreneurs will have to develop and continually update highly detailed (and often interactive) customer databases. In this conceptualization, the most important element of the marketing mix is not *promotion*, it becomes *product (or service)*. The entrepreneur will find it necessary to produce a continual stream of new lines, additions to lines, product and service improvements or revisions, new applications, and repositioning efforts. At the same time process innovation will be vital. This will include new approaches to segmentation, pricing, use of the brand, packaging, customer credit, logistics, design and management of distribution channels, database management, customer communication, and management of customer service levels.

ENTREPRENEURIAL DILEMMAS AND THE FUTURE

George Gilder (1988, p. 49) indicates that "It is the entrepreneurs who know the rules of the world and the laws of God. Thus they sustain the world—they overthrow establishments rather than establish equilibria." Gilder is certainly correct in his characterization of the "entrepreneur as hero," which is the conventional stereotype. Yet, not all entrepreneurs produce dramatic breakthroughs. Ironically, those who do overthrow the establishment frequently find that the returns they achieve can be less than those received by less ambitious entrepreneurs.

This is one of a number of fundamental dilemmas confronting those interested in entrepreneurship. As entrepreneurship plays a more pronounced role in the lives of individuals, organizations, and societies, it is crucial that dilemmas such as these be recognized, and that strategies be developed for addressing them. Below, we have identified five critical dilemmas and some of the issues surrounding each of them.

The Dilemma of Risk versus Return

The relationship between what an entrepreneur does and the outcomes or returns achieved is not a simple one. It is often assumed that major breakthroughs, or higher risk ventures, generate higher returns. But this is not always the case, as returns are influenced by timing, managerial competence, market conditions, and a host of environmental factors. Even if one controls for all of these factors though, doing something that is highly entrepreneurial only raises the possible ceiling on returns if one is successful. Actual returns are unique to the venture.

We believe that the general level of risk facing any entrepreneur will increase in the coming years simply because more entrepreneurship will be occurring. Within this broader context, the probability of failure will be higher for those individuals, organizations, and societies who pursue both very low and very high levels of entrepreneurial intensity (EI). We further believe that the highest returns will come to those who can sustain a balance of degree and frequency of entrepreneurship over time.

The Dilemma of the Individual versus the Team

Entrepreneurship requires a visionary individual with drive and commitment. Entrepreneurship also requires a dedicated team of specialists and generalists. The problem becomes one of emphasizing both individualism and collective teamwork at the same time. Unfortunately, a policy or procedure that incentivizes individual action can serve as a disincentive for collective action. Similarly, a preoccupation with teams will come at the expense of entrepreneurial leadership. Achieving a balance can be tricky.

Nonetheless, in an age of multiple careers and lessened organizational loyalty, the entrepreneur will have to be less of a team dictator and more of a team member. He/she will have to share ownership and control with team members. The objective will be to build an organization based on core competencies and to focus on the continued development of knowledge assets that can deliver these competencies. Thus, the internal team itself becomes fluid or subject to change.

The Dilemma of the Self-Contained Unit versus the Network

As we enter an age where large organizations find that small truly is beautiful, a premium will be placed on being flexible and fast. At the same time, the competitive advantage of small entrepreneurial firms vis-à-vis large corporations will dissipate as the large corporates downsize, restructure, and reengineer. The entrepreneur who is building a venture will need to focus less on accumulating assets and achieving control through ownership and more on building a fluid, adaptable organization that is highly leveraged in terms of financing, buildings, equipment, administrative services, and staffing.

Perhaps the best way to express this is that entrepreneurs will have to think individually, but act collectively. That is, they will best be able to achieve market power through external alliances and networks, not by acquisition or an increase in their physical asset base.

They will effectively gain control by giving up control. Further, external commitments will not be permanent, as individual members of a dynamic network come and go. A new form of barter will arise in terms of what different organizations have to offer to one another in exchange for cooperation.

The Dilemma of Stability versus Turbulence

Entrepreneurship requires both stability and instability. Where there is an established environmental infrastructure (e.g., financial institutions, utilities, transport, distribution channels, courts, police), entrepreneurship is facilitated. Yet, environmental turbulence (e.g., regulatory, technological, market-related, competitive) creates opportunities for proactive entrepreneurs. In fact, there is a circle of turbulence, in that environmental turbulence gives rise to entrepreneurial opportunity, and entrepreneurial behavior in turn produces disruption, or more environmental turbulence. Politicians and economists seem concerned that this cycle will spin out of control, such that unfettered growth will result in rampant inflation and economic chaos. Yet, there is little evidence to support their fears. Periods of uncontrolled inflation and economic instability have typically been the result of far too little entrepreneurial activity, not too much.

There is a related dilemma here, in that entrepreneurship is both constructive and destructive. Entrepreneurs create the new, and in doing so, they preemptorily make existing products, services, and processes obsolete. The copier can still make good copies when it is replaced by a quicker, better machine. In the future, this creative destruction will accelerate, as entrepreneurs find they must continually make their own products obsolete. Along the way, whole new entrepreneurial opportunities will be created for recycling, retrofitting, and identifying alternative distribution channels (reaching new markets) for the products being displaced.

The Dilemma of Success versus Failure

Although it is popular to talk about winners and losers, sustained entrepreneurship is not that simple. Entrepreneurs are often competitive, with a need to win. They are replacing conventional managers who have a need to avoid failure. Yet, many entrepreneurs fail. A considerable number of well-known entrepreneurs experienced failure before ever achieving success. Others can describe an entire portfolio of successes and failures, where one solid hit is followed by a strikeout and two ground outs, and then a home run.

Within failure are the seeds of success. Entrepreneurs must increasingly believe in the successful failure, where lessons from unsuccessful efforts are used to adapt one's concepts and ideas into something that will work. This is important on two levels. A general increase in new product and service introductions and new venture start-ups by definition means a higher failure rate. Similarly, as individuals find themselves doing more entrepreneurial things in their own lives, they will also begin to fail more often. Success will increasingly be a function of one's ability to overcome the psychological fear or avoidance of failure that is ingrained in virtually all of us.

TOMORROW'S ENTREPRENEURS

Given all that has been said about the future, will tomorrow's entrepreneur differ from his/her contemporary counterpart? On some basic issues, one would expect few differences. Entrepreneurs as a group will tend to share certain characteristics (e.g., achievement motivation, internal locus of control, calculated risk-taking). Entrepreneurs as a group will remain passionate about their venture and will be opportunity-driven. As Schwartz (1988, p. 32) has noted, "When the cash register starts ringing, the businessperson feels happy—the entrepreneur feels bored." This will not change. Entrepreneurs as a group will continue to demonstrate significant diversity among their ranks, with a number of different types of entrepreneurs emerging.

However, some changes are also likely. We not only believe that there will be more entrepreneurs, but that all of us will have to find ways to introduce more entrepreneurship into our lives. This means that the pool of entrepreneurs will grow significantly, become even more diverse, and that new categories or new types of entrepreneurs will emerge. The new categories will describe subsets of entrepreneurs found not only in commerce, but in all walks of life.

Other changes are probable as well. Levinson (1997) provides a somewhat normative picture of the future entrepreneur that centers around the concept of balance (e.g., between demands of the venture and one's personal lifestyle, or between company financial performance and a sense of organizational learning and value creation). Table 10.4 includes an outline of Levinson's conceptualization of the twenty-first century entrepreneur.

Our own view is that, in spite of their growing diversity, entrepreneurs will share some additional commonalities. Significantly, we will see the emergence of:

- *The Global Entrepreneur*—There will be a greater awareness of what is happening in other parts of the world, and entrepreneurs will more quickly adapt to or adopt approaches used by others. Entrepreneurs will also focus increasingly on global sources of supply and global markets for their own products. This will be chiefly accomplished through networks and alliances.

- *The Ethnically and Environmentally Conscious Entrepreneur*—Tomorrow's entrepreneurs will define high ethical standards as a key factor in their long-term performance. They will develop a keen sense of their own ethical standards and those of their employees, and these standards will be based on consistent rather than situational behavior guidelines. Similarly, entrepreneurs will be conscious not simply of resource efficiency but of the environmental externalities that result from their businesses. This awareness will include the raw material inputs they use; the disposal or recycling of their unused outputs and waste; the appearance of their physical facilities, equipment, vehicles, and signage; the noise that they generate; and related side-effects of their operations.

- *The Technologically Competent Entrepreneur*—The entrepreneur will understand that technology goes beyond knowing how to turn on his/her own personal computer. As knowledge becomes the key competency, and competitive advantage comes more from speed, adaptability and aggressiveness, the entrepreneur will stress extensive process innovation as new user-friendly technologies are integrated into all aspects of the venture's operations.

- *The Lifestyle-Conscious Entrepreneur*—Raised in a time of relative world peace, limited nuclear threat, global economic growth, free trade, general affluence, and environ-

Table 10.4
The Twenty-First Century Entrepreneur: A Normative View

In the future, entrepreneurs will:

- emphasize balance between the demands or sacrifices of work and the freedom for leisure and lifestyle;

- pursue opportunities based on work that makes him/her happy; will be passionate about the work, while recognizing that the journey is the goal;

- be more concerned with profitability, vitality, quality, learning, and value than growth or size;

- proceed at a steady, planned pace; will work according to a plan; will view stress as an indicator of an unplanned or incorrect approach;

- be disciplined, focused on the task at hand, and concerned more with today than yesterday or tomorrow; will be focused on business strategy as well;

- be team players, dependent upon many others, with an appreciation for mutual dependency;

- emphasize the linking of his/her business to other synergistic enterprises, in the process leveraging resources; as a rule these linkages are not permanent, and many are shorter-term;

- focus on both internal and external flexibility and adaptability.

Source: Adaped from Levinson (1997).

mentalism, tomorrow's entrepreneur will be conscious of quality of life (QOL) considerations. He/she will find ways to enhance QOL through his/her ventures (e.g., working from home or remote locations, creating more holistic work environments that address such issues as daycare, stress on the job, and flextime). He/she will also be more conscious of the value of a private life, time off, adventurous travel, and family and civic involvement.

- *The Multiple Venture Entrepreneur*—The norm for tomorrow's entrepreneur will be a series of entrepreneurial ventures over their lives, and a tendency to have their fingers in multiple ventures at one time. Some of these ventures may have short life spans; others may be ongoing. Stated differently, then, the individual's average EI score will rise, especially in terms of the frequency dimension.

With this last point, we are suggesting a growing emphasis on lifelong entrepreneurship. To truly realize the potential of entrepreneurship as a philosophy, objective, strategy, attitude, and behavioral process—in short, as a source of sustainable advantage—it has to be applied over the entire life cycles of people, organizations, and societies.

TOWARD SUSTAINABLE ADVANTAGE: ENTREPRENEURSHIP AND LIFE CYCLES

The concept of EI is based on the fundamental principle that individuals, organizations, and societies differ in terms of the number of entrepreneurial events they pursue, and the degree to which those events are innovative, involve calculated risks, and are proactive. In Chapter 4, we illustrated the EI concept by showing where a particular person, company, or country might fall in the entrepreneurial grid. In essence, we were assessing entrepreneurial performance at a point in time, or over a finite period of time, such as the past two years.

In the years ahead, we will witness a shift in emphasis toward lifelong entrepreneurship. The concern will be less with achieving something entrepreneurial at one point in one's career or in the life of a company, and more with sustaining it on an ongoing basis. In addition, we will see the role of entrepreneurs change as life cycles evolve.

A life cycle approach attempts to identify major phases of development in the life of a person, product, company, technology, political movement, or national economy. In this book, we have focused upon individuals, organizations, and societies. The developmental life cycle of each are illustrated in Figure 10.2.

The Individual's Life Cycle

Consider the individual. As people evolve through the stages of their lives, changes occur in the relative importance they place on such factors as acceptance, security, materialism, experimentation, structure, diversity, personal

Figure 10.2
Individual, Organizational, and Societal Life Styles

An Individual's Stage in Life	A Company's Stage in the Organizational Life Cycle	A Country's Stage of Societal Development
Childhood	Creativity	Tradition
↓	↓	↓
Adolescence	Direction	Pre-Take-off
↓	↓	↓
Early Adulthood	Delegation	Take-off
↓	↓	↓
Middle-Age Maturity	Integration	Drive to Maturity
↓	↓	↓
Semi-Retirement	Collaboration	Mass Consumption
↓		↓
Retirement/Seniority		Post-Consumption

achievement, partnering, family, roots, and privacy (cf. Sheehy, 1976). The relative importance of frequency versus degree of entrepreneurship is also likely to change as one moves through the stages in Figure 10.2. Selling lemonade in front of one's home as a child and organizing school dances as an adolescent might give way to a period of apprenticeship with an established company, where one experiments with modest process innovations. This might be followed by a period where one champions major innovation within the firm, participates in a business start-up on the side, or simply breaks away and goes it alone. The first independent venture might be followed by participation in a second or third. Later in life, one might help champion social innovation in terms of novel solutions to a problem in the local church or within the community.

Of course, any number of patterns can emerge. By early adulthood, however, one would expect that the individual had begun to develop some semblance of a strategy for entrepreneurship. Also, the relative emphasis on entrepreneurship in one's professional versus family versus social lives can be expected to change over time. For instance, social experimentation might be more in evidence during adolescent and semi-retirement years, while professional experimentation might come more during early adulthood, and again in semi-retirement.

The Organizational Life Cycle

If we turn to the corporation and its organizational life cycle, analogous patterns might emerge. Companies typically start out as fairly creative and entrepreneurial entities. However, the need for controls and structures becomes critical once a certain size is achieved. The organization subsequently evolves through stages, which are disrupted by periodic crises. These crises are addressed over time by alternating between such strategies as delegation or centralization; and the formation of autonomous business units, integrative superstructures, or matrix teams (see Adizes, 1978; Griener, 1972). To address the various crises and organizational requirements that arise, ongoing changes occur in the managerial focus, company structure, leadership style, control system, reward policies, and corporate culture. However, these changes also tend to systematically undermine (or lead to a de-emphasis on) entrepreneurship.

An alternative approach is to strategically manage entrepreneurship, identifying different roles for it, and approaches to it, depending on the stage in the organizational life cycle. Not only will the relative importance of degree and frequency differ over time, but so too will the priority given to product versus service versus process innovation. So, too, might one expect the extent to which entrepreneurship comes from the top, the bottom, or the middle of the company to vary. Further, as a company evolves from being product-driven to production-driven to sales-driven to cost-driven to market-driven, the functional areas within the firm (such as production, research and development, sales, marketing, and finance) that lead the entrepreneurial change can be expected to alternate.

The Societal Life Cycle

Finally, let us briefly examine the ways in which societies evolve. There might first be a pre-development period characterized by a pastoral or nomadic existence. Next would come a stage where society is agriculturally-based, with limited access to technology and a hierarchical social structure based on family and clan. This would be followed by a period of initial (labor-intensive) industrialization and urbanization, which then would become more capital-intensive, with a focus on economies of scale and learning effects. Eventually, society would evolve to a more service-based, and then to a technology-based and knowledge-based foundation (Rostow, 1971; Toffler, 1990).

An interesting parallel perspective can be found in the work of Sirgy and Fox-Mangleberg (1988), who describe societal development in terms of a needs hierarchy. The initial concern is with survival needs, then safety needs, social needs, esteem needs, and finally, self-actualization needs. As societies advance up the hierarchy of needs, the focus changes from a production orientation, to a selling orientation, to a customer-satisfaction orientation, to a societal benefits orientation.

Entrepreneurship not only plays a unique role in each stage of societal evolution, but general levels of entrepreneurial intensity can determine how long a country stays in a particular stage as well as the overall pace of advancement through the various stages. Early stages might find an emphasis on the immigrant as entrepreneur, where much of the entrepreneurial behavior concerns small start-ups (shopkeepers, artisans, brickmakers) and the development of a merchant class. Subsequently, a number of visionary entrepreneurs contribute to a major leap forward by building critical infrastructure (e.g., banks; railroads; core industries such as steel, mining, or automobiles). Later, the entrepreneurs pioneer service innovation (e.g., hotels, package delivery, entertainment) and franchise systems (e.g., fast food, quick copy). This is followed by technology innovations (e.g., computer systems, robotics, lasers, biotechnology). Of course, in every stage one finds shopkeepers, infrastructure pioneers, service innovations, and inventors. However, it is the dominant entrepreneurial focus in any one stage that ultimately defines that stage.

One might further hypothesize that, as societies evolve, there is a change in conceptualization from the entrepreneur as every man (or woman), to the entrepreneur as bold hero, to the entrepreneur as every man (or woman). In a similar vein, early stages might find society preoccupied with frequency of entrepreneurship, the take-off stage with degree of entrepreneurship, and later stages with a balance of frequency and degree.

Lessons can be learned about sustained societal entrepreneurship from the experiences of South Korea, Singapore, and Chile in the latter part of the twentieth century (see Chapter 8). Each country has accelerated its movement through the developmental stages over a 30-year period. Each vividly illustrates both a heightened need and evolving role for entrepreneurship and enlightened government. As a case in point, Singapore initially concentrated on local entrepreneurs to start and grow labor-intensive manufacturing and export businesses. However, this rapidly evolved into an emphasis on technopreneurs, who run world-class, technology-based ventures. The key, of course, is entrepreneurial government, which charts a long-term strategy for societal entrepreneurship.

CONCLUSIONS

These are exciting times to be alive, just as they are very trying times. The competitive environment is hostile and threatening, but it is also filled with opportunity. We live in an age of conflict, turbulence, and paradox. It is an era that can be characterized in many ways, but most importantly, it is the age of entrepreneurship.

We are witnessing what might be called the "democratization of entrepreneurship." Entrepreneurs have always come from all walks of life and pursued all types of ventures. Entrepreneurship is indifferent to race, religion, or age, although some societies have put up discriminatory barriers to certain people doing entrepreneurial things. Yet, in spite of all this, those who actually pursue entrepreneurial ventures have historically represented an extremely small percentage of the total population. This percentage is rapidly increasing and will increase even more in the coming years. Further, in one way or another, entrepreneurship will play an active role in virtually everyone's life.

In this final chapter, we have looked at where emerging opportunities might lie in the new millennium for those who act on their entrepreneurial impulses, and how entrepreneurs themselves can be expected to change. Fundamental dilemmas in the phenomenon of entrepreneurship were identified. The central concept though is the notion of lifetime entrepreneurship. There is a need for individuals, organizations, and societies to develop strategies for managing entrepreneurship over their life cycles. The most common two words in our daily vocabularies must become, what if.

The subtitle of this book contains the words "sustainable advantage." To sustain is to give strength to, encourage, keep from falling, or keep going continuously. Advantage refers to a position that gives one precedence, favorable circumstance, or superiority. Entrepreneurship is the source of strength that allows individuals to continuously put themselves into favorable circumstances, regardless of how unfavorable the surrounding conditions are. It enables companies to move quicker, be more nimble, and arrive in places before customers or competitors have been there. It changes the standard by which societies judge themselves, raising the sights and expectations of all citizens. In modern times, entrepreneurial intensity becomes the compass that will take us to a future of unlimited possibilities, newfound freedoms, and enhanced life satisfaction for every member of the human family.

REFERENCES

Adizes, I. 1978. "Organizational Passages—Diagnosing and Treating Lifecycle Problems of Organizations." *Organizational Dynamics* (Summer), 2–25.

Gilder, G. 1988. "The Revitalization of Everything: The Law of the Microcosm." *Harvard Business Review*, 66 (March–April), 49–61.

Griener, L.E. 1972. "Evolution and Resolution as Organizations Grow." *Harvard Business Review*, 50 (July–August), 37–46.

Handy, C. 1989. *The Age of Unreason*. London: Arrow Books.

Handy, C. 1994. *The Empty Raincoat*. London: Arrow Books.

Hawken, P. 1978. *Growing a Business*. New York: Fireside.

Levinson, J.C. 1997. *The Way of the Guerrilla*. Boston: Houghton Mifflin.

Naisbitt, J. 1994. *Global Paradox*. New York: William Morrow and Co.

Naisbitt, J., and Aburdene, P. 1990. *Megatrends 2000*. New York: William Morrow & Co.

Popcorn, F. 1991. *The Popcorn Report*. New York: Doubleday.

Popcorn, F., and Marigold, L. 1996. *Clicking*. New York: HarperCollins.

Robertson, P. 1996. *The New Millennium*. Dallas: World Publishing.

Rostow, N.W. 1971. *The Stages of Economic Growth*. New York: Cambridge University Press.

Schwartz, B. 1988. "Betting on Yourself." *Lear's* (March–April), 43–44.

Sheehy, G. 1976. *Passages: Predictable Crises of Adult Life*. New York: E.P. Dutton.

Sirgy, M.H., and Fox-Mangleberg, T. 1988. "Toward a General Theory of Social System Development: A Management/Marketing Perspective." *Systems Research*, 5 (2), 115–30.

Toffler, A. 1990. *Power Shift*. New York: Bantam Books.

Suggested Readings

Adizes, I. 1988. *Corporate Lifecycles: How and Why Corporations Grow and Die.* Englewood Cliffs, NJ: Prentice-Hall.

Bird, B.J. 1989. *Entrepreneurial Behavior.* London: Scott, Foresman.

Bygrave, W.D. (ed.). 1977. *The Portable MBA in Entrepreneurship.* New York: John Wiley and Sons.

Bygrave, W.D. 1993. "Theory Building in the Entrepreneurship Paradigm." *Journal of Business Venturing,* 8 (3), 250–280.

Drucker, P. 1985. *Innovation and Entrepreneurship: Practices and Principles.* New York: Harper and Row.

Gartner, W.R. 1985. "A Conceptual Framework for Describing the Phenomenon of New Venture Creation." *Academy of Management Review,* 10 (4), 696–706.

Gartner, W.R. 1988. "Who Is the Entrepreneur? Is the Wrong Question." *American Journal of Small Business,* 12 (4), 33–39.

Gerber, M.E. 1986. *The E-Myth.* Cambridge, MA: Ballinger Publishing.

Gilder, G. 1988. "The Revitalization of Everything: The Law of the Microcosm." *Harvard Business Review,* 66 (March–April), 49–61.

Gilder, G. 1984. *The Spirit of Enterprise.* New York: Simon & Schuster.

Hamel, G., and Prahalad, C.K. 1991. "Corporate Imagination and Expeditionary Marketing." *Harvard Business Review,* 69 (July–August), 81–92.

Hawken, P. 1987. *Growing a Business.* New York: Fireside.

Hisrich, R.D. 1986. *Entrepreneurship, Intrapreneurship and Venture Capital.* Lexington: Lexington Books.

Hood, J., and Young, E. 1993. "Entrepreneurship's Requisite Areas of Development: A Survey of Top Executives in Entrepreneurial Firms." *Journal of Business Venturing,* 8 (2), (March), 115–136.

McMillan, I.C., Block, Z., and Narasimha, P.N.S. 1986. "Corporate Venturing: Alternatives, Obstacles Encountered and Experience Effects." *Journal of Business Venturing,* 1 (2), 177–192.

Miner, J.B. 1996. *The Four Routes to Entrepreneurial Success*. San Francisco: Berrett-Koehler Publishers.

Pinchot III, G. 1985. *Intrapreneuring*. New York: Harper and Row.

Reynolds, P.D. 1987. "Organizations: Predicting Contributions and Survival." In R. Ronstadt et al. (eds.), *Frontiers of Entrepreneurship Research*. Wellesley, MA: Babson College, 584–609.

Roberts, E.B. 1991. *Entrepreneurs in High Technology: Lessons from MIT and Beyond*. New York: Oxford University Press.

Sexton, D.L. and Kasarda, J.D. (eds.). 1992. *The State of the Art of Entrepreneurship*. Boston: PWS-Kent.

Stefflre, V. 1985. "Organizational Obstacles to Innovation: A Formulation of the Problem." *Journal of Product Innovation Management*, 2, 3–11.

Stevenson, H., and Carlos, J. 1990. "A Paradigm of Entrepreneurship." *Strategic Management Journal*, 11, 17–27.

Stevenson, H., and Gumpert, D.E. 1985. "The Heart of Entrepreneurship." *Harvard Business Review*, 63 (March–April), 85–93.

Timmons, J.A. 1990. *New Venture Creation: Entrepreneurship in the 1990's*. Homewood, IL: Irwin Publishing.

Index

About the Author

MICHAEL MORRIS is currently Visiting Professor of Marketing at Georgetown University, after holding the position of Donald Gordon Professor of Entrepreneurship at the University of Cape Town, South Africa. Morris is a founder and Managing Director of PenteVision, an international consulting and executive development firm, and has been personally involved in two entrepreneurial start-ups. He is author of more than 60 articles published in academic journals and author or coauthor of three books, among them *Market-Oriented Pricing: Strategies for Management* (Quorum, 1990).